COMPANY
MEETINGS
HANDBOOK

Sue Lawrence

icsa
The Chartered
Governance
Institute

First published 2020

Published by
ICSA Publishing Limited
Saffron House
6–10 Kirby Street
London EC1N 8TS

Typeset by Paul Barrett Book Production, Cambridge
Edited by Benedict O'Hagan
Cover designed by Anthony Kearney

British Library Cataloguing in Publication Data
A catalogue record for this book is available from the British Library

ISBN 978-1-86072-800-6

Contents

Preface

At the time of writing this book we are moving through the effects of the global coronavirus pandemic, Covid-19. This crisis has resulted in companies having to rapidly adopt new ways of working across their businesses, as well as in terms of their governance and formal meetings.

While the body of this book remains unchanged, Chapter 4 now includes the advice and guidance published by The Chartered Governance Institute and other bodies during this period of uncertainty.

If a positive from the pandemic can be taken, it is that this guidance provides an opportunity to rapidly deploy updated practices for holding meetings that new technology can support and which the industry has long been debating and partially implementing. Legislation supports this ability, while companies will need to ensure that their articles also allow for such usage.

No doubt, after the pandemic, the new normal will embrace more extensive use of technology for larger member meetings as well as meetings of directors, and some of the requirements identified in this book for large meetings will no longer be required for all companies. However, the need to hold meetings to engage with members and document decisions remains a core requirement that benefits from following a robust legal and company framework. This framework, as presented in this book, with some small adjustments, remains as relevant during and after this pandemic as it did before.

Acknowledgements

This book is a refresh and update of *The Law in Practice of Company Meetings* by Andrew C. Hamer, published by The Chartered Governance Institute in 2013. In updating this book, the author drew on her experience of, and fascination in, governance in all its aspects.

In adding specific reference to meetings of bondholders in Chapter 18, personal thanks is also extended for the advice and guidance provided by Helena Giles, Chair of the Association of Corporate Trustees. In addition, thanks are due to individuals who have published articles and advice in light of the Covid-19 pandemic, including Lorraine Young of Board Advisory Services and Tim Beech, Partner, Allen & Overy LLP.

Acronyms and abbreviations

AGM	Annual general meeting
AIM	Alternative investment market
CA 2006	Companies Act 2006
CEO	chief executive officer
CFO	chief financial officer
DTR	Disclosure and Transparency Rules
EEA	European Economic Area
EGM	extraordinary general meeting
ESG	Environmental, social and governance
FCA	Financial Conduct Authority
FRC	Financial Reporting Council
GDPR	General Data Protection Regulation
LR	Listing rules
NED	non-executive director
PSC	person with significant control
RIS	Regulatory Information Service
SID	senior independent director
SPV	Special Purpose Vehicle
UKLA	United Kingdom Listing Authority

Section 1
Introduction to company meetings

1— Introduction

Too often meetings are stale, last too long, lack purpose and merely serve to give attendees a respite from their work rather than being beneficial in themselves.

This book is intended to counteract this by providing an operational framework to meeting governance, thus creating a foundation from which effective meetings can be held. Unfortunately, it is not able to deliver the perfect meeting or able to guide in best practice for making the content and output of meetings beneficial. This can only come from the company itself and the attendees, chair and those that support the meeting. However, delivery of effective, efficient and successful meetings relies on three key areas of focus, namely:

1 Good groundwork ahead of a meeting in setting an appropriate agenda, limiting discussion topics to fill the allotted meeting time, ensuring meeting invites and meeting packs are correct and distributed in good time.
2 Applying good practices in the meeting itself, keeping it on track in terms of agenda topics and timings, engaging all attendees and focussing on deliverables.
3 Following up with minutes, clear of deliverables, agreed individual actions and documented next steps.

Each of these three stages will be covered in the two main sections of this book on internal meetings and shareholder meetings.

Corporate governance

Convening, holding and documenting meetings effectively not only builds a robust corporate governance structure for a company, but it also acts as an audit trail for the future. Too many times decisions made at board meetings have incorrect minutes, or meetings are not held to ratify ad hoc decisions. Quorums at meetings can be challenged resulting in decisions being overturned and the professionalism of directors can be called into question through imperfect processes.

Ensuring clear guidelines for convening, minuting and following up on all meetings is imperative, as is ensuring that the articles of association are followed in respect of formal meetings and that the requirements of the Companies Act are observed. This book references the Companies Act 2006 and relevant updates. It should be noted that companies incorporated before 2006 may specifically reference the Companies Act 1985.

Throughout this book, examples will be included from model form Articles of Association for:

- private companies limited by shares;
- private companies limited by guarantee; and
- public companies.

The most recent published version, dated 28 April 2013, will be referenced. It should be noted that, when applying these principles to a specific company, the articles of that specific company should be referenced. While model form articles are used for the incorporation of most companies, these articles are fixed as at the date of incorporation. Subsequent updates to model articles will not apply to previously incorporated companies. By default, any company incorporated prior to 28 April 2013 will, if referencing the model articles, be referring to older versions, copies of which can be found on the UK government website (www.gov.uk/guidance/model-articles-of-association-for-limited-companies). This clearly evidences the importance of maintaining robust corporate records, including the articles of association, for future reference as well as their significance when planning to hold meetings.

For reference, Appendix 8 provides a simple guide to the differing sections of model articles for private companies limited by shares between those of the 1985 Table A provisions versus the 2006 model articles versus the 2013 model articles.

The application of these processes can be applied to all companies and can be used to support the governance framework for all forms of companies.

This book is split into sections covering (1) general meeting conventions; (2) meetings of directors; (3) general meetings; and (4) other meetings of a company. Throughout the book, reference to member, the standard legal term, can also be replaced with the term 'shareholder'.

Section 1: Introduction to company meetings

After the introduction to this section, Chapter 2 asks whether formal meetings are still required. It then introduces the legal requirements for a company to hold meetings, introducing the relevant requirements under the Companies Act 2006, the articles of association of a company, the UK Corporate Governance Code and other guidelines or frameworks that should be followed. It will also reflect on the prioritisation between each and the impact of subsequent amendments. This general introduction is applicable to all companies and, while UK specific, can be easily replicated for other jurisdictions. Concluding this chapter is an introduction to the importance of the role of the company secretary, whether formally appointed or not, in underpinning the effective application of legal requirements for formal meetings.

Chapter 3 will introduce general concepts of practicalities in respect of meetings in general. As a first step it explains the various types of directors and the extent of their powers, as well as matters that are reserved for the board to action. Thereafter it reflects on operational versus strategic roles, delegation of the role of the executive and the powers that rest with shareholders. Finally, there is an in-depth review of minutes of meetings, their importance as a record of decisions, the format and content, as well as the requirements for their maintenance.

Chapter 4 starts by positioning the current legal framework for communications both to and from a company, explaining the legal framework within which this sits as well as the specifics that need to be adhered to. Given a proportion of internal board and committee meetings are now held virtually, making the most of technological advances, a checklist for holding virtual meetings is included as a reference for their use. Finally, this chapter concludes with considerations up to the end of 2019 on how annual general meetings could utilise technology in holding virtual meetings and the potential issues around voting. It also includes Covid-19 advice on holding shareholder meetings at a time when social distancing measures are in place, with a view to potentially using at least part of these new ways of working after these measures have been removed.

Chapter 5 provides a concluding commentary to Section 1.

Section 2: Meetings of directors

Chapter 6 introduces Section 2 which will focus on internal meetings of directors.

Chapter 7 will specifically cover why and when meetings of the directors should be held, board meeting approvals and delegating authority. The meetings of committees are introduced in more depth in Chapter 21. It also introduces the alternatives to holding a meeting. Written resolutions and their applications are considered in depth, as is the use of informal consent.

Chapter 8 introduces the formal requirements for convening a board meeting including who can call a meeting of directors and the notice requirements such as recipients, content, form and timeline. Setting the agenda is introduced as well as the role of the company secretary when convening a meeting.

Chapter 9 reflects on the actions undertaken at a meeting of the board of directors. Introducing the role of the chair, their role, and duties as well as their appointment. Thereafter, it moves on to quorums, voting and participation in directors' meetings, including the role of alternate directors. The requirements to disclose conflicts of interest is covered as well as the ability to adjourn directors' meetings. Standing orders and internal regulations are introduced as well as the effectiveness of the board. To conclude, the role of the company secretary at any meeting of the board of directors is included, together with a useful checklist.

Chapter 10 follows through with actions to be taken after a meeting has been held, introducing best practice for the content of meeting minutes, as well as their role in providing evidence of the meeting and approvals. The formal approval and signature of meeting minutes is covered as well as requirements for the maintenance of minute books and their certification. Finally, the role of the company secretary in finalising minutes and noting actions to be taken after each meeting is included as a checklist.

Chapter 11 concludes the section with a reflection on the requirements related to meetings of the board of directors.

Section 3: General meetings

Chapter 12 introduces the section and contains an explanation of the difference between shareholders and members as well as the various types of resolutions that could be proposed. It also touches on the use of technology in general meetings. Finally, the conclusion provides a useful reminder of the purpose of general meetings in enabling the board to obtain approval for intended actions through voting on resolutions and the ability of members to challenge the board and hear further about the intentions of the company.

Chapter 13 introduces why and when a general meeting should be convened, firstly introducing the requirements under the Companies Act 2006 and the specific requirements of traded and quoted companies. Thereafter, it recognises that a general meeting is a meeting of members, noting the rights of indirect investors in listed companies, the requirements for written resolutions and unanimous consent. Note is made of when an annual general meeting should be held and the chapter provides further detail of these meetings in general. The ability for members to request inclusion of a specific resolution at the annual general meeting (AGM) is incorporated, including the process to be followed. Finally, the actual business to be covered in the AGM is introduced.

Chapter 14 reflects on the processes and procedures required when convening a general meeting, including its practical organisation, the chair's script and who has the right to attend. Given that meetings of members are an opportunity for disenchanted or activist investors to very publicly raise their personal concerns, whether valid or not, the security of the meeting is covered in detail, including a useful checklist. Notice requirements are noted, including who should receive notice and how, as well as which members are entitled to receive such notice. Special notices are explained as is the content of the notice to be sent, including the specific notice requirements of premium listed companies. Finally, a checklist is provided for company secretaries for convening a general meeting.

Chapter 15 walks through the formalities of the meeting itself, working through the appointment of the chair and their required actions, attendance records, checking the quorum is in place and maintained throughout the meeting. It explains in depth what corporate representative and proxies are, the difference and who they represent when they attend a meeting. The right to attend the meeting and speak is introduced as well as the practicalities and legal standing of voting methodologies at the general meeting. Shareholder remedies in case of disorder are explained as well as the practicalities of adjournment and other procedural motions while at the meeting. Amendments are touched on as is the process for dealing with common items of business such as shareholder resolutions, voting methodologies, proxy voting and meeting quorums.

Chapter 16 introduces the various remedies available to shareholders after the meeting that could make the holding of the meeting or its content subject to challenge. Thereafter, it moves on to the practical actions that need to be taken, starting with the filing of resolutions and introducing the Public Register of members' dissent. Finally, minutes of general meetings are explained and the role of the company secretary after the meeting. As a final reminder, the resolutions that are required to be registered with Companies House are listed.

Chapter 17 provides a brief recap of the significance of general meetings as well as a reminder that these meetings are more than just the practicalities of the formal framework in which they sit; they are an opportunity for the board to showcase the company and its activities to its shareholders.

Section 4: Other company meetings

Chapter 18 reflects on other forms of formal meetings. It briefly refers to dormant companies and special purpose vehicles (SPVs) and their requirements to maintain compliance with the Act and their own articles. It also provides background and insight into meetings of bondholders, which, while following standard company law on the requirements for meetings, also embrace technology to identify bondholders. The Covid-19 pandemic has introduced new meeting methods which may subsequently affect how all companies host meetings. Finally, two other formal meetings are noted: pension scheme boards and employee ownership trust boards.

Chapter 19 sets out the specific requirements for meetings of classes of shareholders, initially explaining the different classes of shares that a company may have and the variation of the rights that may be attached to them. Thereafter, it introduces the special procedural requirements for a variation of class rights meetings and the procedure at these meetings, including notice requirements, the right to call a meeting and member's statements. For the meeting itself, it references the appointment of the chair, quorum requirements, resolutions (including written resolutions), voting, the appointment of proxies and corporate representatives and attendance. Requirements for recording proceedings by keeping minutes and records of class meetings is also incorporated, as well as a section on the classes of members in guarantee companies.

Chapter 20 provides specific insight into sole director and/or sole shareholder meetings. Firstly, it covers sole member meetings which, though it may seem ridiculous, is still a legal requirement, hence the chapter covers general meetings, confirmation of decisions, unanimous consent and written resolutions. It also touches on contracts with sole members who are also a director of a company. The latter part of the chapter focuses on sole director requirements including confirmation of the legal standing of a quorum of one, declaration of interests and minutes of meetings. While sole shareholder and/or sole director companies may see all decision making as part of general company procedures, especially where the two roles are fulfilled by the same individual, it is important to recognise the difference between the two roles and the legislative requirements sitting behind them that must be followed.

Chapter 21 provides specific information on the meetings of committees established by the board which, as a result of their implementation by the board, are meetings of the company. It initially confirms which committees are formal board committees noting their membership, powers and duties. Proceedings at committee meetings are noted including the appointment of a chair, quorum requirements, voting and the disclosure of interests by members. Alternate directors also apply to committees, as do written resolutions, so they are referenced. Thereafter the specifics of the three main committees – audit, remuneration and nomination – are discussed, noting specifically their roles and the requirement to include statements in the annual report of the company.

Chapter 22 provides a brief conclusion to Section 4, reflecting on which meeting principles also apply to other meetings of a company.

Conclusion

The conclusion to the book provides a brief reminder of the purpose of legislation but also an expectation that this book can help in providing a framework and reference source for those who work in some way within the governance of a company. It reminds us that there are two main company meetings: those of the directors of the company and those with shareholders. Having an effective and efficient framework for holding these two types of meeting can underpin and support a company, without detracting from the core business that is required to deliver success.

2 – The legal framework

In order to have effective company meetings that enhance and support a company it is important to understand the legal framework under which meetings are convened, as well as the legal requirements that a company must adhere to when holding meetings. Hence this section introduces this framework as the foundation for its application and the practical aspects that follow.

Are formal meetings still necessary?

The overriding purpose of the law of meetings is to ensure that those who are entitled to participate in the company's decision-making process are given a reasonable and fair opportunity to do so, but also to ensure that decisions can be made by a majority of those who actually choose to participate.

In the eyes of the law, a company is treated as a person and, as such, is able to do anything an individual can do for the purposes of running a business (e.g. own property, enter into contracts, and sue and be sued in its own name). Despite being accorded this status, a company plainly does not have a mind of its own and cannot act without the intervention of human beings. Someone must act and make decisions on its behalf. Who may do so, and how, depends mainly on the Companies Act 2006 and a company's articles of association.

The Companies Act reserves certain matters to the members/shareholders but otherwise leaves matters of internal governance to be determined by the company in its own constitution in the form of articles of association. If the articles do not delegate the company's powers to anyone else, then those powers vest by default in its members. In practice, companies invariably adopt articles of association that delegate wide decision-making powers to the directors. They need not do so. However, it is normally more operationally effective to run a company if certain matters are delegated to the directors.

Articles invariably allow the directors to delegate their own powers to committees or individual executives. Where a power is delegated to an individual, it is obviously not necessary for that person to hold a meeting. However, where a power is vested in a body, it may be necessary to do so. That body could be the company in general meeting (i.e. the members or shareholders) or the board of directors acting under a power delegated to them by the articles.

Where a body (it does not matter which for now) has decision-making powers, a mechanism is required to determine the views of the members of that body on proposals that are put to them. Members of a body will seldom agree on everything unless there is only one member. Accordingly, it is best practice to allow decisions to be taken by a majority, potentially with a higher majority for certain types of important decisions. In some cases, there could be a requirement for the members to make decisions unanimously, although this should be applied with caution. Unanimous decision making enables the minority to obstruct the will of the majority; this would seem to be unfair and could make it impossible for the company to make any decisions.

Decisions made by a majority enable the opportunity for discussion on any proposals by members prior to voting. This allows members to question those making the proposal and give members who oppose the proposal an opportunity to persuade others to vote against it. In the past, the only practical way to ensure that all this happened was to require decisions to be taken at formal meetings. Generally speaking, this is still what the law requires although there are numerous exceptions.

Public companies must still hold a meeting to obtain shareholder approval for certain things (see Appendix 1 for matters reserved for shareholder approval) and must still hold annual general meetings (AGMs).

However, members of private companies can take most decisions without holding meetings. This has been the case since 1989, when the Companies Act 1985 was amended to allow members of private companies to pass written resolutions. In order to do this under the 1985 Act, it was necessary for all members to sign the resolution. In other words, they all had to agree to it. Where this was the case, it obviously did not make sense to require them to hold a meeting to debate the matter.

However, under the Companies Act 2006, members of private companies can now take decisions without holding a meeting even if they are not all of one mind. The 2006 Act written resolution procedure simply requires the requisite majority to consent to the proposal. In other words, the 2006 Act has all but dispensed with the idea that the minority in a private company must automatically be given an opportunity to air their views in an attempt to persuade others of the merits of their case. So, while members' meetings are still necessary for public companies, they are not so for private companies.

Where a company's articles delegate powers to the directors, they must generally exercise those powers collectively in accordance with any decision-making procedures for directors specified in the company's articles. The articles nearly always enable the directors to make decisions by a majority at a properly constituted meeting of directors (known as a board meeting). If a company's articles do not do this, it is possible that the directors would have to make all decisions unanimously. The articles of both public and private companies also normally allow the directors to exercise their powers without holding a meeting, for example by written resolution or unanimous decision. In addition, articles usually authorise the directors to delegate their powers to committees of directors, individual executive directors and other employees and agents.

In practice, it may be possible to run a private company without holding formal meetings of either the members or the directors. This is not the case with public companies, which must still hold an annual general meeting of the members and will probably need to hold fairly regular board meetings. Private companies are not required to hold annual general meetings and, as we have already seen, their members can normally make decisions by written resolution. If the board of directors takes advantage of the procedures in most articles of association which allow them to pass written resolutions, then it is possible that a private company might never need to hold any meeting in the traditional sense.

Holding proper meetings

To ensure that those entitled to participate in a company's decision-making process are given a reasonable and fair opportunity to do so, certain procedures must be followed at meetings. In short, meetings must be properly convened, properly constituted and properly held. They must be called, held and conducted in accordance with the articles, the Companies Acts and the general law of meetings. Although, the procedural requirements for general meetings (meetings of members) are more onerous than those for meetings of directors, the essential principles for both are as follows:

- the meeting must be called by someone with authority to do so and in the correct manner;
- notice of the meeting and the business to be transacted must be given in the correct manner to those entitled to receive it (generally speaking this will be those entitled to vote at the meeting);
- a quorum must be present (i.e. the minimum number of persons necessary to transact business);
- those entitled to attend and vote must be allowed to do so;
- a chair must be elected or appointed;
- the business raised must be within the scope of the notice of meeting;
- the meeting must be conducted properly, particularly in respect of voting; and
- the decisions of the meeting should be recorded.

Failure to conduct a meeting in accordance with these principles, can render the proceedings liable to challenge. It is possible that nobody will challenge their validity. The worst-case scenario for a company is for someone to spot an irregularity but for nobody to be certain if it would affect the validity of the proceedings. Rather than have this uncertainty hanging over its head, a company will often choose to hold another meeting to do things properly. Another option can be for the company itself to seek a court ruling on the validity of the proceedings.

The law of meetings

One of the most difficult aspects of the law relating to company meetings is the complicated hierarchy of rules and procedures. Company meetings are governed by a combination of formal statutory rules, a company's own constitution (primarily its articles of association) and common law rules developed by the courts. Publicly traded companies will also need to comply with additional rules. For example, companies listed on the London Stock Exchange must comply with the Listing Rules and the Disclosure and Transparency Rules. Although failure to comply with these rules will not necessarily directly affect the validity of a meeting or a particular transaction, the Financial Conduct Authority (FCA) may impose sanctions and penalties for non-compliance. Listed companies may also need to have regard to codes of practice, such as the UK Corporate Governance Code.

Statute

The main statutory rules relating to meetings are contained in the Companies Act 2006 ('the Act' or 'the 2006 Act'). Part 13 (Resolutions and Meetings) sets out the main statutory rules governing meetings of members/shareholders and, in the case of private companies, members' written resolutions. The Act deliberately makes very little provision regarding directors' meetings and generally leaves such matters to be determined by a company's articles of association and, in default, the common law.

The provisions of Part 13 were brought into force on 1 October 2007, except for:

(a) section 308 (manner in which notice to be given), section 309 (publication of notice on website) and section 333 (sending documents relating to meetings, etc. in electronic form), which were all brought into force on 20 January 2007 together with the company communication provisions in sections 1143 to 1148 and Schedules 4 and 5 to the Act; and

(b) sections 327(2)(c) and 330(6)(c), which have not been commenced (and probably never will be).

The layout of Part 13 of the Act is summarised in **Appendix 4**. Various other sections of the Act specify the circumstances in which the approval of a company's members/shareholders is required and the type of resolution required. These sections are summarised in **Appendix 1** (Matters requiring members' approval).

The expression 'the Companies Acts' includes:

- the Companies Act 2006;
- Part 2 of the Companies (Audit, Investigations and Community Enterprise) Act 2006;
- the provisions of the Companies Act 1985 that are still in force; and
- the provisions of the Companies Consolidation (Consequential Provisions) Act 1985 that are still in force.

Statutory instruments

The Companies Act 2006 gives the secretary of state power to make regulations and issue orders on certain matters related to company law. The secretary of state is the minister in charge of the government department which has responsibility for company law. At present this is the Department for Business, Energy and Industrial Strategy (BEIS). This was formerly the Department for Business, Innovation and Skills (BIS); prior to that it was the Department for Business, Enterprise and Regulatory Reform (BERR) and, before that, the Department of Trade and Industry (DTI).

Such regulations and orders are referred to collectively as statutory instruments and each one has a unique number. They are often used to make detailed provision on matters governed by the Act. For example, the 2006 Act model articles are prescribed in the Companies (Model Articles) Regulations 2008 which were made under a power given by section 19 of the Act. The unique SI number of these regulations is SI 2008/3229, which indicates that it was the 3,229th SI of 2008 (not all SIs deal with matters of company law).

However, the Act also sometimes gives the secretary of state power to issue regulations that amend its provisions.

Types of company

Several different types of company can be formed under the Companies Acts and each type can be subject to different statutory provisions. It is, therefore, essential to check whether the relevant statutory provisions or procedures are applicable to the type of company you are dealing with. The biggest differences in this regard arise between public and private companies. The rows in the table below show whether a company is public or private. The columns also show other terminology used in the Acts to limit or define the scope of certain provisions. It should be noted that it is no longer possible to form a company limited by guarantee with a share capital (see s. 5).

	Limited company		Unlimited company
	Limited by shares	Limited by guarantee	
Public company	Public limited company (Plc)	–	–
Private company	Private company limited by shares (Ltd)	Private company limited by guarantee (Ltd)	Unlimited company (–)
	Private company limited by guarantee with a share capital (Ltd)		

Common law and precedent

The common law is the body of rules and principles developed by the courts to decide the competing merits of litigants in the absence of any legislative provision or other determining factor. Provisions contained in Acts of Parliament take precedence over any conflicting common law, although in some cases, legislation will specifically state that it is without prejudice to any common law rule. Throughout history, parliament has frequently adopted legislation to codify existing common law rules, although it often takes the opportunity to modify them as well. A recent example of this was the codification in the Companies Act 2006, Part 10 of the common law rules regarding the duties of directors.

A company can exclude the operation of certain common law rules by making alternative provision in its articles of association.

Despite this relatively lowly position in the legal hierarchy, the common law is still of relevance in many areas relating to the law of meetings. For example, the Companies Act does not specify a minimum period of notice for board meetings, nor do most articles. Accordingly, the common law rule applies (i.e. that the notice given must be reasonable in the circumstances). If the articles specified a minimum notice period of seven clear days, that rule would override the common law rule.

The courts are often called upon to rule on the interpretation and application of the Companies Acts and on the precise effect of provisions contained in a company's articles. Decisions in these cases provide precedents which are useful in clarifying the law. Most cases concerning company law are heard initially in the Chancery Division of the High Court. Appeals can be made to the Court of Appeal and, ultimately to the Supreme Court (formerly known as the House of Lords). Generally speaking, decisions taken in higher courts are more influential and act as binding precedents for lower courts. Where the point at issue is the interpretation of EU law, the case may be referred to EU courts and tribunals.

Memorandum of association

UK companies have traditionally had two main constitutional documents: the memorandum of association and the articles of association. Under the Companies Act 2006, a memorandum of association must still be submitted to the Registrar of Companies before a company can be incorporated. However, its importance is much reduced because the only thing that it is allowed to contain is a subscribers' statement.

For a company limited by shares, this statement will do no more than state the fact that each subscriber to the memorandum of association wishes to form a company under the Companies Act 2006 and agrees to become a member of the company. It does not even state how many shares each subscriber will take – this information is provided in a separate document on incorporation.

Under previous Companies Acts, and hence for companies incorporated under previous requirements who have not updated their corporate documentation, the memorandum was required to contain much more detailed information, including:

- the name of the company;
- whether the registered office of the company was to be situated in England and Wales or in Scotland;
- the objects of the company (i.e. the purpose for which it was formed and the company's powers);
- the liability of the members, whether limited by shares, limited by guarantee or unlimited;
- whether it was a public or private company;
- in the case of a company limited by shares, the amount of share capital with which the company proposed to be registered and the division of the share capital into shares of a fixed amount (e.g. the share capital of the company is £100 divided into 100 shares of £1 each); and
- in the case of a company limited by guarantee, the amount that each member guarantees to contribute in the event of insolvency.

Under previous Acts, the memorandum served as an application form during the incorporation process. It determined, amongst other things, what type of company the incorporators wished to be formed and, therefore, which provisions of the Act would apply to it. And, once the company was formed, the memorandum became one of its core constitutional documents, which was capable of amendment. Although the memorandum is still a bit like an application form under the Companies Act 2006, it is no longer capable of amendment. Everything which may need to be amended has been stripped out and is now either superfluous or to be found in the articles of association.

One of the important consequences of this change is that any provision (other than the subscribers' statement) in the memorandum of association of a company that was incorporated under a prior Companies Act is now deemed to form part of its articles of association (s. 28) and to be capable of modification in accordance with the procedures for amendment of the articles set out in sections 21 and 22 of the 2006 Act.

Companies formed on or after 1 October 2009 were incorporated under the Companies Act 2006. Companies formed before that date were incorporated under a previous Act (e.g. under the Companies Act 1985). These are sometimes referred to as 'existing companies' as they were already in existence on 1 October 2009.

Generally speaking, the memorandum provisions of existing companies will continue to have effect even though the Companies Act 2006 does not specifically require a company's articles to make provision in that regard. For example, the objects clause, will still restrict the objects of the company, even though a company's articles are no longer required to include a statement of objects (s. 31).

Articles of association

A company's articles of association (articles) usually contain detailed provisions which govern the conduct of both general meetings and meetings of directors. A company must have articles prescribing regulations for the company (s. 18). A company may alter any of its articles by special resolution (s. 21), unless the article is an entrenched provision, in which case section 22 applies.

A limited company need not submit articles of association with its application for registration. However, if it does not register its own articles, it will be deemed to have adopted the relevant set of model articles prescribed by the Secretary of State (s. 20). Unlimited companies must submit articles of association with their application for registration.

Even if articles are registered, the relevant model articles apply on formation of a limited company in so far as the registered articles do not exclude them (s. 20(1)). Listed companies usually adopt articles which exclude any relevant model articles in their entirety. Many private companies adopt what are known as 'short form' articles. These state that the company has adopted the model articles (or its predecessor, Table A) subject to several express exclusions, modifications or additions. In such circumstances, it is often helpful to produce and hold on file a marked-up copy of the relevant model articles showing which provisions do and do not apply and any relevant modifications or additions. However, it should always be remembered that the 'short form' articles, not the new consolidated version, are registered at Companies House as the company's articles.

It is important to understand that the application of any model articles is frozen at the date of the company's incorporation. The model articles that apply to companies (if any) are those in force on the date of its incorporation. Any subsequent statutory modification of those model articles has no effect on the company's constitution.

The version of model articles reproduced at Appendix 6 is the version prescribed for public listed companies incorporated on or after 28 April 2013.

Table A

Table A is the name that was given to the model articles prescribed for companies limited by shares under previous Companies Acts. When considering meeting provisions, the articles of the particular company should be considered, noting that those companies incorporated using historical model articles will still need to abide by these, subject to any subsequent amendments that may have been made. For reference, we provide here a brief guide to the different Table A articles and their dates of application. Elsewhere in this book, reference is focused on current model articles in place from 28 April 2013, with Appendix 6 providing a ready reference for the comparable sections.

Prior to 1 October 2009, a company limited by shares which did not register its own articles on incorporation was deemed to have adopted the version of Table

A in force at that time. Indeed, the provisions of the relevant Table A in force on the date of a company's incorporation are deemed to apply to that company in so far as its own articles do not exclude or modify them. This remains the case notwithstanding the fact that a different version of Table A may subsequently have been prescribed. Later versions of Table A (or the 2006 Act model articles) only apply to companies incorporated during the period that the relevant version was in force.

Different versions of Table A have been prescribed under each previous Companies Act. For example, a company incorporated under the Companies Act 1948 will be subject to the version prescribed in that Act. A company incorporated under the Companies Act 1985 will be subject to one of the versions of Table A prescribed for the purposes of that Act.

Several different versions of Table A were prescribed for the purposes of companies incorporated under the Companies Act 1985 in the Companies (Tables A to F) Regulations 1985 (SI 1985/805). The different versions were introduced by amendments made to those regulations.

The original version of Table A in those regulations applied from 1 July 1985 to 21 December 2000 inclusive. The original version of Table A in those regulations was amended on 22 December 2000 by the Companies Act 1985 (Electronic Communications) Order 2000 (SI 2000/3373) to facilitate the use of electronic communications. This amended version applied to companies incorporated between 22 December 2000 and 30 September 2007.

Before 1 October 2007, the same version of Table A was used for both public and private companies limited by shares. However, separate versions of the 1985 Table A were introduced for public and private companies incorporated on or after 1 October 2007. These changes were introduced to cater for the fact that, from that date, private companies were no longer required to hold annual general meetings. The new versions were introduced for companies limited by shares incorporated under the 1985 Act on or after 1 October 2007 by the Companies (Tables A to F) (Amendment) Regulations 2007 (SI 2007/2541) and the Companies (Tables A to F) (Amendment) (No 2) Regulations 2007 (SI 2007/2826). However, they ceased to apply for companies incorporated on or after 1 October 2009 as that was the date from which companies began to be incorporated under the Companies Act 2006 and subject to the model articles prescribed under that Act.

For reference for those companies maintaining articles reflecting Table A, Appendix 5 shows the content of current model articles and the location of equivalent provisions in the 1985 Table A, the model articles for private companies limited by shares under the 2006 Act and the current model articles updated in 2013.

Copies of all current and former articles can be found on the UK government website at: www.gov.uk/guidancemodel-articles-of-association-for-limited-companies.

Relationship between Companies Acts and articles

The Companies Act 2006 includes a large number of provisions relating to company meetings. Generally speaking, these override any provisions contained in the articles of association of a company and must, therefore, be followed.

Articles are usually drafted to ensure that no conflicts exist at the time of drafting. However, conflicts can arise subsequently because of later amendments to company legislation or, indeed, as a result of amendments made to the articles in ignorance of the statutory requirements. The Companies Act 2006 made significant changes to company legislation, some of which could override provisions contained in the articles of a company incorporated before the Act came into force.

Changes were also made, for example, to the Companies Act 1985 in 2000 to facilitate the use of electronic communications by companies and their members. These changes enable companies to take advantage of electronic communications, notwithstanding anything to the contrary contained in their articles. This was necessary because, at the time, most articles contained provisions which would otherwise have prevented the use of electronic communications. The relevant provisions of the Companies Act 1985 have now been superseded by the company communications provisions of the Companies Act 2006. Strictly speaking, it is not necessary for any company to amend its articles to bring them into line with any new legislative requirements. However, failure to do so will often lead to confusion as to which rule applies and it is nearly always preferable to have articles which, if followed, ensure compliance with existing legislation.

The position is further complicated by the fact that some of the provisions of the Act only apply if the articles do not make alternative provision (e.g. s. 319 on who may chair a general meeting) while others invalidate the effect of articles not in accordance with certain minimum standards (e.g. s. 327 on the lodging of proxies).

Contractual nature of a company's constitution

The provisions of a company's constitution bind the company and its members to the same extent as if there were covenants on the part of the company and of each member to observe those provisions (s. 33(1)). In addition, money payable by a member to the company under its constitution is a debt due from him to the company; in England and Wales and Northern Ireland, any such debt is of the nature of an ordinary contract debt (s. 33(2)).

Section 17 provides that unless the context otherwise requires, references in the Companies Acts to a company's constitution include the company's articles, and any resolutions and agreements to which Chapter 3 of Part 3 applies, for example the resolutions and agreements which must be filed with the registrar.

Corporate governance

Corporate governance is concerned, among other things, with ensuring that decisions are taken in an appropriate manner by appropriate people after due consideration of the relevant facts. Should a matter be approved by the members? Or is it an area that can safely be left within the remit of the board of directors? If not, should the non-executive directors have some special role? Should the board be able to delegate responsibility to an executive director or a committee of directors? Should members be informed about the decisions taken on their behalf by the directors? And, if so, what action should they be able to take if they are not happy with those decisions?

The answers to these questions will have practical implications for the decision-making structure adopted by companies and the types of meetings that are convened. Codes of practice have emerged largely to fill the gaps left by the Companies Acts. The existence of these gaps is, for the most part, deliberate. UK company law does not tend to interfere in the internal management of companies, mainly in recognition of the fact that it is difficult to find a single solution to suit the needs of all companies. Codes of practice on corporate governance have become highly influential on corporate behaviour generally. They are, however, directed mainly towards listed companies (i.e. companies where the vast majority of members are not involved in the day-to-day management, where highly paid professional managers fulfil that role, and where, on the whole, the members behave as investors rather than owners and are almost totally reliant on information published by the directors when making investment decisions).

Governance guidelines

Governance guidelines and reports in the UK provide a useful reference for the purpose of a board as well as the aims for a robust governance structure. However, they have not been published to provide a practical guide on how to apply governance through meetings and application. As such, the primary reports are listed here for interest without extensive content which can be found by sourcing the documents themselves. It should be noted that these have all been published to be useful and, as such, are a worthwhile support when implementing or reviewing a governance framework or considering the best way to apply the relevant code.

The UK Corporate Governance Code

The UK Corporate Governance Code is published by the Financial Reporting Council (FRC). An independent regulator with delegated powers from the UK its mission is to promote transparency and integrity in business in the UK. The Code, which is reviewed, reported on and updated regularly, includes principles and provisions on:

- board leadership and company purpose;
- division of responsibilities;
- composition, succession and evaluation of the board;
- audit, risk and internal control; and
- remuneration of directors.

However, the code does not provide guidance on the practical application of the principles and provisions in terms of meetings and formal forums. As such, this is a highly beneficial guide to governance in general and serves to underpin best practice without being prescriptive in terms of application.

The Wates corporate governance principles for large private companies

In December 2018 the first Wates corporate governance principles for large private companies was issued, providing similar guidance on best practice for large private companies. Again, this is a highly beneficial reference tool on governance in terms of leadership, board composition, director responsibilities, risk, remuneration and stakeholder engagement. Similarly, this is a beneficial overview of the ethos of good corporate governance without being prescriptive on its application.

The Cadbury and Greenbury reports

Listed companies in the UK have been required to report on their compliance with a corporate governance code since 1992. The first such code was published by a committee chaired by Sir Adrian Cadbury in the *Report of the Committee on the Financial Aspects of Corporate Governance*. This has been amended and renamed several times since 1992, but still forms the basis of the UK Corporate Governance Code.

In February 1995, the Confederation of British Industries (CBI) formed a study group chaired by Sir Richard Greenbury 'to identify good practice in determining directors' remuneration and to prepare a code of such practice for use by UK plcs'. The resultant Greenbury Committee report and related code of practice was published on 17 July 1995. The London Stock Exchange agreed to require UK listed companies to report on their compliance with the Greenbury code and to include in their annual reports a report on directors' remuneration.

All these reports and guidance can be found on the FRC website at: www.frc. org.uk/directors

Types of shareholders

Members are defined as members of the company, not members of the board or members of a committee. It might have been easier for most people to understand if we had said it was about shareholders' decisions. However, it is not just about shareholders' decisions.

Every company must have at least one member. In most cases, the only way to become a member is to become a shareholder. However, this is not true for every company. Companies limited by guarantee can have members who are not shareholders. In fact, it is no longer possible to form a guarantee company with share capital. So, the vast majority of guarantee companies cannot have shareholders. They still have members though and those members still need to make decisions.

This section of the book is not just about how companies with shareholders may make decisions. It is also about how members of companies who are not shareholders may make decisions. That is why we said it was about members' decisions.

Indeed, that is the reason why throughout this book, the term 'member of the company' is used where the word 'shareholder' would seem to be more natural to most. The term 'shareholder' should not really be used unless we are talking about a rule that only applies to companies that have shareholders. If we are talking about a rule that can also apply to companies that have members who are not shareholders, we really ought to use the term 'member'.

As far as companies with a share capital are concerned, it does not really matter which term is used. In such a company, the words 'member' and 'shareholder' can be used interchangeably. Everybody who is a shareholder in such a company is a member and it is not possible to become a member in any other way. So, whenever the word 'member' is used, it is always meant to include 'shareholders' unless otherwise specified.

Obviously, it is important to use the right term when talking about a rule that only applies to companies who do not have shareholders. In this case, we need to say things like 'members of a company without a share capital' or 'members of a guarantee company'. We have aimed to use the correct terminology in these cases and to clarify where different rules apply.

Registered shareholder

If a company has a share capital, the only way to become a member will be to become a shareholder. Some companies incorporated prior to 1981 may have been formed as a guarantee company that also has a share capital, although these are rare and can no longer be formed.

Therefore, when we say 'become a shareholder', we mean become the registered holder of shares in a company. The registered holder is the person whose name is entered in the company's register of members as the holder of the shares. In companies that have shares, people often refer to the register of members as the 'share register'. If a company has more than one class of shares, it will typically keep a separate share register for each class. Where this is the case, each of those registers combine to make up the register of members, which is why every person whose name is entered in any share register as the holder of any type of share automatically becomes a member of the company. The share registers are the company's register of members.

Nominee shareholders and underlying investors

If somebody else holds shares on your behalf, you are not the registered shareholder and are not a member of the company. The person who holds the shares on your behalf is the member and the registered shareholder. People who hold shares through a nominee in this way often think of themselves as shareholders and may even refer to themselves as such. However, they are not shareholders. And if they are not shareholders, they are not members either. They are nothing more than underlying investors. In most cases, a company can choose to ignore the fact that these indirect investors exist and only has to deal with the person who is the registered shareholder. In most cases, underlying investors do not have any enforceable rights against the company. The only rights they will have are those that arise under any agreement they have entered into with the person who is acting as their nominee. These rights are not enforceable against the company but against the nominee.

The reason why we keep saying 'in most cases' is that the Act provides a mechanism to enable underlying investors in listed companies to claim certain 'membership' rights through their nominee. In addition, any company can choose to make provision in its articles to give underlying investors certain 'membership' rights. We tend to refer to people who have such rights as 'indirect investors' to distinguish them from underlying investors who have no rights.

Company secretary

Every public company must appoint a company secretary (s. 271) while private companies are not required to have a secretary but may choose to do so (s. 270). The directors of a public company have a duty to appoint as secretary someone who is capable of carrying out the duties which the post entails (s. 273). Irrespective of this requirement, having a knowledgeable and expert company secretary to apply and support the requirements of the company, including in respect of company meetings and minutes, is invaluable.

The company secretary will normally be responsible for the administration of general meetings, board meetings and other meetings of directors. However, the secretary has no inherent power to ensure compliance with the applicable rules and regulations. They do not even have a right to attend any of these meetings unless they are invited or entitled in some other capacity. The company secretary will, therefore, be totally reliant on the fact that the directors follow their advice or may formally have powers delegated by the directors to them.

The UK Corporate Governance Code states, in supporting principle I, that: 'The board, supported by the company secretary, should ensure that it has the policies, processes, information, time and resources it needs in order to function effectively and efficiently.'

The company secretary should be responsible for advising the board through the chair on all governance matters, including the holding of meetings.

Code provision 16 states:

> All directors should have access to the advice of the company secretary, who is responsible for advising the board on all governance matters. Both the appointment and removal of the company secretary should be a matter for the whole board.

This recommendation has been included in the Code since its inception in 1992. In its report, the Cadbury Committee said:

> The company secretary has a key role to play in ensuring that board procedures are both followed and regularly reviewed. The chair and the board will look to the company secretary for guidance on what their responsibilities are under the rules and regulations to which they are subject and on how those responsibilities should be discharged. All directors should have access to the advice and services of the company secretary and should recognise that the chair is entitled to the strong and positive support of the company secretary in ensuring the effective functioning of the board. It should be standard practice for the company secretary to administer, attend and prepare minutes of board meetings (Cadbury Report, para. 4.25).

Conclusion

As can be seen there is a robust legal foundation for the implementation and practical aspects of company meetings, both those of directors and members. While each company has the flexibility to adapt these to their own requirements as a business and the culture of their company, there are a few areas where there is a legal requirement to comply.

3 – Meetings in practice

Meetings of a company can be split into meetings of the board and meetings that include shareholder attendees. These two forums are covered separately within this book to reference the difference in practical operations in terms of convening the meetings, at the meeting and follow-up reporting and communications. This reflects model articles where there is a differentiation between the two, albeit that there is overlap in some operational matters.

In practice, the majority of meetings are called by the board of directors, whether as part of an annual meeting schedule or for a specific unscheduled purpose. The meeting schedule will reflect the requirement for the company to hold meetings of the board for a specific purpose, as well as to agree and document decisions made by directors to provide an audit trail or formal record. However, there is no legal requirement for a UK company to have a set number of board meetings in any one financial or calendar year.

In smaller companies, meetings may be limited in number and be largely unscheduled reflecting their purpose at any time of the year to approve significant actions, discuss major decisions or document formal approvals. Strategic discussions may be held informally via away days or through meetings including the wider employee base or external contributors. Despite this, there is a benefit to having at least one board meeting diarised and scheduled each year to align with accepting the final accounts of the company prior to submission to Companies House. Further meetings can then be scheduled around this diarised meeting.

The board of directors

The Companies Act 2006 requires every public company to have at least two directors and every private company to have at least one (s. 154). A company can appoint another company as a director. However, at least one director in every UK company must be a natural person (s. 155(1)). An individual under the age of 16 cannot be appointed as a director (s. 157).

The directors usually undertake the day-to-day management of the company on behalf of the members. Although the Act does not specifically require this and does not directly confer any powers of management on the directors, it is drafted on the assumption that they will be responsible for the management of the company. Under common law, a company's powers must be exercised by its members in general meeting unless its memorandum or articles of association provide otherwise.

It would not normally be practicable for a company's business to be managed on a day-to-day basis by the members, particularly if every matter requiring a decision had to be put to a general meeting called and held in accordance with the requirements of the Act. Even in an owner-managed business where there are relatively few members, it would normally be easier for them to manage the company as directors rather than as members. This is mainly because the formalities associated with board meetings not only are less onerous, but also because that is the way most companies are run; doing it any other way would complicate matters unnecessarily and probably involve significant legal expenses.

In practice, the articles of most companies delegate wide powers of management to the directors. Generally speaking, these powers must be exercised by the board of directors collectively (e.g. at a board meeting). However, the articles may allow the directors to make decisions in other ways and invariably allow them to delegate their powers to some other individual or body such as a committee of the board.

In the UK, all directors are usually members of the same board and usually have one vote each. Under this unitary system, each director has an equal say in matters put to the board (although the chair may sometimes have a casting vote). Articles usually allow the board to appoint one or more of the directors to some sort of executive office within the company (e.g. as managing director or finance director) and to delegate any of its powers to them. These executive directors are usually salaried and manage the business of the company on a day-to-day basis under delegated powers. Directors who are not executives are known as non-executive directors.

Boards rarely delegate all their management powers to the executive directors and will normally retain responsibility for certain matters (e.g. the company's strategic direction). Where the board does delegate management powers to executives, it will be responsible for monitoring their performance and setting their pay although, in listed companies, the latter role is often performed by a remuneration committee made up of non-executive directors.

In mainland Europe, two-tier board systems are more common. The company is managed on a day-to-day basis by an executive board which is appointed by, and accountable to, a supervisory board. The supervisory board fulfils the monitoring role performed by non-executive directors in the UK and may include shareholder and employee representatives. The system is appealing to purists as it places the non-executives above the executives in the structural hierarchy. However, it is debatable whether these structural differences make it any easier for the part-time directors to perform their supervisory duties.

One of the main advantages of the unitary system is said to be that it enables the non-executive directors to contribute more effectively to the formulation of the company's strategy and to monitor the performance of the executives; its major disadvantage is that it is more difficult for the non-executive directors to be impartial and independent. The UK Corporate Governance Code is designed to address issues of this nature in the listed company environment and is useful guidance for other large companies.

Directors

Given meetings are primarily called by, or on behalf of, the board of directors, further detail is provided here on the different types of directors.

As a general point it should be remembered that each director is an individual and brings to their role and the board as a collective their own experience, expertise and knowledge. It is the combination of these around the board table and their interactions in meetings that creates and dictates the tone of the leadership and culture of the company. Despite the different types of directors appointed, each has an individual and collective responsibility to understand and deliver this. Too often, companies have failed due to the ineffectiveness of the board. In contrast, a collegiate, effective and focused board can be a leading force to generate success for a company, its employees, shareholders and stakeholders. Hence the impact of having well run, effective meetings should not be underestimated.

Executive directors

An executive director is a director who holds an executive management position within the company. The model articles for private companies provide that directors may undertake any services for the company that the directors decide and are entitled to such remuneration as the directors determine. The appointment of executive directors and the terms of their appointments must, therefore, be approved by a resolution of the board unless the articles specifically allow another person or body to deal with these matters.

Precedent: Board minute of resolution to appoint managing director

There was produced a draft of a service contract between the company and [name] appointing [name] as managing director of the company with effect from [date], on the terms and conditions set out in the service contract.

It was resolved:

THAT [name] be appointed managing director of the company with effect from [date] on the terms set out in the service contract produced at the meeting and that the chair be authorised to sign the service agreement on behalf of the company.

The company's articles usually allow the board to delegate its powers to individual executive directors (pcls 5, clg 5 and plc 5). The terms of any delegation should be approved by a resolution of the board. In delegating its powers, the board may limit the executive's authority by imposing certain conditions. For example, the managing director may be given power to authorise capital expenditure up to a certain value, with any expenditure above that amount requiring board approval. Limits on the authority of individual directors may also be reinforced by the adoption of a schedule of matters reserved to the board.

Non-executive directors

Non-executive directors are directors who have not been appointed to any executive office within the company. The distinction between executive and non-executive directors will not always be clear, particularly where the status of the chair is concerned. The UK Corporate Governance Code recommends as a principle that the board of a listed company should include a balance of executive and non-executive directors (and, in particular, independent non-executive directors) so that no individual or small group of individuals can dominate the board's decision taking (Code principle G).

Whether or not they are independent, non-executive directors participate in the management of the company by attending board meetings and any committees of the board of which they are a member.

Alternate directors

An alternate director is someone appointed by a director to participate in his absence at board meetings and who may also have power to participate in his stead in any other directors' decision-making processes provided for by the articles. As the Act does not authorise a director to appoint an alternate or a proxy, a director may only appoint an alternate if the articles make specific provision to that effect.

An alternate director should receive notice of all meetings being held, whether or not they will be attending. It is possible to appoint another director as an alternate director or another candidate. The latter can be used to introduce a deputy or other colleague into the functioning of the board to support potential succession planning.

De facto directors

De facto directors are people who act as directors and are held out to be directors by the company through their title, even though they have never actually been legally appointed as directors or have ceased to be directors. A company will normally be bound by the acts of any such director, although they would not be authorised to call a board meeting or invited to attend board meetings as a director. Companies seeking to build an organisational structure using the title of director should be mindful of the implied and actual impact on the company that the acts of these individuals may have, particularly in their communications outside the company.

In the UK, the easiest way to confirm if an individual is a director or a de facto director, is to check the publicly available records of the company at Companies House.

Shadow directors

A shadow director is a person in accordance with whose instructions the directors of the company are accustomed to act. A person is not deemed to be a shadow director by reason only that the directors act on advice by him in a professional capacity (e.g. as a lawyer, accountant or financial adviser). Typically, a shadow director will be a shareholder or person of significant influence over the company through historical ties.

Extent of the directors' powers

In order to decide whether a decision is within the directors' powers and thus whether a formal meeting should be convened the following issues need to be addressed:

- A transaction will not be within the powers of the directors if it is not within the powers of the company.
- Member/shareholder approval may be required under the Companies Acts (or under other applicable legislation, rule or code), or under the company's articles of association, or by virtue of a shareholders' agreement. See **Appendix 1** for examples of matters that require shareholder/member approval.
- If the articles give the directors power to manage the company and the decision concerns the management of the company, the directors may act under those powers unless:
  - some other provision in the articles restricts their powers in relation to the matter concerned; or
  - the members have given the directors a valid instruction which restricts their freedom to act.
- If the decision does not concern the management of the company, the directors cannot act unless there is a special power in the articles which authorises them to do so.
- If the decision relates to a matter which would otherwise constitute a breach of their fiduciary duties, the directors cannot act unless the articles allow them to do so (e.g. fix their own remuneration).

It is important to note that a company will normally be bound by transactions with third parties entered into by the directors on its behalf even though the directors may have exceeded their powers. It is equally important to note that the directors have a duty to act within their powers and can be sued by the company for any losses it suffers as a result of any breach of that duty.

Matters reserved for the board

No matter how effective a board of directors may be, it is not possible for it to have hands-on involvement in every area of the company's business. An effective board controls the business but delegates day-to-day responsibility to the executive management.

That said, there are a number of matters which are required to be or, in the interests of the company, should only be, decided by the board of directors as a whole. It is incumbent upon the board to make it clear what these matters reserved for the board are.

As a minimum, matters that are reserved for the board would cover:

- the acquisition and disposal of assets of the company or its subsidiaries that are material to the company;
- investments;
- capital projects;
- authority levels;
- treasury policies; and
- risk management policies.

In addition, the board has responsibility for health and safety in the company and should ensure that this is reported on at each meeting.

Ultra vires and the objects clause

A company's constitution may include an objects clause which limits or defines the purposes for which the company was formed. Historically, all companies were required to include an objects clause in their memorandum of association. Under the Companies Act 2006, a company's articles may still include a statement of objects but need not do so. If they do not, the company's objects are deemed to be unrestricted (s. 31(1)). The statement of objects can no longer be included in the memorandum of association and any objects clause in the memorandum of association of a company incorporated under a prior Act is now deemed to form part of its articles (s. 28).

Historically, the objects clause had the effect of limiting the powers of the company and rendering any acts of the company or its directors in excess of those powers unenforceable. In practice, companies often attempted to draft objects clauses that placed no restriction whatsoever on the company's objects or powers. However, a company could, if it chose to do so, try to limit the purposes for which it should be used. For example, if the clause stated that the object of the company was to build and operate a railway, the company and its directors would have no power to do anything else. Such a company could not provide banking services and any transaction by the company with a third party in connection with banking would, therefore, be *ultra vires* (i.e. beyond the company's powers) and invalid.

Historically, a third party was deemed to have notice of any such limitations, and be bound by them, by virtue of the fact that the constitutional documents containing the objects clause were filed and made available for inspection at Companies House. However, various statutory modifications have reduced the impact of the *ultra vires* rule in recent years.

These rules are now contained in sections 39–42 of the 2006 Act. Section 39(1) provides that the validity of an act done by a company shall not be called into question on the ground of lack of capacity by reason of anything in its constitution. Section 40 provides that in favour of a person dealing with a company in good faith, the power of the directors to bind the company, or authorise others to do so, is deemed to be free of any limitation under the company's constitution.

Nevertheless, a member of the company may still bring proceedings to restrain an act which is beyond a company's capacity (s. 40(4)). In addition, it remains the duty of the directors to observe any limitations on their powers flowing from the company's constitution (s. 40(5)). Accordingly, the directors may still be held liable to compensate the company if it suffers a loss as a result of an *ultra vires* transaction approved by them. By participating in an *ultra vires* act, the directors are in breach of their duty to act within their powers under section 171.

The directors effectively bear most of the risks of an *ultra vires* transaction. However, the court can relieve the directors of their liability if it is satisfied that they have acted honestly and reasonably and ought fairly to be excused (s. 1157). In addition, the members may ratify any act of the directors which was beyond the capacity of the company (s. 239).

Dealing with urgent business

It is recommended that, in drawing up a schedule of matters reserved for the board, companies should also establish procedures for dealing with matters which need to be dealt with urgently between regular board meetings. These procedures should balance the need for urgency with the overriding principle that each director should be given as much information as possible, the time to consider it properly and an opportunity to discuss the matter prior to the commitment of the company. This is an important discipline because boards rarely meet more than once a month and urgent matters can arise with alarming frequency. There is not much point in having a schedule of matters reserved to the board if the board is constantly being asked to ratify things that have already happened. If the board wants to have the last word on the matters included in the schedule, it may need to meet more frequently and be prepared to hold ad hoc meetings to deal with urgent matters. It will not always be necessary or appropriate to hold an emergency board meeting. This would usually be reserved for matters of the utmost importance, such as the launch by another company of a takeover bid. Other arrangements can be adopted to deal with less important (but no less urgent) matters. These procedures could include some sort of informal consultation process conducted by email or telephone, or a written resolution procedure. If the matter is considered to be routine, and discussion is not thought to be necessary, one could question why it has been included as a matter reserved for the board in the first place, and whether it might not be better in the future to delegate such matters to a committee or individual.

The purpose of any informal consultation process will normally be to establish whether there is any substantial opposition to the proposal. Where this proves to be the case, it may be necessary to consider holding a formal board meeting. It is important to remember in this regard that, under most articles, any director can call a board meeting and that an informal consultation process will not normally constitute a valid board decision. In most cases, directors who oppose a proposal will not insist on a board meeting being held where it is clear that they are in the minority. However, they may take some convincing that they are in a minority, may genuinely believe that they can persuade the other directors of the merits of their case and may sometimes insist on a board meeting merely as a delaying tactic.

Generally speaking, it will be the chair who is expected to decide, within any guidelines set by the board, what procedures should be followed in cases where an urgent decision is required, and what action to take where a proposal proves to be controversial.

When making urgent decisions, special care should be taken to ensure that the directors have made any necessary declarations of interest before the company enters into the relevant transaction or arrangement. It will not normally be possible for the directors to make any new declarations using the general notice procedure as there will not normally be another board meeting before the company enters into the transaction. Accordingly, directors will need to declare any new and relevant interests in accordance with the written notice procedures provided for in section 184. The interests of the directors need to be borne in mind for the purposes of determining whether the board is capable of making a decision on the urgent business and whether there is in fact a valid majority in favour of the proposal.

If the method by which any urgent decision was reached does not constitute a valid decision-making process under the articles, the board should ratify the decision at its next meeting. If the decision was approved using a valid decision-making process, it should still be recorded, possibly by being noted in the minutes of the next board meeting, or if it was passed under some sort of written resolution procedure, in the usual manner adopted for such resolutions.

Operational versus strategic

The focus of the board of directors can be split into those that are primarily focused on operational matters and those that have more strategic aims. In practice, the two are often combined, which can result in one or other of the topics being lost in discussion. Too often, board meetings revolve around operational matters to the detriment of the board considering strategy, future-looking activities, market changes or other significant matters.

Board meetings also need to meet their oversight responsibilities, either directly in themselves or through delegation to a committee constituted to act on their behalf. However, it should be remembered that the board of directors cannot delegate their responsibilities in their entirety and board meetings need to reflect the continued ownership. As an example, the board cannot delegate their responsibilities for health and safety. Whereas they may delegate the operational application to a committee, every board meeting should accept the report of that committee and consider it in the context of their overall responsibility and ownership.

Holding effective board meetings with a differentiation between operational oversight and strategic direction are key to ensuring that meetings are effective and the governance framework that is in place is beneficial to the company as a whole.

Delegation

The board has the ability to delegate certain powers so, in the context of this book, this means that the convening, holding and minuting of meetings held by a forum with delegated powers has equal importance with that of a board meeting. However, for clarity it should be noted that the delegated forum does not have the right to convene a board meeting directly themselves.

To provide greater clarity, further background on the ability to delegate powers from the board is provided here.

Articles usually allow boards to delegate their powers. If no such provision is made, no such delegation is allowed.

The power to delegate to a committee cannot be used for an improper purpose (e.g. to exclude one or more of the directors from the forum where the board's decisions are taken).

The model articles provide that (pcls, clg and plc 5):

5.— (1) Subject to the articles, the directors may delegate any of the powers which are conferred on them under the articles—

(a)   to such person or committee;

(b)   by such means (including by power of attorney);

(c)   to such an extent;

(d)   in relation to such matters or territories; and

(e)   on such terms and conditions;

as they think fit.

> (2)   If the directors so specify, any such delegation may authorise further delegation of the directors' powers by any person to whom they are delegated.
>
> (3)   The directors may revoke any delegation in whole or part, or alter its terms and conditions.

Exclusive authority

It should be noted that where the board delegates its powers, it still retains the authority to exercise them itself. Thus, unless the articles provide otherwise, the board retains collateral power to act even though it has delegated those powers to a committee or person. Accordingly, even if it has delegated to a committee to the exclusion of its own powers, it could revoke that authority and act itself.

Sub-delegation

Committees and executive directors cannot sub-delegate their powers unless authorised to do so by the board. This does not mean that a committee may not ask one or more of its members to make recommendations to a future meeting of the committee, as long as the committee takes the final decision. It also does not limit the ability of the board to set up a group-wide structure which defines a primary committee and sub-committees thereunder. This would be most effective where a company is large, complex in structure or has international businesses with local management responsibilities.

Where no specific provision is made in the articles to allow sub-delegation, it is assumed that the directors have this power as part of their general authority to delegate. Even if this is not the case, the apparent lack of sub-delegated authority may be of little consequence because of general agency principles, the indoor management rule and the possibility that the person exercising the powers may be deemed to be authorised to do so under the articles. One of the rare circumstances in which these principles might not necessarily apply is where the act complained of involves a possible breach of directors' duties.

Restrictions on power to delegate

Although articles usually state that the directors may delegate 'any of their powers', this may not include special powers given to the directors by the articles (e.g. the power to fix the remuneration of directors). This is a difficult area and the answer will depend on the construction of the articles in each case. What is beyond doubt is that the general power to delegate will, unless otherwise stated, cover the powers given to the directors under the general management clause.

The model articles allow the directors to delegate 'any of the powers which are conferred on them under the articles' (art. 5). This would appear to allow them to delegate any special powers given to them under the articles.

Executive committee

It is worth noting here the role of the board versus that of the executive committee – if there is one. The executive committee, with a membership of the senior executive directors and other operational senior leaders is a committee of the board with specific delegated authorities related to the operations of the company.

Meetings of the executive committee should be administratively supported and documented in the same way that the board is; however, the board has oversight of the executive and is the primary decision-making forum. The board will also have the benefit of non-executive directors and, in most cases, an independent chair, to bring breadth to the strategic discussions and company oversight.

In smaller companies there is no differentiation between the executive committee and the board and the two function as a single forum. Where there is a separate executive committee, reference herein to internal board meetings are to those where a quorum is met, with further detail provided on the quorum for internal meetings.

Shareholder powers

Articles invariably contain a provision (known as the general management clause) which substantially reverses the common law rule that the company's powers must be exercised by the members in general meeting. Without such a clause it would be almost impossible for the directors to perform their operational duties.

The model articles note that (pcls, clg and plc 3 and 4):

Directors' general authority
3.   Subject to the articles, the directors are responsible for the management of the company's business, for which purpose they may exercise all the powers of the company.

Shareholders' reserve power
4.— (1)   The shareholders may, by special resolution, direct the directors to take, or refrain from taking, specified action.
      (2)   No such special resolution invalidates anything which the directors have done before the passing of the resolution.

It should be noted that a general management clause giving the directors all powers 'necessary in the management of the company' does not authorise them to present a winding-up petition without the approval of the members because winding up is not connected with the management of the company. Although, directors now have a statutory power to apply for a compulsory winding up under the Insolvency Act 1986, their powers may be subject to other limitations where this type of wording is adopted. Modern articles seek to avoid this problem by conferring powers on the directors without the condition that they be exercised in the management of the company.

Under a general management clause it is usually safe to assume that the directors can do anything the company can do as long as they are not prevented from doing that thing by the Act or another provision in the articles (or a memorandum provision now deemed to form part of the articles). The directors may not do anything which would be a breach of their fiduciary duty to the company unless the articles give them specific powers in that regard (e.g. pay themselves a salary). In addition, they may not delegate their powers unless the articles so provide.

Subject to the provisions of the Act

All powers conferred on the directors by the articles are subject to the provisions of the Companies Act 2006, regardless of whether this is stated in the articles. Thus, the directors cannot exercise any of the company's powers which are reserved to the members by the Act and must comply with the requirements of the Act when exercising their powers. For example, the directors cannot authorise loans above a certain amount to one of their number without the approval of the members. For further examples of transactions which require member approval, see Appendix 1 which shows the type of resolution required for various types of business at general meetings.

Increasingly under law and general business expectations, directors are required to have regard to the interests of various stakeholders, not just shareholders. This would include employees, suppliers, their community and the environment as a whole.

Subject to the articles

The general management clause is normally expressed as being subject to other provisions in the articles of association or, in the case of older companies, in the memorandum of association (which will now be deemed to form part of the articles by virtue of section 28). These may include provisions which:

- limit the capacity of the company and, therefore, the directors (e.g. an objects clause);
- limit the powers of the directors but not the members (e.g. a limit on directors' borrowing powers);
- reserve certain powers to the members (e.g. to approve the payment of dividend although the articles may allow the directors to pay an interim dividend without reference to the members);
- determine the procedures which the directors must follow when exercising their powers (e.g. regulation of proceedings at meetings of directors);
- allow the directors to delegate their powers;

- relax the conditions members must satisfy in order to exercise certain statutory rights; and
- provide additional procedures for removal of directors (e.g. by extraordinary resolution).

Directions given by members

Unless the articles contain some special provision allowing the members to give directions, the only way they can interfere in the exercise by the directors of their powers is to alter the articles in such a way that those powers revert back to the company in general meeting

Most articles provide an alternative method for the members to give instructions to the directors. Whether or not such provision is made, the members may achieve the same result by proposing and passing a special resolution (which requires a 75% majority) to amend the articles so that, for example, the powers revert back to the company in general meeting. Having done that, they need only pass an ordinary resolution (50% majority of those voting) to approve the proposed course of action.

In the case of the model articles (art. 4), the members may give the directors binding instructions by passing a special resolution. As the articles can be amended by special resolution, this does not place them in a significantly stronger position than if no such provision was made. The only real advantage is that it is not necessary for the resolution giving directions to be framed as an amendment of the articles. This allows the members to give directions in a specific instance without limiting the directors' powers generally. Although such a resolution would not, if passed, constitute an amendment to the articles, a copy of it would have to be filed at Companies House and attached to any copy of the articles issued after it had been passed.

Prior acts of directors not invalidated

Most articles make some provision to ensure that prior acts of the directors are not invalidated by any subsequent direction by the members (model articles plc 4(2)). This type of provision ensures that the members cannot reverse a decision of the directors which has already been acted upon. Without it, third parties could never be sure that the company would be bound by the acts of its directors.

Culture

It should also be remembered that the tone and culture of a company emanates from the top, evidenced by the actions of, and interactions within and without, the board. An efficient board, delegating powers, focusing on effective oversight rather than board ownership, and continued emphasis on opportunities and the future will create a powerful leadership team and governance framework.

The combination of all elements of effective governance evidenced by effective and efficient board protocols and procedures will cascade through a company to efficient and effective operations of the company itself. By setting the tone and expectations from the top, the board will lead by example. Conversely, diluted, long, ineffective or turbulent board meetings will be replicated in internal communications and other forums thus wasting time and energy and losing the engagement of employees at all levels.

Hence creating an effective framework for the operations of the board has a dual purpose of creating effective leadership and setting a positive culture for the company. While the operations of meetings may seem solely administrative in nature, their effective implementation can have a much wider beneficial effect.

This section will provide an outline of how board meeting operations can be effectively implemented so that its application becomes process driven enabling board meetings to focus on content.

Governance framework

Best practice is for a company to have a written governance statement that documents the purpose of the company, the framework of its governance and provides an overview of the core meetings and their purpose. This should also capture the interaction between legal entities or governance forums within an organisation, such as committees of the board.

By having this framework documented, the priority of meetings and their hierarchy in the organisation of a company is then clear. For example, does a risk committee of the board have priority on risk matters to a divisional or subsidiary board? If so, how do they interact and when should the main board be consulted or overrule actions of any of the more junior forums.

Within this framework, it may also be beneficial to document the standard operations of each meeting in terms of:

- membership and invited attendees;
- number of meetings per year;
- standard agenda items;
- attendance expectations (e.g. all members need to attend at least 75% of meetings otherwise their membership will be reviewed); and
- operational support for each meeting, documenting which function supports each meeting.

Items included in a governance statement should reflect the articles of the company in terms of operational application and any related points.

Even without a formal governance statement, a company can rely on its articles to provide the framework for meetings. Although it should be noted that articles tend to be read for reference as and when required rather than creating the foundation for meeting operations.

Subsidiary board meetings

Given that most large – and some smaller – companies have more than one legal entity under a parent or holding company umbrella, the interaction and prioritisation of legal entity meetings should be made clear. Defining the primary company for decision making will enable a clearer application of governance requirements.

If a parent company in a structure defines the strategic direction of the group, board meetings of subsidiary companies are likely to be operational in nature, functioning in a similar capacity to committees. Strategy in these companies would be escalated to the parent company board, while application of this group strategy may be discussed and agreed at subsidiary board meetings. This assumes that the subsidiary boards have different memberships to the parent company board.

Similarly, it should be made clear when and how escalation of delegation should be undertaken between the main board and subsidiary boards.

Committee meetings

An effective board, especially within a large or complex company, will utilise committees to delegate discussions and, in some cases, authority. This enables the board to cover a wider spectrum of topics utilising the expertise in the relevant forum. An audit committee benefits in having the majority, if not all, of its members coming from a financial background with expertise in finance and its applications, often evidenced by formal financial qualifications. A main board with a similar membership might stifle discussion of broader topics or may limit it to financial matters. Hence, implementing committees may enhance the ability of the main board to widen its discussion.

FRC guidance provides extensive guidance on the application, implementation and content of committees, particularly in terms of audit remuneration and nomination committees.

Standardisation

The expectation is that subsidiary and committee meetings would be convened, held, documented and supported in the same way as company board meetings.

Subsidiaries will have their own articles to reference in terms of the operations of their meetings and these should be balanced and standardised with those of the parent company. Care should be taken when standardising subsidiary board meetings where the parent company is non-UK based to ensure that requirements of the articles or law are not inadvertently ignored due to group standardisation or expectations. Equally, the flexibility of subsidiary board meetings should be applied to ensure that they are consistent with group expectation without creating duplication or contention between the two forums.

Despite no reference to committee meetings in the model articles, reference to board meetings herein can equally be applicable. It is imperative that minutes of committee meetings are kept to evidence decisions being made or escalated to the board to ensure an audit trail for future reference. It is also important that any of these decisions are kept within the guidelines included in the terms of reference of the committee and that delegated authority is clear and not over-stepped by the committee.

Electronic meetings

As a general rule, it is rare for companies to specifically enable general meetings to be held electronically, while conversely, standard board meetings are frequently held electronically with dial-in facilities. In the case of the latter, one constriction may be that of local legislative requirements or a need to recognise a physical base for the company evidenced by physical board meetings for tax purposes.

Holding general meetings electronically is restricted more by law and standard articles, although increasingly companies are adding the ability to hold electronic general meetings in their articles.

For the purpose of this introduction, it can be assumed that electronic means can be used for board meetings. Further detail on virtual meetings can be found in Chapter 4.

Minutes

The Act requires minutes to be kept of general meetings and meetings of directors and records to be kept of members' written resolutions and any informal decisions of sole members. Although this may, at times, seem a burdensome requirement, the company stands to benefit if it is done properly. Minutes signed by the chair are deemed to be evidence of the proceedings. In other words, if the company produces a set of minutes signed by the chair, those minutes are taken as evidence that the meeting actually took place properly and as evidence of the decisions taken at that meeting. Unless other evidence to the contrary is submitted during legal proceedings, the company will not need to tender any other evidence in support of the minutes.

Because the primary purpose of the minutes and records is to provide evidence of the decisions taken, it is essential that they accurately record those decisions. As a rule of thumb, this means they should contain sufficient information to enable a person who did not attend to ascertain what decisions were taken.

General duty to prepare and keep

Every company must keep the following records:

(a) minutes of all proceedings at meetings of directors (s. 248);
(b) minutes of general meetings:

      –   copies of any written resolutions of the members; and
      –   a record of any decisions taken by the sole member of a company (s. 355);
(c) minutes of any class meetings:
      –   copies of any written resolutions of a class of members; and
      –   a record of any decisions taken by the sole member of a class (s. 359).

The main purpose of these requirements could be said to be to ensure that a proper record is kept of the decisions made by and on behalf of the company by its members or directors as proof of those decisions and the fact that they were properly made. For this purpose, the records are given special evidential status. However, a subsidiary purpose in all cases is that certain people are given the right to inspect the records the company is required to keep.

Minutes of directors' written resolutions and unanimous decisions

The requirement in section 248 to keep minutes of proceedings at directors' meetings does not include a requirement to keep records of decisions made by directors as written resolutions; or unanimous decisions under procedures provided for by a company's articles; or of decisions made informally under the principle of unanimous consent. None of these decisions would normally be made at a meeting of directors and it would appear that, unlike minutes of meetings, even if records of these decisions are kept, they may not be afforded any special evidential status under section 249.

    The parallel requirements relating to members do require records to be kept of written resolutions, which are then afforded special evidential status (see below). The fact that the Act does not do so in relation to directors' decisions taken outside meetings cannot be viewed as an oversight because the model articles prescribed under the Act require the directors to keep a record of any such decisions for at least ten years. The reason why the Act makes no provision in this regard, but does in relation to members' written resolutions, is probably because it makes direct provision on the procedures to be followed for members' written resolutions but does not do so with regard to directors' written resolutions and informal decisions. The procedures to be followed in the case of directors' decision making are generally governed by the articles and the common law rather than the Act.

    This suggests that, even now, there may be some advantage to be gained from using the traditional decision-making method of holding a directors' meeting and preparing a set of minutes rather than using any other decision-making procedures because the minutes of such meetings are afforded special evidential status by the Act. It should be noted, however, that the records of written resolutions and unanimous decisions may still be given special evidential status by the courts under the common law.

    The model articles for private companies require the directors to ensure that the company keeps a record of every unanimous or majority decision taken by the directors for at least ten years from the date of the decision recorded (pcls 15 and clg 15). The model articles for public companies require the company secretary to ensure that the company keeps a record in writing of all directors' written resolutions for at least ten years from the date of their adoption (plc 18(4)). The relevant records are required to be kept 'in writing'. However, under all three versions of the model articles, this means in hard copy or electronic form. Unlike the model articles for private companies, the model articles for public companies do not specifically require minutes of directors' meetings to be kept and presumably rely on the statutory requirement in this regard.

Notwithstanding the fact that the articles may require records of directors' written resolutions and unanimous decisions to be kept, no offence will be committed if they fail to do so. However, the lack of evidence or an audit trail may have a detrimental impact on the ability to rely on records in the case of other proceedings.

Retention of minutes and related records

The 2006 Act imposes a minimum retention period of ten years in relation to minutes and other records to which sections 248 and 355 apply. This retention period only applies to records relating to meetings held, resolutions passed, or decisions made on or after 1 October 2007. Any records relating to earlier meetings, resolutions or decisions must be kept in accordance with the requirements of the Companies Act 1985 so should be retained permanently (i.e. for at least the life of the company and possibly beyond in view of the provisions of sections 1024 to 1034 (restoration to the register) and regulation 3A of the Insolvency Regulations 1994).

Notwithstanding, the fact that records kept under the provisions of the 2006 Act can now be kept for as little as ten years, it is still strongly recommended that they be kept for considerably longer, if not permanently. The reduction of the retention period in the 2006 Act seems to have been made in anticipation of reform to the law governing limitation of actions. The law generally restricts the time in which it is possible to commence civil legal proceedings. The relevant time limit in each case is known as the limitation period.

Irrespective of the legal issues involved, it is hard to imagine any company wishing to dispose of records such as minutes, which will often form an invaluable historical record and contain potentially useful business information. As far as company secretaries are concerned, the minutes could be invaluable if it ever proved to be necessary to re-construct the company's registers and records.

It is arguable whether it is necessary to keep the original signed copies of minutes if they have been stored electronically. However, if minutes are still manually signed, it may be advisable to keep the original copies for at least the minimum ten year period required for records held in accordance with the 2006 Act.

Form in which minutes and records should be kept

Records required to be kept under the 2006 Act in relation to meetings held, resolutions passed or decisions made on or after 1 October 2007 must be kept in the form and manner prescribed by the provisions of the 2006 Act on company records in sections 1134–1138.

Section 1134 states that for the purposes of these requirements company records means 'any register, index, accounting records, agreement, memorandum, minutes or other document required by the Companies Acts to be kept by a company' and 'any register kept by the company of its debenture holders'.

Section 1135 states that the company records may be kept in hard copy or electronic form and may be arranged in such manner as the directors of the company think fit, provided that the information is adequately recorded for future reference (s. 1135(1)). Where the records are kept in electronic form, they must be capable of being reproduced in hard copy form (s. 1135(2)). Failure to comply with these requirements is an offence for which any officer in default may be fined (s. 1135 (3) and (4)).

Where a company's records are kept otherwise than in bound books, adequate precautions should be taken to guard against falsification and to facilitate the discovery of falsification (s. 1138(1)). Failure to comply with this requirement is also an offence for which any officer in default may be fined (s. 1138(2) and (3)).

The requirements of sections 382–383 of the Companies Act 1985 still apply in relation to minutes of general meetings held, members' resolutions passed, and decisions of sole members made before 1 October 2007 and to the inspection and copying of those records. This requires minutes of general meetings to be entered in books kept for that purpose and this rule must still be assumed to apply for minutes required to be kept under that section of the 1985 Act. Section 382A of the 1985 Act requires a record of any members' written resolution passed before 1 October 2007 (and of the signatures) to be entered in a book in the same way as minutes of general meetings.

Minute books

Minutes were traditionally handwritten in bound books kept for that purpose. Although it is still perfectly acceptable to record minutes in this manner, it is far more likely that minutes will be produced as a printout of a word-processor file or stored and shared electronically. Where bound books are still used, the printout or typed-up copy of the minutes can then be pasted in the serially numbered pages of the bound minute book. Copies of other resolutions or records can also be produced in the same manner and pasted into the bound minute book.

Minute books specifically designed for purpose often include pages that allow an index to be created. Many company secretaries use these to index the minutes by subject and names mentioned. Although there is no legal requirement to do this, it is considered good practice and will be particularly helpful when it is necessary to refer (e.g. to decisions of the directors which have the effect of modifying the company's articles (e.g. by setting the quorum for directors' meetings)).

Many companies use loose-leaf minute books. Although this is allowed under the Act, additional precautions must be taken to guard against falsification as they are not bound books. If a loose-leaf minute book is used, it is preferable (but not essential) to use one which has a locking device either in the spine or between the covers. Strict control should be exercised over access to the keys to the minute book and any duplicates should be lodged in a secure place such as a safe or safety deposit box. When a loose-leaf folder is used, the pages should be serially numbered at the time of insertion in the binder, normally under the control of the secretary or the person acting as the secretary to the relevant body. The minuted items are also usually numbered consecutively from one meeting to the next so as to prevent the insertion of a false set of minutes.

All minute books, whether bound books or loose-leaf folders, should be kept in a secure place. Ideally this should be a robust, lockable and fire-proof filing cabinet or safe to which access is restricted. This is of even greater importance if minutes are kept in an ordinary unlockable, loose-leaf folder.

Separate minute books would normally be used to keep minutes of general meetings and meetings of directors, with subsidiary minute books being used for each board committee. The items minuted at meetings would normally be numbered consecutively from No 1 onwards throughout each minute book. One would normally expect the minutes of meetings to be entered in the minute books in date order, and the appearance of any minutes out of order could give rise to questions as to their veracity should the minute book ever need to be tendered as evidence in legal proceedings.

If for any genuine reason, including oversight, it is necessary to insert a set of minutes or a record in a minute book out of date order, it would be advisable for some sort of reference to be included in a subsequent set of minutes of that body confirming that the minutes are genuine and explaining the reason for the insertion. This might also be necessary if two sets of minutes have used the same serial numbers. In either case, the very least that should be done is for a note to be included in the minute book by the chair or the secretary explaining the reason for the discrepancy.

Increasingly companies are using electronic board portals to collate board packs, support meetings and enable effective minute taking. Such electronic formats also enable minutes and other meeting records to be stored electronically through third-party suppliers thus reducing the need for in-house support and expertise. Increasingly, these are being used by larger companies where the duplication of electronic and hard copy records must be documented and managed effectively.

Guarding against falsification

Minutes may not be acceptable as evidence unless adequate precautions have been taken to guard against falsification and to facilitate its discovery. In a judgment prior to the current legislation, a loose-leaf minute book was rejected on the basis that: 'anyone wishing to do so . . . can take a number of leaves out and substitute any number of other leaves. It is a thing with which anyone disposed to be dishonest can easily tamper'. Although the law allows companies to use loose-leaf minute books, their content could easily be challenged if it could be proved that the security measures taken to guard against falsification were inadequate.

Some or all of the following safeguards should be adopted where minutes are kept in minute books:

- sequential numbering of the minutes of each type of meeting (e.g. if the last minute of the first meeting of company's board of directors is numbered minute 20, the first minute of the second meeting of the board of directors should be numbered minute 21 and so on);
- the chair should initial every page;
- pages should be numbered sequentially on specially printed paper;
- when pasted into bound books or onto number sheets, the chair's signature and initials should start on the printed sheet and run on to the bound page;
- the minute book should be kept in a safe (preferably fireproof) with restricted access;
- a lockable binder should be used, particularly for minutes kept in a loose-leaf folder; and
- minutes of general meetings and board meetings should be kept in separate books or folders to prevent members (who are entitled to inspect the minutes of general meetings) from gaining access to the minutes of meetings of directors and managers.

It should be noted that serially numbering minutes does not of itself prevent falsification, particularly where the series is started again each year or the minutes are kept in a loose-leaf folder. Where a loose-leaf folder is used, the original pages can simply be removed and new ones inserted with false minutes or records which utilise the same serial numbers. Where the numerical series is started again at the beginning of each year (e.g. by using a system such as 2009/0001 for the first minute in the year 2009 and 2010/0001 for the first minute in the year 2010) it would, in theory, be possible for somebody to insert a false set of minutes at the end of each year unless some system is used to record the fact that a particular minute or record is the last entry for that year. It would be even worse if the numbering system was based on the month in which the meeting was held (e.g. 2009/03/0001 for the first minute of a meeting held in March 2009). Using numbering based on years, months or dates will undoubtedly make cross-referencing and indexing easier but may also make it easier for a person to falsify the minutes. Accordingly, if any such system is used, even greater precautions should be taken to guard against falsification, such as the use of bound books, lockable folders and the initialling of each page by the chair.

Electronic minutes and records

If minutes are kept in electronic form they must still be authenticated by the chair to be treated as evidence of the proceedings under section 249 (minutes of directors' meetings) or section 356 (minutes of general meetings and records of resolutions). Any doubts over the admissibility of electronic signatures in legal proceedings for these purposes have been removed by the Electronic Communications Act 2000. Accordingly, the chair could apply an electronic signature to a file containing the minutes which could then be stored on a computer. As the security of the technique used to apply the electronic signature could have a bearing on the weight the courts give to the minutes, it would be preferable for the chair to use the most modern cryptographic techniques to do this.

Different considerations arise where it is proposed, for example, to scan manually signed minutes for retention in computerised form and to destroy the original paper copies. Where this is done, the electronic image may ultimately need to be tendered in evidence in court, as secondary evidence of the signature of the minutes and of their contents. To ensure that it is acceptable as evidence in this regard, it will be essential to follow the British Standards Institute's Code of Practice for Legal Admissibility of Information Stored Electronically.

If minutes are kept in computerised form, they must still be capable of being reproduced in hard copy form (s. 1135(2)) for at least ten years (or indefinitely if they are 1985 Act records). Ideally, whenever a new computer system or new software is adopted, checks should be carried out to ensure that the files containing the minutes can still be read. If not, it may be possible to convert them into a suitable format. However, if this is not possible (e.g. because doing so would compromise the electronic signature), it may be necessary to retain the old hardware and software forever. These considerations will obviously be less of a problem for minutes and records kept under the 2006 Act regarding meetings and decisions made on or after 1 October 2007 as these only need to be kept for ten years. Nevertheless, many companies will probably wish to keep these records for longer than the ten-year minimum prescribed by the Act.

Modern electronic storage systems and board portals have the added benefit of creating an audit trail of document amendments thus enabling clear oversight of changes and providing a guard against unauthorised changes.

Inspection of minutes and other records

The records required to be kept under section 355 of the 2006 Act (i.e. minutes of general meetings held, records of members' resolutions passed, and decisions of sole members made on or after 1 October 2007) must be made available for inspection in accordance with section 358 of the 2006 Act. Section 358 only requires records relating to the previous ten years to be made available for inspection. No company will have ten years' worth of records that have to be made available for inspection under this rule until October 2017. All minutes of general meetings held, records of resolutions passed, and decision of sole members made before 1 October 2007 must be made available for inspection and copying under the rules set out in section 383 of the Companies Act 1985 (i.e. permanently).

Any 2006 Act records relating to the previous ten years must be made available for inspection to members without charge:

(a) at the company's registered office; or
(b) at a place specified in regulations under section 1136 (known as the single alternative inspection location or SAIL) (s. 358).

A company must give the registrar notice of the place at which the records are kept available for inspection, and of any change in that place, unless they have at all times been kept at the company's registered office (s. 358(2)). The regulations made under section 1136 allow a company to make its company records available for inspection at a single location other than its registered office (see the Companies (Company Records) Regulations 2008 (SI 2008/3006)). That location must have been notified to the registrar of companies and must be situated in the same part of the United Kingdom as the company is registered (reg. 3 of SI 2008/3006).

Any member may require a copy of any of these 2006 Act records on payment of a fee (s. 358(4)) which is prescribed under regulation 4 of the Companies (Fees for Inspection and Copying of Company Records) Regulations 2007 (SI 2007/2612).

Members are entitled to be provided with copies of minutes of general meetings within 14 days of making a request. If the company wrongly refuses to allow an inspection or fails to provide copies of the minutes within the proper time, any officer in default can be fined (s. 358(5) and (6)). In such circumstances, the court may order an immediate inspection or direct that the desired copies be sent (s. 358(7)).

Members are entitled to be accompanied by an advisor when they inspect the minutes of general meetings.

The requirements of sections 382 to 383 of the 1985 Act still apply in relation to the records which must be kept of minutes of general meetings held, members' resolutions passed, and decisions taken before 1 October 2007 and to the inspection and copying of those records.

Section 383 of the 1985 Act requires the books containing the minutes of proceedings of general meetings of the company (which should also include records of members' written resolutions) to be kept at the company's registered office and to be open to the inspection of any member without charge (s. 383(1), 1985 Act). It should be noted that section 383(1) does not allow the inspection place to be anywhere other than the company's registered office, although the provisions of the 2006 Act and the Companies (Company Records) Regulations 2008 (SI 2008/3006) may prevail in this regard and enable the records to be made available either at the registered office or some other place notified to the registrar.

Under section 383(3) of the 1985 Act, members are entitled on payment of a prescribed fee to be furnished with a copy of any minutes of general meetings (and presumably any written resolutions included in the minute book) within seven days of making a request. The relevant fee for these purposes is 10p per 100 words or part thereof. This is different to the prescribed fee under the Companies Act 2006, which is 10p per 500 words (plus expenses). The fee for the purposes of 1985 Act records is prescribed in paragraph 3(b) of Schedule 2 to the Companies (Inspection and Copying of Registers, Indices and Documents) Regulations 1991, which continues to apply in respect of requests relating to minutes of general meetings which are subject to section 383 of the Companies Act 1985 by virtue of paragraph 40(2) of Schedule 3 to the Companies Act 2006 (Commencement No. 3, Consequential Amendments, Transitional Provisions and Savings) Order 2007 (see reg. 5(3) of the Companies (Fees for Inspection and Copying of Company Records) Regulations 2007 (SI 2007/2612)).

Common inspection and copying rules

The Companies (Company Records) Regulations 2008 (SI 2008/3006) (the Records Regulations 2008) set out the obligations of companies in relation to company records (including minutes of general meetings and records of resolutions, etc.) in respect of which there is a right of inspection. The following rules apply to inspection and copying under section 358 of the 2006 Act.

A private company is required to make its company records available for inspection for at least two hours between 9 am and 5 pm on a working day. A person wishing to inspect the records of a private company is required to give the company at least 10 working days' notice of the working day on which they wish to carry out their inspection. However, they only need to give two days' notice if they wish to inspect the records during the notice period of a general meeting or a class meeting or during a period for agreeing a written resolution under section 297(1) of the Act, provided that the two-day notice period given for their inspection request both begins and ends during the relevant period. The person wishing to inspect is also required to specify in both cases the time at which he wants to start his inspection on the relevant day, which must be between the hours of 9 am and 3 pm. The company is then required to make its records available for inspection for at least two hours from the time specified (reg. 4 of the Records Regulations 2008).

A public company is required to make its company records available for inspection between 9 am and 5 pm on every working day (reg. 5 of the Records Regulations 2008).

A 'working day' is defined for these purposes in section 1173(1) of the 2006 Act as a day that is not a Saturday or Sunday, Christmas Day, Good Friday or any day that is a bank holiday under the Banking and Financial Dealings Act 1971 in the part of the United Kingdom where the company is registered.

A company is not required to present a company record in a different order, structure or form to the one set out in that record (reg. 6(1) of the Records Regulations 2008). A person may make a copy of a company record but a company is not required to assist that person in making that copy (reg. 6(2) of the Records Regulations 2008). However, nothing in the regulations prevents a company from providing more extensive facilities than those provided for in the regulations (see s. 1137(5)(a)).

The regulations also expand upon the obligations of companies in relation to the provision of copies of company records. The terms 'hard copy form', 'electronic copy form' and related expressions are defined in section 1168 of the Act. Company records may be kept in hard copy or electronic form provided that the information is adequately recorded (see s. 1135(1)) but if kept in electronic form, they must be capable of being reproduced in hard copy form (see s. 1135(2)).

A person who requests a hard copy of a company record must be supplied with a hard copy (reg. 7 of the Records Regulations 2008). A person who requests an electronic copy of a record must be supplied with an electronic copy unless the record is only kept in hard copy (reg. 8(1) and (2) of the Records Regulations 2008). The company can decide the electronic form in which it will supply the record (reg. 8(1) of the Records Regulations 2008) (subject to s. 1168(5) and (6) which imposes conditions relating to the form and legibility of the copy).

Where a company provides a copy of a company record in electronic form to a company member or debenture holder, it is not then obliged to send a hard copy of that record to such a person free of charge (reg. 8(3) of the Records Regulations 2008). Regulation 8(3), in conjunction with section 1143, disapplies section 1145 of the Act.

A company is not required to present information in a copy of a company record in a different order, structure or form to the one set out in that record (reg. 9 of the Records Regulations 2008).

Meetings of directors

It is standard practice to distribute copies of the minutes to the directors before the next meeting or with the papers for the next succeeding meeting. In addition, however, directors have a common law right to inspect the minutes and may be accompanied by an advisor when they do so.

Members, creditors and members of the public are not entitled to inspect nor to take copies of the minutes of meetings of directors or managers.

Inspection by auditors

A company's auditors have a right of access at all times to the company's books, accounts and vouchers (in whatever form they are held) and such information and explanations necessary for the performance of their duties as auditors (s. 499). The company's books presumably include all of the company's statutory books and records, including any minutes and records the company is required to keep under ss 248 or 355. The auditors' letter of engagement will normally make some reference to the obligation of the company to make these and other records available for inspection.

Approval and signature by chair

Minutes are evidence of the proceedings of the relevant meeting once they have been signed by the chair of that meeting or by the chair of the next succeeding meeting (ss 249 and 356).

Companies are given considerable leeway in the methods which they can adopt for approving the minutes with the recommendation that boards should establish written procedures with regard to minutes of board meetings. Although minutes which have not been signed by the chair may be admissible as evidence of the proceedings, they will certainly not be accorded the same weight if they were ever challenged.

General meetings

It is standard practice for the minutes of general meetings to be signed shortly after the meeting by the person who acted as the chair of the meeting. This is often done at the first available board meeting so as to allow the other directors to make any comments but also so that an entry may be made in the board minutes to the effect that they were duly signed. If this procedure is followed, it is not necessary to seek the approval of the members at the next general meeting nor, indeed, to refer to the minutes of the previous meeting at all.

If the person who acted as the chair of the meeting is unable or unwilling to sign the minutes, they should be signed by the chair of the next general meeting.

If it is not possible to adopt this procedure, then the minutes may need to be read at the next general meeting (they cannot be taken as read unless all the members have received a copy) and a resolution put to the meeting that they be approved.

Meetings of directors

Board minutes are usually distributed in draft form to the directors for comment and signed by the chair of the next succeeding board meeting. They are often included in the agenda papers for the meeting at which they are to be approved, particularly if any changes have been made to the first draft as a consequence of comments by directors. At the meeting, the minutes are usually taken as read and a motion is put recommending their adoption as a true and accurate record of the proceedings of the meeting to which they refer. If approved, they should be signed immediately by the chair who need not have been present at the original meeting.

The chair may, however, sign the minutes before the next succeeding meeting of the board and need not necessarily give the other directors an opportunity to comment on them before doing so. This will rarely be necessary and any chair who follows this procedure should be prepared to explain to his fellow directors why he departed from the usual practice and expect to have the minutes scrutinised more closely than might normally be the case. If this procedure is followed and the directors disagree with the chair's interpretation of the proceedings, they could pass a resolution to that effect which would be recorded in the minutes of that meeting. The minutes which were the subject of the disagreement should not be altered although it might be sensible for the secretary to make a marginal note in the original minutes cross-referring to the subsequent decision.

In the unlikely event that the chair refuses to sign the minutes, it should be recorded in the minutes of the next meeting that they were approved as a true record by the other directors who were present at the original meeting, if that was the case.

Amendment of minutes

Alterations can be made to the minutes before they have been signed as an accurate record by the chair. The directors may wish to amend the company secretary's original draft and may request the chair to amend the draft that is put before them at the next board meeting. Once the minutes have been included in the papers for a board meeting, best practice dictates that they should be amended by long hand or typed entries on the original copy and each amendment should be initialled by the chair before signing the minutes themselves. It may not be practical to follow precisely the same procedures where the minutes are to be kept on a computer and signed by the chair electronically.

Alterations should not be made after the minutes have been signed by the chair. If the directors present at a subsequent meeting disagree with a decision taken at a previous meeting that is properly recorded in signed minutes, they should pass a further resolution rescinding or amending their previous decision which should be recorded in the minutes of that meeting. Similarly, if it is discovered after the minutes have been signed that they are inaccurate, a further resolution should be passed and recorded in the minutes of the meeting at which the inaccuracy was raised.

Details which were not available at the meeting should not be inserted in the minutes (e.g. the date of a call). Equally, attendees should not be able to add content to the minutes that was not made at the meeting (e.g. adding personal comment on a subject matter after further consideration post the meeting) as minutes should be an accurate record of decisions and, where included, the discussion held at the meeting.

However, resolutions documented in the minutes can be framed so that they allow a director or the secretary to action a matter which is contingent upon further details being available.

Who should take the minutes?

Preparing minutes of company meetings is one of the company secretary's core duties. If the company secretary is not available, it normally falls to the deputy or assistant secretary to undertake the task. Although not good practice, there is nothing to prevent someone else performing these functions. Where the named company secretary is also a director of the company and in attendance at the meeting in their role as director, it is preferable to have an alternate taking the minutes to enable the director who is also the company secretary to fully engage in the meeting in their role as director.

The company secretary and the directors can be fined for any default by the company of the provisions of the Act relating to the maintenance of minutes (s. 248(3) and (4) and section 355(3) and (4)). Although the directors share responsibility with the company secretary (if any) for ensuring that minutes are kept, it is difficult for anyone to contribute effectively to the business of the meeting if they are also required to record the proceedings. It could also be argued that they lack the impartiality which the secretary can provide when drafting the minutes.

It is quite common for company secretaries to use an assistant to help take notes of the proceedings. This allows them to concentrate more on their advisory role during the meeting. It is also increasingly common for a recording or transcript of the meeting to be made to assist in the preparation of the minutes. This can be particularly helpful at AGMs where it is often difficult for the secretary to record all the names of speakers from the floor and, sometimes, difficult to understand the meaning of their questions or statements.

It should also be noted that transcripts and recordings of meetings can be tendered as evidence during legal proceedings to rebut the evidence of the minutes. These would have to be disclosed during the discovery process prior to those proceedings. Where meetings are being recorded, to comply with legislation, it should be noted at the outset of the meeting that this is being done so that all attendees have prior knowledge and can object if they so wish. Care should also be taken when keeping audio copies of meetings to ensure that this complies with application legislation.

Content and style

Different people often have different views about what took place at a meeting. These views tend to become even more polarised as those present become blessed with the benefit of hindsight. There is little point holding formal meetings if no-one can remember what was decided at the meeting. The decisions taken must be recorded and those present should confirm that the record properly reflects what was decided. Preparing minutes is, therefore, an essential part of the decision-making process.

The art of preparing minutes is not simply doing so concisely, accurately and clearly in the shortest possible time, although achieving these objectives requires a degree of aptitude. It is knowing when to sacrifice or adapt these principles. Detailed explanations may sometimes be required. On other occasions, brevity will be the only way to document the discussions held.

In some companies as house style is followed that either requires concise minutes or, conversely, dictates that every detail of each discussion is incorporated in the minutes. Hence, although certain conventions are normally followed, the presentational style can be tailored. What can never be compromised, however, is the principle that the minutes should contain an accurate record of the decisions taken. It may be beneficial to briefly confirm how each decision should be documented with the chair at the time the decision is finalised in the meeting. In this way all attendees will also hear how a decision will be documented in the minutes.

Although the minutes should represent a true and accurate record of the proceedings of the meeting, it is neither necessary, nor is it desirable, to include a transcript of the proceedings, unless this is a requirement of the company itself. The minutes should record the decisions taken and provide sufficient background to those decisions. Many different styles of presentation may be adopted provided that the minutes include the following basic elements:

- name of the company;
- type of meeting (e.g. annual general meeting (AGM) or audit committee);
- place where the meeting was held;
- day of the meeting (optional);
- date of the meeting;
- time of the meeting (optional, but see below);
- names and/or numbers present (see Record of attendance below);
- record of the proceedings; and
- chair's signature.

Time of the meeting

Although it may not be strictly necessary to include the time of the meeting, there may be good reason to do so. If the time of the meeting is included in the heading of the minutes, it ought to state the actual time that the meeting started, rather than the time the meeting was meant to start. It may be necessary to record the time a meeting started as evidence that one meeting took place before another where, for example, the business at the second meeting was conditional upon approval being obtained at the first. It may also be necessary to record the time certain decisions were made, for example for tax purposes.

Record of attendance

There is no need to keep a separate record of attendance at either general or board meetings unless the articles so provide. However, it is important to include sufficient details in the minutes to show that a quorum was present for each item of business or, where relevant, that a disinterested quorum was present. It should also be clear from the minutes who chaired the meeting. This is normally done by adding the words 'chairperson' or 'chair' next to the name of the relevant person. If someone other than a director chairs a general meeting, this should also be apparent from the minute referring to the election of the chair.

Best practice, whether required or not, is to include the names of the directors present at meetings (including general meetings) to be included in the minutes of that meeting. If a director attends for only part of a meeting, this should be recorded in the minutes, normally by annotating the list of directors present with the words such as 'for minutes 23 to 34 only'. By doing so, it should be clear whether or not a disinterested quorum was present throughout the meeting. It should be assumed that the director who was present when a decision was made was present for that item unless he absents himself from participating in that decision, which he may sometimes do on the basis that he has not participated in the discussion.

Although it is not necessary to record in the minutes of general meetings the names of the members present at the meeting, it is essential to record the numbers present or represented so that the minutes prove that a quorum was present for each item of business.

Record of proceedings

The record of the proceedings should include the text of any resolutions put to the meeting and the result of any vote. It should also include a record of any amendments and procedural resolutions proposed at the meeting and the results of any vote on them. Any rulings made by the chair should also be recorded (e.g. on a demand for a poll). If a resolution is passed on a show of hands it is only necessary to state that the chair declared the resolution carried. If a poll is called and taken, the number of votes for and against should be included in the minutes together with a statement as to whether the resolution was or was not carried.

Precedent: Board minute reflecting resolution to allot securities via vote

The chair proposed as a special resolution:

THAT the authority and power conferred on the Directors by Article [No.] (Authority to allot securities) of the Articles of Association of the Company be renewed for the period expiring on the date of the annual general meeting of the Company to be held in [year + 1] and that:

a   for the purposes of Article [No.], the prescribed amount for the above period shall be [amount 1] and

b   for the purposes of the proviso to Article [No.], the aggregate nominal amount of equity securities allotted wholly for cash during such period, otherwise than as mentioned in such proviso, shall not exceed [amount 2].

[Name], a member of the company, proposed an amendment the effect of which would have been to substitute [amount 3] as the prescribed amount for the purposes of Article [No.]. The chair ruled the amendment out of order and explained that it was not possible to amend the substance of a special resolution.

After further discussion, the chair put the resolution to the meeting and declared it carried.

[Name], a member of the company, and [name], a proxy representing a member of the company, demanded a poll on the resolution. The chair informed the meeting that the demand was valid and that a poll would be held immediately at which representatives of the company's auditors would act as scrutineers. After the chair informed the meeting of the poll procedures, voting papers were issued and collected by the company's registrars.

The results of the poll were as follows:

For: 13,567,342
Against: 1,003,231
Votes withheld: 4,006

All papers presented at the meeting should be clearly identified in the minutes and retained for reference. In the interests of brevity, it is possible to refer in the minutes to papers presented at the meeting which contain the detailed proposals, rather than reproduce the proposals in full. Any such document should be initialled by the chair for the purpose of identification and the minutes should record that fact. However, it should be noted that minutes are not user friendly at the best of times and it will not help matters if readers have to make continuous reference to other documents in order to discern what decisions were taken. In addition, documents which are essential to understand the record of decisions taken in the minutes should be retained in the same way and for as long as the minutes themselves.

Precedent: Minute of papers presented to the meeting

There was produced and discussed a document prepared by [name] entitled 'Going greener' (Board paper 94/12), on the company's environmental policy. It was resolved:

> THAT no decision could be made to implement the proposals in the paper without detailed costings. The chair requested the presenter to resubmit the proposals at the next board meeting together with a schedule of the projected costs of implementing each of the recommendations for each of the company's subsidiaries.

Registers which may form a subset of the minutes

It is relatively common for certain matters that would otherwise need to be recorded in the minutes of directors' meetings to be included in registers specifically kept for that purpose. Examples include:

(a) registers of documents sealed;
(b) registers of transfers;
(c) registers of allotments; and
(d) registers of disclosures by directors of interests in transactions or arrangements.

For example, where the articles require the board to authorise the use of the company seal, approval may be obtained and recorded in the minutes by making reference to entries in the sealing register. Where such registers are used, they should be treated as a subset of the minutes, accorded the same sort of security and retained for at least as long as the original minutes which refer to them.

Matters which must be recorded in board minutes
Contract with sole member who is also a director

Where a limited company having only one member enters into a contract with the sole member who is also a director of the company and the contract is not entered into in the ordinary course of the company's business, the company must, unless the contract is in writing, ensure that the terms of the contract are either:

(a) set out in a written memorandum; or
(b) recorded in the minutes of the first meeting of the directors of the company following the making of the contract (s. 231).

If a company fails to comply with this section an offence is committed by every officer of the company who is in default, and they may be fined (s. 231(3) and (4)).

However, failure to comply with this requirement in relation to a contract does not affect the validity of the contract (s. 231(6)), and nothing in section 231 should be read as excluding the operation of any other enactment or rule of law applying to contracts between a company and a director of the company (s. 231(7)).

Declarations of interest

If a director makes a declaration of interest at a meeting of directors under section 177 (proposed transactions or arrangements) or section 182 (existing transactions or arrangements), the declaration must be recorded in the minutes as part of the proceedings.

In addition, if a director makes a declaration of interest:

(a) by giving notice in writing in accordance with section 184 hc must send the notice to the other directors. In addition the making of the declaration is deemed to form part of the proceedings at the next meeting of the directors after the notice is given, and the provisions of section 248 (minutes of meetings of directors) apply as if the declaration had been made at that meeting (s. 184(5));

(b) by general notice in accordance with section 185, the notice is not effective unless it is given at a meeting of the directors or the director takes reasonable steps to secure that it is brought up and read at the next meeting of the directors after it is given (in either case, one would expect the minutes to record the fact that the director had given general notice of an interest) (s. 185(4));

(c) under section 182 (duty to declare interest in existing transaction or arrangement) and the director is the sole director of a company that is required to have more than one director, the declaration must be recorded in writing and the making of the declaration is deemed to form part of the proceedings at the next meeting of the directors after the notice is given, and the provisions of section 248 (minutes of meetings of directors) apply as if the declaration had been made at that meeting (s. 186(1)).

Conclusion

The general principles of having effective meetings of a company, with records that clearly document the proceedings and that are available for subsequent review, underpins good governance of a company. While not the driving force for business success, ineffective meetings, poor tone from the top or, conversely, too much time and resources spent on meetings can be severely detrimental to a company's success. It may seem that meetings are purely administrative, but their use and the interaction of attendees during the meetings can have a powerful and positive influence on the business.

4 – Communication, technology and virtual meetings

At a time of great uncertainty as seen globally as a result of Covid-19, companies and their directors will need to focus on making the critical decisions that will enable them to get through the period with least disruption. From a governance perspective, the impact of this crisis has served to rapidly escalate the implementation of virtual meetings and the use of technology to support continued effectiveness.

The expectation is that, once these new ways of working are implemented, they may become normalised with legislation needing review to ensure it meets the requirements to both monitor and underpin the use of technology in the governance space. In the meantime, legislation covers the requirements for communications, the methods of communication and framework in which it sits.

This chapter will initially position the current communications legislation and its application. Thereafter, it will introduce guidance for virtual board and committee meetings. Finally, it will present the challenges and considerations for considering virtual annual general meetings (AGMs), the current thinking and updated advice as a result of Covid-19.

On this latter point, The Chartered Governance Institute, working alongside reputable advisers and government departments, has provided timely guidance for companies needing to hold AGMs during the crisis as well as further guidance on holding virtual board and committee meetings. This chapter replicates and draws heavily on these guidance notes to provide a framework for virtual meetings for companies to adopt. It should be noted that, as a first step, companies should ensure that their articles enable the use of technology and virtual meetings noting that, while most recently incorporated companies do have this ability, those with older version articles would benefit from update or clarification. In this respect, reference to, and alignment with, the section on communication is advisable.

It is also worth noting one other technological advancement that can be beneficially implemented at AGMs and that is the use of electronic voting. The ability for attendees at a physical meeting to be able to vote electronically has enabled much faster responses to votes, and greater efficiency in meetings as a result. No longer just used in TV gameshows, their implementation can enable meetings of large groups of members to be more efficiently monitored and tracked for voting results during the meeting.

This chapter is separated into:

- communication and the current legislation;
- virtual board and committee meetings; and
- virtual annual general meetings.

While the impact of Covid-19 will dissipate over time, the guidance provided gives a thought-provoking list of considerations for companies seeking alternate ways to hold meetings with multiple stakeholders, whether members or bondholders. As such, the majority of the guidance has been provided within this chapter for consideration of options.

Communication under the law

The provisions of the Companies Act 2006 that specify the permitted methods of communication both to and from companies are known as the 'company communications provisions'. The relevant provisions in Part 37 (ss 1143–1148) and Schedules 4 and 5 of the Act came into force on 20 January 2007. They make hard copy the default method of communication, but allow electronic communications to be used where the intended recipient has agreed to accept communications in that manner.

The company communications provisions have effect 'for the purposes of any provision of the Companies Acts that authorises or requires documents or information to be sent or supplied by or to a company' (s. 1143(1)). However, their application in this regard is subject to any requirements imposed, or contrary provision made, by or under any enactment (s. 1143(2)) and, in relation to documents or information to be sent or supplied to the registrar, subject to the provisions of Part 35 (s. 1143(3)). For the purposes of subsection (2), a provision in any other enactment is not to be regarded as contrary to the company communications provisions by reason only of the fact that it expressly authorises a document or information to be sent or supplied in hard copy form, in electronic form or by means of a website (s. 1143(4)).

The company communications provisions do not apply to any documents or information required to be sent under other legislation or rules (e.g. the Listing Rules), unless those things can also be interpreted as being required or authorised under the Companies Acts. Even where something seems to be required or authorised by the Companies Acts, care needs to be taken to ensure that there is nothing in the other legislation or rules which overrides the company communications provisions. The requirements of the Stock Transfer Act 1963 are a good example of this. Section 770 of the 2006 Act prohibits a company from registering a transfer of shares without 'a proper instrument of transfer'. Instruments of transfer are, therefore, documents required to be sent to companies under the Companies Acts. However, section 1 of the Stock Transfer Act 1963 prescribes the stock transfer form as the proper instrument of transfer for non-CREST transactions, and requires such forms to be executed under hand. Accordingly, the company communications provisions do not apply in this regard.

Specific provision is, of course, often made in other legislation to enable documents or information to be sent electronically. This is certainly the case with regard to the additional matters that listed companies are required to send to investors under the Listing Rules and the Disclosure and Transparency Rules.

Except where the Act specifically allows contrary provision to be made (e.g. in relation to deemed delivery), the company communications provisions are intended to override anything in a company's articles dealing with the methods of communications to be used in relation to documents or information required or authorised to be sent by or to a company under the Companies Acts. They do not override article provisions in relation to communications not required or authorised under the Companies Acts. For example, the company communications provisions would not apply in relation to any requirement in a company's articles requiring directors to resign by giving 'notice in writing' or any requirement to submit a letter of request to the company on transmission. The question as to whether electronic communications can be used for these purposes would need be determined in accordance with the company's articles and the general law. Articles sometimes require things to be done 'in writing'. Unless the term 'in writing' is expressly stated in the articles to include by electronic means, it is usually assumed to mean in paper form. The model articles define the term 'writing' as 'the representation or reproduction of words, symbols or other information in a visible form by any method or combination of methods, whether sent or supplied in electronic form or otherwise'.

If the articles do not specify the form in which a document or information must be sent by a member to the company and the relevant document or information is not required or authorised to be sent by that member under the Companies Acts, the company can generally choose whether to require it to be sent in hard copy or electronic form and whether to require the original or allow a copy to be sent.

Application to directors
Section 1148(3) clarifies that the company communications provisions apply to documents or information sent or supplied by or to the directors of the company acting on behalf of the company. This ensures that formal notices addressed to the directors (such as a demand for a requisitioned meeting) are brought within the ambit of the company communications provisions, together with communications made by directors on behalf of the company. It does not, however, necessarily extend the ambit of the company communications provisions to all communications between the company and its directors, unless those are required or authorised under the Companies Acts.

On this basis, it is doubtful whether, for example, the company communication provisions are intended to apply to communications connected with board meetings because the Companies Acts do not particularly require or authorise companies to hold board meetings except, say, to approve the accounts.

Documents sent to or by a company and from one company to another

Under the company communication provisions, different rules apply depending on whether documents or information are sent *to a company* or *by a company*. The different rules are set out in separate schedules to the Act:

- Schedule 4 sets out the rules for documents and information required or authorised to be sent *to a company* (e.g. by a member).
- Schedule 5 sets out the rules for documents and information required or authorised to be sent *by a company* (e.g. to a member or debenture holder).

Making separate provision in this manner immediately raises the question as to which rules apply where something needs to be sent by one company to another. Section 1144(3) specifies that the rules in Schedule 5 apply in these circumstances. As a consequence, the rules in Schedule 5 apply not only where a company needs to communicate with a corporate shareholder or director, but also where that corporate shareholder or director needs to communicate with the company.

Somewhat surprisingly, the practical application of the rules in Schedule 5 to communications by a corporate shareholder or director with the company turn out to be exactly the same as the rules in Schedule 4 for communications by an individual. Accordingly, it is easier to understand the company communications provisions if you assume that:

(a) the rules in Schedule 4 apply to communications sent *to* a company by its shareholders, directors and debenture holders (whether they are individuals or companies); and

(b) the rules in Schedule 5 apply to communications sent *by* a company to its shareholders, directors and debenture holders (whether they are individuals or companies).

Right to hard copy version

Section 1145 gives individual members or debenture holders the right to require that any document received electronically be sent without charge by the company in hard copy within 21 days of a request.

Definitions

Section 1148 of the 2006 Act defines various terms for the purposes of the company communications provisions. An 'address' includes a number or address used for the purposes of sending or receiving documents or information by electronic means. 'Company' includes any body corporate. 'Document' includes a summons, notice, order or other legal process and registers.

Section 1168 defines 'hard copy' and 'electronic form' as follows:

- Hard copy means 'on paper or similar form capable of being read'.
- Electronic form means by 'electronic means (for example, by e-mail or fax)' or 'by any other means while in an electronic form (for example, sending a disc by post)'.

Documents or information sent in electronic form must enable the recipient to retain a copy and read it with the naked eye (s. 1168(5) and (6)).

Given the prevalent use of technology it can be assumed that the electronic transmission of a scanned document would fall under the definition of a hard copy document, albeit that it is communicated electronically.

Authentication requirements

Section 1146 of the 2006 Act sets out the authentication requirements for documents sent to a company that the Companies Act requires to be authenticated (e.g. a meeting requisition). Hard copy documents are sufficiently authenticated if signed by the person sending or supplying them. Documents sent in electronic form are sufficiently authenticated:

(a) if the identity of the sender is confirmed in a manner specified by the company; or

(b) where no such manner is specified, the communication contains or is accompanied by a statement of the identity of the sender and the company has no reason to doubt the truth of that statement.

It follows from these rules that companies can specify the type of authentication required for any methods of electronic communication that they allow, for example by requiring shareholders to provide a unique shareholder reference number or to include password protected access to website-based records.

Deemed delivery

Section 1147 of the 2006 Act sets out when documents or information authorised or required by the Companies Acts to be sent by a company are deemed to have been delivered in the absence of contrary provisions in a company's articles or a relevant agreement or contract. The rules do not apply to any documents or information sent to a company, unless perhaps the other person sending the documents or information is another company.

Subject to any modification by a company's articles or a relevant agreement or contract, section 1147 provides that documents and information:

(a) sent by post are deemed to be delivered 48 hours after they were posted provided the company can show that they were properly addressed, pre-paid and posted;

(b) sent in electronic form are deemed to have been received by the intended recipients 48 hours after they were sent provided the company can show they were properly addressed; and

(c) sent or supplied via a website are deemed to have been received by the intended recipient when first made available on the website or, if later, when the recipient received (or is deemed to have received) notice of the fact that the material was available on the website.

In calculating the period of hours for the purposes of section 1147, no account may be taken of any part of a day that is not a working day. A 'working day' is defined in section 1173 of the 2006 Act for these purposes as a day that is not a Saturday or Sunday, Christmas Day, Good Friday, or any day which is a bank holiday in the part of the United Kingdom where the company is registered.

Section 1147 has effect:

(a) in its application to documents or information sent or supplied by a company to its members, any contrary provision of the company's articles;

(b) in its application to documents or information sent or supplied by a company to its debenture holders, any contrary provision in the instrument constituting the debentures;

(c) in its application to documents or information sent or supplied by a company to a person otherwise in his capacity as a member or debenture holder, any contrary provision in an agreement between that person and the company (s. 1147(6)).

Schedule 4 – Documents sent or supplied to a company

Schedule 4 of the 2006 Act sets out the methods by which documents and information may be sent or supplied to a company by any person other than another company. The methods include:

- hard copy form by hand or by post (Schedule 4, Pt 2, paras 2–4);
- electronic form, provided that the company has agreed or can be deemed to have agreed (Schedule 4, Part 3, paras 5–7); and
- any other form agreed by the company (Sch. 4, Pt 4, para. 8).

Although company-to-company communications are governed by Schedule 5, the practical application of those rules to communications sent to a company by its corporate shareholders or debenture holders is essentially the same as the application of the rules in Schedule 4 for individuals.

Hard copy form

Under Schedule 4, paragraphs 2–4, hard copy documents and information may be sent or supplied to a company by hand or by post:

- to an address specified by the company for that purpose;
- to the company's registered office; or
- to an address to which any provision of the Companies Acts authorises the document or information to be sent or supplied.

Hard copy for these purposes means 'on paper or similar form capable of being read' (s. 1168). It is worth noticing in this regard that where the Act uses the expression 'in writing' it should no longer be assumed that this means in hard copy form.

The rules in Schedule 5, paragraphs 2–4, which would apply when a company in its capacity as a corporate member wishes to send hard copy communications to the company of which it is a member, are essentially the same as those in Schedule 4 for natural persons.

For the purposes of Schedules 4 and 5, a person posts a document by posting a pre-paid envelope containing the document or information (Sch. 4, para. 3(2) and Sch. 5 para. 3(2)). At first sight, this would seem to preclude the use of pre-paid cards. However, these would probably fall within the provisions on other agreed forms of communication in Schedule 4, paragraph 8, and Schedule 5, paragraph 15, particularly where the company has sent a reply-paid card for use by members. By sending such a card for their use, the company would undoubtedly be deemed to have agreed to accept communications from them in this manner.

Using electronic communications to send documents or information to a company

Part 3 of Schedule 4 covers the use of electronic communications by individuals for the purposes of sending documents or information to a company. Although Part 3 of Schedule 5 deals separately with the use of electronic communications between companies, its application is essentially the same in relation to communications by a corporate member or debenture holder with the company in which it holds shares or debentures.

Schedule 4, paragraph 6 provides that a document may only be sent or supplied to the company in electronic form if:

- the company has agreed (generally or specifically) to allow it to be sent in that manner; or
- it can be deemed to have so agreed by virtue of a provision in the Companies Acts (e.g. s. 333).

It is not necessary for the members to pass any resolution or for provision to be made in a company's articles to enable electronic communications to be used for this purpose. A company can signify its agreement to accept communications in electronic form in other ways, and can be deemed to have done so in relation to a meeting if it includes an address capable of being used for that purpose in the notice or proxy forms sent to members.

The document or information must be sent to an address specified by the company for this purpose, or deemed to have been so specified (e.g. by virtue of s. 333 (Sch. 4, para. 7(1)). However, where the document is sent or supplied in electronic form by hand or by post, it must be delivered to an address that would be valid if it were in hard copy form (Sch. 4, para. 7(2)).

Using other methods for sending documents or information to a company

Schedule 4 provides that a document or information that is sent to a company by any other means is validly sent if it is sent in a form or manner that has been agreed by the company (Sch. 4, para. 8). Schedule 5 makes similar provision regarding the use of other methods of communication for the purposes of documents and information sent by corporate members or debenture holders (Sch. 5, para. 15).

As mentioned above, these provisions would almost certainly serve to authorise the use by members of reply-paid cards supplied to them by the company.

Schedule 5 – Communications by a company

Schedule 5 of the 2006 Act sets out the methods by which documents and information may be sent or supplied by a company to shareholders, debenture holders, directors and other persons. The available methods include:

- hard copy form by hand or by post (Sch. 5, Pt 2, paras 2–4);
- electronic form, provided that the intended recipient has agreed or can be deemed to have agreed (Sch. 5, Pt 3, paras 5–7);
- communications by means of a website (Sch. 5, Pt 4, paras 8–14); and
- any other form agreed by the company (Sch. 4, Pt 5, para. 15).

Hard copy form

Part 2 of Schedule 5 sets out the methods that may be used by a company for hard copy communications, including the methods of delivery and the addresses that can be used for these purposes. Hard copy is defined for these purposes as being 'on paper or similar form capable of being read' (s. 1168).

Hard copy documents or information must be either handed by the company to the intended recipient or sent or supplied by hand or by post (Sch. 5, para. 3(1)). Posting is defined for these purposes as posting a pre-paid envelope containing the document or information. This definition would appear to prevent a company from using a post card to send documents or information to its members or debenture holders without first obtaining their consent. As discussed above, it would not prevent the company from providing pre-paid cards for them to use to return information to the company.

The addresses that may be used by a company for communications in hard copy form include:

- an address specified for the purpose by the intended recipient;
- in the case of a company, its registered office;
- in the case of a member of the company, the address shown in the register of members;
- in the case of a director, the address shown in the register of directors; and
- an address to which any provision of the Companies Acts authorises the document to be sent (Sch. 5, para. 4(1)).

There may sometimes be more than one address that a company can use to send hard copy communications to certain recipients. For example, a director may have provided the company with an address to be used for general communications purposes, but the company could still validly serve a document on that director by sending it to the service address recorded in the register of directors.

A company can use the intended recipient's last known address where it is unable to obtain an address specified by them for the purpose (Sch. 5, para. 4(2)).

Communications by a company in electronic form

Part 3 of Schedule 5 covers the use of electronic communications by a company. It states that a company can only send or supply a document or information in electronic form to a person who has agreed (generally or specifically) to receive it in that manner or to a company that is deemed under the Companies Acts to have so agreed (Sch. 5, para. 6). The document or information may only be sent by electronic means to an address specified for the purpose by the intended recipient, or where the recipient is a company, deemed by a provision of the Companies Act to have been so specified (Sch. 5, para. 7(1)). Where a document or information is sent in electronic form by hand or by post, it must be either handed to the intended recipient or sent to an address that could be validly used for hard copy communications (Sch. 5 para. 7(2)).

Website communications by a company

Part 4 of Schedule 5 allows a company to send or supply a document or information by making it available on a website and notifying the intended recipient of the fact that it has done so. A document or information made available on a website for these purposes must be made available in a form, and by a means, that the company reasonably considers will enable the recipient to read it with the naked eye and retain a copy of it (Sch. 5, para. 12). The company must also notify the intended recipient that the document or information has been made available on the website, give the address of the website, the place on the website where it may be accessed, and how to access the document or information (Sch. 5, para. 13).

The company must make the document available on the website throughout the period specified by any applicable provision of the Companies Acts or, if no such period is specified, for a period of 28 days commencing on the date that the notification is sent (Sch. 5, para. 14(1)). The document or information is taken to be 'sent' on the date the notification is sent, or if later, on the date that the document or information becomes available on the website (s. 1147). Any failure to make the document or information available throughout the relevant period can be disregarded if it is made available on the website for part of that period and the failure is wholly attributable to circumstances that it would not be reasonable to have expected the company to prevent or avoid (Sch. 5, para. 14(2)).

Website communications can only be used if the intended recipient:

- has agreed (generally or specifically) to receive the document or information in that manner (Sch. 5, para. 9(a)); or
- can be deemed to have so agreed by not responding to a consultation conducted in accordance with either Schedule 5, paragraph 10 (members and indirect investors) or Schedule 5, paragraph 11 (debenture holders) (Sch. 5, para. 9(b)).

A company that wishes to use website communications for Companies Act purposes need not have authority in its articles to do so, or pass an ordinary resolution of its members to that effect, unless it wishes to take advantage of the deemed consent provisions in Schedule 5. Unless it does one of these things, it must obtain the individual consent of the intended recipient to the use of website communications. This means that the intended recipient must have positively elected to receive website communications.

The deemed consent provisions in Schedule 5, paragraph 10 can only be used if the members have resolved that the company may send or supply documents or information to the member's company by making them available on a website or the articles contain provisions to that effect.

> **Precedent: Resolution to authorise the use of electronic communications**
>
> THAT the company be and is hereby generally and unconditionally authorised to use electronic communications with its shareholders and in particular authorised to send or supply documents or information to its shareholders by making them available on a website.

If this authority is in place, then the company can conduct a consultation whereby members can be deemed to have agreed to opt for website communications if they fail to respond to a consultation for this purpose within 28 days. The consultation must be clear about the effect of a failure to respond and cannot be conducted more than once in any 12-month period. This type of consultation can also be used to ascertain the wishes of a person nominated by a member to enjoy information rights under section 146 or any person nominated by a member in accordance with the company's articles to enjoy or exercise any rights of the member.

Schedule 5, paragraph 11 provides a similar procedure for website communications with debenture holders, which allows the company to deem those debenture holders who do not respond to a consultation within 28 days to have elected to receive website communications. In this case, the relevant debenture holders must have passed a resolution allowing the company to use website communications or the relevant instrument creating the debenture must contain provision to that effect.

Companies that were using website communications under the 1985 Act regime could continue to do so for the documents covered by the consent given under the 1985 Act without taking any further action. No resolution would be required to take advantage of the deemed consent consultation procedures if the company's articles already made provisions allowing it to send or supply documents or information to members by website. However, if the articles only covered certain documents, a new resolution would be required to provide general cover for other documents to be provided via the website communication method.

Other methods of communication by a company

Part 5 of Schedule 5 provides that a document or information that is sent or supplied otherwise than in hard copy, electronic form or via a website is validly sent if sent in a form or manner agreed by the intended recipient.

Communications with joint holders

The rules in Schedule 5, paragraph 16 regarding communications with joint holders of shares or debentures apply subject to any contrary provision in a company's articles. They provide that anything to be agreed or specified by the holder must be agreed or specified by all the joint holders (Sch. 5, para. 16(2)) and that anything required to be sent or supplied to the holder may be sent or supplied to each of them or to the first-named holder in the relevant register (Sch. 5, para. 16(3)).

Communications with shareholders in the event of death or bankruptcy

Documents or information required or authorised to be sent to a member who has died or has been declared bankrupt may be sent to the persons claiming to be entitled to the shares in consequence of the death or bankruptcy either by name or by the title of representatives of the deceased, or trustee of the bankrupt, or by any like description (Sch. 5, para. 17). This rule also has effect subject to any contrary provision in a company's articles.

Sending documents relating to meetings in electronic form

Section 333 of the 2006 Act provides that where a company has given an electronic address in a notice calling a general meeting (or a class meeting (see s. 335)), it is deemed to have agreed that any document or information relating to proceedings at that meeting may be sent by electronic means to that address (subject to any conditions or limitations specified in the notice).

Similarly, if a company includes an electronic address in an instrument of proxy or proxy invitation sent out by the company, it is deemed to have agreed that any document or information relating to proxies may be sent by electronic means to that address (subject to any conditions or limitations specified in the 'notice').

Documents relating to proxies for the purposes of section 333 include proxy appointments, any documents necessary to show the validity of the appointment, and any notice of termination of the authority of the proxy (s. 333(3)).

'Electronic address' is defined, for the purposes of section 333, as including any address or number used for the purpose of sending or receiving documents or information by electronic means (s. 333(4)).

Traded company: duty to provide electronic address for receipt of proxies

A traded company must, when sending out an instrument of proxy for the purposes of a general meeting or issuing an invitation to appoint a proxy for those purposes, give an electronic address for the receipt of any document or information relating to proxies for the meeting (s. 333A(1)). In doing so, a traded company is deemed to have agreed that any document or information relating to proxies for the meeting may be sent by electronic means to that address (subject to any limitations specified by the company when giving the address) (s. 333A(2)).

Documents relating to proxies for the purposes of section 333A include proxy appointments, any documents necessary to show the validity of the appointment, and any notice of termination of the authority of the proxy (s. 333A(3) and section 333(3)).

'Electronic address' is defined for the purposes of section 333A as including any address or number used for the purpose of sending or receiving documents or information by electronic means (ss 333A(3) and 333(4)).

Electronic communications under the Listing Rules and Disclosure and Transparency Rules

The Listing Rules (LR) and the Disclosure and Transparency Rules (DTR) both require issuers whose shares or debt securities are traded on a regulated market in the UK to send certain additional information to holders of those securities.

LR 1.4.9G confirms that issuers can use electronic means to send documents required under the Listing Rules to security holders 'in accordance with DTR 6.1.8R'. DTR 6.1.7G also confirms that issuers can use electronic means to send information to shareholders or debt security holders. Accordingly, issuers must comply with DTR 6.18R in order to use electronic communications for the purposes of the Listing Rules and the Disclosure and Transparency Rules.

DTR 6.1.8(1) requires issuers to obtain the consent of the members in general meeting before using electronic communications for these purposes (the Companies Act 2006 only requires shareholder approval, as a body, if the company wants to take advantage of the deemed consent to website communications method of consultation).

Shareholder consent to the use of website communications obtained under the Companies Act 1985 regime could be carried over to the new regime (see Transitional Provision 12 in the DTR Sourcebook Transitional Provisions).

DTR 6.1.8(2) stipulates that the use of electronic means must not depend on the location of the seat of residence of the shareholders and other persons. As this rule is based on an EU Directive requirement, it requires issuers who wish to use electronic communications to offer that option to all members or debt security holders based in the EEA.

DTR 6.1.8(3) requires identification arrangements to be put in place so that the shareholders, debt security holders or other persons entitled to exercise or to direct the exercise of voting rights are effectively informed.

DTR 6.1.8(5) requires any apportionment of the costs entailed in conveying information by electronic means to be determined by the issuer in compliance with the principle of equal treatment set out in DTR 6.1.3R.

For issuers that are not subject to the company communications provisions in Schedule 5 of the 2006 Act, DTR 6.1.8(4) provides that shareholders, debt security holders and certain indirect investors must be:

(a) contacted in writing to request their consent for the use of electronic communications and if they do not object within a reasonable period of time, their consent can be considered to have been given; and

(b) able to request at any time in the future that information be conveyed in writing.

Schedule 5 of the Act also requires a company to obtain the individual consent of the intended recipient to the use of electronic communications. That consent must be given specifically (Sch. 5, para. 9(a)) except where the person fails to respond to a consultation regarding website communications conducted in accordance with the requirements of Schedule 5, paragraph 10 (in the case of members) or Schedule 5, paragraph 11 (in the case of debenture holders), in which case they may be deemed to have consented to receive communications from the company in that manner.

Elections to receive electronic communications
A company must continue to send hard copies of any documents or information to any member, debt security holder or indirect investor who is entitled to receive

them under the Companies Acts, unless that person has agreed that they may be sent electronically. The Act provides two options in this regard:

(a) a company may use electronic communications to send a full electronic version of the document to a person who has provided it with an address for that purpose (e.g. an email address); and

(b) alternatively, a company may simply notify a person that the relevant documents have been published on a website together with details of how they may be accessed.

A company cannot use either of these methods without the agreement of the person concerned, although that agreement may be deemed in the case of website communications if a person fails to respond in time to a consultation conducted in accordance with either Schedule 5, paragraph 10 (members) or Schedule 5, paragraph 11 (debenture holders) of the 2006 Act.

Where consent is required to use non-hard copy communications, the Act does not require companies to obtain a person's written consent. Members could, therefore, be allowed to signify their consent in some other way (e.g. by registering on a website or sending an email). Ideally, members should be required to authenticate their election in some way, potentially through their access to the website and provision of a password.

There is nothing in the Act to prevent a person from electing to receive certain types of document one way and others in a different manner. A company need not, however, allow a person to make such an election. Indeed, a company need not provide members with any choice at all as to the available methods. It could, for example, decide to publish the documents on a website and only offer members the opportunity to receive notifications of the fact that the information has been so published and how to find it.

Listed companies will not only need to obtain the consent of members for the various statutory purposes but also in respect of documents which they are required to send pursuant to the Listing Rules and the Disclosure and Transparency Rules.

A consultation regarding the use of website communications, whereby those who do not respond within 28 days can be deemed to have agreed to accept electronic communications, can only be conducted if the members have resolved that the company may send or supply documents or information by making them available on a website or the articles contain provisions to that effect. Under Schedule 5, paragraph 10 such a consultation with members or indirect investors must be clear about the effect of a failure to respond and cannot be conducted more than once in any 12-month period.

Schedule 5, paragraph 11 provides a similar procedure for website communications with debenture holders, which allows the company to deem those debenture holders who do not respond to a consultation within 28 days to have elected to receive website communications. In this case, the relevant debenture holders must have passed a resolution allowing the company to use website communications or the relevant instrument creating the debenture must contain provision to that effect.

Companies will need to comply with applicable data protection rules and practices when collecting, storing and using information provided by members, debenture holders or others for the purposes of electronic communications. Details of elections made by members and any electronic addresses provided by them should not be entered in any of the statutory registers in a manner which would require their disclosure to people inspecting the register. As the Act does not require these details to be entered in any statutory register, they are not covered by any of the applicable data protection exemptions for statutory registers.

Precedent: Form of a specimen data protection statement

DATA PROTECTION STATEMENT

A. The identity of the Data Controller
    The company is a Data Controller for the purposes of the Data Protection Act 1998. This means that it is responsible for making decisions about how your personal data will be processed and how it may be used.

B. Use of your personal data
    The company will record any election you make on this form and any information which you provide that is necessary for the company to give effect to that election. The data will be used to determine what methods the company may use to serve documents and notices on you and the address that should be used for that purpose. The company will use any email address you supply only to send company documents connected with your election.
    The company will disclose to [its registrars], some or all of the data you provide. The registrars will use that data solely for the purposes of distributing documents connected with your election. In addition, the company will receive certain administrative data from its registrars, which it has created for the purposes of carrying out its function as registrar and which relates to your shareholding.

C. Security of your personal data
    The company has put in place appropriate technical and organisational measures to prevent the unauthorised or unlawful processing of your personal data. These include restricted access to databases that contain personal data, access restricted by password authentication and training of personnel on the rules of data protection and obligations of confidentiality.

D. Updating your personal data
    Under the Data Protection Act you have the right to be told what personal data the company holds about you and to request that it be updated. This may be done by contacting: [name and address].

Indirect investors

The default right given to indirect investors is for documents and information to be supplied by means of a website. If the nominated person is to receive hard copies of the documents, they must have asked the registered holder to nominate them to receive a hard copy and must have supplied an address for this purpose. The nomination given to the company by the registered holder must then indicate that the investor wishes to receive hard copy communications and give the address supplied by that person. As an alternative, a person nominated to receive web-based communications only may directly revoke the implied agreement to receive web-based communications and thus become entitled to receive hard copy (see s. 147(6)). The fact that a person may be nominated to receive hard copy communications does not prevent the company from making use of the electronic communications provisions and seeking to obtain that person's agreement to the use of website communications (s. 147(4)).

Amending articles for electronic communications

Articles can sometimes give the impression that it is not possible for either the company or its members to use electronic communications. This is because they require various things to be done 'in writing' without defining what the term means. In the past, the term 'in writing' was used in articles and legislative provisions to indicate that a thing had to be done in hard copy form (e.g. paper form) rather than, say, orally. Accordingly, whenever the term 'in writing' is used, people like to see something that confirms that it can also be done 'electronically'.

The Companies Act 2006 provides confirmation that things that are required or authorised to be sent by or to a company can be sent electronically as long as the intended recipient has agreed to accept communications in that manner. Accordingly, the Act overrides any possible obstacle caused by the meaning of the term 'in writing' in a company's articles, but only in relation to things that are required or authorised to be done under the Act. Most things that a company is required to do under its articles are also things that it is either required or authorised to do under the Act. However, several of the things that members are required to do under the articles are not specifically required under the Act or necessarily authorised to be done under it, except in the sense that the Act does not prohibit a company from requiring members to do these things. On the whole, this does not matter because they are not normally the sort of things that companies would necessarily want members to be able to do electronically. For example, a company would not normally be willing to accept a scanned copy of a share certificate to be submitted with a share transfer.

If the articles do not specify the form in which a document or information must be sent by a member to the company and the relevant document or information is not required or authorised to be sent by that member under the Companies Acts, the company can generally choose whether to require it to be sent in hard copy or electronic form and whether to require the original or allow a copy to be sent.

Although the 2006 Act allows a company to take advantage of electronic communications without first amending its articles, it is probably preferable to do so.

Electronic signatures

Section 7 of the Electronic Communications Act 2000 ('the ECA 2000') makes provision for the admissibility in legal proceedings of:

- an electronic signature incorporated into or logically associated with a particular electronic communication or particular electronic data; and
- the certification by any person of such a signature.

An electronic signature (or any certification thereof) is admissible as evidence in relation to any of the following questions regarding the authenticity or integrity of a communication or data:

(a) whether the communication or data comes from a particular person or other source;
(b) whether it is accurately timed and dated; and
(c) whether it is intended to have legal effect.

In addition, references to the integrity of any communication or data are references to whether there has been any tampering with or other modification of the communication or data (ECA 2000 s. 15(2)).

An electronic signature is defined in section 7(2) of the Electronic Communications Act 2000 as:

so much of anything in electronic form as:
(a) is incorporated into or otherwise logically associated with any electronic communication or electronic data; and
(b) purports to be used by the individual creating it to sign.

Section 7(3) of the Electronic Communications Act 2000 provides that an electronic signature can be certified by any person if that person (whether before or after the making of the communication) has made a statement confirming that:

(a) the signature,
(b) a means of producing, communicating or verifying the signature, or
(c) a procedure applied to the signature, is (either alone or in combination with other factors) a valid means of signing.

Definition of electronic communications

An 'electronic communication' is defined in section 15 of the Electronic Communications Act 2000 as:

a communication transmitted (whether from one person to another, from one device to another or from a person to a device or vice versa)

(a) by means of an electronic communications network; or

(b) by other means but while in an electronic form.

'Electronic communication' means a communication transmitted (whether from one person to another, from one device to another or from a person to a device or vice versa):

(a) by means of an electronic communications network; or

(b) by other means but while in an electronic form.

It should be noted that the definition of an electronic communication in the Electronic Communications Act 2000 does not have any particular relevance for the purposes of the company communications provisions of the Companies Act 2006, which adopt a slightly different phraseology with their own distinct definitions. It is questionable, therefore, whether it would be appropriate to use some of the above methods for Companies Acts purposes, particularly those which are of an ephemeral nature.

However, the admissibility of electronic signatures in legal proceedings may be of significance in the following areas covered by this book:

■ the retention of signed minutes in computerised form;

■ the authentication of proxy appointments made using electronic communications; and

■ the authentication of other electronic communications sent by or to the company.

Virtual board and committee meetings

This content was abstracted from The Chartered Governance Institute's *Good Practice for Virtual Board and Committee Meetings*, March 2020 guidance note which was prepared with the assistance of Lorraine Young Board Advisory Services and a working group comprising members of The Chartered Governance Institute. The full document can be found on the website of The Chartered Governance Institute at: www.icsa.org.uk/knowledge/resourcesgood-practice-for-virtual-board-and-committee-meetings

There are a few key points that underpin the successful implementation of virtual meetings and their subsequent use, namely:

■ The choice of the right communication channel is vital – if the technology does not work well the meeting will be harder to run, will likely last for longer than is optimal and will be less effective. An audio call or telephone conference will be less risky, but a video conference is more engaging if you can get it to work well.

- Virtual meetings need to be well structured and avoid unnecessary complexity – it is entirely possible to hold an effective meeting by virtual means. However, it should be structured more simply than a face-to-face meeting and should recognise the constraints of technology. If necessary, the board has alternative ways to make decisions.
- Preparation is key.
- The chair will need additional techniques to run an orderly meeting, allowing adequate debate and obtaining the sense of the meeting.
- 'Ground rules' for participants should be circulated to all those joining the meeting in good time beforehand.
- Clear instructions on accessing the meeting system or app are essential – not all participants will be familiar with the technology. Give everyone clear instructions in advance about how to access and use the meeting app and offer individual practice calls if necessary.
- Good boardroom practices are even more necessary for virtual meetings than for those held face to face.

Initial considerations
Choice of platform
Most boards are used to holding meetings by telephone conference call to deal with urgent items of business which arise between scheduled meetings. It is also possible to use a virtual meeting application or app. There are other ways to effect board decisions without holding a meeting and the pros and cons of these are covered below.

Validity
The Companies Act 2006 generally facilitates e-communications. You should also check the articles of association for any provisions on telephone or video conferencing. If necessary, the articles should be updated.

Before the meeting
There are a number of practical matters to attend to before the meeting.

Setting up the meeting or call
The call or virtual meeting needs to be set up and invites sent out. Helpful tips are:

- Schedule shorter meetings and include breaks – People's attention span is shorter on the phone or on an app than in person. If some people only join for specific items, try to arrange these straight after a break to minimise disruption.

- Take account of different time zones – If participants are on different time zones, ensure the correct time is shown on invitations and agendas. If necessary, make the start time in each location clear on the agenda.
- Circulate the link and dial in details for the meeting – on the meeting invitation, on the agenda and by email. You could also circulate them again an hour before the meeting, so they are easily to hand.
- The company secretary (or their designate) should act as host – They should also have all of the access codes/PINs to hand and should open the call 10–15 minutes before the start time to allow a prompt start and deal with any issues with the technology.
- Issue clear joining and conduct instructions – Ensure everyone has clear instructions about how to join the meeting and use the key features of the app (such as muting and unmuting their microphone) and offer them a practice run. The platform you are using may allow you to mute individual lines and you should know how to do this if needed.
- Offer dial-in numbers with freephone and local call rate numbers – Make clear which number to use from mobile phones to avoid heavy network charges. If using an app, explain that the dial in numbers should be used as a backup if there are issues with the technology.
- Review start times – Experience has shown that there may be issues with starting calls at peak times, due to bandwidth limitations. Consider scheduling meetings just before or just after the hour or half hour (e.g. have a start time of 9:50 or 10:10 rather than 10:00).
- Use audio-only calls for large meetings – Video links may impair connectivity, and for large meetings it may be impractical to have everyone present by video.
- Have IT support on standby – Ensure they are immediately available if there is a problem.

Supporting the chair
- Communication – Agree with the chair beforehand how you will communicate with each other during the meeting if you need to. Text messaging will probably be the quickest and most reliable means.
- Attenders – Make sure you and the chair have a list of all those due to attend the meeting so that either or both of you can check who is on the call.
- Use a timed agenda – Give presenters an approximate time when they will be asked to join the meeting. They should not join early; it is best to message them when you are ready for them to join. To ensure confidentiality, if the technology permits, ask them to wait in the 'virtual lobby' until needed.
- Outcomes – Make sure it is clear what the board is being asked to do for each agenda item.

During the meeting
Absence
Any apologies for absence should be recorded. If anyone is unable to attend, the chair should speak to them before the meeting to get their views, answer any questions and to pass on any comments they may have at the meeting. The chair or company secretary should also contact them after the meeting to advise them of the outcome. If they are too unwell to provide any input beforehand, the meeting can still go ahead validly, provided it is quorate. Follow-up can then be done once they have sufficiently recovered.

If the chair is indisposed, someone else will need to take on this role.

Attendance
A virtual meeting app may allow the person hosting the meeting (and other participants) to see who is present at the meeting, when they leave and others join, and who is speaking. It may also be possible to message other participants and to mute lines if needed.

If such a facility is not available to everyone, the chair or the company secretary should do a roll call at the start, to ensure everyone is present. They should also request that participants advise if they have to leave the call (this could be by messaging the company secretary to avoid disrupting the meeting).

Everyone should attend the meeting from a quiet place, to avoid distraction, and should be on mute unless speaking.

At the end of the meeting (under 'Any Other Business') the chair should ask participants by name if they have any other matters to raise. This also allows the company secretary to check if everyone is still on the call.

Quorum
If the above process is followed, it should be possible to ensure a quorum is present on the call at all times. If the meeting is not quorate it should be adjourned and reconvened when everyone can be present.

Papers
- Portals, PDFs and security – If everyone is working away from the office, it may not be practical or possible to send out paper packs. Many boards already use electronic board portals or email board packs in pdf form to directors. Board portals are relatively secure but if papers are circulated by email, there are risks with using (usually non-executive) directors' personal email addresses if they are not linked to secure domains. Alternatives could be to allocate the directors a company email address – but make sure that they can access this easily – offer assistance if required. If possible, papers emailed to directors should be password protected and the password notified separately.

- Agenda – Suggest to participants (and particularly the chair) that they print off the agenda for the meeting so that they can follow it easily. If the board pack is in pdf format, the agenda should include page numbers for each item for quick reference.
- Screen sharing – Some of the virtual meeting apps allow documents to be shared on screen during the call to ensure that everyone is on the same page (or slide). If this facility is not used, the presenter should indicate which slide or page number they are on as they move through their presentation.

Communication during the meeting

- Communication between participants during a meeting – Some virtual meeting apps have a messaging facility which participants can use to indicate to the chair that they wish to speak on an item and with which the chair can acknowledge this wish. This messaging may not be private, it may be visible to all on the call. Everyone should be given instructions about how to use this facility and told who can view their messages.
- Private communication during a meeting – Private messaging may be available within the app but, if not, then text messaging is probably the quickest and most reliable system. Whichever option you choose, make sure you agree with the chair beforehand how you will communicate with each other during the meeting.

Chairing

- Alternate chair – If the chair is unable to attend the meeting due to illness or other reason, the articles will normally provide that the directors choose one of their number to chair. You may wish to arrange this in advance of the meeting. The company secretary should provide advice and guidance as needed to the alternate chair, particularly if they are less experienced in the role.
- The role of the chair – This is to run the meeting, ensure a good debate, obtain the view of the meeting and reach a decision (if one is required). Allowing everyone to have their say and facilitating an effective debate can be challenging when the meeting is being held over the phone or internet.
- Ground rules – You should circulate ground rules for participants. There is a risk of people talking over one another and/or accidentally interrupting and people not speaking at all. It is of primary importance during board calls and virtual meetings for participants to defer to the chair and for the chair to be proactive in leading and managing the meeting, assisted by the company secretary. The chair should also ensure that they proactively seek engagement and contributions from all attendees as the agenda progresses ensuring that all views are aired.

Meeting management

- The chair needs to be exceptionally clear about leading the meeting through the agenda and handing over to each presenter. Even if there is a video link there will not be the normal lines of sight and in a telephone conference call it can be even harder for participants to keep track of what is going on.
- Words may have to replace what would normally be obvious when the meeting is held face to face.
- Presenters should be clear about when they have completed their slot.
- The chair should invite questions at the end, rather than during the presentation.
- For each item, the chair may wish to ask that directors indicate if they would like to speak on the item. They can then be invited to speak in turn to allow orderly debate.
- Before moving on to the decision making, the chair should ensure everyone has had the chance to comment or ask their question, by checking if there are any further questions, maybe inviting individual participants to comment if they have not already done so.

Clarity of decision making

Board papers should indicate whether a decision is required or if the item is for noting/information only. The chair should determine the sense of the meeting by asking everyone to indicate their support or if the matter is not thought to be contentious, they could ask for any indications of dissent. The usual nods or show of hands will need to be replaced by spoken assent (or dissent). Some virtual meeting apps may have a facility for an electronic voting process if a formal vote is needed.

At the end of the item, the chair should state clearly what the board has just decided/noted. If the chair does not do so and the minute taker is unsure of what has been agreed, they must ask at that point before the meeting moves to the next item.

If there is no consensus then, as with a physical meeting, it is up to the chair to determine the best course of action. This might be for the executive to return to the next meeting with more information or an updated proposal or for the item to be deferred for a longer period of time, or dropped entirely.

Technical considerations

- Audio is more reliable than video – A fast and stable internet connection is required for virtual meeting apps, or the meeting could be disrupted. If there are issues with internet connectivity or if the directors are not familiar with the technology, an audio call may be better than a video conference. However, video conferences are more engaging.
- Participants may need two screens for video – For video calls, participants may require more than one screen or device – one for reading their papers and

another for any video input from the call/messaging functions and so on. If this is not easy to achieve, then an audio call/telephone conference may be a better option.

- Running the technology – The company secretary should run the technical aspects of the call, rather than the chair. If the meeting has a lot of participants, it may be better for the company secretary to appoint a designate to deal with any technical issues or to communicate with the directors and the chair during the meeting.
- Minute the meeting as usual – Do not record it – recording board and committee meetings is not generally recommended. Refer to The Chartered Governance Institute's guidance on minute taking for more information.
- Have IT support on standby throughout the meeting – Ensure prompt assistance with any technical issues can be obtained.

After the meeting

Ask for feedback and see what can be improved next time. Make sure you address any issues in good time before the next meeting. Update your ground rules if necessary.

Alternatives to meetings

Written resolutions

If face-to-face meetings are not possible, the technology fails or is not practicable, most articles of association allow board decisions to be made by written resolution. This might be unanimous or by a particular majority of the board. The exact wording of the resolution can be circulated by email and agreement given under the e-communications provisions of the Companies Act 2006. It is not necessary for each director to print out the resolution, sign it and scan it back.

Any written resolution should still be recorded and, if consent is by email, then a copy of the email agreement from each director should be put in the minute book.

Email 'meetings'

This is not the same process as circulating a written resolution by email, described above. This would be where a proposal is circulated by email and people communicate their views over the email with an indication as to whether they support the proposal. This is not ideal since those participating cannot communicate to everyone else at the same time and there may be delays between the messages – in effect, it is not a meeting. People may change their views as the 'conversation' progresses and the end/decision point may not be clear.

If a matter requires discussion it should be discussed with the board all together at the same time. If the matter is more straightforward, then the written resolution procedure can follow on from any proposal which is communicated by email.

Delegation to a committee

If it is impossible for the board to have a call or virtual meeting, then the matter could be delegated to a committee of any two or three directors. This can be effected by the written resolution procedure outlined above.

It is better not to specify only named individuals as members of the committee, in case they are unable to participate. A safer option is to say (for example) 'any two directors' and add in any preferences such as 'at least one of whom must be a Non-Executive Director'.

Subsequent ratification

This is where a decision is taken informally, with the intention that it is ratified at a future board meeting. This is not ideal as circumstances may change and some directors may change their mind about ratifying the original 'decision'. It is better to follow up any informal communication by following the written resolution procedure outlined above.

Virtual annual general meetings

The benefit of having an AGM for companies to engage with members and, conversely, for members to be able to hold the board of directors to account has long been recognised and accepted. However, the format for this meeting has been a subject of discussion for some time, especially with the advent of new technology to support alternate ways of communicating and the geographical spread of members of some companies.

Unlike virtual meetings of directors and committees, implementing virtual AGMS for large companies is considerably more complex despite the advances in technology that could support them. While arranging virtual attendance and presenting at the meeting are relatively straightforward, the ability of members to vote on resolutions being presented is more difficult without the use of proxies.

Smaller companies, or those with a small number of members, could implement virtual AGMS, subject to their articles. If this is possible, the guidance for virtual board and committees meetings noted above is a useful starting point for their implementation and practical use.

Potential revisions to the use of annual general meetings

In August 2016, the Registrars Group of The Chartered Governance Institute presented a paper on potential revisions to the use of AGMs, including the use of virtual meetings. Within this it was noted that the idea of a virtual AGM where the structure of the meeting is the same as currently, but the shareholders 'attend' and vote, not at a physical meeting but through a combination of tele-conferencing, webinar and electronic voting application is currently permissible, if the company's constitution allows.

Virtual meetings have the advantage of there being no need to hire a venue and the attendant costs which accompany that, such as security, catering, travel etc. However, there are additional considerations which result from this format, including enhanced telephony provision and contingency because of the fear that the meeting could be invalidated by such a failure, requiring adjournment and reconvening with the attendant costs and embarrassment. This can erode the risk assessment/cost–benefit of not having to hold a physical meeting.

While this approach is feasible for smaller companies, particularly those who are relatively recent start-ups or have just gone public, the constitutional change required for long-established companies, having entrenched shareholder bases, with higher levels of more mature individual shareholders will be more difficult, costly because of the extended communication programme, and risks potential adverse publicity by taking such a step into the unknown, especially if there is a viable alternative.

Jimmy Choo PLC amended their articles in 2015 in order to facilitate the change and delivered the company's first electronic AGM – which is how they chose to describe it – on 15 June 2016. They were seeking a way of increasing investor access to their AGM while saving travel costs for investors, as well as the cost to the company of hiring a venue and collecting the board in one physical location.

The AGM was much better attended than Jimmy Choo's first physical AGM in 2015, which evidences the greater appeal and accessibility of an electronic AGM. Peter Harf, Chairman of Jimmy Choo plc, added: 'We are very pleased with the outcome of this process, which achieved its aim of broadening shareholder access to our AGM in the most convenient way possible.'

Splitting meetings and voting

In addition, the Registrars Group paper proposed having a separate shareholder meeting during which management, members of the board and members could discuss issues relating to the company ahead of a vote.

Currently most companies have meetings with large investors at which presentations are made, discussions held, and questions asked about performance and strategy. Not all the directors are present; those who are will depend upon the circumstances of the company at that moment but, as well as the CEO and chairman, may include some or all of the finance director, the senior NED, Audit & risk committee chair etc. Such meetings are seen as an essential ingredient of shareholder engagement and stewardship.

In this scenario, the business of the AGM – the resolutions which are currently required to be put before the meeting – would be subject to a vote which was entirely separate from the meeting. There is an argument to say that such a vote should ideally be held within a certain period of the shareholder meeting. This would allow informed voting based on 'attendance' at the shareholder meeting or perusal of any internet-based output from it.

Advantages include:

- Simplifying the process by removing potential duplications (shareholders who have submitted a proxy and then attend) and not collating proxies and votes at the meeting.
- The cost savings and process simplification of not having to carry out the count at the meeting venue, remote from the registrars' systems.
- Potential benefits due to changes in the voting, as compared to the original proxy appointment.
- Vote confirmation would be simplified as there would be a direct correlation between the receipted instruction and the vote on the resolution.

While splitting the meeting into two was proposed as an option, the progression towards holding virtual AGMS without this option has progressed more rapidly due to the impact of Covid-19 and related prohibitions from meeting in person. The implementation of virtual AGMs, as first evidenced by Jimmy Choo, is conceptually an easier action to implement.

Covid-19 advice

The Covid-19 pandemic has left companies with a requirement to hold AGMs within a specific timescale with a dilemma as to how to proceed. An initial guidance paper was produced jointly by Slaughter and May and The Chartered Governance Institute on 16 March 2020. This guidance offered suggestions reflecting UK company law and associated regulation. It noted that companies would need to consider their own individual circumstances, including their articles and any other relevant matters. The guidance provided the following options:

- Adapt the basis on which you hold the AGM.
- Delay convening the AGM, if notice has not yet been issued.
- Postpone the AGM, if permitted under the articles.
- Adjourn the AGM.
- Conduct a hybrid AGM, if permitted under the Articles.

Given that the situation has continued to evolve after the publication of the guidance and the restrictions on meetings have been increased, the ability to implement a short-term delay has become impractical. Considerations of longer-term potential solutions of holding a hybrid AGM utilising elements of virtual meeting technology already used for directors' meetings has become more relevant. As was previously noted, precedents have been set by companies such as Jimmy Choo for holding full virtual AGMs, as long as the technology can be applied.

In the guidance, it was noted that virtual-only meetings are not viable for most companies given they may not constitute valid meetings. However, if the articles allow this, companies can conduct a hybrid AGM (a combination of a physical and electronic meeting).

If a company has already issued its AGM notice for a physical-only meeting but its articles allow a hybrid AGM, it can change to a hybrid AGM. An announcement should be made to reflect this decision and the website should be updated.

Companies conducting a hybrid AGM should make shareholders aware that they can participate fully in the AGM electronically. Holding a hybrid meeting in itself will not preclude the ability of shareholders to attend in person, therefore, the measures under 'Adapt the basis on which you hold the AGM' should also be considered.

It should be noted that, if a company has a limited number of members, it may be possible to hold a full virtual AGM, following the guidance on virtual meetings of directors.

Guidance on virtual AGMs

In light of increased Covid-19 restrictions, a further guidance note was prepared and published on 26 March 2020 by Linklaters LLP, Slaughter and May, Clifford Chance LLP, Freshfields Bruckhaus Deringer LLP and The Chartered Governance Institute, with the support of the Financial Reporting Council, the City of London Law Society Company Law Committee, GC100 – the Association of General Counsel and Company Secretaries working in FTSE 100 Companies, the Investment Association and the Quoted Companies Alliance.

This set out their views regarding how listed companies incorporated under the UK Companies Acts might implement contingency plans in light of the prohibitions on meeting in the absence of any relevant legislative changes. The Department for Business, Energy and Industrial Strategy has also reviewed this guidance note.

Checking relevant provisions of a company's articles and co-ordinating with registrars and venue providers is key, as is ensuring shareholders are kept regularly updated and are given their right to vote. The guidance note offered suggestions reflecting UK company law and associated regulation.

The guidance consisted of a number of frequently asked questions and their answers, which are replicated here:

1   Can a general meeting of a listed UK public company be validly held while the restrictions on meeting are in force?

   Yes, but general meetings will have to be held in a different way while the restrictions are in force. While the requirements of a valid general meeting are in part determined by a company's articles (and will, therefore, need to be checked on a case-by-case basis), the majority of listed UK public companies should be able to hold a valid general meeting in the manner described below.

2 Are shareholders generally able to attend general meetings while the restrictions are in force?

Not in person. The restrictions prohibit public gatherings of more than two people. The only exceptions to this are where the gathering is of people who live together or where the gathering is 'essential for work purposes' (noting that workers should try to minimise all gatherings). Attendance at a general meeting by a shareholder (other than one specifically required to form the quorum for that meeting) is not 'essential for work purposes'.

Shareholders should, of course, be encouraged to vote by proxy. Companies may want to encourage the submission of questions for the board of directors in writing with the answers to be published in whatever manner companies determine, for example on the company website.

Companies should make it clear in their notice of meeting, or by RIS announcement and by updating the information on their website where the notice of meeting has already been published, that public gatherings of more than two people are not permitted under the 'Stay at Home' measures and that, therefore, shareholders are not allowed to attend the meeting in person. This wording should be unambiguous (i.e. stronger than merely recommending that shareholders not attend) and should make it clear that anyone seeking to attend the meeting will be refused entry to the meeting and that shareholders should vote by proxy. Information should also be offered about how shareholders can remain engaged through voting and ask questions of directors. It should, however, also note that the current situation is evolving and that further announcements may be required.

3 Can a company prevent shareholders and proxies from attending a general meeting?

Yes. The chair of a general meeting of a UK public company has broad common law powers to preserve order at that meeting, ensure the safety of the attendees and allow the business of the meeting to be transacted. These are likely to be backed up by express powers to do the same in the company's articles.

As the attendance of more than two people at a general meeting (other than where this is essential for work purposes) is not permitted under the restrictions, not to mention unsafe for the attendees, the chair of a general meeting should exercise those powers to exclude excess attendees. This means that any of those whose presence is not 'essential for work purposes' should be excluded, once two people (including the chair of the meeting) are present. This allows a public company to hold a general meeting 'behind closed doors' and to carry out the business of that meeting, provided a quorum can be established and maintained, and provided the other requirements of a general meeting are observed.

For some companies, it may be necessary to have additional personnel at the location of the meeting (if not in the room where it is held) to ensure its proper conduct and safe operation (such as technicians, if there is to be a webcast, and/or security staff) but this should be kept to the minimum and only where this is essential for work purposes.

4 How will a quorate general meeting be held, if shareholders are not able to attend?

The quorum for a general meeting is typically set out in a public company's articles (or is determined to be two members present in person or by proxy by section 318(2) of the Companies Act 2006). This quorum may be satisfied by two director and/or employee shareholders of the company attending the meeting, with resolutions being passed by the proxy votes of those who have not been able to attend in person (or by appointing one of those employees as a corporate representative under section 323 of the Companies Act 2006) and the votes of those in attendance.

This might be achieved by, for example, an executive director and the company secretary being present at the general meeting, provided that each is a member, a corporate representative or appointed as a proxy. The fact that their presence is necessary in order for a quorum to be formed means that their presence is 'essential for work purposes' (and, therefore, permitted), especially given they are both employees and the company needs to deal with the business of the meeting.

All, or almost all, companies should be able to form a quorate meeting in this way. In some situations (for example where the meeting venue is unavailable), it may be necessary for a quorate meeting to be formed at another location which is under the control of the company. In extreme situations, this might be at the home of a director or employee, with that director or employee and a fellow householder (if not shareholders themselves) being appointed as proxies or corporate representatives. This is clearly permitted under the restrictions, but the appropriate process for changing the venue of a general meeting would need to be followed as described below.

Of course, all appropriate social distancing measures should be observed by the small number of attendees at a physical meeting. For example, the meeting should be no longer than is required and if those attending are not from the same household, they should maintain at least the recommended minimum degree of physical separation.

5 What if the quorum requirement is more than two?

The articles of some public companies require more than two shareholders to be present for a meeting to be quorate. However, these members may typically be present either in person or represented by proxy. In this case, two natural persons will need to be present in person as described above in order to constitute a 'meeting', but one of them (for example, the person who chairs the general meeting) might be appointed as proxy for other members in order to fulfil the quorum requirement.

If, unusually, a quorum requires the physical presence of more than two persons, then additional members or proxies may be required to attend in person. This is likely to be limited to a very small number of companies and the number of people required to be present in any one place is likely to be very small (in single figures) and should be kept to the minimum necessary to enable the meeting to proceed. Again, all appropriate social distancing measures should be observed.

6   Who will chair a general meeting?

The articles will determine who chairs a general meeting. They typically provide that the chair of the board or, in the absence of the chair of the board, another director shall preside as chair of the meeting. It may be helpful for a director to attend as part of the quorum so that it is clear who shall act as chair of the meeting. Alternatively, articles may allow for any member to be elected to act as the chair of the meeting by a resolution of the company passed at that meeting.

To make sure that the chair of the meeting can exercise all proxy votes submitted, companies should make sure that the form of proxy appoints the chair of the meeting (and not the chair of the board or a specific director who may on the day be unable to attend). Where shareholders have already appointed someone other than the chair of the meeting as their proxy, they should be encouraged to submit a new proxy form appointing the chair of the meeting instead (as it is unlikely that the original proxy will be permitted to attend unless she/he is someone required to form part of the quorum for the meeting). Where proxy forms allow someone other than the chair of the meeting to be appointed (as they normally do), shareholders should be encouraged to appoint the chair of the meeting, given that any other proxy may well not be permitted to attend the meeting.

7   Will the other directors be allowed to or expected to attend the general meeting?

There is no legal requirement for directors (other than those whose presence may be required to form a quorate meeting as described above) to attend a general meeting and their attendance would not be permitted under the restrictions in place. It would, however, be possible as an option for them to dial in to the meeting if the company considers that this is helpful for running the meeting, although it is not required.

8   Where should general meetings be held if the planned venue is unavailable or otherwise inaccessible?

Companies that have already convened a general meeting for a venue that has since become unavailable will need to find an alternative venue. If the company's articles allow the board to postpone the meeting or move its location to an alternative venue, they should consider exercising this power to move the meeting to a more controlled venue, such as the company's head office. While some companies may ordinarily have security concerns (especially if their general meetings are normally very well-attended or if they operate in contentious sectors) the fact that the meeting may be held behind closed doors should mitigate these concerns.

Companies that do not have articles provisions that enable them to postpone their meeting or switch to an alternative venue should, in law, adjourn the meeting from the planned venue to an alternative venue. If practicable, it is accepted that this could be achieved by the small number of employees/others who plan to form a quorum attending the planned venue (or close to it – e.g. outside the door) and adjourning to another suitable venue, where the meeting would be held as described above. Where this is not practicable, companies should take advice on the best course of action in the circumstances, while always preserving the safety of the directors and employees involved and complying with prevailing government rules.

Conclusion

While legislation is adapting to keep pace with the developing technology available to companies, the speed of this development means that they will both inevitably be playing catch up. The Covid-19 pandemic has facilitated the greater use of technology, albeit that elements of it, such as virtual board meetings and the use of board portals, were already in use across the majority of companies.

In general, legislation and its application to company meetings can be seen to be relatively flexible given its aim is to facilitate greater and more effective communication between companies and their shareholders.

5 – Section 1 conclusion

The framework for company meetings is incorporated under law and in the articles of a company. While the Company Act 2006 is overarching in its application, it would be too simplistic to assume that all companies use both it and the model articles introduced in 2013. In practice, the articles of a company are those in use at their time of incorporation and may, or may not, have been updated and adapted since such time.

Putting in place a framework for effective meeting processes can start with the legislation and general guidance. It would then need to be checked against the particular articles of the company before having final sign off.

Many may believe that meetings of the board are too formulaic and rigid in their format and remit. While legislation does provide some rigour that must be followed, its application can reflect the culture and requirements of each individual company, in the same way that articles can be adapted where required to meet specific requirements. Having said that this is possible, it may not be advisable, given the act and model articles have been drafted to create a robust but flexible framework that should be suitable for the majority of companies without being too rigid.

Even with the rapid development and implementation of new technology, legislation and articles remain flexible enough to enable implementation; it is the wider infrastructure that sometimes prevents rapid deployment, whether this is recognising members, ensuring security of data or creating equal access for all.

This book, and this section in particular, provides both the foundation for implementation and also areas for thought and consideration as to where the framework for meetings of the future may go aligned to new possibilities opened up by technology and new ways of working and interacting. If an audit of the application of these frameworks is needed it should focus on the resources and time spent on meetings. If this is excessive there is room for improvement to enable the purpose of the company to be the driving factor, not the framework of meetings and governance which should sit beneath it in a positive support role.

Section 2
Meetings of directors

6 – Section 2 Introduction

Introduction to meetings of the board of directors

This section focuses on internal meetings of directors, their purpose, when they should be called, the practical aspects of convening internal meetings, actions at the meeting and subsequent reporting. For clarity, this introduction also provides background on the powers conferred on both the company itself as well as its directors, plus the members' ability to become involved where they disagree with the board. For context, explanations of the number of directors and their quorum is also explained.

Delegation of director responsibilities to committees and further background on meetings of committees is included in Chapter 21.

Powers to Act

Directors derive their powers from provisions that are usually contained in a company's articles of association and from common law. Generally speaking, they must exercise those powers collectively at a board meeting. However, articles normally allow the directors to act by written resolution and to delegate their powers to some other body or person.

The procedures to be followed at meetings of directors are determined largely by a company's articles of association. The Companies Act 2006 interferes very little in this area, however, where the articles are silent on any matter, the common law will apply. Where the topic is included, articles usually provide that the proceedings of committees of directors are governed by the same rules as board meetings.

The courts will not necessarily invalidate a transaction merely because the directors failed to follow proper procedures, particularly where the directors could rectify that failing by holding a proper meeting. The courts will not, however, normally tolerate such failures where a director is interested in the transaction.

It is beneficial when considering internal board meetings to differentiate between items that need board discussion and approval and those that can be delegated. Too often board meetings are held for operational matters that are not board decisions, thus creating an ineffective governance structure that occupies senior board members in ineffective meetings without clear purpose. This limits their ability to perform as leaders, reduces the resources available, diminishes focus on strategy, and allows the company to drift.

Conversely, having too few board meetings or delegating all responsibilities to management of the business can result in the leadership and oversight role of the board becoming ineffective with managers effectively running the business without direction, formality or guidance.

Adopting and maintaining a healthy governance structure with meaningful board meetings, clear delegation and effective interaction ensures that the framework enhances the company instead of being detrimental.

This section will reflect on why and when board meetings should be held to create an effective governance framework that enhances the company and supports business success. Thereafter the practicalities of meeting protocols and best practice will be covered in detail to enable practical application. Before then it is worth providing more detail on what happens if directors fail to comply with their fiduciary duties.

Failure to comply

Although the directors have a duty to act in accordance with the provisions of the company's articles of association in order to avoid personal liability, their failure to do so will not always invalidate a transaction, at least as far as innocent third parties are concerned. Protection against defects in the decision-making process is provided by statute, articles and the common law where, for example:

- the directors act beyond the company's powers;
- the directors act beyond their powers;
- there is a defect in the appointment or qualification of a director;
- the directors fail to follow proper procedures;
- under the principle of unanimous consent, where the directors fail to follow the proper formal procedures but can be shown to have all agreed informally to the proposed transaction; and
- the number of directors is less than the minimum prescribed by or in accordance with the articles.

In relation to meetings of the company or the board, the above-noted criteria are key areas for the company board members and their support team to ensure that guidelines are in place and that they are followed. Specifically, the appointment of directors also has a knock-on effect on the confirmation of a quorum, as does the prescribed number of directors.

Acts beyond the company's capacity

The validity of an act done by a company cannot be called into question on the grounds of lack of capacity by reason of anything contained in the company's constitution; for example, the objects clause or statement of objects (s. 39(1)). A member may still bring proceedings to restrain the doing of an act which is beyond the company's capacity; but no such proceedings shall lie in respect of an act to be done in fulfilment of a legal obligation arising from a previous act of the company (s. 40(4)).

It remains the duty of the directors to observe any limitations on their powers flowing from any limitation on the company's capacity (s. 171) and action by the directors which, but for section 39(1), would be beyond the company's capacity may only be ratified by an ordinary resolution of the company passed in accordance with section 239.

Acts beyond the powers of the directors

In favour of a person dealing with a company in good faith, the power of the board of directors to bind the company, or authorise others to do so, is deemed, by virtue of section 40, to be free of any limitation under the company's constitution. Limitations under the company's constitution are deemed to include limitations deriving from a resolution of the company in general meeting or a meeting of any class of shareholders or from any shareholders' agreement (s. 40(3)). This section does not apply where a director is a party to the transaction (s. 41) (see below).

A person is not bound to make any enquiries as to the limitations on the powers of the board to bind the company or authorise others to do so, is presumed to have acted in good faith unless the contrary is proved, and is not to be regarded as acting in bad faith by reason only of his knowing that an act is beyond the powers of the directors under the company's constitution (s. 40(2)).

A member may still bring proceedings to restrain the doing of an act which is beyond the powers of the directors provided that the act is not required to be done in fulfilment of a legal obligation arising from a previous act of the company (s. 40(4)).

The liability incurred by the directors, or any other person, by reason of the directors' exceeding their powers is also not affected (s. 40(5)). The company could, therefore, sue the directors itself. This is most likely to occur if a new board has been appointed or the company is in insolvency as the incumbent directors rarely initiate action against themselves. However, if the directors refuse to take action against themselves, the shareholders might be able to bring a derivative action on behalf of the company.

Although it is possible for an act by the board of directors which is not beyond the powers of the company but which is beyond the board's powers to be ratified by an ordinary resolution of the company in general meeting after the event, it is not possible to authorise such acts in advance.

Where a director is party to a transaction

Section 40 is qualified with respect to transactions to which directors or their associates are a party by section 41. It provides that where the board of directors exceeds its powers under the company's constitution and one of the parties to the transaction with the company is a director of the company or its holding company or an associate of such a director, the transaction will be voidable at the instance of the company (s. 41(2)). This means that, assuming the transaction is still capable of being rescinded, the company can decide whether to treat it as void or to enforce its contractual rights. Whether or not the transaction is avoided, the director or his associate will be liable to account to the company for any gain which he has made directly or indirectly by the transaction and to indemnify the company for any loss or damage resulting from the transaction (s. 41(3)).

The transaction ceases to be voidable if:

■ restitution of any money or other asset which was the subject of the transaction is no longer possible; or
■ the company is indemnified for any loss or damage resulting from the transaction; or
■ rights acquired in good faith for value and without actual notice of the directors' exceeding their powers by a person who is not a party to the transaction would be affected by the avoidance; or
■ the transaction is affirmed by the company in general meeting, by ordinary or special resolution or otherwise as the case may require (s. 41(5)).

A person other than a director of the company is not liable if he shows that at the time the transaction was entered into he did not know that the directors were exceeding their powers (s. 41(5)). Section 41 does not affect the rights of an innocent party to a transaction and such parties may apply to the court for an order affirming, severing or setting aside the transaction (s. 41(6)).

Defects in appointment of qualification of directors
CA 2006, section 161

Section 161 of the Companies Act 2006 serves to validate the acts of a person acting as a director notwithstanding that it is afterwards discovered:

(a) that there was a defect in their appointment;
(b) that they were disqualified from holding office;
(c) that they had ceased to hold office; and
(d) that they were not entitled to vote on the matter in question.

This allows third parties to deal with the company through its directors without having to investigate whether they have been properly appointed.

Anyone seeking to rely on such provisions must have acted in good faith. It is particularly important to note that the defect must have been discovered 'afterwards'. A person who merely has notice of the facts which give rise to the defect will not be prevented from relying on them unless they are also aware of the consequences of those facts. The requirements of good faith will normally prevent a director from benefiting under such provisions.

Number of directors less than prescribed minimum and quorum
Articles commonly require a company to have a minimum number of directors as well as specifying a quorum for meetings of directors. No such provision is made in any of the model articles. It is not uncommon for a company's articles to set out a higher and more straightforward minimum requirement.

Such requirement can cause problems because, under the common law, if the articles prescribe a minimum number of directors and the actual number of directors falls below that minimum, the continuing directors cannot exercise any of their powers even though there are sufficient of them to form a quorum.

A question that begs to be asked is whether there is any point prescribing a minimum number of directors if the articles say that such a minimum can be ignored? The best answer that can be given is that the remaining directors may have a general duty to take steps to fill the vacancies so as to bring their number back to the prescribed minimum. In other words, they could not continue indefinitely to operate below the prescribed minimum. It may also be that if they fail to fill the vacancies, the members in general meeting may do so in default regardless of anything in the articles to the contrary.

The articles of a company with four equal shareholders might require a minimum of four directors, the implication being that each of the members will be appointed as a director. The promoters or incorporators of a company may set a high figure to give the impression that the company is more respectable and that the executive directors will be monitored by an independent element on the board.

In reality, prescribing a minimum number of directors in the articles that is higher than the statutory minimum is likely to cause more problems than it is worth and it is notable that no minimum number is prescribed in any of the model articles.

Number of directors falls below quorum
Articles which allow the directors to act notwithstanding any vacancy in their number do not operate where the number of directors is less than that required to constitute a quorum unless specific provision is made. Modern articles usually give the continuing directors limited powers to act in these circumstances (see, e.g. reg. 90 of Table A above). Because of the words 'falls below' in regulation 90, this type of article can only be relied upon if the minimum number of directors prescribed by the articles has at some time been reached.

Even if a company's articles make no provision for a minimum number of directors, they will normally give the directors limited powers to act where there are not sufficient to form a quorum. The powers given will normally be exclusively related to making further appointments to bring the number back up to the quorum. This is the case with the model articles for private companies which provide (pcls and clg 11(3)):

> 11 (3) If the total number of directors for the time being is less than the quorum required, the directors must not take any decision other than a decision—
>   (a) to appoint further directors, or
>   (b) to call a general meeting to enable the shareholders to appoint further directors.

The model articles for plcs make similar provision but provide for different rules depending on whether there is only one remaining director or more than one (plc 11). Some companies have adopted articles which go further by giving the continuing directors power to act where there is a matter which must be dealt with urgently.

7 – Why and when to convene a board meeting

There are no fixed rules regarding the convening of formal board meetings with the model articles permitting company directors to reach decisions by any other means, provided they can communicate effectively with each other. Accordingly, decisions may be reached through electronic means as well as physically. Written resolutions of directors are permitted by the model articles and additional articles could be included to enable approval by a majority rather than all. The key is to ensure that all directors can participate on decision making and related exchanges of views and debate.

Although the day-to-day operations of a company will be left to the executive team and management, the board as a collective sets the culture, values and behaviours of the business. Formal meetings of the board display this leadership role in action and ensure that all board members continue to function as a cohesive team. Board meetings are also the forum used to discuss and agree strategy and purpose, as well as maintaining oversight of finance and risk. Practically this is also the forum where matters of policy are debated and approved.

Why and when to convene a formal board meeting

Having clear guidelines on what should be approved at a board meeting and what topics the board should retain responsibility for creates a framework for agreeing why and when a board meeting should be held. This starts with matters reserved for the board (see Chapter 3 and Appendix 1) and extends to those matters that the board believes they should keep full ownership of beyond standard matters.

Where the company is listed, the board should be mindful of those matters that must be approved by members rather than the board of directors. Appendix 1 provides a list of matters requiring approval by resolution, differentiating between differing types of resolution.

Where the company is privately held, this list also provides a useful list of matters that would be expected to be approved by the shareholder or the board of directors, or a combination of both. In practice, a number of these are operational, such as appointing auditors, while others are more strategic such as approving an acquisition or divestment.

In practice, the board should convene on a regular basis with a standing agenda to cover their main responsibilities. There is no defined requirement for scheduling board meetings; however, best practice is quarterly, allowing the company to function between meetings without too intrusive board oversight while providing sufficient frequency to ensure operational effectiveness and strategic development.

In practice, all companies will have a requirement to hold meetings of the board to agree and document decisions made by directors to provide an audit trail or formal record. However, there is no legal requirement for a UK company to have a set number of board meetings in any one financial year.

Board meeting approvals

There are several actions of a company that require director approval which is best evidenced by a formal board meeting being held and minutes being documented, including:

- to approve incorporation of the company;
- to appoint or remove directors of the company;
- to amend the statutory records and documents of the company, such as to change the registered address;
- payment of dividends; and
- to accept and approve the annual statutory accounts.

It is also important to reflect on when a board meeting is not required and whether delegation of responsibilities and authorities creates a more effective organisation or, conversely, creates a board in name only with no ownership. Getting the balance between the two is important to create an effective governance structure and its application will be specific to each company. This will be based on type, size, ownership, breadth, leadership style, management capabilities and a wide range of cultural impacts.

Delegating authority

Boards can delegate authority, particularly in respect of operational matters. Where this is done, best practice is for each formal board meeting to ratify the actions taken since the last meeting. This has a dual purpose in that it provides an audit trail of oversight and provides those undertaking actions on behalf of the board with the comfort that their actions have been approved. Ratification may take the form of simple approval of actions taken or a more in-depth review of the authorities being applied. The differentiation between light-touch approval and in-depth review should be based on the complexity or impact of the authority.

Even if the route of light-touch ratification is taken it benefits having an annual in-depth review of the actions taken and the authority under which these actions are taken, given this is part of the framework that enhances the company and supports business success. For example, if a board has delegated signing authority to an individual, role or team under a power of attorney, an annual re-issuance of such power of attorney – including a review of its effectiveness – would ensure board oversight of its use is being maintained. Interim board meetings can then ratify the use of the power of attorney through confirming a submitted register of use.

Where a board has delegated authority to a formal committee, the board should receive regular reports from the committee at their meetings. The board should then review the report and ensure the continued effectiveness of the committee. What should not happen is a duplication of discussions at board and committee level, otherwise the benefit of the committee is lost. The terms of reference of the committee by the board should be reviewed on an annual or three-year cycle, depending on its purpose. Further information on committee meetings can be found in Chapter 21.

Written resolutions

Most articles make specific provision enabling the directors to act by written resolution even though it is established that they may act outside formal board meetings if they all agree. This is partly because of the uncertainties in the common law but also because articles usually provide a slightly more relaxed regime.

A written resolution enables a board to agree a resolution without the need to meet, whether physically or virtually. The resolution can be set out in writing and approved by all directors independently. This method should obviously only be used where the resolution is uncontentious or a formality and all directors are in agreement.

Sample format for a written resolution

Written resolution of the directors

XYZ LIMITED

Pursuant to the authority given by article [no.] of the company's articles of association, we, the undersigned, being all the directors of XYZ Limited [entitled to receive notice of a meeting of directors (option under Table A)] [eligible to vote on the following resolution had it been proposed at a directors' meeting (option under the model articles)], hereby resolve THAT . . . [insert resolution]

[Date]

[Signatures]

Model articles for private companies

The model articles for private companies provide as a general rule that the directors must take decisions either by a majority at a meeting or as a unanimous decision in accordance with Article 8 of the model articles for private companies which provides that:

Unanimous decisions

8.— (1) A decision of the directors is taken in accordance with this article when all eligible directors indicate to each other by any means that they share a common view on a matter.

(2) Such a decision may take the form of a resolution in writing, copies of which have been signed by each eligible director or to which each eligible director has otherwise indicated agreement in writing.

(3) References in this article to eligible directors are to directors who would have been entitled to vote on the matter had it been proposed as a resolution at a directors' meeting.

(4) A decision may not be taken in accordance with this article if the eligible directors would not have formed a quorum at such a meeting.

Article 8 allows the directors to signify their consent to a unanimous decision in a variety of ways. All that is required is that they must have indicated to each other in some way that they share a common view on the matter. This could, for example, be done at a face-to-face meeting, a series of face-to-face meetings, by a chain of emails, telephone conversations, or using the more traditional method of a written resolution. The article would seem to require the directors to share a common view and to have indicated that view to each other. Accordingly, unlike the common law principle of unanimous consent, it does not necessarily allow any of the directors to be deemed to have acquiesced in the decision. Neither, however, should the article necessarily be considered to exclude the common law principle of unanimous consent, which could still serve to validate decisions not made in accordance with the articles.

It should be noted, however, that although it is not necessary under article 8 for the directors to agree to a decision in writing, they are required to ensure that the company keeps a written record of every unanimous decision taken by them for at least ten years from the date of the decision (pcls and clg 15).

The record of the decision kept for these purposes need not be signed by all the eligible directors but probably ought to be authenticated by a director (preferably the chair) or the company secretary (if the company has one). Nevertheless, it is almost certainly preferable for the copy of the decision retained for these purposes to be signed by all the eligible directors because this will then serve as evidence of their agreement.

Article 8 makes it clear that the unanimous decision-making procedure may not be used if the number of directors able to participate in the decision would not have been sufficient to form a quorum at a meeting of directors. Directors who would not have been entitled to vote on the matter had it been proposed as a resolution at a directors' meeting cannot be counted for these purposes. Effectively, directors who would not have been eligible to vote on the matter at a board meeting (e.g. because of a personal interest) are not required to consent to the decision and the fact that may have purported to consent to it (or, perhaps, even to oppose it) is irrelevant for the purposes of determining whether the decision is valid.

It should be noted that 'in writing' is defined for the purposes of the model articles in article 8 (1) (defined terms) as 'the representation or reproduction of words, symbols or other information in a visible form by any method or combination of methods, whether sent or supplied in electronic form or otherwise'. Accordingly, it is not necessary for the purposes of a written resolution under art. 8 for directors to sign a hard copy of the resolution under hand. Any method of signature, including some sort of electronic signature, would suffice for these purposes. Indeed, in the case of a written resolution sent to a director by email, it is likely that an emailed reply clearly signifying consent would be satisfactory for these purposes, although it would obviously be preferable for evidential purposes if that email was signed using a proper electronic signature.

Model articles for public companies

The model articles for public companies also allow the directors to act without holding a meeting by the more traditional method of passing a written resolution (plc 7, 17 and 18). The plc model articles make far more detailed provision about who may propose a directors' written resolution and the procedures that must be followed in this regard.

Proposing directors' written resolutions

17.—(1) Any director may propose a directors' written resolution.

(2) The company secretary must propose a directors' written resolution if a director so requests.

(3) A directors' written resolution is proposed by giving notice of the proposed resolution to the directors.

(4) Notice of a proposed directors' written resolution must indicate—

(a) the proposed resolution, and

(b) the time by which it is proposed that the directors should adopt it.

(5) Notice of a proposed directors' written resolution must be given in writing to each director.

---

(6) Any decision which a person giving notice of a proposed directors' written resolution takes regarding the process of adopting that resolution must be taken reasonably in good faith.

Adoption of directors' written resolutions

18.—(1) A proposed directors' written resolution is adopted when all the directors who would have been entitled to vote on the resolution at a directors' meeting have signed one or more copies of it, provided that those directors would have formed a quorum at such a meeting.

(2) It is immaterial whether any director signs the resolution before or after the time by which the notice proposed that it should be adopted.

(3) Once a directors' written resolution has been adopted, it must be treated as if it had been a decision taken at a directors' meeting in accordance with the articles.

(4) The company secretary must ensure that the company keeps a record, in writing, of all directors' written resolutions for at least ten years from the date of their adoption.

The requirement in article 17(4) that notice of a proposed directors' written resolution *must* indicate the time by which it is proposed that the directors should adopt it seems pernickety at best, when one considers that article 18(2) specifically states that it is immaterial whether any director signs the resolution before or after the time by which the notice proposed that it should be adopted. Technically, this means that a written resolution that does not state a time by which it is proposed it should be adopted might be defective even though any such statement is largely superfluous. Hopefully, should this issue ever be raised in litigation, the courts will adopt a common-sense approach and rule that the absence of any proposed deadline in the notice should be taken for the purposes of article 17(4) to mean that there was no deadline.

It should be noted that 'in writing' is defined for the purposes of the model articles in article 1 as 'the representation or reproduction of words, symbols or other information in a visible form by any method or combination of methods, whether sent or supplied in electronic form or otherwise'. Accordingly, notice of the resolution may be given in either hard copy or electronic form. In addition, the fact that directors are required by article 18(1) to sign a copy of the resolution does not mean that this must be done by signature under hand on a hard copy version. Any method of signature, including electronic signature, would suffice for these purposes. Indeed, in the case of a written resolution sent to a director by email, it is likely that an emailed reply clearly signifying consent would be satisfactory for these purposes, although it would obviously be preferable for evidential purposes if that email was subsequently validated by formal signature.

Under the model articles for public companies, an alternate director may sign a written resolution, but only if it is not signed or to be signed by that person's appointor (plc 26(3)). For these purposes, it is probably safe to say that the signature of an alternate can be ignored if the resolution is also signed by his appointor. An alternate is presumably entitled to receive notice of any proposed written resolution under plc 26(1) and will be subject to the same restrictions as his appointor regarding his participation in a decision made by written resolution (plc 26(2)(c)) as well as potentially being excluded from participating on his own account (plc 26(2)(a)).

Practical points on written resolutions

Most company secretaries prefer to obtain all the necessary signatures of the directors on the same day. If that is not possible, it is normally preferable to send out copies and obtain all the relevant signatures as quickly as possible. It is quite common for copies of the written resolution to be faxed or emailed to the directors and for the directors to be asked to fax back a signed copy or email their consent to the company on the same day.

There is nothing to prevent the inclusion in articles of procedures to enable the directors to pass resolutions in writing where, for example, only three out of four directors or a certain percentage of them sign it.

Example wording for article enabling written resolution approval by majority

A resolution in writing signed or approved [by fax or by any electronic system or by telephone and subsequently confirmed in writing or by fax or by electronic systems] by not less than [90%] of the directors [and] entitled to vote thereon shall be as valid and effectual as a resolution duly passed at a meeting of the directors and may consist of several documents or other such forms of approval in the like form each signed or so approved by one or more directors.

Provision can also be made to allow directors to sign, approve or signify their agreement to written resolutions by methods other than a normal signature under hand on a hard copy version. The model articles achieve this by adopting a much wider definition of the term 'in writing' than might be traditionally applied.

Effective date and minutes

It must be presumed that a written resolution will not be effective until the last director required to sign it has done so.

It is not necessary to keep original signed copies of a directors' written resolution, although it may be sensible to do so for evidential purposes. It is not particularly clear from section 248 whether it is necessary to keep a record of written resolutions or unanimous decisions in the same way as is required with regard to minutes of meetings of directors. However, the model articles require companies to do so (pcls 15, clg 15 and plc 18(4)). The record kept for these purposes need not be the original signed copies (although they would be satisfactory). A record of the fact that a resolution had been passed or decision made in accordance with the relevant article would suffice for these purposes, although that record probably ought to be authenticated by a director (preferably the chair) or the company secretary (if the company has one).

Circulation of written resolutions proposed by the directors

There are circumstances where written resolutions proposed by the directors must be circulated to the members and section 291 of the 2006 Act applies to the circulation of a written resolution proposed by the directors. The company must send or submit a copy of the resolution to every eligible member by:

(a) sending copies at the same time (so far as reasonably practicable) to each of them in hard copy form, electronic form or by means of a website; or
(b) if it is possible to do so without undue delay, by submitting the same copy to each eligible member in turn (or different copies to each of a number of eligible members in turn); or
(c) by a combination of the above methods.

The copy of the resolution must be accompanied by a statement informing the member how to signify their agreement to the resolution and the date by which the resolution must be passed if it is not to lapse.

Failure to comply with section 291 is an offence but does not affect the validity of the resolution if passed (s. 291(7)).

Special procedures apply to pass certain resolutions as written resolution. These adaptations generally require the same information to be circulated with the written resolution as would have been included in any notice had it been proposed at a general meeting. The relevant requirements are contained in the sections of the Act which impose the general requirements for that type of resolution, rather than in Part 13, Chapter 2. Examples of where special procedures are required include:

(a) a resolution approving a director's long-term service contract under section 188;
(b) a resolution approving a director's loan, quasi loan or credit transaction under sections 197, 198 or 201 respectively;
(c) a resolution to disapply pre-emption rights under section 571.
(d) a resolution under section 694 conferring authority to make an off-market purchase of the company's own shares (see s. 696);
(e) a resolution under section 697 conferring authority to vary a contract for an off-market purchase of the company's own shares (see s. 699);

(f) a resolution under section 700 releasing a company's rights under a contract for an off-market purchase of the company's own shares (see s. 699); and

(g) a resolution giving approval under section 716 for the redemption or purchase of company's own shares out of capital (see s. 718).

Further detail on written resolutions proposed by members can be found in Chapter 13.

Maintaining copies of written resolutions

Every company must keep copies of all resolutions of members passed otherwise than at general meetings, so resolutions passed as written resolutions should also be kept (s. 355(1)(a)).

In relation to resolutions passed on or after 1 October 2007, the copies must be kept for at least ten years from the date of the resolution (s. 355(2)).

Copies of resolutions passed before that date must be kept permanently because they are still required to be kept in accordance with the requirements of section 382A of the Companies Act 1985.

The company secretary (if any) and the directors can be fined for any default regarding compliance with the requirements of section 355 of the 2006 Act and section 382A of the 1985 Act relating to the maintenance of these records.

Evidential status of copies of written resolutions

Section 356 confers special evidential status on copies of resolutions kept in accordance with section 355. A record of a resolution passed otherwise than at a general meeting, if purporting to be signed by a director of the company or by the company secretary, is evidence (in Scotland, sufficient evidence) of the passing of the resolution (s. 356(2)). Where there is a record of a written resolution of a private company, the requirements of the Act with respect to the passing of the resolution are deemed to be complied with unless the contrary is proved (s. 356(3)).

Section 382A(2) of the 1985 Act makes similar provision regarding records kept in accordance with the requirements of that Act.

Informal consent

If the directors unanimously agree on a particular course of action, there is no need for that decision to be taken at a formal meeting of directors. However, it is unwise to rely on this common law rule, particularly where the articles provide an alternative method of acting without holding a meeting (e.g. by passing a written resolution).

It is always preferable to retain some evidence of the fact that all the directors agreed to act in a certain way. One of the dangers of relying on the principle of unanimous consent is that it might be difficult to prove that there was indeed unanimity, although this can sometimes be inferred from the fact that a director did not object within a reasonable time.

Creating and keeping an audit trail of unanimous consent may be best served by having approval in writing through email or other written communication. A complete record could then be created by using this as the foundation for written consent, thus negating any future potential for retracting consent or challenging the decision.

Conclusion

As has been seen, board meetings should be held to agree and approve decisions made by directors, with the minutes of such meetings providing the documentary evidence of such that can be referred to at a later stage if required. They should also be used as a forum to discuss and agree the delegation of authority to any other individual or forum, such as a committee.

It should not be forgotten that the board should also be leading the business and setting the strategy for the future. The application of this strategy can be documented in a business plan, the actions under which may form part of the delegations agreed at the board meeting.

In some circumstances, it may be more advantageous to use written resolutions rather than have the formality of a board meeting, although these should not take the place of all board meetings, unless there is a sole director (see Chapter 20). This chapter has provided detail on the use of written resolutions, however it should be remembered that the function of the board is best served as a collective of experts above and beyond just approvals and this cannot be accessed without the directors meeting for discussion, challenge and agreement.

8 – How to convene a board meeting

Most matters concerning proceedings at meetings of directors are determined by the articles of the company and, in default, by reference to the common law. Although companies have considerable freedom to establish their own internal board procedures, most have historically adopted the provisions contained within model articles. These model articles, whether the current version or historical ones that companies may have in place, provide a valuable framework for meetings of the board and, as a minimum, create a framework to underpin company specific requirements. They also provide a default position for those without the impetus, for whatever reason, to establish their own procedures. For smaller companies still using historical articles, such as Table A, and without the resources or time to create a framework, it may be beneficial to amend and adopt current model articles or, as a minimum, adopt the meeting framework from current model articles. Appendix 5 provides a comparison between Table A and current model articles.

This chapter concludes with a checklist for the company secretary or others who may be supporting meetings of the board of directors.

Collective exercise of powers

As a general rule, the directors must exercise their powers collectively (i.e. at a properly convened and constituted meeting of the board of directors). However, there are noted exceptions that enable powers to be exercised either in a different forum or manner if:

■ the articles allow them to delegate their powers (e.g. to a committee);
■ the articles allow them to make decisions in some other way (e.g. by written resolution); and
■ the directors all agree, in which case they may act informally.

It should be noted that the last points still provide the board with a way to exercise their powers as a collective, while the first point is a delegation outside of this collective. It should always be remembered that there are certain matters that must be reserved for the board (see Chapter 3). Here, while a committee or other alternative forum could discuss and advise on such topic, any decisions must be made by the board.

Where the directors are required to act collectively as a board, unanimity is not required. Under common law, decisions may validly be made by a majority of the directors who are present at board meetings, provided that there are sufficient directors to form a quorum. Under common law, a quorum exists where a majority of the directors are present at the meeting. Thus, if there are nine directors, five must be present to form a quorum. If five attend a meeting only three of them (i.e. one third of the directors in total) need to vote in favour of a proposal to bind the company. If seven attend, four must vote in favour, and so on. The common law principle that a majority of the directors present may bind the company is usually adopted in the articles. However, the articles usually specify a different quorum for meetings of directors and frequently allow them to alter that quorum.

Who can call a meeting of directors?

Articles usually provide that any director may call a meeting of directors and that the company secretary at the request of a director shall do so (e.g. pcls 9 and reg. 88 of Table A). Accordingly, a director can normally call a meeting by giving due notice of it to the other directors or by authorising or instructing the company secretary (if any) to give notice of it.

In practice, it is usual for boards of directors to fix the dates of meetings in advance so that the directors can plan their diaries. However, there may be occasions when an additional meeting is needed to deal with urgent business. Any additional meetings are usually called by the chair, and any director wishing to call a meeting would normally be expected to consult the chair first. This ensures that the chair is kept fully informed of the circumstances and may enable an alternative solution to be found, such as the use of a written resolution. If approached, the company secretary should seek to persuade a director to follow this course of action. Although the company secretary cannot refuse to call a meeting if instructed to do so by a director, it is advisable to inform the chair at the earliest opportunity if the director decides not to follow this advice.

Date, time and place

Generally, the directors can hold their meetings wherever they wish, including overseas. However, if the court is satisfied that a particular venue was chosen to ensure that certain directors were unable to attend, it may prevent the meeting from taking place or subsequently declare the proceedings invalid.

The person calling the meeting should specify the date, time and place at which it is to be held as this information must be given in the notice of the meeting. If a director instructs the company secretary to call a meeting, they may specify these matters or leave them to be settled by the secretary, perhaps after contacting the other directors to find the most suitable time and place.

Boards often meet at some regular date, time and place that most of the directors find convenient, (e.g. the second Thursday of each month at the company's registered office). They sometimes go so far as to include this in the board's internal procedures or standing orders. It would be very unusual for such a provision to find its way into a company's articles and almost certainly would be ill-advised.

Notice

The Act makes no provision with regard to notice of directors' meetings. Under the common law, reasonable notice of a meeting must be given to all the directors, although it may not always be necessary to give notice of the business. If proper notice is not given, the meeting and any business transacted at it is liable to be declared invalid. Although articles can modify the basic common law principles, they very rarely do so to any significant extent.

The courts are often reluctant to intervene in disputes regarding the adequacy of the notice given for meetings of directors, particularly where it is evident that a clear majority of the directors were in favour of the business conducted and that, if the meeting was declared invalid, they would simply go back to the office and make exactly the same decision again, albeit by following proper procedures. In addition, those who wish to complain about the adequacy of notice are expected to take prompt action, otherwise the courts may rule that they are deemed to have acquiesced to the irregularity.

Recipients of notice

As a general rule, notice must be given to all the directors. However, notice need not be given where:

- it can have no effect;
- all the directors agree to waive it;
- the articles specifically provide that it need not be given.

Where articles make provision for the appointment of alternate directors, they usually make provision requiring notice of meetings to be given to any alternates in respect of any meeting which the person who appointed them would be entitled to attend (e.g. plc 26). Even if the articles make no such provision, alternate directors are probably entitled to receive notice of such meetings under common law principles.

Notice need not be given where the directors have agreed amongst themselves (or the articles prescribe) that meetings shall be held on a regular basis at a fixed time and place (e.g. on the first Thursday each month at 4.00pm at the company's registered office). In such circumstances, notice would, however, need to be given for any meeting held at a different time or place.

Waiver of notice

Unless the articles provide otherwise, directors cannot waive in advance their right to receive notice of a meeting. All three versions of the model articles make specific provision to allow directors to waive notice (pcls 9(4), clg 9(4) and plc 8(6)) by providing that:

> Notice of a directors' meeting need not be given to directors who waive their entitlement to notice of that meeting, by giving notice to that effect to the company not more than 7 days after the date on which the meeting is held. Where such notice is given after the meeting has been held, that does not affect the validity of the meeting, or of any business conducted at it.

Notice can be waived if all the directors are present and agree to hold a board meeting without notice. In *Smith v Paringa Mines Ltd* [1906] 2 Ch 193, the two directors of a company met in the offices of one of them. The director who was the chair proposed the appointment of a third director. Despite the objection of the other director to this appointment, the chair declared the resolution carried by his casting vote. The appointment was held to be valid as they were both deemed to have agreed to treat their meeting as a board meeting. In *Barron v Potter* [1914] 1 Ch 895, a similar chance meeting between the directors of a company was held to be invalid as a board meeting as the director who proposed and purported to pass (by virtue of his casting vote) resolutions appointing new directors knew that the other director did not wish to attend any board meeting with him.

Length of notice

There is no strict rule as to the length of notice required for meetings of directors although there is an underlying assumption that it must be reasonable according to the circumstances of the company or the meeting concerned. Where the board of directors all work in the same office, reasonable notice may well be two to three hours. Where the directors are spread across different countries, notice would have to take into account time differences and local holidays. Where the directors normally meet on a quarterly basis only and do not work at the same location, the reasonable notice may be two weeks or more.

In practice, standardised meeting schedules are often agreed at the beginning of the calendar year so that all directors have them in their diaries and can work round the dates. Frequently the time, place and date of the next board meeting is also noted and agreed at the end of each board meeting with the meeting minutes being a record and reminder of such. As can be seen, it is impossible to define what is reasonable in every case, or state conclusively the circumstances in which the notice given might be deemed unreasonable.

It is fairly safe to assume that reasonable notice was given if none of the directors object or they all attend the meeting. However, it does not necessarily follow that the notice given was unreasonable merely because a director objects. If a director does object to the notice given, the other directors should consider their position very carefully, taking into account all the other relevant factors. These might include:

(a) the length of notice usually given for similar meetings in that company; and

(b) the nature and urgency of the business to be transacted.

It goes without saying that the courts are more likely to intervene if it can be inferred that the purpose of calling the meeting at relatively short notice was to exclude a particular director from the decision-making process. A director should register his or her objection to the length of notice given immediately and should commence legal proceedings as soon as possible, otherwise the courts may refuse to intervene.

Content of notice

As a minimum, the notice must include the date, time and place of the meeting. It need not necessarily state the nature of the business to be transacted. However, where notice of the business is given, it must not be deliberately misleading. In *Re Homer District Consolidated Gold Mines, ex parte Smith* (1888) 39 ChD 546, a board meeting was called at very short notice and a resolution was passed to rescind a decision made at a meeting held only two weeks previously. The notice of the meeting was held to be invalid for several reasons, one of which was that it was misleading in so far as it did not mention this item of business.

Sample notice of a board meeting

XYZ LIMITED

[Address]

[Date]

To the directors of XYZ Limited

Notice of board meeting

A meeting of the directors of the company will be held at [place] on [date] at [time].

[Signature]

Secretary

By order of the chair

In practice, detailed notice of the business of board meetings and board committees is usually given in the agenda papers circulated prior to the meeting.

Form of notice

Articles often specify the manner in which required notice must be given. However, they usually state that these rules do not apply to meetings of directors.

The model articles prescribed under the 2006 Act basically follow the common-sense approach that notice can be given using any method agreed by the director (see pcls 48, clg 34 and plc 79). They each provide:

1 Subject to the articles, anything sent or supplied by or to the company under the articles may be sent or supplied in any way in which the Companies Act 2006 provides for documents or information which are authorised or required by any provision of that Act to be sent or supplied by or to the company.

2 Subject to the articles, any notice or document to be sent or supplied to a director in connection with the taking of decisions by directors may also be sent or supplied by the means by which that director has asked to be sent or supplied with such notices or documents for the time being.

3 A director may agree with the company that notices or documents sent to that director in a particular way are to be deemed to have been received within a specified time of their being sent, and for the specified time to be less than 48 hours.

In each case, sub-article (1) suggests that documents or information sent by or to the company *under the articles* can be sent in any manner provided for by the 2006 Act (i.e. under company communications provisions). This is useful because the company communications provisions of the Act only apply automatically to documents or information required or authorised to be sent under the Act. Without such an article they would not necessarily extend to documents or information required or authorised to be sent under the articles alone.

It is doubtful whether a notice of a directors' meetings is a document that is required or authorised to be sent by a company under the Act. There is no doubt whatsoever that such a notice is something that is required or authorised to be sent under the model articles (see pcls 9, clg 9 and plc 8). However, it is not necessarily something that is required or authorised to be sent by the company. The model articles provide that any director may call a directors' meeting by giving notice of the meeting to the other directors or by authorising the company secretary (if any) to give such notice. In other words, it is the director who wants to call the meeting who must give notice of it. One could, of course, argue that the director who calls the meeting is acting on behalf of the company, and that the company communications provisions therefore apply to such notices by virtue of sub-article (1). If so, this would mean that notices of directors' meetings can be sent in any form permitted by Schedule 5 of the Act, which sets out the rules for communications by a company. Under those rules, hard copy is the default method of communication. However, electronic, website and other methods of communication can be used if the intended recipient (i.e. a director) has agreed to accept service in that manner.

The 2006 model articles do not require notices of directors' meetings to be sent in accordance with the company communications provisions in Schedule 5 of the Act. In all three versions of the model articles, sub-article (2) provides that any notice or document to be sent or supplied to a director in connection with the taking of decisions by directors *may also* be sent or supplied by the means by which that director has asked to be sent or supplied with such notices or documents for the time being. The words 'may also' in sub-article (2) seem to confirm that sub-article (1) is meant to apply to notices of directors' meetings, in which case it may seem somewhat superfluous to say that they can be sent in some other way because the company communications provisions allow documents or information to be sent by a company in any manner provided the recipient has agreed to accept service in that manner. However, sub-article (2) is not superfluous in so far as it relates to things that may, in practice, need to be sent to the directors in connection with a meeting (e.g. the agenda papers) that are not required to be sent *under the articles*. The model articles require notice of a directors' meeting to be given and state that the notice must specify the date, time and place of the meeting and how the directors may participate in it. The model articles do not require notice of the business to be given or agenda papers to be sent out.

The use of the words 'director has asked' in sub-article (2) implies that a director must have agreed beforehand to the method of communication used. The fact that a director has asked the company to send notices and other documents in a particular way does not necessarily preclude the company from sending them in some other way, provided that the method it uses is effective under any applicable rules. For example, the fact that a director has asked for documents to be sent by email would not necessarily preclude the company from providing them in hard copy form. The fact that a director has provided an address to which such hard copy documents should be sent would not necessarily preclude the company from sending them to the address recorded in the Register of Directors as his service address, if that was different. Under the company communications provisions, the address shown in the Register of Directors (i.e. the directors' service address) is the default address to be used for the service of hard copy communications on a director. The company can also use another address provided by the director for that purpose, but the company communications provisions do not seem to require it to do so (Sch. 5, para. 4(1)).

It is easy to imagine situations in which the court might, if asked, rule otherwise in this regard, particularly where the manner in which notice was given was deliberately chosen to ensure that the director did not, in practice, receive it in time. This could easily happen where a director has provided the company's registered office as his service address but has asked for notices and board agenda papers to be sent to his home address. Unless he regularly attends the registered office and opens his mail, he will not necessarily be aware of the fact that a notice has been sent to him via the registered office. Naturally, directors are meant to make arrangements to ensure that documents served on them at their service address are brought to their attention. If a director nominates the company's registered office as his service address, the assumption must presumably be that somebody from the company will do this. If nobody from the company bothers to do so, or somebody decides deliberately not to do so, in respect of a notice of meeting (which could be viewed as being sent by or on behalf of the company), it would seem to be unfair for the company to be able to claim that the notice had been validly served.

Following this line of reasoning, it would seem to be advisable for a company to use the method of communications that a director has asked it to use, and to notify him using that method if anything has been sent using a different method.

Deemed delivery

Section 1147 provides that documents and information sent by post or electronically are deemed to have been received after 48 hours. In calculating the period of hours for these purposes, no account may be taken of any part of a day that is not a working day.

The deemed delivery rules in section 1147 form part of the company communications provisions of the Act. Accordingly, they only apply for the purposes of any provision of the Companies Acts which requires or authorises documents or information to be sent or supplied by a company (s. 1143). They do not apply to notices, agenda papers or documents sent to directors unless those things are required or authorised to be sent under the Companies Acts. Section 169 provides a good example of a notice that is required under the Act to be sent by a company to a director. It requires the company to notify a director of the fact that someone intends to propose a resolution at a general meeting to remove them as a director. The Act makes no provision whatsoever with regard to the notice that needs to be given for a meeting of directors. This is an area that is governed by a company's articles and the common law. Accordingly, the company communications provisions of the Act do not apply unless the articles say otherwise.

As we have already seen, all three versions of the model articles (see sub-article (1) of pcls 48, clg 34 and plc 79) do seem to apply the company communications provisions of the Act to anything that is required under the articles to be sent to a director, and that this does include notices of meetings (see pcls 9, clg 9 and plc 8), but not necessarily the agenda papers. Where the company communications provisions are deemed to apply (e.g. for documents such as notices), this means that the rules in section 1147 regarding deemed delivery apply. As we have already seen, the application of the default rules in section 1147 can be varied with the agreement of the director (see s. 1147(6)(c)). However, the model articles also provide (see sub-article (3) of pcls 48, clg 34 and plc 79) that a director may agree with the company that notices or documents sent to him in a particular way are to be deemed to have been received within a specified time of their being sent, and for the specified time to be less than 48 hours. This is consistent with the rules in section 1147, but also enables the company to reach agreement regarding the delivery of documents that are not subject to these rules.

Any company whose articles make different provision from the statutory rules on deemed delivery in section 1147 (e.g. by making provision for deemed service after 24 hours for documents sent by first class post) may no longer be able to apply those rules to documents required or authorised to be sent to directors under the Companies Acts because the default rules in section 1147 (where they apply) can only be varied with the agreement of the director concerned. Such articles will still be effective in relation to any document or information that must be sent to the directors under the articles if it is not required or authorised to be sent under the Act.

Practical issues

It is common practice to schedule regular board and board committee meetings for the forthcoming year. This allows the directors to organise their diaries so that they can attend meetings. The schedule is normally appended to or included in the minutes of a board meeting. This satisfies the common law requirements as to notice provided that a copy is sent to each director and it shows the date, time and place of each meeting (see, however, the additional requirement in the model articles that the notice should specify how directors may participate in the meeting (if at all) without being present at the place where it is to take place). It is not strictly necessary to give every piece of information at the same time. However, each of the necessary components must be given within reasonable time before the meeting. It is also normal for a copy of the agenda for the meeting to be circulated to each director prior to the meeting. As this would normally specify the date, time and place of the meeting and any other necessary details, it will also serve as notice of the meeting provided that it is sent out early enough to comply with the requirement that notice must be reasonable in the circumstances.

For small companies with relatively few directors, it may not be necessary or possible to plan so far ahead. Meetings may simply be called on an ad hoc basis at relatively short notice. Even in large public companies it is sometimes necessary to hold additional board meetings to deal with matters which cannot wait until the next scheduled meeting. In such circumstances, it is a good practice for the chair or the company secretary to contact each director to explain the circumstances and to offer a range of possible dates for the meeting, making it clear that the one on which the most are able to attend will be chosen. Once this has been done, each director should be notified of the finally agreed date, time and venue in the usual manner.

The agenda

The agenda is an ordered list of the business to be transacted at a meeting. Although it is not strictly necessary to give notice of the business to be transacted at meetings of directors, it is normal for an agenda to be prepared and sent to each director prior to the meeting, together with any supporting papers that may be necessary to facilitate discussion of that business. If an agenda is sent to the directors prior to the meeting, it will constitute notice of the business and, as such, the rule that it must not be deliberately misleading will apply.

If the notice of meeting includes notice of the business to be transacted, that part of the notice can be referred to as the agenda.

Items of business on the agenda are usually placed in the order that the business is to be taken at the meeting, although the board is not obligated to take them in that order.

Standard agenda items include, but are not limited to:

- appointment of the chair;
- apologies for absence;
- notification of any conflicts of interest;
- ratification of actions taken on behalf of the board since the last meeting;
- review of agreed actions from previous meeting;
- acceptance of reports;
- any other business; and
- confirmation of date, time and place of next meeting.

As can be seen, these standard items are practical in their focus and, while they may bring some discussion, they are focused on the operational aspects of the company.

Example: Agenda for board meeting of a public company

XYZ PLC

Agenda for board meeting to be held at [place] on [date] at [time]

Item		Agenda paper
1.	Minutes of previous meeting	
	To approve the minutes of the board meeting held on [date].	2020/04-01
2.	Management accounts	
	To consider:	
	(a) a list of bank balances as at [date];	2020/04-02a
	(b) cash flow statements for the period to [date];	2020/04-02b
	(c) financial statement as at [date].	2020/04-02c

3.	Audit committee To note the minutes of the [audit] committee meeting held on [date], and the committee's recommendations regarding the financial statements.	2020/04-03
4.	Annual report and accounts To approve the directors' report, [directors' remuneration report], chair's statement, corporate governance reports, statement of directors' responsibility, and annual accounts for the financial year ended [date].	2020/04-04
5.	Dividend To recommend a final dividend of [ ]p per share recommended therein (making a total dividend of [ ]p per share for the year) be approved and that, subject to approval by the company in general meeting, such dividend be paid on [date] to shareholders registered at the close of business on [date].	2020/04-5
6.	Preliminary announcement To authorise the release of the preliminary announcement of the results for the year ended [date].	2020/04-6
7.	Sealing To authorise the affixing of the common seal of the company to the documents set out against items Nos . . . to . . . inclusive in the sealing register.	2020/04-7 briefly explains each transaction
8.	Future meetings To confirm the dates (and general themes) of future board meetings.	2020/04-8

[Date]

[Secretary]

By order of the chair

Most companies would also add a section for discussion of strategy, business plans, risks, opportunities and forward-looking developments. Hence, while the formal agenda will incorporate actions, an active chair will ensure that the board is also discussing the wider environment and business strategy.

Under the Act (s. 172) directors have a responsibility to promote the success of the business, acting in good faith and for the benefit of stakeholders. In doing so they should have regard for:

(a) the likely consequences of any decision in the long term;

(b) the interests of the company's employees;

(c) the need to foster the company's business relationships with suppliers, customers and others;

(d) the impact of the company's operations on the community and the environment;

(e) the desirability of the company maintaining a reputation for high standards of business conduct; and

(f) the need to act fairly as between members of the company.

By building in a wider discussion of the strategy of the business, in relation to all stakeholders, not just shareholders, the directors can evidence, through the discussions held at their board meetings and the minutes thereafter, that they are, in part, meeting these directors' responsibilities through their discussion and subsequent actions.

Agenda for first board meeting

The agenda of the first board meeting of a company on incorporation is relatively standard and serves to create the format of subsequent agendas in terms of the layout of the document.

Example: Agenda for first board meeting (private company)

XYZ LIMITED

Agenda for board meeting to be held at [place] on [date] at [time]

1. To produce the certificate of incorporation and a copy of the memorandum and articles of association as registered.

2. To note that the first directors of the company named by the subscribers in the documents delivered to the Registrar of Companies with the memorandum of association are: [names].

3. To consider and, if thought fit, resolve that [name of director] be appointed chair of the board.

4. To note that [name] was named by the subscribers as secretary in the documents delivered to the Registrar of Companies and to consider and, if thought fit, resolve:

   THAT the appointment of [name] as secretary be confirmed at a salary payable from [date] at the rate of [amount] per annum, such appointment being terminable by [period] notice in writing given by either party to the other at any time.

5. To consider and, if thought fit, resolve:

   THAT the situation of the company's registered office shown in the documents delivered with the memorandum to the Registrar of Companies (namely, [address]) be confirmed.

6. To consider and, if thought fit, resolve:
   THAT the seal, of which an impression is affixed in the margin hereof, be adopted as the common seal of the company.
7. To consider opening a bank account with [name of bank] and, if thought fit, resolve:
   [Resolutions in accordance with bank's printed form for opening an account.]
8. To consider and, if thought fit, resolve:
   THAT [name] be appointed auditors of the company.
9. To produce and read to the meeting declarations made by the directors of interests in transactions or arrangements pursuant to sections 177 and 182 of the Companies Act 2006.
10. To produce forms of application for 98 shares of £1 each in the capital of the company, together with cheques for a total of £100, being payment in full for the said shares and the two shares taken by the subscribers to the memorandum of association.
    To consider and, if thought fit, resolve:
    (a) THAT 49 shares of £1 each, fully paid and numbered 3 to 51 inclusive, be allotted to [applicant 1];
    (b) THAT 49 shares of £1 each, fully paid and numbered 52 to 100 inclusive, be allotted to [applicant 2];
    (c) THAT all the shares of the company shall henceforth cease to bear distinguishing numbers;
    (c) THAT the undermentioned share certificates drawn in respect of subscribers' shares and the allotments made by resolutions (a) and (b) above be approved and that the common seal be affixed thereto:
    No. 1   [applicant 1]   50 shares
    No. 2   [applicant 2]   50 shares
11. To consider fixing dates for future board meetings.

Any other business

In view of the fact that it is not necessary to give notice of the business to be transacted at board meetings, it would seem to be perfectly in order for business not included in the notice or the agenda to be raised under the heading 'any other business'. Two qualifications must be made to this principle. The first is that the notice may be deemed to be invalid if the item is omitted so as to mislead members of the board that it will not be raised. The second is that it is unreasonable to expect the directors to make reasoned decisions if they are not given sufficient time to consider the merits of a proposal or the opportunity to consider any alternative proposals.

Some chairs refuse as a matter of principle to put matters raised under 'any other business' to a vote until the following meeting. In practice, however, it may sometimes be necessary to do so, for example where the matter is urgent and must be dealt with before the next meeting. This is unlikely to present a problem if the matter is uncontroversial and all the directors are happy for the business to be dealt with in this manner. It is obviously more risky if any of the directors object at the meeting or if the chair is aware that the proposal is controversial and would probably have been opposed by directors who are not present. Allowing the business to be dealt with in these circumstances could be risky because the absent directors might seek to reverse the decision at the next meeting or via legal proceedings. Accordingly, the chair should consider whether there might be a better way of dealing with the business. If the matter is urgent, this could include the possibility of holding another unscheduled board meeting or dealing with the business as a written resolution. If the matter is not urgent, it will nearly always be better to postpone any decision until the next scheduled meeting.

Practical agenda issues

It is normal for the agenda to refer only briefly to the nature of the business to be transacted. For most items, the agenda will make some reference to supporting papers which contain the detailed proposals. If the business can be described accurately and briefly, the substance of the resolution to be put at the meeting may be included in the agenda. Even then, however, there may be some supporting papers and, if so, the agenda should include some reference to them. The overall objective when preparing the agenda should be to keep it as short as possible. This enables the directors to assess the business of the meeting at a glance.

Where supporting papers are required, they should be clearly identified, numbered and placed in the order in which they appear on the agenda. This task normally falls to the company secretary, who should ensure that all reports and papers have been submitted and are listed in the proper form on the agenda.

The agenda and supporting papers should be sent in good time before the meeting so that the directors have sufficient time to read them. Many directors will not do this until the very last minute regardless of when they receive the board papers. However, they tend to forget this when they receive the board papers late and will not normally hesitate to complain. Most companies aim to get the agenda papers for board meetings out or in the hands of the directors about a week before the meeting, although the bottom line for company secretaries will often be to ensure that the papers arrive so that they are in the hands of the directors at least 48 hours prior to the meeting.

Many companies now send out the agenda and the agenda papers in electronic form or use software products and board portals. However, it should be remembered that board members will each have their own methods and preferences for accessing and reading board papers. Companies utilising electronic board systems may still have board members who print their copies for reference and referral. As such, individual preference for format, as well as associated issues of security and confidentiality should be considered and accommodated. In particular, it should be noted that electronic security measures must be adopted by senders and recipients. Equally, content may be confidential to the board both in terms of restricting content within the company as well as externally. However, human error can never be avoided, as evidenced by politicians attending confidential meetings with printed documents tucked under their arms with the content headlines visible to photographers and reporters. Whatever the format of distribution and the preference of attendees, the agenda should be easy to navigate, and recipients should be reminded of their duties in terms of security and confidentiality.

As a principle, the board should be supplied in a timely manner with information in a form and of a quality appropriate to enable it to discharge its duties. Primary responsibility for ensuring that this is done is usually allocated to the chair and, although 'management' has an obligation to provide accurate, timely and clear information, directors should seek clarification or amplification where necessary.

The company secretary will clearly have a major role to play in ensuring that good information flows within the board and its committees, and between senior management and non-executive directors.

Role of the company secretary

The following checklist is adapted from The Chartered Governance Institute's *Company Secretary's Handbook*, 12th edition, Chapter 9: Directors' meetings and resolutions.

Prior to the board meeting, the company secretary should ensure the following tasks are done:

☑ Issue a call for board papers to relevant directors, and others responsible for preparing the reports to the meeting, including updates from relevant staff or committees on progress on actions previously agreed by the board. Where relevant, ensure that a list of all matters to be ratified at the formal board meeting is also provided.

☑ Send a notice to each director stating the time, date and place of meeting with a copy of the agenda and supporting papers, noting that these may be sent in electronic form or via a board portal if in use.

☑ If any of the company's managers are to attend the whole or part of the meeting, for example the company's accountant, they should also be advised of the meeting and sent a copy of the agenda and supporting papers. If they are to attend only part of the meeting, they should be sent the papers for the relevant items only.

☑ It is sensible for the company secretary to ensure that spare copies of the agenda and supporting papers are available at the meeting itself.

☑ In preparing the agenda for the meeting, the company secretary should consider those items that come up on a recurring basis, for example a half-yearly staff report, and if necessary, remind the appropriate department to have the report ready in time for circulation with the agenda. Matters on which no decision was reached at a previous meeting or which were deferred from a previous meeting should also be included in the agenda as should any actions agreed at prior meetings and their progress.

☑ Sometimes the supporting papers will incorporate a formal resolution, which the board is to be asked to pass. This will save time when the minutes of the meeting are prepared.

☑ Just before the meeting, arrangements should be made to ensure that everything necessary for the meeting is ready in the boardroom. It is also usual to have a copy of the company's articles of association, the Companies Act and other relevant material in the boardroom, in case it is necessary to refer to them during the meeting.

☑ In the case of listed companies, the opportunity is often taken to have schedules of transfers available for inspection by board members. For those companies with an active share register, these summaries will usually be restricted to the largest transfers, as otherwise the reports would be too lengthy to be of any use.

Conclusion

The practicalities of convening a meeting of the board of directors can become standard within most companies, becoming an administrative task that replicates the previous meeting. On occasion, preferably annually or when a new company secretary or chair is appointed, it is beneficial to review and refresh the process to ensure that it still meets the requirements of the company. In particular, the notice periods for meetings can often slip, whether for regular or ad hoc meetings, which may result in attendance being sporadic.

The agenda should also be reviewed and refreshed on a regular basis to ensure that it is fit for purpose and that each item has had sufficient time to be concluded. When reviewing the agenda, it is also beneficial to consider if a particular topic is becoming dominant and whether, for the benefit of the other agenda items, it may be useful to propose implementing a committee to cover the topic or to delegate its review to an existing committee or forum.

Hence, while the process of convening a meeting of the directors is formulaic, its effectiveness needs to be constantly monitored.

9 – At a directors' meeting

This chapter covers the practicalities when at a meeting of directors, specifically looking at the practicalities of:

- chairing the meeting and the role of the chair, as well as resolutions where no chair is present;
- the quorum for meetings of directors;
- voting processes and procedures;
- participation in directors' meetings.;
- the appointment of alternate directors, although their benefit has been significantly reduced with the implementation of virtual meetings;
- conflicts of interests and the processes for their declaration;
- adjournments of directors' meetings; and
- standing orders and the application of internal regulations.

As a final point, board effectiveness is considered with specific reference to the guidance available under the Financial Reporting Council's (FRC) Guidance on Board Effectiveness which, while noting that governance arrangements are ultimately for individual boards to decide, provides useful guidance and best practice, including for effective boards and their meetings.

Chairing the meeting

Formally appointing the chair should be the first agenda item of all board meetings. Where the board has a formal chair role it is clear the incumbent will be appointed to chair the meeting. However, even if this is the case, the board minutes should reflect the fact that the chair has been appointed and note their name.

As was seen when convening a meeting, the chair has already influenced the formalities of the board meeting through setting the agenda and its order of discussion.

Role of the chair

The role of the chair within a board meeting is primarily to:

- follow the agenda;
- ensure sufficient discussions are held without limiting the full agenda through focus on one item;
- ensure all board members have the opportunity to contribute;
- accept, or decline, additional topics brought to the meetings;
- maintain the timekeeping of the meeting;
- adjourn the meeting, whether briefly or to another day.

Duties of the chair

In theory, the duties of the chair at a meeting of directors are largely the same as those of the chair of a general meeting. However, meetings of directors are usually a lot less formal than general meetings. Decisions are often reached on a consensual basis and the chair is less likely to be called upon to exercise formal control over the proceedings.

The chair of the board is invariably elected by the board members and, in theory, can be removed by them. Unless the chair is a majority shareholder or they have been appointed by a majority shareholder, their position as the chair of the board (and, therefore, chair of the meeting) may, therefore, be slightly more tenuous. Accordingly, at meetings of directors the chair tends to act more as a facilitator or arbiter, as opposed to an autocrat or judge.

The common law duties of the chair are primarily to ensure that:

(a) the meeting is properly conducted;
(b) all directors are given a fair opportunity to contribute to the deliberations;
(c) the sense of the meeting is properly ascertained and recorded; and
(d) order is preserved.

The chair's authority is derived from the body which made the appointment. In other words, by electing an individual as chair, the directors are deemed to have conferred all the powers necessary to fulfil the role. At general meetings, the chair is deemed to have authority to rule on points of order and on other incidental questions that may arise during the meeting. It may also be the case at meetings of directors although, if challenged at the meeting, it may sometimes be prudent for the chair to bend to the will of the majority. If called upon to make a ruling that may affect the outcome of a meeting of directors, the chair clearly ought to try to make an impartial decision based on the facts. However, if they do not do so and their decision is challenged, there is no guarantee that the courts will intervene. The law takes a surprisingly pragmatic approach to procedural irregularities that occur in the decision-making process of directors. The courts invariably refuse to intervene where it is clear that, if they did, the directors would merely make exactly the same decision again, albeit in accordance with proper procedures. It would be wrong to suggest that this means that a chair who is, say, also a majority shareholder, can ride completely roughshod over the views of the other directors. However, it probably does mean that the chair can give due regard to the will of the majority. After all, if the chair totally ignores this factor, it is likely that they are merely delaying the inevitable. In making a judgement, the chair should consider whether any legal challenge would succeed.

Articles sometimes give the chair the power to determine certain matters. This is normally the case with regard to any question as to the right of a director to vote, where their ruling in relation to any director other than himself will normally be final and conclusive (pcls 14, clg 14 and plc 16). The chair's role in this regard will be particularly important where the articles provide that a director who has a material interest in a transaction cannot vote on it. The chair will often be called upon to decide whether a director's interest is material.

In the unlikely event that a meeting is disorderly, the chair probably has inherent power to adjourn the meeting for the purposes of restoring order. Otherwise, the power to adjourn will rest with the meeting and the chair should not adjourn or close the meeting without the consent of the meeting until all business has been transacted.

The chair's governance role

Most articles allow any director to call a meeting. In practice, it will be the chair who usually decides whether meetings are necessary and who settles the agenda. In doing so, they will take account of the views of other directors (particularly the chief executive) and the advice of the company secretary (particularly on formal items of business, but also on matters of governance).

Principle F of the UK Corporate Governance Code states that the chair leads the board and is responsible for its overall effectiveness in directing the company. They should demonstrate objective judgement throughout their tenure and promote a culture of openness and debate. In addition, the chair facilitates constructive board relations and the effective contribution of all non-executive directors, and ensures that directors receive accurate, timely and clear information.

In application, the FRC's Guidance on Board Effectiveness notes that the chair is pivotal in creating the conditions for overall board and individual director effectiveness, setting clear expectations concerning the style and tone of board discussions, ensuring the board has effective decision-making processes and applies sufficient challenge to major proposals. It is up to the chair to make certain that all directors are aware of their responsibilities and to hold meetings with the non-executive directors without the executives present to facilitate a full and frank airing of views.

The FRC's Guidance on Board Effectiveness expands upon this by suggesting that the chair's role includes:

- setting a board agenda primarily focused on strategy, performance, value creation culture, stakeholders and accountability, and ensuring that issues relevant to these areas are reserved for board decision;
- shaping the culture in the boardroom;
- encouraging all board members to engage in board and committee meetings by drawing on their skills, experience and knowledge;
- fostering relationships based on trust, mutual respect and open communication, both in and outside the boardroom, between non-executive directors and the executive team;
- developing a productive working relationship with the chief executive, providing support and advice, while respecting executive responsibility;
- providing guidance and mentoring to new directors as appropriate;
- leading the annual board evaluation, with support from the senior independent director as appropriate, and acting on the results; and
- considering having regular externally facilitated board evaluations.

The same guidance states that the chair should ensure that:

- adequate time is available for discussion of all agenda items, in particular strategic issues, and that debate is not truncated;
- there is a timely flow of accurate, high-quality and clear information;
- the board determines the nature, and extent, of the significant risks the company is willing to embrace in the implementation of its strategy;
- all directors are aware of and able to discharge their statutory duties;
- the board listens to the views of shareholders, the workforce, customers and other key stakeholders;
- all directors receive a full, formal and tailored induction on joining the board; and
- all directors continually update their skills, knowledge and familiarity with the company to fulfil their role both on the board and committees.

Appointment of the chair

Articles usually specify the method by which the chair of the board of directors is to be appointed. For example, the model articles for private companies (pcls 12 and clg 12) in respect of chairing directors' meetings provide that:

1 The directors may appoint a director to chair their meetings.
2 The person so appointed for the time being is known as the chair.
3 The directors may appoint other directors as deputy or assistant chair to chair directors' meetings in the chair's absence.
4 The directors may terminate the appointment of the chair, deputy or assistant chair at any time.
5 If neither the chair nor any director appointed generally to chair directors' meetings in the chair's absence is participating in a meeting within ten

minutes of the time at which it was to start, the participating directors must appoint one of themselves to chair it.

The main objective of these provisions is to avoid the need to elect a chair at each meeting of directors. A director appointed to the office of 'chair' or 'chair of the board of directors' has a right to chair any meeting of directors that he attends until removed from that office.

If, unusually, the articles make no provision regarding the appointment of the chair, the directors present at each meeting may elect one of their number to chair it.

If the office of chair is unsalaried, a director is not deemed to have an interest in his or her appointment to that office and may, therefore, vote on a resolution to that effect. Where the office is salaried, a director will have a personal interest and may be prevented by the articles from voting on their own appointment. The same principles apply to any resolution to remove the chair. A salaried chair can, therefore, be removed more easily than an unsalaried chair.

Problems appointing a chair

Under most articles, the person appointed as 'chair' or 'chair of the board of directors' is automatically entitled (until removed from office):

- to chair subsequent meetings of directors;
- to a casting vote at any meeting of directors; and
- to chair general meetings of the company.

The ability of the chair to exercise a casting vote at board meetings could easily tip the balance of power and it is not unusual for the directors to be unable to reach agreement on the appointment of a chair for this reason. In these circumstances, the directors may prefer at each board meeting to elect one of their number as 'chair of the meeting', leaving the office of 'chair' or 'chair of the board of directors' vacant, and to determine the issue of who is to chair general meetings on a case-by-case basis in accordance with the articles. Any person elected as the 'chair of the meeting' would, however, still have a casting vote at a meeting of directors because articles usually confer that right on the 'chair of the meeting' rather than on the 'chair of the board of directors'.

Where the articles confer a casting vote on the chair of the meeting in this manner, it is not uncommon for the directors to be unable to agree on the appointment of a chair, particularly where there is an even number of directors who are equally divided in a power struggle. To avoid this problem, it may be advisable at the outset to remove the chair's right to a casting vote by amending the articles.

In the event of complete deadlock, it may be possible for the directors to appoint someone as chair of the meeting on the condition that they refrain from exercising the right to a casting vote, the assumption being that the person appointed will automatically be removed if he attempts to do so. It might, however, be safer not to appoint a chair or to invite someone who is not a director to chair or act as a facilitator at meetings.

No chair

There would seem to be no logical reason why the board of directors should not be able to operate without a chair. Most articles merely provide that the directors 'may' appoint one of their number to be chair (pcls 12, clg 12 and plc 12). This would seem to imply that they need not do so. The chair is said to derive authority from the meeting. If no chair is appointed, the meeting simply retains those powers itself. Matters which the chair would normally be called upon to decide could be resolved by the meeting itself.

The board may also act without a chair by way of written resolution in accordance with any provisions of the articles in that regard, or by a unanimous decision (preferably evidenced in writing) if the articles do not specifically provide for written resolutions.

Chair not present

Articles commonly provide that if the chair of the board is not present within a specified time after the scheduled start of the meeting, the directors may elect one of their number to chair the meeting. If the chair of the board subsequently arrives, the person elected is under no obligation to vacate the chair, although it is normal practice to do so.

Quorum

The quorum is the minimum number of directors who must be present and entitled to vote at a meeting of directors so it can transact business. A quorum must be present for each item of business considered and a director who is not entitled to vote (e.g. because he is interested in the transaction) cannot be counted in calculating whether a quorum exists for that item.

The quorum is normally fixed by the articles. If these are silent on the matter, the basic common law rule is that the quorum is a majority of the directors.

Articles normally give the directors limited powers to act where their number (i.e. the total number of directors in office and not merely the number present at the meeting) falls below the number fixed as the quorum.

Quorum fixed by or in accordance with the articles

Articles invariably specify the quorum for meetings of directors or a method of fixing one. For example, pcls 11, clg 11 and plc 10 all provide:

1   At a directors' meeting, unless a quorum is participating, no proposal is to be voted on, except a proposal to call another meeting.

2 The quorum for directors' meetings may be fixed from time to time by a decision of the directors, but it must never be less than two, and unless otherwise fixed it is two.

If the articles do not fix or provide for a method of fixing a quorum, the quorum for meetings of directors will be a majority of the directors currently holding office or, where it can be shown that a standard practice has evolved over time, the number of directors who usually act in conducting the business of the company. It goes without saying that where the articles make no provision, it is safer to assume that the quorum is a majority of the directors. It is worth noting that if the articles do not specify the quorum, the number required to form a quorum under the common law (being a majority of the directors) automatically falls as the number of appointed directors falls.

Where the articles do not specify a quorum but provide a method for fixing one, for example by a resolution of the directors, the quorum will be a majority of the directors until such time as alternative provision is made by that method. However, where the articles allow the directors to fix their own quorum and no resolution to that effect has ever been passed, the majority rule may be dispensed with if a court is satisfied that there was an understanding between all the directors which was followed. Again, it would always be safer to assume that the quorum is a majority of the appointed directors unless the alternative quorum has been applied for a number of years.

Changing the quorum

Where the articles give the directors power to fix or alter the quorum, they may only exercise that power if they act in accordance with the existing rules and procedures governing their meetings, including the existing quorum requirements. In other words, they cannot change the quorum unless there is a quorum under the existing rules.

If the articles allow the directors to fix or alter the quorum, they may do so by a written resolution as long as the articles allow them to act in this manner. It is doubtful whether such a resolution would be valid, however, if there were insufficient directors to form a quorum under the existing rules.

If the quorum is fixed by the articles and they make no separate provision for alteration, the quorum can only be changed by passing a special resolution at a general meeting to amend the relevant article.

Disinterested quorum

Under common law, a quorum must be present for each item of business at a meeting and only those entitled to vote may be counted in calculating whether a quorum exists. These principles apply to meetings of directors unless they are specifically excluded by the articles.

This rule can be of critical importance because articles frequently prohibit a director from voting at a meeting of directors on any matter in which he has a material interest (see Voting at a directors' meeting below). Where such restrictions operate, a quorum may, in fact, be present for some but not all items of business. Care should, therefore, be taken to check that a competent or disinterested quorum exists for each item of business.

The courts do not look favourably on techniques used by directors to avoid the operation of rules restricting their right to vote on matters in which they have an interest. Two such techniques were rejected in a case where a company's articles allowed directors to contract with the company but not to vote on any such contract. The quorum for board meetings had been fixed at three by the directors under powers given to them by the articles. At a meeting attended by four directors, a contract in which two of them were interested was passed by two separate resolutions. Each interested director voted only on the resolution concerning the other director. These resolutions were held to be invalid because there was, in reality, only one item of business. Treating it as two separate resolutions was merely a device to avoid the operation of the articles (this rule could prevent directors from voting on a number of separate resolutions to take out directors' and officers' insurance cover for each director where only one policy to cover them all is to be taken out). At a subsequent meeting attended by three directors, those present voted to reduce the quorum to two so as to allow a resolution to be passed issuing a debenture to one of the directors present. The resolution to alter the quorum was also held to be invalid because its sole purpose was to enable something to be done indirectly which could not be done directly. In this case, the reason for altering the quorum was blatantly obvious. If it could be shown that the quorum was altered for other legitimate reasons, the resolutions at this second meeting may well have been valid.

Where articles prohibit a director from voting on any transaction in which he is interested, they usually specify some exceptions to that rule, and make provision to allow the members in general meeting to suspend or relax the operation of the rules by ordinary resolution (see pcls 14, clg 14 and plc 16). If it is not possible for the directors to make a decision on a matter themselves, they should seek a dispensation from the members under these procedures and/or consider proposing a suitable amendment to the articles to remove the obstacle (e.g. by widening the list of exceptions).

For small owner-managed companies, it is usually sensible to exclude or modify the relevant model articles to allow the directors to vote on any matter irrespective of any interest they may have in it.

From a practical perspective, it is not necessary for a director who is unable to vote because of a material conflict to leave the meeting while the matter is being decided. A director can, of course, choose to do so. However, it is doubtful whether the other directors can force him to. It has been held that a director who is not entitled to vote at a board meeting cannot be excluded from the meeting. It may sometimes be in the interests of the conflicted director to leave the meeting to avoid coming into possession of confidential information that might place him in a difficult position. This sort of situation can arise with regard to proposals for management buyouts where it may also be thought necessary to withhold certain board papers from the conflicted directors.

Practical issues when fixing a quorum

Generally speaking, it is preferable to fix a low quorum as this facilitates the conduct of the board's business. If the quorum is too high, one or more of the directors may be able to obstruct the board by deliberately absenting themselves from meetings. A director cannot be forced to attend board meetings against his will. In *Barron v Potter* [1914] 1 Ch 895, the quorum was two and Barron, one of only two directors, refused to attend board meetings. Had he done so, Potter, the other director who was entitled to a casting vote as chair, would have been able to appoint his own nominee as an additional director. Potter tried to hold a board meeting at a railway station and again at the company's offices during which he purported to propose and carry with his casting vote a resolution to appoint his nominee as an additional director. Barron made it clear that he refused to attend board meetings and it was held that he could not be forced to do so against his will. The appointment by Potter was, therefore, invalid.

In *Re Opera Photographic Ltd* (1989) 5 BCC 601, a director tried to prevent the board from convening a general meeting to remove him as a director by absenting himself from board meetings, thereby making it impossible to obtain a quorum at board meetings. The court ordered that a general meeting be called. In *Barron v Potter*, it would have served no purpose for Potter to apply to the court for an order calling a general meeting. Barron had already requisitioned a general meeting to appoint new directors at which he would have been in the majority. Potter's only chance of success was, therefore, to entice Barron to attend a board meeting at which he had the casting vote.

Thus, although a director may be able to obstruct the business of the company by absenting himself from board meetings, the will of the majority will nearly always prevail as they will be in a position to remove him or to appoint additional directors unless the director has special class rights which enable him to veto appointments and removals.

It is, of course, sometimes desirable to establish a deadlocked company (e.g. where two members hold the same number of voting shares and are the only directors). In this case, it will be necessary to remove the chair's casting vote at board and general meetings and fix a quorum of two at board meetings. If the directors fail to agree, it would serve no purpose to apply to the court to call a general meeting as the balance of power would be the same.

The advantages of setting a relatively low figure as the quorum are plain. The other directors cannot call a meeting without giving reasonable notice. If the meeting is called to deal with routine or uncontroversial business, only sufficient directors to form a quorum need attend. However, whether all the directors attend or not, when an important or controversial item of business is considered, the will of the majority and not the minority will hold sway.

Number below quorum

Articles which allow the directors to act notwithstanding any vacancy in their number do not allow them to act where their number falls below that required to constitute a quorum. This issue is, however, normally addressed in modern articles.

The 2006 Act model articles for private companies state that the directors may only hold a meeting of the directors in order to appoint sufficient directors to make up a quorum or to call a general meeting to enable the members to appoint further directors (pcls 11(3), clg 11(3)). The model articles for public companies also make similar provision but distinguish between the situation where there is only one director and where there is more than one (plc 11).

Voting

The rules on voting at directors' meetings are based on the common law but are subject to modification by the articles. Board meetings are usually conducted with less formality than shareholder meetings. Decisions are normally reached by consensus and matters are rarely put to a formal vote because it will normally be apparent without doing so which side would win.

When a resolution is put to a vote, each director will have one vote unless the articles provide otherwise. Questions are usually decided on a majority of votes cast for or against the resolution, although the articles may require a special majority for certain types of business. Most articles restrict the right to vote where a director has a personal interest in the matter under consideration. The chair is commonly given a second or casting vote to be used in the event of a deadlock.

The model articles make specific provision with general rules for voting at directors' meetings (plc 13) stating that:

1 Subject to the articles, a decision is taken at a directors' meeting by a majority of the votes of the participating directors.
2 Subject to the articles, each director participating in a directors' meeting has one vote.
3 Subject to the articles, if a director has an interest in an actual or proposed transaction or arrangement with the company:
   (a) that director and that director's alternate may not vote on any proposal relating to it, but
   (b) this does not preclude the alternate from voting in relation to that transaction or arrangement on behalf of another appointor who does not have such an interest.

Method of voting

Articles rarely specify the method of voting. Voting is normally conducted by a show of hands or some other simple method of counting with each director having one vote. This method may not be satisfactory if any of the directors is entitled to more than one vote (e.g. a personal vote plus acting as an alternate for another director). A director who is present at the meeting and who has more than one vote has a right to have each of those votes counted and may have a right to demand a poll if they are not counted. Hence, the method of voting used should take account of the fact that some directors may have more votes than others. It is not necessary to follow the formal procedures used at company meetings. Voting papers could be used where it is difficult for the chair to calculate the true number of votes for and against the resolution on a show of hands, although in practice, this is unlikely to be required at a meeting of directors.

Chair's casting vote

Unless the articles so provide, the chair has no right to a casting vote. Under most articles the person who acts as the chair of a meeting of directors is given a casting vote. The model articles under the 2006 Act provide for a casting vote but state that this does not apply if the chair is not to be counted under the articles as participating in the decision-making process for quorum or voting purposes, for example due to a conflict of interest (pcls 13, clg 13 and plc 14). Although older articles may not make direct provision on this matter, it may be sensible to apply the same principle.

A casting vote may only be used where there has already been a vote and the number of votes for and against the resolution are exactly equal. It cannot be used where there is a majority in favour or against in order to manufacture a tie.

It is not necessary for the chair to use any casting vote in the event of a tie. Indeed, it may be preferable not to do so if the chair wishes to remain impartial. The chair need not use the casting vote in the same way as their original vote on the resolution.

In exercising a casting vote the chair can follow one of two guiding principles (which are quite capable of producing opposite results). The first, which is adopted by the Speaker of the House of Commons, is that the casting vote should be used to preserve the status quo. This may mean voting for or against the resolution depending on which way the resolution is worded. The second, which is perhaps more commonly applied, is that the chair should use the casting vote in the best interests of the company. Clearly this second principle is more subjective than the first and depends on the chair's view of what is in the interest of the company.

Record of votes

It is not normal to record the number of votes cast for and against a proposal in the minutes of directors' meetings. However, directors have a right to have their opposition to a resolution recorded in the minutes regardless of whether a formal vote was put to the meeting. Their purpose in doing so will normally be to minimise their potential liabilities in respect of the decision. If the minutes record the fact that they opposed the decision, they are unlikely to share liability with the other directors if it turns out to be a poor decision.

Restrictions on voting

Articles frequently impose restrictions on the right to vote where a director has an interest in the subject of the resolution and provide that a director prohibited from voting shall not be counted in determining whether there is a quorum for that item of business (pcls 14, clg 14 and plc 16). However, provided that a quorum exists there is nothing to prevent the other directors from entering into a contract in which a director is interested.

Practical issues

It is difficult to frame many of the issues discussed at board meetings as formal resolutions and it can sometimes be counter-productive to do so. When the chair feels that a consensus has been reached, they should attempt to summarise it. This gives the other directors an opportunity to object to that interpretation and is obviously helpful for the secretary in preparing the minutes. What often happens, however, is that the chair ends the discussion by saying: 'I think we are all agreed on that subject and suggest we move on to the next item of business.' In such circumstances, if one were to go round the table asking each director what they thought had been agreed, each one would probably give a different answer. The other directors should not allow the chair to get away with this, although it is often left to the secretary to ask the chair to summarise what has been decided so that it can be properly recorded in the minutes.

Participation in meetings

Under common law, it is necessary for a director to attend a meeting in person to participate in it and be counted in the quorum. In addition, there is no common law right for a director to appoint a proxy. Articles commonly vary these rules by allowing directors to appoint an alternate, who may then participate in meetings on their behalf if they are unable to do so themselves. In practice, it is often easier for a director who is unable to attend a meeting to participate virtually via telephone or audio-visual links, and articles often make specific provision to allow this. Where this is the case, there will not normally be any need for a director to appoint an alternate.

The 2006 Act model articles allow directors to participate in meetings using conference call technology. The model articles for public companies also allow directors to appoint an alternate, whereas the model articles for private companies do not. The usual provisions on alternate directors were omitted from the private company model articles as a simplification measure.

Methods of participation allowed under model articles

	In person	Conference calls	Alternate director
Model articles for a private company limited by shares	✓	✓	✗
Model articles for a private company limited by shares	✓	✓	✗
Model articles for a public company	✓	✓	✓

Virtual attendance

It is common for companies to enable directors to participate virtually in board meetings. The question as to whether participation in this manner is effective will depend, in part, on whether the company's articles of association make specific provision allowing directors to do so and, in the absence of any such provision, the relevant common law rules. Those common law rules were developed long before this type of technology became available, in an era where directors could only participate in meetings by gathering in person at the time and place specified in the notice of meeting. Recent cases suggest that the courts are willing to adapt the old rules to reflect modern technological developments. However, for the avoidance of doubt, it is better to adopt articles which specifically authorise directors to participate in this manner and which avoid any of the potential pitfalls that could arise under the common law.

All three versions of the model articles make specific provision for participation by directors in meetings from multiple locations and thus imply the use of technology and holding virtual meetings, specifically (pcls 10, clg 10 and plc 9) as follows:

1 Subject to the articles, directors participate in a directors' meeting, or part of a directors' meeting, when—
   (a) the meeting has been called and takes place in accordance with the articles, and
   (b) they can each communicate to the others any information or opinions they have on any particular item of the business of the meeting.
2 In determining whether directors are participating in a directors' meeting, it is irrelevant where any director is or how they communicate with each other.

3 If all the directors participating in a meeting are not in the same place, they may decide that the meeting is to be treated as taking place wherever any of them is.

Such articles need to clarify that directors who are in contact with the meeting by these other means may be counted in the quorum and may vote notwithstanding the fact that they are not personally present at the location where the meeting is taking place because there is a long-standing common law rule that would seem to suggest otherwise. Best practice is to reflect attendance at meetings in the minutes and noting next to each attendee's name how they attended.

In practice, the votes of directors in communication by other means will not always affect the outcome of any vote. In any case, there are a number of reasons to suppose that the courts would give effect to a decision carried on a formal vote by directors who were not physically present at the meeting. Logic suggests that in these circumstances the will of the majority should prevail no matter how it is expressed (i.e. whether in person or by telephone). It should also be noted that the courts are often reluctant to intervene in what they consider to be internal irregularities where it is obvious that the directors would merely make the same decision again (albeit by following proper procedures). Procedures adopted by the board may also be saved by the type of article which states that the directors may otherwise regulate their proceedings as they see fit.

Where no specific provision is made in a company's articles to allow for participation in directors' meetings by other means, the best solution is to amend the articles so that they do. However, failing that, it is suggested that the chances of any intervention by the court would be reduced by the inclusion in the notice of meeting a statement describing how participation in the meeting may be effected, for example either by personal attendance at a specified location or by being in contact with the people at that location via a communications facility. In addition, it might be worth examining the company's articles on alternate directors under which it may be possible for each director not physically present to appoint the chair of the meeting to act as their alternate and to vote in accordance with their instructions during the meeting.

It should be noted that the principle of unanimous consent could also serve to validate decisions of directors not taken in accordance with the usual procedures required by the Act or the company's articles.

Series of electronic contacts

A decision made by a series of one-to-one telephone calls or email exchanges will normally be valid under the principle of unanimous consent if all the directors agreed to that decision. However, this method of decision making should not be relied upon to make decisions by a majority, unless the articles make specific provision in this regard.

The notion that a series of one-to-one telephone calls or email exchanges should be treated as a meeting would stretch the common law concept of a meeting too far. Even with the ability to share and comment on documents, the method does not allow a simultaneous transfer of views or discussion of the topic. There would be no meeting of minds at a particular point in time. Those who were contacted first may have changed their minds by the time the chair has spoken to the last director. They might also have reached a different conclusion if they had heard the views of other directors. The same might be true of those who were contacted later in the series of calls if the chair fails to explain adequately the views of the minority.

Some companies have adopted articles which specifically allow board decisions to be reached in this manner. On the whole, such a method of decision making is only suitable for issues which are simple or mere formalities. When using this type of decision-making process, special care will always need to be taken to ensure that directors have made any necessary declarations of interest.

Alternate directors

Directors who are also major shareholders will often wish to ensure that their views are represented at board meetings even though they are unable to attend or participate themselves. This is also the case in joint venture companies where each of the joint venture partners normally has the right to appoint a fixed number of directors and would normally want to ensure that they are fully represented at board meetings.

Under common law there is no automatic right to vote by proxy. The Act confers a statutory right on the members to vote by proxy but does not make similar provision with regard to the directors. Thus, a director who is unable to attend or participate in a meeting of directors will be unable to vote at that meeting unless the articles provide otherwise.

The 2006 Act model articles for public companies provide a mechanism which allows directors to appoint another person to attend and vote in their stead at board meetings. A person so appointed is known as an alternate director (plc 25–27).

The 2006 Act model articles for private companies do not make any provision for the appointment of alternate directors. The relevant provisions were deliberately omitted to keep the private company model articles as simple as possible. The decision to do so was made easier because the model articles specifically allow directors to participate in meetings via conference calls. Accordingly, it was thought that they would be less likely to need to appoint alternates. This is almost certainly true. In any case, it is relatively easy for a private company incorporated under the 2006 Act to make provision in its articles for alternate directors by adopting provisions similar to those in the public company model articles.

The model articles for public companies provides that alternate directors may be appointed and removed by notice to the company signed by the director making or revoking the appointment, or in any other manner approved by the directors. However, it additionally requires the board to approve by resolution any appointment of a person as an alternate director where the person nominated is not already a director of the company (plc 25). Such approval is not required where another director is appointed.

A person appointed as an alternate director is regarded as a director for Companies Act purposes. Accordingly, if the person appointed is not already a director of the company, the usual formalities for appointment of a new director should be followed, for example notification of appointment to the Registrar of Companies and entry in the register of directors.

A person who holds office only as an alternate director shall, if his appointor is not present, be counted in the quorum (plc 26(3)). It should be noted in this regard that it is the alternate who is counted in the quorum rather than the person who appointed him. Thus, if two directors appoint the same alternate, that alternate can only be counted in the quorum once. If they had each appointed a different person, then both alternates could be counted in the quorum. The model articles for public companies clarify this by providing that an alternate cannot be counted as more than one director for the purposes of the quorum. It should also be noted that the relevant provision of the model articles only applies to a person who holds office only as an alternate director. In other words, if a director appoints another director as his alternate, that other director cannot be counted twice in the quorum. He will be counted in his own capacity as a director but not in his capacity as an alternate for any other director.

An alternate director can vote at a meeting of directors in the absence of his appointer (plc 26(3)). The model articles make special provision to clarify that where an existing director acts as an alternate director, any vote that he is entitled to cast as an alternate is in addition to any vote he is entitled to cast in his own right. The wording of the model articles for public companies in this regard clarify that such a director is entitled to an additional vote for each appointor (plc 15). It should be noted that the model articles for public companies specifically deal with the situation where two or more directors appoint the same person as their alternate where that person is not a director. It is not entirely clear whether such a person would be entitled to one vote on behalf of each appointor. An alternate director may also sign a written resolution instead of his appointor (see plc 26(3)).

Under the model articles for public companies, alternate directors are deemed to be directors, deemed responsible for their own acts and defaults and deemed not to be the agents of the person who appointed them (plc 26(2)). Thus, the chair need not be concerned as to whether the alternate is voting in accordance with the instructions of his appointor.

Under the model articles for public companies, alternate directors are given the same rights, in relation to any directors' meeting or directors' written resolution, as their appointor (plc 26(1)) but are also made subject to the same restrictions (plc 26(2)(c)). Those restrictions will include limitations on the right to vote where a conflict of interest arises under plc 16. However, they will also be disqualified from voting where the director who appointed them is disqualified.

Despite the option to appoint an alternative director, given the ability for directors to attend meetings virtually, the majority of companies no longer see the benefit when compared to the requirements to formally appoint alternative directors, notify their appointment to Companies House, include all alternate directors in notifications for meetings as well as the additional administrative burden of differentiating between directors and alternative directors.

Conflicts of interests

Directors have a statutory duty to declare the nature and extent of any direct or indirect interest they may have in any:

(a) *proposed* transaction or arrangement with the company (s. 177); and

(b) *existing* transaction or arrangement with the company (s. 182).

At its most basic, a 'transaction or arrangement with the company' includes any contract between the company and a third party. A director could be interested in such a contract directly as the other contracting party, or indirectly (e.g. because they are a shareholder of another company (or partner in a firm) which is a party to the contract). Strictly speaking, a director's duty of disclosure under these provisions also extends to other non-contractual arrangements that the company may enter into. Rather than try to define what these might be, it is safer to assume that directors must disclose their interest in anything that the company does unless that thing is covered by a statutory exception.

The requirement to disclose interests in *proposed* transactions or arrangements is, perhaps, easier to understand than the requirement to disclose interests in *existing* ones. It is obvious that the board of directors should be made aware of the fact that one of the directors has an interest in a *proposed* contract or arrangement before they decide whether the company should enter into it. If the director's interest is material, it should put them on alert as to whether the company is getting the best deal, particularly if the director concerned has been involved in negotiating the deal and appears to be promoting it.

It is also essential that directors make the necessary declarations if the company's articles prohibit a director who has such an interest from participating in any decision on that matter at a meeting of directors. The chair and secretary of the meeting need to be able to work out who can vote, who can be counted in the quorum, and whether the meeting is able to make a decision on the proposal.

It is not necessarily as clear why the directors need to know about a director's interests in *existing* transactions or arrangements (i.e. those that the company has already entered into, possibly even before the director was appointed). The justification for this could partly be to ensure that the board does not inadvertently place a director in charge of managing an existing contractual relationship if he has a material interest in that contract. The board also needs to know if a director might have an interest in promoting the continuation or renegotiation of an existing contract or arrangement.

The easiest way of recognising such an interest by a director is to acknowledge any director conflicts of interest at the outset of each meeting, thus capturing any existing interest in the topics under discussion (see below, Methods of making a declaration). It should be noted that disclosing an interest does not automatically exclude a director from a discussion once their conflict is noted. However, the chair should be mindful of their interest during the relevant discussion and when making any related decision or taking a related vote.

Breach of conflict of interest

A breach by a director of the duty of disclosure under section 177 in relation to a *proposed* transaction or arrangement is not a criminal offence but gives rise to potential civil liability on the part of the director to account to the company for any profits he may have made from the transaction and potentially renders the contract voidable at the instance of the company.

A breach of the second duty under section 182 regarding an *existing* transaction or arrangement is a criminal offence (s. 183) but does not give rise to the same civil remedies as the first. It may seem strange that a breach of the first duty relating to *proposed* transactions is not a criminal offence. It should be noted that under the 2006 Act, any failure by a director to disclose an interest in a *proposed* transaction will, if the company enters into that transaction and the director's interest remains undisclosed, become a failure to disclose an interest in an *existing* transaction, which will then attract potential criminal penalties. However, no offence is committed if the company does not enter into the proposed contract or arrangement.

No declaration is required under either of the requirements of any interest of which the director is not aware or if the director is not aware of the transaction or arrangement in question – a director is treated as being aware of matters of which he ought reasonably to be aware. There is also no need to declare an interest:

(a) if it cannot reasonably be regarded as likely to give rise to a conflict of interest;

(b) if, or to the extent that, the other directors are already aware of it – for this purpose, the other directors are treated as aware of anything of which they ought reasonably to be aware); or

(c) if, or to the extent that, it concerns terms of his service contract that have been or are to be considered by a meeting of the directors, or by a committee of the directors appointed for the purpose under the company's articles.

In the case of a *proposed* transaction or arrangement, a director is required to declare the nature and extent of his or her interest to the other directors before the company enters into the transaction or arrangement (s. 177).

In the case of an *existing* transaction or arrangement, a director is required to declare the nature and extent of their interest to the other directors as soon as is reasonably practicable (s. 182). However, the requirement to make a declaration interest in an *existing* transaction or arrangement under section 182 does not apply if it has already been declared as an interest in a *proposed* transaction or arrangement under section 177. Effectively, a declaration of interest in a *proposed* contract or arrangement carries forward as a declaration of interest in an *existing* contract or arrangement if the company enters into that contract or arrangement.

Methods of making a declaration

In the case of an interest in a *proposed* transaction or arrangement (s. 177), the declaration may (*but need not*) be made:

(a) at a meeting of the directors;
(b) by notice in writing to the directors in accordance with section 184; or
(c) by general notice in accordance with section 185.

In the case of an *existing* transaction or arrangement, the declaration *must* be made using one of the three methods mentioned above.

If a declaration of interest proves to be, or becomes, inaccurate or incomplete, a further declaration must be made. Information regarding the extent of a director's interest will most likely need updating. Directors may not always remember to do this or even realise that they have to. Accordingly, it is good practice for the secretary to issue regular reminders and to ask directors to check whether the interests they have declared need to be updated. When doing so, care should be taken to ensure that the directors understand that they have an ongoing duty to declare (and update) their interests, and that they should not do so only in response to a reminder.

General notice

The method that directors most commonly use to make a declaration of interest is to give general notice in accordance with section 185. Under this method, the director gives notice to the other directors of the fact that he or she:

(a) has an interest (as a member, officer, employee or otherwise) in a specified body corporate or firm and is to be regarded as interested in any transaction or arrangement that may, after the date of the notice, be made with that body corporate or firm; or
(b) is connected with a specified person (other than a body corporate or firm) and is to be regarded as interested in any transaction or arrangement that may, after the date of the notice, be made with that person.

A general notice must state the nature and extent of the director's interest in the body corporate or firm or the nature of their connection with any specified person. It will not be effective unless it is given at a meeting of the directors, or the director concerned takes reasonable steps to secure that it is brought up and read at the next meeting of the directors after it is given. Subject to these conditions, a general notice is a sufficient declaration of interest in relation to the matters to which it relates. It is particularly important in this regard that the details regarding the nature and extent of a director's interests are kept up to date.

General notice need not be given in writing. It can, for example, be given orally at a board meeting. However, it is usual for directors to make such notifications in writing as they will often be quite detailed. Whether the notice is given in writing or orally, the fact that it has been given should be recorded in the minutes of the relevant board meeting at which it was given, brought up or read out.

Example: Declaration of director's interest

Director's interests – General notice of interests in transactions or arrangements

The Directors

.... Limited/plc

Pursuant to section 185, Companies Act 2006, I give notice that I have the interest in each of the companies or firms listed below which is shown against its name below and that I am to be regarded as interested in any transaction or arrangement which may, after the date hereof, be made with any of those companies and firms.

Name of company or firm	Nature and extent of interest

I also give notice under that section that I am connected with each of the person(s) listed below and am to be regarded as interested in any transaction or arrangement which may, after the date hereof, be made with any of the undermentioned persons.

Name of person	Nature of connection with that person
(Date)	(Signature)

One obvious weakness with the general notice procedure is that a director may have made the declaration a long time ago. Although that declaration (if kept up to date) will ensure that he has complied with his statutory duties, the other directors may not necessarily remember what interests the director declared. Accordingly, when a transaction is raised at a board meeting, they may not necessarily remember that that the director has an interest in it unless they are reminded of that fact. Although it is not necessary for statutory purposes for a director to remind the board of an interest that has already been declared, it will often be necessary for him to do so to enable the chair of the meeting to decide whether the director can participate in the decision under any relevant article provisions.

Notice in writing

A director may also make a declaration by giving notice in writing in accordance with section 184. Under this method, the director concerned must send the notice to the other directors either in hard copy form (by hand or by post) or, if the recipient has agreed to receive it in electronic form, in an agreed electronic form sent by agreed electronic means. The notice must disclose the nature and extent of the director's interest and, if it relates to a *proposed* transaction or arrangement, must be given before the company enters into the relevant transaction or arrangement. A declaration made by notice in writing is then deemed to form part of the proceedings at the next meeting of the directors after the notice is given and must be minuted accordingly. It is good practice to raise the fact that such a declaration has been made at the meeting.

Declaration made at a meeting of directors

A director may make a declaration of interest for the purposes of sections 177 and 182 at a 'meeting of directors'. Such a declaration would typically be made orally, although there is no reason why a director should not table a written declaration of interest at the meeting. The declaration would have to comply with all the usual requirements (e.g. disclose the nature and extent of the director's interest and, for the purposes of a proposed transaction, be made before the company enters into that transaction). Subject to these conditions, a declaration of interest made at a meeting of directors will suffice even though some directors may have been absent from the meeting and may not, therefore, be aware that one was made. It is not necessary for the company to wait until the absent directors have been informed of the interest before entering into the transaction.

Declarations of interest made at a meeting of directors form part of the proceedings of that meeting and should, therefore, be minuted. If this is done properly and the minutes are circulated to the directors, those who were absent will be put on notice that a director declared an interest at the meeting. However, as mentioned above, the validity of the declaration does not depend on this being done.

Consequences of breach

The consequences of a breach of section 177 in relation to a proposed transaction or arrangement are the same as would apply if the corresponding common law rule or equitable principle applied (s. 178).

The basic common law position on directors' conflicts of interest is that they can only be ratified by the company in general meeting, unless the articles provided otherwise.

The law leaves it up to the members to decide whether to impose any further restrictions on the directors in the company's articles.

Hence, in general, any breach of disclosure rules by a director would be a breach under law.

Adjournment

Articles rarely make specific provision with respect to adjournment of directors' meetings other than to state that the directors may adjourn. As a result, the common law rules on adjournment will normally apply and the power to adjourn will rest with the meeting. It is not possible to adjourn a meeting that never actually started. A meeting cannot start unless there is a quorum. If a quorum is not obtained, the meeting cannot, therefore, be adjourned, unless the articles make some sort of provision for automatic adjournment in these circumstances. Although articles do this for shareholder meetings, they rarely make similar provision for meetings of directors. Accordingly, if a quorum is never obtained, a new meeting must be called.

If a quorum is present, the directors may adjourn. In practice, it is unusual for directors' meetings to be adjourned for more than a couple of hours, perhaps to allow lunch to be taken or further negotiations to take place before a final decision is made. Strictly speaking, there is no need to give notice of an adjourned meeting, but it is normal practice to notify directors who were unable to attend the original meeting, if only to ensure that there is a quorum at the adjourned meeting. The quorum required at an adjourned meeting will be the same as the original meeting.

Where a meeting is adjourned temporarily within the same day, the minutes should reflect the point in the discussion when the meeting was adjourned and pick up in the same document when it reconvenes. Where a meeting is adjourned to a different day, perhaps due to overrun on the agenda, a different set of minutes should be produced.

Standing orders and internal regulations

Boards frequently adopt standing orders or internal regulations which govern their own conduct and procedures. These will often seek to ensure that the directors comply with any relevant article provisions but also cover a range of matters not specifically governed by the articles, such as:

- length of notice for board meetings;
- location and frequency of meetings;
- requirements to give notice of business and circulate an agenda;
- procedures for the approval and circulation of the minutes of meetings; and
- schedule of matters reserved to the board.

Articles frequently include a provision which confirms that the directors may regulate their proceedings as they think fit, provided they comply with any other relevant article provisions. This is almost certainly the case even if the articles do not make specific provision in this regard. Although it is always better for the board to adopt written procedures, the courts will often take into account informal practices and procedures that may have been adopted over time.

Standing orders and internal regulations typically require things to be done in a manner that would not necessarily be required under the articles or the common law. For example, they could specify a minimum notice period for board meetings. They obviously cannot be used to override things that are either required under the articles or not permitted. It is possible that they could be used to override something that is required under the common law. However, it would be impossible to predict with any certainty whether they would be effective in this regard, so this is something that should be avoided.

Assuming that any regulations adopted by the directors are consistent with the articles and any common law requirements, the question arises as to whether the directors must comply with them and what the consequences would be if they do not. Much will depend on the way they are drafted. If they are framed as a code of best practice (in other words, they are aspirational rather than mandatory), they are unlikely to be enforceable under law. If, however, they are drafted as regulations and are clearly intended to be mandatory, it is arguable that the directors should comply with them. This does not necessarily mean that every decision taken by the board in breach of its own internal procedures will be invalid as it is obviously within the directors' powers to ratify a decision that has not been made in accordance with its own procedures. It would be up to a director to object to any breach of internal procedures. If nobody did, it is likely that they would all be deemed to have acquiesced to the irregularity. However, if a director does object to an irregularity, then the chair should probably seek to ensure that a majority of the directors are happy for the decision to be taken. It may not be sufficient for the chair to obtain the agreement of the directors who attend the meeting unless a majority of the directors are actually present. Notwithstanding the fact that a quorum may be present, it would not make sense for a minority to override any procedural rules adopted by the majority.

A director wishing to challenge the validity of a decision in legal proceedings on the basis of a breach of internal regulations would need to act quickly to avoid being deemed by the court to have acquiesced in the irregularity. A court would not intervene if the decision had already been ratified by the directors and would be unlikely to declare any decision invalid where it is clear that a majority of the directors are in favour of it because any irregularities could be cured by the board going through the proper process.

Board effectiveness

The FRC's Guidance on Board Effectiveness suggests that well-informed and high-quality decision making is a critical requirement for a board to be effective. Boards can minimise the risk of poor decisions by investing time in the design of their decision-making policies and processes, especially those undertaken in general meetings.

Meeting regularly is essential for the board to discharge its duties effectively and to allow adequate time for consideration of all the issues falling within its remit. Ensuring there is a formal schedule of matters reserved for its decision will assist the board's planning and provide clarity to all over where responsibility for decision-making lies.

For significant decisions, a board may wish to consider extra steps, for example:

■ describing in board papers the process that has been used to arrive at and challenge the proposal prior to presenting it to the board, thereby allowing directors not involved in the project to assess the appropriateness of the process before assessing the merits of the project itself;

■ where appropriate, putting in place additional safeguards to reduce the risk of distorted judgements by, for example, commissioning an independent report, seeking advice from an expert, introducing a devil's advocate to provide challenge, establishing a specific sub-committee, and convening additional meetings; or

■ ensuring that board minutes document the discussion that led to the decision, including the issues raised and the reasons for the decision.

In addition, the guidance recommends that once a significant decision has been made and implemented the board may find it useful to review both the effectiveness of the decision-making process and the merits of the decision itself where it considers it relevant. This could also be considered as part of the board evaluation process.

Role of the company secretary

The following checklist is adapted from The Chartered Governance Institute's *Company Secretary's Handbook*, 12th edition, Chapter 9: Directors' meetings and resolutions:

- For incorporation in the minutes, take a note of those directors present and report any apologies for absence.
- Ensure that a quorum is present. If any item in which a director has an interest is to be considered, ensure that there will still be an independent, disinterested quorum to deal with it.
- Take notes during the meeting on any consideration made by the board and of its decisions reached, together with appropriate justification, if necessary. The minutes should not be a verbatim record of what is said. If they were, this could cause complications. If a decision is unclear, complicated or has been contentious, confirm the wording of the decision to be incorporated in the minutes with the chair at the meeting so that all those present are aware of how it will be documented. However, do not interrupt the flow of the meeting by requesting approval of a long description. Clarification on this would be better sought after the meeting.
- It is usual to note in the minutes the arrival of any director after the proceedings have started or the departure of a director before the meeting has ended.
- The chair may ask the company secretary to advise on any point of procedure regarding the conduct of the business of the meeting, but it would be appropriate for the company secretary to intervene in the meeting (unless they are themselves a director) only if the board were proposing to do something that was unlawful or contrary to the company's articles of association.
- If a manager is to be called in for discussion of a specific item, ensure that they are ready to be called when that item is reached on the agenda.
- If any confidential papers are left behind on the board table by the directors, these should be collected by the company secretary before staff come in to clear the room.
- If the meeting is temporarily adjourned, ensure the meeting room remains closed and that confidential materials are not left open. Ensure that the time for the meeting to restart is clearly communicated before any attendees leave the meeting room. Ensure that any attendees who have joined by electronic means are aware of the time that they should re-join the meeting.

Conclusion

As can be seen, the chair of any meeting of directors is a key individual in both ensuring that the board is effective and that individuals contribute. Its effectiveness is a combination of the application of the formal requirements as well as their practical application during the meeting.

The formalities for ensuring that a quorum is present are relatively straightforward once checked against the articles of the company. However, this may also extend to ensuring that directors are aware of their responsibilities in attending and participating. Some companies set guidelines, whether formally or informally, on the number of meetings that a director should attend during the year. Others specify that a director should not miss more than one formal meeting per year, excluding purpose-specific ad hoc meetings. Given their ability to attend meetings virtually, with less expectation of attending every meeting in person, there are fewer reasons why a director should regularly miss meetings.

Noting conflicts of interest at the start of every meeting ensures that it is captured and updated. In some cases, a list of other appointments is kept by the company secretary and confirmed at the start of each meeting to ensure the point is covered.

While the purpose of this book and the content of this chapter reflects the framework for meetings of directors, good conduct during the meeting by all attendees is imperative to ensuring that each meeting is effective and purposeful. This does not mean that it should be soulless or formulaic. One of the chair's roles is to ensure that all attendees have the opportunity to contribute whether in agreement or challenge. By building mutual respect and trust any board can become the collective leaders that a company needs to be successful, and creating this is a requirement for all attendees. If the framework for the meeting provided here is adopted and implemented as a support, the purpose and actions of the meeting, rather than the processes, can take centre stage.

10 – After the meeting

As internal meetings, there is little reporting of the meeting beyond capturing the content via the minutes, ensuring that draft minutes are circulated for comment and are maintained appropriately. Hence, the majority of this chapter will cover the requirements of minutes and the importance of ensuring that their content provides an effective audit trail of decisions made and discussions held.

Finally, a checklist for company secretaries is included as a reminder of the required actions after each directors' meeting has been held.

Minutes

Every company must keep minutes of all proceedings at meetings of directors (s. 248(1)). Minutes of meetings of directors held on or after 1 October 2007 must be kept for at least ten years from the date of the meeting (s. 248(2)). Minutes of directors' meetings held before that date should be kept in accordance with the requirements of section 382 of the Companies Act 1985 (see Sch. 3, para. 19 to the Companies Act 2006 (Commencement No. 3, Consequential Amendments, Transitional Provisions and Savings) Order 2007 (SI 2007/2194)). This means that they should be kept permanently.

The company secretary (if any) and the directors can be fined for any default by the company of the provisions of the Act relating to the maintenance of these minutes and records under section 248(3) (or s. 382 of the 1985 Act).

Minutes may be kept in electronic as well as physical form, noting that internal company procedures may have different retention policies for documents in general. It is common for retention policies to maintain electronic records for six years in accordance with relevant legislation. Hence, exceptions are required for minutes to ensure that the data is kept for the relevant timescale.

Content of minutes

As the primary purpose of the minutes and records is to provide evidence of the decisions taken at a meeting, it is essential that they accurately record those decisions. As a rule of thumb, this means they should contain a record of the decisions reached at the meeting together with sufficient of the discussions to enable the sense of the meeting to be established. Any specific disagreement by a director with a particular resolution or course of action should be recorded.

For public companies, while dividends should be approved at the general meeting, the payment of interim dividends can be approved by a directors' meeting, as long as sufficient funds are available to pay such a dividend. Clearly the minutes of that meeting should include reference to the discussion confirming that there are sufficient funds and payment of an interim dividend will not financially disadvantage the company.

Precedent: Minutes of board resolution to pay an interim dividend

It was resolved:

THAT an interim dividend for the year ended [date] of [7] pence per share on the ordinary shares of [25] pence each be paid on [date] to shareholders registered at the close of business on [date].

It should be noted that companies that have external regulations will often have particular requirements for their directors' minutes to include more detail of discussions leading up to decisions.

Minutes should reflect the proceedings at the meeting. Subsequent additions, comments or changes of decisions should not be included as they are, by their nature, not relevant to the minutes of the specific meeting.

Minutes of first board meeting

The minutes of the first board meeting of a company on incorporation are relatively standard and serve to create the format of subsequent minutes in terms of the layout of the document.

Example: Minutes of first board meeting (private company)

XYZ LIMITED

Minutes of a board meeting held at [place] on [date] at [time]

Present: [name] (chair)

            [name]

In attendance: [name] (secretary)

1. There were produced the certificate of incorporation and a copy of the memorandum and articles of association as registered.

2. It was noted that the first directors of the company named by the subscribers in the documents delivered to the Registrar of Companies with the memorandum of association are: [names].

3. It was resolved:
   THAT [name of director] be appointed chair of the board.

4. It was noted that [name] was named by the subscribers as secretary in the documents delivered to the Registrar of Companies and resolved:
   THAT the appointment of [name] as secretary be confirmed at a salary payable from [date] at the rate of [amount] per annum, such appointment being terminable by [period] notice in writing given by either party to the other at any time.

5. It was resolved:
   THAT the situation of the company's registered office shown in the documents delivered with the memorandum to the Registrar of Companies (namely, [address]) be confirmed.

6. It was resolved:
   THAT the seal, of which an impression is affixed in the margin hereof, be adopted as the common seal of the company.

7. It was resolved:
   THAT a bank account be opened with [name of bank] and ... [Resolutions in accordance with bank's printed form for opening an account.]

8. It was resolved:
   THAT [name] be appointed auditors of the company to hold office until the conclusion of the first general meeting at which accounts are laid before the company.

9. There were produced and read to the meeting notices given by [names of directors] pursuant to sections 177 and 182 of the Companies Act 2006. The secretary was instructed to enter details of the declarations in a register that is to be kept for this purpose.

10. There were produced forms of application for 98 shares of £1 each in the capital of the company, together with cheques for a total of £100, being payment in full for the said shares and the two shares taken by the subscribers to the memorandum of association.
    It was resolved:
    (a) THAT 49 shares of £1 each, fully paid and numbered 3 to 51 inclusive, be allotted to [applicant 1].
    (b) THAT 49 shares of £1 each, fully paid and numbered 52 to 100 inclusive, be allotted to [applicant 2].
    (c) THAT all the shares of the company shall henceforth cease to bear distinguishing numbers.

(d) THAT the undermentioned share certificates drawn in respect of subscribers' shares and the allotments made by resolutions (a) and (b) above be approved and that the common seal be affixed thereto:

No. 1   [applicant 1]   50 shares
No. 2   [applicant 2]   50 shares.

11. It was resolved that the next meeting of the board of directors would be held at [place] on [date] at [time].

[Signed]

[Chair]

Evidential status of minutes of meetings of directors

Minutes of meetings of directors recorded in accordance with section 248 are evidence of the proceedings at the meeting if purporting to be authenticated by the chair of the meeting or the chair of the next directors' meeting (s. 249(1)). Where minutes have been made of the proceedings of a meeting of directors in accordance with the Act, then, until the contrary is proved:

(a) the meeting is deemed duly held and convened;
(b) all proceedings at the meeting are deemed to have duly taken place; and
(c) all appointments at the meeting are deemed valid (s. 249(2)).

Approval and signature of minutes of meetings of directors

Board minutes are usually distributed in draft form to the directors for comment and signed by the chair of the next succeeding board meeting.

Distribution in draft form usually takes place as soon as possible following the completion of the meeting to ensure that directors can comment when the proceedings are fresh in their minds. There is no requirement for all directors to comment on the content at such time although, in practice, if minutes are to be tabled at the next meeting for approval and ratification by signing, it is difficult to justify the incorporation of additional comments at such a late stage. Directors should be encouraged to comment within a reasonable timeframe of the distribution of the draft minutes so that any significant comments can be incorporated.

To facilitate this, they are often included in the agenda papers for the meeting at which they are to be approved, particularly if any changes have been made to the first draft as a consequence of comments by directors. At the meeting, the minutes are usually taken as read and a motion is put recommending their adoption as a true and accurate record of the proceedings of the meeting to which they refer. If approved, they should be signed immediately by the chair who need not have been present at the original meeting.

The chair may, however, sign the minutes before the next succeeding meeting of the board and need not necessarily give the other directors an opportunity to comment on them before doing so. This will rarely be necessary and any chair who follows this procedure should be prepared to explain to his fellow directors why he departed from the usual practice and expect to have the minutes scrutinised more closely than might normally be the case. If this procedure is followed and the directors disagree with the chair's interpretation of the proceedings, they could pass a resolution to that effect which would be recorded in the minutes of that meeting. The minutes which were the subject of the disagreement should not be altered although it might be sensible for the secretary to make a marginal note in the original minutes cross-referring to the subsequent decision.

In the unlikely event that the chair refuses to sign the minutes, it should be recorded in the minutes of the next meeting that they were approved as a true record by the other directors who were present at the original meeting, if that was the case.

Maintenance of minute books

Companies are required by section 248 to maintain minutes of all meetings of the directors and for these to be available for inspection by any director. There is no provision or right for the members to have access to minutes of the meetings of the directors. Conversely, members can request to see minutes of members meetings. The taking of minutes, and their maintenance and safekeeping, is one of the core duties of the company secretary.

Certification of minute books

Where a third party, such as the company's bank or landlord, requests to see a copy of a particular board resolution, it is clearly not advisable to submit the entire minutes of that particular meeting or even a particular page, as these may contain confidential information. In such circumstances, it is normal for the resolution in question to be reproduced as a separate document and for the company secretary or a director to certify the extract as a true copy of the original minute.

Role of the company secretary, after the meeting

The following checklist is adapted from The Chartered Governance Institute's *Company Secretary's Handbook*, 12th edition, Chapter 9: Directors' meetings and resolutions.

Tasks and actions of the company secretary after the meeting:

1 (Listed, AIM and ISDX companies only) If the company has made a decision with regard to the payment of a dividend on the company's ordinary shares, yearly or half-yearly accounts have been approved or a decision for the appointment or resignation of a director, a regulatory information service should be advised immediately by telephone or fax (Listing Rule 9.7.2). If necessary, a regulatory information service should be advised of any decision to make an issue of shares or debentures or to postpone the payment of a preference dividend or of interest (Listing Rule 9.6.4, 9.7.2.2).

2 Make a list of any actions that have been agreed at the meeting, the person or committee responsible for delivery and the due date and ensure that this is updated with progress prior to the next meeting. This list should add to actions agreed at previous meetings to ensure that none are overlooked. Reference to the date of the meeting where the action was agreed as well as the relevant meeting minute number provides a simple action checklist numbering system

3 The company's managers, or if relevant, any committee of the board, should be notified in writing of any action which the board require them to take, for example by sending a memorandum, letter or email to the managers concerned or the chair of the relevant committee.

4 Make a note of any item that has been deferred for future consideration to ensure that it is not overlooked.

5 If the directors have asked for a report on a specific subject to be prepared for their next meeting, ensure that the manager responsible for preparing it has been notified.

6 Prepare the minutes of the meeting, showing the names of the directors present, those whose apologies were noted, and the arrival and departure of any director who was not present at the beginning or end of the meeting.

7 The procedure to be followed after preparation of the minutes will vary from company to company. However, it is usual to send a copy of the draft minutes to the chair for their initial comments. On receipt and incorporation of these, the draft minutes should be sent to every director present with a request that they return any comments by a given date, following which the minutes can be prepared in their final form for distribution to all directors, including those that were not present at the meeting.

8 If a director makes a comment about the wording of a particular minute after the final draft has been circulated, the alteration should be agreed with the chair, who will then mention the amendment at the subsequent board meeting before signing the minutes. Since the chair has agreed the amendment, it is unlikely that any director present at the subsequent board meeting will object to the alteration. Other than obvious mistakes, alterations

should be confined to what was said rather than what any particular director meant to say or, on reflection, would have preferred not to say.

Conclusion

This chapter has focused on the production and content of the minutes as a record of the discussions and agreements made at the meeting. Their content and purpose as a record should not be underestimated given they may, in the future, provide evidence required to substantiate decisions or defend claims. Attendees should ensure that they capture the decisions made as they see them. Where a director believes they are not representative, either of the meeting or their personal contribution, they should as a starting point, discuss this with the company secretary and chair.

Each company and/or company secretary will have their own style and format for meeting minutes and there is no 'correct' way to record the content of meetings; some can be extensive replications of the full discussion, while others limit their content to the decisions agreed. It should be noted that certain minutes may be required to be circulated externally, either in full or as an abstract, as proof of a decision being approved.

Minutes can also provide a useful history of a company documenting as they do the appointments and removals of directors, decisions made, acquisitions approved and divestments agreed. As well as an audit trail of decision such as these, they also provide a timeline for developing and changing strategies for the company, with resultant success capable of being tracked back via minutes to effective board discussions and meetings.

11 – Section 2 conclusion

Having effective meetings of directors underpins the success of a company. However, ensuring that the process and implementation of meetings and their support is appropriate is key to ensuring that good governance does not become the main focus of the company and its leadership.

Conversely, poorly implemented meeting frameworks can provide future issues for a company with little or no audit trail of decisions made, limited discussion or challenge of business decisions and a lack of leadership from the board.

Balancing the processes to ensure its effectiveness can serve to support the business in the long term as well as create a positive leadership culture. The framework for internal meetings and any defined processes and procedures should be suitable for the particular company with limited guidance or legislative expectations on its implementation. The culture of the business as well as the leadership style will dictate whether these processes need to be prescriptive or light touch. Equally, the membership of the board and their expectations will create a leadership and meeting framework that meets their requirements as well as that of the company.

Those supporting the board in their meetings should provide clarity on what must be undertaken and what is a company decision. Supporting or creating the framework for internal meetings and making the processes efficient and effective will ensure that the framework is applied in a positive manner.

Section 3
General meetings

12 – Section 3 Introduction

Section 3 deals with the formal meetings held by a company with their members or shareholders.

Specifically, in this section we will look at why and when a formal shareholders' meeting should be held, what the processes are for convening a meeting, proceedings at the meetings and the follow-up requirements. In addition, we will touch on the alternatives to holding a formal meeting of shareholders and the rights of those shareholders to call a meeting themselves.

First, it is useful to clarify the difference between members and shareholders as well as the different types of resolutions that a company may seek to pass at a general meeting. Finally, we will touch on the emergence of hybrid meetings which combine physical and virtual meetings and the developments that are being seen in this area.

Members or shareholders?

While common language references shareholders rather than members of a company, there are distinct differences between the two which are worth understanding.

Every company must have at least one member. In most cases, the only way to become a member is to become a shareholder. However, this is not true for every company. Companies limited by guarantee can have members who are not shareholders. In fact, since 1980, you can no longer form a guarantee company with a share capital. Hence, the vast majority of guarantee companies cannot have shareholders and instead have members who still need to make decisions on behalf of the company.

This section is not just about how companies with shareholders may make decisions. It is also about how members of companies who are not shareholders may make decisions. That is why the term 'members' has been used rather than the more narrowly defined 'shareholder'.

There may be some companies or actions that are specific to either members or shareholders, however the majority of applications can be applied to both.

As far as companies with a share capital are concerned, it does not really matter which term we use. In such a company, the words 'member' and 'shareholder' can be used interchangeably. Everybody who is a shareholder in such a company is a member of it, and it is not possible to become a member in any other way. So, whenever we use the word 'member' it is always meant to include 'shareholders' unless otherwise specified.

Registered shareholder

If a company has a share capital, the only way to become a member will be to become a shareholder. The registered holder is the person whose name is entered in the company's register of members as the holder of the shares. In companies that have shares, people often refer to the register of members as the share register. If a company has more than one class of shares, it will typically keep a separate share register for each class. Where this is the case, each of those registers combine to make up the register of members. This is why every person whose name is entered in any share register as the holder of any type of share automatically becomes a member of the company. The share registers are the company's register of members.

Nominee shareholders and underlying investors

It follows that, if somebody else holds shares on your behalf, you are not the registered shareholder and not a member of the company. It is the person who holds the shares on your behalf who is the member and the registered shareholder. People who hold shares through a nominee in this way often think of themselves as shareholders and may even refer to themselves as shareholders. However, they are not. And if they are not shareholders, they are not members either. They are nothing more than underlying investors. In most cases, a company can choose to ignore the fact that these indirect investors exist. In most cases, the company only has to deal with the person who is the registered shareholder. In most cases, underlying investors do not have any enforceable rights against the company, the only rights being those that arise under any agreement they have entered into with the person who is acting as their nominee. These rights are not enforceable against the company but against the nominee.

The reason why we keep saying 'in most cases' is that the Act provides a mechanism to enable underlying investors in listed companies to claim certain 'membership' rights through their nominee. In addition, any company can choose to make provision in its articles to give underlying investors certain 'membership' rights. We tend to refer to people who have such rights as 'indirect investors' to distinguish them from underlying investors who have no rights.

Types of resolutions

Resolutions can be split into special resolutions and ordinary resolutions, with Appendix 4 providing a list of each in respect of most companies.

The type of resolution required to deal with an item of business is determined primarily by the Companies Act 2006 but can also depend on other factors. For each type of resolution, there are different requirements with regard to the majority required to pass it and there can be different notice requirements.

Part 13, Chapter 1 of the Act sets out the general provisions about resolutions. Section 281 provides that a resolution of the members (or of a class of members) of:

(a) a private company must be passed:
   (i) as a written resolution in accordance with the Companies Act 2006, Part 13, Chapter 2, or
   (ii) at a meeting of the members (to which the provisions of the Companies Act 2006, Pt 13, Ch. 3 apply) (s. 281(1)).
(b) a public company must be passed at a meeting of the members (to which the provisions of the Companies Act 2006, Pt 13, Ch. 3 and, where relevant, Pt 13, Ch. 4 of that Act apply).

Section 281(4) provides that nothing in Part 13 of the 2006 Act affects any enactment or rule of law as to:

- things done otherwise than by passing a resolution;
- circumstances in which a resolution is or is not treated as having been passed; or
- cases in which a person is precluded from alleging that a resolution has not been duly passed.

Ordinary resolutions

As a general rule, unless the Companies Acts or a company's articles specify otherwise, all business at general meetings may be dealt with by ordinary resolution, although listed companies may also need to have regard to the requirements of Financial Conduct Authority (FCA) Rules and guidance issued by institutional investors.

Where a provision of the Companies Acts requires a resolution of the company or of the members (or a class of members) and does not specify what type of resolution is required, an ordinary resolution will suffice unless the company's articles require a higher majority (or unanimity) (s. 281(3)). Anything that may be done by ordinary resolution may also be done by special resolution (s. 282(5)). However, a thing that is required to be done by special resolution cannot be done by ordinary resolution even if it is passed by the requisite majority of at least 75% because a special resolution must be proposed as a special resolution.

An ordinary resolution is defined in section 282 of the Act. In simple terms it is a resolution of the members (or a class of members) which may be passed by a simple majority (s. 282(1)).

A written resolution is passed by a simple majority if it is passed by members representing a simple majority of the total voting rights of eligible members (s. 282(2)).

A resolution passed at a meeting on a show of hands is passed by a simple majority if it is passed by a simple majority of the votes cast by those entitled to vote (s. 282(3)).

A resolution passed on a poll taken at a meeting is passed by a simple majority if it is passed by members representing a simple majority of the total voting rights of members who (being entitled to do so) vote in person or by proxy on the resolution (s. 282(4)).

It should be noted that an abstention or vote withheld on a resolution proposed at a meeting (whether on a show of hands or on a poll) is not considered to be a vote for these purposes. Accordingly, an ordinary resolution proposed at a general meeting will be passed if the number of votes cast in favour of the resolution exceeds the number against. However, failure to vote on a proposed written resolution has the same effect as voting against it.

Articles sometimes purport to give the chairman of the meeting a casting vote in addition to any other vote he may have if the outcome of a vote on either a show of hands or a poll is a tie. The continuing validity of any such provision is open to some doubt.

A copy of some, but not all, ordinary resolutions must be filed at Companies House. The table in Appendix 1 shows the matters that require member or shareholder approval under the Act and other sources, what sort of resolution is required and whether the resolution must be filed at Companies House.

Special resolutions

A special resolution is defined in section 283 as a resolution of the members (or a class of members) of a company passed by a majority of not less than 75% (s. 283(1)).

A written special resolution is passed by a majority of not less than 75% if it is passed by members representing not less than 75% of the total voting rights of eligible members (s. 283(2)).

Where a resolution of a private company is passed as a written resolution, the resolution is not a special resolution unless it stated that it was proposed as a special resolution, and if the resolution so stated, it may only be passed as a special resolution (s. 283(3)).

A resolution passed at a meeting on a show of hands is passed by a majority of not less than 75% if it is passed by not less than 75% of the votes cast by those entitled to vote.

A resolution passed on a poll taken at a meeting is passed by a majority of not less than 75% if it is passed by members representing not less than 75% of the total voting rights of the members who (being entitled to do so) vote in person or by proxy on the resolution (s. 283(5)).

Where a resolution is passed at a meeting:

(a) the resolution is not a special resolution unless the notice of the meeting included the text of the resolution and specified the intention to propose the resolution as a special resolution; and

(b) if the notice of the meeting so specified, the resolution may only be passed as a special resolution (s. 283(6)).

The intention to propose a resolution as a special resolution should be clearly stated in the notice calling the meeting. The notice should also include either the text or substance of the resolution.

Similarly, a copy of every special resolution passed by a company must be filed at Companies House within 15 days of it being passed (ss. 29 and 30) (see Chapter 10: After the meeting).

For a table showing items of business which must be passed by members as a special resolution, see Appendix 1.

Extraordinary resolutions

The 2006 Act makes no specific provision for extraordinary resolutions. However, they are preserved by virtue of paragraph 23 of Schedule 3 to the Third Commencement Order (SI 2007/2194) (as amended by paragraph 2 of Schedule 5 to the Fifth Commencement Order (SI 2007/3495)). Subsection (1) of paragraph 23 provides that any reference to an extraordinary resolution in a company's memorandum or articles of association or any contractual provision continues to have effect and shall be construed in accordance with section 378 of the Companies Act 1985 as if that section had not been repealed. Subsection (2) of paragraph 23 provides that Chapter 3 of Part 3 (resolutions affecting a company's constitution) of the 2006 Act applies to any such extraordinary resolution. Accordingly, a copy of any such extraordinary resolution must be filed at Companies House.

An extraordinary resolution will be invalid if the notice does not specify the intention to propose it as an extraordinary resolution and if it does not state the text or entire substance of the proposals to be submitted.

There are no specific requirements as to the period of notice which must be given for extraordinary resolutions. Accordingly, the period of notice required will be determined by the requirements for the type of meeting at which the resolution is to be proposed.

Unanimous consent of members

The unanimous consent of members is required for a company to do the following:

(a) to insert or amend entrenched provisions in a company's articles (s. 22);
(b) to re-register a private limited company as unlimited (s. 102);
(c) to re-register a public limited company as unlimited (s. 109);
(d) to hold an annual general meeting (AGM) of a public company at short notice (s. 337).

Date a resolution is passed

The date of passing a resolution will be the date of the meeting or, if the resolution was passed at an adjourned meeting, the date of the adjourned meeting (s. 332). Where the business of a meeting is suspended for the purposes of calculating the results of a poll conducted at the meeting, the date of the resolution will be the date of the meeting at which the poll was taken. Where the business of a meeting is suspended for the purposes of conducting a poll on a later date, the date of the resolution will be the date of the meeting at which the poll was taken or, if later, the result ascertained.

If a resolution is passed as a written resolution, it is passed on the date that it was agreed to by the last member required to agree to it to pass it.

Electronic general meetings

Several UK-listed companies have, in the last few years, considered using electronic general meetings, while market and global impacts have driven more companies to consider and, where possible, adopt their use. However, typically, the general meeting is still an important opportunity for shareholders to come together in one physical location and hear directly from the company's directors. Companies considering the use of electronic meetings, either fully electronic or a hybrid version, should consider how they will deal with these in planning for all general meetings and, in particular, for their AGMs.

There are a number of key topics to consider, some of which are listed here.

Printing and postal delays

It is likely that many companies, particularly those with a large retail shareholder base, still need to send out a number of hard copy notices of meetings and their accompanying documents. The Companies Act 2006 and Financial Conduct Authority (FCA) Rules encourage communication by electronic means but UK issuers can only take full advantage of these provisions if they have obtained the specific consent of individual shareholders. Companies should work with their registrar to check on the timetable and logistics for getting the necessary documents printed and sent out on time.

It is helpful to note that, even if there are printing or posting delays for whatever reason, most listed companies should have more time than they need to fulfil their legal obligations to give the notice of meeting (21 working days for the AGM and 14 for most other types of general meeting, not counting the days when the notice is given or when the meeting is actually held). Issuers usually comply with best practice recommendations for shareholders to receive meeting documents roughly one month (20 working days) before the AGM. In addition, companies are not responsible for making sure that the notice of the meeting is actually received by the shareholders as they can rely on provisions in the Companies Act and in their articles of association for the notice to have been deemed to have been received by a certain date.

Care should be taken that the printed materials that are posted to shareholders are the same as those posted electronically and that there is no mismatch between the two that could cause confusion or, if significant, lead to a potential claim for miscommunication or an attempt to undermine any approval process.

Quorum and attendance

The quorum requirement should be checked, but for a UK company is likely to be relatively low. It should, therefore, be possible to satisfy this and hold a valid meeting, even if the number of physical attendees is low but is enhanced by those attending virtually. However, where votes are to be cast, it should be checked at the outset of the meeting that not only is there a quorum present, but that those individuals counting towards the quorum are also capable of voting whether physically present or attending virtually.

It is best practice to ensure, wherever possible, that board members and those who may be called on to formally contribute, such as auditors or other advisers, can attend in person. If not, their ability to both attend and contribute virtually should be checked before the commencement of the meeting.

Electronic meetings

Some companies have amended their articles to allow for meetings to be held by electronic means, as well as in a physical place. A minority of companies may have articles which allow them to hold general meetings that are entirely electronic or 'virtual-only'. However, the standard investor guidance recommends that a physical place of meeting should always be provided. In any case, an option for all companies is to proceed with the meeting at the physical place as normal, while suggesting to shareholders that they should consider not turning up in person on the day, although they do, of course, have a right to do so.

All shareholders should also be encouraged to exercise their rights to appoint a proxy and to submit questions to the board in advance of the meeting (e.g. via an online portal or using a dedicated email address).

In addition, companies that do not currently do so should consider live-streaming the meeting on the company's website and/or making a recording available afterwards. In such case, communications should make clear that these facilities are provided for information purposes only and not as a formal part of the meeting.

> **Example: Electronic meetings**
>
> As a professional provider of support services to companies, Computershare themselves host their AGM both physically in person in Australia as well as electronically, providing access to their shareholders worldwide. Their most recent AGM 2019 was broadcast as a webcast with virtual attendance and presentations added to their website. To participate, shareholders had to download an app. This then allowed them to view a live webcast of the meeting, submit questions for the directors and submit votes in real time. The webcast was also recorded and made available as a video to be viewed at any time.
>
> More details can be seen here: https://www.computershare.com/corporate/ investor-relations/events/annual-general-meetings

Forms of electronic meetings, the technology available to support them and the ability for presenters and shareholders to contribute effectively are being developed rapidly with the need for legislation and individual company articles to enable their use.

Conclusion

Annual general meetings of members exist to provide two functions:

- to seek shareholder approval for certain matters as required by the Companies Act and/or Listing Rules; and
- to give an opportunity for shareholders to hold the directors to account for the running of the company.

This chapter has given an overview of the format of the approvals which require approval at such meetings, in the form of resolutions. It will be seen from the subsequent chapters that, while there is a clear legislative framework to be adopted in the practice of holding meetings of members, the second point of enabling the members to hold the directors to account is more flexible and will be reflected in the interactions during the meeting itself, whether they are supportive of, or combative against, the board and their actions.

At its heart, the meeting is providing the board with an opportunity to have formal approval of actions being taken in the form of resolutions, but also seeking to explain their strategy to deliver further success which would enhance the value of shares for those same members.

13 – Why and when to hold a general meeting

Under law, members of a company primarily make decisions by passing resolutions, usually when tabled at a general meeting of the members. Alternate options for decision making include written resolutions. However, the majority of formal decision making via resolution at large companies, and by law all public companies, will be undertaken by presenting the resolutions to the members at a formal general meeting and for them to be voted on. For smaller companies and particularly those with a single member, written resolutions are more likely to be used. Specific requirements for single member companies can be found in Chapter 20.

For those convening member meetings, Part 13 of the Companies Act 2006 sets out the formal methods by which members may pass resolutions with most meetings of the members or shareholders being held as general meetings. As such, the relevant clauses of Part 13 are listed within this chapter for reference. The full act can be found on the UK government website at: www.legislation.gov.uk/ukpga/2006/46/contents.

Companies can be required to hold meetings that are not general meetings (e.g. meetings of a specific class of members, where these exist). For ease of reference, class meetings are covered separately in Chapter 19.

Where resolutions are passed in accordance with Part 13, it is not necessary for all the members to participate in the decision or for them all to agree with it. Resolutions may be passed by a majority, with this majority not always required to be the same percentage. For example, certain matters must be passed as a special resolution which requires a 75% majority, while others may be passed by a simple majority within a quorum. As such, Chapter 15, will provide further detail on both quorums and voting during the meeting.

Decision-making methods

Part 13 of the Companies Act 2006 sets out the main statutory rules governing the methods by which members of a company may make decisions and begins (at s. 281) by saying that a resolution of the members of a private company (or of a class of members) *must* be passed either:

(a) as a written resolution in accordance with Part 13, Chapter 2; or
(b) at a meeting of the members.

However, for public companies, it states that a resolution of the members (or of a class of members) *must* be passed at a meeting of the members. In other words, a public company cannot take advantage of the statutory written resolution procedures in Part 13, Chapter 2.

Although the Act does not say so explicitly, it also recognises that members can also make unanimous decisions without following the usual formalities. The purpose of holding a meeting or circulating a written resolution is to discover whether the necessary majority are in favour of a proposal. Where it is clear that all the members agree, it is arguable that they should be able to dispense with these formalities. This is the underlying foundation of the common law principle of unanimous consent. This common law rule is preserved by section 281(4). However, the principle can sometimes prove to have rocky foundations. The courts will not always apply it to rectify procedural irregularities, particularly where the members were not given the necessary information upon which to base their decision. It is far safer, therefore, for a company to make decisions by passing formal resolutions in accordance with the requirements of the Act.

It should be noted in this regard that, although an informal decision is capable of having the same effect as a resolution, it is not treated under the Act as a resolution. That is why section 281 does not say that a resolution can be passed as an informal decision. The best way to understand this is to say that all resolutions must be passed in accordance with the Act but that decisions do not necessarily have to be made by passing a resolution. One could argue that the Act is almost deliberately misleading in this regard. The government did consider making it more explicit in the Act that members can make decisions informally. However, it decided not to do so. The principle of unanimous consent is meant to be a closely guarded secret. On the whole, it is better if people who run companies are unaware that it exists as it is much safer for them to make decisions by passing resolutions in accordance with the Act. It is impossible to write a book about meetings without referring to the principle of unanimous consent. However, it gives the author no pleasure to think that, having explained it, readers might use it in preference to the procedures for passing resolutions under the Act. It is best to view the principle of unanimous consent as something that may get you out of a sticky situation when you have accidentally failed to do what was required in order to pass a resolution. Otherwise, it is best to forget that it exists. Unfortunately, this is not an easy thing to do. The principle just has too many memorable features, the most memorable of which is probably that it can apply in the absence of unanimity.

Part 13 of the Companies Act 2006

Part 13 of the Companies Act 2006, which is the relevant section for general meetings, is divided into Chapters as follows:

Chapter No.	Subject	Section Nos
Chapter 1	General provisions about resolutions	281–287
Chapter 2	Written resolutions	288–300
Chapter 3	Resolutions at meetings	301–335
Chapter 4	Public Companies: Additional requirements for AGMs	336–340
Chapter 5	Additional requirements for quoted companies	341–354
Chapter 6	Records of resolutions and meetings	355–359
Chapter 7	Supplementary provisions	360–361

Most of the provisions of Part 13 were brought into force on 1 October 2007, although section 333 (sending documents relating to meetings etc. in electronic form) was brought into force on 20 January 2007 together with the company communication provisions in sections 1143 to 1148 and Schedules 4 and 5 of the Act. Part 9 of the Act (ss 145 to 153) on indirect investor rights was also brought into force on 1 October 2007.

From 1 October 2007, separate versions of Table A for public and private companies came into force to cater for the fact that private companies were no longer required to hold annual general meetings (AGMs) from that date and to reflect the provisions of Part 13 of the Companies Act 2006 on resolutions and meetings that were commenced on that date. The amended versions of Table A only applied to companies incorporated between 1 October 2007 and 30 September 2009 and did not affect any company with articles already based on a previous version of Table A.

From 30 April 2013, companies were incorporated under new model articles prescribed for the purposes of the Companies Act 2006. The three different versions for private companies limited by shares, private companies limited by guarantee and public companies can be found at Annexes C2, C3 and C4 respectively. Annex C1 shows a comparative table of contents for the three different versions of the model articles. A comparative of the contents of Table A articles against model articles can be found in Appendix 6.

Traded and quoted companies

Various provisions on resolutions and meetings in Part 13 of the Act only apply to 'traded companies' or 'quoted companies'.

Traded companies

A 'traded company' is defined in section 360C (for the purposes of Part 13 only) as 'a company any shares of which carry rights to vote at general meetings and are admitted to trading on a regulated market in an EEA State by or with the consent of the company'. This is similar to (but not exactly the same as) the definition of a 'traded company' used for the purposes of the annual return in Part 24 of the Act. The fact that a company is a 'traded company' for the purposes of the annual return, does not necessarily mean that it is a 'traded company' for the purposes of Part 13. The Part 13 definition requires the company's voting shares to be listed. For the purposes of Part 24, it does not matter whether the shares that are listed are voting shares.

The overwhelming majority of companies which fall within the definition of a traded company for the purposes of Part 13 will be public companies. However, it is also technically possible for a private company to be a traded company.

Quoted companies

Various provisions of the Act apply to quoted companies only. The term 'quoted company' was first introduced to define the type of company that must prepare a directors' remuneration report. However, it is now used for other purposes. The original definition in Part 15 of the Act (at s. 385) only applies for the purposes of Part 15. Accordingly, it has to be defined again if it is used for any other purpose. However, whenever it is used, the relevant definition always refers to the original definition in section 385 of Part 15. In other words, the same definition is used throughout the Act (see, e.g., the definition in Part 13, s. 361).

Section 385 of the Act defines a quoted company as a company whose equity share capital:

(a) has been included in the official list in accordance with the provisions of Part 6 of the FSMA 2000 (i.e. is officially listed in the UK); or
(b) is officially listed in a European Economic Area (EEA) State; or
(c) is admitted to dealing on either the New York Stock Exchange or the exchange known as Nasdaq.

The 'official list' is maintained in the UK by the Financial Conduct Authority (FCA) in accordance with section 103(1) of the FSMA 2000. It should be noted that a UK company will be a 'quoted company' if any of its shares are listed. The shares need not be voting shares. The Listing Rules provide additional requirements for listed companies in terms of reporting, including reporting related to meetings of listed companies.

Meetings of members

The two primary meetings of members of a company are the general meeting and a class meeting of holders of a specific class of shares. While class meetings are introduced here, greater detail can be found in Chapter 19.

General meetings

Meetings of the members or shareholders of a company are usually referred to as 'general meetings'. However, it would be wrong to suggest that every meeting of members or shareholders will necessarily be a general meeting. A general meeting is a meeting of the members or shareholders who are entitled to make decisions on behalf of the company. This may not necessarily include all members or shareholders as some may not be entitled to vote. A general meeting is a meeting of the members who are entitled to vote. It is those members who collectively represent the mind of the company and who can make decisions on its behalf. Those decisions can be described as a decision of the company in general meeting.

The AGM is a type of general meeting that certain companies (e.g. public companies) are required to hold. General meetings are sometimes referred to as company meetings or shareholder meetings. Reference within this section to general meetings should, unless specified otherwise, include AGMs.

A matter which requires the approval of the members in a general meeting can be dealt with either at a general meeting called for that purpose or, if the company holds an AGM, at the AGM. Private companies are not normally required to hold AGMs unless their articles expressly require them to do so. Nevertheless, a private company will need to hold a general meeting to deal with business which needs member approval if it is not able to dispose of it by written resolution.

As public companies are required to hold an AGM, they will only need to call other general meetings throughout the year to deal with business which cannot wait for it. It is not necessary for a public company to lay its accounts, reappoint auditors or fix their remuneration at the AGM. The Act simply requires accounts to be laid at a general meeting and for the auditors to be reappointed at that meeting. In other words, this can be done at any general meeting.

Class meetings

Many of the rules and procedures applicable to general meetings also apply to class meetings. A class meeting can be described as a meeting held to obtain the approval of a class of members or shareholders rather than the approval of all the members or shareholders who would be entitled to vote at a general meeting. If all the members of the company have exactly the same rights or they all hold exactly the same shares which confer exactly the same rights, the company will probably never need to hold a class meeting. However, if a company has members who have different rights (or different interests), it may occasionally need to hold a separate meeting to determine the views of those people. The main reason why a company would need to hold a class meeting is to obtain the approval of a particular class of members or shareholders to a proposal to change their rights. Any such proposal would need the approval of the members in general meeting and the separate approval of the members of that class.

Say, for example, a company had a class of non-voting shares that paid a fixed dividend each year. It would be unfair if the shareholders with voting shares were able to pass a resolution at a general meeting to reduce the dividend payable on the non-voting shares without the consent of the holders of those shares. The Act does not allow this. The non-voting shareholders would be required to approve the change. The rules governing class meetings and class rights are covered separately in Chapter 19.

It should be noted that, where there is only one class of shares, a, general meeting is, by default, also a class meeting. This should be remembered if at any point a company decides to issue additional share classes, at which point the differentiating voting rights of the various share classes should be clear and will drive the requirement for any separate class meetings.

Court meetings

The court can sometimes direct that a company must hold a meeting of members. This could be a general meeting or a class meeting. Generally speaking, the court will order that the meeting be held in accordance with normal procedures. However, it can direct that different procedures be followed. If so, the meeting must be held in accordance with the directions of the court. This is, in reality, the only practical difference between court meetings and other meetings.

It should also be noted that in connection with a scheme of arrangement, the court may sometimes direct that a separate meeting be held to obtain the approval of members with different interests even though they are notionally all members of the same class or hold shares of the same class.

Paper meetings

Companies often view the requirement to hold general meetings as an unnecessary administrative burden. Many prepare minutes of meetings which have not actually taken place. This practice is sometimes referred to as holding a 'paper meeting', a name which gives it a false aura of legality. In reality, a paper meeting is no better than no meeting at all. The fact that a set of minutes have been prepared recording that a meeting has been held and that certain decisions have been made does not make it true. Although minutes are evidence of the proceedings it would not take much to undermine their status as evidence. Where minutes are submitted as evidence in legal proceedings, somebody who is listed as being in attendance at the meeting is usually required to swear an affidavit that the meeting actually took place. If you are not prepared to perjure yourself in legal proceedings, you should not get involved in writing minutes of meetings that did not take place.

The fact that no meeting actually took place does not necessarily mean that all the decisions recorded in the minutes will be invalid. It is possible that they will be capable of validation under the principle of unanimous consent. Whether or not this is the case, the fact that you have had to admit that no meeting took place is not going to do much to improve your credibility as a witness.

Paper meetings are, therefore, something that should be avoided at all costs. In the case of a private company, if it is not possible to hold a meeting, it is better to make the decision by written resolution. Even if you are relying on the principle of unanimous consent, it is pointless to lie about the fact that a meeting took place. It is far better to simply record the fact that the members have made the decision informally, and even better from an evidential perspective, to get them all to sign it to confirm that they have done so, or to get them signify their agreement in some other way that can be kept (e.g. by email).

Other meetings

Many of the common law principles that apply to general meetings will also apply to meetings of debenture holders and meetings in insolvency. These are not covered in this book as they are not governed by the Companies Acts. Meetings in insolvency are governed mainly by insolvency law. Meetings of debenture holders will be governed mainly by the debenture instrument or trust deed.

Historically, companies could also hold extraordinary general meetings. However, these are no longer required and, as such, they have not been included. Companies should instead utilise general meetings for presenting any matters to the members.

Some older articles refer to the AGM as the 'ordinary meeting' and any other general meeting as an 'extraordinary meeting'. However, the Companies Act 2006 no longer makes this distinction and, as such, these terms are no longer applicable. The Act instead refers to the AGM and general meetings and reference herein to general meetings should be inferred to include both.

Listed companies: Rights of indirect investors

Sections 146–151 of the 2006 Act, which apply to companies whose shares are admitted to trading on a regulated market (such as the London Stock Exchange main listed market but not AIM), provide that shareholders (such as nominee companies) who hold shares on behalf of other persons may nominate them to receive certain information rights. The information rights concerned include the right to receive copies of all documents sent to shareholders generally (or to members of the relevant class of shares), including reports and accounts and any summary financial statements (see s. 146(3)).

The nomination(s) must be communicated to the company by the registered holder of the shares and not, for example, by the investment manager who operates the nominee company concerned. They must also relate to all, and not part only, of the information rights. The default right given by a nomination is for the documents to be supplied by means of a website – if the nominated person is to receive hard copies of the documents, he must have asked the registered holder to nominate him, hence a nominee company cannot make a 'blanket' nomination to receive hard copy for all its indirect investors. To be included in the nomination, the indirect investor must have made a specific request for hard copy and must have supplied an address for this purpose.

The nomination given to the company by the registered holder must then indicate that the person nominated wishes to receive hard copy communications and give the address supplied by that person. As an alternative, a person nominated to receive web-based communications only may directly revoke the implied agreement to receive web-based communications and thus become entitled to receive hard copy (see s. 147(6)). These provisions of the 2006 Act come into force on 1 October 2007 so as to enable nominations to be given and recorded (and if the company so wishes, acted on) but a company was not required to act on a nomination until 1 January 2008 (see SI 2007/2194, Sch. 3, para. 3).

The fact that a person may be nominated to receive hard copy communications does not prevent the company from making use of the electronic communications provisions and seeking to obtain from that person actual or deemed agreement to website-based communications (s. 147(4)).

Information rights are enforceable by the registered member, not by the nominated person, as if they were rights under the articles.

Where a copy of a notice of meeting is sent to a nominated person as part of the information rights this must be accompanied by a statement that:

(a) he may have a right under an agreement between him and the member by whom he was nominated to be appointed, or to have someone else appointed, as a proxy for the meeting; and

(b) if he has no such right or does not wish to exercise it, he may have a right under such an agreement to give instructions to the member as to the exercise of voting rights.

The copy notice may also not include the statement of member's rights in relation to appointment of proxy (prescribed by s. 325) or that statement must indicate that it does not apply to the nominated person (s. 149).

A nomination may be terminated by the registered member or the nominated person, and automatically ceases if the registered member or the nominated person dies, becomes bankrupt, or subject to a winding-up order. The company may also ask a nominated person if the nomination is to continue. If a reply is not received to that inquiry within 28 days, the nomination is terminated. This will be a useful procedure to 'clean up' the nomination records periodically but such an inquiry may not be made of a nominated person more than once in any 12-month period (s. 148).

Should a member have nominated more persons than the number of shares he holds, the effect of all his nominations is suspended while that situation continues (s. 148(5)).

Sections 152 and 153 make it easier for registered members to exercise rights in different ways to reflect the underlying holdings and allow indirect investors to participate in, for example, requests for resolutions at the AGM. Section 152 provides that a member can choose to split their holding, and exercise rights attached to shares in different ways. This is to assist members who hold shares on behalf of more than one person, each of whom may want to exercise rights attaching to their shares in different ways (so, for example, it enables votes to be cast in different ways). If the member does not make it clear to the company in what way they are exercising their rights, the company can assume that all rights are being dealt with in the same way.

Indirect investors' and the '100 shareholders' test

Section 153 deals with provisions where the shareholder threshold required to trigger a right is 100 shareholders holding £100 each on average of paid-up capital. Indirect investors are enabled to count towards the total subject to certain conditions, intended to ensure that only genuine indirect investors are allowed to count towards the total, that the same shares cannot be used twice and that the indirect investor's contractual arrangements with the member allow the former to give voting instructions. Section 153 applies in relation to:

- section 314 (power to require circulation of statement);
- section 338 (public companies: power to require circulation of resolution for AGM);
- section 338A (traded companies: members' power to include matters in business dealt with at AGM);
- section 342 (power to require independent report on poll); and
- section 527 (power to require website publication of audit concerns).

It requires a listed company to act under any of those sections if it receives a request in relation to which the following conditions are met:

(a) it is made by at least 100 persons;
(b) it is authenticated by all the persons making it;
(c) in the case of any of those persons who is not a member of the company, it is accompanied by a statement—
    (i) of the full name and address of a person ('the member') who is a member of the company and holds shares on behalf of that person,
    (ii) that the member is holding those shares on behalf of that person in the course of a business,
    (iii) of the number of shares in the company that the member holds on behalf of that person,

  (iv) of the total amount paid up on those shares,

  (v) that those shares are not held on behalf of anyone else or, if they are, that the other person or persons are not among the other persons making the request,

  (vi) that some or all of those shares confer voting rights that are relevant for the purposes of making a request under the section in question, and

  (vii) that the person has the right to instruct the member how to exercise those rights;

(d) in the case of any of those persons who is a member of the company, it is accompanied by a statement—

  (i) that he holds shares otherwise than on behalf of another person, or

  (ii) that he holds shares on behalf of one or more other persons but those persons are not among the other persons making the request;

(e) it is accompanied by such evidence as the company may reasonably require of the matters mentioned in paragraphs (c) and (d);

(f) the total amount of the sums paid up on—

  (i) shares held as mentioned in paragraph (c), and

  (ii) shares held as mentioned in paragraph (d),

  divided by the number of persons making the request, is not less than £100;

(g) the request complies with any other requirements of the section in question as to contents, timing and otherwise.

The Chartered Governance Institute guidance on indirect investors

The Chartered Governance Institute has published guidance on the rights of indirect investors (Guidance Note: Indirect Investors — Information Rights and Voting) which members can access via their website at: www.icsa.org.uk/knowledge/resources/indirect-investors-information-rights-and-voting.

Articles can make provision for indirect investors

Other provisions in Part 9 (which apply to all companies, not just to those traded on a regulated market) are designed to make it easier for investors to exercise their governance rights where they hold through a nominee. Section 145 removes any doubts as to the ability of a company to make provision in its articles for underlying beneficial owners to exercise membership rights. It provides that where a company makes provision, through its articles, to extend rights to those holding shares through intermediaries, the provision is legally effective in relation to a non-exhaustive list of various statutory requirements. The articles may specify that this entitlement can apply only to certain rights or to all rights, except the right to transfer the shares. Where a company makes relevant provision in its articles, all the references to 'member' in the Companies Acts' provisions (relative to the specified rights) should be read as if the reference to member was a reference to the person or persons nominated by the member. Non-members will not be given direct enforceable rights against the company. They may only enforce their rights through the member whose name is on the register and who has the right to enforce the articles. Companies appear to be taking a very cautious approach to the question of whether their articles should give rights to indirect investors as envisaged in this section.

Written resolutions and unanimous consent

Written resolutions are a means for a private company to pass resolutions without the formality of a general meeting. Hence, for the majority of private companies, particularly those who only have a few members, the written resolution process is likely to be used in the majority of cases, as holding a members' meeting is a much more time-consuming process.

With a few exceptions, the members of a private company may pass any resolution that could be put to a general meeting by written resolution. The exceptions are:

- removal of a director under section 168; and
- removal of an auditor under section 510.

Written resolutions may be proposed by the directors using the procedure set out in section 291 and are covered in Chapter 7. Written resolutions by the members using the procedure set out in sections 292–295 (s. 288) are covered here.

In general, a copy of the proposed written resolution must be sent by post or electronic means to all members entitled to attend and vote at a general meeting. A member signifies their agreement to a written resolution by returning to the company a document in hard copy or electronically, identifying the resolution and signifying their consent. A written resolution is then approved when the requisite majority of members have signified their agreement, votes being calculated according to the number of shares held by each member. If agreement has not been given within 28 days from the date the resolution was circulated, it is deemed to have lapsed and any consent given after that date has no effect.

Copies of written resolutions circulated to members must also be sent to the company's auditor if it has one.

It is not necessarily safe for a public company to assume that it can rely on any such written resolution procedures in its articles. Under the common law principle of unanimous consent, it may not always be necessary to go through the usual process of holding a meeting and passing a formal resolution, if it can be shown that all the members who would have been entitled to vote agreed with the decision. However, although this common law principle is often applied to rectify procedural failings, it is not always safe to rely on the fact that a court will accept this given there is no specific ability for a public company to act by written consent.

Resolutions proposed by members

Any member or members of a private company together holding not less than 5% of the total voting rights of the company may also request that a statement of not more than 1,000 words be circulated with the proposed resolution. The company's articles may provide for a share ownership threshold of less than 5% (s. 292).

A company need not comply with such a request if the resolution, on being passed, would be ineffective by reason of inconsistency with legislation or the company's constitution or if it is frivolous, vexatious or defamatory (s. 292).

Where a valid request is received, copies of the proposed resolution and any accompanying statement must be circulated to all eligible members at the same time in hard copy, in electronic form or by means of a website within 21 days of receiving the request (s. 293).

The cost of circulating the proposed resolution and any statement must be met by those requesting the resolution and, unless the company has previously agreed to do so, it need not comply with the request unless sufficient funds are deposited by those requesting the resolution to meet the expenses (s. 294).

The company or other aggrieved person may apply to the court for an order not to comply with the request to circulate the proposed resolution and any statement on the grounds that the rights conferred by section 292 are being abused (s. 295).

Members' written resolutions

A resolution agreed to by a private company as a written resolution in accordance with Part 13, Chapter 2 of the Act has effect as if it was passed by the company in general meeting, or a meeting of the relevant class of members, and any reference in any statute to a meeting at which a resolution is passed or to members voting in favour of a resolution shall be construed accordingly.

A provision of the articles of a private company is void in so far it would have the effect that a resolution that is required by or otherwise provided for in an enactment could not be proposed and passed as a written resolution (s. 300). It should be noted that a written resolution is defined for these purposes as a resolution of a private company proposed and passed in accordance with Part 13, Chapter 2 of the Act.

Example: Members' written resolution

...............................LIMITED

[Address]

Circulation Date: [Date].

We, the undersigned, being members of the Company eligible to vote on the proposals at the time and date of circulation, hereby pass the following resolution(s) pursuant to sections 288 to 300 of the Companies Act 2006:

As a Special Resolution

THAT ... ...

As an Ordinary Resolution

THAT ... ...

(Signatures)   (Date of signature)

Notes:

1. Members may signify their agreement to the resolution by returning a hard copy of the resolution signed by them (or on their behalf) to the company at the address shown above. Agreement may also be signified by email as follows: ...

2. The proposed resolution(s) will lapse if not passed within the period of 28 days beginning with the circulation date shown above.

Resolutions which may not be passed as written resolutions

Written resolutions may not be used to remove a director or auditor from office before the expiry of his period of office (s. 288(2)).

It may or may not be possible for a private company to hold an AGM by written resolution. This was not possible under the Companies Act 1985 which actually required a meeting to be held, unless the company had dispensed with that requirement under the elective regime. Private companies are no longer required by the Companies Act 2006 to hold AGMs and they will only be required to do so if their articles expressly require it. Depending on the construction of the articles, it may be possible to hold such a meeting and to transact any business by written resolution, although this may not be popular with the members. It is also debatable whether a private company required by its articles to lay its accounts before the members in general meeting could do this by written resolution. It would seem odd if this is the case, as the main purpose of laying accounts is not to approve them (this is done by the directors) but to make them an item of business at a meeting so as to enable them to be discussed at that meeting.

Date written resolution passed

A written resolution will be passed when the required majority of eligible members have signified their agreement to it (s. 296(4)).

Electronic communications

Where a company has given an electronic address in any document containing or accompanying a written resolution, it is deemed to have agreed that any document or information relating to that resolution may be sent by electronic means to that address subject to any conditions or limitations specified in the document (s. 298).

If a company sends a written resolution or a statement relating to a written resolution to a person by means of a website, the resolution or statement is not validly sent unless it is available on the website throughout the period beginning with the circulation date and ending on the date the resolution lapses under section 297 (s. 299).

Form of written resolution

Although the members may sign or authenticate separate documents, each document should accurately state the terms of the resolution. In practice, this means that the wording of the resolution on each document should be identical. It is preferable if the form of words which precede the substantive resolution make it clear that the resolution is being proposed as a written resolution under the statutory procedures.

Filing and recording of written resolutions

Written resolutions need only be filed at Companies House if they have effect as a resolution which needs filing in itself.

It should also be noted that it is not a requirement of the Act that the original signed copies of the resolution be filed at Companies House. All that needs to be filed is 'a copy' of the resolution certified by a director or the secretary.

Example: Specimen copy of a written resolution for filing at Companies House

[Company Number]

RESOLUTION OF

XYZ LIMITED

On the .... day of .... 20..., the following resolution(s) were duly passed by a written resolution of the members of the Company pursuant to sections 288 to 300 of the Companies Act 2006:

As a special resolution

[Text of resolution]

As an ordinary resolution

[Text of resolution]

[Signed]

[Secretary/Director]

[Date]

A company is required to keep a record of every written resolution and to make those records available for inspection and copying.

Example: Record of a Written Resolution

Record of a written resolution of XYZ LIMITED

The following resolution(s) was/were passed as a written resolution on [date], being the date on which the written resolution was signed by the last member required to do so in order to pass the resolutions:

A copy of the resolution was delivered to the auditors on [date].

The signatories to the resolution were:

[Names of directors]

Signature

[Director/Secretary]

[Date]

Copies to auditors

A private company's auditors (if any) will have a right to be sent all communications required to be circulated to the members under Part 13, Chapter 2 of the 2006 Act in relation to a written resolution (s. 502). This will include the proposed written resolution itself, any statement by the members and any additional documents required to be circulated with the resolution.

Example: Letter to auditors to accompany a copy of a written resolution

[On the company's headed stationery]

To: The Auditors

Proposed written resolution

We enclose a copy of a resolution which it is proposed to be agreed as a written resolution of the above-named company in accordance with Chapter 2 of Part 13 of the Companies Act 2006 ('the Act') [together with the documents which are required by the Act to be circulated with it to members of the company]. This copy is being sent to you for your information in accordance with the requirements of section 502(1) of the Act. No action on your part is required. However, if you would like to discuss any matter regarding the proposed resolution that concerns you as the company's auditors, please do not hesitate to contact me.

Yours faithfully,

Secretary

On behalf of XYZ Limited

There is no suggestion in the 2006 Act that failure to send a copy of such communications to the auditors will invalidate the resolution. The relevant provision is merely expressed as a right given to the auditors rather than as a condition that must be complied with in order to pass a written resolution. Under the 1985 Act, failure to send a copy of a written resolution to the auditors was an offence. This is no longer the case under the 2006 Act.

Members' power to propose written resolutions

The members of a private company may require the company to circulate a written resolution and to circulate with it a statement of not more than 1,000 words on the subject matter of the resolution.

A company is required to circulate the resolution and any accompanying statement once it has received requests to do so from members representing not less than 5% of the total voting rights of all members entitled to vote on the resolution or such lower percentage specified for this purpose by the articles (s. 292(4)(5)). The requests may be made in hard copy or electronic form, must identify the resolution to which it relates together with any accompanying statement, and be authenticated by the person or persons making it (s. 292(6)).

If the members have deposited or tendered a sum to pay the expenses of circulating the resolution, the company must circulate it to all eligible members in accordance with the requirements of section 293. Copies may be sent in hard copy or electronic form, by means of a website or, if it is possible to do so without undue delay, by submitting the same copy to each eligible member in turn, or a combination of these methods (s. 293(2)).

The resolution must be circulated to members not more than 21 days after the obligation under section 292 arises (s. 293(3)) and be accompanied by guidance as to how to signify agreement to the resolution and the date by which it must be passed if it is not to lapse (s. 293(4)). Failure to comply with the circulation requirements in section 293 is an offence but does not invalidate the written resolution concerned if it is passed.

The expenses of circulating a written resolution must be paid for by the members making the request unless the company resolves otherwise (s. 294(1)). Unless the company has previously so resolved, it is not bound to comply with a request unless those requesting the resolution deposit with it or tender a sum reasonably sufficient to meet its expenses in doing so (s. 294(2)).

The company or any other person claiming to be aggrieved may apply to the court for an order preventing the circulation of a statement made in connection with a written resolution. The court may order the members who requested that the statement be circulated to pay the whole or part of the company's costs on such an application (s. 295).

Written resolutions and related articles – private companies

The articles of a private company, particularly those under Table A, may include a clause which appears to provide a different procedure for passing a written resolution of the members to that under company law. However, the Act would take precedence.

It should be noted that section 281(1) of the Act states that a resolution of the members (or of a class of members) of a private company must be passed either:

(a) as a written resolution in accordance with Part 13, Chapter 2; or
(b) at a meeting of the members (to which the provisions of Part 13, Chapter 3 apply).

Accordingly, the statutory written resolution procedures for private companies should always be used in preference to any provisions of the articles.

Written resolutions and related articles – public companies

The articles of a public company could also include an article similar to regulation 53 of Table A. Public companies cannot pass written resolutions under the statutory procedures in Part 13, Chapter 2 of the Act. Section 380(2) of the Act states that a resolution of the members (or of a class of members) of a public company must be passed at a meeting of the members (to which the provisions of Part 13, Chapter 3 and, where relevant, Chapter 4 of the Act apply). Accordingly, it is dangerous for a company to rely on any written resolution procedure in its articles. Such procedures might be valid under the common law principle of unanimous consent if unanimity is, in fact, required under the relevant article procedure. However, it is not normally sensible for a public company to rely on on such articles or the principle of unanimous consent. It should be noted that the 2006 Act model articles for public companies do not make any provision regarding members' written resolution, and that regulation 53 was dispensed with for public companies with effect from 1 October 2007.

Unanimous consent rule

Under the common law principle of unanimous consent, members may act informally without holding a meeting if they unanimously approve the transaction in some other manner, whether in writing or orally. In *Re Express Engineering Works Ltd* [1920] 1 Ch 466, five directors who were the only shareholders of the company, resolved at a board meeting to purchase some property from a syndicate in which they each had an interest. The company's articles disqualified directors from voting on any contract in which they were interested. The liquidator subsequently sought to have the transaction set aside on the basis that the directors were precluded from voting and that the members were only capable of acting at a properly constituted general meeting. The Court of Appeal held that although the meeting was referred to in the minutes as a board meeting, the unanimous informal consent of the five as the members of the company was capable of binding the company.

Provided all the members assent and the transaction is within the company's powers, the members may assent at different times.

In *Cane v Jones* [1981] 1 All ER 533, it was held that an agreement signed by all the shareholders that the chair should cease to be entitled to use his casting vote, had the same effect as a special resolution altering the articles to that effect, and it was immaterial that the statutory obligation to file such resolutions had not been complied with.

The fact that the informal consent of members must be unanimous was emphasised in *EBM Co Ltd v Dominion Bank* [1937] 3 All ER 555. In this case, there were five shareholders, three of whom held over 99% of the shares. The other two shareholders had one share each. A resolution of the three major shareholders was held not to bind the company in relation to security given to a bank for a loan despite the fact that the other two holdings were insignificant.

Exceptions

Generally speaking, it is not a good idea to rely on the unanimous consent rule as a routine method of decision making. It is, for example, infinitely preferable for a private company to act by written resolution in accordance with the statutory provisions. The courts tend to apply the rule to rectify defects in the decision-making process in owner-managed companies which arise out of ignorance of the proper procedures. They also tend not to look too kindly on its deliberate use. For example, the courts will not apply the rule so as to enable the members to do something they would not have been able to do at a meeting.

In addition, courts will not necessarily apply the rule where legislation requires certain formalities to be carried out in order for the resolution to be effective. The general approach in this regard appears to be that the rule will not apply where these formalities cannot be waived by the current members or where the formalities are designed to protect third parties. However, it is not always easy to predict how the courts will apply these general principles.

In *Re Duomatic Ltd* [1969] 1 All ER 161, directors' salaries were paid without being authorised by a resolution of the shareholders as required by the articles. It was held that the agreement of the two directors who held all the voting shares amounted to an informal ratification of the payment of unauthorised salaries even though they had never constituted themselves as a shareholders' meeting. The fact that they had neither informed nor sought the agreement of the sole holder of the company's preference shares had no bearing because all that was required was the unanimous agreement of the members entitled to vote. However, the court came to a different conclusion in the same case in relation to a payment made to a director for loss of office because statute required particulars of the proposed payment to be disclosed to the members and no such disclosure had taken place with regard to the preference shareholder.

When annual general meetings should be held

There are different requirements for private companies, private listed companies and public companies with regard to holding an AGM which are covered here. In addition, members of a company have the right to request a meeting to be held to present a particular resolution, in addition to the general calling of an AGM by the company itself.

Annual general meetings – private companies

Subject to the exceptions noted below, private companies are no longer required to hold an AGM. The underlying requirements of the Companies Act 1985 for private companies to hold an AGM (s. 366), to lay their accounts at a general meeting (s. 241), and to reappoint auditors annually (s. 385,) were repealed on 1 October 2007.

The 2006 Act requires public companies to hold an AGM but does not generally do so for most private companies. There are just two exceptions to this rule, namely that:

- a private company must continue to hold AGMs if any provision of its articles 'expressly' requires it to do so; and
- a private company which is also a traded company is required by the Act to hold AGMs.

Members of private companies holding as little as 5% of the voting rights may requisition a general meeting and propose written resolutions. These rights are clearly meant to act as a substitute for the right to propose resolutions at an AGM.

Requirement to hold AGMs under the articles

Any provision in a private company's memorandum or articles that 'expressly' requires the company to hold an AGM will continue to have effect. The word 'expressly' must be stressed here and confirms, for the avoidance of doubt, that provisions commonly found in company articles specifying that one or more directors are to retire at each AGM are not to be treated as a provision 'expressly' requiring the company to hold an AGM. This means that for most private companies, the requirement to hold an AGM ceased after 1 October 2007.

However, any company with articles similar to regulation 47 of the 1948 Act Table A , which states: 'The company shall in each year hold a general meeting as its annual general meeting in addition to any other meetings in that year ...', will have to continue holding AGMs until such time as they amend or delete the relevant article.

It should be noted that none of the provisions of the Act regarding AGMs will apply to any such meeting held by a private company unless it is directly required under the Act to hold an AGM because it is a traded company (see below). As a result, it may not even be clear whether there are any time limits for holding the meeting unless the articles so provide. It should be noted in this regard that older articles are more likely to adopt the formula of requiring a meeting to be held as the AGM at least once every calendar year with not more than 15 months between meetings.

In the absence of any other provisions in its articles, a private company required by its articles to hold an AGM will need to hold and call the meeting in accordance with the requirements of the Act on general meetings of private companies in Part 13, Chapter 3 of the 2006 Act. For example, under the Act the minimum notice period will be 14 clear days unless the articles provide otherwise. In addition, a private company that is required by its articles to hold AGMs may find that there is no business that needs to be transacted at that meeting. There is nothing in the Act that requires a private company to do anything at such a meeting (unless it is a traded company). Accordingly, everything will depend on the articles, which could, for example, require some of the directors to retire by rotation at each meeting or require the company to lay its accounts before the members at a general meeting or allow the members to propose AGM resolutions (members of private companies having no statutory rights in this regard).

This all suggests that a private company that wishes to continue holding AGMs may need to modify its articles to ensure that there is some purpose in doing so and that the meeting is called and held in the appropriate manner. Its articles could, for example, be modified to require the company to lay its accounts before the members, reappoint auditors annually at a general meeting, etc.

Private traded company required to hold AGMs

As mentioned above, a private company which is a traded company must also hold AGMs (s. 336(1A)). This requirement derives from amendments made to the Act by the Companies (Shareholders' Rights) Regulations 2009 (SI 2009/1632) in August 2009 for the purposes of implementing the EU Shareholders' Rights Directive (2017/828) which requires all traded companies to hold AGMs. A traded company is defined for these purposes as a company whose voting shares are traded on a regulated market with the consent of the company (see s. 360C). Most people would probably refer to these companies as 'listed companies'. However, it would only include a company whose voting shares are traded on the main market of the London Stock Exchange, which is a regulated market, and not those traded on the Alternative Investment Market (AIM), which is not a regulated market.

Most listed companies are, of course, public companies. Private companies cannot make a public offer of their shares. Accordingly, it is not normally possible to gain admission without converting into a public company if there is any sort of public offer involved. However, as long as there is no public offer, it would appear that the shares of a private company could technically be admitted to trading on a regulated market. Although this will rarely (if ever) happen in practice, it explains why the requirement to hold an AGM was extended by the directive to private companies which are also traded.

Any private company incorporated in the UK that is also a traded company must hold an AGM within nine months of its year-end (rather than the six-month time limit for public companies) in addition to any other meetings held during that period (s. 336(1A)). The minimum notice period for the meeting will be 21 clear days (ss 307A and 360). The notice must state that the meeting will be held as the AGM (s. 337(1)), include the date time and place of the meeting (s. 311(1)), state the general nature of the business (s. 311(2)), and include the matters specified in s. 311(3) for inclusion in the notice by traded companies and the statement required by s. 337(3) regarding the rights of members under section 338A to require the company to include a matter in the business to be dealt with at the meeting.

The company must also publish on a website before the meeting the matters specified in section 311A and make facilities available to enable members to appoint proxies via a website and publish details of the address of that website (s. 333A).

The members of the company have a right to ask questions at the AGM (and any other general meeting of the company) in accordance with section 319A and to require the company to include matters (other than resolutions) in the business to be dealt with at the meeting (s. 338A). The results of any poll taken at a general meeting of a private company that is a traded company must be published on a website (s. 341(1A)) and, if the company is also a quoted company, the members will also have a right to require an independent report on any poll taken at a general meeting (s. 342).

Other than matters validly proposed by members, it is not clear from the Act what the business of the AGM of a private company which is a traded company should be.

It should be noted that a number of the above requirements apply to any general meeting held by a private company that is a traded company and not just to the AGM.

All references herein to AGMs and their administration should be read as including the requirements for traded private companies, unless otherwise noted as different.

Annual general meetings – public companies

Public companies are still required to hold an AGM (s. 336). The meeting must be held within the six-month period beginning with the date following their accounting reference date/year-end (s. 336(1)). For example, if a company's year-end is 31 December, its AGM must be held by 30 June.

If a company fails to comply with the above requirements, an offence is committed by every officer in default for which the punishment is a fine (s. 336(3) and (4)).

However, a company which fails to comply following a change in its accounting reference date effected by shortening the previous accounting period is not treated as being in breach if it holds an AGM within three months of the change (s. 336(2)).

A notice calling an AGM of a public company must state that the meeting is an AGM (s. 337(1)). The company must give at least 21 days' notice of the meeting (s. 307(2)). The notice required is clear days by virtue of section 360. Shorter notice may be given of the AGM of a public company which is not a traded company if all the members entitled to attend agree (s. 337(2)).

The requirement to hold an AGM is not satisfied by holding a general meeting during the period in question, even if the business at that meeting is the same as that which would normally be dealt with at the AGM. Section 337 requires the notice of meeting to specify that the meeting will be held as the AGM.

Members of public companies have a right to require the company to circulate resolutions for consideration at the AGM. This right is not extended to members of private companies that are traded companies. However, members of traded companies (whether public or private) have a right to require the company to include matters of business (other than resolutions) on the AGM agenda.

Where a notice calling an AGM of a traded company is given more than six weeks before the meeting, the notice must include:

- if the company is a public company, a statement of the right under section 338 to require the company to give notice of a resolution to be moved at the meeting and a statement of the right under section 338A to require the company to include a matter in the business to be dealt with at the meeting; and
- if the company is a private company, a statement of the right under section 338A to require the company to include a matter (other than a resolution) in the business to be dealt with at the meeting (s. 337(3)).

Annual general meetings in general

Date of annual general meeting following a change of accounting reference date

Problems can arise with respect to the date of the AGM when a company changes its accounting reference date and, in doing so, shortens its current financial year. The timing of the change may be such that the company finds itself automatically in breach of the normal requirement to hold an AGM.

The Act provides that a company which fails to comply with the usual time limit for holding an AGM following a change in its accounting reference date effected by shortening the previous accounting period is not treated as being in breach if it holds an AGM within three months of the change (s. 336(2)).

Requirement to hold annual general meeting following conversion

It can be difficult to decide whether it is necessary to hold an AGM following conversion of a company's status from public to private and vice versa, or whether an offence has been committed if one is not held. If a private company is re-registered as a public company and the period within which it must as a public company hold an AGM has not expired, it could (and probably should) hold an AGM within that period. However, if it converts after the time limit for holding an AGM has already expired, it is impossible for it to comply fully with the requirement to hold it. If it is impossible to comply, it could be argued that it is not necessary to comply.

On the other hand, if a public company has failed to hold an AGM within the period, it will already have committed an offence that presumably would not be extinguished by re-registering as a private company. However if it re-registers as a private company before the expiry of the period for a public company to hold an AGM, no offence would have been committed, and the re-registered company would not (as a private company) be required to hold an AGM in that year, unless one of the usual exceptions for private companies applies.

Circulation of members' annual general meeting resolutions by a public company

Members of public companies have a statutory right under section 338 to require the company to give notice of resolutions which the members intend to propose at AGMs. This right is not extended to the members of a private company even if the company is required to hold AGMs by the Act (because it is a traded company) or under its articles.

However, members of traded companies (whether public or private companies) have a statutory right to require the company to include in the business to be dealt with at the AGM a matter (other than a proposed resolution) which may properly be included in the business (s. 338A).

In addition, members of all companies have a statutory right to have statements circulated by the company in connection with any business that is to be dealt with at any general meeting (ss 314–316).

Annual general meeting notices of traded companies

If the AGM notice of a traded company is given more than six weeks before the meeting, it must (if the company is a public company) contain a statement regarding members' rights under section 338 to require the company to give notice of a resolution to be moved at the meeting and (whether the company is public or private) contain a statement regarding members' rights under section 338A to require the company to include a matter (other than a resolution) in the business to be dealt with at the meeting (s. 337(3)).

Documents to be displayed at the annual general meeting

Companies used to be required to display a number of documents at the AGM. Most of these have now been abolished.

For example, under the Companies Act 1985, companies were required to keep a register of directors' interests in shares or debentures of the company (s. 325) and to make that register available for inspection at the AGM (para. 29 of Sch. 13). However, this requirement was abolished with effect from 6 April 2007 to coincide with the abolition of the requirement to keep the register.

The Companies Act 2006 still requires directors' service contracts to be made available for inspection, but not at the AGM (s. 228). The Listing Rules used to require listed companies to make copies of directors' service contracts available for inspection at the AGM for at least 15 minutes prior to and during the meeting. However, this requirement was abolished in 2005. The Listing Rules also used to require the notice convening the AGM to contain a note informing members as to when and where directors' service contracts would be made available for inspection. This requirement was deleted in June 1996.

The UK Corporate Governance Code requires the terms and conditions of appointment of non-executive directors to be made available for inspection by any person at the company's registered office during normal business hours and at the AGM (for 15 minutes prior to the meeting and during the meeting).

In practice, the only other documents that are likely to have to be put on display any more are those which the company has said it will display in the notice of the meeting, which could include, for example, copies of the articles where the company proposes to adopt an entirely new version.

Members' requests to include resolutions

Conditions for valid members' request

Members of a company may request the company to include a specific resolution in the AGM under section 338. The members may not require the company to give notice of a resolution or other matter of business unless the resolution can be properly moved at the meeting or the matter of business can be properly included in the business of the meeting.

A resolution may properly be moved at an AGM unless it would, if passed, be ineffective (whether by reason of inconsistency with any enactment or the company's constitution or otherwise), it is defamatory of any person, or it is frivolous or vexatious (s. 338(2)).

A company is required to give notice of a resolution under section 338 once it has received requests to do so from:

(a) members representing not less than 5% of the total voting rights of all the members who have a right to vote on the resolution at the AGM to which the requests relate (excluding any voting rights attached to shares held in treasury); or

(b) at least 100 members who have a right to vote on the resolution at the AGM to which the requests relate and hold shares in the company on which there has been paid up an average sum, per member, of not less than £100 (s. 338(3)).

It should be noted that under (a) above, the validity of the demand must be determined by reference to the number of members who would have been entitled to vote if the meeting had been held on the date of the requisition. Thus, if preference dividends are in arrears on the date of the requisition and the company's articles give preference shareholders the right to vote in such circumstances, the requirements for a valid requisition will be more onerous.

In relation to (b) above, the number of shares which members must hold is calculated according to the nominal value of the shares. For example, if the nominal value is £1, each member must hold on average 100 fully paid shares. If the nominal value is 25p, each member must hold, on average, 400 shares.

It should be noted that any indirect investors in a company whose shares are admitted to trading on a regulated market are also able to participate in a request under section 338 for the purposes of determining whether the 100 members test is satisfied (s. 153).

Time limit for making the request

A request under section 338 must be received by the company at least six weeks before the meeting to which it relates, or if later, the time at which notice is given of that meeting (s. 338(4)). A company is not bound to comply with a demand made after the later of the above. In practice, the later of the two will normally be the time at which notice is given in view of the statutory requirement to give 21 clear days' notice of an AGM, which normally works out at just over three weeks. It should be noted that notice will not be given until it is deemed to have been served and that due allowance will need to be made for the relevant service period. In practice, this means that a valid request can not only be made after the notices have been printed but can also be made for a short period after the notices have been sent out, that period being the applicable service period under the Act or the company's articles.

Although it will not normally be very relevant for the purposes of determining whether a request has been validly made, it should be noted that the requirements of section 360 regarding clear days apply for the purposes of determining whether a request has been received six weeks before the meeting. In practice, this means that the six-week time limit will not be satisfied unless the members submit their request to the company at least 42 clear days before the meeting.

Form of the request

A request under section 338 may be in hard copy or electronic form, must identify the resolution of which notice is to be given, and must be authenticated by the person or persons making it.

Example: Members' request for AGM resolution

The Directors

XYZ plc

[Registered office address]

We the undersigned being [members of the Company representing not less than five per cent of the total voting rights of all the members having at the date hereof a right to vote at the next annual general meeting of the company][1,] hereby require you pursuant to section 338 of the Companies Act 2006 to give to the members entitled to receive notice of the next annual general meeting notice of the following resolution, which it is intended to move thereat as an [ordinary resolution/special resolution] [, and pursuant to section 314 of the Companies Act 2006 to circulate to the members entitled to have notice of the meeting sent to them the annexed statement with respect to the matter referred to in the proposed resolution]:

[ORDINARY/SPECIAL] RESOLUTION

[Text of resolution]

[STATEMENT IN SUPPORT]

[Text of statement of not more than 1,000 words]

[A cheque for £ .... is enclosed to meet the company's expenses in giving effect to this requisition.]

[Signed]   [Address]

[Date]

Notes:

1. The precise form of words will depend on the condition the members satisfy.

2. Listed companies cannot charge members for circulating an AGM resolution.

The usual rules set out in the company communications provisions of the 2006 Act determine the manner in which the request must be served on the company whether it be in hard copy or electronic form.

Company's duty on receipt of a members' request

On receipt of a valid request, a company has a duty to give a copy of the resolution to each member of the company entitled to receive notice of the AGM in the same manner as notice of the meeting, and at the same time as, or as soon as reasonably practical after, it gives notice of the meeting (s. 339(1)).

Example: Requisitioned resolution in notice of annual general meeting

To consider the following resolution intended to be moved at the meeting as a special resolution, notice of which is given by the company pursuant to section 338 of the Companies Act 2006 at the request of certain members:

SPECIAL RESOLUTION

[Text of resolution]

The company need not, however, comply with the request of the members if they are liable to pay the company's expenses in complying with the request under section 340(2) and have not deposited or tendered a sum reasonably sufficient to do so (s. 339(2)).

Although the Act imposes the duty to circulate the requisitioned resolution on the company, it will fall to the directors to ensure compliance; it is noteworthy that it is the officers who are liable to a fine in default (s. 339(4)).

Notice of the resolution must be given to the members entitled to receive notice of the AGM as determined by the Act and the company's articles of association. In addition, a copy should also be sent to:

(a) the directors (s. 310(1));
(b) any indirect investors (s. 146(3));
(c) the company's auditors who are entitled to receive all notices of, and other communications relating to, any general meeting which a member of the company is entitled to receive (s. 502(2)); and
(d) any other persons entitled to receive notices under the articles.

Members who are not entitled to have the notice sent to them but who are entitled to receive notice by some other means (e.g. holders of bearer shares who are entitled to be given notice by advertisement) must be given notice of the resolution in any manner permitted for giving such members notice of meetings.

Accidental failure to give notice of a requisitioned resolution to one or more members is disregarded for the purpose of determining whether notice of the resolution is duly given (s. 313). It should be noted that this provision applies to notice of a requisitioned resolution given under section 339 notwithstanding anything in a company's articles.

The business which may be dealt with at an AGM includes a resolution, for which notice is given by the company in accordance with section 339 (s. 339(3)).

It should be noted that, under section 338, the members may only require a public company to give notice of a proposed resolution in respect of the AGM. A public company is not required to include such a resolution in the notice of any other general meeting to be held before the next AGM. If the members are not prepared to wait, they should requisition a general meeting under section 303, assuming that they are able to satisfy the conditions.

Cost of circulating a members' resolution

Under the 1985 Act, the right to requisition AGM resolutions was rarely exercised in practice, probably because the cost of exercising it fell upon the members themselves (unless the company in general meeting resolved otherwise). Under the 2006 Act, the company must bear the costs of circulating a resolution if a valid request is made before the end of the financial year preceding the meeting. However, if a valid request is made after the year-end, the resolution need not be circulated unless:

(a) those requesting the resolution have, within the time limits for making a valid request, 'deposited' or 'tendered' a sum reasonably sufficient to meet the company's expenses in circulating the resolution (s. 340(2)). The clear days rule in s. 360 applies for the purposes of determining whether they have done this within the six-week time limit, if that time limit applies; or

(b) the company resolves otherwise (e.g. decides not to require those making the request to pay its costs).

It is obviously difficult for those making the request to make an accurate assessment of the company's costs and they may seek guidance from the company before depositing it. If there is a dispute between the company and the requestors as to the sum required, the directors would be well advised to give effect to the requisition as they could be liable to a fine for failing to comply with the requirements of section 339 if a court takes the view that the sum deposited or tendered by the requestors was reasonably sufficient.

The cost of giving effect to a request should not be prohibitive if it is deposited in time for inclusion in the notice calling the AGM. If the company has already printed the notice at the time of the deposit, it should attempt to minimise the cost of giving effect to the request by printing the resolution separately rather than, for example, having the original notice reprinted, particularly if that notice is embodied in the annual report and accounts. If a company does decide to reprint the notice, it does not necessarily follow that it may require the requestors to pay the whole of its costs of doing so.

In practice, the company (i.e. the directors or an authorised officer) may sometimes agree to give effect to a request without charge to the requestors. The requestors should still offer to pay any reasonable costs the directors may decide to impose in their original request to ensure that the directors have a duty to circulate the resolution. They may not have a duty to circulate a resolution for which the members are potentially liable to pay the costs unless the members indicate that they are willing to bear those costs. Also, if the directors subsequently agree to waive the costs and proceed to circulate the resolution, the company could not then require the requestors to pay the company's costs.

If the directors do not agree to waive the costs, the requestors can include in their request a resolution to be put to the AGM that the company should bear the costs. If such a resolution is passed, the requestors will not be liable to pay the company's costs under section 340(2)(a). Requestors sometimes try to achieve this by embodying a proposal regarding costs in the requested resolution. This has the advantage of ensuring that they will not be required to pay if the resolution is passed. However, it may be preferable, from their point of view, for the proposal to be drafted as a separate requested resolution, particularly where their main proposal is one which requires a special majority, because the resolution regarding costs need only be passed as an ordinary resolution.

However, even if they do this, they must deposit or tender with the request a sum reasonably sufficient to meet the company's costs (on the basis that their resolution regarding costs may be defeated), unless the company has previously resolved that the expenses of circulating the resolution (or perhaps more likely, members' resolutions generally) should not be borne by the requestors.

Best practice is that, unless the company agrees at the outset to absorb all the costs of circulation, members' resolutions should automatically be accompanied (in any notice) by another resolution giving shareholders the opportunity to decide whether the company or the requestors should bear the relevant costs. If the directors feel that any particular case does not justify the adoption of such a resolution, they should, however, be free to recommend a vote against it. Companies should also consider including members' resolutions in the notice without charge.

Trading companies – members' powers to include other matters in AGM business

Members of traded companies (whether public or private) may require the company to include in the business to be dealt with at the AGM, a matter (other than a proposed resolution) which may properly be included in the business (s. 338A).

This right enables members to raise matters not already included on the agenda for the meeting (or not within the scope of the notice) without the need to frame the business as a resolution. For example, the members could require the directors to include an item enabling the discussion of the company's ethical policies at the meeting. Although the members of a traded company could probably raise this matter in the general question and answer session which occurs when the meeting considers the annual report (and may even have a right to do so under s. 319A), they would inevitably draw more attention to the issue by making it a formal agenda item, particularly if they also required the company to circulate a statement in connection with the business. It should also be noted that a requisition under section 338A could be used in an attempt to ensure that the directors have an obligation to answer questions put to them at the meeting on the matter under section 319A, which only applies in relation to business being dealt with at the meeting.

Section 388A(2) provides that a matter may properly be included in the business at an AGM unless it is defamatory of any person or it is frivolous or vexatious. The question as to whether a matter proposed by members is defamatory, frivolous or vexatious will be for the company to judge, at least initially. However, if a company wrongly refuses to include an item on these grounds, the members could take legal action to enforce their rights. It should also be noted that if the company fails to comply with a valid request, the directors and officers may be guilty of an offence (s. 340A(3)). Accordingly, the directors would need to be pretty sure of their grounds before refusing to comply with such a request. As no resolution needs to be proposed (or can be proposed) for the purposes of section 338A, it seems likely that the courts would take a fairly stringent approach to any refusal to comply with a request.

It is assumed that members of a traded company could not add an item (other than a resolution) to the agenda under section 338A and then seek to propose a resolution in connection with that business at the meeting on the basis that their resolution is within the scope of the notice.

Members' rights – statement in annual general meeting notice

If the AGM notice of a traded company is given more than six weeks before the meeting, it must contain a statement regarding members' rights under section 338A to require the company to include a matter (other than a resolution) in the business to be dealt with at the meeting (s. 337(3)). If the traded company is also a public company, it must also include a statement of members' rights to propose resolutions under section 338.

Conditions for valid member request

The conditions for a valid request under section 338A are summarised below. It should be noted that they are almost identical to the conditions for proposing a resolution at the AGM of a public company under section 338. Accordingly, much of the discussion of relating to a request under section 338 will also be relevant to requests made under section 338A.

A traded company is required to include a matter which may properly be included in the business to be dealt with once it has received requests that it do so from:

(a) members representing at least 5% of the total voting rights of all the members who have a right to vote at the meeting to which the requests relate; or

(b) at least 100 members who have a right to vote on the resolution at the AGM to which the requests relate and hold shares in the company on which there has been paid up an average sum, per member, of at least £100 (s. 388A(3)).

Indirect investors may join in making such a request under section 153.

A request under section 388A may be made in hard copy or electronic form, must identify the matter to be included in the business, must be accompanied by a statement setting out the grounds for the request, and must be authenticated by the person or persons making it (s. 388A(4)).

The request must be received by the company not later than six weeks before the meeting to which it relates, or, if later, the time at which notice is given of that meeting. In practice, the clear days rule in section 360 applies for the purposes of calculating the six-week period. Accordingly, it should, therefore, be interpreted as meaning 42 clear days before the meeting.

Company's obligations

Section 340A(1) provides that a company that is required under section 338A to include any matter in the business to be dealt with at an AGM must:

(a) give notice of it to each member of the company entitled to receive notice of the AGM in the same manner as notice of the meeting and at the same time as, or as soon as reasonably practicable after, it gives notice of the meeting; and

(b) publish it on the same website as that on which the company published the information required by section 311A.

However, the company's duty to circulate is subject to compliance by the requestors with any duty under section 340B(2) to deposit or tender of sum in respect of expenses of circulation.

If a company fails to comply with a valid request, an offence is committed by every officer in default for which a fine may be imposed (s. 340A(3) and (4)).

Cost of circulation

Section 340B provides that the expenses of the company in complying with a request under section 340A to circulate a matter (other than a resolution) need not be paid by the members who requested the inclusion of the matter in the business to be dealt with at the AGM if requests sufficient to require the company to include the matter are received before the end of the financial year preceding the meeting.

Where this is not the case, the expenses of the company in complying with the request must be paid by the members who requested the inclusion of the matter unless the company resolves otherwise. And unless the company has previously so resolved, it is not bound to comply with the request unless there is deposited with or tendered to it, not later than six weeks (i.e. 42 clear days) before the AGM to which the requests relate, or if later, the time at which notice is given of that meeting, a sum reasonably sufficient to meet its expenses in complying with the request (s. 340B(2)).

Business of the annual general meeting

There are only two things that the Act actually requires to be dealt with at the AGM:

- resolutions proposed by shareholders; and
- a resolution to allow a traded company to hold general meetings at 14 days' notice.

The Act does not require anything else to be done at the AGM or prescribe that anything else can only be done at the AGM. Nevertheless, it does still have a big influence on the type of business which is normally put before the meeting. This is partly because all public companies must at some stage after their year-end:

- lay their accounts before the members at a general meeting (s. 437);
- appoint or reappoint auditors at that meeting (s. 489(2));
- fix the auditors' remuneration at that meeting (s. 492); and
- if the company is a quoted company, put the directors' remuneration report prepared by the directors to members for approval at that meeting (s. 439).

The meeting at which all these matters must be dealt with, for example the meeting at which accounts are laid, is referred to in section 437 as the 'accounts meeting'. The accounts of a public company can be laid either at the AGM or at a separate general meeting called for that purpose. If they are laid at the AGM, that meeting will also be the 'accounts meeting'. If they are not, a separate general meeting will need to be held.

Although the accounts need not be laid at the AGM, it is plainly sensible to do so to avoid having to hold another general meeting. A company must still hold an AGM even if it is not held as the accounts meeting. The fact that the deadline for holding AGMs and the normal deadline for filing the accounts of a public company are now the same makes it all the more likely that the company will be able use the AGM as its accounts meeting.

If a company is required by law to hold a meeting of shareholders as its AGM, it is also sensible to take the opportunity that the meeting presents to deal with other items of business that need shareholder approval. In addition, the company's articles may require certain matters to be dealt with at the AGM (e.g. the re-election of directors retiring by rotation, etc.).

All these factors combine to make the business of the AGM fairly predictable and, in practice, the meeting will probably deal with some or all of the following items:

- laying of the accounts;
- appointment of the auditors and fixing their remuneration;
- in the case of a quoted company, the directors' remuneration report;
- appointment of directors;

- reappointment of directors retiring by rotation;
- approval of any final dividend recommended by the board;
- renewal by ordinary resolution of the directors' authority to allot shares in accordance with section 551 (if required);
- special resolution to disapply pre-emption rights in accordance with section 571 (if required);
- authority to buy-back own shares (if required);
- special resolutions to amend articles of association (if required);
- in the case of a traded company, a resolution to enable the company to give 14 days' notice of any general meeting held in the following year (s. 307A);
- other business required by the articles to be conducted at the AGM;
- any other business which needs shareholder approval and which it is convenient to deal with at the meeting; and
- resolutions validly proposed by the members.

No business to be transacted

If the accounts are not ready to be laid at the AGM, the only business to be conducted could be the reappointment of directors retiring by rotation in accordance with the articles of association. If the articles make no such provision or none of the directors are subject to retirement by rotation, there may be no business to be transacted. Nevertheless, a meeting must still be held and notice must be sent to members (indicating, if necessary, that no business is to be proposed by the directors). Members may still have the right to propose resolutions and other agenda items themselves. Even if they do not do so, some might still attend the meeting to seek an explanation as to why the accounts are not ready.

In practice, it may be difficult to obtain a quorum where there is no business to be transacted. The meeting may never actually be properly held or never be properly completed because of the rules on adjournment in the company's articles in these circumstances. Nevertheless, it is submitted that the directors will have done their duty under the Act and need not make any other attempt to hold the meeting unless it is necessary to enable appointments or reappointments of directors to take place in accordance with the articles.

Effectiveness of the annual general meeting

The purpose of holding AGMs has been called into question on a number of occasions in recent years. This has already resulted in legislation to allow most private companies to dispense with holding AGMS completely. However, questions have even been raised with regard to value of AGMs for listed companies. The Cadbury Committee observed that: 'If too many Annual General Meetings are at present an opportunity missed, this is because shareholders do not make the most of them and, in some cases, boards do not encourage them to do so' (Cadbury Report, para. 6.7).

Over the years there has been considerable dialogue and proposals discussing the benefit of AGMs and whether they should still be required. However, the basic concept that it is an opportunity for the company to be visible to, and challenged by, their shareholders remains as true now as it has ever been. Previous frustrations that institutional investors were largely silent attendees or, in some cases, non-attendees, has largely dissipated as these members have seen the benefit of challenging the company.

Social media has also increasingly challenged the actions of companies in respect of society, the environment and their wider contribution. As a consequence, AGMs tend to now be opportunities for the leadership of a company to showcase the positives of the company as well as accept challenge and discussion on a wide range of topics.

Despite this widening focus, the register of shareholder dissent now maintained by the Investment Association (see Chapter 16, Member dissent – The Public Register) still showcases that the majority of shareholder dissent focuses on remuneration and the appointment of directors. Additionally, analysis of online annual reports recognises that the most-read page of the report is not financial but is, instead, the report of the remuneration committee.

The consensus of opinion is that there continues to be a benefit to holding an AGM, including:

■ to give members an opportunity to question the directors face-to-face regarding their stewardship of the company, particularly in the context of the company's published accounts and, in the case of a quoted company, the directors' remuneration report; and

■ to allow members to debate resolutions proposed by the directors or as members' resolutions before voting on them.

Company secretaries sometimes cite as evidence of the AGM's effectiveness the fact that, when taking decisions on certain policies and strategies, directors often consider whether they would feel comfortable justifying their proposed course of action at the AGM. The attendance of the press at listed company AGMs also means that directors are held accountable to a wider audience.

Conclusion

As can be seen, there are different types of meetings that a company can hold with their members. In addition, members have the right to request a meeting be held in certain circumstances.

Before moving on to the practicalities of why and when to hold an AGM, this chapter covered the option to pass resolutions by written resolution, whether proposed by the board or by members.

Thereafter, greater detail has been provided on the purpose and content of the AGM given this is the primary forum for member engagement with the board.

This focused on the legal and practical requirements for a physical meeting of members. The increasing use of technology and the potential for this to be fully or partially included in AGMs is covered in part in later chapters of this section as well as in Chapter 4.

14 – Convening a general meeting

This chapter will cover the practicalities and legal framework for convening a general meeting, specifically covering:

- calling a general meeting;
- the practical organisation of a general meeting;
- providing a chair's script: What it should contain;
- who has the right to attend;
- security at the general meeting;
- giving notice, to whom and how;
- members entitled to receive notice;
- special notices;
- content of the notice, with practical examples;
- premium listed company notice requirements as detailed in the Listing Rules; and
- the role of the company secretary in preparing the annual general meeting (AGM).

The final section provides a useful checklist extracted on the role of the company secretary when preparing for the AGM, which can be used for all general meetings. This is an extract from The Chartered Governance Institute's *Company Secretary's Handbook*, 12th edition.

As well as having the benefit of a company secretary, larger companies may delegate all or some of the organisation of a general meeting to a specialist third-party provider, often their registrar. However, even when outsourcing the process, it is invaluable to understand the various requirements and at what stage they should be considered so that the company retains oversight of the process.

Smaller companies, or those with larger in-house teams, may prefer to undertake the process themselves, either to the full extent of the below or capturing the key elements as provided.

Calling a general meeting

Unless the time and place at which meetings are to be held each year is fixed, someone must be given the power to call meetings (i.e. to direct that a meeting will be held at a certain time and place to consider certain business). A general meeting must be convened (called) by a person or body with appropriate authority otherwise the meeting and any business transacted at it will be invalid.

Meetings convened by the board of directors

Under section 302 of the Act, directors of a company may call a general meeting hence current model articles do not specify this. Previous articles, prior to this inclusion in the Act, empowered directors in this matter and this should be confirmed when convening meeting of companies incorporated before this date. It would not normally be considered best practice for the directors to delegate responsibility for calling general meetings, albeit that the practicalities of calling the meeting would not be undertaken by the directors themselves.

A directors' resolution calling a general meeting should state the date, time and place of the meeting and its purpose. A draft copy of the notice together with any additional documents which will accompany it should also be approved by the board. The board should also authorise someone (usually the secretary) to sign and issue the notice to all those entitled to receive it.

A further board meeting would be needed to approve the addition of any further item of business or to amend the substance of the notice.

Ratification of invalid notice

Notice of a general meeting given by any person without the sanction of the directors or other proper authority will be invalid. This is the case even if it was issued by the secretary in response to a valid requisition by the members. However, a meeting called without proper authority will be valid if it is ratified before the meeting by the body with authority to call the meeting (e.g. the board of directors). Thus, a notice issued by a director or the company secretary without the authority of the board will be valid if it is subsequently ratified prior to the general meeting by the directors at a properly convened and constituted meeting of the board.

However, a general meeting convened or ratified by an irregularly constituted board (e.g. at an inquorate meeting) would still be invalid.

Practical procedures for convening a general meeting

In practice, a proof of the general meeting notice is usually tabled at the board meeting held to approve the report and accounts, and its contents are used to frame the appropriate board resolution convening the meeting. The board resolution should specify the date, time and place as well as the business to be transacted. The directors should also authorise the secretary to sign the notice and send copies to all persons entitled to receive it (e.g. the members and the auditors as well as anyone else specified in the articles).

> **Example: Board resolution to convene an annual general meeting**
>
> It was resolved:
>
> THAT an Annual General Meeting of the Company be convened and held at [place] on [date] at [time] for the following purpose:
>
> 1. To receive the accounts and the reports of the directors and auditors for the financial year ending [date].
>
> 2. To reappoint ABC as auditors until the conclusion of the next meeting at which accounts are laid and to authorise the directors to fix their remuneration.
>
> 3. To authorise the directors to allot shares pursuant to section 551 of the Companies Act 2006.
>
> THAT the secretary be authorised to sign the notice on behalf of the board and to issue notices accordingly, together with a form of proxy in accordance with the proof print submitted to and approved by this meeting.

As soon as the proof print of the report and accounts has been approved by the directors, the balance sheet, directors' report and auditors' report should be signed and dated by the appropriate people. A further copy should be prepared with the names of the signatories and the dates on which they signed inserted at the appropriate points. This copy can then be printed for inclusion in the notice together with final copies of the notice itself and, if necessary, any circular or proxy cards.

The notice usually goes out under the name of the secretary who signs 'by order of the board'. It is usually dated for the day on which it is sent out and this date can be included in the proofs sent to the printers even though the notice may not yet have been physically signed. It is, however, also common for the notice to be signed and dated on the day it is approved by the board. Strictly speaking, the date on the notice should be the date on which it was actually signed. Accordingly, if it is to show the date on which the notice is to be sent out, it should also be signed on that date.

If accounts are to be laid at the general meeting, copies of the report and accounts must be sent to members not less 21 days before the meeting. As members must be given 21 clear days' notice of the general meeting it is sensible to send both together. The notice of the meeting can be incorporated in the document containing the annual report and accounts.

Issues convening meetings
Number of directors below quorum
The model articles for public companies allow two or more members to call a general meeting (or instruct the company secretary to do so) for the purpose of

appointing one or more directors if the company has fewer than two directors, and the director (if any) is unable or unwilling to appoint sufficient directors to make up a quorum or to call a general meeting to do so (plc 28).

However, it only operates to allow the members to call general meetings for the purposes of appointing additional directors where the number of directors has fallen below two and only operates as a fallback to the powers given to any remaining director(s) to appoint sufficient directors or call a general meeting to do so (plc 11).

Private companies – death of all members and directors

Under the model articles for private companies, where, as a result of death, a private company has no members or directors, the personal representatives of the last member to die has the right, by notice in writing, to appoint a person to be director (pcls and clg 17(2)). Any director so appointed would then be able to exercise the statutory power to call general meetings.

Director refuses to attend board meetings

In small companies, it is not unusual for directors who are vehemently opposed to a particular proposal supported by the other directors to attempt to frustrate the will of the majority by refusing to attend board meetings. If their presence is necessary in order to form a quorum, this tactic will prevent the other directors approving a proposal. Although it may not be the intention of the dissident director(s) to prevent the calling of a general meeting, this is often one of the side effects of such tactics. If they are not opposed to calling a meeting, and assuming the articles allow this, it might be possible to call the meeting by written resolution. The members could requisition a general meeting under section 303 and, if the directors do not convene a meeting within 21 days, convene a meeting themselves in accordance with section 305. If all else fails, an application may need to be made to the court under section 306.

Directors refuse to call meeting

Where the directors refuse to call a general meeting, the members can requisition one under section 303 and convene it themselves if the directors fail to do so within 21 days. Any director or member may apply to the court for an order in respect of a general meeting.

Powers of the court to call a general meeting

If, for any reason, it is impracticable to call a general meeting, or to conduct the meeting in the manner prescribed by the company's articles or the Act, the court may order a meeting of the company to be called, held and conducted in any manner it thinks fit (s. 306). The court may make such an order on the application of any member who would be entitled to vote at the meeting or any director. In doing so, the court may give such ancillary or consequential directions as it thinks fit (s. 306(3)), which may include a direction that one member present in person or by proxy be deemed to constitute a meeting (s. 306(4)). Any meeting called, held and conducted in accordance with an order of the court made under section 306 is deemed for all purposes to be a meeting of the company duly called held and conducted (s. 306(5)).

These powers have been exercised where it was impracticable to hold a meeting with a quorum in accordance with the articles and where the directors, being minority shareholders, failed to call a general meeting (including an AGM) thus preventing the majority shareholder from exercising his right to remove them. The court has also used these powers to direct that a vote be taken by postal ballot because previous general meetings had been disrupted by protesters in such a violent manner that it was likely that most ordinary members would not attend any future meetings.

The court may also convene a meeting under section 896 where a compromise or arrangement is proposed between the company and its creditors.

Members' request for a general meeting

The members of a company have a right to request a general meeting to be held at the company's expense. They must satisfy certain conditions, some of which vary according to the type of company. The normal procedure is for the members to submit their request and, if the request is valid, for the directors to call the meeting. However, if the directors fail to do so within a specified time, those requesting the meeting may call the meeting themselves and recover their expenses from the company.

Members of public companies (but not private companies) can also require the directors to include a specific resolution on the agenda of the AGM. Members of private companies (but not public companies) can also propose written resolutions.

Conditions for member demand – percentages

The directors of a company are required by section 303 to convene a general meeting of the company on receipt of a valid demand. A demand will not be valid unless it is made by:

(a) members representing at least 5% of such of the paid-up capital of the company as carries the right of voting at general meetings of the company (excluding any paid-up capital held as treasury shares); or
(b) in the case of a company not having a share capital (for example a company limited by guarantee), members who represent at least 5% of the total voting rights of all the members having a right to vote at general meetings.

It should be noted that these percentage requirements in the Act were amended by the Companies (Shareholders' Rights) Regulations 2009 (SI 2009/1632) with effect from August 2009 and that the Act previously required such demands to be supported by members holding at least 10% of the paid-up capital-carrying voting rights or, in the case of a company without a share capital, at least 10% of the voting rights, although this was reduced in both cases to at least 5% for private companies in certain circumstances.

The reduction made by the regulations from 10% to 5% for public companies means that it is almost as easy for the members to requisition a general meeting as it is for them to propose resolutions at an AGM, although the requirements for proposing an AGM resolution are still slightly less strict in that they provide for an addition test for making a valid demand (i.e. the 100-member test), which does not apply for requisitioning a general meeting.

In calculating whether a valid demand has been made by members of a company with a share capital, the critical factor is the amount of paid-up capital held by the members rather than the number of votes attached to those shares. Where all the shares are of equal value and carry the same number of votes, this calculation will be simple. However, care should be taken to ensure that shares which confer the right to vote in limited circumstances are included in the calculation if those circumstances operate at the time of the deposit. For example:

> ABC plc has a share capital of 5,000 £1 ordinary shares and 2,000 £1 preference shares. The preference shareholders only have a right to vote if their dividends are in arrears. As long as the preference dividends are not in arrears, any ordinary shareholder(s) holding 250 or more shares can requisition a meeting. If the dividends are in arrears, a member(s) holding 350 or more shares (either ordinary shares, preference shares or a combination of the two) would be needed.

It should be noted that articles commonly remove the right to vote when any calls on a share are unpaid (plc 41).

Articles cannot impose more stringent conditions than those established under section 303. They may, however, provide a less-stringent regime.

Conditions for member demand – form of request

The request may be made in hard copy or electronic form and must be authenticated by the person or persons making it (s. 303(6)). If the request is made in hard copy form, it must be delivered to the company in accordance with the relevant company communications provisions. These would require it to be deposited at the registered office of the company. In addition, it would need to be signed by those members requesting it and, in the case of joint holders, the requisition must be signed by each of them. A request may consist of several requests in like form each signed by one or more of those requesting it. This allows a master document to be prepared and for copies to be circulated to members for signature.

Example: Member requisition for general meeting

The Directors

XYZ plc

We the undersigned, being members of XYZ plc holding in the aggregate [number] ordinary shares of £1 each out of the issued and paid-up capital of [number] ordinary shares of £1 each, require you, pursuant to section 303 of the Companies Act 2006, to convene a general meeting of the company for the purpose of considering the following resolutions, which will be proposed as ordinary resolutions:

1. THAT [name A] be appointed a director of the company.

2. THAT [name B] be appointed a director of the company.

[Signatures]   [Addresses]

[Date]

(Note: If (unusually) the company's articles provide a more relaxed regime for a members' requisition and the members are unable to meet the statutory requirements, the wording of the requisition should refer to the relevant article.)

Conditions for member demand – purpose of the meeting

The request must state the general nature of the business to be dealt with at the meeting and may include the text of a resolution that may be proposed and is intended to be proposed at the meeting (s. 303(4)).

According to section 303(5), a resolution may be proposed at a meeting unless:

(a) it would, if passed, be ineffective (whether by reason of inconsistency with any enactment or the company's constitution or otherwise);

(b) it is defamatory of any person; or

(c) it is frivolous or vexatious.

These rules can cause considerable difficulty for those requesting the resolution who may not have sufficient legal knowledge to be able to frame their request in a manner which is legally effective. It would appear from the above rules, that the directors would have an obligation to call a meeting as long as the request states the general nature of the business, even though none of the resolutions may be properly proposed. However, even this might not be the case.

It has been held that the board cannot refuse to act on a request unless its objects cannot legally be carried into effect.

There will be circumstances in which it is sufficient for those submitting the request to set out the general nature of the business. In normal circumstances that is all that will be required in order to give valid notice of business to be transacted at a general meeting. This is all that is required by section 311(2), which applies subject to any provision of a company's articles. Most articles also only require notice of the general nature of the business to be given. However, they can contain exceptions which may serve to trip up the members. Even though those submitting a request may not always need to include the text of a resolution in their request, they will need to prepare draft resolutions that can be proposed at the meeting in order to put their objects into effect. Hence, it may sometimes be necessary for the submission to include the proposed resolution to the company before the notice is sent out. This will always be necessary if, for example, the business must be proposed as a special resolution. Such a resolution cannot validly be passed unless the notice of the meeting included the text of the resolution and specified the intention to propose it as a special resolution (s. 283(6)).

The directors have no obligation to help those submitting a request to draft their request or any of the related resolutions, although if they had been found to be deliberately obstructive, any subsequent legal case may be more likely to find in favour of those requesting the proposal.

Directors' duty on receipt of valid request

On receipt of a valid request, the directors must, within 21 days, convene a general meeting to be held on a date not more than 28 days after the date of the notice of the meeting (s. 304(1)). These requirements are intended to prevent the directors defeating the objects of those submitting the request by delaying the calling or holding of the meeting.

If the requests received by the company identify a resolution intended to be moved at the meeting, the notice of the meeting must include notice of the resolution (s. 304(2)). The business that may be dealt with at the meeting includes a resolution of which notice is given in accordance with section 304 (s. 304(3)).

If a resolution is to be proposed as a special resolution, the directors are treated as not having duly called the meeting if they do not give the required notice of the resolution in accordance with section 283.

If the directors do not properly comply with any of the above requirements, those submitting the request may convene the meeting themselves (see below).

When it convenes the meeting, the board may add other items to the agenda for the requested meeting by giving notice in the normal manner. However, a member cannot raise any other matter at the meeting which was not specified in the request. For example, a member may not propose a resolution to remove a director at a requested meeting where that was not one of the objects of the original request.

In practice, when convening a requisitioned meeting, the directors will probably want to send a circular with the notice to the members explaining the circumstances in which the meeting was being called and stating whether or not they support the proposals to be considered at the meeting. Given that the board did not convene the meeting themselves, it is probable that the directors will oppose the proposals and may seek the support of the members to enable them to be defeated. The result would usually depend upon the measure of support given by proxy votes to each side.

If the directors proceed to call the meeting, the notice will be in the same form as for a general meeting convened by the directors in the usual way.

Example: Notice of meeting requested by members

XYZ Plc

NOTICE IS HEREBY GIVEN that, pursuant to a requisition dated [date] made in accordance with the provisions of section 303 of the Companies Act 2006, and deposited at the registered office of the company on [date of deposit], a General Meeting of the company will be held at [place] on [date] at [time] for the purpose of considering the following resolutions, which will be proposed as ordinary resolutions:

RESOLUTIONS

1. THAT [name A] be appointed a director of the company.

2. THAT [name B] be appointed a director of the company.

[Signatures and names]   [Addresses]

[Date]

Notes

1. A member entitled to attend and vote at the meeting is entitled to appoint one or more proxies to attend and vote on his or her behalf. A proxy need not also be a member. A member may appoint more than one proxy in relation to the meeting provided that each proxy is appointed to exercise the rights to a different share or shares held by the member.

2. To be effective the form of proxy must be completed in accordance with the instructions and received by the company no later than 48 hours before the time for which the meeting is convened.

(The notice would normally be accompanied by an explanatory letter from the requisitionists and a form of proxy in their favour.)

Failure to convene a requested meeting

If, on receipt of a valid request, the directors do not properly convene a meeting in accordance with the requirements of section 304, those requesting the meeting (or any of them representing more than one half of their total voting rights) may themselves call a general meeting (s. 305(1)). The meeting must be called for a date not more than three months after the date on which the directors become subject to the requirement to call a meeting (s. 305(3)).

The meeting must be called in the same manner, as nearly as possible, as that in which meetings are required to be called by directors of the company (s. 305(4)). In order to do this, those requesting the meeting will need to obtain a list of members of the company and a copy of its articles of association, and ensure that they comply with any relevant article provisions together with any applicable rules of the Companies Act 2006.

Where the request received by the company includes the text of a resolution intended to be proposed at the meeting, the notice of the meeting must include notice of the resolution (s. 305(2)). The business which may be dealt with at the meeting includes a resolution of which notice is given in accordance with this section 305 (s. 305(5)).

Any reasonable expenses incurred by the members requesting the meeting by reason of the failure of the directors duly to call a meeting must be reimbursed by the company (s. 305(6)). Any sum so reimbursed shall be retained by the company out of any sums due, or to become due, from the company as fees or other remuneration in respect of the services of those of the directors that were in default (s. 305(7)).

Requisition of a meeting by a resigning auditor

An auditor may resign his office by giving the company notice in writing to that effect together with a statement of circumstances (ss 516 and 519). If the statement is of circumstances which the auditor believes should be brought to the attention of members, he may deposit at the same time a signed requisition calling on the directors of the company to convene an extraordinary general meeting for the purpose of receiving and considering his explanation of the circumstances of his resignation (s. 518(2)). The auditor also has a right to have a statement in writing of the circumstances connected with his resignation circulated to the members before any meeting convened on his requisition.

The directors must, within 21 days from the date of the deposit of the requisition, proceed to convene a meeting for a day not less than 28 days after the notice convening the meeting is given (s. 518(5)) and are liable to a fine if in default. However, the auditor has no right to convene a meeting themselves if it is in default.

Organising general meetings

This section deals with some of the more practical aspects of organising an AGM, although many of the issues raised will also be relevant to other meetings. It also includes a practical checklist for organising AGMs.

Checklist for AGM

The checklist below gives an easy reference for those individuals tasked with the practicalities of convening a general meeting or for those with oversight of a third-party provider of services acting on behalf of the company.

Actions, dates and practicalities should be checked against the Act as well as the articles of the company to ensure that they meet required protocols.

Date of meeting

- Calculate last date on which AGM must be held.
- Choose a suitable date or range of possible dates before the last date.
- Consult chair and other relevant personnel.
- Fix date and inform relevant company personnel and external advisers, e.g. registrars, auditors, solicitor, broker, PR consultants, etc.
- If a suitable opportunity arrives, inform the members.

Venue

- Estimate likely attendance numbers.
- Determine other requirements, e.g. location, cost, etc.
- Select and visit potential venues.
- Assess general suitability of each venue.
- Assess suitability for security purposes.
- Provisionally book preferred venue.
- Consult chair (and any other directors who wish to be consulted).
- If they approve, book venue and obtain confirmation of booking.
- Agree and sign contract.
- Obtain map of venue location and travel instructions.

Other arrangements

- Make arrangements for
  - catering (if required);
  - security and stewards;
  - audio visual equipment (if required);
  - voting equipment (if required);
  - printing of signs for AGM;
  - stage design (if required); and
  - display stands (if required).

Planning the AGM mailing

- Calculate last date notice must be sent out bearing in mind:
  - notice requirements;

- – requirement for clear days' notice;
- – date notice deemed given if sent by post or electronically; and
- – application of UK Corporate Governance Code recommendation.
- Set date for posting of notice and accounts (preferably before last date).
- If not possible within time limit, consider trying to obtain consent to short notice, otherwise change date of AGM.
- Set dates for:
  - – final draft of notice;
  - – finalisation of accounts and audit;
  - – board meeting to approve accounts and convene AGM;
  - – printing of notice, proxies, circulars, accounts and other documents to go with AGM mailing (inform printers); and
  - – printing of address labels (if by registrar, inform registrar stating where they are to be sent).

Drafting the notice, etc

- Prepare rough outline of business to be transacted at the AGM.
- If listed, check whether the notice and any accompanying circular will need to be approved by the United Kingdom Listing Authority (UKLA) before it is sent out;
- Check whether special notice is required for any resolution.
- Check type of resolution (ordinary, special) required for each item of business to be proposed.
- Calculate which (if any) of the directors must retire by rotation.
- Confirm that auditors are willing to be reappointed.
- Check whether directors' authority to allot needs to be renewed.
- Include any valid resolutions or statements submitted by members.
- Draft the AGM notice and circular.
- If a traded company, make preparations for publication of notice and other statements on website.
- Draft proxy cards and prepare website facilities for proxy appointments (if required).
- Draft attendance card (if required).
- Draft invitation to members to submit questions in advance (if required).

Board meeting to convene AGM and approve results and dividends

- Prepare and send out notice of board meeting including resolutions:
  - – to approve report and accounts;
  - – to authorise signing of accounts and reports;
  - – to recommend a dividend;
  - – to convene the AGM and approve business;
  - – to authorise secretary to sign and send out notices, etc.;

- – to recommend the appointment of any directors (if articles require);
- – to approve the release of any preliminary announcement or results announcement (listed plc only); and
- – to nominate director to act as chair of the general meeting in the absence of the chair of the board.
■ Immediately before meeting check again for any valid members' resolutions and include in papers put to the board.
■ Hold board meeting and pass resolutions.

Immediately after the board meeting

■ Release any preliminary announcement (listed plc only).
■ Balance sheet signed by a director.
■ Directors' report signed by a director or secretary.
■ Auditors' report signed by auditors.
■ Notice signed and dated by secretary.
■ Calculate required number of copies of:
  - – annual report (including extra copies); and
  - – notice, circular and proxy cards.
■ Final proofs of report and accounts, proxy cards, notice, etc. sent to printers with instructions as to numbers required.

Sending out the notice

■ Send report and accounts, notice, etc. to persons entitled to receive them.
■ File annual report at Companies House.
■ Send report and accounts to others on mailing list kept for that purpose.
■ If a traded company, publish notice and other statements on website.
■ Make available any website facilities for making proxy appointments.

Miscellaneous matters

■ Make arrangements to enable the payment of the dividend (if subsequently approved).
■ Calculate cut off time for valid proxies and, if necessary, inform registrars.
■ Monitor proxies received.
■ If necessary, contact major shareholders to encourage submission of proxies.
■ At appropriate time on cut-off date for proxies prepare:
  - – schedule of proxies appointed for the use of staff on the registration desk; and
  - – schedule of voting instructions for the chair where the member has appointed chair as proxy.
■ Print voting cards and poll cards (if required).

Preparations immediately before AGM

- Arrange for proposers and seconders of resolutions (as required).
- Finalise chair's agenda/script (see Appendix 2).
- Prepare AGM briefing document (see Appendix 10).
- If members were invited to submit questions in advance, prepare answers.
- Brief chair.
- Rehearse questions and answers.
- Allocate following duties to staff and brief accordingly:
  - registration;
  - poll;
  - roving microphone; and
  - stewards and security.
- Rehearse AGM.
- Confirm final arrangements with venue, security staff, registrars, etc.
- Make arrangements for the release of an announcement if it is intended to reveal price-sensitive information at the meeting (listed plc only).

Day of the AGM

- Things to take to the meeting:
  - directors' service contracts/non-executive directors' terms of appointment;
  - spare copies of report & accounts and notice;
  - chair's agenda/script (plus copies for other directors who are to propose resolutions);
  - questions and answers script;
  - memorandum and articles of association (indexed);
  - consolidated version of Companies Act 2006 (as amended);
  - a textbook on the law and procedures of meetings;
  - summary of proxies received;
  - original proxy forms and summary sheets;
  - register of members (usually supplied by registrar);
  - attendance sheets for members, proxies and corporate representatives, and guests;
  - notepads, pens and pencils;
  - name plates for top table and name badges;
  - reserved seats signs;
  - voting cards;
  - calculator with printed roll for counting votes on a poll;
  - telephone numbers of crucial participants.
- Final briefing of staff.
- Check that quorum present.
- Open meeting and conduct business (see Chair's script at Appendix 2).
- Record proceedings.

After the meeting

- Prepare minutes for signature by chair.
- Take actions required as a result of resolutions passed.
- Authorise payment of dividend.
- File any necessary copies of resolutions at Companies House.
- Announce results of resolutions and send copies of resolutions sent to the UK Listing Authority (listed plc only).
- Publish the results of any poll on a website (quoted companies only).
- Publish results of any independent report on a poll on a website.
- Respond to shareholder questions raised at meeting.
- Review the organisation of the AGM.
- Book venue for next AGM.

Location of meeting

Generally speaking, it is preferable to hold general meetings in the country of incorporation. However, the directors may determine the place at which the meeting shall be held and, in the absence of fraud, their decision cannot be challenged. The directors must, therefore, exercise their power to select the place of the meeting in the best interests of the company. If they call a meeting to be held at a time and place which clearly restricts the ability of a significant proportion of the members to attend, their decision is liable to challenge.

These rules would not prevent a UK registered company holding a meeting outside the UK if, for example, the majority of its shareholders were resident in the country in which the meeting was to be held or that country was the most convenient for the members as a whole. Some companies hold their meetings in multiple locations at the same time, which may not necessarily be in the same country.

Choosing a date for the general meeting

Before choosing a date for the general meeting, it is necessary to calculate the last date on which the meeting must be held. For public companies required to hold an AGM under the Act, this is now a very simple process as the meeting must now be held within six months of the year-end (or nine months in the case of a private company that is a traded company). Any date during that period may be chosen and it does not matter how long there is between each AGM or whether, by selecting a certain date, no AGM will be held in any particular calendar year. Although the meeting is still frequently called the AGM, it is not necessary for a meeting to be held annually.

Under the Companies Act 1985, companies were required to hold an AGM in each calendar year with not more than 15 months being allowed to elapse between the date of one AGM meeting and the next. Newly registered companies were required to hold their first AGM within 18 months of incorporation and, as long as they complied with this requirement, were not required to hold one in the year of incorporation or the following year (s. 366, 1985 Act).

Under the 2006 Act, a company may not be required to hold an AGM in a particular year, perhaps because its year-end falls in the second half of the year or because it has extended the accounting period by changing its accounting reference date. For example, a public company with a 30 September year-end could choose to hold its AGM for the financial year ending 30 September 2020 in December 2020, but choose to hold its next AGM in January 2022.

A company incorporated under an earlier Act may find that its articles follow the traditional model by requiring an AGM to be held once every calendar year. A company required by the 2006 Act to hold an AGM must comply with the timing requirements of the Act in order to avoid committing an offence. However, it should also seek to comply with the requirements of the articles, particularly where a proportion of the directors are required to retire by rotation at each AGM. Failure to hold a meeting in any particular year could cause complications in this regard. In the long term it might be better for such a company to delete the AGM timing requirements from its articles or to bring them in line with the Act. However, there is no particular reason why a private company that wishes to continue holding AGMs, despite not being required to do so by the Act, should not continue to do so in accordance with the old timing model.

It obviously makes sense for a public company to aim for an AGM date which allows the report and accounts to be laid before the meeting and it may be advisable to delay the meeting in order to do so (if that is possible in view of the above requirements). Public companies must lay their accounts before the members in general meeting no later than the end of the period for filing them with the registrar of companies. This period is normally six months after the year-end (ss 437 and 442). However, this will not always be the case. For example, the company may apply to the Secretary of State for a filing extension and the filing deadline may be different for the company's first accounts or, if it subsequently changes, its accounting reference date (see below).

The existence of other companies within the group that are required to hold an AGM may influence the choice of date. It may be desirable to hold the AGMs of these companies on the same day, particularly if the membership of each company is similar.

Listed companies will often seek to avoid holding their AGM on the same date as, or before, other companies in the same sector. Other factors that may determine the date chosen might include the availability of the chair and other directors, the availability of a suitable venue, and the availability of the auditors, registrars and other advisors. To ensure that all these factors can be co-ordinated, it may be necessary to begin planning the AGM a long way in advance. Many listed companies book the venue of their AGM up to two years in advance.

Finally, it should not be forgotten that 21 clear days' notice of the AGM must be given unless the consent of all the members to shorter notice can be obtained.

Traded companies are not allowed to hold a meeting with less than 21 days' notice. If the accounts which are to be laid at the meeting are sent out less than 21 days before the meeting, separate consent will also be required (s. 424(4)).

Estimating attendance

Ideally, the venue for a general meeting should be capable of accommodating all the members. For companies with few members, this is relatively easy to arrange. However, for companies with thousands of shareholders, this is impractical. Instead, the company secretary must try to predict the number of members and guests likely to attend. The starting point for this exercise for an AGM will normally be to examine attendance levels in previous years. If the number of shareholders has increased or decreased significantly, appropriate adjustments should be made.

If the company's results are not as good as expected or it has been the subject of adverse press comment, the proportion of members attending will probably be higher than normal. Numbers will also increase where food and drink or company products are offered for the first time. An interesting or unusual venue may also attract more shareholders as may a change of venue to a location which is more accessible.

Whatever figure is finally arrived at, most company secretaries tend to add a little extra for contingency purposes. Preparations for the meeting are usually made a long way in advance and it is sensible to assume that something may subsequently happen which increases shareholder attendance.

Some companies conduct surveys of a sample of their members to estimate the likely attendance. Others ask shareholders to confirm electronically or return a reply-paid card if they intend to attend. Such methods usually produce a forecast which is higher than the actual attendance on the day. To this extent, they can be a useful guide to the absolute maximum attendance, particularly for a newly listed company or one which has recently undergone a major change in its shareholder base (e.g. following a takeover or merger). One company which asked all its members to return a card indicating whether they would attend, found that the responses tallied almost exactly with the actual attendance. However, on analysing the responses, it found that this was because the number of shareholders who said they would attend but did not turn up was practically the same as the number who did not respond but attended on the day.

Having determined the maximum number of members for whom accommodation will be provided, additional provision should be made for guests, the press and employees.

Room size

If the estimate of the maximum attendance differs greatly from the normal attendance, the prime consideration may be flexibility. A large room capable of being partitioned off may be preferable to separate overspill rooms which need to be connected by audio visual links to the main meeting room. However, the use of visual links could also enable a company to make use of multiple venues, either in the same building, differing cities or countries as well as sharing for online connectivity.

It is usual, and best practice, for the board of directors to be seated with the chair, facing the shareholders. The company secretary will usually be seated on the top table or platform next to the chair so that they can discretely provide support on governance matters during the meeting. Some companies also invite the audit partner and the company's solicitor to sit on the top table. Some venues have built in stage areas and platforms. However, the seating capacity of the room may depend on the size of the platform required. It is becoming increasingly common for each director to have a screen which is used to display either the running order or information compiled by researchers which may be helpful for the directors when answering questions from shareholders. The chair may make use of an autocue facility.

Other factors influencing the choice of venue

Several other factors will influence the choice of venue and some of these are considered below. It can be useful to produce a checklist of the company's main requirements prior to considering venues so that it is easier to compare the suitability of the various venues considered both prior to visiting and when visiting a short-list of options.

Availability

The meeting room(s) should be booked to allow for the possibility that the meeting may take longer than expected. Nothing is likely to annoy shareholders more than for discussion to be cut short because the room must be vacated. Indeed, the chair may find it necessary to adjourn the meeting in such circumstances which could be both costly and embarrassing. Adequate time must also be allowed to set up the room before the meeting and for taking down any stage designs and displays after the meeting. This may mean booking the room for the day before the meeting and for a few hours after the meeting is due to close.

Terms of licence

The terms and conditions of the venue (e.g. dress codes, security checks, etc.) should be checked to ensure that they are not inconsistent with the company's legal obligations to admit all shareholders. Problems can also arise if it is not possible for the company to restrict public access to the meeting venue.

Location

Is the venue easily accessible by road and public transport? Does it have access for the disabled? The Chartered Governance Institute's Guide to Best Practice for AGMs recommends that the venue for the AGM should be accessible by attendees who have disabilities and have facilities for those with poor hearing.

Noise levels

Is the room relatively soundproof? The most common problem within hotels and conference centres is that rooms are occupied by multiple users or are situated next to the kitchen and catering staff where noise carries easily. Partitioned rooms should be avoided unless you can afford to reserve the whole suite as it is inevitable that the adjoining section(s) will be hired by people whose activities involve making a great deal of noise. Although the partitions themselves are normally soundproof, the connecting doors frequently are not. Also check whether the owners intend to do any building, decorating or repairs around the date of the meeting. The venue may look wonderful when you book it. Things could be very different on the day. If possible, obtain a written undertaking that no such work will be carried out on the day.

Lighting, heating and air conditioning

Can the lights, heating and air conditioning be adjusted easily and are they sufficient? In many venues access to these controls is restricted. If so, will a member of staff be available to make the necessary adjustments?

Layout

Other questions regarding the layout of the venue which may need to be resolved include:

- What seating arrangement can be provided comfortably (e.g. theatre, classroom, or boardroom styles)?
- Can areas be cordoned off for different classes of members or non-members?
- Are the seating arrangements comfortable?
- Will everyone be able to see the presenters and/or the screen if one is being used?
- Will roving microphones for questions be able to easily and quickly access the whole room?
- Do the facilities enable adequate security arrangements to be put in place?

Registration and help desks

In addition to the main meeting room, the venue will need to have a suitable area for registration. Ideally, it should not be possible for members to gain entry to the meeting room without passing through the registration area. If there is more than one entrance to the venue, the registration area might need to be located immediately outside the entrance to the meeting room. The size of the registration area will depend on the number of members and guests that are expected to attend. It may need to be large enough to accommodate several registration desks and the company's registrars may need power points if they plan to access the register of members using computer equipment.

Many companies provide shareholder help desks to deal with members' enquiries about dividends and other issues relating to their shareholdings. Retail and consumer companies often establish separate help desks to deal with enquiries which are customer related. By doing so, members are less likely to raise these issues at the meeting and the chair is able to refer a member who asks such a question to the relevant help desk. If these facilities are to be provided, they will need to be situated in a prominent position, perhaps in the foyer and reference should be made to them at the outset of the chair's speech.

Security

Space may be needed for security checks to be carried out prior to registration to prevent members bringing into the meeting any objects which could be used to disrupt the meeting (e.g. banners, missiles, whistles, klaxons, etc. (see below)).

Sound system and recordings

Sound equipment may be necessary for the top table and for taking questions from the floor. It should be remembered that the acoustics in an empty room are far better than when it is full of people. If the meeting room is large, it will almost certainly be necessary to provide some means of amplification for shareholders who wish to ask questions during the meeting. This can be done using roving microphones. If microphones are not provided, the chair should be briefed to repeat or summarise the questions put from the floor before answering them.

It is often beneficial to record the proceedings (including questions from the floor) so that a transcript can be made. The company may also wish to make arrangements for the proceedings to be recorded for electronic transmission so that shareholders who were unable to attend can watch remotely. Given current technology, some companies also use this method to live stream their meetings so that shareholders can watch real time. In this scenario, accessibility and attendance limited to shareholders and other authorised attendees should be incorporated into the process for initially viewing.

All those who will be speaking should liaise with sound system staff with regard to personal microphones and their use, including sound checks prior to the commencement of the meeting.

Refreshments

Where refreshments are provided, they are normally served in a separate room so that the catering staff do not disrupt the meeting. Exhibitions of company products or its history could also be placed in this area or in the main meeting room.

Directors' room

The availability of a meeting or preparation room for the directors and an office for the meeting organisers should also be considered.

Staff

Are the staff friendly and helpful? Do they have sufficient staff to cater for your needs? Will a manager be on hand throughout the meeting to handle any problems?

Toilet and cloakroom facilities

The standard of both the ladies and the gents' toilets should be checked. It may also be necessary to provide facilities for members to leave their coats and baggage, particularly if certain items are not allowed to be taken into the meeting. It is also worth checking whether the venue will staff the cloakroom or if it is the responsibility of the hirer.

Other facilities

The availability of telephone, internet, fax and photocopying facilities may be important to the organisers and to members attending.

Webcasts

Larger listed companies tend to make their AGM available on a live video webcast (usually via the company's website). This obviously enables a much wider audience to view the proceedings but does not always allow them to participate. Where the proceedings are being recorded, but particularly where they are being filmed, it is usual to warn shareholders in advance in the AGM circular and at the start of the meeting. Where viewers are able to submit questions electronically in real time, it is beneficial to have an individual tasked with monitoring these to pass on to the chair or other relevant person to ensure that they are addressed during the meeting.

Some companies also make an edited version of the live video webcast (possibly including the chair's statement, other presentations made by operational managers and the general question and answer session) available shortly after the meeting on their website.

Use of websites

Companies are required or authorised to use websites for a variety of purposes connected with general meetings. Indeed, for those who use communications via website as their default method of communicating with shareholders, the content and design of the company's website has become a very important issue.

Websites are required or authorised to be used for the following purposes.

Traded companies are required under section 311A to publish the following information on their websites throughout the period beginning with the first date on which notice of the meeting is given and ending with the conclusion of the meeting and to include in the notice a statement giving details of the website on which the information is published (s. 311(3)):

- the matters set out in the notice of the meeting;
- the total numbers of shares in the company (and shares of each class) in respect of which members are entitled to exercise voting rights at the meeting, ascertained at the latest practicable time before the first date on which notice of the meeting is given; and
- the totals of the voting rights that members are entitled to exercise at the meeting in respect of the shares of each class.

A traded company must also ensure that any members' statements regarding audit concerns (under s. 527), members' resolutions (under s. 388) and members' matters of business (under s. 388A) received by the company after the first date on which notice of the meeting is given are made available on a website. This information must be made available as soon as reasonably practicable. It should be noted in this regard that any such statements, resolutions and matters of business received before that date will also be published on the website as they will be expected to form part of the notice of meeting.

The above information must be made available on a website that is maintained by or on behalf of the company and identifies the company (s. 311A(2)). Access to the information on the website, and the ability to obtain a hard copy of the information from the website, must not be conditional on payment of a fee or otherwise restricted (s. 311A(3)). The information must be made available on the website throughout the period of two years beginning with the date on which it is first made available in accordance with section 311A (s. 311A(4)). Failure to do so does not affect the validity of the meeting or of anything done at the meeting (s. 311A(7)), but is an offence (s. 311A(8)) for which any officer in default may be fined (s. 311A(9)). However, any failure to make information available throughout the two-year period is disregarded if the information is made available on the website for part of that period and the failure is wholly attributable to circumstances that it would not be reasonable to have expected the company to prevent or avoid (s. 311A(5)).

Quoted companies and traded companies are required to publish the results of any poll on their website. Quoted companies are also required to publish any independent report on a poll on their website.

Quoted companies may be required by members satisfying the requirements of section 527 to publish on a website a statement by them relating to the audit of the company's accounts which are to be laid before the next accounts meeting (including the auditor's report and the conduct of the audit) or, where applicable, any circumstances connected with an auditor of the company ceasing to hold office since the previous accounts meeting at which accounts were laid.

Traded companies are not required to answer questions at general meetings if the answer has already been given on the company's website in the form of an answer to a question (s. 319A). This means that listed companies will need to create a specific Q&A section on their websites to which shareholders who ask questions at the meeting may be referred if necessary.

A traded company must give an electronic address that can be used by members for the purposes of appointing proxies either on the website maintained for the purposes of section 311A or in every instrument of proxy sent out by the company for the purposes of a general meeting of the company, and every invitation to appoint a proxy issued by the company for the purposes of such a meeting (s. 333A(1)). This address must, for all practical purposes, be a website address where it is possible for members to appoint proxies. This service is normally provided by a company's registrars and it is likely that the address provided will link directly to them, although it could direct the members to the company's website first. If a traded company does not offer the facility to vote by electronic means to all members who hold shares that carry rights to vote at general meetings, it must give 21 days' notice of all meetings (s. 307A).

Just about the only thing that is not required to be published on a traded company's website is the minutes of the meeting. The results of any poll must be published on the website but not any vote on a show of hands. Listed companies are required to announce the fact that certain resolutions have been passed under the Listing Rules. This announcement is normally made available somewhere on the company's website. However, it is not always easy to find, and it might be easier for shareholders if the page on the company's website dealing with the AGM for that year contained a link to the announcement. There is no particular reason why the minutes of the meeting should not be made available on the website as well, although companies tend not to do this.

Electronic meetings

Section 322A(1) provides that a company's articles may contain provision to the effect that on a vote on a resolution on a poll taken at a meeting, the votes may include votes cast in advance. Section 322A(3) allows a company to impose the same maximum time limits on voting in advance as are allowed for appointing proxies. However, it does not require those time limits to be imposed.

With the rapid development of electronic voting systems, it is now also possible for attendees to vote electronically, either when physically attending the meeting or when joining the meeting virtually.

Section 360A specifically provides that nothing in Part 13 (meetings and resolutions) of the Companies Act 2006 shall be taken to preclude the holding and conducting of a meeting in such a way that persons who are not present together at the same place may by electronic means attend and speak and vote at it.

Section 360A(2) further provides that, in the case of a traded company, the use of electronic means for the purpose of enabling members to participate in a general meeting may be made subject only to such requirements and restrictions as are necessary to ensure the identification of those taking part and the security of the electronic communication, and that are proportionate to the achievement of those objectives. It is assumed that this provision is intended to prevent some shareholders from being excluded from participating in a meeting by electronic means on any other grounds right from the start, rather than to prevent the chair of the meeting imposing rules of conduct that could, for example, curtail their right to participate in some respects and which could ultimately result in their expulsion.

As electronic meetings are becoming more prevalent, it is necessary to adopt a flexible and workable solution for enabling all members, whether attending in person or virtually, to have the right to speak. Modern articles nearly always interpret this as requiring a person to be heard by others participating in the meeting. This could be enabled by utilising electronic bulletin boards, real-time question submissions or other online facilities, monitored and contributed by a representative at the meeting. One of the problems for large companies may be the volume of contributions and the practical management of these submissions. It should be noted, however, that the right to speak does not necessarily always guarantee that all shareholders who wish to do so will be afforded that opportunity. Accordingly, there would appear to be no reason why any online contributions should not be moderated, subject to the application of the rules regarding shareholders' questions.

It is arguable that, irrespective of section 360A, there is nothing in the Act to prevent a company from holding electronic meetings. However, it is also undeniable that it would be extremely expensive and difficult to do so for a company with a large number of shareholders, and that modifications would need to be made to the company's articles (e.g. to cater for this method of participation for the purposes of voting, speaking, attendance and quorum requirements and to prevent the proceedings from being invalidated by any failure of communications). In practice, it might be easier for a company with relatively few shareholders to run electronic meetings, especially with the reducing cost of implementation and availability of technology.

The chair's script

It is sensible for the chair to follow a basic script at a general meeting, which should be drafted on the assumption that everything will run smoothly. The chair should also have several additional scripts to hand for dealing with other situations that may arise, especially where specific protocols need to be followed. These could include scripts for:

- dealing with a demand for a poll from the floor;
- the conduct of a poll;
- proposing an adjournment or dealing with such a proposal from the floor;
- dealing with disorder;
- dealing with amendments; and
- procedural resolutions for the management of the proceedings.

Examples of various chair's scripts (including a script for an AGM) can be found in Appendix 2.

If possible, the chair should be given the opportunity to rehearse the script and should be thoroughly briefed on the actions they should take if anything unusual happens. Many companies also try to anticipate questions which shareholders may ask and prepare answers to these hypothetical questions.

Other things that the chair needs to know

It is obviously helpful if the chair knows how meetings should be run. However, even the most experienced chair will need a bit of help occasionally, and it is normally the company secretary who will sit next to the chair at the meeting ready to offer that help if it is required, particularly in respect of procedural requirements that must be followed.

It is not necessarily as easy as it looks to chair a meeting, particularly where things are not going to plan. The secretary should not sit idly by if the chair takes a wrong turn, although their input should be carefully provided to ensure it adds value without detracting from the purpose and flow of the meeting. This can be avoided to a certain extent by preparing a good script and briefing the chair on a range of other matters before the meeting.

Such a briefing should cover the basic concepts of the law of meetings and, in particular, the specific requirements of the company's articles. In preparing such a briefing, it is a good idea to produce a marked-up copy of the articles, which highlights any provisions that may no longer apply because of subsequent statutory modifications.

The briefing should probably cover, but not necessarily be limited to, matters such as:

- The chair's duties.
- The chair's powers under the general law and under the articles.
- What quorum is required for the meeting to proceed to business, and who can be counted for the purposes of calculating whether that quorum has been obtained?
- What should the chair do if a quorum is not obtained at the time specified in the notice for the start of the meeting?
- What should the chair do if a quorum was present at the start of the meeting but is subsequently lost?
- Who has a right to attend and what measures have been put in place to ensure that only those who have that right or have been invited to attend are allowed to gain admittance?
- Who has a right to speak?
- What method of voting will be used for substantive and procedural resolutions?
- Who has a right to vote on a show of hands?
- Who can make a valid demand for a poll?

- Who has a right to vote on a poll?
- Have any members appointed the chair of the meeting as their proxy and, if so, for each resolution what are the total number of votes that they have instructed him or her to cast in favour, against or withhold and the total number for which they have given him or her discretion as to how to vote?
- What procedures should be followed if someone proposes an amendment to a substantive or procedural resolution?

Right to attend

Company meetings are private meetings and, as such, the company is bound to admit only those who are legally entitled to attend. The right to attend usually goes hand-in-hand with the right to vote. However, the Act gives various people a statutory right to attend and the articles may allow others to attend or give the chair discretion in this regard

Members and corporate representatives

Voting at general meetings is usually conducted by a show of hands or a poll. Both methods require the presence of the person voting (or their proxy). It follows that, in order to exercise their right to vote, the members must also have a right to attend the meeting. However, a member who does not have a right to vote may still have a right to attend the meeting, unless the articles provide otherwise.

Companies whose shares have been admitted to CREST may specify in the notice a time, not more than 48 hours before the time fixed for the meeting, by which a person must be entered on the relevant register of securities in order to have the right to attend and vote at the meeting.

A member who persistently disrupts the meeting may be ejected. However, a member who is wrongfully excluded from a meeting, and thereby prevented from voting, may be able to challenge the validity of the proceedings. For example, it would be wrong to exclude a person without the backing of some sort of court order merely because they have disrupted previous meetings.

Care should be taken to ensure that a member's right to attend is not prejudiced by the terms and conditions imposed under the licence to use the venue where the meeting is to be held (e.g. it would be unwise to choose a venue which imposes a dress code). Some companies have taken powers in their articles that allow them to exclude members who refuse to comply with conditions imposed for the purposes of security (e.g. electronic screening and prohibitions on taking hand baggage into the meeting).

Joint holders

Where shares are registered in the names of joint holders each of the joint holders is a member of the company and is, therefore, entitled to attend the meeting unless the articles provide otherwise. Articles commonly make special provision to enable the company to determine which vote should be accepted if more than one of the joint holders tenders a vote. In the absence of anything in a company's articles on voting by joint holders, section 286 of the Act applies, whereby only the vote of the senior holder who votes (and any proxies duly authorised by them) may be counted by the company. For this purpose, the senior holder of a share is determined by the order in which the names of the joint holders appear in the register of members.

The rules do not restrict the right of each of the joint holders to vote at the meeting. So any one of them could turn up and vote. Even if more than one of the joint holders attends, the company cannot predict which, if any of them, will tender a vote. All the company knows is that if more than one of them tenders a vote, only the vote of the senior holder can be accepted.

Death or bankruptcy

Articles commonly provide that a person who becomes entitled to a share in consequence of the death or bankruptcy of a member shall not be entitled to attend or vote at any meeting of the company or of the holders of any class of shares until he has been registered as the holder of the share (pcls 27 and plc 66).

Corporate representatives

Corporate representatives are deemed to have the same rights as individual members by virtue of section 323. Accordingly, they have the same right to attend as an individual member. However, they should be required to provide evidence of their appointment before being admitted.

Proxies

Proxies have a statutory right to attend on behalf of those who appointed them (s. 324). If the person who appointed the proxy is not entitled to attend, their proxy will not be entitled to attend. Any proxy appointed by a member may attend even if the member who appointed them attends the meeting. If the member does not vote, the proxy may do so.

Indirect investors

Investors who hold shares through an intermediary or nominee do not have a right to attend unless the registered shareholder appoints them as a proxy or corporate representative. A company's articles may allow members to identify another person or persons to enjoy or exercise all or any specified rights of a member, which could include the right to vote (s. 145). In order to exercise the right to vote it would normally be necessary to confer rights of attendance as well, unless the right to vote was restricted to voting in advance. Companies sometimes allow indirect investors to attend general meetings as guests without conferring upon them any rights, although there would seem to be no reason why the chair should not also allow them to speak at the meeting in these circumstances.

Auditors

A company's auditors have a statutory right to receive notice of any general meeting of the company and to attend and speak at any such meeting on any part of the business which concerns them as auditors (s. 502(2)). The rights conferred by section 502(2) are also extended to:

(a) an auditor who has been removed from office in relation to any general meeting at which his term of office would otherwise have expired or at which it is proposed to fill the vacancy caused by his removal (s. 513); and

(b) a resigning auditor in relation to a meeting convened on his requisition or at any general meeting at which his term of office would otherwise have expired or at which it is proposed to fill the vacancy caused by his resignation (s. 518(10)).

Directors

Directors do not have a statutory right to attend general meetings, except where a resolution to remove them is to be proposed under section 168 (s. 169(2)). However, directors who are members (or a representative or proxy of a member) will have a right to attend in that capacity.

It is highly likely that a director who is not a member has a common law right to attend, although that right may be subject to the will of the meeting. It would be odd if a director who was not a member but who had, for example, been appointed as the chair of the board of directors (and therefore, under the company's articles, as the chair of the general meeting) did not have a right to attend. Equally, any director who is also the chair of a committee of the board may be expected to attend in order to answer any questions on the operations and effectiveness of that committee.

To remove any doubt on the matter, articles usually state that directors who are not members shall be entitled to attend and speak at meetings of the company (pcls 40, clg 26 and plc 32). There is some doubt as to whether a director who is not a member could enforce such a right as he is not a party to the contract which is deemed to exist between the members and the company by virtue of the articles. His exclusion from the meeting would be unlikely to invalidate the proceedings except in the case of a resolution to remove him as a director. Any right which a director has to attend a meeting must presumably be subject to the usual rules on ejection on the grounds of disorderly conduct.

Company secretary

The company secretary has no statutory right to attend general meetings. Articles rarely address the subject. However, in view of the role and the value that they bring to proceedings, it would be unusual for the secretary to be excluded from the meeting.

Other classes of member
All members have the right to attend general meetings unless the articles provide otherwise. Where a company has more than one class of shares, it is usual for the articles to specify the voting rights of each class. For example, preference shareholders are not usually entitled to vote at general meetings unless their dividends are in arrears. If they are not entitled to vote, they would not normally be entitled to attend. Members of a class will, of course be entitled to attend meetings of their own class.

Attendance by invitation
It is normal for a public company to invite its lawyers, specialist advisers, brokers, analysts, press representatives, etc. These invitations are usually issued by the secretary on behalf of the company. The presence at a meeting of persons not entitled to be present or to vote does not invalidate the meeting.

Under the model articles, the chair of the meeting is given specific power to permit any person who is not a member of the company or otherwise entitled to attend and speak, to attend and speak at a general meeting (pcls 40(2), clg 26(2), plc 32(2)). Where the articles make no such provision, the chair can undoubtedly allow other people to attend. However, his power to do so might be subject to the will of the meeting, which could decide otherwise. The inclusion of a power in the articles means that the decision as to who can and cannot attend lies solely with the chair of the meeting, who may obviously revoke any permission previously given and who will undoubtedly take into account the views of the members in deciding whether or not to do so. If a person who is an invited guest refuses to leave upon being asked to do so, reasonable force may be used to eject them.

Companies should employ some method of ensuring that people attending by invitation cannot vote on any resolution (e.g. by issuing voting cards to the members or restricting electronic voting methods to members) or are not counted when a vote is taken (e.g. by physically placing them in a separate area).

Record of attendance
A record should be kept of the names of the members, proxies and corporate representatives who attend any general meeting. The record is used primarily to ensure that a quorum is present throughout the proceedings. Totals of the members, corporate representatives and proxies present should be calculated and shown in the minutes. The record of attendance can also be useful in helping to reconcile the votes cast on a poll. In theory, no-one should vote on a poll unless they are present in person or represented by a proxy, corporate representative or, in the case of a company whose articles allow voting in advance, they have voted in advance or the company has adopted electronic voting.

Listed companies usually send each shareholder an attendance card or electronic code with a unique bar-coding and request members to produce it on arrival at the meeting. The information on the attendance card is scanned and fed into a computer which holds details of the register of members. The computer is then able to calculate the number of members present in person or by proxy and to print out a list of attendees. This also enables the company to identify whether certain shareholders are present, for example institutional investors or members who represent pressure groups.

Maintaining the attendance list throughout the meeting also enables its update if members leave the meeting. This can be particularly important for votes cast after their departure where the result of the vote is marginal.

Attendance

Traditionally, the right to attend a meeting and to participate in it could only be exercised by turning up in person at the designated venue. However, modern articles allow the use of multiple locations which need not necessarily be in the same country and for virtual attendance. For example, the model articles provide that, in determining attendance at a general meeting, it is immaterial whether any two or more members attending it are in the same place as each other, and that two or more persons who are not in the same place as each other attend a general meeting if their circumstances are such that if they have (or were to have) the right to speak and vote at that meeting, they are (or would be) able to exercise them (pcls 37, clg 23 and plc 29). This provision is also reflected in the provisions of the model articles on the quorum at general meetings, which provide that no business other than the appointment of the chair of the meeting is to be transacted at a general meeting if the *persons attending it* do not constitute a quorum (pcls 38, clg 24 and plc 30). This means that even where the quorum is two, the two people who must attend the meeting in order for it to transact any business do not have to be in the same place.

Under the model articles, the directors may make whatever arrangements they consider appropriate to enable those attending the meeting to exercise their rights to speak and vote at it. However, those arrangements must enable a person who has the right to speak at the meeting to communicate to all those attending the meeting, during the meeting, any information or opinions which he has on the business of the meeting. The arrangements must also ensure that a person who has the right to vote is able to do so during the meeting on resolutions put to the vote at the meeting, and ensure that their vote can be taken into account in determining whether or not such resolutions are passed at the same time as the votes of all the other persons attending the meeting.

Section 311 requires the notice of any general meeting to state the place of the meeting. Accordingly, where attendance at different locations is allowed, it must be necessary for the notice to state each of those locations. This would seem to preclude the use of certain types of electronic communications which might enable people to attend from unpredictable locations. However, section 360A(1) provides that nothing in Part 13 of the Act shall be taken to preclude the holding and conducting of a meeting in such a way that persons who are not present together at the same place may by electronic means attend and speak and vote at it.

In the case of a traded company, the use of electronic means for the purpose of enabling members to participate in a general meeting may be made subject only to such requirements and restrictions as are:

(a) necessary to ensure the identification of those taking part and the security of the electronic communication; and

(b) proportionate to the achievement of those objectives.

Security

Security is not normally a problem for private companies. However, for companies which are in the public eye, it is an increasingly important issue. Pressure groups frequently disrupt meetings of listed companies in order to gain publicity for their cause. In the current political and social environment, companies can no longer discount the possibility of terrorist attack or the possibility that a member or customer with a grudge against the company will behave in a violent manner at the meeting. Many companies now invest a considerable amount of time and money on security measures to counter these threats.

The company's main line of defence is the registration process. Some listed companies still allow members of the public to attend their AGMs without an invitation. However, more and more are restricting entry for the purposes of security and require people wishing to gain entry to prior register their intention to attend and prove their identity on attendance. If nothing else, the venue chosen for holding the meeting will often impose strict security and requires prior notification of the list of attendees.

Companies that face disruption need to be prepared to tackle it in a professional and measured manner, especially now that personal mobile devices can post actions immediately that would be seen beyond the confines of the meeting itself. For those companies where disruption may occur, a security checklist is included.

Proof of identity

Proof of identity for security purposes is often a requirement from the management of the venue where the meeting is being held so can be aligned to the requirements of the company related to record keeping of member attendance and record-keeping of non-member attendees.

A company may refuse to admit members who cannot provide satisfactory evidence of their identity. If it were otherwise, the company would be forced to admit two people claiming to be the same member. The same can be said with regard to proxies and corporate representatives.

Most members will have no difficulty satisfying any reasonable request made by the company. This might include the production of a passport, driving licence or some other document evidencing their identity. A company could, although it is becoming rare, also accept the confirmation of an individual's identity by someone else who is known to the company. It is also arguable that anyone who is able to furnish accurate information about their holding (e.g. full name, address, size of holding, date of purchase of shares, mandate details, etc.) should also be admitted. In cases of doubt, it is wise to err on the side of caution as the exclusion of a person entitled to attend and vote could render the meeting liable to challenge. However, admitting people who are not entitled to attend, and allowing them to vote, could be considered just as dangerous.

If proof of identity is required, security and registration staff should be properly briefed. The procedures which should be followed before refusing entry to a person who would be entitled to attend if able to prove their identity should be approved by the chair. Indeed, it may be preferable to refer difficult cases to the chair or a senior representative appointed by them to act in this function. In cases of doubt, the person could be admitted but asked to sit in a specially allocated area. If that person's vote would have affected the outcome on a show of hands, the chair may need to make a ruling on the validity of their vote, which under most articles will be deemed to be conclusive. Alternatively, the chair could demand a poll (if the articles so allow) in the hope that this will resolve the difficulty. This would also enable the company to take further steps to establish the identity of the person claiming to be a member, etc. If the result of the poll is affected by the disputed votes, the chair will have to make a ruling on their validity. The courts have endorsed the use by the chair of a 'conditional' casting vote where the validity of some votes had been in doubt and it was not clear whether the vote was tied.

Attendance cards

Some companies send shareholders attendance cards, either electronic or printed, and request that they produce them on arrival in order to gain entry to the meeting. The main advantage of this system is that it helps to speed up the registration process. It does, however, have several weaknesses. The first of these is that attendance cards actually facilitate impersonation where no other identity checks are made. In addition, a company cannot refuse to admit members merely because they are unable to produce an attendance card, unless the articles specify this as a condition of entry or the chair is able to do so under powers conferred by the articles. Even then, it would be unreasonable not to allow members who cannot produce their attendance cards to prove their identity in some other way. However, it would not be unreasonable to impose more exacting standards on members who do not bring their attendance cards than those who do.

Companies sometimes request proxies and corporate representatives to bring the member's attendance card with them. If the member has appointed more than one proxy or corporate representative, it will be impossible for them all to do so.

They should, therefore, be allowed to prove their identity in some other way. In the case of corporate representatives, they should also be required to produce evidence of their authority at the meeting.

Security checks

Some companies have taken specific powers in their articles to refuse entry to members who fail to comply with certain conditions of entry. The model articles make no specific provision in this regard, although they do provide that the directors may make whatever arrangements they consider appropriate to enable those attending a general meeting to exercise their rights to speak or vote at it (pcls 37(3), clg 23(3) and plc 29(3)). However, even if the articles do not make specific provision with regard to security, the company can (and perhaps should) take reasonable security measures, particularly where it has reason to believe that the meeting might be disrupted or that the safety of those attending might be at risk.

The chair has a duty to preserve order at meetings and to ensure the business of the meeting is properly conducted. Security procedures such as screening devices and baggage searches are now a commonplace and a legitimate method of ensuring that the meeting is not disrupted and that it is able to complete its business. Many listed companies deliberately hold their meetings at venues which have built-in security screening at the point of entry. Anyone wishing to attend must pass through an electronic screening device and have their baggage inspected. A company can legitimately exclude a person who refuses to be screened if the purpose of that screening is to ensure the safety of other members present and to prevent disorder at the meeting. If a person refuses on medical grounds to be screened electronically, they should still be prepared to submit to some sort of manual screening.

With the advent of mobile devices capable of taking photographs, videos or recordings of proceedings, it is less prevalent to see attendees denied access as a result of attempting to take cameras and recording equipment into the meeting. However, the start of the meeting should include an announcement as to their use, including noting that continual flash photography could disrupt the meeting and that recordings of the proceedings in its entirety should not be made. Where a meeting is being recorded either for company purposes or to share electronically either in real time or subsequent to the meeting, all attendees should be notified of this fact.

Security checklist for AGM

While most meetings will proceed with minimal disruption, in some sectors and for some companies, it is preferable to be overly prepared than have to react after the event. The following checklist is based on material produced by company secretaries of companies whose meetings have been disrupted by protesters and demonstrations.

Planning the meeting

Make someone responsible for security.

- Identify issues which are likely to be controversial, e.g.
  - any company issues likely to lead to demonstrations;
  - any staff issues likely to lead to demonstrations;
  - any shareholder issues likely to lead to demonstrations;
  - any active shareholder protest groups;
  - any known agitators likely to attend; and
  - any historical issues which have arisen at company meetings.
- Consider issuing a statement concerning any controversial or difficult issues prior to the meeting to diffuse potential protests.
- Notify the local police of security concerns and request their availability.
- Persuade the chair to rehearse any complications.
- If professional cameras and tape recorders are not to be allowed in and the use of personal mobile devices is to be restricted, the notice to shareholders should include this information.
- Be aware of the possibilities for various forms of protest and take appropriate precautions, for example:
  - irrelevant questioning;
  - mass sit-in;
  - noise disturbance during the meeting;
  - storming the platform;
  - handcuffing to immovable objects;
  - protests outside the venue; or
  - abseiling from the roof.

The AGM venue

- Ensure that the company's security staff are involved in selecting the venue and co-ordinate with them.
- Can entry to the venue be controlled with limited access points?
- Consider which access routes to the meeting hall are to be used.
- Is there a clear route for the directors to the meeting hall from the venue of any pre-meeting get-together? Can they enter and leave the room by a separate exit which is easily accessible from the stage?
- Is physical security satisfactory?
- Are there any areas which are always open to the public?
- Who else has booked conference facilities on the same day?
- Does the venue have adequate security procedures, e.g. to deal with bomb alerts?
- Does it have a security manager or other in-house security staff?
- Has the venue hosted company meetings before?
- What are the normal arrangements for dealing with disturbances?

- Where does the venue boundary meet the public highway?
- Is there a tannoy system?
- Does it have a controlled car parking area?
- Is it possible to erect barriers at the venue entrance and reception areas to control the flow of attendees?
- Is the reception area large enough to accommodate all attendees before entering the meeting hall?
- Are the toilets inside the secure area or will attendees need to go through security checks each time they enter the hall?
- Check availability of discrete exits to remove demonstrators.
- Are the seats fixed?
- Are the handrails or other fittings removable?
- Are there any balconies or other public areas from which items could be thrown, banners displayed or photographers planted?

Precautions

- Prevent demonstrators erecting banners on the stage by using floral arrangements or guards.
- Thoroughly search the meeting area before commencement of meeting for suspicious objects and then secure until access is opened for the meeting.
- Conduct regular security patrols.
- Consider personal searches, including metal detectors. If detectors or scans are to be used, ensure that trained staff are employed to operate them.
- Consider inspection of baggage and/or barring of baggage from the meeting hall. If baggage is not allowed in, consider providing clear plastic folder for documents.
- Establish a policy on:
  - cameras and videos;
  - recording equipment;
  - mobile telephones; and
  - access for TV/radio crews.
- Display clear notices detailing the items not allowed in the meeting.
- Arrange for secure storage of items not allowed into the meeting.
- Alert venue staff to any person who may be carrying anything unusual.
- Send out invitation cards, either electronic or printed, which must be presented to gain access to the meeting. In the event of failure to produce an invitation, entry to the meeting should only be permitted on production of identification, personal verification by a known third party or, for shareholders, identification on the share register.
- Organise a system of security passes for all attendees and staff.
- Rotate the colour of passes each year.

- Prepare a script for the chair to follow in the event of disruptions, covering ejection of protesters by stewards and/or adjournment of the meeting.
- Use radio mikes to prevent attachment or damage to cables.
- Ensure that radio microphones do not interfere with security radio network and vice versa.
- Use hands-free radios for security guards.
- Have the following equipment available:
  - large bolt cutters
  - solvent for superglue
  - smother blankets for smoke bombs
  - tools to remove handrails.
- Bring spare clothes for chair in case missiles thrown.
- Consider videoing the proceedings.
- Have staff who have received first-aid training standing by.

Demonstrators

- Identify known activists.
- Review recent purchases of small number of shares, paying particular attention to purchases of one share. Obtain details of purchaser (and, if off-market, the transferor) and obtain background information on them if possible (some registrars have compiled a database of shareholders who are known to be connected with certain groups).
- Alert staff on the registration desk of suspects' names.
- Obtain copies of questions if possible.
- Be positive with demonstrators – they will attempt to intimidate or antagonise.
- Consider delaying opening doors to meeting hall until, say, half-an-hour before the start of the meeting. This may prevent potential agitators obtaining pole positions.
- Consider refusing entry to any press not authorised by the company's PR department.
- Protest groups often pre-warn the press. The company's PR department may be able to find out whether this has happened from its press contacts.

Staffing

- If necessary, engage additional security staff and ensure that the security staff includes a number of women. Use well-trained staff.
- Arrange protection for chair, directors and senior executives especially during period of mingling with shareholders.
- If there is risk of violence to the chair or other speakers, access to the rostrum should be restricted by security staff facing the audience.

- Consider the need to have extra security staff available but hidden in the immediate vicinity of the meeting hall.
- Stewards and security staff should be briefed and given a checklist on the arrangements for, and their powers for dealing with, disturbances.
- Place staff on every door leading to the meeting hall and only allow persons with the requisite pass to enter the hall.
- Arrange for venue's own security staff to be present to help in fire or bomb emergencies.
- Consider how security staff (company's own staff, external staff and venue staff) are to be dressed – high or low profile.
- Clearly identify the role of all staff involved.
- Establish with the venue's management that, if necessary, they will deal with the removal of demonstrators from their property to the public highway boundary.
- If staff demonstrations are anticipated, arrange for an industrial relations manager to be available to meet with staff representatives.
- Use staff as fillers to occupy areas of seating and/or form barriers.

Giving notice

There are clear guidelines for providing notice of a general meeting within legislation. In addition, the notices published by listed companies provide an easy reference for the format of notices.

Length of notice

Subject to the exception noted below in relation to traded companies, a general meeting of a private company (other than an adjourned meeting) must be called by notice of at least 14 clear days (s. 307(1)).

Subject to the exception noted below in relation to traded companies, a general meeting of a public company (other than an adjourned meeting) must be called by notice:

- of at least 21 days in the case of an AGM; or
- of at least 14 days, in any other case (s. 307(2)).

The number of days in each case means clear days (s. 360).

A company's articles may specify a longer period of notice than the statutory minimum for any type of general meeting (s. 307(3)). However, unless the members consent to receive short notice in accordance with the statutory requirements, meetings called with less than the notice required by the Act or the articles (if they specify a longer period of notice), will be invalid.

Notice requirements for general meetings of traded companies

Section 307A(1) provides that a general meeting of a traded company must be called by notice of:

- at least 21 days in the case of an AGM; and
- in any other case, at least 14 days if two conditions are met, and at least 21 days if they are not.

The number of days in each case is clear days (s. 360).

The conditions for calling general meetings at 14 days' notice are:

- *Condition A*: that the company offers the facility for members to vote by electronic means accessible to all members who hold shares that carry rights to vote at general meetings. This condition is met if there is a facility, offered by the company and accessible to all such members, to appoint a proxy by means of a website; and
- *Condition B*: that a special resolution reducing the period of notice to not less than 14 days has been passed at the immediately preceding AGM, or at a general meeting held since that AGM.

In the case of a newly incorporated company which has not yet held an AGM, condition B is modified to require only that a special resolution reducing the period of notice to not less than 14 days has been passed (s. 307A(4)).

The articles of a traded company may require a longer period of notice than that specified in subsection (1).

Where a general meeting is adjourned, the adjourned meeting may be called by shorter notice than required by subsection (1). But in the case of an adjournment for lack of a quorum, this exemption applies only if:

- no business is to be dealt with at the adjourned meeting the general nature of which was not stated in the notice of the original meeting; and
- the adjourned meeting is to be held at least 10 days after the original meeting.

The rules in section 307A do not apply in relation to a general meeting of a traded company that is an opted-in company (as defined by s. 971(1)), where:

(a) the meeting is held to decide whether to take any action that might result in the frustration of a takeover bid for the company; or
(b) the meeting is held by virtue of section 969 (power of offeror to require general meeting to be held).

Clear days

Section 360 provides that any reference in the following provisions to a period of notice, or to a period before a meeting by which a request must be received or sum deposited or tendered, is to clear days. A clear day is defined as a period of the specified length excluding the day of the meeting, and the day on which the notice is given, the request received or the sum deposited or tendered:

■ section 307(1) and (2) (notice required of general meeting);
■ section 307A(1), (4), (5) and (7)(b) (notice required of general meeting of traded company);
■ section 312(1) and (3) (resolution requiring special notice);
■ section 314(4)(d) (request to circulate members' statement);
■ section 316(2)(b) (expenses of circulating statement to be deposited or tendered before meeting);
■ section 337(3) (contents of notice of AGM of traded company);
■ section 338(4)(d)(i) (request to circulate member's resolution at AGM of public company);
■ section 338A(5) (request to include matter in the business to be dealt with at AGM of traded company);
■ section 340(2)(b)(i) (expenses of circulating statement to be deposited or tendered before meeting); and
■ section 340B(2)(b) (traded companies: duty to circulate members' matters for AGM).

This provision is not capable of modification by a company's articles in its application to the above provisions. However, a company's articles will often make the same provision and may extend the rule to other requirements in the articles.

Where it is not clear whether a notice requirement means clear days, it is always safer to assume that it does and, subject to any applicable provision of the articles, to apply the formula adopted in section 360.

Date of service

Under the clear days rule, a notice period cannot start running until the day after notice is given. Notice is not given until it has been served on all of the intended recipients (or can be deemed to have been served). The rules concerning deemed service or delivery in this regard are set out in section 1147 of the company communications provisions of the 2006 Act. However, the rules set out in section 1147 are capable of modification by a company's articles and frequently are modified.

Subject to any such modification by a company's articles, section 1147 provides that:

■ notices sent by post which are properly addressed, pre-paid and posted are deemed to be delivered 48 hours after they were posted;
■ notices sent in electronic form that the company is able to show were properly addressed are deemed to have been received by the intended recipients 48 hours after they were sent; and

- notices given via a website are deemed to have been received by the intended recipient when first made available on the website or, if later, when the recipient received (or is deemed to have received) notice of the fact that the material was available on the website.

In calculating the period of hours for the purposes of section 1147, no account may be taken of any part of a day that is not a working day. A 'working day' is defined in section 1173 of the 2006 Act for these purposes as a day that is not a Saturday or Sunday, Christmas Day, Good Friday, or any day which is a bank holiday in the part of the United Kingdom where the company is registered.

The model articles prescribed under the 2006 Act make no separate provision regarding deemed delivery. Accordingly, the provisions of section 1147 apply by default.

Subject to the articles, notices in hard copy form that are handed to the intended recipient or supplied by hand to their address can be assumed to be served immediately. Notices given by advertisement are deemed to have been served the day after the newspaper is published, unless the articles provide otherwise.

Proof of service

The rules in section 1147 regarding deemed delivery and service only apply where the company can show that notices sent by post were properly addressed, pre-paid and posted and that any notices sent in electronic form were properly addressed.

When notices are sent by post, there is, of course, a danger that some may be lost and not delivered. To avoid the possibility of a meeting being invalidated for this reason, articles sometimes provide that proof that an envelope containing a notice was properly addressed, stamped and posted shall be conclusive evidence that the notice was given. When sending out written notices of meetings, it is advisable to obtain and retain a receipt (proof of posting) from the Post Office for this purpose. For companies with large shareholder registers, this may be impractical and an undertaking by the registrars that the proper procedures were followed will probably be sufficient.

With the increasing use of electronic notifications, proof of delivery via electronic means may be obtained by the registrar through keeping records of undeliverable emails that can provide an audit trail of non-delivery. This is preferable to requesting a read receipt of documents, given there is no specific requirements that shareholders read the received information, merely that they have received it and can act on the content if they so wish.

Practical calculation of the timing of notices

The date by which notices should be sent out needs to be calculated carefully in accordance with the above rules to ensure that proper notice is given. If the date of the meeting is already known it is necessary to work backwards from that date to establish the latest date by which the notices should be posted or served. The basic rules are that:

- the statutory period of notice commences the day after the notice has been served or is deemed to have been served on the member; and
- the meeting must be held after the last day of the period of notice required by statute or, if longer, by the articles.

To take an example, a public company which has adopted the model articles in full must post the notice of its AGM at least 24 days before the date of the meeting. If the notices were posted on 1 April they would be deemed to have been served 48 hours later (i.e. on 3 April). The period of 21 days' notice would not commence until 4 April, the first clear day, and would expire on 24 April. The earliest date that the meeting could be held would, therefore, be on 25 April, the first clear day after the notice period has expired.

The same principles would apply to an extraordinary general meeting, and notices would have to be posted a minimum of 17 days before the date of the meeting.

Consent to short notice

The members of a company may consent to receive less than the statutory minimum period of notice required under the Act. Different rules apply as to the majority that is required to consent to short notice depending on the type of meeting that is being held and the type of company that is proposing to hold it.

These concessions are useful where it is not possible to give the minimum period of notice required by section 307(1) or (2) (or by the articles) and where an item of business needs to be expedited quickly. In practice, advantage of the concessions may be taken only by companies with a relatively small number of members.

Separate consent is no longer required to propose special resolutions because the Companies Act 2006 no longer imposes any requirements as to the period of notice that should be given for this type of resolution. However, it may not be possible to give less than 14 days' notice of resolution that is subject to the special notice rules.

It is not necessary for consent to be given in writing. Consent could, for example, be given by a suitably authenticated electronic communication.

Short notice consent – annual general meetings

An AGM of a public company that is not a traded company may be called with less than 21 days' notice if all the members entitled to attend and vote give their consent (s. 337(2)). If accounts are to be laid at the AGM of a public company, consent will probably also need to be given to accept the report and accounts less than 21 days before the meeting. The consent of all the members of a public company is required to do this, whether the accounts are to be laid at the AGM or a general meeting (s. 424(3) and (4)).

The Act makes no provision to enable the AGM of a traded companies (whether public or private) to be held at short notice. Section 337(2) only applies to public companies that are not traded companies.

Short notice consent – general meetings

In the case of any other general meeting of a non-traded company, consent to short notice must be agreed to by a majority in number of the members having a right to attend and vote at the meeting, being a majority who:

- in the case of a private company, together hold not less than 90% of the share capital giving the right to attend and vote at the meeting (excluding any shares held in treasury);
- in the case of a public company, together hold not less than 95% of the share capital giving the right to attend and vote at the meeting (excluding any shares held in treasury); or
- in the case of a private company not having a share capital, together represent not less than 90% of the total voting rights (s. 307(5) and (6)).

It should be noted that the majority required is calculated by reference to the rights of all the members (excluding any treasury shares) and not simply by reference to the rights of those who actually attend the meeting. Where a majority of 95% is required, one member cannot form a majority in number and overrule the minority in this regard. However, a sole member would clearly be able to satisfy the requirements for both AGMs and extraordinary general meetings.

Section 307A, which sets out the notice requirements for general meetings of traded companies (whether public or private), makes no provision to enable meetings of such companies to be held at short notice.

Resolutions subject to the special notice rules

The Act makes no provision for consent to short notice of resolutions requiring special notice, for example a resolution to remove the auditors or a director. This is logical because the special notice requirements are intended to allow the auditors or the director concerned to prepare a statement for circulation to the members. It would appear that the requirement to give at least 14 days' notice of a resolution which requires special notice (see s. 312(3)) would prevent such a resolution from being proposed at a meeting called at shorter notice unless notice of the resolution had been given earlier than the notice of meeting, which would seem impracticable.

Consent to short notice – practical points

In practice, consent to short notice will only be useful to companies with relatively few members (e.g., small private companies and subsidiaries). General meetings of traded companies cannot be called at short notice. It is not necessary for the members' consent to be given in writing. A resolution passed by the appropriate majority at the start of the meeting will suffice. Consent may be given in hard copy or electronic form in accordance with the usual rules under the company communications provisions. It is advisable to obtain the consent of members prior to the meeting. It may prove to be impossible to obtain the necessary majority at the meeting perhaps because some members do not attend or have not submitted proxies. Consent in writing is preferable as a method of proving compliance with the requirements of the Act. Where a meeting has been held at short notice, the minutes should record that fact, together with the fact that consent has been received by the requisite majority or, where applicable, all the members. Any form(s) of consent signed by the members could be entered in the minute book as proof for this purpose. Consents given in electronic form (e.g. by email) could also be printed out and included, or referred to in the minutes.

By consenting to short notice in accordance with the statutory provisions, the members do not consent to receive no notice at all. Some notice, however short, must be given prior to the meeting and that notice must be served in a manner allowed by the articles, unless all the members attend the meeting.

As a final point of detail, notice still needs to be given to any person entitled to receive it who is not entitled to vote at the meeting. This would include the auditors, if any, who have a statutory right to receive any notice of general meeting. Although the Act does not require the agreement of the auditors for a meeting to be held at short notice, it may be advisable to obtain from the auditors a letter of non-objection to the short notice. This may help to avoid any possibility of subsequent objection being taken to the proceedings of the meeting on procedural grounds; companies must send a copy of the notice of all general meetings to the auditors under section 502 and under that provision the auditors have the right to attend all general meetings and to be heard on matters that concern them as auditors.

Form and manner in which notice may be served

The company communications provisions of the 2006 Act (ss 1143 to 1148 and Schs 4 and 5) determine the form and manner in which notices of general meetings may be served. In summary, these allow notice to be given:

- in hard copy form;
- in electronic form, provided the intended recipient has agreed to accept service in this manner;
- via a website, provided the intended recipient has agreed to accept service in this manner (or can be deemed to have agreed); and
- by any other means agreed to by the intended recipient.

Many of the company communications provisions set out in the Act override any contrary provisions in a company's articles, hence they override any provision in a company's articles which state that notice of general meetings must be given 'in writing', which in the absence of any definition in the articles is traditionally interpreted as meaning in hard copy form. This means that any company may serve notice in any manner allowed under the company communications provisions, provided it complies with any of the relevant conditions imposed by those provisions.

The company communications provisions of the Act provide a complete regime for the service of notices and other documents and information. Accordingly, the model articles make no further provision other than to extend the rules, subject to any other provision made in the articles, to 'anything sent or supplied by or to the company under the articles' (pcls 48, clg 34 and plc 79).

The company communications provisions have effect for the purposes of any provision of the Companies Acts that authorises or requires documents or information to be sent or supplied by or to a company (s. 1143(1)). A notice of general meeting is something that is required by the 2006 Act to be sent to certain people by the company (e.g. under s. 310 (members and directors), s. 146 (indirect investors) and s. 502 (auditors)). Accordingly, the company communications provisions have effect with regard to notices of general meetings sent by a company to any of those persons. They will also apply with regard to notices sent to any other person entitled to receive notice under the articles, if they extend the rules to notices sent to such persons.

The only provisions of the company communication provisions that are expressed as being subject to a company's articles are:

(a) section 1147 (deemed delivery of documents and information);
(b) Schedule 5, paragraph 16 (documents and information to be supplied to joint holders of shares or debentures); and
(c) Schedule 5, paragraph 16 (documents and information to be supplied in respect of a deceased or bankrupt shareholder).

It should be noted that, except in the two circumstances in (b) and (c) above, the company communications provisions do not determine to whom notice should be sent and that even in this case those provisions are expressed as being subject to the articles. However, other provisions of the Act do specify who is entitled to receive notice, although in the case of the members, section 310 is capable of modification by the articles.

Nevertheless, many of the company communications provisions can be viewed as being permissive in so far as they allow companies to send notices in certain ways but do not necessarily require them to do so. For example, although a company can send notices by email to members who have agreed to accept service in that manner, it is under no obligation to do so. It must, however, give notice in some manner and the default will be in hard copy form in accordance with the company communications provisions unless the intended recipient has agreed otherwise.

Written notice

If notice is given in writing, it must be given in the manner required for hard copy communications under the company communications provisions of the 2006 Act. Accordingly, written notice must be served either personally or by post. For these purposes a document or information is sent by post if it is sent in a pre-paid envelope containing the document or information to the person. Service by post includes ordinary and registered post and by recorded delivery.

The address which may be used for this purpose is one of the addresses specified in Schedule 5, paragraph 4 of which includes an address specified for this purpose by the intended recipient:

- an address specified for this purpose by the intended recipient;
- to a company at its registered office;
- to a person in his capacity as a member of the company at his address as shown in the company's register of members;
- to a person in his capacity as a director of the company at his address as shown in the company's register of directors; and
- to an address to which any provision of the Companies Acts authorises the document or information to be supplied or sent.

Articles sometimes allow notices to be served by advertisement. This is clearly necessary for companies which allow members to hold shares in bearer form. However, the ability to give notice by advertisement can also be useful in the event of a postal strike. It has been held that a provision in a company's articles which stated that notices shall be deemed to have been served a certain period after posting did not apply where disruption to the postal service was such that placing the letters in a letter-box could not reasonably be expected to result in delivery to members within that time. Public companies are increasingly taking power in their articles to give notice by advertisement in such circumstances. Such articles need to be carefully worded to ensure that they apply where there is only a partial disruption of the postal service. The Listing Rules used to require notices given by advertisement to be inserted in at least one national newspaper. However, this requirement was deleted in January 2000.

Giving notice electronically

Under the company communications provisions of the 2006 Act, a company can give notice of a general meeting via a website or by electronic communications, such as email, notwithstanding any provision to the contrary in its articles, provided that person has agreed (or can be deemed to have agreed) to accept service in that manner.

Persons entitled to receive notice

Notice of a general meeting of a company must be sent to the following persons under the Act:

- every member of the company (s. 310(1)(a)), although this requirement is subject to any enactment and any provision of the company's articles (s. 310(2));
- every person who is entitled to a share in consequence of the death or bankruptcy of a member (s. 310(2)), although this requirement is subject to any enactment and any provision of the company's articles (s. 310(2));
- every director of the company (s. 310(1)(b), although this requirement is subject to any enactment and any provision of the company's articles (s. 310(2));
- the company's auditors, if any (s. 502(2)); and
- in the case of a company whose shares are traded of a regulated market, any indirect investors (s. 146).

Articles do frequently modify the statutory requirement to give notice of general meetings to every member. Where the articles are silent on the matter, notice must be given to every member of the company (s. 310(1)). This does not necessarily include each person who is a joint shareholder (see below). However, it would include members whose calls are in arrears or who are resident abroad, and the holders of all classes of shares whether or not they have a right to attend and vote. Articles usually modify or exclude the rights of these members to receive notice (see below).

Auditors have a statutory right to receive notices of meetings and any other communications relating to any general meeting which a member is entitled to receive (s. 502(2)). An auditor who has been removed under section 510 retains the rights conferred by section 502(2) in relation to any general meeting at which his term of office would otherwise have expired, or at which it is proposed to fill the vacancy caused by his removal. An auditor who has resigned from office under section 516 also retains the rights conferred by section 502(2) in relation to any general meeting requisitioned by him in connection with his resignation and any general meeting at which his term of office would otherwise have expired or at which it is proposed to fill the vacancy caused by his resignation (s. 518(10)).

A listed company must provide information to shareholders on the place, time and agenda of meetings, the total number of shares and voting rights, and the rights of holders to participate in meetings.

Restrictions on right to receive notice

Articles often specify who is entitled to receive notice of general meetings. For example, they may provide that, subject to any restrictions imposed on shares, notice shall be given to all the members, all persons entitled to a share in consequence of the death or bankruptcy of a member, the directors and the auditors. It should be noted that this includes nearly all of the persons required to be given notice by the default statutory provisions. Model articles do not include this language, presumably on the grounds that it would be superfluous to repeat the statutory obligations.

It should be noted that a person may have a right to receive notice but not a right to attend or vote at the meeting. A person may also have a right to attend and vote at a meeting but not to receive notice of it (e.g. a member whose registered address is outside the UK). The following restrictions on the right to receive notice of meetings are commonly found in the articles.

Joint shareholders

Articles often provide that notice sent to the joint holder whose name stands first in the register of members in respect of the joint holding shall be sufficient notice to all the joint holders. Companies often allow joint shareholders to split their holding, if it is capable of being split, so that two or more accounts are entered in the register of members each with a different name as the first named holder. By doing so, each joint holder whose name stands first in one of the accounts in the register is assured of receiving notice of any meeting.

If the articles make no provision as to joint shareholders, then paragraph 16 of Schedule 5 to the Act applies, which provides anything authorised or required to be sent or supplied to joint shareholders may be sent or supplied either to each of the joint holders, or to the holder whose name appears first in the register of members. This statutory provision is expressed as being subject to anything in a company's articles, although it would be unusual for articles to make any provision.

Death or bankruptcy of a shareholder

The default position with regard to persons entitled to a share as a result of the death or bankruptcy is that they should be sent notices (s. 310(2)). This is reinforced by paragraph 17 of Schedule 5 to the Act, which provides that documents or information required or authorised to be sent or supplied to a member who has died or has been declared bankrupt may be sent or supplied to the persons claiming to be entitled to the shares in consequence of the death or bankruptcy by name, by the title of representatives of the deceased, trustee of the bankrupt, or by any like description, at the UK address supplied for the purpose by those so claiming. But until such an address has been so supplied, a document or information may be sent or supplied in any manner in which it might have been sent or supplied if the death or bankruptcy had not occurred. Paragraph 17 is expressed as being subject to anything in the company's articles and includes definitions of bankruptcy for the purposes of the statutory rules.

Persons entitled to a share in consequence of the death or bankruptcy of a shareholder are sometimes referred to as 'transmittees' in articles. Articles normally provide that they are bound by any prior notices served on the member (pcls 29 and plc 68).

Address not within the United Kingdom

A member whose registered address is not within the UK may not be entitled to receive notices unless he has given the company a UK address at which notices may be served. However, electronic transmission of notices may make this exclusion redundant.

Calls unpaid

Articles commonly restrict the rights of members whose calls are in arrears to vote at a general meeting (plc 41). Such members must still be given notice of that meeting unless the articles specify otherwise, although model articles for public companies are silent on this point.

Preference shareholders

It is common for companies with preference share capital to restrict the rights of preference shareholders to receive notice of, attend and vote at general meetings. However, the model articles for public companies make no such provision and any company which intends to issue preference shares and wishes to restrict these rights will need to make provision in its articles accordingly.

Typically, the preference shareholders might be entitled under the articles to receive notice of any general meeting at which it is proposed to wind up the company or where a resolution is to be proposed that will affect the rights and privileges of the preference shareholders. Where the right to receive dividends is cumulative, the preference shareholders will normally be entitled to receive notice of (and to attend and vote at) general meetings if those dividends are in arrears for a specified period (normally six months).

Where preference dividends are payable each year out of profits earned in that year only, it is considered that dividends are not in arrears for a particular year where there were no profits in that year. Accordingly, preference shareholders had no right to receive notice.

Non-voting shares and other classes of share

However, if a separate class of shares is established which gives the holders the right to vote at general meetings, there may be no need to make special provision as to notices under the Act and most articles they would be entitled to receive notices of general meetings anyway. If, however, any class of non-voting shares is established, it would be usual for the articles to exclude the right of the holders to receive notices. This would normally be done in one of the articles which establishes the rights of the holders of that type of share.

Holdings in CREST

Companies whose securities have been admitted to CREST may set a record date for determining entitlement to receive notice of meetings. The date must not be more than 21 days before the date on which the notices are sent out (i.e. the actual date of posting and not necessarily the date of signing shown on the notice). If a company sets such a record date, only those members whose names have been entered on the relevant register of securities at the close of business on that date will be entitled to receive notice (Uncertificated Securities Regulations 1995, 1995/3272, reg. 34). Boards may set a record date by including in their resolution to approve the notice something along the following lines (although no reference needs to be made in the notice itself to this resolution):

> For the purposes of regulation 34 of the Uncertificated Securities Regulations 1995 the members entitled to receive notice of [description of meeting] shall be those entered on the company's register of [members/ other securities] at the close of business on [date].

Special notice

Certain resolutions cannot validly be proposed at a general meeting unless special notice has been given in accordance with the requirements of section 312. Special notice is required by the Act in relation to the following resolutions:

- to remove a director by ordinary resolution before the expiration of his period of office or to appoint somebody instead of a director so removed at a meeting at which he is removed (s. 168);
- to remove an auditor before the expiration of his term of office (ss 510 and 511); and
- resolution at a general meeting of a company whose effect would be to appoint a person as auditor in place of a person (the 'outgoing auditor') whose term of office has ended, or is to end (s. 515).

Any such resolution will be invalid unless notice of the intention to propose it has been given to the company at least 28 clear days before the meeting at which it is to be proposed. Subject to one exception, this is the case whether the resolution is to be proposed by a dissident member or to be included in the notice of a general meeting at the instigation of the board of directors. The exception to the rule is that if after notice of the intention to propose the resolution has been given to the company, a meeting is called for a date 28 days or less after the notice has been given, the notice will be deemed to have been properly given, though not within the time required (s. 312(4)). It should also be noted that, provided it is served at least 28 clear days before the meeting, special notice may be validly served on the company after the notice of meeting has been circulated. The 28-day notice period specified in section 312(1) means clear days by virtue of the application of section 360.

It can be implied from the words used in the Act that special notice must be given to the company by someone who would be entitled to propose the resolution at a general meeting. Plainly, this includes any member, but might also, at a stretch, include the person who will chair the general meeting (usually the chair of the board of directors). However, if the resolution is to be proposed at the instigation of the board, it is infinitely preferable for a member (e.g. a director who is a member) to give the necessary notice to the company.

Company's obligations on receipt of special notice

On receipt of notice of the intention to propose one of the above resolutions, the company must comply with certain additional requirements which differ according to the subject of the resolution. For example, on receipt of special notice of the intention to propose a resolution to remove an auditor, the company must immediately send a copy of the notice to the auditor named in the resolution. The auditor concerned then has a right to have a statement circulated with the notice of the meeting (s. 511).

Where practicable, the company must give its members notice of any such resolution at the same time and in the same manner as it gives notice of the meeting. Where that is not practicable, the company must give its members notice at least 14 clear days before the meeting by advertisement in a newspaper having an appropriate circulation, or in any other manner allowed by the company's articles (s. 312(3). The requirement to give 14 clear days' notice arises by virtue of the application of sections 397 to 312(3).

It would appear that the requirement to give at least 14 days' notice of a resolution which requires special notice would prevent such a resolution from being proposed at a meeting called at shorter notice unless notice of the resolution had been given earlier than the notice of meeting, which would seem impracticable.

There is nothing in section 312 that requires a company to convene a meeting to consider a resolution for which special notice has been given. A public company will eventually need to hold an AGM. However, a private company might never hold a meeting at which such a resolution could be proposed unless the member also gave notice under section 303 requiring it to hold a general meeting for that purpose.

A company is not obliged to include in the notice of the meeting a resolution submitted by a member, or to give members notice of it in any other manner, unless the member who submitted it has also satisfied the conditions of either section 303 (members' power to require the directors to call a general meeting) or section 338 (public companies: members' power to require circulation of resolutions for AGM).

A member who cannot comply with the usual conditions for requisitioning a meeting or an AGM resolution, cannot force the company to include the resolution in the notice of the meeting or to give notice of it in any other manner. A company may, of course, choose to include the resolution on the agenda even though the member has not satisfied these conditions and, if it does, it must allow the member to propose the resolution at the meeting.

The Act makes no provision for a penalty in the event of a failure by the company to give notice of the resolution in accordance with section 312. It is not particularly clear whether a resolution subject to the special notice rules can be proposed if the company has not given notice of it to the members in accordance with section 312. Section 312(4) rectifies any failure on the part of a member to give special notice of the intention to propose the resolution at least 28 clear days before the meeting where, after receiving the special notice from the member, the company calls a meeting for a date 28 clear days or less after it received the special notice. In other words, it prevents a company from manipulating the requirements of section 312 to avoid any obligation it may otherwise have to give notice of the resolution. It should also be borne in mind that if such a resolution were to be requisitioned under section 338 in relation to the AGM of a public company, it would be an offence for the company to fail to give notice of it in accordance with the requirements of that section.

Circulation of members' statements

The members of both public and private companies may require the company to circulate to its members a statement of not more than 1,000 words with respect to a matter referred to in a proposed resolution to be dealt with at a general meeting or any business to be dealt with at the meeting (s. 314). The statement could be made by members in connection with a meeting or resolution requisitioned by them or in connection with an item of business proposed by the directors.

The member or members making the request must represent at least 5% of the total voting rights of all the members who would be entitled to vote on the resolution at the AGM (excluding any rights attached to treasury shares). Alternatively, the requisition will also be valid if made by at least 100 members who would have the right to vote on the resolution and hold shares on which there has been paid up an average sum, per member, of at least £100.

The request may be made in hard copy or electronic form, must identify the statement to be circulated, must be authenticated by the person or persons making it, and must be received by the company at least one week before the meeting to which it relates (s. 314(4)). The requirements of section 360 regarding clear days' notice apply for the purposes of the request by members. In practice this means that a company need not comply with such a request unless it is received at least seven clear days before the meeting.

On receipt of a valid request, the company must send a copy of the statement to every member entitled to receive notice of the meeting in the same manner and at the same time as, or as soon as reasonably practicable after, it gives notice of the meeting (s. 315(1)).

Cost of circulating a statement

A public company must bear the costs of circulating the statement if it relates to the company's AGM and is received before the end of the financial year preceding the meeting (s. 316(1)). In all other cases, a company need not circulate the statement unless those requesting the resolution deposit or tender within the time limit for making a valid request a sum reasonably sufficient to meet the company's expenses in circulating the statement (s. 316(2)). It should be noted that the requirements of section 360 regarding clear days' notice also apply for the purposes of determining whether the members have deposited or tendered the necessary sum. In practice this means that they will need to do so at least seven clear days before the meeting.

Although a requisition requiring a statement to be circulated can be deposited after the notice has been sent out, the cost of circulating it at this late stage will obviously be greater, even if primarily distributed electronically. Unless the directors agree to waive the costs of circulating a statement, those requesting the resolution will have no choice but to pay them. If the requested statement is deposited at least six weeks before the meeting, they could, however, also request a resolution proposing that the company bears its own costs in giving effect to the requisitioned statement.

It should be noted that as an alternative to requisitioning a statement under section 314, any member may (on payment of the prescribed fee) demand a copy of the company's register of members and use the names and addresses of the members to circulate a statement to all or part of the members. This may well be cheaper if it is only necessary to target, say, shareholders holding more than 5% of the company's equity. However, it should be noted that requirements under legislation for the protection of data, such as the General Data Protection Requirements (GDPR) would also need to be accommodated in the release of such information.

Abuse of rights under section 314

If the court is satisfied that the rights conferred by section 314 are being abused it may, on the application of the company or any other aggrieved person, order that the company is not bound to circulate any such statement and that those requesting the resolution pay the whole or part of the company's costs on such an application, even if they are not parties to the application (s. 317).

Accidental failure to give proper notice

Unless all the members actually attend, the failure to give proper notice to any person entitled to receive it invalidates the meeting. However, the Act provides that accidental failure to give notice of a general meeting or a resolution intended to be moved at a general meeting to one or more persons shall be disregarded for the purpose of establishing whether notice of the meeting or resolution (as the case may be) is duly given (s. 313(1)). Except in relation to notice given under section 304 (notice of meetings required by members), section 305 (notice of meetings called by members) and section 339 (notice of resolutions at AGMs proposed by members), this rule is capable of modification by a company's articles.

On the whole, articles do not particularly seek to modify this rule but may include provisions which have largely the same effect. Such an article may serve to validate a meeting for which notice had not been given to several members because the address plates for those members had inadvertently been separated from the rest because their dividends had been returned uncashed.

However, a deliberate failure to send a notice to a member will not be validated even if the company had reason to believe that the notice would not reach the member at his registered address. Once it is shown that some members were not given notice, the onus lies with those claiming that the meeting was valid to show that the omission was accidental.

Some companies have adopted articles which provide that a member shall not be entitled to receive notice if on the three most recent occasions on which they were sent documents by the company, they were returned undelivered, unless they have subsequently confirmed their address or notified a new address.

Articles commonly provide that a member present, either in person or by proxy, at any meeting of the company or of the holders of any class of shares shall be deemed to have received notice of the meeting and of the purposes for which it was called. Even without such a provision a member who was present and voted at a meeting of which irregular notice had been given may be deemed to have acquiesced in the irregularity.

Failure to deliver notices in electronic form may be avoided by tracking delivery without receipt of an undeliverable response. Keeping an audit trail of such responses, as well as validating these against those details provided by members, would also provide evidence that the notice had been sent with good faith to addresses provided.

Contents of notice

Notice of a general meeting must include:

- the name of the company (reg. 6(1) of the Companies (Trading Disclosures) Regulations 2008 (SI 2008/495);
- the type of meeting (e.g. whether the meeting is a general meeting or an AGM in accordance with s. 337(1) or a class meeting) (see below);
- the time and date of the meeting (s. 311(1)(a));
- the place of the meeting (s. 311(1)(b));

- the general nature of the business to be dealt with at the meeting (s. 311(2)(a)) (in relation to a company other than a traded company, this requirement has effect subject to any provision of the company's articles;
- the full text of any resolution to be proposed as a special resolution (s. 283(6)), extraordinary resolution (s. 378, 1985 Act), elective resolution (s. 379A, 1985 Act), or as an ordinary resolution for which special notice is required (s. 312(2));
- state on whose authority it is issued, for example the board, requisitioning members, court, etc. and the name of the person who signed it on their behalf, for example the name of the director or secretary;
- be dated; and
- include with reasonable prominence a statement of a member's right to appoint a proxy under section 324 and any more extensive rights conferred by the company's articles to appoint more than one proxy (s. 325(1)).

At least one copy of the notice should be signed by or on behalf of the person or body under whose authority it is issued. In practice, it is normally signed and dated by the secretary or one of the directors above the words 'By order of the board'. The original signed copy should be retained by the company for evidential purposes. Copies of the notice sent to shareholders do not need to be signed but should include the name and position of the person who signed it on behalf of the board. It is helpful if the notice can be dated for the day on which it is to be posted or the advertisement is to be placed. However, this is not strictly necessary and will not always be possible in view of the fact that it should be dated for the day on which it is actually signed.

Although the Act and most articles only require the notice to specify 'annual general meetings' as such, it is plainly sensible to specify 'general meetings' as such. Although the Act no longer uses the term 'extraordinary general meeting', some articles still specify that any meeting other than the AGM shall be known as such. Where this is the case, it is sensible to describe the meeting in the notice as an 'extraordinary general meeting'. Where the articles do not make such provision, it is probably better to refer to the meeting as a 'general meeting', although the word 'meeting' would probably also suffice; the assumption being that it must be a general meeting if it is not specified as an AGM. Plainly, the words used to describe a class meeting should attempt to define the class of members that will be meeting and should not be described as a general meeting.

A notice will be invalid if it states that the meeting will only be held in certain pre-determined circumstances (e.g. on the passing of a resolution by members of a different class) unless the articles specifically allow such notices to be given. However, resolutions may be included in the business of a meeting which are contingent upon other events.

Notices may be required by the Act to be accompanied by certain statements. In the case of a listed company, the issuer must provide information to holders on the total number of shares and voting rights and the rights of holders to participate in meetings (DTR 6.1.12R).

Additional content requirements for publicly traded companies
This paragraph sets out the additional content requirements for notices of meetings issued by companies that are publicly traded. Any company subject to these rules must also comply with the requirements set out above.

Additional requirements of the Act for traded companies
The Act imposes a number of additional requirements on traded companies. A traded company is defined for these purposes in section 360C.

Under section 311(3), every notice of general meeting of a traded company must include:

(a) a statement giving details of the website on which the information required by section 311A (traded companies: publication of information in advance of general meeting) is published;

(b) a statement that the right to vote at the meeting is determined by reference to the register of members and of the time when that right is determined in accordance with section 360B(2);

(c) a statement of the procedures with which members must comply in order to be able to attend and vote at the meeting (including the date by which they must comply);

(d) a statement giving details of any forms to be used for the appointment of a proxy;

(e) a statement of the procedure for doing so (including the date by which it must be done and details of any forms to be used) where the company offers the facility for members to vote in advance (see section 322A) or by electronic means (see s. 360A); and

(f) a statement of the right of members to ask questions in accordance with section 319A (traded companies: questions at meetings).

Under section 337(3), if the AGM notice of a traded company is given more than six weeks before the meeting, the notice must include a statement regarding members' rights under section 338A to require the company to include a matter (other than a resolution) in the business to be dealt with at the meeting and, if the company is a public company, a statement of members' rights to propose resolutions under section 338.

Any notice of meeting of a traded company must state the general nature of business of the meeting (s. 311(2)(a)).

Example: RNS Notice on London Stock Exchange or Publication of AGM

1   Notice of AGM

Released 16:25 23-Mar-2020

 PHOENIX GROUP

RNS Number : 2654H
Phoenix Group Holdings PLC
23 March 2020
LEI: 2138001P49OLAEU33T68

PHOENIX GROUP HOLDINGS PLC
2019 Annual Report and Accounts and 2020 AGM

Phoenix Group Holdings plc (the 'Company') has today posted to shareholders the following documents:

- 2019 Annual Report and Accounts
- Notice of 2020 AGM
- Form of Proxy for the 2020 AGM

In accordance with Listing Rule 9.6.1, a copy of each of these documents has been submitted to the UK Listing Authority via the National Storage Mechanism and will shortly be available for viewing at www.morningstar.co.uk/uk/nsm.

Copies of these documents will also be available later today on the company's website at www.thephoenixgroup.com.

The Company's AGM will be held at Saddlers' Hall, 40 Gutter Lane, London, EC2V 6BR on Friday 15 May 2020 at 10.00 a.m. (British Summer Time).

Warnings for indirect investors

If a listed company is required under section 146 to send a notice of meeting to an indirect investor, the version of the notice sent to that person must state that they may have the right to be appointed as a proxy by the registered shareholder, and that they may be able to give voting instructions to the registered shareholder (who would then aggregate the votes and lodge them with the company) (s. 149(2)). The word 'may' has to be used as it is at the discretion of the registered shareholder whether to offer any of these voting facilities.

Furthermore, under section 149(3) the standard proxy statement in any notice of general meeting, which tells the registered shareholder that he can appoint a proxy, must either:

(a) be omitted from the version sent to indirect investors; or
(b) contain the statement that it does not apply to them.

Note on possible audit concerns: quoted companies

Under section 529, a quoted company must, in any notice of a meeting which is to be held as the accounts meeting, draw attention to the possibility of a statement being placed on a website pursuant to members' requests under section 527, that members may make such a request free of charge, that a copy of any such statement will be forwarded to the company's auditors and that any published statement will form part of the business which may be dealt with at the meeting.

Members satisfying the requirements of section 527 may require a quoted company to publish on a website a statement relating to the audit of the company's accounts which are to be laid before the next accounts meeting (including the auditor's report and the conduct of the audit) or, where applicable, any circumstances connected with an auditor of the company ceasing to hold office since the previous accounts meeting at which accounts were laid. Should a valid request for the publication of such a statement be received, the company must, within three working days of receipt, publish the statement on a website and forward a copy of it to its auditors. Any statement published on a website under these rules forms part of the business which may be dealt with at the next accounts meeting.

Companies with securities admitted to CREST

A company whose securities, both equity and debt, have been admitted to CREST, may specify in the notice a time by which a person must be entered on the relevant register of securities in order to have the right to attend and vote at the meeting (Uncertificated Securities Regulations 2001, reg. 41 (SI 2001/3755)). This may not be more than 48 hours before the time fixed for the meeting, although in calculating this limit, no account need be taken of any part of a day that is not a working day. It should be noted that the effect of this rule is almost identical to section 360B(2) of the Act (which applies to traded companies only). The only difference between the two provisions is that the former applies to a potentially wider range of companies (including AIM companies whose securities have been admitted to CREST).

Both provisions allow a snapshot of the register to be taken at a particular point prior to the meeting to be used for the purpose of verifying attendance and voting rights at the meeting. This is necessary because CREST operates on a real-time basis, which means that the dematerialised part of the register can alter right up to the meeting and during its course.

Wording in any notice should also include provisions concerning possible adjournment. This is necessary because the cut-off point for the original meeting would not necessarily apply on an adjournment – the cut-off point for the adjournment could not, under the Uncertificated Securities Regulations, be more than 48 hours before the time of the adjourned meeting.

The Uncertificated Securities Regulations also allow companies whose securities have been admitted to CREST to establish a record date for the purposes of determining entitlement to receive notice of a meeting. This date must be not more than 21 days before the date on which the notices are sent out (i.e. the actual date of posting – not just the date of signing shown on the notice).

In order to take advantage of this concession, the board of such a company should, when approving the notice of meeting, include in its resolution something on the following lines:

> For the purposes of regulation 41 of the Uncertificated Securities Regulations 2001 the members entitled to receive notice of [the AGM for 20...] shall be those entered on the company's register of members at the close of business on ..... 20...

No reference needs to be made in the notice itself to this aspect.

The company should agree the date to be stated in the resolution with its registrars (which should, of course, be the date at which the registrars will be preparing their label run for the meeting notice mailing).

To avoid possible legal disputes, it would be advisable for such a board resolution to be passed even if, as a courtesy, the company sends copies of the notice of meeting to persons who are only entered on the register during the notice period preceding the meeting.

Additional content requirements under the Listing Rules and the Disclosure and Transparency Rules

A notice of general meeting is a 'circular' for the purposes of the Listing Rules. Accordingly, it must comply with the requirements for circulars in Chapter 13, including the basic requirements for all circulars and any specific requirements for notices, some of which depend on the business to be transacted.

A listed company must provide information in the notice of any general meeting on the total number of shares and voting rights and the rights of holders to participate in meetings (DTR 6.1.12R). This is useful for anybody who is appointed as a proxy as it helps them to calculate whether they have a notifiable voting interest (3% or more) for the purposes of DTR 5.

Information to be published on a website by a traded company before a general meeting

Section 311A requires a traded company to publish the following information on a website before any general meeting:

- the matters set out in the notice of the meeting;
- the total numbers of shares in the company, and shares of each class, in respect of which members are entitled to exercise voting rights at the meeting; and

- the totals of the voting rights that members are entitled to exercise at the meeting in respect of the shares of each class.

The matters must be made available on the website throughout the period beginning with the first date on which notice of the meeting is given and for a period of two years thereafter (s. 311A(4)). Members' statements, members' resolutions and members' matters of business received by the company after that date must be published as soon as reasonably practicable and be available on the website for the remainder of that period (s. 311A(4)). The number of shares and voting rights must be ascertained at the latest practicable time before the first date on which notice of the meeting is given (s. 311A(6)).

Failure to comply with the requirements of section 311A regarding website publication is an offence but does not affect the validity of the meeting or of anything done at the meeting (s. 311A(7)–(9)).

Notice of the business

Section 311(2) requires a company to state in any notice of a general meeting the general nature of any business to be transacted at that meeting, but allows this rule to be modified by a company's articles if the company is not a traded company. Most articles which make any provision in this regard also require notices to state the general nature of the business to be transacted, although it is not uncommon to find articles that distinguish between 'ordinary business' and 'special business' in this regard. The requirement for the notice to state the general nature of the business was not included in any previous Companies Acts. However, it could be said to represent what was the position under the common law. Accordingly, previous common law cases will still be highly influential in determining whether a company has complied with the requirement.

It should be noted that, under the common law, the adequacy of the notice regarding the explanation of the business is judged separately for each item of business. If no explanation and no notice of the business is included in a notice of meeting, it is possible that the whole of the notice could be declared invalid. However, the fact that the explanation for one item is found to be inadequate does not necessarily mean that the whole notice would be declared invalid or that the other items of business could not be properly transacted.

The requirement to state the general nature of the business should not be viewed simply as a requirement to state the text of the resolutions. It is not necessary to give the exact text of the resolutions to be proposed at a general meeting in the notice, unless specifically required by the Act, for example in relation to special resolutions and ordinary resolutions that require special notice. It is possible to state the general nature of the business without stating the exact text of the resolutions. Although it is normal to give the text of the resolutions in the notice, it is important to understand that this may not necessarily suffice for the purposes of the requirement to state the general nature of the business. Some sort of explanation of the business may also be required. Under the common law, the notice must give a 'fair and candid and reasonable explanation' of the purposes for which the meeting is called.

Notices are not construed with excessive strictness and their content will depend on the particular facts in each case. The test the courts apply is what the notice would fairly convey to an ordinary person. In determining the validity of the notice the courts often apply the absent shareholder test. In that would a shareholder on reading the notice understand its content sufficiently to confidently leave the decision to the majority vote or, conversely, could the content be misleading or unclear in its content to such an extent that the absent shareholder is unaware of what they have left to the majority vote.

Common law recognises the concept of an explanatory circular. Indeed, it has been suggested that it is desirable to supplement the notice with an explanatory circular where the business is complex or important. Where a circular is sent with the notice, it will normally be read in conjunction with the notice in order to determine whether adequate notice of the business has been given. The same is true of the directors' report and accordingly any other document sent with the notice.

Business which has not been sufficiently notified or which is substantially different from that notified cannot be validly transacted. However, amendments which are relevant to, and arise fairly out of, an item of business of which notice has been given may be proposed at the meeting (e.g. a notice 'to elect directors' is sufficient for the meeting to elect directors up to the number permitted by the articles even though the notice only named one director). However, amendments may not generally be made to the substance of resolutions proposed as special, extraordinary or resolutions requiring special notice.

The business actually carried out must substantially correspond to what was included in the notice. If notice is given of a single resolution which contains more than one proposal, it is not possible to adopt only part of it, because it is impossible to know how many shareholders were satisfied with the arrangement as proposed and, therefore, who abstained from attending the meeting. Where notice is given of a meeting to consider resolutions for reconstruction and for winding up as incidental thereto, and only a resolution to wind up was passed, it would be held to be invalid as it resulted in a position fundamentally different from that contemplated by the notice. However, where the notice specified several separate resolutions and one of those was to wind up the company, that resolution would be effective even though the other resolutions which were concerned with the sale of the undertaking and consequent reorganisation, would be found to be ultra vires and, therefore, void. The difference between these two cases is that in the first the notice implied that a resolution to wind up would only be passed as part of the whole reconstruction. In the second, the notice of the resolution to wind up was capable of standing in its own right. It follows that if it is intended to make a resolution contingent on the passing of another resolution, this should be done either by combining the two proposals in one resolution or clearly stating in the notice that the resolution is (or resolutions are) contingent upon the passing of another resolution(s).

Best practice would always to be to combine inter-twined resolutions as one resolution, therefore requiring all or none to be passed. Where resolutions stand independently, the notice should differentiate each resolution so that they can be passed as stand-alone items with all or some only being passed.

Distribution of price sensitive (inside) information

The Disclosure and Transparency Rules (DTR) impose a general obligation on the part of listed companies to notify a Regulatory Information Service (RIS) as soon as possible of any inside information that directly concerns it as an issuer unless it is entitled to delay disclosure (DTR 2.2.1). Inside information is defined for these purposes in section 118C of the Financial Services and Markets Act (FSMA) 2000 as information of a precise nature that:

(a) is not generally available;
(b) relates, directly or indirectly, to the issuer; and
(c) would, if generally available, be likely to have a significant effect on the price of its securities.

A company may delay disclosure of inside information under DTR 2.5.1 so as not to prejudice its legitimate interests provided that:

(a) such omission would not be likely to mislead the public;
(b) any person receiving the information owes the issuer a duty of confidentiality, regardless of whether that duty is based on law, regulations, articles or contract; and
(c) the issuer is able to ensure the confidentiality of the information.

For the purposes of applying DTR 2.5.1, legitimate interests may, in particular, relate to negotiations where the outcome or normal pattern of the negotiations could be affected by public disclosure and decisions or contracts made by the management body that need the approval of another body of the issuer in order to become effective (DTR 2.5.3).

The DTR include formal guidance on various aspects of a listed company's obligations of disclosure, including specific guidance on the meaning of inside information (see DTR 2.2.3–2.2.10).

The UKLA has also published informal advice on good practice for dealing with inside information – see List! Issue 9 (July 2005) which states (at para. 3):

3.1 We encourage issuers to make the most of opportunities to communicate with investors. An issuer may reinforce its corporate messages in non-technical terms and provide indicators of its future direction through its annual report, the chair's address to the AGM, a web-cast or a conference call.

3.2 If a meeting is to be held (e.g. with shareholders, analysts or a press conference), issuers should consider in advance how to respond to questions designed to elicit inside information. While the AGM is an opportunity for investors to discuss with directors issues affecting the company, arrangements should be made for any inside information that is to be discussed at the meeting to be included in an announcement via a Regulatory Information Service (RIS) at or before the start of the meeting. If inside information is inadvertently released, the issuer should fully disclose it in line with DR2.6.2R.

In order to comply with these requirements, it is usual for listed companies to release a copy of the chair's address via their RIS immediately prior to the meeting, particularly where this includes updated trading information. However, this will not be necessary if the chair merely recites information already published in the annual report. It may also be necessary to release the text of any presentations to be made by operational managers. As these presentations and the chair's address will be prepared before the meeting, it will be possible to take advice from the company's advisers on the action which should be taken where there is any doubt, although most listed companies probably err on the side of disclosure these days.

The rules prohibiting the selective disclosure of price sensitive information also tend to inhibit the ability of directors to answer shareholders' questions at general meetings. Indeed, they are sometimes accused of emasculating one of the main purposes of the AGM (i.e. to enable shareholders to hold the directors accountable for their stewardship of the company). This feeling may have arisen amongst shareholders because directors often cite these rules as the reason for not answering certain questions even though commercial confidentiality is probably the primary reason. The acid test in this regard is whether the directors would have answered the question if there were no rules on the release of price sensitive information. In most cases, the answer would probably be no.

Nevertheless, the DTR do impose limitations on listed companies which are predisposed towards answering shareholders' questions. And the main problem which the directors will face is trying to decide at the meeting whether the answer which they would like to give would constitute price sensitive/inside information.

Issuers must establish effective arrangements to deny access to inside information to persons other than those who require it for the exercise of their functions within the issuer (DTR 2.6.1). They must also have in place procedures that enable public disclosure to be made via an RIS as soon as possible in the event of a breach of confidentiality (DTR 2.6.2).

If in the course of a general meeting, previously unpublished price-sensitive/inside information is inadvertently disclosed, it will, of course, be necessary for a listed company to make an announcement as soon as possible. It should also be noted that the results of resolutions taken at general meetings may in themselves be price sensitive information, particularly where a resolution has been defeated. A listed company must notify an RIS as soon as possible after a general meeting of all resolutions passed by the company (other than resolutions concerning ordinary business passed at an AGM) (Listing Rule 9.6.18) and must send copies of all resolutions (other than those concerning ordinary business) to the Financial Conduct Authority (FCA) without delay after the relevant meeting (Listing Rule 9.6.2).

Ordinary and special business

Some companies may still have articles which distinguish between ordinary and special business. These are usually based on regulation 52 of the 1948 Table A which defines special business as any business

> that is transacted at an extraordinary general meeting, and also all that is transacted at an annual general meeting, with the exception of declaring a dividend, the consideration of the accounts, balance sheets, and the reports of the directors and auditors, and the election of directors in the place of those retiring and the appointment of, and the fixing of the remuneration, of the auditors.

Any resolution which is not special business will be ordinary business.

Regulation 50 of the 1948 Table A provides that in the case of special business the notice shall specify 'the general nature of that business'. Thus, it must give a 'fair and candid and reasonable explanation' of the business to be transacted and give all material information to enable it to be understood.

No such requirement exists with regard to ordinary business and the effect of such provisions is to enable notice of AGMs to be given without setting out the nature of the ordinary business. The members are assumed to know that matters of ordinary business may be dealt with at the meeting by virtue of the articles.

In practice, most companies with such articles specify the nature of both ordinary and special business in any notices. Indeed, although articles may distinguish between ordinary and special business, they may still require the general nature of ordinary business to be specified in the notice. Whether or not this is the case, it would be impracticable for a listed company to do otherwise. This is because section 311(2) specifies that a traded company must specify the general nature of the business in the notice. In addition, the form of proxy sent to members must allow them to instruct their proxy how to vote on all resolutions intended to be proposed at the meeting (Listing Rules, para. 13.28), and it would be confusing for members if resolutions were included on the proxy form but not in the notice.

Premium listed company notice requirements

Any circular that a company with a premium listing of equity shares sends to holders of its listed securities must comply with the requirements of Chapter 13 of the Listing Rules (LR 13). A circular is defined for the purposes of the Listing Rules in the Handbook Glossary as

> any document issued to holders of listed securities *including notices of meetings* but excluding prospectuses, listing particulars, annual reports and accounts, interim reports, proxy cards and dividend or interest vouchers.

The requirement to send a circular arises most frequently in connection with matters that require shareholder approval, whether under the Act or the Listing Rules. Every notice of meeting sent to shareholders is a circular. As such, every notice of meeting must comply with the basic requirements for circulars in LR 13. One of those requirements is that the notice must be accompanied by an 'explanatory circular'. LR 13 sets out the minimum disclosures that should be made in the 'explanatory circular'.

The general purpose of the Listing Rules in this regard is to ensure that the purpose and effect of any business proposed at a meeting is properly explained and that shareholders are given all necessary background information.

Types of approved circulars

Specifically, LR 13. 2.1 states that a listed company must not circulate or publish any of the following types of circular unless it has been approved by the FCA:

1 a class 1 circular; or
2 a related party circular; or
3 a circular that proposes the purchase by a listed company of its own shares which is required by n LR 13.7.1R(2) to include a working capital statement; or
4 a circular that proposes a reconstruction or a refinancing of a listed company which is required by n LR 9.5.12R to include a working capital statement; or
5 a circular that proposes a cancellation of listing which is required to be sent to shareholders under n LR 5.2.5R(1); or
6 a circular that proposes a transfer of listing which is required to be sent to shareholders under n LR 5.4A.4R(2).

Contents of circulars

Every circular sent by a listed company to holders of its listed securities must (LR13.3.1):

(a) provide a clear and adequate explanation of its subject matter giving due prominence to its essential characteristics, benefits and risks;

(b) state why the security holder is being asked to vote or, if no vote is required, why the circular is being sent;

(c) if voting or other action is required, contain all information necessary to allow the security holders to make a properly informed decision;

(d) if voting or other action is required, contain a heading drawing attention to the document's importance and advising security holders who are in any doubt as to what action to take to consult appropriate independent advisers;

(e) if voting is required, contain a recommendation from the board as to the voting action security holders should take for all resolutions proposed, indicating whether or not the proposal described in the circular is, in the board's opinion, in the best interests of security holders as a whole;

(f) state that if all the securities have been sold or transferred by the addressee the circular and any other relevant documents should be passed to the person through whom the sale or transfer was effected for transmission to the purchaser or transferee;

(g) if new securities are being issued in substitution for existing securities, explain what will happen to existing documents of title;

(h) not include any reference to a specific date on which listed securities will be marked 'ex' any benefit or entitlement which has not been agreed in advance with the RIE on which the company's securities are or are to be traded;

(i) if it relates to a transaction in connection with which securities are proposed to be listed, include a statement that application has been or will be made for the securities to be admitted and, if known, a statement of the following matters:

– the dates on which the securities are expected to be admitted and on which dealings are expected to commence;

– how the new securities rank for dividend or interest;

– whether the new securities rank equally with any existing listed securities;

– the nature of the document of title;

– the proposed date of issue;

– the treatment of any fractions;

– whether or not the security may be held in uncertificated form; and

– the names of the RIEs on which securities are to be traded.

(j) if a person is named in the circular as having advised the listed company or its directors, a statement that the adviser has given and has not withdrawn its written consent to the inclusion of the reference to the adviser's name in the form and context in which it is included; and

(k) if the circular relates to cancelling listing, state whether it is the company's intention to apply to cancel the securities' listing.

Further specified information is required for circulars of a particular type and are in addition to the above core requirements. These include, but are not limited to, meetings to acquire or dispose of property, allot shares, amend employees' share schemes and appoint independent directors.

Submission of documents

All listed companies, not just those that are premium listed, must forward to the FCA, for publication through the document viewing facility, two copies of all circulars, notices, reports or other documents to which the Listing Rules apply, at the same time as any such documents are issued (LR 14.3.6(1)).

The role of the company secretary

Preparation for an annual general meeting of a public company

As well as the routine business of AGMs outlined above, it is also routine business for companies with the appropriate provision in their articles to pass an ordinary resolution giving authority to the directors to offer shareholders the option to receive the whole or any part of their dividends in new ordinary shares rather than in cash.

Other items of non-routine business, for example alteration of articles, should be described in a separate circular to members dispatched with the notice of the meeting.

The venue for the meeting will probably have been fixed several months in advance, and the date of the AGM included in the programme of board meetings for the year and previously approved by the directors. Following receipt of the audited accounts, the following matters should be undertaken by the company secretary.

- It is quite common for the report and accounts to incorporate the notice of the meeting as well as the chair's statement. Three proof copies of the booklet containing the notice of meeting and the accounts will be required, and all three copies will require signature for each of the reports.
- Send another copy of the report and accounts with the names of the signatories and dates printed within it to the company's printers for a final proof prior to running off the bulk supply for dispatch to shareholders.
- Advise the company's registrar (either the company's own in-house registrar or a firm of service registrars) of the amount of the recommended dividend, if any, in order that they may prepare the dividend warrants for dispatch to shareholders following approval at the AGM.
- If a dividend is to be paid, the company should also arrange with its bankers for a dividend account to be opened, in which the money required to pay the dividend will be placed.

- Prepare proxy forms for dispatch with the report and accounts to shareholders. These can be either separate cards inserted in the booklet or a tear-out page in the booklet.
- The report and accounts will normally be sent directly to shareholders by the company's printers. They should be instructed as to the date on which posting should take place and whether the document is to be sent by first- or second-class post. The names of the signatories on the bulk printed supply should be printed in exactly the same way as the original signatures on the three signed copies (e.g. 'Albert Smith' and not 'A. Smith').
- One of the three signed copies of the report and accounts booklet will be placed in the company's directors' board minute book, one copy will be retained by the company's auditors and the third copy will be sent to the Registrar of Companies. The signed copy of the report and accounts for the Registrar of Companies could be sent either at the same time that these are dispatched to members or at a later date, within the time allowed by section 442.
- It is usual to invite the company's solicitor to attend the meeting. The company's auditors are entitled to attend under section 502(2).
- The forms of proxy returned by shareholders should be checked against the register of members. A report on the result of the proxy count should be made available for the board after the expiry of the deadline for receipt of proxies (usually 48 hours before the time of the meeting).
- Consider the preparation of ballot papers in case a poll is demanded (for more detail, see below). It might be prudent to do this if many proxy cards have been returned with votes against any particular resolution(s).
- If the chair is going to make remarks at the meeting, additional to those contained in their statement in the report and accounts, prepare copies to give to the company's press agents at the meeting and, for Listed, AIM or NEX companies, to send simultaneously to a regulatory information service (see DR 2.2.1).
- A copy of the register of members should be available at the AGM. This is required in case it is necessary for persons attending the meeting to be identified, to ensure only those entitled to attend are present.
- Provide attendance sheets for shareholders, the press, proxies and representatives of corporate shareholders who are attending the meeting under authority of section 323.
- Make available for inspection copies of the directors' service contracts.
- Prepare an order of proceedings, setting out the various resolutions to be passed at the meeting. There is no requirement for resolutions to be seconded and it is perfectly in order for the chair of the meeting to propose all resolutions with no seconder.
- From the outset, always bear in mind practical considerations, such as making room bookings in good time, checking catering arrangements and finding out whether a photographer or video-conferencing facility is needed.

Conclusion

This chapter has provided extensive detail of the requirements needed to hold a meeting, including the practicalities of calling a meeting as well as the preparation and support for the chair prior to the meeting.

An attendee's right to attend has also been covered to reflect those that are invited to attend and those that should be excluded. All members have a right to attend, even if they only hold one share, albeit that such a shareholding would have little effect on any of the proceedings. Small shareholdings may reflect contentious activists so this chapter also covered in some detail elements of security required for some companies in relation to physical meetings given they can be an opportunity to showcase dissent not just of the company but frequently the sector in which they operate or their practices relating to their community or the environment.

Notice requirements and distribution of materials prior to the meeting have also been explained capturing the practical actions that need to be undertaken before the day of the actual meeting.

15 – At the general meeting

This chapter provides further detail on actions taken during the general meeting including:

- the appointment of the chair and their required actions during the meeting;
- quorum;
- corporate representatives;
- proxies;
- voting;
- the right to attend and speak;
- shareholder remedies in the case of dissent;
- adjournment;
- other procedural motions;
- amendments; and
- dealing with common items of business.

Appointment of the chair

Formal appointment of a chair for the meeting is the first agenda item for all meetings, despite the fact that the chair of any meeting will have worked with the company secretary and any other advisers in setting the agenda for the meeting.

Given the importance of the role, it is common for the articles to determine who should chair the general meeting rather than leave it open to appointment at the outset or rely on voting by attending members, albeit that members have a residual right to elect a chair at each meeting as well as the ability to remove a chair not appointed under the articles.

The authority, role and responsibility of the chair are relatively clear, however, there are specific requirements detailed under law and under model articles that are required to be adhered to.

In addition, there are specific requirements if a chair is to be removed either during or after a meeting and before any adjourned meeting.

A general meeting cannot proceed without a chair for legal and practical reasons. There must be an individual to lead on the agenda, put motions to the meeting, declare the results of voting, and rule on points of order.

The Act includes two specific provisions regarding the appointment of a chair, both of which are expressed as being subject to any provision of a company's articles:

(a) a member may be elected to be the chair of a general meeting by a resolution of the company passed at the meeting (s. 319); and

(b) a proxy may be elected to be the chair of a general meeting by a resolution of the company passed at the meeting (s. 328).

A corporate representative would also be entitled to act as the chair of a general meeting under this default statutory regime on the basis that any such representative is entitled to exercise the same powers on behalf of the corporation as the corporation could exercise if it were an individual member of the company (s. 323(2)).

Articles usually provide an alternative regime for the appointment of the chair. They normally provide for general meetings to be chaired by the person (if any) who has been appointed as chair of the board of directors, but also make provision for another person to be appointed if the chair of the board is not present or is unwilling to act (pcls 39, clg 25 and plc 31). In the following example taken from the model articles for private companies limited by shares, references to 'the chair' are to 'the chair of the board':

31.(1) If the directors have appointed a chairman, the chairman shall chair general meetings if present and willing to do so.

(2) If the directors have not appointed a chairman, or if the chairman is unwilling to chair the meeting or is not present within ten minutes of the time at which a meeting was due to start—

(a) the directors present, or

(b) (if no directors are present), the meeting, must appoint a director or shareholder to chair the meeting, and the appointment of the chairman of the meeting must be the first business of the meeting.

(3) The person chairing a meeting in accordance with this article is referred to as 'the chairman of the meeting'.

It can be seen that articles normally allow the directors to decide who will chair general meetings and it is unusual for anyone other than a director to be chosen by them to do so. The only occasion on which the members would normally get to elect a chair is where there are no directors present or willing to act. Where no director is willing to chair the meeting, articles often require a 'member' or 'shareholder' to be appointed or elected to act as chair. It is somewhat surprising that the model articles prescribed under the 2006 Act use this formula in view of the default provision in section 328 which states that a proxy may do so, subject to anything in the company's articles on the matter. The words 'member' or 'shareholder' in the model articles would appear to exclude the possibility that a proxy may be appointed. However, it is submitted that this is not necessarily the case. It has been held that the word member (or shareholder) must include a proxy where the articles say that proxies can be counted in calculating whether there is a quorum and only proxies are present. There is no particular reason to suppose that a proxy could not also chair the meeting if duly elected to do so even if there were members present. In the same case, it was held that a person who is neither a member, corporate representative or a proxy may take the chair at the start of the meeting to preside over the election of a chair. However, the court held that the rulings of such a person (who in this case was largely self-appointed) were liable to challenge in the courts irrespective of anything contained in the articles (e.g. on the validity of any votes tendered in the election process).

Any objection to the appointment of a chair at a meeting should be made immediately as any irregularity in the nomination may be cured by the acquiescence of those present.

Removal of the chair

A chair elected by the meeting, for example when no director is present or willing to act in that capacity, may subsequently be removed by a motion of no confidence in the chair. If such a resolution is proposed, the chair should step down until the result of the vote is determined.

Where the chair is appointed in accordance with the articles, the removal of the chair by attendees is not possible as their removal would result in them being reappointed under the terms of the articles.

Chair's duties

The individual appointed as the chair of the meeting is deemed to have been given authority by the meeting to regulate its proceedings. As this is a form of delegated authority, the chair must still act in accordance with the wishes of the majority at the meeting, unless exercising a power conferred by statute or the company's articles of association, or one which the courts have ruled can be exercised by the chair without reference to the members (e.g. the power to adjourn to restore order).

The chair has an overriding duty to act in good faith in the best interests of the company and is formally responsible for:

- the proper conduct of the meeting;
- the preservation of order;
- ensuring that all views are given a fair hearing; and
- ensuring that the content of the meeting is properly recorded.

Proper conduct of the meeting

The chair must ensure that the meeting is conducted in accordance with the requirements of the Act, the company's articles of association and any applicable common law rules, and will normally be guided in this respect by the company secretary and other formal advisers.

The chair should not open the meeting before the time specified in the notice and should, as far as possible, ensure that the meeting starts on time and that all the business on the agenda is transacted. The start of the meeting can be delayed in certain circumstances, the most obvious is where there is no quorum, with the delayed start enabling the attendance by latecomers. The chair can also legitimately delay the meeting to allow members who arrived on time to register and gain admittance. In general, best practice is to limit any delay to a maximum of 30 minutes. Issues requiring longer to be resolved should be dealt with via an adjournment, which is implemented through the start and immediate adjournment and close of the meeting (see section later in this chapter on Adjournment).

The chair may rule on any question raised from the floor relating to the conduct of the meeting. If their decision is challenged, the matter should be put to the meeting and decided by the majority of those present. It is relatively unusual for matters to get to this stage because either the chair or the objectors will often give way if they sense that the mood of the meeting is against them. Any formal vote on such matters would normally be decided on a show of hands by a simple majority. If that vote went against the chair, or was inconclusive, they could consider calling a poll, assuming they have power to do so under the articles.

If the chair conducts the meeting in a certain way or makes a ruling that is not challenged at the meeting, the members present may be deemed to have acquiesced or consented to that conduct. In *Carruth v Imperial Chemical Industries Ltd* [1937] AC 707, the directors convened an extraordinary general meeting of the company and two meetings of different classes of shares to be held on the same day and at the same venue to approve a reduction of capital. As one meeting finished, the next meeting started and each meeting was attended by each of the different classes of member. The resolution of one class of members was challenged on the ground that people who were not members of that class were present at the meeting. The resolution was held to be valid and Lord Russell said:

> There are many matters relating to the conduct of a meeting which lie entirely in the hands of those persons who are present and constitute the meeting. Thus it rests with the meeting to decide whether notices, resolutions, minutes, accounts, and such like shall be read to the meeting or be taken as read; whether representatives of the press, or any other persons not qualified to be summoned to the meeting, shall be permitted to be present, or if present, shall be permitted to remain; whether and when discussion shall be terminated and a vote taken; whether the meeting shall be adjourned. In all these matters, and they are only instances, the meeting decides, and if necessary a vote must be taken to ascertain the wishes of the majority. If no objection is taken by any

constituent of the meeting, the meeting must be taken to be assenting to the course adopted.

It should be noted that certain procedural matters have to be dealt with by a formal resolution and that it is preferable to deal with procedural matters that may be critical to the outcome of the meeting as a formal resolution. This topic is discussed further later in this chapter in relation to procedural motions, adjournments and amendments.

The chair cannot close the meeting until all the business has been dealt with. In *National Dwelling Society Ltd v Sykes*, the chair wrongly refused to accept an amendment to a resolution to receive the report and accounts and closed the meeting before all the business had been transacted. The members elected another chair to transact the unfinished business and adjourned the meeting. It was held that the chair had acted outside his powers by closing the meeting without its consent before the business had been completed and that the meeting could go on with the business for which it had been convened and appoint another chair to conduct that business.

Fair hearing of opinions

The chair should seek to ensure that all members who hold different views on a resolution before the meeting are given a fair hearing. To do otherwise would defeat one of the objects of holding the meeting. In particular, the chair should not curtail the debate unless the minority has had a reasonable opportunity to put its views.

The amount of time that should be made available for debate will vary depending on the nature of the business and the number of people wishing to speak on it. This does not mean that the discussion should be allowed to go on forever. Shortly before closing the debate, the chair should ask members to refrain from speaking unless they have a different point to make. Although it not an easy thing to do without causing offence, the chair should at this point cut short any speaker who is repeating a point made earlier in the debate in order to ensure that those with different views are given a fair hearing. When the chair considers that a full range of views have been expressed, they may seek to curtail discussion and put the resolution to a vote. If any member objects, the chair could seek the consent of the meeting by proposing a formal 'closure motion', that the question before the meeting be now put to the vote (see Appendix 2 for an example of a chair's script). However, the chair may be justified in putting the resolution to the vote without obtaining the consent of the meeting if the minority have been given a fair hearing and/or the members present are filibustering (trying to prevent the completion of the business of the meeting). This is only sensible if the chair is confident that he has the support of the majority or that the resolution would be carried (or defeated, as the case may be) on a poll, if one was called.

Sense of the meeting

The chair has a duty to ensure that the sense of the meeting is properly ascertained with regard to any question which is properly before the meeting. In doing so the chair should put resolutions to a vote, ensure that the votes are properly counted and declare the results of that vote.

In order to prevent issues regarding the precise number of votes cast for and against the resolution being reopened after the meeting, section 320 provides that a declaration by the chair of the result of a show of hands is conclusive evidence that the resolution has or has not been passed, or passed with a particular majority, without proof of the number or proportion of the votes recorded in favour of or against the resolution (s. 320(1)). In addition, an entry in the minutes of a general meeting in respect of a declaration by the chair as to the result of a show of hands is conclusive evidence of that fact without such proof (s. 320(2)).

Every company is required to produce and keep minutes of all proceedings of general meetings. The directors can be fined for any default by the company of the provisions of the Act relating to the maintenance of minutes. The chair can be said to have a special duty in this regard in so far as minutes signed by the chair of the meeting are evidence of the proceedings.

Chair's powers

The chair is given the following powers under statute and the general law:

(a) to make a conclusive declaration of the result of any vote taken on a show of hands;
(b) to make rulings on the conduct of the proceedings;
(c) to adjourn the meeting for the purpose of restoring order;
(d) to adjourn the meeting to facilitate its conduct or to conduct a poll; and
(e) to order the ejection of members who are disrupting the proceedings.

In addition, a company's articles of association may give the chair power to:

(a) call a poll;
(b) rule conclusively on the validity of any votes tendered at the meeting;
(c) rule conclusively on the validity of proposed amendments; and
(d) make security arrangements for general meetings.

The articles may also purport to give the chair a casting vote in the event of a tie. Such a power cannot be exercised in relation to a meeting of a traded company and may not be valid for other types of company. The chair should seek clarification before the meeting as to whether there are any circumstances in which he may exercise any such power.

Additional chairs

Where a meeting is held at more than one location, it will be necessary from a practical perspective for someone to be appointed to facilitate or chair the proceedings at any of the other locations. It would also be advantageous if that person could be given certain powers that assist in the conduct of the proceedings and the maintenance of order at those subsidiary proceedings.

It is probably within the chair's power to delegate some aspects of his authority for these purposes without any specific provision being made in the company's articles. In the case of the model articles, the directors are given power to make whatever arrangements they consider appropriate to enable those attending a general meeting to exercise their rights. However, some companies have decided to make specific provision with regard to the powers of additional chairs.

Where a meeting is also being held virtually, the chair should ensure they have direct communication during the meeting with the individual tasked with ensuring the online broadcast aligns to the physical meeting and the virtual attendees can contribute.

Quorum

The quorum is defined as the minimum number of attendees entitled to vote who must be present or represented at a meeting in order for it to transact any business (being present may also include presence via electronic methods if the company's articles allow it).

The minimum number of members to be present is usually stated in the articles of the company. By default, where no number is specified therein reference should be made to the Companies Act, which states that there should be two (unless there is only one member, see Chapter 20). As an example, model articles for private companies limited by shares do not specify the quorum for general meetings although, conversely, they do specify the quorum for a meeting of directors – care must be taken to reference the correct quorum needed for the type of meeting being held.

Example: The reference to quorum in all three Model Articles

Quorum for General Meetings

No business other than the appointment of the chair of the meeting is to be transacted at a general meeting if the persons attending it do not constitute a quorum.

In this example the quorum would, by default, be that specified in the Companies Act 2006 section 318, namely:

'In any other case, subject to the provisions of the company's articles, two qualifying persons present at a meeting are a quorum, unless—

(a) each is a qualifying person only because he is authorised under section 323 to act as the representative of a corporation in relation to the meeting, and they are representatives of the same corporation; or

(b) each is a qualifying person only because he is appointed as proxy of a member in relation to the meeting, and they are proxies of the same member.'

The quorum is distinct and separate from the votes entitled to be cast or counted when a vote of a specific resolution is held (see Voting later in this chapter).

A proxy attendee, representing a member, is counted as a representative, unless the articles state otherwise. Where an attendee is representing more than one member, their attendance will be counted once for each member they are representing. Hence, while a visible count of attendees may indicate that a quorum has not been reached, the attendance by an individual representing more than one member would negate the visible headcount and could reflect that a quorum has been met. However, it should be noted that a meeting cannot be held with only one attendee, even if that attendee is the representative of, or has a proxy for, multiple members (unless there is only one member, see Chapter 20).

Articles usually require a meeting to be automatically adjourned if a quorum is not met within a certain time after the stated start time of the meeting, unless there have been multiple adjournments or the meeting is being held by court order. Equally, the quorum should be maintained throughout the meeting.

It should be noted that, in counting a quorum, each individual is representing a shareholding, they are not representing each share. Hence, for example, a proxy of a member at the meeting counts in the quorum as the same single attendee as a representative of a corporate member, no matter what their respective shareholding. Share ownership itself is relevant when the actual votes are taken (see later in this chapter).

Who may be counted in the quorum?

For the purposes of confirming a quorum, a 'qualifying person' means:

(a) an individual who is a member/shareholder of the company;
(b) a person authorised to act as the representative of a corporate member in relation to the meeting; or
(c) a person appointed as proxy of a member/shareholder in relation to the meeting.

It should be noted that, where two or more attendees are representing the same corporate member or have been appointed as the proxy of the same member/shareholder, then their attendance would be counted as a single representative.

Accordingly, any member, corporate representative or proxy may be counted in the quorum unless a company's articles provide otherwise.

A secondary query is whether a member must also be entitled to vote to be counted as part of the quorum. Under common law, to be counted in the quorum, a person must first and foremost be eligible to vote. However, a member may be ineligible to vote for a variety of reasons or may be eligible to vote for only part of their shareholding. These specifics are covered under Voting (see below). For the purposes of counting the quorum, an attendee should be counted if they hold at least some shares with voting rights, unless the quorum is required for a specific class of shares which the attendee neither holds nor represents.

More than one person

A quorum may exist even though the actual number of attendees is less than the number specified as the quorum by the articles. This is because a person may represent more than one member (e.g. an attendee may be representing more than one member as a representative or proxy or may be in attendance in their own capacity as well as acting on behalf of others, such as being a trustee).

However, this rule is subject to the basic common law principle that for a meeting to take place there must be at least two people in attendance. Thus, a meeting attended by only one member who held proxies for all the other members would be invalidly constituted. Similarly, where a company's articles provided that two or more members present in person or by proxy shall be a quorum, one member present in his own capacity and in his capacity as the first-named trustee for holdings under a trust and as proxy for another member would not constitute a valid meeting.

The exception to the requirement to have at least two attendees is where there is only one shareholder (see Chapter 21) or if it has been held in relation to specific share classes where there is only one holder of all the class shares. In this latter case, this does not apply where all the shares in a public company fall into the hands of a single member. In these circumstances the correct procedure would be for the member to transfer at least one share into the name of another person (normally a nominee) so that a meeting may be held. If this is not possible, an application should be made to the court for an order that a meeting may be held with a quorum of one.

Failure to obtain a quorum

There will invariably be times when a quorum is not met at a meeting which negates the ability for the meeting to start, let alone for any resolutions to be approved. In some cases, a quorum for a specific item may not be met where a differently defined quorum is required, such as a resolution for specific classes of shares. Alternatively, the initial quorum may not be maintained throughout the meeting due to attendees departing.

What happens if there are not sufficient attendees to form a quorum at the time appointed for the start of the meeting? How long should the start of the meeting be delayed to enable attendees to arrive so that a quorum can be obtained? What happens if it is not? Is the meeting automatically dissolved or can it be assumed to have been adjourned? These are questions that are normally, but not always, answered in a company's articles.

Example: Model Articles

Adjournment

If the persons attending a general meeting within half an hour of the time at which the meeting was due to start do not constitute a quorum, or if during a meeting a quorum ceases to be present, the chair of the meeting must adjourn it.

Practically, the adjournment of a meeting through lack of a quorum is implemented by the chair of the meeting. Hence the meeting is formally opened, albeit with a noted start time 30 minutes after that originally scheduled to accommodate late arrivals. The first action will be to appoint a chair of the meeting. The chair will then note that the meeting has been adjourned to a subsequent date, time and place, or to a date, time and place to be specified by the directors subsequent to this adjourned meeting. Creating formal minutes of this adjourned meeting, signed by the chair, will create a simple but beneficial audit trail of the adjournment through lack of quorum which then enables any future review to easily identify the reason for a subsequent meeting being called.

It is not particularly clear what happens if nobody turns up at all, or if nobody who turns up has power to adjourn the meeting because they were not appointed or elected as the chair of the meeting. It is probable that in any of these circumstances the meeting could be deemed to have been either dissolved or adjourned indefinitely to a date, time and place to be determined by the directors. And subsequently communicated to all members.

If the meeting continues without a quorum being present, any business transacted at such meeting could be subsequently challenged and potentially over-ruled, thus negating the meeting and its outcomes. Hence, ensuring that the quorum is present is a necessary process that should be completed at each formal meeting of members.

The quorum required for the adjourned meeting will be the same as for the original meeting. However, it is not unusual for this rule to be modified so that if, at the adjourned meeting, a quorum is not present within a certain time, the members present will form a quorum, unless there is only one member present.

As a last resort, if it has become impossible to obtain a quorum to transact the required business, a company can apply for a court order to call a meeting without a quorum. However, in this extreme example, care should be taken to ensure that this is not being used as a way to circumvent the approval of resolutions by a quorum of members as this could lead to greater legal challenge and risk.

Failure to maintain a quorum

For all meetings, a quorum must be present for each item of business throughout the meeting.

This implies that a meeting should be automatically adjourned if, during a meeting, the quorum is no longer in place. However, practical application may enable that a quorum should be maintained until such time as any agenda items requiring member voting is complete. Practically, the absence of a quorum following completion of such items, with only housekeeping remaining on the agenda, may not require a continued quorum and would be difficult to challenge as would a temporary absence of a quorum during non-voting resolutions. The latter may occur where the quorum is close to its minimum limit and one or more attendee(s) has to step out of the room temporarily. The chair may or may not want to note the absence and subsequent meeting of a quorum in the minutes, depending on the stage of the meeting agenda or the item(s) being discussed. Best practice would be to note any temporary absence of a quorum to avoid any potential future claim of being inquorate.

An alternative to a temporary mid-meeting lack of quorum, is to adjourn for a brief period to allow the members to address any outside business, before convening again after such brief respite.

In an attempt to avoid this issue altogether, articles sometimes provide that a quorum need only be present at the time when the meeting proceeds to business requiring a vote. This type of article allows for temporary absences and also prevents a dissenting minority obstructing the transaction of business by leaving the meeting once they realise things are not going their way. It would obviously serve little purpose to have such an article unless the quorum is higher than two.

Abuse of quorum requirements

In extreme circumstances, if a minority shareholder attempts to frustrate the will of the majority by refusing to attend a meeting, thereby preventing the formation of a quorum, the company may seek court direction to order the holding of a meeting and direct that the quorum for that meeting shall be less than the number normally required. The court will only do so where the quorum is a fixed number of shareholders and the minority shareholder's ability to prevent the holding of meetings is merely a consequence of the number of shareholders there are at that time. It will not do so where the articles specifically provide that a meeting shall not be quorate without the presence of that shareholder (see below).

Seeking court redress to hold a meeting with a reduced quorum should not be seen as an opportunity to proceed with a meeting without full notice to all shareholders or as an opportunity to circumvent full member consideration of the resolutions.

Special quorum requirements

The quorum requirements can be used to protect the interests of certain shareholders. The articles, or a shareholders' agreement, may provide that a quorum shall not exist unless a particular member or the holder of particular class of shares is present.

These special requirements can also be restricted to certain types of business decisions, such as the appointment and removal of directors. Such provisions will usually be framed so that they attach special rights to a certain class of shares. The courts have held that where they apply to a named shareholder, that shareholder will be treated as having class rights which may not be modified unless the proper procedures for variation are followed.

Corporate representatives and proxies

Corporate representatives and proxies effectively fulfil the same function, attending meetings on behalf of members to vote on their behalf. In practice, they represent two distinct categories of members:

- A corporate representative represents the interest of corporate members; while
- A proxy represents the interests of individual members at a meeting.

These should not be confused with the role of a trustee attending a meeting to represent shares held under a trust to which they are appointed and for which they would vote in relation to the best interests of the beneficiaries of the trust.

Equally, they are not the same as an attendee with power of attorney who may, or may not, have the authority to attend a meeting but would have personal discretion to vote on any matters. In general, members should only appoint either a proxy or a corporate representative to attend a formal meeting if they are unable to attend themselves.

Both a proxy and a corporate representative serve the same purpose in enabling a member to exercise their right to vote on any resolutions set to members at a meeting despite them being unable to attend the meeting in person. The main difference between the actions of these two agents is that the appointment of a corporate representative does not have to be notified in advance.

This section will walk through both the requirements for a proxy and that of a corporate representative.

Corporate representatives

A company which is a member of another company (e.g. an institutional investor) clearly cannot attend and vote in person at general meetings. In order to place them on the same footing as individual members, a corporation which is a member of another company is allowed to appoint one or more persons to act as its representative(s) at any meeting of the company (s. 323). This right is also extended to class meetings by virtue of sections 334 and 335. A person so appointed by a company is usually known as a corporate representative.

The right to appoint a corporate representative is extended by section 323 to any corporation that is a member of a UK company. For these purposes, a corporation includes any corporate body (whether or not a company within the meaning of the Companies Act 2006) which has separate legal personality. This includes overseas companies but does not include a corporation sole or a partnership that, whether or not a legal person, is not regarded as a body corporate under the law by which it is governed (s. 1173).

Appointment of corporate representatives

A corporation may appoint a person as its corporate representative by a resolution of its board of directors or other governing body (s. 323(1)). For these purposes, the words 'other governing body' can include a liquidator (*Hillman v Crystal Bowl Amusements and Others* [1973] 1 WLR 162, CA).

Unlike the appointment of a proxy, the Act is relatively brief on the appointment of a corporate representative, limited to one section.

Section 323 Representation of corporations at meetings

1   If a corporation (whether or not a company within the meaning of this Act) is a member of a company, it may by resolution of its directors or other governing body authorise a person or persons to act as its representative or representatives at any meeting of the company.

2   Where the corporation authorises only one person, he is entitled to exercise the same powers on behalf of the corporation as the corporation could exercise if it were an individual member of the company.

3   Where the corporation authorises more than one person, any one of them is entitled to exercise the same powers on behalf of the corporation as the corporation could exercise if it were an individual member of the company.

4   Where the corporation authorises more than one person and more than one of them purport to exercise a power under subsection (3)— (a) if they purport to exercise the power in the same way, the power is treated as exercised in that way, (b) if they do not purport to exercise the power in the same way, the power is treated as not exercised.

There is no formal requirement for a corporation to deposit a form of appointment prior to the meeting. The articles of listed companies normally specify that a corporate representative may be required by the company to produce evidence of his authority on admission or at any time during the meeting or in connection with the exercise of any right to vote on a poll.

Precedent: Article on corporate representative

Any corporation which is a member of the company may by resolution of its directors or other governing body authorise such person as it thinks fit to act as its representative at any meeting of the company, and any person so authorised shall be entitled to exercise the same powers on behalf of the corporation which he represents as that corporation could exercise if it were an individual member of the company, but such representative may be required to produce evidence of such authorisation on admission or at any time during the meeting or in connection with the exercise of any right in respect of such meeting, including without limitation participation in a poll on any resolution. Any such authorisation in writing purporting to be signed by an officer of or other person duly authorised for the purpose by the said corporation shall be conclusive evidence of the authority of the representative to act on behalf of the corporation.

Even though a company's articles may not make specific provision in this regard, a company can and should take steps to ensure that those who attend and vote are eligible to do so. For individual shareholders and creditors, proof of identity will be sufficient for these purposes. Clearly this will not be enough in the case of a corporate representative who must, in addition, be required to provide evidence of their authority, otherwise it would be possible for anyone to turn up off the street and claim to be a corporate representative.

Evidence of appointment should be produced by the representative on entering the meeting, unless it has previously been lodged. As it would appear that a resolution of the board of directors of the member company or other governing body is required, the evidence could be provided in the form of a certified copy of the relevant resolution. The resolution can be authenticated (certified) by any director, secretary or other authorised officer of the company.

The appointment of a representative may relate to a specific meeting or, as is commonly the case, may be of more general application.

Precedent: Board minute of member company authorising a representative

It was resolved:

THAT [name A] or, failing him, [name B] or, failing her, [name C] be appointed, pursuant to section 323 of the Companies Act 2006, to act as the company's representative at any meeting of the members or creditors of other companies in which the company is or may become interested as a member or creditor.

or

It was resolved:

THAT the following persons be appointed, pursuant to section 323 of the Companies Act 2006, to act as the company's representative at the general meeting of [name of company] to be held on [date] (or any adjournment thereof) in respect of the number of shares shown next to their respective names:

[name A], or failing him, [name B]	12,000 shares
[name C]	24,000 shares
[name D] and [name E] jointly	30,000 shares
[name F]	over the balance of the company's holding.

In practice, registrars will accept a letter certifying the appointment provided it was an original, on the registered member's stationery and signed by an authorised signatory. It further suggests that, for the sake of clarity, such a letter would be expected to state the name of the registered shareholder as it appears on the share register. It should also give the designation (if any) of the shareholder's account, confirm the name of the appointee, state the date that the board resolution was passed and the number of shares to be voted if less than the total holding.

Precedent: Letter appointing corporate representative

[Headed notepaper of company making the appointment]

[Date]

To the Directors of [name of company]

Confirmation of appointment of corporate representative

It is hereby certified that the person or persons named below were appointed by a board resolution of the above-named company dated [date] pursuant to section 323 of the Companies Act 2006 to act as the company's corporate representative(s) at the [annual] general meeting of [name of company] to be held on [date] in respect of the number of shares shown next to their respective names.

Names	Number of shares
[corporate representative A]	23,090
[corporate representative B]	the balance of our holding

It is hereby certified that the authority of any person appointed to act as the company's corporate representative other than those named above, and any evidence of that person's authority, is [hereby revoked/shall continue to have effect] in respect of the abovementioned meeting.

Signed

[Director/Secretary/Authorised Officer]

[The above letter must be an original, on the registered member's stationery and signed by an authorised signatory.]

Who may be appointed

A person appointed as a corporate representative need not be a member of the company. One might have thought, however, that the Act would require the person appointed to be an individual rather than another company, but this is not the case. The Act allows any 'person' to be appointed, which includes another company, although any such company will no more be able to attend meetings than the original corporate member. The fact that it does so may require a more liberal interpretation of the powers of a corporate representative because the only way a corporate representative that is a company could exercise the powers of the member would be if it was itself able to appoint individuals as representatives to act on its behalf, possibly as proxies or corporate representatives. If this is not the case, the appointment of another company as a corporate representative would be totally ineffective.

Rights of corporate representatives

Under section 323(1), a corporate member may authorise a person to act as its corporate representative 'at any meeting of the company'. Where the corporate member authorises only one person as its corporate representative, that person is entitled to exercise the same powers on behalf of the corporate member as the corporate member could exercise if it were an individual member of the company (s. 323(2)). This is also generally the case where more than one representative is appointed, although the rule is subject to certain modifications.

It should be noted that the powers that the corporate representative may exercise under the Act are not the general powers of the member but the powers that the member could exercise 'at any meeting of the company' if it were an individual member of the company.

There is no doubt whatsoever that these powers include the power to attend, speak, propose resolutions (including procedural resolutions and amendments to resolutions), chair the meeting, vote on a show of hands or on a poll, and to join in a demand for a poll. These are all things that can be done at the meeting.

A corporate representative must also be counted as a member for the purposes of calculating whether there is a quorum.

It is less clear whether a corporate representative can exercise powers that are incidental to the meeting, such as the right to appoint a proxy or, if the corporate representative appointed by the member is itself a company, appoint a corporate representative. The appointment of a proxy or corporate representative is normally something which a member must do before the meeting rather than 'at the meeting'. While true that this could not be done, best practice would be to accept any such appointment made at the meeting by a formally appointed corporate representative.

To avoid any potential uncertainty, it would be preferable for the corporate member to confer express authority on its corporate representative in this regard. This is sometimes done by granting a power of attorney to the corporate representative. Unless something like this is done, the corporate representative may find it difficult to satisfy a request from the company holding the meeting for evidence of authority, particularly in relation to the appointment of a proxy, where articles tend to be more specific. If the corporate representative is unable to provide such evidence, the company could argue that the corporate member ought to take steps itself to appoint a proxy or a different corporate representative. Assuming that there is still time to do so, this could be viewed as a sensible course of action on the part of the company. If there is not, the company chair might need to be asked to make a ruling on the validity of the appointment (and any votes cast under it).

Multiple corporate representatives

The 2006 Act was drafted with the deliberate intention of enabling the appointment of multiple corporate representatives. This is something that was not thought possible under the Companies Act 1985. By allowing multiple appointments, the 2006 Act ensures, for example, that a nominee company holding shares for a number of underlying investors can appoint a different person to represent each underlying holding if so desired.

Subsequent revisions further clarified the rights of multiple corporate representatives under the Companies (Shareholders' Rights) Regulations 2009 (SI 2009/1632) with effect from 1 August 2009 (see below under 'Designated corporate representative').

A person authorised by a corporation is entitled to exercise (on behalf of the corporation) the same powers as the corporation could exercise if it were an individual member of the company (s. 323(2)). This rule generally applies where the corporation has appointed one or more representatives but is subject to the following modifications where more than one representative is appointed.

The first modification is that, on a vote taken on a show of hands, each authorised person has the same voting rights as the corporation would be entitled to (s. 323(3)). Thus, if the corporate member would have been entitled to vote on a show of hands, so will each of its corporate representatives, with each one having the same number of votes as the corporate member (i.e. normally one each). If the corporate member would not have been entitled to vote on a show of hands, neither will any of its corporate representatives.

The second modification is that, in any case other than a vote on a show of hands, where more than one corporate representative for the same member purports to exercise a power under section 323(2) in respect of the same shares, that power is treated as exercised if they purport to exercise it in the same way as each other but not if they purport to exercise the power in different ways to each other (s. 323(4)).

It is important to recognise that a power will only be treated as not exercised if the representatives exercise it in different ways over the same shares. If a corporate member appoints multiple representatives but each one represents a different block of shares, they may each validly exercise their powers in different ways. However, if any of them represent the same holding, and more than one of them attempts to exercise any of the members' powers, they must exercise those powers in the same way. It should be noted that in these circumstances it is not necessary for them to exercise the member's powers jointly. Any one of them may validly exercise the member's powers as long as the others do not attempt to exercise those powers in a different way.

Designated corporate representative

It should be noted that section 323 was amended on 1 August 2009 by the Companies (Shareholders' Rights) Regulations 2009 (SI 2009/1632) and did not originally clarify that each representative has a vote on a show of hands or that any other powers which multiple corporate representatives purported to exercise in different ways would only be invalid if they were exercised over the same shares.

The original wording of section 323 caused concern among institutional shareholders as it was thought that the possibility of multiple representatives' votes being treated as void could prevent the practice of treating designated accounts as separate shareholders for the purposes of voting and prevent different corporate representatives being appointed to represent a different part of a pooled account.

It is recommended that shareholders who wish to appoint multiple representatives should do so as proxies rather than corporate representatives. Under the 2006 Act, shareholders may appoint multiple proxies, each of whom may now speak and vote on a show of hands (as well as a poll) at meetings, and the only advantage provided by the appointment of a corporate representative is that they may register at the meeting itself and do not need to be notified in advance.

Proxy

A proxy is a person appointed by a member of a company, to attend, speak and vote on their behalf at a meeting of the company (including any adjournment) but for no other purpose. The proxy does not have to be a member of the company, an employee or relative of the shareholder. The proxy may also be a named function rather than an individual (e.g. the proxy may appoint the chair of the meeting to vote on their behalf).

Where a member owns multiple share classes, they may appoint more than one proxy to represent them for each class of shares, as long as it is clear which shares each proxy is representing. They may also split their ownership in a single share class amongst multiple proxies, again as long as it is clear which shares are being presented by each proxy.

The word 'proxy' is commonly used to describe the person appointed by a member, the form for the appointment sent to members and the votes held by a proxy (e.g. those held under proxy by the chair of the meeting). Only the first of these is strictly correct. A proxy is a person appointed by a member to attend and vote on their behalf. To avoid confusion, the instrument of appointment can be referred to as the 'proxy form' and votes cast by a proxy as 'proxy votes'.

Rights of proxies

Proxies have a statutory right to attend, speak and vote on behalf of the members who appointed them and also have the right to ask for or join in a call for a poll. The right to attend will, however, be subject to the usual rules on ejection in cases of severe disorder.

Given the purpose of their appointment, a proxy must attend the meeting in person in order to vote. Equally, if the meeting is adjourned, their appointment as a proxy continues to be valid for the subsequent meeting, unless the articles of the company specifically request a new proxy form to be submitted for any subsequent meetings. The model articles do not have this requirement.

Historically, proxies were entitled to vote on a poll but not on a show of hands. The restriction on voting on a show of hands was normally imposed by a company's articles and not by anything in the Companies Acts. The default position under the 2006 Act is that proxies have a statutory right to vote on a show of hands but that this right is subject to any provision of the company's articles.

In practice, a vote, either by a show of hands or verbally, is used at the meeting where the expectation is for the outcome to be clear (e.g. in relation to housekeeping of a company). Where the outcome of a resolution is expected to be contentious or close, a poll should be used. The difference is that a vote will evidence the decision of the quorum as a collective. A poll will take into account the various shares held by those appointed.

Confusion may occur where a proxy is representing the interests of more than one member with such member's votes to be cast opposingly. However, given the use of a vote by show of hands is unlikely to be contentious this should not be an issue. More recent advances in electronic voting at meetings may allow for a greater use of polls and the ability of a proxy representing multiple members to be able to vote according to their individual requests.

Statement in the notice of the meeting

A statement must be included with reasonable prominence in the notice of every meeting of a company which informs the members of their statutory right to appoint a proxy (or proxies) under section 324 and of any other more extensive rights conferred by the company's articles to appoint more than one proxy (s. 325). The statement is usually positioned at the end of the notice and must either be omitted or modified in any version of the notice sent by a listed company to anyone nominated as an indirect investor.

Invitations to appoint a proxy

The Act does not require companies to send proxy forms to members, although listed companies are required to do so under the Listing Rules. Notices of meetings convened by the court are normally required by the court to be accompanied by proxy forms. A company's articles could also require proxy forms to be circulated with the notice of any meeting, although this is very rare.

Any company may, however, issue proxy forms to members at the company's expense. Generally, any expenses incurred in good faith in the best interests of the company to secure votes in support of the directors' policy are payable out of the funds of the company. Thus, the directors may send proxy forms made out in their own names to shareholders accompanied by a stamped addressed envelope to encourage a greater response.

Invitations to appoint a person (e.g. the chair) or one of a number of persons may only be issued at the company's expense if they are sent to all the members entitled to receive notice of the meeting (s. 326(1)). For the purposes of section 326(1), an invitation will include any proxy form with the name of a person already inserted as the proxy or any document, circular or letter inviting members to appoint a particular person or persons as their proxy. An officer of the company who knowingly or wilfully permits the issue of invitations to selected members is liable to a fine. This does not prevent a company from issuing to a member at his request a form of appointment naming the proxy or a list of persons willing to act as proxy provided that form or list is freely available on request to all other members entitled to vote at the meeting (s. 326(2)).

It should be noted that section 326 does not prevent anyone (including the directors) from soliciting proxies at their own expense.

Invitations by traded companies

A traded company must provide an electronic address for the receipt of any document or information relating to proxies for a general meeting (s. 333A) and must do so either:

- by giving it when sending out an instrument of proxy for the purposes of the meeting or issuing an invitation to appoint a proxy for those purposes; or
- by ensuring that it is made available, throughout the period beginning with the first date on which notice of the meeting is given and ending with the conclusion of the meeting, on the website on which the information required by section 311A(1) is made available.

Appointment of a proxy

The relationship between a member and his proxy is one of principal and agent. In the normal course of events, an agent can be appointed either in writing or orally or by any other legal method, including the use of electronic communications. Although a person may validly appoint an agent without notifying anyone of the appointment, third parties usually demand to see evidence of the agent's authority to ensure that the principal will be bound by the acts of his purported agent. Companies usually require members to notify proxy appointments well in advance of the meeting so that they can check the validity of the appointment, but also so that they know in advance who must be admitted to the meeting and who may be excluded. If prior notification were not required, the company would have to try to check the validity of appointments at the meeting.

In the normal course of events, proxy forms provide evidence that any poll called at a meeting was properly conducted and that the votes cast by proxies on behalf of members were valid. They could, however, be used by someone seeking to challenge the result to show that some fraud had been committed (e.g. that their signature had been forged). Whether this would have any effect on the outcome of the meeting will depend partly on whether the company's articles give the chair power to rule on the validity of votes cast at the meeting. However, the courts would be unlikely to allow a company to rely on such an article where the company (or the chair) was a party to the fraud.

Form and method of appointment

The Act does not generally dictate how proxies must be appointed except for traded companies, where section 327(A1) specifies that appointments must be made 'in writing' which, in the context of the Act, means in hard copy or electronic form, as opposed to, say, orally. The Act does, however, impose certain restrictions on provisions which may be contained in a company's articles regarding how far in advance of the meeting any notice of appointment or revocation must be lodged with the company and does provide that, in certain circumstances, a company will be deemed to have agreed to accept electronic appointments.

Modern articles usually require appointments to be made in writing or electronically. Older articles may specify that appointments must be made in writing. Even where this is the case a company may allow appointments to be made electronically by virtue of the company communications provisions and section 333 of the 2006 Act which together have the effect of overriding any such barrier in the articles regarding electronic appointments where the directors have indicated in documents such as notices or proxy forms relating to the meeting that appointments may be made electronically. The company communications provisions apply to documents or information required or authorised to be sent or supplied by or to a company under the Companies Acts (see s. 1143). Members are entitled under the Act to appoint proxies, and companies are entitled under the Act to require evidence of appointment. Accordingly, it is arguable that completed proxy forms are documents which are, at the very least, authorised under the Act to be sent to a company. If this is the case, Schedules 4 and 5 of the Act apply. These allow documents or information to be sent or supplied to the company in electronic form if the company has agreed (generally or specifically) that it may be sent in that form (and has not revoked that agreement) or is deemed to have so agreed by virtue of a provision of the Companies Acts.

Section 333(1) provides that where a company has given an electronic address in a notice calling a meeting, it is deemed to have agreed that any document or information relating to proceedings at the meeting may be sent by electronic means to that address (subject to any conditions or limitations specified in the notice).

In addition section 333(2) provides that, where a company has given an electronic address in an instrument of proxy sent out by the company or in an invitation to appoint a proxy issued by the company in relation to the meeting, it is deemed to have agreed that any document or information relating to proxies for that meeting may be sent by electronic means to that address (subject to any conditions or limitations specified in the notice). Section 333(3) clarifies that the documents relating to proxies that may be sent by electronic means in these circumstances include:

(a) the appointment of a proxy in relation to a meeting;
(b) any document necessary to show the validity of, or otherwise relating to, the appointment of a proxy; and
(c) notice of the termination of the authority of a proxy.

Section 333(4) clarifies that, for the purposes of section 333, 'electronic address' means any address or number used for the purposes of sending or receiving documents or information by electronic means.

Traded companies must allow electronic appointments
If a traded company does not offer the facility to vote by electronic means to all members who hold shares that carry rights to vote at general meetings, it must

give 21 days' notice of all meetings (s. 307A). This condition is met if there is a facility, offered by the company and accessible to all such members, to appoint a proxy by means of a website (s. 307A(2)).

A traded company is, in any case, required by section 333A(1) to provide an electronic address for the receipt of any document or information relating to proxies for a general meeting and must do so either:

- by giving the address when sending out an instrument of proxy for the purposes of the meeting or issuing an invitation to appoint a proxy for those purposes; or
- by ensuring that it is made available, throughout the period beginning with the first date on which notice of the meeting is given and ending with the conclusion of the meeting, on the website on which the information required by section 311A(1) is made available (s. 33A(2)).

In either case, the company is deemed to have agreed that any document or information relating to proxies for the meeting may be sent by electronic means to the address provided (subject to any limitations specified by the company when providing the address) (s. 333A(3)).

For the purposes of section 333A, the terms 'documents relating to proxies' and 'electronic address' have the same meaning as they do for section 333 (see above).

Subject to any limitations specified by the company, it would seem that compliance with section 333A will almost certainly result in compliance with the condition in section 307A regarding electronic proxy appointments which must be satisfied for a traded company to hold general meetings at less than 21 days' notice.

Other general rules regarding appointments

It is not necessary for a named person to be nominated as proxy as long as the person appointed is capable of being identified. Members may, for example, nominate 'the chair of the meeting' as their proxy.

Articles usually allow the appointment of a proxy to be executed on behalf of a member. In these circumstances, they normally require the authority under which the person executed the instrument of appointment (for example, a power of attorney) or a copy of it, to be deposited by the deadline for deposit of the instrument of proxy. Articles sometimes give the directors power to dispense with this requirement.

Electronic appointments

Unless a company is a traded company it need not allow members to make appointments using electronic communications. If it chooses not to do so, appointments must be made in accordance with its articles, which will normally, by default, require the appointment to be made in writing (which is normally taken to mean in hard copy form). The model articles provide that proxies may only validly be appointed by a notice in writing (pcls 45, clg 31 and plc 38). However, under the model articles, the words 'in writing' mean in hard copy or electronic form (see the definition in pcls, clg and plc 1).

A company could be unwittingly forced to accept electronic appointments if it includes an electronic address in the notice of meeting or any proxy form or proxy invitation sent to members, in which case it may very well be deemed to have agreed to allow members to use that address to make proxy electronic appointments by virtue of section 333. The biggest danger here would be to give an email address in any document which could be deemed to form part of the notice (which could include almost any document sent out with the notice, including the report and accounts) without specifying that it may not be used to make proxy appointments.

Electronic appointments under the model articles

Under the model articles, the proxy notice (whether in hard copy or electronic form) must:

(a) state the name and address of the shareholder appointing the proxy;
(b) identify the person appointed to be that shareholder's proxy and the general meeting in relation to which that person is appointed;
(c) be signed by or on behalf of the shareholder appointing the proxy, or be authenticated in such manner as the directors may determine; and
(d) be delivered to the company in accordance with the articles and any instructions contained in the notice of the general meeting to which they relate (pcls 45(1), clg 31(1) and plc 38(1)).

Neither of the model articles for private companies impose any conditions as to the time limit for delivering proxy notices. Accordingly, it must be assumed that there is none unless one can be imposed by the directors in the instructions contained in the notice.

The model articles for public companies do make provision requiring proxy notices to be submitted in advance.

No provision for electronic proxy appointments

Although it is not necessary for a company to amend its articles before allowing members to make proxy appointments by email or via a website (or any other electronic method), it is desirable.

The articles of nearly every company incorporated before 22 December 2000 will, unless subsequently amended, probably require proxy appointments to be made in hard copy form. With the prevalence of electronic communications and its rapid development, it is advisable for any outstanding articles requiring only hard copy form to be updated.

Generally speaking, if a company wishes to allow members to make proxy appointments using some form of electronic communications, it should notify them of the fact that this facility is being made available and specifically notify them of the address to be used for this purpose. In practice, this address will normally be the address of the company's website (or possibly an email address). However, the definition of electronic communications is so wide that members could conceivably be allowed to use other methods of communication, including the telephone, text message or a fax. An address in these cases would mean a telephone number.

Although the Act does not require companies to send proxy forms to members, it can be said to authorise them to do so. Accordingly, it can be assumed that the company communications provisions apply to proxy forms and that they may be sent to a member by electronic means or via a website provided that the member has agreed (or can be deemed to have agreed) in accordance with the normal rules.

In practice, most companies will probably only want to allow members to use methods of electronic communication which enable the company to ensure that the member uses its standard form of appointment and provides all the information necessary to ensure that the appointment is valid. Generally speaking, it has been found that the best way of achieving this is to provide some web-based method of appointment, although other workable methods could be devised.

Authentication/execution

If a company intends to allow members to make electronic proxy appointments, it will need to devise a method of authentication. Where appointments are made in writing, they are authenticated by being executed (i.e. by the signature of an individual or the seal of a company). Although a company will often have no way of knowing whether the signatures on proxy forms are genuine, the existence of signed proxy forms enables this to be established after the event, should the need arise. They also provide the basis on which the chair would make any ruling on the validity of votes tendered by proxy.

The company communications provisions of the 2006 Act provide that a document or information sent or supplied in electronic form is sufficiently authenticated:

- if the identity of the sender is confirmed in a manner specified by the company; or
- where no such manner has been specified by the company, if the communication contains or is accompanied by a statement of the identity of the sender and the company has no reason to doubt the truth of that statement (s. 1146(3)).

It should be noted that section 1146(3) does not make reference to the manner of authentication specified in a company's articles but simply to the manner specified by the company. Accordingly, a company will presumably be bound to accept electronic appointments authenticated in the manner specified in any notice of meeting or proxy form or on a website provided by the company for the purpose of making proxy appointments even though that method of authentication may not appear to comply with any relevant article.

However, where a document or information is sent or supplied by one person on behalf of another, section 1146(3) it does not override any provision of a company's articles under which the company may require reasonable evidence of the authority of the former to act on behalf of the latter (s. 1146(4)).

A company could, in theory, allow members to notify proxy appointments electronically without providing any authentication at all. In other words, it could simply trust to luck that there will be no challenge as to the validity of any votes. Should there be a challenge, the chair might find it difficult to rule on the validity of votes tendered by proxy in this manner. Any decision could conceivably be challenged in legal proceedings even where the articles provide that the chair's ruling shall be conclusive in this regard. It is submitted, therefore, that members should be required to provide some sort of authentication when making electronic proxy appointments.

The closest equivalent to a manual signature for these purposes is the so-called 'electronic' signature. Under the Electronic Communications Act 2000, electronic signatures are now admissible as evidence in legal proceedings.

Instead, most companies will probably require members to authenticate their appointment by confirming a unique identification number which the company or its registrars has allocated to them for these purposes, or which it may have already allocated for some other purpose. For example, most service registrars allocate a unique reference number to each shareholder which is often printed on share certificates and proxy forms. For reasons of security and practicality, it may be preferable to allocate a separate identification number for the purposes of electronic communications.

It should be noted that, with the increased use of websites containing information and personalised logins to such sites, the risk surrounding invalid authentication or validation of a proxy by a member is considerably diminished.

Appointments in hard copy form

Where a company decides not to allow appointments of proxies to be made electronically, all appointments will probably need to be made in hard copy form. The articles of any company incorporated before 22 December 2000 will (unless subsequently amended) probably still require proxy appointments to be made in writing. Where the expression 'in writing' is used in articles without being defined, it is normally assumed that it means in hard copy form. Appointments will need to be made in hard copy form under the model articles where a company decides not to allow electronic appointments. Under the company communications provisions of the 2006 Act, it is not possible for a company to refuse to accept appointments solely on the basis that they are made in hard copy form. In other words, it is not possible to insist that all appointments are to be made electronically.

Older articles sometimes require the instrument appointing a proxy to be attested (e.g. to be signed in the presence of a witness). An instrument of proxy which does not comply with such a requirement contained in the articles, will be invalid and a proxy cannot attest his or her own appointment in such circumstances.

Proxies – model articles

The model articles provide that proxies may only validly be appointed by a notice in writing and refer to the instrument of appointment as a defined term of 'proxy notice' (pcls 45, clg 31 and plc 38). Under the model articles, the words 'in writing' mean in hard copy or electronic form (see the definition in pcls, clg and plc 1). The proxy notice must:

(a) state the name and address of the shareholder appointing the proxy;
(b) identify the person appointed to be that shareholder's proxy and the general meeting in relation to which that person is appointed;
(c) be signed by or on behalf of the shareholder appointing the proxy, or be authenticated in such manner as the directors may determine; and
(d) be delivered to the company in accordance with the articles and any instructions contained in the notice of the general meeting to which they relate (pcls 45(1), clg 31(1) and plc 38(1)).

The company may require proxy notices to be delivered in a particular form and may specify different forms for different purposes (pcls 45(2), clg 31(2) and plc 38(2)).

Proxy notices may specify how the proxy appointed under them is to vote (or that the proxy is to abstain from voting) on one or more resolutions (pcls 45(3), clg 31(3) and plc 38(3)).

If a proxy notice is not executed by the person appointing the proxy, it must be accompanied by written evidence of the authority of the person who executed it to do so on the appointor's behalf (pcls 46(4), clg 32(4) and plc 39(8)).

Section 1146 provides that a document or information sent or supplied by a person in hard copy form to a company is sufficiently authenticated if it is signed by the person sending or supplying it.

Additional rules regarding proxies for listed companies

The Disclosure and Transparency Rules (DTRs) require listed companies to issue a proxy form either on paper or, where applicable, by electronic means, to each person entitled to vote at a meeting of shareholders or a meeting of debt security holders (DTR 6.1.5(2) and 6.1.5(3)).

The proxy form must be made available either together with the notice concerning the meeting or after the announcement of the meeting (DTR 6.1.5(3)). Shareholders and debt security holders must not be prevented from exercising their rights by proxy, subject to the law of the country in which the issuer is incorporated (DTR 6.1.5(1)).

The proxy forms must make provision for 'at least three-way voting' – with provision for members to indicate which way their votes are to be cast on all resolutions other than those relating to the procedure of the meeting (Listing Rule 9.3.6). This rule requires listed companies to make provision for abstentions or a 'vote withheld' options on proxy forms in addition to the usual for and against options.

In addition, Listing Rule 9.3.6 requires proxy forms to state that if the form is returned without an indication as to how the proxy shall vote on any resolution, the proxy will exercise his discretion as to how he votes and as to whether or not he abstains from voting.

Listing Rule 9.3.6 also used to require proxy forms to state that a shareholder is entitled to appoint a proxy of his own choice (e.g. somebody other than a director named in the printed form) and should provide a space for the name of such a proxy. Although this requirement was deleted in August 2007, listed companies still comply with it.

If the resolutions to be proposed include the re-election of retiring directors and the number of retiring directors standing for re-election exceeds five, the proxy form may give shareholders the opportunity to vote for or against (or abstain from voting on) the re-election of the retiring directors as a whole but must also allow votes to be cast for or against (or for shareholders to abstain from voting on) the re-election of the retiring directors individually (LR 9.3.7).

Proxy forms which comply with the requirements of Chapter 13 of the Listing Rules and which have no unusual features (e.g. see the three-way proxy precedent below) do not need to be approved by the UK Listing Authority before they are dispatched. However, two copies must be lodged with the Financial Conduct Authority) (FCA) no later than the date on which they are dispatched to holders of the relevant securities. It is difficult to say what might be considered an unusual feature on a proxy form.

Precedent: Three-way proxy that complies with the Listing Rules

XYZ plc

FORM OF PROXY FOR USE AT [ANNUAL] GENERAL MEETING

I/We (Block Capitals, please), ...
.... being a member/members of
the above-named Company, hereby appoint the chair of the meeting* ....
.... as my/our proxy to
vote for me/us on my/our behalf at the Annual General Meeting of the Company to
be held at 12 noon on .... day, the .... day of .... 20......... , and
at any adjournment thereof.

I/We hereby authorise and instruct the proxy to vote on the resolutions to be proposed
at such meeting as indicated in the boxes below. Unless otherwise directed, the proxy
will vote or abstain from voting as he or she thinks fit. Should any resolutions, other
than those specified, be proposed at the meeting, the proxy may vote thereon as he
or she thinks fit.

Signature ....

Dated .... 20........

[* Delete if it is desired to appoint any other person and insert his or her name and
address in the space provided.]

Please indicate with an X in the spaces below how you wish your votes to be cast.

		For	Against	Votes withheld
Resolution 1	To receive the report and accounts			
Resolution 2	To approve the directors' remuneration report			
Resolution 3	To declare a final dividend			
Resolution 4	To re-elect [name A] as a director			
Resolution 5	To re-elect [name B] a director			
Resolution 6	To re-elect [name C] a director			

		For	Against	Votes withheld
Resolution 7	Reappointment of auditors			
Resolution 8	Share buyback			
Resolution 9	Directors' authority to allot shares (Section 551)			
Resolution 10	Disapplication of pre-emption rights			
Resolution 11	Notice of general meetings			

Date

Signature

NOTES

1. A member may appoint a proxy of his own choice. If such an appointment is made, delete the words 'the chair of the meeting' and insert the name of the person appointed proxy in the space provided.
2. Appointing a proxy does not prevent a member from attending the meeting in person if he so wishes.
3. If the appointer is a corporation, this form must be under its common seal or under the hand of some officer or attorney duly authorised in that behalf.
4. In the case of joint holders, the signature of any one holder will be sufficient, but the names of all the joint holders should be stated.
5. If you wish your proxy to cast your votes for or against a resolution you may insert an 'X' in the appropriate box. If you do not want your proxy to vote on any particular resolution, you may insert an 'X' in the 'Vote withheld' box. A 'Vote withheld' is not a vote in law and will not be counted in the calculation of votes 'For' and 'Against' a resolution. If you do not indicate how your proxy is to vote, you will be deemed to have authorised your proxy to vote or to withhold your vote as your proxy thinks fit. Your proxy will also be entitled to vote at his or her discretion on any other resolution properly put before the meeting.
6. Particulars of the directors standing for re-election are set out on pages x to x of [circular/annual report].
7. To be valid, this form must be completed and deposited at the registered office of the Company not less than 48 hours before the time fixed for holding the meeting or adjourned meeting.

Abstention boxes on proxy forms

As noted above, listed companies are required under the Listing Rules to provide for three-way voting on proxy forms. If members voting by proxy wish to abstain on a resolution, they must specifically instruct their proxy not to vote. In practice, where a traditional two-way proxy form is used, if a member marks a proxy card 'abstain', the company (or its registrar) should count this as an abstention. However, many shareholders do not know that this option is available or assume that not ticking 'for' or 'against' is an abstention.

Leaving the voting instructions on a two-way proxy form blank does not necessarily constitute an abstention because the standard wording on proxy forms provides:

> I/We hereby authorise and instruct the proxy to vote on the resolutions to be proposed at such meeting as indicated in the boxes below. Unless otherwise directed, the proxy will vote or abstain from voting as he or she thinks fit.

This is the formula used in the two-way proxy form in Table A, so there is nothing unusual about it. Even if a shareholder gives voting instructions for some of the resolutions but not others, those for which he or she has given no instructions will be deemed to be a discretionary proxy.

Time limit for deposit of proxies

A company may require proxy appointments (and any document relating to or necessary to show the validity of any such appointment) to be lodged or delivered by a specified time before the meeting. This is normally done to allow the validity of the instruments to be checked and the votes for and against the resolution to be counted before the meeting. If no such provision is made in the articles, the company must accept a vote tendered by proxy at the meeting even though the proxy is unable at the meeting to establish his authority.

In the case of a traded company, the appointment of a person as proxy must be notified to the company in writing and where such an appointment is made, the company may not require to be provided with anything else relating to the appointment other than reasonable evidence of the identity of the member and of the proxy, the member's instructions (if any) as to how the proxy is to vote, and where the proxy is appointed by a person acting on behalf of the member, the authority of that person to make the appointment (s. 327(A1)).

Section 327(2), which applies to all companies, provides that any provision of a company's articles will be void in so far as it would have the effect of requiring the appointment of a proxy or any document necessary to show the validity of, or otherwise relating to, the appointment of a proxy to be received by the company or another person earlier than:

(a) in the case of a meeting or adjourned meeting, 48 hours before the time for holding the meeting or adjourned meeting;

(b) in the case of a poll taken more than 48 hours after it was demanded, 24 hours before the time appointed for the taking of the poll.

Section 327(2)(c) which would, in the case of a poll taken not more than 48 hours after it was demanded, make it illegal to require a proxy to be delivered before the time at which the poll was demanded, has not been commenced and, according to a government statement, will never be commenced.

In calculating the above periods, no account shall be taken of any part of a day that is not a working day (s. 327(3)). This means, for example, that a company's articles may require proxies to be delivered more than 48 hours before a meeting if the meeting takes place on a Monday or Tuesday, in which case some of the 48 hours would fall on non-working days.

The model articles for private companies do not impose any conditions as to the time for delivering proxy notices. Accordingly, it must be assumed that there is no time limit unless one can be imposed by the directors in the instructions contained in the notice. It is far from clear whether this is actually allowed and a person whose proxy vote was excluded on this basis might be able to challenge the validity of the proceedings.

The model articles for public companies do make provision requiring proxy notices to be submitted in advance. Any notice of a general meeting must specify the address or addresses ('proxy notification address') at which the company or its agents will receive proxy notices relating to that meeting, or any adjournment of it, delivered in hard copy or electronic form (plc 39(1)). A proxy notice must be delivered to a proxy notification address not less than 48 hours before the general meeting or adjourned meeting to which it relates (plc 39(3)). However, in the case of a poll not taken during the meeting but taken not more than 48 hours after it was demanded, the proxy notice must be delivered under the above rules or at the meeting at which the poll was demanded to the chair, secretary or any director (plc 39(5)). In the case of a poll taken more than 48 hours after it is demanded, the notice must be delivered to a proxy notification address not less than 24 hours before the time appointed for the taking of the poll (plc 39(4)).

Most older articles require proxies to be deposited not less than 48 hours before the time for holding the meeting or adjourned meeting, and make no provision for excluding hours which fall on non-working days (e.g. reg. 62 of Table A). In these circumstances, if a meeting is held on a Monday or a Tuesday, it will normally be necessary for someone to be present at the nominated office at the deadline to ensure that proxies delivered after that time are not accepted.

Proxy forms received after the time specified in the articles will not be valid for that meeting and should not be accepted under any circumstances.

Registrars Group guidance note on proxy voting

The Chartered Governance Institute Registrars Group published a guidance note in March 2012 entitled 'Practical Issues around Voting at General Meetings', which remains relevant. It seeks to explain some of the practical processes used by company registrars to determine the voting rights of members and proxies and the validity of proxy voting instructions at general meetings. The main objective of the guidance is to ensure that investors are aware of what they need to do to ensure that their votes are counted. In this regard, it recommends that investors should:

(a) lodge their proxies and proxy instructions as early as possible before the deadline so as not only to maximise the chances of valid receipt and reconciliation but also to enable the company to enter into a dialogue with the investor should it choose to do so;

(b) make use of any proxy facilities provided through CREST to communicate with the company or, if that is not possible, any website facility provided by the company; and

(c) seek to avoid using more than one of the available methods for notifying proxy appointments and instructions in respect of the same holding.

The guidance also explains what registrars normally do when trying to reconcile invalid proxy voting instructions.

Proxies on a poll

A proxy delivered after the time specified in the articles will not be valid on the suspension of business for the purposes of taking a poll unless the articles expressly allow proxies to be deposited at a specified time before the poll is taken (e.g. reg. 62 of Table A and plc 39). It should be noted in this regard that a poll directed to be taken on a later date is not treated as an adjournment but rather as a suspension of the proceedings, which is why separate provision needs to be made in articles of association in this regard. The model articles for public companies only impose the condition that the proxy be delivered not less than 24 hours before the time for taking the poll (plc 39(4)). Accordingly, proxies submitted late for the original meeting will be valid on the poll.

The model articles for private companies do not make any special provision for proxies on a poll because they require all polls to be taken immediately. It should also be noted, however, that they do not impose any time limits on the submission of proxies. Accordingly, a member could presumably deliver a proxy at any time before the meeting and, subject to any instructions contained in the notice of meeting, deliver that proxy at the meeting (see pcls 45(1) and clg 31(1)).

Revocation of proxies

Section 330(A1) provides that in the case of a traded company, the termination of the authority of a person to act as proxy must be notified to the company in writing. This provision was inserted by the Companies (Shareholders' Rights) Regulations 2009 (SI 2009/1632) in order to comply with an EU directive and may very well have a bearing on the application of the common law rules regarding revocation of proxies.

Section 330 also makes other provision regarding termination of a proxy's authority. These other rules apply to all companies (whether traded or otherwise).

Section 330(2) provides that the termination of the authority of a person to act as proxy does not affect whether he counts in deciding whether there is a quorum at a meeting, the validity of anything he does as chair of a meeting, or the validity of a poll demanded by him at a meeting, unless the company receives notice of the termination before the commencement of the meeting.

Section 330(3) provides that the termination of the authority of a person to act as proxy does not affect the validity of a vote given by that person unless the company receives notice of the termination before the commencement of the meeting or adjourned meeting at which the vote is given or, in the case of a poll taken more than 48 hours after it is demanded, before the time appointed for taking the poll.

Section 330(4) provides that, if the company's articles require or permit members to give notice of termination to a person other than the company, the references above to the company receiving notice have effect as if they were or (as the case may be) included a reference to that person.

The above rules have effect subject to any provision of the company's articles which has the effect of requiring notice of termination to be received by the company or another person at a time earlier than that specified in those subsections (s. 330(5)). However, any provision of a company's articles is void in so far as it would have the effect of requiring notice of termination to be received by the company or another person earlier than:

- in the case of a meeting or adjourned meeting, 48 hours before the time for holding the meeting or adjourned meeting; and
- in the case of a poll taken more than 48 hours after it was demanded, 24 hours before the time appointed for the taking of the poll (s. 330(6)).

In calculating the periods mentioned above, no account shall be taken of any part of a day that is not a working day (s. 330(7)). It should be noted that section 330(6) (c), which would in the case of a poll taken not more than 48 hours after it was demanded, invalidate any provision in a company's articles which required notice of termination to be given before the time at which the poll was demanded, has not been commenced and is never likely to be.

Subject to the statutory rules on revocation for traded companies, it is arguable that the appointment of a proxy in relation to a share will automatically be revoked (terminated) on the registration of a transfer of that share. Revocation may also be automatic in certain other circumstances (see below). Revocation can also be effected by notifying the company that the appointment has been revoked or that the authority under which the instrument of proxy was signed has been revoked (e.g. the revocation of a power of attorney). A proxy which is expressed as being irrevocable cannot be revoked.

Articles usually require notice of revocation to be given before the meeting or the time appointed for the taking of a poll. Under the model articles, a proxy appointment may be revoked by delivering to the company a notice in writing given by or on behalf of the person by whom or on whose behalf the proxy notice was given (pcls 46(2), clg 32(2) and plc 39(6)). In this case, 'in writing' means in hard copy or electronic form (pcls, clg and plc 1). However, notice of revocation can only be submitted in electronic form if the company has provided an address for that purpose (or can be deemed to have done so). Under the model articles for private companies, a notice revoking a proxy appointment only takes effect if it is delivered before the start of the meeting or the adjourned meeting to which it relates (pcls 46(3), clg 32(3)). The model articles for public companies make the same provision but also provide that a notice revoking a proxy appointment will take effect, in the case of a poll not taken on the same day as the meeting or adjourned meeting, if it is delivered before the time appointed for taking the poll to which it relates (plc 39(6) and (7)).

A proxy may vote on behalf of the member who appointed him even though that member attends the meeting. However, the proxy is impliedly revoked if the member votes in person. This will be the case even where the articles require notice of revocation to be given to the company a specified period before the meeting.

Under the model articles, a person who is entitled to attend, speak or vote (either on a show of hands or on a poll) at a general meeting remains so entitled in respect of that meeting or any adjournment of it, even though a valid proxy notice has been delivered to the company by or on behalf of that person (pcls 46(1), clg 32(1) and plc 39(2)).

The execution and deposit of a second or later instrument of proxy in respect of the same holding within the time allowed under the articles will act as a revocation of any previous appointment where members are entitled to appoint only one proxy (e.g. in the case of a company limited by guarantee). This may also be the case where the deadline for appointments has expired, which could result in the member not being represented at the meeting. Where more than one appointment is made within the period specified by the articles, the company should accept the last appointment to the exclusion of the first. Where it is not possible to determine when each proxy was executed, the company may need to resolve the matter in some other way, e.g. by assuming that the appointment last received was the last to be executed or that an electronic appointment received on the same day takes precedence over a hard copy appointment.

Where members are entitled to appoint more than one proxy, the deposit of a second instrument appointing a different person will not always be conclusive evidence of the intention to revoke the original appointment, except, perhaps, where the second appointment is accompanied by new voting instructions.

The ability to appoint more than one proxy allows nominee companies to appoint separate proxies to attend and vote on behalf of the various underlying holders. Several instruments of appointment, each representing different shares within the same registered holding, can be deposited. However, if the sum of the parts exceeds the whole, the company will obviously need to find some way of limiting the number of votes cast. It might inform the various proxy holders in the hope that they are able to come to an arrangement between themselves. If all the proxies attempt to vote, the company must scale down the votes of one or more of the proxies. One way of doing so might be to assume that the last proxy submitted had the effect of revoking (either in whole or in part) one or more of the previously submitted proxies on a first in first out basis.

Personal representatives

The death or insanity of a member automatically revokes any appointment by that person of a proxy unless the articles provide otherwise. Any transfer which occurs by operation of law could also potentially have this effect. Articles sometimes specifically provide that any proxy appointed by a member will still be valid in these circumstances unless the company receives notice of the event giving rise to revocation (e.g. the death of that member).

Precedent: Article on non-revocation of proxies

A vote given in accordance with the terms of an instrument of proxy shall be valid, notwithstanding the previous death or insanity of the principal or revocation of the proxy, or of the authority under which the proxy was executed, or the transfer of the share in respect of which the proxy is given, provided that no intimation in writing of such death, insanity, revocation or transfer shall have been received by the Company at the Office (or other place in the United Kingdom specified pursuant to Article [No.]) before the commencement of the meetings or adjourned meeting at which the proxy is used.

Even if the articles do not do so, it is difficult to see how the company (and the chair of the meeting in particular) can do anything other than assume that all proxies are valid unless the company has been given satisfactory evidence to the contrary. The validity of votes tendered in these circumstances might fall to be decided by the chair under (and the decision saved by) any provision on objections to the validity of votes (pcls 43, clg 29 and plc 35).

A person who becomes entitled to a share in consequence of the death or bankruptcy of a member will not normally be entitled to attend or vote at any meeting of the company until they are registered as the holder of the share (pcls 27(3) and plc 66(2)). It follows that such a person will not be entitled to appoint a proxy until registered as the holder. A proxy appointed by the deceased member will also no longer be valid, although in the absence of any provision in the articles, it is questionable what evidence the chair ought to require. A rumour in this regard would presumably not be sufficient. If the shareholder died in front of the chair's own eyes, it would be difficult for him to ignore that fact.

Change of voting instructions

Members may issue their proxy with voting instructions or change any voting instructions previously given to their proxy at any time before a vote is taken. This may cause particular problems for companies which issue two-way or three-way proxy forms inviting members to appoint the chair of the meeting as their proxy. Unless the articles provide otherwise, the chair should act on any change of instructions received in respect of those shares up to the time that the poll is taken.

It is common practice for chairmen to seek to deter members from demanding a poll by indicating at the meeting the number of proxies which they hold for and against the resolution, the implication being that the result is a foregone conclusion. In fact, the chair can never be certain of the result of a poll until it is actually taken because his authority as a proxy may be revoked by a member voting in person at the meeting (unless perhaps it is a traded company, in which case under section 330(A1) it appears that revocation may only be effected by notice in writing) and members may alter their instructions at any time prior to the taking of the poll.

Joint shareholders

Section 286 provides that in the case of joint holders of shares of a company, only the vote of the senior holder who votes (and any proxies duly authorised by him) may be counted by the company. It also provides that for these purposes, the senior holder is determined by the order in which the names of the joint holders appear in the register of members. The model articles rely on this statutory provision. However, section 286 is expressed as being subject to any provision of a company's articles. Accordingly, if a company's articles make any other provision, which would be unusual, they will override the statutory rules in this regard.

Proxies' obligations and discretions
Statutory obligation

Section 324A provides that a proxy must vote in accordance with any instructions given by the member by whom the proxy is appointed. The Act does not, however, specify what the consequences might be if the proxy does not do so.

A person who agrees to act as a proxy is considered to be the legally constituted agent of the member who makes the appointment. However, the relationship of principal and agent can only be established by the consent of the principal and the agent. Thus, a person appointed by a member as his proxy need not act in that capacity unless there is a binding contract between the parties or the proxy has a legal or equitable obligation to do so.

Where there is a contractual agreement to vote in a certain way, the court may enforce that contract by mandatory injunction. The member may also be entitled to damages for any loss he incurs as a result of his proxy failing to vote in accordance with instructions in breach of a contractual or fiduciary duty.

The statutory requirement on the part of a proxy to vote in accordance with any instructions given by the member who appointed him cannot generally be viewed as anything other than a requirement not to vote in a manner which is contrary to any instructions given by the member. It almost certainly does not give rise to a duty on the part of a named proxy to attend the meeting but could conceivably give rise to a duty to vote if in attendance and able to do so (on the basis that a failure to vote could have the effect of enabling other members to achieve a result that is different from the one desired by the member and could, therefore, be interpreted as being similar to voting in a manner which is contrary to the member's instructions). This interpretation would probably be more strictly applied where the person appointed as a proxy was a director or the chair of the meeting. Any failure by such a person to vote in accordance with a member's instructions could render the proceedings liable to challenge if the outcome of the vote would have been different. However, it is far from clear whether this would be the case if the person who failed to vote was not under any fiduciary duty or not connected with the company.

It is exceedingly doubtful whether section 234A imposes any duty on the company to ensure that proxies (other than those appointing the chair of the meeting or a director) do not vote in a manner which is contrary to any instructions given by the member. In practice, even if the company has notice of the instructions given by the member to his proxy, it cannot be certain that the member has not issued revised instructions. Accordingly, it would seem to be dangerous for the company to refuse to accept proxy votes on these grounds.

Chair's obligations

The position of the chair of the meeting in relation to proxies is particularly important. Most two-way or three-way proxies name 'the chair of the meeting' as the default proxy. Accordingly, the vast majority of shareholders appoint the chair as their proxy. By doing so they at least ensure that their nominated proxy attends the meeting. They also secure the added benefit of appointing a person who has a duty to ascertain the sense of the meeting.

Proxies' discretion

Section 324A provides that a proxy must vote in accordance with any instructions given by the member. Accordingly, where a member issues voting instructions, the extent of the proxy's discretion will depend on the wording of those instructions and the form of appointment.

Under the model articles, proxy notices may specify how the proxy appointed under them is to vote (or that the proxy is to abstain from voting) on one or more resolutions (pcls 45(3), clg 31(3) and plc 38(3)). The member may also give their proxy discretion as to how to vote on any resolution, as long as the terminology in the proxy form is clear and states that, in the absence of any instructions, the proxy may vote as they think fit or abstain from voting. This should also specify in relation to which resolution the proxy has discretion to vote.

Best practice is also to include language on whether the proxy has discretion on any resolutions brought to the meeting that the member has not specified on their proxy form or was unaware when appointing the proxy and submitting the proxy form. The proxy would then be expected to reflect the same decision process for administrative amendments or procedural resolutions made at the meeting.

Model Articles: Listed Companies

Section 33

(3) Proxy notices may specify how the proxy appointed under them is to vote (or that the proxy is to abstain from voting) on one or more resolutions.

(4) Unless a proxy notice indicates otherwise, it must be treated as—
   (a) allowing the person appointed under it as a proxy discretion as to how to vote on any ancillary or procedural resolutions put to the meeting, and
   (b) appointing that person as a proxy in relation to any adjournment of the general meeting to which it relates as well as the meeting itself.

A more difficult question is whether the proxy can also vote on resolutions which come before the meeting of which the member has had no notice, such as amendments, proposals to adjourn, etc. Modern forms of proxy attempt to cater for this by using words such as:

> I/We hereby authorise and instruct the proxy to vote on the resolutions to be proposed at such meeting as indicated in the boxes below. Unless otherwise directed, the proxy will vote or abstain from voting as he or she thinks fit. Should any resolutions, other than those specified, be proposed at the meeting, the proxy may vote thereon as he or she thinks fit.

Where this form of words is used, there can be no doubt that the proxy has complete discretion when voting on amendments, adjournments, etc. Whether the proxy should follow any guiding principles in determining how to vote on such matters is a difficult question. The answer is probably no where there is no contractual or fiduciary relationship between the proxy and his appointor. However, where such a relationship exists, the proxy presumably has a duty to act in the best interests of his appointor. It is arguable that the chair of the meeting is in such a position, particularly where the company has issued proxy forms inviting members to appoint him as their proxy. The difficulties this can cause can be demonstrated by the chair's options on a proposal to adjourn.

The approach taken by most chairs on a proposal from the floor to adjourn is to assume that those members who have given instructions to vote in favour of the remaining resolutions proposed in the notice of meeting approve of the conduct of the business before the meeting at this time, and accordingly, would wish to vote against the proposal to adjourn. The chair might also cast against the proposal those votes where he has been given discretion how to vote and abstain in relation to those members who have instructed him to vote against any of the remaining resolutions proposed in the notice of meeting. However, the chair can hardly be expected to follow these guiding principles where he has proposed an adjournment to facilitate the conduct of the meeting. In such circumstances, he will normally assume that those who have instructed him to vote in favour of the resolutions would vote in favour of the adjournment. If the resolution is passed on a show of hands and would, in view of his discretionary votes be passed on a poll, it would appear that he would not be under any obligation to demand a poll.

Likewise, chairs nearly always assume that those who have issued instructions to vote in favour of a resolution would wish to vote against any amendment to that resolution. This will normally be sufficient to defeat any amendment. However, they would probably not want to do so with regard to an amendment which was being proposed or supported by the board or was an amendment for purely administrative reasons. Modern articles commonly require proposals to amend resolutions to be notified in advance of the meeting. This enables the chair to take legal advice before the meeting on any proposed amendments and, almost certainly, serves to minimise the number of amendments proposed. In view of the fact that the vast majority of votes at meetings of listed companies are cast by proxy and the fact that a proxy has no real way of knowing how his appointor would have voted, this is perhaps a sensible precaution and provides an audit trail for any future challenge.

Limitation of liability in connection with proxies
It is clear that a proxy has certain duties and could incur certain liabilities if they fail to perform those duties according to the instructions they have received. Although these liabilities might be difficult for a shareholder to establish, some companies have adopted articles which seek to limit the liability of directors and others involved in the proxy process although these as yet are not incorporated into the model articles.

Proxy advisers
Professional firms of proxy advisers have gained momentum as shareholders have sought their services, particularly investment firms with significant holdings across multiple listed companies where they lack the resources to attend every

meeting. Prevalent in the United States, proxy advisers attend meetings on behalf of shareholders, either attending and voting on their instruction or, on occasion, acting under more general guidelines. A study by Stanford University Graduate School of Business in 2018 noted the influence that proxy advisory firms have in the US market. In summary, they noted that their standards were beneficial while their influence was not as significant as thought.

However, increased use of their services means that the same resource and time constraints that impact institutional shareholders are starting to impact on advisory firms. This reducing resource and time availability might compel proxy advisory firms to employ more rigid and, therefore, arbitrary standards that are less accommodating to situational information that is unique to a company's situation, industry, size, or stage of growth.

The use of proxy advisers in the UK is less prevalent, although there is no doubt that, if there is a need, their services will become more prevalent.

Validity of proxies and their destruction

All decisions on the validity of proxies fall to the chair to decide, or more prevalently the company secretary or registrar on their behalf. No proxy should be rejected if it has been properly executed merely because there may be a belief that it has been obtained by misrepresentation or because it contains a minor error, for example it refers to the meeting as an annual general meeting (AGM) instead of an extraordinary general meeting.

However, in ruling on the validity of proxies, the chair is effectively ruling on the validity of votes and is, therefore, protected by any article which provides that the chair's ruling on any question of the validity of votes shall be final and conclusive.

Model Articles

Errors and disputes

1   No objection may be raised to the qualification of any person voting at a general meeting except at the meeting or adjourned meeting at which the vote objected to is tendered, and every vote not disallowed at the meeting is valid.
2   Any such objection must be referred to the chair of the meeting whose decision is final.

Maximum validity and destruction of proxies

Some companies have adopted articles which limit the period of validity of a proxy. This type of article tends to go hand-in-hand with those that allow proxy appointments to be destroyed after a certain period, in which case it is sensible to limit their validity to that period. No such provision is made in both cases under either the model articles for private companies. However, the model articles for public companies do allow proxy notices to be destroyed a year after the end of the meeting to which they relate (plc 82(1)(e)).

Where no provision is made by the articles allowing for destruction of proxies, it is still normal practice to destroy them after one year. However, one of the benefits of having an article provision in this regard will be that it will also normally provide that it shall be conclusively presumed in favour of the company that any such document destroyed was valid.

Best practice, if there is no reference in the articles, is to destroy the proxies after one year as long as there is no pending business or potential claim resulting from the meeting.

Voting

Every member of a company has the right to vote (s. 284). However, the section in which this is stated has effect subject to any provisions of a company's articles (s. 284(4)). Accordingly, the regime established in that section is only the starting point and is capable of modification by a company's articles.

Section 284 provides that, on a vote on a resolution on a show of hands, every member present in person has one vote. On a vote on a resolution taken on a poll at a meeting:

(a) every member of a company having a share capital shall have one vote for each share held (or, if the company's shares have been converted into stock, one vote for each £10 of stock held); and,

(b) every member of a company limited by guarantee shall have one vote (s. 284).

The model articles prescribed under the 2006 Act rely on the default rules in section 284 but include certain restrictions and variations. However, older articles often override section 284 completely by setting out an alternative regime for the voting rights of members. This is usually done in an article which sets out the basic voting rights of members, which are expressed as being subject to any other restrictions or enhancements set out in the articles. As such, the articles of the company should be reviewed in this respect.

A members' right to vote may also be restricted in other ways or be disregarded for certain purposes, notwithstanding the provisions of the company's articles.

Membership

The register of members is evidence of membership for the purpose of voting. The subscribers to the memorandum of association become members on incorporation and no entry on the register of members is required (s. 112(1)). Every other person who agrees to become a member, and whose name is entered in the register of members, is a member of the company (s. 112(2)).

The holders of preference shares or any other class of shares are members of the company for these purposes. However, their right to vote may be restricted by the articles of the company. The same principles apply with respect to guarantee companies where every class of member will have a right to vote unless the articles provide otherwise.

The default position is that it is the members in the register on the day of the meeting who have the right to vote. However, companies may sometimes be allowed to use a prior record date for the purposes of determining voting entitlements.

Stock

The references to stock in section 284 are to shares converted into stock. It is no longer possible under the Companies Act 2006 to convert shares into stock (s. 540(2)), although it is still possible to convert stock back into shares (s. 620). However, because there are still a few long-established companies that have stock instead of shares, section 284 still makes reference to it.

All listed companies used to have to convert their shares into stock to allow trading to take place on the London Stock Exchange. This was necessary because a company's shares had to be individually numbered, which would have made it virtually impossible to keep track of who owned each of those individually numbered shares, and to enter those numbers on share certificates, where the shares were publicly traded. Accordingly, companies used to convert their shares into stock, which did not have to be numbered, and parcels of that stock that were traded on the markets rather than the shares. It has not been necessary for listed companies to do this for many years because all companies are allowed to decide not to have individually numbered shares as long as all the shares (or shares of the same class) have the same rights and are fully paid (s. 543).

Bearer shares

A bearer share is a share which is evidenced by a certificate which does not show the name of the holder and which can be transferred by the holder to another person by giving up possession. In the Act, these types of instrument are referred to as 'share warrants'. Although a company will know who it issued the original share warrant to, it will, for obvious reasons, have no idea who currently retains possession of it or who is entitled to exercise any of the rights attached to the shares represented by the warrant. Accordingly, the register of members is normally amended to record the fact that a share warrant has been issued and to ensure that no person is named in the register as the holder of the shares specified in the warrant to ensure that they are not treated as members for the purposes of section 112. The articles of companies that issue bearer shares will normally make special provision to enable the holders to exercise their rights. These normally involve depositing their certificates at a nominated bank or depositary before the meeting. The company will usually be required to publish notices of meetings by advertisement in national newspapers and explain the procedure which holders must follow in order to exercise their right to vote at the meeting.

Precedent: Article on bearer shares

(A) A Bearer may at any time deposit the Share Warrant together with a written declaration specifying his name and postal address at such place as the Directors may from time to time appoint (or, in default of such appointment, at the Transfer Office), and, so long as the Share Warrant remains so deposited, the depositor shall have the same right of signing a requisition for calling a meeting of the Company, of giving notice of intention to submit a resolution to a meeting, of attending and voting, giving a proxy and exercising the other rights and privileges of a member at any meeting held after the expiration of forty-eight hours from the time of deposit, as if from the time of deposit his name were inserted in the Register as the holder of the shares specified in the deposited Share Warrant. Not more than one person shall be recognised as depositor of any Share Warrant. Every Share Warrant which shall have been so deposited as aforesaid shall remain so deposited until after the conclusion of the meeting (including any adjournment) at which the depositor desires to attend or to be represented. Save as otherwise expressly provided, no person shall, as bearer of a Share Warrant, be entitled to sign a requisition for calling a general meeting;

(B) In the case of any notice or document or other communication with members or any class of members, it shall be sufficient, so far as any Bearer is concerned, to advertise the notice, document or other communication once in a leading London daily newspaper, and such other newspapers (if any) as the Directors may from time to time determine, and to give a postal address (and, if the Directors see fit, the address of a website) where copies of the notice, document or other communication may be obtained by any Bearer.

Freedom to exercise voting rights

A member has a right to have any votes tendered accepted at a meeting of the company and a refusal to accept those votes may invalidate the resolution. A member's vote is a property right which, as a general rule, can be exercised at that person's complete discretion. In casting their votes members are free to use their own judgement and act in their own interests even though those interests might conflict with the general interests of the company.

A director who is also a member can exercise his votes against a resolution which the court has ordered the company to effect given they are as a person owing no fiduciary duty to the company and who is exercising their own right of property to vote as they think fit. The fact that the result of the voting at the meeting will bind the company cannot effect the position that, in voting, he is voting simply in exercise of his property rights.

A member may contract to vote in a certain way or at the direction of a third party (e.g. under a shareholders' agreement). The obligations under any such contract can be enforced by mandatory injunction provided that the contract is for consideration and the member continues to hold the shares. The company (unless it is a party to the contract) need only be concerned that the person tendering the vote is entitled to do so and not with the obligations of that person to vote in a certain way.

A member may vote in favour of a resolution in which he has a financial interest even if he is a director of the company as he is voting as an individual member not in his role as director.

The rules are, of course, subject to certain exceptions, including:

(a) the requirements of the Act regarding resolutions to ratify a breach of conduct by a director and certain resolutions connected with the purchase by a company of its own shares or payment for a purchase or redemption out of capital; and

(b) the common law requirement that members must exercise the power to alter the articles of association in good faith for the benefit of the company as a whole.

Restrictions on voting

The following paragraphs summarise the restrictions that can apply to the right of a member to vote. These restrictions may arise under a statutory provision or the company's articles, or by virtue of a court order. Companies have considerable discretion in determining who may vote and under what circumstances. The statutory rights of members as stated in section 284 are capable of modification by a company's articles and are frequently modified, particularly where there is more than one class of share in issue.

Restrictions on the right to vote can usually be found in articles which establish the rights of any class of members but may also be found in articles that deal with the transmission of shares, the non-payment of calls on shares and joint shareholders. Articles may impose other restrictions and it is important to examine them carefully to ascertain the true position.

Members represented by proxy

A company's articles may restrict the right of a member who is represented by a proxy to vote on a show of hands. The default position under the Act is that proxies have a right to vote on a show of hands. However, this rule is capable of modification by a company's articles).

The model articles (plc 38) clarifies the ability of a proxy to vote:

(3) Proxy notices may specify how the proxy appointed under them is to vote (or that the proxy is to abstain from voting) on one or more resolutions.

(4) Unless a proxy notice indicates otherwise, it must be treated as—

    (a) allowing the person appointed under it as a proxy discretion as to how to vote on any ancillary or procedural resolutions put to the meeting, and

    (b) appointing that person as a proxy in relation to any adjournment of the general meeting to which it relates as well as the meeting itself.

Proxies have a statutory right to vote on a poll and to demand (or join in any demand) for a poll, and these rights cannot be excluded by the articles.

Record dates for traded companies and securities admitted to CREST

A company whose shares (or other securities) have been admitted to CREST may specify in the notice a time, not more than 48 hours before the time fixed for the meeting, by which a person must be entered on the relevant register of securities in order to have the right to attend and vote at that meeting (or meeting of the holders of those securities) (Uncertificated Securities Regulations, reg. 34).

Such a provision is necessary because CREST operates on a real time basis and the dematerialised part of the register could be changing right up to (and even during) the meeting.

As regulation 34 uses the expression 'a time', it is best practice to give a specific time in the notice rather than to use an expression like 'the close of business' given the international distribution of owners across various time zones. Where the meeting is to be held on a Monday or a Tuesday, the notice could specify, say, 11.00 pm GMT on the Sunday preceding the meeting or a time early on Monday morning before any entries will have been made on the register.

Suggested form of wording

Record date for attendance and voting

To be entitled to attend and vote at the meeting (and for the purpose of the determination by the company of the number of votes they may cast), members must be entered on the company's register of members at [time and date not more than 48 hours before the time fixed for the meeting] ('the specified time'). If the meeting is adjourned to a time not more than 48 hours after the specified time applicable to the original meeting, that time will also apply for the purpose of determining the entitlement of members to attend and vote (and for the purpose of determining the number of votes they may cast) at the adjourned meeting. If, however, the meeting is adjourned for a longer period then, to be so entitled, members must be entered on the company's register of members at the time which is [number of hours, e.g. 48] before the time fixed for the adjourned meeting or, if the Company gives notice of the adjourned meeting, at the time specified in that notice.

In addition, the Act specifies that a traded company must determine the right to vote at a general meeting of the company by reference to the register of members as at a time (determined by the company) that is not more than 48 hours before the time for the holding of the meeting (s. 360B(2)). In calculating this period, no account is to be taken of any part of a day that is not a working day (s. 360B(3)).

A traded company is defined by section 360C as a company which has shares that carry rights to vote at general meetings and are admitted to trading on a regulated market in an European Economic Area (EEA) State by or with the consent of the company. Most UK companies that fall within this definition will also be subject to the rule in the Uncertificated Securities Regulations by virtue of the fact that their shares will have been admitted to CREST. It should be noted that, for the moment, those regulations do not allow any part of a day that is not a working day to be excluded for the purposes of calculating the 48-hour time limit. However, the regulations may ultimately be amended to bring them into line with section 360B, which was introduced to comply with an EU directive on shareholders' rights. It should also be noted that the regulations may apply to a wider range of companies than section 360B. For example, they apply to Alternative Investment Markets (AIM) companies whose shares are admitted to CREST. Such companies are not traded companies for the purposes of section 360B because AIM is not a regulated market.

Section 360B(1) provides that any provision of a traded company's articles is void in so far as it would have the effect of:

- imposing a restriction on a right of a member to participate in and vote at a general meeting of the company unless the member's shares have (after having been acquired by the member and before the meeting) been deposited with, or transferred to, or registered in the name of another person; or
- imposing a restriction on the right of a member to transfer shares in the company during the period of 48 hours before the time for the holding of a general meeting of the company if that right would not otherwise be subject to that restriction. In calculating this period, no account is to be taken of any part of a day that is not a working day (s. 360B(3)).

Record dates generally

Companies whose shares are held in CREST do not need to make provision in their articles to enable a record date to be used for the purposes of determining the right to attend and vote at general meetings because they are allowed by law to do so. Companies that are not publicly traded do not normally need to use a record date for these purposes as they would not normally have any difficulty calculating voting and attendance rights on the basis of the register on the day of the meeting. In order to use a record date, it would be necessary for a company that was not a CREST participant to make some sort of provision in its articles.

Record dates can also be used for other purposes such as calculating dividend entitlements and the right to receive notices. In most cases, the record date will be set before the usual date for calculating entitlements. However, in the case of dividend entitlements, the record date used is usually later than the date of the meeting held to approve the dividend.

Special voting rules imposed by statute for certain resolutions

The Act sometimes requires the votes of certain members or the votes attached to certain shares to be disregarded in determining whether the requisite majority required to pass certain resolutions has been obtained. These restrictions apply in the following cases:

(a) an ordinary resolution of the company to ratify conduct by a director amounting to negligence, default, breach of duty or breach of trust in relation to the company (s. 239(2)), in which case the director's votes in favour are disregarded;

(b) any special resolution giving authority for off-market purchase of own shares (s. 694(2)), to vary a contract for off-market purchase (s. 697), or to release company's rights under contract for off-market purchase (s. 700), in which case any votes attached to the shares which are the subject of the resolution are disregarded if they are cast in favour of the resolution;

(c) a special resolution authorising a payment out of capital for the redemption or purchase of own shares (ss. 713 and 716), in which case any votes attached to the shares which are the subject of the resolution are disregarded if they are cast in favour of the resolution.

In each of the above cases, votes in favour of the resolution must be disregarded but votes against the resolution can be counted and could be used to help defeat the resolution. In the case of the resolutions regarding the purchase of owns shares, a member is allowed to use any other shares he holds (i.e. shares which are not the subject of the proposed buy-back) to vote either for or against the resolution. It should also be noted that the same restrictions apply where any of the above resolutions are passed as a written resolution.

Joint holders

Where members are allowed to hold shares jointly, the default position under the Act is that only the vote of the senior holder who votes (and any proxies duly authorised by him) may be counted by the company. Seniority for these purposes is determined by the order in which the names appear in the register of members (s. 286). Although this provision is capable of modification by a company's articles, it is very rare for a company's articles to do so. The model articles rely on the statutory provision in this regard and make no separate provision about the votes of joint shareholders.

Joint holders may be able to circumvent these restrictions by having their holdings split into two or more joint holdings, each having a different person registered as the senior joint holder. By doing so, the joint holders gain an advantage with respect to voting on a show of hands and, in most cases, satisfying the requirements for demanding a poll.

Death and bankruptcy

Most articles restrict the right of a person who becomes entitled to a share in consequence of the death or bankruptcy of a member to attend and vote at any meeting of the company. Under the general law a personal representative is entitled to be registered as the holder of shares in the absence of any provisions to the contrary. Articles usually provide that a personal representative or a trustee in bankruptcy may, upon providing satisfactory evidence of appointment, elect to become the holder of the share (by giving notice to that effect) or to have some other person registered as the holder (by executing an instrument of transfer). In addition, they usually provide that personal representatives or trustees in bankruptcy shall not be entitled to attend or vote until they have been registered as the holders of the share (pcls 27(3), and plc 66(2)).

If a company continues over a period of time to send notices of meetings and proxy forms to personal representatives or trustees in bankruptcy who have not elected to become the holders of the shares or to have them registered in the name of someone else, it is possible that the company may be stopped from denying their right to attend and vote because it has created a reasonable expectation on their part that they may attend and vote. It is questionable whether a company should stop sending notices of meetings and proxy forms in these circumstances, unless the articles allow. However, it would be sensible to include with any such documents a letter or note warning the representatives or trustees that they will not be entitled to vote without taking further action in accordance with the articles.

Normally the death of a member automatically revokes the appointment by that person of a proxy. However, articles sometimes provide that any proxy appointed by a member who subsequently dies will be valid unless the company receives notice in writing of the death of that member.

Personal representatives are entitled to determine the order in which their names appear on the register of members.

A bankrupt who remains registered as a member of the company is entitled to vote at general meetings but must vote in accordance with the directions of his trustee. It should be noted, however, that the company is not bound to ensure that those instructions have been followed.

Mental or physical incapacity

Articles sometimes make provision regarding voting by members who are suffering from some sort of mental incapacity. However, no specific provision in this regard is included in any of the model articles prescribed under the 2006 Act, although they do require any proxy form not executed by the person appointing the proxy (in this case the incapacitated member), to be accompanied by evidence of the authority of the person who executed it (pcls 46(4), clg 32(4) and plc 39(8)).

In England and Wales, appointment orders will be made by the Court of Protection under the Mental Capacity Act 2005. The Court of Protection may make orders appointing a 'deputy' (formerly termed a 'receiver') to deal with the income or property of a person who, in the judgment of the court, lacks capacity. Such orders may authorise the deputy (or deputies) to receive all income of the person and give such other directions as are appropriate at the time. Orders will vary in their terms, and particular care should be taken to ensure that all acts by the deputy in connection with the shareholding are within his powers as expressed in the order appointing him. The order received in the first instance may, for example, relate only to income from the shareholding, leaving other aspects to be dealt with in subsequent orders or directions.

All orders will bear the official seal of the Court. The administrative aspects of Court of Protection orders are dealt with by the Public Guardianship Office. The equivalent Scottish document is known as an appointment of guardian.

If a Court of Protection order is received for registration, the existence of the order, together with the name and address of the deputy (or deputies) and the date of registration should be entered in the register of members. Future communications to the shareholder should be addressed to the deputy, who should be described as 'deputy (appointed by the Court of Protection) for ... '. However, the account of the shareholder in the register of members should remain in the same position, as legally the person lacking capacity is still the registered shareholder.

A Court of Protection order will continue in force until the death of the shareholder concerned (unless the order is earlier revoked and the deputy is discharged by the Court). On the death of the shareholder, the order will lapse and the powers of the deputy terminate, whereupon the company may then take the usual action in relation to a deceased shareholder on proof of death.

It should be noted that the Mental Capacity Act 2005, which came into force on 1 October 2007 and applies only in England and Wales, enables individuals to grant a lasting power of attorney which will continue in force even if they should lose their capacity. Such powers do not become effective until they been registered with the Public Guardian. The prescribed form for lasting powers of attorney, and the procedure for registration, is set out in the Lasting Powers of Attorney, Enduring Powers of Attorney and Public Guardian Regulations 2007 (SI 2007/1253).

Enduring powers of attorney created before 1 October 2007 under the Enduring Powers of Attorney Act 1985 and not revoked are still valid (subject to certain conditions) but, if the donor of the power has become mentally incapable, must be registered with the Public Guardian before they can be used. See Schedule 4 of the

Mental Capacity Act 2005 for the detailed provisions governing such enduring powers.

Calls unpaid

Articles commonly restrict the voting rights of members in respect of shares on which calls or other sums presently payable have not been paid. The scope of the restrictions which can be imposed vary and care should be taken to ensure that the power to disenfranchise is properly exercised. The model articles for private companies limited by shares do not make any such provision, presumably because all shares are meant to be issued fully paid (pcls 21).

Where the articles do include such a restriction, they will normally provide that no voting rights attached to a share may be exercised unless all amounts payable to the company in respect of that share have been paid (e.g. reg. 57 of Table A and plc 41). However, regulation 65 of the 1948 Table A provides that no *member* shall be entitled to vote at any general meeting unless *all* calls or other sums presently payable by him in respect of shares have been paid. In other words, a member will be disqualified from voting even if a call on only one of his shares remains unpaid. Modern articles often impose similar restrictions but give the directors the option not to enforce them.

Precedent: Article: Voting Rights where a Call is Unpaid

No member shall, unless the Board otherwise determines be entitled to vote at a General Meeting either personally or by proxy, or to exercise any privilege as a member unless all calls or other sums presently payable by him in respect of shares in the Company have been paid.

Failure to respond to section 793 inquiry

Public companies often take power in their articles to disenfranchise shares held by a member who has not replied to a notice served under section 793 of the 2006 Act inquiring as to any beneficial interests in shares.

Precedent: Article of public company removing voting rights for failure to respond to a section 793 notice

(A) If any member, or any other person appearing to be interested in shares held by such member, has been duly served with a notice under Section 793 of the Companies Act 2006 and is in default for the Designated Period in supplying to the Company the information thereby required, then the Directors may in their absolute discretion at any time thereafter by notice (a 'Direction Notice') to such member direct that in respect of the shares in relation to which the default occurred (the 'Default Shares') (which expression shall include any further shares which are issued in respect of such shares) the member shall not (for so long as the default continues) nor shall any transferee to whom any of such shares are transferred (other than pursuant to an approved transfer or pursuant to (C) below) be entitled to vote either personally or by proxy at a general meeting of the Company or a meeting of the holders of any class of shares of the Company or to exercise any other right to attend or vote at general meetings of the Company or meetings of the holders of any class of shares of the Company.

(B) The Company shall send to each other person appearing to be interested in the shares the subject of any Direction Notice a copy of the said notice, but the failure or omission by the Company to do so shall not invalidate such Direction Notice.

(C) Where the Default Shares represent at least 0.25 per cent of the issued shares of that class then the Direction Notice may additionally direct:

(i) that any cash dividend or other such money, or shares issued in lieu of a dividend, which would otherwise be due in respect of each of the Default Shares shall (in whole or any part thereof) be retained (or, as the case may be, not issued) by the Company without any liability to pay interest thereon when such dividend or other money or shares is finally paid or issued to the member; and/or

(ii) that no transfer of any of the shares held by such member shall be registered unless:

(a) the member is not himself in default as regards supplying the information required and the transfer is of part only of the member's holding and when presented for registration is accompanied by a certificate by the member in a form satisfactory to the Directors to the effect that after due and careful enquiry the member is satisfied that no person in default as regards supplying such information is interested in any of the shares the subject of the transfer; or

(b) the transfer is an Approved Transfer.

(D) Any Direction Notice shall have effect in accordance with its terms for so long as the default in respect of which the Direction Notice was issued continues and (unless the Directors otherwise determine) for a period of one week thereafter but shall cease to have effect in relation to any Default Shares which are transferred by such member by means of an Approved Transfer. The Directors may at any time give notice cancelling a Direction Notice.

(E) For the purpose of this Article:

(i) a person shall be treated as appearing to be interested in any shares if the member holding such shares has given to the Company a notification under the said Section 793 which either (a) names such person as being so interested or (b) fails to establish the identities of those interested in the shares and (after taking into account the said notification and any other relevant Section 793 notification) the Company knows or has reasonable cause to believe or suspects on reasonable grounds that the person in question is or may be interested in the shares;

(ii) the Designated Period is twenty-eight days from the date of service of the notice under the said Section 793 except that if the Default Shares represent at least 0.25 per cent. of the issued shares of that class, the Designated Period is fourteen days from such date; and

(iii) a transfer of shares is an Approved Transfer if but only if:

(a) it is a transfer of shares to an offeror by way or in pursuance of acceptance of a take-over offer for a company (as defined in Section 974 of the Companies Act 2006); or

(b) the Directors are satisfied that the transfer is made pursuant to a sale of the whole of the beneficial ownership of the shares to a party unconnected with the member and with other persons appearing to be interested in such shares; or

(c) the transfer results from a sale made through a Recognised Investment Exchange.

(F) Nothing contained in this Article shall limit the power of the Directors under the Companies Act 2006.

The Listing Rules require that where such power is taken in the articles of a listed company, the sanction may not take effect earlier than 14 days after the service of the section 793 notice. In addition, any sanctions imposed must cease after not more than seven days after:

(a) receipt by the issuer of notice that the shareholding has been sold to an unconnected third party through a RIE or an overseas exchange or by the acceptance of a takeover offer; or

(b) due compliance, to the satisfaction of the issuer, with the notice under section 793 (Listing Rule 9.3.9).

A company can apply to the court for an order imposing certain restrictions on shares (including the removal of voting rights) where a person has failed to give the information required following service of a section 793 notice (s. 794) .

Non-voting or restricted voting shares

Articles usually provide that the company may issue more than one class of shares with such rights and restrictions as may be determined by ordinary resolution or by the directors. Shares will be of a different class if they give their holders different rights from other shares. The rights of the holders will typically be set out in the resolution creating the class or set out in the articles of association. A company may issue non-voting shares or shares with restricted voting rights. Preference shares are an example of a class of shares with restricted voting rights (see below).

Preference shares

Preference shares are perhaps the most common class of shares issued in addition to the ordinary shares. They usually have priority over the ordinary shares with respect to the payment of dividends and repayment of capital on winding up. The holders are usually entitled to a fixed rate of dividend and are not normally entitled to vote unless those dividends are in arrears by more than six months.

Enhanced voting rights

The articles may give members enhanced voting rights in certain circumstances. The most common example is as a protection for a founder member against removal as a director of a private limited company.

Precedent: Article giving enhanced voting rights

(a) Subject to sub-paragraphs (b) and (c) below, on a show of hands every member who (being an individual) is present in person or (being a corporation) is present by a duly authorised representative, not being himself a member, shall have one vote and on a poll every member shall have one vote for every share of which he is the holder.

(b) If at any general meeting a poll is duly demanded on a resolution to remove a director from office, the director named in the resolution shall be entitled to [number] votes for each share of which he is the holder.

(c) If at any general meeting a poll is duly demanded on a resolution to delete or amend the provisions of this article, every director shall have [number] votes for each share of which he is the holder if voting against such a resolution.

The method employed in the above precedent article does not create a different class of shares – any member who is a director will be entitled to more votes per share on a resolution to remove him as a director or to amend the article conferring those rights. Normally, the number of extra votes will be sufficient to defeat the other members. If the membership of the company subsequently changes, it may be necessary to amend this type of article to preserve that position.

If it is intended to give some but not all members protection against removal as a director, it is necessary to give those members a different class of shares with different voting rights.

Voting on a show of hands

Under the common law, voting is conducted on a show of hands at a meeting unless there are regulations or enactments to the contrary. The Act is drafted on the assumption that voting will proceed first by some means other than a poll, and the articles of most companies adopt the common law practice. There is, however, no statutory requirement to do so and a company's articles could provide, for example, that voting shall be conducted by a poll on all substantive resolutions. In the US, voting at general meetings of listed corporations must be conducted in this way and many UK listed companies now adopt this practice.

However, the articles of most companies provide that a resolution put to the vote at a general meeting shall be decided on a show of hands unless a poll is duly demanded (pcls 42, clg 28 and plc 34).

Under the common law, each member present has one vote on a show of hands regardless of any other factors such as the number of shares held or the fact that they may be attending in more than one capacity.

The default rule of one vote for each member present in person in section 284(2) also applies in relation to a single corporate representative appointed by a corporate member by virtue of the fact that such a representative is deemed under section 323 to have the same rights as a member who is an individual. However, if a corporate member appoints multiple representatives, each representative has the same voting rights as the corporation would be entitled to on a show of hands (s. 323(3)). It should be noted that the statutory rules regarding corporate representatives are not capable of modification by the articles except to the extent that the articles may exclude or enhance the voting rights of the member (and therefore the corporate representative). Accordingly, under the above formula, any modification made by a company's articles to the default 'one member one vote' rule would also apply to both single and multiple corporate representatives.

Section 285 of the Act also gives proxies a statutory right to vote on a show of hands. However, the relevant provisions are expressed as being subject to anything in a company's articles and may, therefore, be modified or excluded. Section 285(1) provides that, on a vote on a resolution on a show of hands at a meeting every proxy present who has been duly appointed by one or more members entitled to vote on the resolution has one vote. This means that, subject to the articles, if a member who is entitled to vote appoints multiple proxies, each proxy for that member has a right to one vote on a show of hands. Under section 285(1), a person who has been appointed as the proxy of more than one member entitled to vote on the resolution would have only one vote if instructed by all those members to vote in the same way. However, section 285(2) provides that if the proxy has been instructed by one or more of those members to vote for the resolution and by one or more other of those members to vote against it, he shall have one vote for and one vote against the resolution on a show of hands. This rule may or may not apply where a proxy has been instructed to vote one way by certain members and is inclined to vote the opposite way on behalf of other members who have given him discretion as to how to vote.

It should be noted that all three versions of the model articles prescribed under the 2006 Act rely totally on the statutory default provisions with respect to voting on a show of hands. However, older articles may make separate provision. Where they do so, they will usually provide something along the lines that 'subject to any rights or restrictions attached to any shares, on a show of hands every member who (being an individual) is present in person or (being a corporation) present by a duly authorised representative, not being himself a member entitled to vote, shall have one vote'. It should be noted that section 323 modifies this rule so far as multiple corporate representatives of the same member are concerned, who are each given a right to vote on a show of hands by that section where the member who appointed them has a right to vote. Articles on voting on a show of hands may or may not allow proxies to vote on a show of hands. Older articles are often silent on the matter. Total silence on matters of voting will mean that the default statutory rules apply. However, in the example quoted above, it is arguable that the failure to mention proxies in the list of those entitled to vote on a show of hands means that the articles override the statutory rules.

As can be seen, voting on a show of hands does not necessarily proceed strictly on the basis of one member one vote (a member who appoints multiple proxies or corporate representatives may secure the right to more than one vote). Neither can it be said to proceed strictly on the basis that each person present who is entitled to vote gets only one vote (although this is closer to the truth it is not always true because a proxy representing more than one member may be able to vote both for and against the resolution). These anomalies do not really matter because voting on a show of hands is not intended to be a perfect democratic process. In a company with a share capital each of the members may hold different numbers of shares or have different voting rights which are not taken into account on a show of hands. It is, of course, possible that the result of a vote would be different if these factors were taken into account and it is for this reason that members are given the right to demand a poll, a method of voting that ensures that they are taken into account.

Nevertheless, voting on a show of hands is clearly a much quicker method of voting and is ideally suited to situations where resolutions are passed without any opposition and with a clear majority either for or against.

Declaration by chair of results on a show of hands

On a vote on a resolution at a meeting on a show of hands, a declaration by the chair that the resolution has or has not been passed, or passed with a particular majority, is conclusive evidence of that fact without proof of the number or proportion of the votes recorded in favour of or against the resolution (s. 320(1)). An entry in respect of such a declaration in minutes of the meeting recorded in accordance with section 355 is also conclusive evidence of that fact without such proof (s. 320(2)). Section 320 does not have effect if a poll is demanded in respect of the resolution (and the demand is not subsequently withdrawn).

Articles sometimes duplicate the effect of section 320, however, the statutory provision cannot be overridden by a company's articles.

A declaration made by the chair in good faith under section 320 will be conclusive and will prevent the question being reopened in legal proceedings. This is so even where there is evidence that the chair's declaration was wrong, unless there is evidence of fraud or manifest error.

Voting on a poll

A poll is a vote conducted by voting papers (or some equivalent electronic method) rather than by a show of hands. The voting rights of members on a poll will be determined by the articles and, in default, by the Act. Generally speaking, for a company with a share capital, members will be entitled to one vote for each share held, although members holding certain shares may have no votes and others may have enhanced voting rights. This normally means that members with larger holdings of ordinary shares will have a greater say in the result than they would on a show of hands. In addition, a show of hands does not necessarily reflect the fact that a person may be voting as the proxy or representative of more than one member.

In the case of a company without a share capital (e.g. a guarantee company), the members will normally have no more votes on a poll than they do on a show of hands. However, the outcome of a vote on a show of hands may still be different to the outcome of a vote taken on a poll because some of the people able to vote on a show of hands may be acting as the proxy or representative of several members. This is not reflected when they vote on a show of hands but is when a vote is taken on a poll.

Irrespective of anything contained in a company's articles, votes may be tendered on a poll either by the member in person, by a corporate representative or by a proxy.

On a poll, all or any of the voting rights of a member may be exercised by one or more duly appointed proxies (s. 285(3)). However, where a member appoints more than one proxy, this does not authorise the exercise by the proxies taken together of more extensive voting rights than could be exercised by the member in person (s. 285(4)).

A corporate representative is entitled to exercise (on behalf of the corporation) the same powers at a meeting as the corporation could exercise if it were an individual member of the company (s. 323(2)), and is, therefore, authorised to vote on a poll on its behalf.

On a poll taken at a meeting of the company or a meeting of any class of members, a member entitled to more than one vote need not, if they vote, use all their votes or cast all the votes they use in the same way (s. 322).

Poll procedures

Under the common law, where the method of voting used at a meeting is a show of hands, any person who is entitled to vote at a meeting may demand a poll. This common rule applies to company meetings unless the articles provide otherwise.

In practice, articles frequently modify the conditions which a person must satisfy in order to make a valid demand for a poll. In a large company with many thousands of shares, it would be ludicrous for one member holding only one share to be allowed to demand a poll without the support of other members. On the other hand, it would not be fair if the conditions made it almost impossible for the members to demand a poll. To ensure that this does not happen, the Act provides certain safeguards regarding the conditions for making a valid demand (see below), and, perhaps more importantly, states that a provision in a company's articles will be void in so far as it excludes the right to demand a poll on any question other than a resolution to elect the chair of the meeting or to adjourn the meeting (s. 321(1)). The model articles allow a poll to be demanded on both the election of the chair and a resolution to adjourn. However, those for public companies require any poll demanded on these questions to be taken immediately (plc 37(4)). The model articles for private companies require all polls to be taken immediately (pcls 44(4), clg 30(4)).

Valid demand

A poll may be demanded either on or before the declaration of the result of a show of hands by any person or persons entitled under the articles to do so. This will usually include the chair, members (whether represented in person or by proxy or a corporate representative) satisfying certain conditions, and, in some cases, the directors.

Under section 321(2), a provision contained in a company's articles will be void in so far as it would have the effect of making ineffective a demand for a poll:

(a) by not less than five members having the right to vote on the resolution; or
(b) by a member or members representing not less than 10% of the total voting rights of all the members having the right to vote on the resolution (excluding any voting rights attached to any shares in the company held as treasury shares); or
(c) by a member or members holding shares in the company conferring a right to vote on the resolution, being shares on which an aggregate sum has been paid up equal to not less than 10% of the total sum paid up on all the shares conferring that right (excluding shares in the company conferring a right to vote on the resolution which are held as treasury shares).

If an article is deemed to be void under section 321(2), the common law right to demand a poll will apply whereby one member may make a valid demand.

A proxy has the right to demand or join in the demand for a poll (s. 329). In applying the provisions of section 321(2) (requirements for effective demand), section 329(2) provides that a demand by a proxy counts:

(a) for the purposes of the 'not less than five members' test, as a demand by the member;
(b) for the purposes of the '10% of voting rights test', as a demand by a member representing the voting rights that the proxy is authorised to exercise; and
(c) for the purposes of the '10% of paid up share capital conferring the right to vote' test, as a demand by a member holding the shares to which those rights are attached.

It is questionable whether two or more proxies appointed by the same member can defeat any provision regarding the specific number of members who must join in a demand for a poll. Section 329(2) only applies for the purposes of determining whether the provisions in a company's articles are valid. It suggests that demands by proxies for the same member do not need to be treated as demands by different members but as demands by the same member. However, the answer will depend on the precise wording of a company's articles.

Articles often relax the conditions for a valid demand (e.g. they may enable a valid demand to be made by two (rather than five) members having the right to vote at the meeting). It has been held that where the articles state that 'members' holding a certain percentage of shares may demand a poll, a single member holding that percentage may demand a poll. In particular, this is the case if the company's articles stated in the definitions section (usually the first article) that words in the singular should be taken to include the plural and vice versa. Most articles track the wording of section 321 to avoid any problem in this regard.

In the absence of any provision to the contrary in the articles, joint holders should be counted as a single member for the purposes of demanding a poll.

The chair has no right to direct that a poll be taken unless it is duly demanded or he is given that power by the articles. Articles usually give the chair the power to demand a poll (pcls 44(2), clg 30(2) and plc 36(2)). The chair of the meeting will, however, usually be entitled to demand or join in a demand for a poll in his capacity as a proxy. Where the chair has the power to call a poll, he must exercise that power if it is necessary to ascertain the true sense of the meeting. For example, where the chair has been instructed by proxies to vote in a certain way and those votes, if cast, would produce a different result from the one on the vote on a show of hands, he has a duty to demand a poll.

Special rules

The Act provides that different rules shall apply when deciding whether a valid demand has been made in certain circumstances. These rules override any provision of a company's articles. For example, at a class meeting held to consider a variation of rights, any member of that class, whether present in person or by proxy, may demand a poll (s. 334(6) – meetings relating to class of shareholders and s. 335(5) – class meetings of companies without a share capital).

In addition, any member, whether present in person or by proxy, may demand a poll in the following circumstances:

(a) on any special resolution under section 694 giving authority for an off-market purchase of own shares (s. 695(4)(b)), under section 697 to vary a contract for an off-market purchase (s. 698(4)(b)), or under section 700 to release a company's rights under a contract for an off-market purchase (s. 700(5));

(b) on a special resolution under section 716 approving a payment out of capital for the purchase or redemption of the company's own shares (s. 717(4)(b)).

Withdrawal of demand

Articles usually provide that a demand for a poll may, before the poll is taken, be withdrawn but only with the consent of the chair (pcls 44(3), clg 30(3) and plc 36(3)).

Under the common law, the result of a show of hands ceases to have any effect once a valid demand for a poll has been made. Unless provision is made in the articles, it is arguable that it would be dangerous for the chair to assume that the previous vote on a show of hands was still valid and safer for him not to consent to the withdrawal of the demand and to proceed with the poll. Another possibility is that if a valid demand for a poll is withdrawn, the chair could call for another vote on a show of hands to be taken. However, it would be slightly disturbing if the outcome of this second show of hands was different to the first. If that were to happen, it would suggest that a poll probably would have been the most desirable option and the chair might reasonably be expected to call one himself at this juncture if he has the power to do so.

If the chair does decide to take any previous vote on a show of hands as the result of the vote on that resolution, it is suggested that he should make a declaration to that effect and if he has not already done so, declare the resolution carried or not carried, as the case may be. In view of the statutory provisions regarding any such declaration by the chair, this would be conclusive evidence that the resolution has or has not been passed, or passed with a particular majority, without proof of the number or proportion of the votes recorded in favour of or against the resolution (s. 320(1)). This provision does not have effect if a poll is demanded in respect of the resolution (and the demand is not subsequently withdrawn) (s. 320(3)). However, it must still be assumed to apply where a demand for a poll has been made but subsequently withdrawn.

If a poll demanded before a vote on a show of hands is subsequently withdrawn, it is plainly necessary to put the resolution to a vote by a show of hands. The model articles do not bother making any provision in this regard.

Conduct of poll

Articles usually specify the manner in which the poll is to be conducted or who may determine the manner in which it is to be conducted. The model articles for private companies require all polls to be taken immediately in such manner as the chair of the meeting directs (pcls 44(4), clg 30(4)).

The model articles for public companies do not require polls to be taken immediately, except on a resolution to adjourn or to appoint a chair of the meeting (plc 37(4)). They provide that any other poll shall be taken as the chair directs within 30 days, that he may appoint scrutineers (who need not be members) and that the result of the poll shall be deemed to be the resolution of the meeting at which the poll was demanded (plc 37).

A poll cannot be taken on a number of resolutions together. In other words, the members must be given an opportunity to vote for or against each resolution separately. This does not mean that separate voting papers must be used for each resolution as long as the voting papers allow members to vote for some resolutions and against others.

Precedent: Voting Card for use by Members and Corporate Representatives

VOTING CARD

For the [Annual] General Meeting of

XYZ PLC

held on [date]

(To be used as instructed by the chair)

Name of shareholder (in Block Capitals)

. . . .

Signature . . . .

Number of shares voted (see note 1) . . . .

		For	Against	Votes withheld
Resolution 1	To receive the report and accounts			
Resolution 2	To approve the directors' remuneration report			
Resolution 3	To declare a final dividend			

		For	Against	Votes withheld
Resolution 4	To re-elect [name A] as a director			
Resolution 5	To re-elect [name B] a director			
Resolution 6	To re-elect [name C] a director			
Resolution 7	Reappointment of auditors			
Resolution 8	Share buyback			
Resolution 9	Directors' authority to allot shares (Section 551)			
Resolution 10	Disapplication of pre-emption rights			
Resolution 11	Notice of general meetings			

Notes
1. It is not necessary to complete the number of shares voted, provided that your vote is being given in respect of the entire holding of the member.
2. If you wish to cast all the votes covered by this voting form in the same way, you may do so by placing an X in the appropriate column above. If you place an X in more than one column for any resolution, your vote(s) on that resolution will not be counted.
3. If you wish to cast your votes in different ways, you may do so by indicating the number of votes cast 'for' or 'against' or the number of votes withheld in the appropriate columns.
4. A 'vote withheld' on any resolution is not a vote in law and will not be counted for the purposes of determining whether or not that resolution has been passed by a particular majority.

Precedent: Voting card for use by proxies on a poll

VOTING CARD

For the [Annual] General Meeting of

XYZ PLC

held on [date]

(To be used as instructed by the chair)

Name of proxy . . . .

(In Block Capitals)

Signature of proxy . . . .

Name of shareholder represented . . . .

(In Block Capitals)

Number of shares represented by proxy . . . .

[The rest of the voting card will be the same as for shareholders above.]

Voting card for use by chair on a poll

CHAIR'S VOTING CARD

For the [Annual/Extraordinary] General Meeting of

XYZ PLC

held on [date]

Signature of chair of meeting . . . .

See attached sheet for names and holdings of shareholders represented.

Number of votes

		For	Against	Votes withheld
Resolution 1	To receive the report and accounts			
Resolution 2	To approve the directors' remuneration report			
Resolution 3	To declare a final dividend			
Resolution 4	To re-elect [name A] as a director			
Resolution 5	To re-elect [name B] a director			
Resolution 6	To re-elect [name C] a director			
Resolution 7	Reappointment of auditors			
Resolution 8	Share buyback			
Resolution 9	Directors' authority to allot shares (Section 551)			
Resolution 10	Disapplication of pre-emption rights			
Resolution 11	Notice of general meetings			

Where the articles allow the chair to determine the method of taking the poll but also require the personal attendance of the voter or the proxy appointed, the chair has no right to direct that the poll be taken by voting papers to be returned by members through the post.

Unless the articles specify the length of time for which the poll is to continue, the chair should not close it as long as votes are still being tendered. Where the articles provide that a poll shall be taken 'in such manner as the chair may direct', the chair may direct that it be taken immediately. However, where the articles provided for a poll to be taken at a time and place to be fixed by the directors within seven days of the meeting, the chair cannot direct that a poll be taken immediately.

The model articles for public companies provides that a demand for a poll shall not prevent the continuance of a meeting for the transaction of any business other than the question on which the poll was demanded (plc 37(6)).

Notice of a poll

A poll taken at a later date is deemed to be a continuance of the original meeting. The original meeting is deemed to have been suspended rather than adjourned and it is not necessary to give any notice unless the articles so require. Articles often contain provisions which specify when notice of a poll must be given. Plainly, this is not necessary for the model articles for private companies, which require all polls to be taken immediately. However, the model articles for public companies provide that no notice need be given of a poll not taken forthwith if the time and place at which it is to be taken is announced at the meeting at which it is demanded, but that in any other case at least seven days' notice specifying the time and place at which the poll is to be taken must be given to all the members (including those who did not attend the meeting) (plc 37(7) and (8)). If the chair does not announce the date and time of the poll at the meeting, it follows that it cannot be held for at least eight days and then only if proper notice has been given.

Procedure on a poll

The procedure for conducting a poll will obviously depend in part on any specific provision made in that regard by a company's articles. Accordingly, the following outline is only provided as a guide and should be read in conjunction with any article provisions governing voting by shareholders on a poll.

Action before the meeting

- A summary should be produced of the total proxy votes given in favour of the chair for each resolution indicating the number of votes he has been instructed to cast for or against the resolution, any votes withheld and the number of votes where the chair has been given discretion as to how to vote.
- A summary should also be produced of any proxies given in favour of other persons together with any voting instructions (if any).

- In the case of a listed company, it will be necessary to amalgamate the two summaries in order to prepare a schedule of votes tendered by proxy for the purposes of the disclosures required to be made at the meeting in accordance with the recommendations of the UK Corporate Governance Code.
- Appoint the people who will conduct any poll which is taken and/or act as scrutineers (usually employees of the company or its solicitors, registrars or auditors) and arrange for their attendance.
- In the case of a quoted company, monitor whether a valid demand for independent report on a poll has been made and take action accordingly.
- Prepare voting papers.
- Draft script for chair.
- Ascertain the conditions under which a valid demand may be made and brief chair accordingly.
- Brief staff and scrutineers and liaise with any independent assessor.
- Obtain an up-to-date list of members entitled to vote (or if class meeting, members of that class) and annotate which, if any, are not entitled to vote owing to some special restriction and which, if any, are entitled to any enhanced voting rights.

When a poll is demanded

- If appropriate, the chair may suggest the demand be withdrawn in view of proxy position.
- If not withdrawn, take the names of those making the demand and check against the register of members whether they satisfy the conditions for a valid demand.
- If the demand is not valid or it is withdrawn, the chair should rule accordingly and proceed with the business:
  - if the demand was made before a vote was taken on a show of hands, the chair may invite members to vote on the resolution in that manner and declare the result accordingly or decide to continue to proceed with the poll; and
  - if the demand was made after the chair had declared the result of the vote on a show of hands, the chair may decide to continue to proceed with the poll or to proceed with the business.

If demand valid

- The chair should advise the meeting of the validity of the demand.
- The chair should announce when the poll will be held. Depending on the articles and the nature of the business, this may be:
  - immediately;
  - at the conclusion of meeting; or
  - at a later date.

- If the poll is to be held later (i.e. not immediately), the chair should proceed to next item of business.

Holding a poll
- The chair should explain the procedure for the taking of the poll.
- Voting papers should be issued to all those entitled to vote.
- The chair should complete voting forms in respect of proxy votes held by him.
- Completed voting papers should be collected.
- Each voting paper should be checked for completeness.
- Where the votes are given by proxy:
  - check that person voting has been validly appointed as a proxy; and
  - that proxy has followed member's instruction, if any.
- Any voting paper not on the face of it valid should be referred to the scrutineers (if any). In cases of doubt the chair should be asked to make a ruling.
- Verify holdings against the register of members (or the list of entitlements to vote prepared before the meeting).
- Eliminate votes given by proxy (including those given to the chair in that capacity) where the member voted in person on the poll.
- If a member has appointed more than one proxy, ensure that the total number of votes cast does not exceed that members' holding. Refer any problems to the chair.
- Count the votes for and against.
- Prepare a summary of the votes cast for and against in person and by proxy, votes withheld, abstentions and spoilt votes.
- Scrutineers to sign summary and certify the result of the poll.
- Report the result to the chair.

Declaration of result of poll
- At the meeting:
  - if the poll was directed to be taken at a later time, the meeting should be resumed at the appointed time and the result declared; or
  - if the poll was taken immediately, the chair to announce result when other business completed.
- If the resolution is passed, a copy of it may need to be filed at Companies House and, in the case of listed companies, with the UK Listing Authority.

Voting on a poll: votes cast in advance
A company's articles may contain provision to the effect that on a vote on a resolution on a poll taken at a meeting, the votes may include votes cast in advance (s. 322A(1)). This provision was introduced by the Companies (Shareholders' Rights) Regulations 2009 (SI 2009/1632) to comply with a requirement of the Shareholders' Rights Directive. The ability to vote in advance

on a poll is already provided by the system which enables members to appoint the chair of the meeting as their proxy and to instruct him how to vote. Accordingly, it is not clear what advantage would be gained by a company or its members from a separate system allowing votes on a poll to be cast in advance.

If such a system for voting in advance is provided for in a company's articles, it must comply with certain conditions. The condition in section 322A(2) only applies to companies that are traded companies. It provides that any article relating to voting in advance at a general meeting may be made subject only to such requirements and restrictions as are necessary to ensure the identification of the person voting, and that are proportionate to the achievement of that objective. However, it also clarifies that nothing in this rule affects any power of a company to require reasonable evidence of the entitlement of any person who is not a member to vote. A traded company for these purposes is defined in section 380C as a company any shares of which carry rights to vote at general meetings and are admitted to trading on a regulated market in an EEA state either by or with the consent of the company.

The condition in section 322A(3) applies to any company which makes provision in its articles for voting in advance. It provides that any provision of a company's articles is void in so far as it would have the effect of requiring any document casting a vote in advance to be received by the company or another person earlier than:

- in the case of a poll taken more than 48 hours after it was demanded, 24 hours before the time appointed for the taking of the poll; or
- in the case of any other poll, 48 hours before the time for holding the meeting or adjourned meeting.

In calculating the above periods, no account may be taken of any part of a day that is not a working day (s. 322A(4)).

Results of a poll

The date of a resolution passed on a poll is the date the result of the poll is ascertained. Articles may seem to override this rule by providing that the result of the poll shall be the decision of the meeting in respect of the resolution on which the poll was demanded (plc 37(3)). However, all this type of article provision probably does is enable a meeting to be closed pending the outcome of the poll. It is feasible that a company's articles could provide that the date of a resolution passed on a poll is deemed to be the date on which the poll was taken or the date on which voting on the poll closed. However, this is not normally considered necessary because the company will normally seek to ensure that the results of the poll are determined on the day it is taken or on the day that voting on it was closed.

Probably the least satisfactory aspect of voting on a poll rather than a show of hands, is the fact that the result of the poll is rarely known until after the meeting.

This often means that the members who attended the meeting will have no idea whether the resolution has been passed or defeated, let alone how many votes were cast for or against it. The only exception would appear to be where the articles require a poll to be taken immediately. In some cases, for example, on a poll on a resolution to adjourn or to appoint a chair of the meeting, the requirement that the poll be taken immediately implies that the result must also be determined before the meeting can progress. However, there is no reason why this should be the case for any other poll taken under the model articles for private companies, which require all polls to be taken immediately. In practice, unless there is a good reason why the business of the meeting should be suspended until the outcome of the vote on the poll is determined, it is suggested that once the poll has been taken, the meeting may proceed to the next item of business and the results of the poll can be declared as and when they become available.

There is no requirement to notify members of the results of the poll. This is the case even with regard to the members who demanded it. This is not to say that the company should refuse to reveal the results of the poll. The result must be recorded in the minutes and any member may request a copy of the minutes. In addition, if the resolution is one which must be filed at Companies House, the fact that it has been passed will become a matter of public record.

Quoted companies are required to publish the results of any poll on a website. Listed companies must announce the results of resolutions passed at any meeting of the company and file copies of any such resolutions with the UK Listing Authority.

There is no reason why a company should not notify the results of a poll to the members who demanded it. However, a publicly traded company should bear in mind that the result may be price-sensitive information and it may, therefore, need to be announced before the members are notified. Some companies advertise the results of the poll in a newspaper.

A company may, if it so desires, inform the members how particular votes were cast. It has been held that this is not confidential information and that the company has a right to the information if the poll is conducted by independent scrutineers.

Website publication of poll results and independent reports on a poll
Quoted companies – website publication
Quoted companies are required to disclose on a website the results of any poll taken at a general meeting, specifying the number of votes cast for and against (s. 341).

The information required to be made available under section 341 must be made available on a website maintained by or on behalf of the company as soon as reasonably practicable and be kept available for two years after publication (s. 353).

Traded company website publication requirements

Under section 341(1A) a traded company must publish the following information on its website in relation to a poll taken at a general meeting:

(a) the date of the meeting;
(b) the text of the resolution or, as the case may be, a description of the subject matter of the poll;
(c) the number of votes validly cast;
(d) the proportion of the company's issued share capital (determined at the time at which the right to vote is determined under section 360B(2)) represented by those votes;
(e) the number of votes cast in favour;
(f) the number of votes cast against; and
(g) the number of abstentions (if counted).

The company must comply with this requirement by the end of the 16-day period beginning with the day of the meeting, or, or if later, the end of the first working day following the day on which the result of the poll is declared (s. 341(1B)).

The information must be made available on a website maintained by or on behalf of the company and be kept available for two years after publication in accordance with section 353.

Independent report on a poll

Members of quoted companies are given a right to require an independent scrutiny of any polled vote, with the scrutineer's report having to be disclosed on the company's website (ss 342–354). The directors are required to obtain an independent report if they receive requests to do so from members representing 5% of the total voting rights or at least 100 members holding on average £100's worth of share capital each. A request may be made in hard copy or electronic form, must identify the poll or polls to which it relates and must be received by the company not later than one week after the date on which the poll is taken.

On receipt of a valid request, a company must appoint an independent assessor to prepare a report who meets the requirements of section 344 as to independence and has no other role in relation to any poll on which he is to report (e.g. collecting and counting votes) (s. 343). These rules will prevent a company from appointing its registrar as the independent assessor.

In his report, the independent assessor is required to state:

(a) whether the procedures adopted in connection with the poll or polls were adequate;
(b) whether the votes cast were fairly and accurately recorded;
(c) whether the validity of members' appointments of proxies was fairly assessed;
(d) whether the notice of meeting complied with section 325;

(e) whether there was any breach of section 326 (company sponsored invitations to appoint a proxy).

Sections 348 and 349 give the independent assessor a right to attend the meeting and a right of access to relevant information.

Where an independent assessor has been appointed to report on a poll, the company must make the following information available on a website (s. 351):

(a) the fact of his appointment and his identity;
(b) the text of any resolutions or a description of the subject matter of the poll(s) to which his appointment relates; and
(c) a copy of his report.

The information required to be made available under section 351 must be made available on a website maintained by or on behalf of the company as soon as reasonably practicable and be kept available for two years after publication (s. 353).

Chair's casting vote

Articles may purport to give the chair a casting vote. None of the model articles do so as it is thought that the chair's casting vote is incompatible with the provisions on voting and resolutions in the 2006 Act. Previous articles may include this provision and should be checked in reference to the specific company.

Where a company's articles provide for the chair to have a casting vote and that article is still effective, they will normally make provision similar to regulation 50 of the original version of the 1985 Table, which states:

> 50. In the case of an equality of votes, whether on a show of hands or on a poll, the chair shall be entitled to a casting vote in addition to any other vote he may have.

The circumstances in which it is reasonable for the chair to use his or her casting vote on a show of hands are fairly limited. It is submitted that, in most cases, in order to ascertain the true sense of the meeting, the chair should exercise the power to demand a poll rather than use the casting vote, particularly where proxies are being held on behalf of the members. A casting vote cannot be used to manufacture a tie.

The chair should use their casting vote in the best interests of the company. This is, of course, a vague duty and it is unlikely that the chair will be entirely impartial. In Parliament, the Speaker normally uses his or her casting vote to maintain the status quo. This would normally entail voting against the resolution as most seek to change the status quo. However, in these circumstances, it is not necessary for the chair to do anything because the resolution would not be passed if the number of votes cast both for and against it were the same.

The existence of a chair's casting vote could, in certain circumstances, be intended to ensure that one group of shareholders is able to hold sway over another. For example, a company may have been established with two groups of shareholders each holding an equal number of shares but with one group holding 'A ordinary shares' and the other 'B ordinary shares'. The 'A ordinary shareholders' may have been given the right to appoint three directors and the 'B ordinary shareholders' the right to appoint only two directors. This would mean that the 'A ordinary shareholders' would be able to determine who is appointed chair of the board of directors and, therefore, who will chair general meetings and get the casting vote. In other words, the whole structure of the company's shares is designed to ensure that one group of shareholders has more control than the other. In these circumstances, one might reasonably expect the chair to exercise his casting vote in the interests of his own group of shareholders.

The courts have endorsed the use by the chair of a 'conditional' casting vote where the validity of some votes had been in doubt and it was not clear whether or not the vote was tied.

Objections to qualification of voter

Articles usually provide that objections to the qualification of any voter must be raised at the meeting at which the vote objected to is tendered and that every vote not disallowed at the meeting shall be valid. Objections made in due time are normally required to be referred to the chair whose decision shall be final and conclusive (pcls 43, clg 29 and plc 35).

(1) No objection may be raised to the qualification of any person voting at a general meeting except at the meeting or adjourned meeting at which the vote objected to is tendered, and every vote not disallowed at the meeting is valid.

(2) Any such objection must be referred to the chair of the meeting whose decision is final.

Right to attend and speak

The primary purpose of holding general meetings is to enable the members to make decisions by a majority or special majority after listening to, or participating in, a debate on each proposal.

Where voting is allowed to be conducted without holding a meeting, for example by a written resolution of a private company, the members are given no formal opportunity to judge, question or challenge the proposition or to listen to the arguments of those who may oppose the proposals. As such, all members do not have an equivalent opportunity to be involved. In practice, by allowing members of private companies to take majority decisions by written resolution, it is assumed that members of private companies are able to communicate with each other outside the confines of a general meeting or have a single consistent way of thinking. This is likely to be the case in private companies with relatively few members. The rights of the minority are protected to a certain extent by having the ability to circulate their own written resolutions (accompanied by a statement) and to demand that a general meeting be held. However, although they are entitled to have a statement circulated in connection with any business proposed at a general meeting, they are not entitled to do so in connection with a written resolution proposed by the directors or another member.

A general meeting is an opportunity for both sides to put their case to the floating voter. Where all or most of the members attend, the debate may have an influence on the final outcome. In practice, the outcome is often determined in advance by the votes given by proxy before the meeting. In the case of listed companies, it is not uncommon for the proxy votes in favour of resolutions proposed by the board to exceed the total number of votes held by all the members actually present at the meeting and the proxy votes cast against the resolution. In other words, even if a speaker persuaded everyone at the meeting to oppose a resolution, it would still be carried on a poll called by the chair. Nevertheless, this does not mean that the chair would be justified in curtailing debate on the issues. A member who has appointed a proxy could attend and vote at the meeting in person, and in so doing, would override any voting instructions given to his proxy. It is also possible for a member to issue new voting instructions any time before the vote is taken. These two factors mean that the outcome will not always be a foregone conclusion.

Members entitled to attend and vote at general meetings have a common law right to speak at the meeting. Whether a member who is entitled to attend but not to vote is entitled to speak is a moot point. This will be relevant where the articles provide that the vote of the senior joint holder shall be accepted to the exclusion of all others but do not restrict the other joint holders' right to attend meetings of the company. The question may also be relevant for a member who has been disenfranchised for some reason (typically, in the case of listed companies, for failing to respond to a s. 793 notice). In practice, most companies allow members who are entitled to attend to speak even though they may not be entitled to vote, as this ensures that all views are aired. Hence this is undoubtedly the most pragmatic and safest course of action.

Formally, a corporate representative is deemed to have the same rights that the corporate member who appointed him would have if it were an individual member by virtue of section 323. Accordingly, a corporate representative will have the right to speak if the corporate member would have been so entitled.

Potentially, all proxies have the right to speak at a meeting. A member has a right to appoint another person as his proxy to exercise all or any of his rights to attend and to speak and vote at a meeting of a company (s. 324(1)). Assuming that the member does actually appoint the proxy to speak on his behalf, the proxy will have a right to speak. However, it may be possible for a member to appoint a proxy to exercise his right to attend or vote without giving him the right to speak.

Indeed, it may be possible for a member to appoint a proxy to attend and speak on his behalf, but not to vote. If a member has appointed a proxy to speak on his behalf, the proxy will undoubtedly have a right to do so. Even if a proxy has not been appointed to speak on behalf of the member, he will have a statutory right to demand or join in a demand for a poll if he was authorised under the terms of his appointment to vote on that matter (s. 329).

Although it would be unusual to do so, there is nothing to prevent the articles restricting the rights of members who are entitled to attend and vote from speaking at the meeting. A member's right to speak is a common law right and, as such, is capable of modification by the articles. The Act would not prevent this provided that the restrictions were applied to members rather than being directed at proxies or corporate representatives. Under the Act, proxies only have the same rights as the member who appointed them, and corporate representatives the same rights as the corporation would have if it were an individual member. Accordingly, if the rights of the member were restricted, then the rights of their proxies or corporate representatives would be similarly restricted.

Directors are given a statutory right to speak on a resolution to remove them as directors (s. 169(2)). Apart from this, directors who are not members or a corporate representative or proxy of a member do not have a statutory right to speak at meetings. However, articles usually give directors who are not members the right to speak (pcls 40, clg 26 and plc 32). Where they are silent on the matter, it is possible that the meeting could refuse to allow directors to speak if they are not otherwise qualified to do so. Clearly, this is not something which the members would normally wish to do. In practice, directors will normally be invited by the chair to speak as and when necessary, and it should be assumed that they may do so unless the meeting objects. It should also be noted that directors, and if different, the chair of any committee, would be expected to attend and respond to any direct questions from members that they have direct responsibility for.

The model articles provide that the chair of the meeting may permit any other person who is not a member of the company or otherwise entitled to attend and speak, to attend and speak at a general meeting (pcls 40(2), clg 26(2), plc 32(2)). This is a sensible provision and one which companies with older articles might sensibly adopt. Where the articles make no such provision, the chair undoubtedly can invite other people to attend and speak. However, his power to do so might be subject to the will of the meeting, which could decide otherwise. The inclusion of a power in the articles means that the decision as to who can and cannot attend and speak lies solely with the chair of the meeting, who clearly may revoke any permission previously given and who will undoubtedly take into account the views of the members in deciding whether or not to do so.

Auditors have a statutory right to speak on matters which concern them as auditors (s. 502(2)). This right is preserved in certain respects in the case of auditors who have been removed before the expiry of their period of office (s. 513) and resigning auditors (s. 518(10)).

Common law restrictions of the right to speak

The members' right to speak will always be subject to any reasonable limitations imposed by the chair or the meeting itself. Under the common law, the chair has a duty to ensure that all shades of opinion on a resolution before the meeting are given a fair hearing. In particular, the chair should seek to ensure that the minority has had a reasonable opportunity to put its views. This does not mean that all those who hold those views must be allowed to speak. It will suffice if members representing the range of views on a resolution have been allowed to do so.

The chair also has a duty to ensure that all the business before the meeting is conducted. In order to facilitate the conduct of the meeting, the chair may, if the meeting does not object, apply various rules of debate. The most commonly applied is that speakers must confine themselves to the subject of the resolution before the meeting. This is particularly appropriate where a member is speaking on a matter which will be the subject of a subsequent resolution put to the meeting. From a practical point of view, it is normal for the chair to inform speakers that they will be given an opportunity to raise these matters at the appropriate time and to ask them to keep to the subject of the resolution.

It is not so easy to apply this rule where a member wishes to raise a matter which, strictly speaking, is not on the agenda. Here the chair ought, perhaps, to allow slightly more leeway, particularly if other members want to speak on the same subject. In reality, it is often difficult for the chair to rule that an issue raised by a member has no connection with the resolution before the meeting. Experienced speakers will normally be able to manufacture a reason why the point they wish to make is relevant and the chair cannot really decide whether their contribution is relevant without giving them an opportunity to state their case. In such circumstances, it might be advisable for the chair to allocate time at the end of the meeting to discuss the issues raised.

Another rule of debate which is sometimes applied is that no person other than the proposer of the resolution may speak more than once in connection with it. In the context of general meetings, this may not always be appropriate. For example, members who exercise their right to speak by asking a question probably ought to be given an opportunity to comment on any answer given. Ordinarily, there is no reason why a member who has spoken previously should not be allowed to respond to comments made by other speakers, particularly if that member is in the minority. It may, however, be appropriate to apply this rule where there is only limited time available for debate and there are still several members who wish to speak. In addition, there will always come a point where a member has had a reasonable opportunity to make his or her point. The chair need not allow a member to make the same points over and over again or to speak for an inordinate length of time.

The amount of time which should be made available for debate will vary depending on the nature of the business and the number of people wishing to speak on it. This does not mean that the discussion should be allowed to go on forever or that everyone who wishes to speak must be allowed to do so. Shortly before closing the debate, the chair should ask members to refrain from speaking unless they have a different point to make. Although it is not an easy thing to do without causing offence, the chair should, at this point, cut short any speaker who is repeating a point made earlier in the debate in order to ensure that those with different views are given a fair hearing. When the chair considers that a full range of views have been expressed, he may seek to curtail the discussion and put the resolution to a vote. If several members object, the chair could seek the consent of the meeting by proposing a formal 'closure motion' (e.g. that the question before the meeting now be put to the vote). If the resolution is defeated on a show of hands, the chair could, if the articles so provide, demand a poll on the question and would be justified in casting votes given to him as proxy in favour of the substantive resolution in favour of the formal closure motion.

Shareholder questions

In exercising their right to speak, members may ask questions that are relevant to the business in hand. Whether or not the company has a legal obligation to respond, it is usual for the chair and the directors to do so in order to explain their point of view and to persuade the members to support the resolution before the meeting. It is reasonable on this basis for the chair to refuse to answer questions that are not pertinent to the business in hand.

It is also reasonable for the directors to refuse to divulge commercially sensitive information and for listed companies to be cautious about disclosing potentially price-sensitive information in any answer without taking steps to release the information to the market by way of an announcement. Within these constraints, one might expect the directors to do their best to answer questions. However, they may simply not know the answer. On occasion, their lack of knowledge or refusal to disclose information may be sufficient to turn the meeting against them. The members could, for example, decide that they cannot be expected to make a decision on the resolution without certain information and may use one of the procedural resolutions to defer consideration of the matter until a later date. All these factors mitigate towards a tendency on the part of the directors to be co-operative and to strive to answer relevant questions to the satisfaction of the members present. However, the fact that the chair may be certain of the outcome of the meeting by virtue of proxies lodged in favour of a resolution before the meeting can breed complacency in this regard, particularly at meetings of listed companies.

Public companies are required to 'lay' their accounts before the company in general meeting (s. 437). Private companies are no longer required to do so by the Act but may be required to do so under their articles. The requirement to 'lay' accounts is nothing more than an obligation to make them an item of business at the meeting. This is traditionally done by making the accounts the subject of a resolution; the company lays the accounts before the members who are asked to vote to 'receive' them. It does not really matter how the resolution is framed or whether it is defeated. The accounts will still have been laid before the meeting and will still be the company's statutory accounts. On this basis, it can be seen that the sole purpose of the requirement to lay the accounts is to make them an item of business upon which discussion, debate and questions may ensue. In practice, it affords the members an opportunity to question the directors on their stewardship of the company. No other purpose is served by laying the accounts except where a resolution is put to the members in connection with them, other than that it enables the members to signify a vote of no confidence in the directors.

In practice, when the meeting moves to the business of the report and accounts, the chair will normally invite questions and comments from the floor. Questions and debate are usually allowed on a broad range of issues because it is difficult to define the scope of the meeting at that point. Almost any subject raised by a member could have an impact on the financial performance of the company. It is at this stage that most general questions are asked of the executive, frequently with focus on reports of key committees such as the remuneration committee or the Environment, Social and Governance committee, given their direct connection to topics of wide relevance. The chair would, however, be justified in refusing to allow questions or discussion on a matter which has already been dealt with in a previous item of business or that will be the subject of a subsequent item of business at the meeting.

The following recommendations on the subject of shareholder questions and debate provide a useful guide:

- Boards should provide adequate time for shareholder questions at AGMs.
- When moving the adoption or receipt of the accounts, the chair should allow shareholders to raise questions on any item concerning the company's past performance, its results and its intended future performance. However, the directors need not answer questions which are irrelevant to the company or its business or which could result in the release of commercially sensitive information. Nor should they disclose price-sensitive information unless it can be done in compliance with the Listing Rules and guidance regarding the release of price-sensitive information.
- The chair should allow time for questions to be answered by directors or, if relevant, the chair of any committees that report in the annual report, as well as questions specifically on the accounts.
- Before each resolution is put to the vote, the chair should explain again its purpose and effect. If necessary, he should elaborate on the information previously provided in the explanatory circular which accompanied the notice of the meeting. He should also invite shareholders to speak.
- Where concerns are raised by a shareholder at the AGM and the chair undertakes to consider them, the shareholder should subsequently be sent a full report of the action taken.

- When a particular issue has been raised by a shareholder, the chair may assist the flow of the meeting by inviting other shareholders who wish to speak on the same subject to do so at that time.

Some companies include in the documents sent to shareholders prior to the AGM an invitation to submit questions in advance of the meeting. This enables them to select the most common questions and provide an answer for each one at the meeting. Answers can be given orally by the chair or the relevant director, or they can be distributed to shareholders in the form of a printed question-and-answer sheet. The latter allows more detailed information to be provided in numerical or graphical form and enables the chair to refer questioners who raise similar issues at the meeting to the relevant written answer.

Of course, giving shareholders the opportunity to raise questions in advance of the AGM may not always assuage all their concerns. Questions on broadly the same subject may arrive in 40 or 50 different forms for the company to co-ordinate into a single response. Such a reply may satisfactorily answer most points but is unlikely to address them all. Companies are recommended to invite shareholders to submit questions in advance, as this makes structuring the AGM more manageable. Companies themselves should decide how best to convey the invitation. However, at no time should inviting questions in advance be deployed by companies as a method of manipulating the AGM by requiring written notice of questions; nor is it intended to replace spontaneity at the AGM, which should be one of its greatest attributes.

Traded companies – questions at meetings

Section 319A(1) provides that at a general meeting of a traded company, it must answer any question relating to the business being dealt with at the meeting put by a member. However, no such answer need be given:

- if to do so would interfere unduly with the preparation for the meeting, or involve the disclosure of confidential information;
- if the answer has already been given on a website in the form of an answer to a question; or
- if it is undesirable in the interests of the company or the good order of the meeting that the question be answered.

It should be noted that section 319A is framed so as to impose duties on the traded company and makes no provision to enable members to enforce any consequent rights they may have. Members may presumably do so by some sort of injunctive relief. However, there is absolutely no suggestion that any failure on the part of a company to answer questions will have any effect on the validity of the business transacted at the meeting.

It should also be noted that there is no restriction on members asking questions which they are aware cannot be answered. By merely asking a question in a specific way, awareness of the topic is raised, which may, in some instances, be a sufficient purpose to justify asking the question.

Any rights which shareholders have under section 319A(1) are severely limited by subsection (2) and it is doubtful whether the requirements do anything other than codify what companies already do. A possible cause for concern could be where the company does not know the answer to the question and cannot refuse to answer it on any of the grounds in subsection (2). In such circumstances, the company could presumably give a holding answer (e.g. 'We don't know, but we'll get back to you on that one if you provide us with your details [and/or publish the answer on our website])'.

Another concern could be that section 319A may make it difficult for the chair to curtail the debate until all the members who want to ask a question have done so. It is not difficult for a speaker to frame his speech in the form of a question. General meetings in Germany have been known to go on through the night because German company law gives members an unrestricted right to speak. In the UK, it is very likely that the courts would support any company which sought to curtail the debate after giving members a reasonable opportunity to speak and ask questions, and would not look kindly on behaviour by the members which could be interpreted as filibustering. The curtailment of questions and debate in these circumstances would presumably fall within the exception provided in section 319A regarding the 'good order of the meeting'.

Disorder at the meeting

Disruption at general meetings is nothing new, and the common law has developed various rules that enable the chair to deal with it. A skilful chair can sometimes avoid undue disruption by dealing with dissident members firmly, politely and fairly and with good humour. Even if this has no effect on the dissident members, it will probably ensure that the chair retains the support of the meeting should further action need to be taken. If the dissident members persist in their disorderly conduct to such an extent that the meeting is no longer able to transact the business before it, the chair may either order the ejection of those who are causing the disorder or adjourn the meeting in an attempt to restore order.

Preservation of order

The chair's primary responsibility is to ensure that all the business before the meeting is properly and fairly transacted. This is unlikely to be achieved if the meeting is constantly disrupted by dissident members. The chair is, therefore, responsible for the preservation of order at the meeting and should seek to ensure that it is conducted without undue disruption.

A skilful chair can sometimes avoid undue disruption by dealing with dissident members firmly, politely, fairly and with good humour. Even if this has no effect on the dissident members, it will probably ensure that the chair retains the support of the meeting should further action need to be taken.

Where it is known that a group of shareholders is likely to attempt to disrupt the meeting, the chair may take preventative action before the meeting (e.g. to prevent members entering the hall with klaxons, tape recorders, banners, and any other objects which would be used for disruption).

Adjournment to restore order

If there is persistent and violent disorder, the chair has a right – and may even have a duty – to adjourn the meeting to restore order. In *John v Rees* [1969] 2 WLR 1294, Megarry J explained this principle as follows:

> The first duty of the chair of a meeting is to keep order if he can. If there is disorder, his duty, I think, is to make earnest and sustained efforts to restore order, and for this purpose to summon to his aid any officers or others whose assistance is available. If all his efforts are in vain, he should endeavour to put into operation whatever provisions for adjournment there are in the rules, as by obtaining a resolution to adjourn. If this proves impossible, he should exercise his inherent power to adjourn the meeting for a short while, such as 15 minutes, taking due steps to ensure as far as possible that all persons know of this adjournment. If instead of mere disorder there is violence, I think that he should take similar steps, save that the greater the violence the less prolonged should be his efforts to restore order before adjourning. In my judgment, he has not merely a power but a duty to adjourn in this way, in the interests of those who fear for their safety. I am not suggesting that there is a power and a duty to adjourn if the violence consists of no more than a few technical assaults and batteries. Mere pushing and jostling is one thing; it is another when people are put in fear, where there is heavy punching, or the knives are out, so that blood may flow, and there are prospects, or more, of grievous bodily harm. In the latter case the sooner the chair adjourns the meeting the better. At meetings, as elsewhere, the Queen's Peace must be kept.
>
> If then, the chair has this inherent power and duty, what limitations, if any, are there upon its exercise? First, I think that the power and duty must be exercised bona fide for the purpose of forwarding and facilitating the meeting, and not for the purpose of interruption or procrastination. Second, I think that the adjournment must be for no longer than the necessities appear to dictate. If the adjournment is merely for such period as the chair considers to be reasonably necessary for the restoration of order, it would be within his power and his duty; a long adjournment would not. One must remember that to attend a meeting may for some mean travelling far and giving up much leisure. An adjournment to another day when a mere 15 minutes might suffice to restore order may

well impose an unjustifiable burden on many; for they must either once more travel far and give up their leisure, or else remain away and lose their chance to speak and vote at the meeting.

Powers of ejection

Members may be expelled from a meeting if they seriously interfere with the business of the meeting. 'The power . . . of suspending a member guilty of obstruction or disorderly conduct during the continuance of [a meeting] is . . . reasonably necessary for the proper exercise of the functions of any . . . assembly' (*Barton v Taylor* (1886) 11 App Cas 197, per Lord Selborne at p. 204).

If possible, the chair should seek the consent of the meeting before ordering that a person be expelled. In practice, it will rarely be possible to take a vote on the matter and the chair must rely on his innate authority to take action to preserve order at the meeting. Expulsion should only be used as a last resort or in cases of severe disorder. Members should, if possible, be warned of the consequences of their actions. If they continue to disrupt the meeting, they should be given an opportunity to leave voluntarily. If they refuse to do so, they can be forcibly ejected, although only reasonable force should be used. If unnecessary force is used, the person removed will have a cause of action for assault against the persons responsible. This may include the chair as the person who authorised their removal.

See **Appendix 2** for an example of chair's scripts dealing with disorder.

Adjournment and other procedural motions

Meetings are called to deal with items of business. The resolutions that are proposed in connection with each item of business (e.g. a resolution to appoint a director) are known as substantive resolutions because they concern the substance of the meeting, the reason why it was called.

By contrast, procedural motions or resolutions (sometimes referred to as 'formal motions') are used to regulate or facilitate the conduct of the meeting (e.g. matters of procedure). It would be hoped that nobody would call a meeting only to debate matters of procedure.

The distinction between procedural motions and substantive resolutions can sometimes be blurred, mainly because the outcome of the meeting can be affected by procedural motions. For example, a proposal to amend a substantive resolution can be characterised as a procedural motion. The fact that it can alter the substance of the original resolution and thereby affect the outcome of the meeting does not mean that it cannot be properly viewed as a procedural motion. Indeed, it is better to view things the other way. The reason why certain things must be done by way of a procedural resolution is precisely because they are capable of affecting the outcome of the meeting. A decision to adjourn is capable of affecting the outcome of the proceedings. That is why it must normally be proposed as a formal resolution.

The terminology used to describe procedural motions is often old-fashioned and obscure, with no clear definition for the terminology. Provided that the intention of the motion is clear, there is little benefit from insisting that it be used. Indeed, it is probably more likely to cause confusion.

As procedural motions relate to the conduct rather than the substance of the meeting, no prior notice is normally required or, indeed, could normally be given. Although the chair is the person who is most likely to propose a procedural resolution, any member, representative or proxy entitled to vote and speak at the meeting may do so.

One common exception to this rule is that a company's articles may require members to notify the company in advance of any amendments they wish to propose. The purpose of such rules is to give the company enough time to work out whether the amendment can be properly proposed. Articles do not normally require the company to notify members of any amendments that it has decided to accept or that it intends to propose itself, nor does the common law.

Decisions on procedural resolutions are usually taken, at least initially, on a show of hands at the meeting. A poll can be demanded unless the articles provide otherwise, which they occasionally do for certain types of procedural resolution. Even if the articles do not prohibit a poll on a procedural resolution, they may require any poll that is demanded on certain procedural matters to be taken immediately (e.g. the election of the chair). Articles that may appear to require all resolutions to be taken on a poll typically only apply to substantive resolutions. It is possible that they may also apply to procedural motions. However, this will probably not be by design but as a consequence of bad drafting. In practice, a poll is only likely to be implemented if the show of hands did not provide a clear approval or dissent.

Formal motions, implied consent or a ruling by the chair

It is not necessary for all matters of procedure at general meetings to be decided by a procedural or 'formal' motion. No decision is required if the procedure that is being followed is in line with the fundamental expectations as to how a meeting should be run under the company's articles and any applicable common law rules. However, some sort of decision will be required if the chair or anybody else wants to depart from those fundamental rules or principles, assuming that it is possible to do so.

Examples of these fundamental rules and principles would include (but not necessarily be limited to) the expectation that:

(a) the meeting will start at the appointed time;

(b) the meeting will deal with all the business on the agenda in the order that it appears on the agenda;

(c) resolutions included in the notice will be put to the meeting in the form that they appear in the notice;

(d) that members have the right to speak; and

(e) the meeting will continue until all the business has been completed.

Although these can be described as fundamental expectations, some are not as critical in terms of the outcome of the meeting as others. As we will see, the chair can usually make informal rulings on minor matters of procedure himself. However, decisions on matters of procedure which could potentially affect the outcome of the meeting usually have to be dealt with as a formal motion. For example, the chair clearly cannot propose a resolution that is materially different from that which was included in the notice without proposing a formal amendment. To do so would be against the fundamental expectations as to how a meeting should be run and could materially affect the outcome of proceedings. Amendments that materially affect the substance of a resolution must always be proposed as a formal motion. It may not be necessary to do so to correct a minor clerical error or spelling mistake. However, it is always better to do so because it is difficult to say for certain that a formal motion is not required unless it is a patent error.

A resolution to adjourn must usually be proposed as a formal resolution because it involves a change to one of the fundamental expectations and could affect the outcome of the meeting. The same would also be true of any decision not to propose a resolution. These are not minor matters of procedure that fall within the chair's powers. They can materially affect the outcome of the meeting. Accordingly, they should be proposed as a formal motion.

The mere fact that some procedural matters have to be dealt with by proposing a procedural motion helps to explains why people sometimes refer to them as 'formal motions'.

It is inevitable that there will be some grey areas where it is difficult to decide whether a formal motion is actually necessary. After all, we are dealing with the common law. For example, it could be argued that the order in which the items on agenda are taken will not normally affect the outcome as long as all the items are dealt with eventually. However, the fact is that the order in which the items are taken can affect the outcome, and the normal expectation is that if you issue an agenda, you will follow it. Accordingly, if you want to change the order of the items, it is sensible to obtain the consent of the meeting before doing so. The right and proper way of doing this is to propose and pass an appropriate procedural resolution. However, where the matter is not as critical to the outcome of the proceedings, it may be sufficient for the chair to draw attention to the action he is proposing to take, and to ask if there are any objections. It would definitely be wrong for the chair to change the order of the agenda without at least having obtained the implied consent of the meeting in this way. If there is a good reason to change the order, it is highly unlikely that anybody would object. However, if the reason for changing the order was to try to prevent a particular item from being dealt with, or to ensure that it can be dealt with while certain people are not there, you might reasonably expect some members to object. If anybody does object, the chair would be well-advised to put the matter to a formal vote, from both a political and legal perspective.

The chair also tends to use this technique when dealing with minor matters of procedure that will not necessarily affect the outcome of the meeting. It is accepted under the common law that the chair may make rulings on minor matters of procedure and points of order. However, it is important to understand that the courts view the chair's authority in this regard as a form of delegated authority that is vested in them by the meeting but, critically, not to the exclusion of its own powers in this regard. In other words, unless the chair has an inherent or specific power to make a ruling on a matter of procedure, their rulings can be overturned by the meeting. On this basis it is arguable that the chair should inform members of any rulings that they propose to make on matters of procedure that depart from the norm, and offer them the opportunity to object where it is within their power to overrule any decision. In practice, it will not necessarily be critical if the chair does not do so on minor matters of procedure. The acid test for the chair is whether the thing that they are proposing to do could affect the validity of the proceedings. If so, it should not really be treated as a minor matter. At the very least, the chair should offer members the opportunity to object and ensure that the minutes record the fact that they did so. Although this is far better than doing nothing, it would be much safer for the chair to propose a formal motion where the matter is potentially critical, and for the fact that they did so to be recorded in the minutes, along with the fact that it was passed. Even though this is the safest course of action, companies often seem to be reluctant to do it. Where this is the case, it is normally because they are seeking to avoid the possibility of a poll being demanded on the matter. This could raise some very difficult issues for the chair regarding the proper use of any proxy votes they may have.

It is fairly obvious that the chair need not worry as much about minor matters of procedures that will not affect the outcome of the meeting or the validity of the proceedings. Almost by definition, it will not make much difference whether the chair asks members whether they have any objections to any rulings made in this regard. As an example, it is highly unlikely that the validity of the proceedings will ever be affected by the fact that somebody has been allowed to speak who did not have the right to speak. Accordingly, it would not normally make any difference whether the chair had sought permission from the members before inviting such a person to speak. If the chair had invited thousands of non-members and invited them to speak in an attempt to prevent the members from speaking, things might be different.

Although it may not always be necessary for the chair to ask whether there are any objections to his rulings on minor matters of procedure, it is normally considered polite to do so. However, if the chair did so on every trivial matter he might appear obsequious or, at the very least, unconfident in his role and unclear on his authority.

Adjournment

Under the common law, the right to adjourn any meeting (including a general meeting of a company) is vested in the meeting itself. If the chair, contrary to the wishes of the majority, purports to halt the proceedings before the business of the meeting has been completed, the meeting may elect a new chair and continue to transact the unfinished business. These basic common law rules are subject to a number of exceptions and modification by the articles. Articles usually contain detailed provisions setting out when, how and by whom general meetings can be adjourned (see below).

The purpose of an adjournment is to enable the meeting to be reconstituted at some time in the future. When a meeting has been adjourned it has not been permanently dissolved or closed. The proceedings have merely been suspended. A meeting may be adjourned:

(a) for a fixed interval of time (e.g. for 15 minutes) or until a specified time (e.g. 3.30 pm) on the same day;

(b) to another place (maybe with a brief interval to allow everyone to get there);

(c) to a fixed time on a specified date and at a named place;

(d) for an unspecified period not exceeding a given maximum;

(e) until a time and place to be specified by a person or body;

(f) indefinitely (in which case the meeting is said to be adjourned *sine die*).

Legally, there is not much difference between an adjournment to a time and place to be specified and an indefinite adjournment. In both cases, the adjourned meeting could be reconvened by the relevant convening body. However, the former tends to be used where it is intended to reconvene the meeting, whereas meetings tend to be adjourned *sine die* where there is no such intention. There is no reason why the convening authority should not change its mind and proceed to reconvene a meeting that has been adjourned *sine die*.

Adjournment when there is no quorum

Articles usually make provision as to what happens (or should happen) where a quorum is never obtained or ceases to exist at some point during a meeting. Under Table A, meetings are liable to be adjourned automatically in these circumstances. Under the model articles, the meeting probably enters into a state of paralysis and should be adjourned by the chair. It is worth noting when considering this area that it is possible (although unusual) for a general meeting to be quorate for certain items of business but not others even though the same number of members are present throughout.

Adjournment – Table A Articles

Regulation 40 of Table A sets out the quorum requirements at general meetings (normally two persons entitled to attend and vote). However, regulation 41 of Table A provides:

> 41. If such a quorum is not present within half an hour from the time appointed for the meeting, or if during a meeting such a quorum ceases to be present, *the meeting shall stand adjourned to the same day in the next week at the same time and place or to such time and place as the directors may determine*.

The provision found in the model articles, noted below, is preferable in some respects to regulation 41 of Table A, but maybe not in others. A meeting will be adjourned automatically under Table A to the same time and same place even if nobody turns up. It will be automatically adjourned again if nobody turns up at the designated time the following week, the next following week, and so forth. In fact, under Table A, a meeting can never be ended through adjournment and will continue until such time in the future that members attend.

The automatic nature of an adjournment under Table A can be seen as an advantage in that it enables the meeting to be held the following week if so desired without any action on the part of the chair or the directors. However, this could also be viewed as a disadvantage because members who are able to form a quorum might be able to turn up at the same time and place on the same day in any future week, elect their own chair and proceed to transact the business of the meeting.

Another thing that is tricky about regulation 41 of Table A is that the meeting is adjourned automatically unless it is adjourned to some other time or place by 'the directors'. Normally, when articles use the word 'directors', it is interpreted as meaning the board of directors and not an individual director. This may mean that a valid decision of the directors is required to prevent a meeting being automatically adjourned under regulation 41 of Table A. This is not necessarily a problem where a quorum is never obtained because the meeting will automatically stand adjourned to the same time and place the following week and the directors will have time to decide if they wish to adjourn it to another time or place before the adjourned meeting takes place. However, it can cause a problem if a quorum ceases to exist in the middle of the meeting. In these circumstances it may be desirable to be able to declare a temporary adjournment, particularly where the absence of a quorum is only expected to be temporary. It is possible that the word 'directors' might be capable of being interpreted more flexibly for the purposes of regulation 41 of Table A. The directors could, for example, be deemed to have delegated their authority to determine such matters to the chair. Alternatively, the term 'directors' could be interpreted as meaning the 'directors present at the general meeting' in these circumstances or to include the chair acting individually. In any case, any decision made at the general meeting could be ratified by the board at a later date and could, in the absence of any such ratification, be saved by the principle of unanimous consent. One thing that regulation 41 of Table A definitely does not allow, however, is for a member who is not a director, but who has been elected as chair of the meeting, to adjourn the meeting to some other time and place where a quorum ceases to exist unless this is viewed as something that the chair has an inherent power to do. It should also be noted that the meeting itself, being inquorate, cannot resolve to adjourn in these circumstances, unless it does so immediately prior to the event giving rise to the lack of a quorum.

Adjournment – Model articles

The model articles provide (pcls 41(1), clg 27(1) and plc 33(1)) that:

(1) If the persons attending a general meeting within half an hour of the time at which the meeting was due to start do not constitute a quorum, or if during a meeting a quorum ceases to be present, *the chair of the meeting must adjourn it.*

Under these model articles, general meetings are not automatically adjourned and resurrected on a weekly basis where a quorum is neither obtained nor maintained. Instead, they provide that the chair of the meeting 'must' adjourn it in these circumstances (pcls 41(1), clg 27(1) and plc 33(1)). This opens a number of questions regarding the formality of adjourning the meeting.

The first question is what happens if the person who was meant to chair the meeting does not turn up but somebody else does? The answer here is that, under the model articles, the meeting can still appoint a chair even though it is not quorate (see pcls 38, clg 24 and plc 30); any person eligible to be elected as the chair of the meeting and who is so elected could then proceed to adjourn the meeting to a date, time and place of their choosing.

The next question is what happens if nobody turns up at all or if nobody who has power to do so actually adjourns the meeting? The position here is less clear, however, it should be noted that until a quorum is present, no meeting technically exists. Hence, fresh notices will have to be sent out if it is desired to proceed with the business for which the meeting was convened. It should be remembered that the meeting can be convened within 30 minutes of the original start time to allow members who are late to attend and a quorum to be achieved. Therefore, this automatic process of the meeting not having been recognised should only be followed when such time for delay has passed.

On this basis, it is reasonable to assume that, under the common law, a meeting would be deemed to have been dissolved if a quorum was still not present after 30 minutes. However, the model articles say that if a quorum is not present within 30 minutes, the chair must adjourn it. So, if a member has attended a meeting called under the model articles which turns out to be inquorate, he will probably be expected to attend for at least 30 minutes and to wait and see what ruling the chair may make regarding the adjournment of the meeting. If this member is aware that nobody at the meeting is in a position to act as chair to make the necessary adjournment declaration, he would presumably be quite justified in deciding to leave on the assumption that the meeting has failed and that there will be no adjournment. It may well be, therefore, that if nobody adjourns the meeting in accordance with the articles, it will be deemed to have been dissolved (i.e. is no longer capable of being held). This would mean that a new meeting would have to be convened to transact any of the business.

Other interpretations are possible, including one where the meeting continues in existence but in a state of paralysis which can only be cured by a decision of the chair that it be adjourned and subsequently reconvened, or by the subsequent attendance of a quorum. If it can be cured by a decision to adjourn made after the event by the person who would have been entitled to chair the meeting (e.g. the chair of the board of directors) fresh notice would have to be given of the meeting if it were to be held more than 14 days after the original meeting. If the paralysis can be cured by the attendance of a quorum, this would mean that a quorum of members could turn up at the venue for the meeting at any time in the future and proceed to elect a chair and transact the business of the meeting. It is not even certain whether the rule regarding notice of any continuation of an adjourned meeting would apply in these circumstances, because the meeting will never have been properly adjourned, although it is possible that it might be deemed to have been adjourned out of neglect.

This solution does not seem very satisfactory when applied to a meeting at which a quorum was never obtained but might be more so where a meeting starts out with a quorum, but that is not maintained. Say this only happens on a temporary basis during a meeting and the chair does not notice it. It would be far more sensible to assume that the business transacted in the absence of a quorum was invalid because the meeting was in a state of paralysis, but that any business transacted if and when the quorum was restored, was valid. For this to work, it can be seen that the temporary state of paralysis has to be capable of being cured by the re-establishment of a quorum and not depend upon the fact that the chair has adjourned the meeting properly. In the absence of an adjournment declared by the chair, a dissolution in these circumstances would invalidate all the business of the meeting transacted after a quorum ceased to exist. It is possible that the principles that apply where a quorum is never obtained are different from those that apply to situations where a quorum has ceased to exist. In the latter case, it is suggested that in the absence of any action to adjourn by the chair of the meeting, the meeting continues but enters into a state of paralysis which can be converted into an adjournment at any time by the chair of the meeting but which can also be cured by the re-establishment of a quorum. This sits more naturally with the notion that it is possible for the quorum requirements to be satisfied for certain items of business at a general meeting but not for others because a member might be disqualified from voting on certain resolutions. This never arises by virtue of any statutory prohibition but could arise by virtue of some additional provision in a company's articles.

In view of the difficulties that can arise in these circumstances where a general meeting is not properly adjourned, it is understandable why the model articles say that the chair of the meeting *must* adjourn it.

Authority to adjourn

Articles usually contain detailed provisions setting out when, how and by whom general meetings can be adjourned. Regulation 45 of Table A states:

> **45.** The chair may, with the consent of a meeting at which a quorum is present (and shall if so directed by the meeting), adjourn the meeting from time to time and from place to place, but no business shall be transacted at an adjourned meeting other than that business which might properly have been transacted at the meeting had the adjournment not taken place. When a meeting is adjourned for fourteen days or more, at least seven days' notice shall be given specifying the time and place of the adjourned meeting and the general nature of the business to be transacted. Otherwise it shall not be necessary to give any such notice.

This type of article leaves the matter of adjournment in the hands of the meeting. The chair must adjourn the meeting if a resolution to adjourn is duly passed.

If, however, a company's articles provide that the chair may adjourn with the consent of the meeting, and omit the words 'and shall if so directed by the meeting') the chair can refuse to adjourn despite the fact that a resolution to adjourn has been passed by the meeting.

Some articles give the chair power to adjourn without the consent of the meeting. The model articles follow the same formula as Table A, but also provide that the chair may adjourn a general meeting at which a quorum is present if it appears to him that an adjournment is necessary to protect the safety of any person attending the meeting or ensure that the business of the meeting is conducted in an orderly manner (pcls 41, clg 27 and plc 33). This modification can be said to summarise the chair's inherent power to adjourn under the common law (see below).

Chair's inherent power to adjourn

The chair has inherent power to adjourn to facilitate the conduct of the meeting, both to preserve order in the meeting and to regulate the proceedings to give all persons entitled a reasonable opportunity of voting. He is to do the acts necessary for those purposes on his own responsibility, and subject to being called upon to answer for his conduct if he has done anything improperly.

It is also possible for a chair to adjourn a meeting to enable a poll to be conducted even though the company's articles may state that the chair could only adjourn with the consent of the meeting. For example, the chair could adjourn the meeting to take a poll on a resolution to adjourn the meeting. Quite naturally, those seeking to oppose the resolution to adjourn would object. However, the chair has the power to adjourn the meeting in the first place, thus effectively side lining those opposed to the adjournment.

Most articles which allow a poll on a resolution to adjourn, state that the poll must be taken immediately (see below).

The chair could also adjourn the meeting if the venue was too small to accommodate the attendees or communications with any overflow room were inadequate or did not enable members to adequately join in the meeting. However, modern technology largely overcomes the potential issues of an inadequate meeting venue. The application for adjournment could equally be applied if a meeting was, in part or in whole, being held virtually and contact was lost or continually being interrupted.

The model articles potentially give the chair power to adjourn for these purposes, although it is debatable whether any such articles would prevent the courts from interfering if the nature of the adjournment did not actually facilitate the effective conduct of the meeting.

Adjournment to restore order
The chair has inherent power to adjourn if there is persistent and violent disorder, but for no longer than is necessary to restore order.

Resolution to adjourn
Except where the chair exercises an inherent power to adjourn, or a power given to him under the articles, a formal resolution to adjourn the meeting must be proposed and passed by the meeting. The resolution can be proposed by the chair or a member from the floor.

A meeting may be adjourned for as long as necessary, although it may be necessary under the articles to give notice if it is adjourned for longer than a certain number of days. A meeting may also be adjourned to another place. If the purpose of the adjournment is to restore order or, in the case of virtual meetings, to enable a technical issue to be resolved, an adjournment of 15 minutes may suffice. It is not necessary to state specifically that it will be reconvened at the same place in these circumstances. In the absence of anything to the contrary in a resolution to adjourn, it can be assumed that the adjourned meeting will take place at the same place as the original meeting.

An indefinite adjournment may be appropriate where it is not known when the unfinished business can be dealt with, in which case the meeting is said to have been adjourned *sine die*. If an adjournment is not planned or expected, the company is not likely to have made arrangements to reserve a venue for the adjourned meeting. In these circumstances the original meeting may have to be adjourned to a time and place to be determined by the directors.

Poll on a resolution to adjourn

Section 321 provides members with a statutory right to demand a poll. However, section 321(1) specifically allows a company's articles to exclude that right on a resolution to adjourn. Most articles do not do so. However, both Table A and the model articles for public companies require a poll on a resolution to adjourn to be taken forthwith/immediately, while the model articles for private companies require all polls to be taken immediately. If the right to demand a poll on a resolution to adjourn is excluded, a dissident minority may be able to obstruct the will of the majority by packing the meeting and proposing a long adjournment to prevent a poll being conducted on a resolution to which they are opposed. Under Table A and the model articles, the chair would be entitled to demand a poll on the question of adjournment which would be taken forthwith. The chair would normally cast those proxies which he holds in favour of the substantive resolution against the resolution to adjourn.

Notice of adjourned meeting

Under the common law, there is no need to give notice of an adjourned meeting if the resolution to adjourn specifies the time and place at which the meeting is to be held. Articles usually modify this rule by requiring notice to be given of any meeting which is adjourned for longer than a specified period. For example, model articles, (plc 33(5)) states:

> If the continuation of an adjourned meeting is to take place more than 14 days after it was adjourned, the company must give at least 7 clear days' notice of it (that is, excluding the day of the adjourned meeting and the day on which the notice is given)—
> (a) to the same persons to whom notice of the company's general meetings is required to be given, and
> (b) containing the same information which such notice is required to contain.

Under this rule and the equivalent provision in Table A, notice must be given where the adjournment is for 14 days or more. Notice must also be given in both cases where a meeting has been adjourned indefinitely *(sine die)* or to a time and place to be specified by the chair or the directors.

Business of an adjourned meeting

Where a resolution is passed at an adjourned meeting, it is treated for all purposes as having been passed on the date on which it is in fact passed, and not on any earlier date (s 332).

Articles normally provide that no business may be transacted at an adjourned general meeting which could not properly have been transacted at the meeting if the adjournment had not taken place (pcls 41(6), clg 27(5) and plc 33(6)).

Attendance, voting and proxies at an adjourned meeting

A member who was not present at the original meeting may attend and vote at the adjourned meeting. An instrument of proxy deposited in time for the original meeting is also valid for any adjournment of that meeting on the basis that the adjourned meeting is merely a continuation of the original meeting.

Proxies submitted after the deadline for the original meeting are not valid for the adjourned meeting unless the articles make provision to that effect. Most articles provide that a proxy lodged at least 48 hours before an adjourned meeting will be valid for that meeting. Proxy forms usually state that the appointment is made in respect of the original meeting 'and any adjournment thereof'. A proxy appointment made in this form submitted the appropriate number of hours before the adjourned meeting would be valid even though it was not submitted in time for the original meeting.

Postponement

Once a meeting has been duly called, it is not possible to postpone it unless allowed by the articles. Thus, the meeting should be held at the appointed time and place. If the chair and the directors fail to attend, the members present can elect their own chair and proceed to transact the business of the meeting. If nobody attends or there is no quorum, the meeting may be adjourned automatically under the articles. The correct procedure is, therefore, to open the meeting in the normal way and, if appropriate, to adjourn it to another time or place or, if the purpose of the meeting is redundant, to close it after passing a resolution not to put any of the business to a vote.

The immediate adjournment procedure was used by two major listed companies in the 1990s after their AGM venues were destroyed by a terrorist bomb in London. Both companies advertised the change of venue in national newspapers prior to the meeting and posted staff at access points to the original venue to direct members to the new venue. The chair and sufficient members to form a quorum held a meeting as close as possible to the original venue at the appointed hour and immediately adjourned to the new venue. Had there been any contentious business at either meeting, the safest course of action might have been to adjourn the meeting for longer and to give notice to the members in accordance with the articles. To prevent any problems in this regard, some companies now include articles which allow the directors to postpone and change the place of the meeting.

Other procedural motions

There are a variety of other procedural motions that may need to be proposed at a general meeting. It is not necessary to use old-fashioned language and terminology when proposing procedural motions. Indeed, it is almost certainly better not to. It is necessary for procedural motions to be drafted carefully to ensure that they achieve their intended purpose. It is also important for the chair to ensure that members understand the consequences of any procedural motion before it is voted upon. If the motion is proposed from the floor, the chair may need to invite the proposer to explain the intended consequences, and may need to help the member draft a motion that achieves those consequences.

Motion to appoint or remove the chair

Any motion to appoint or remove a chair of the meeting is a procedural motion. The ability of the members to propose such motions will depend on the procedures in the articles on the appointment of the chair. If it is allowed at all, a proposal to remove the chair is traditionally framed as a motion of no confidence in the chair. One of the possible reasons for this is to avoid confusion with a motion 'that the chair leave the chair', which is apparently similar to a motion to adjourn *sine die* (until further notice). It would be easy for such a motion to be confused with a motion to remove the chair. Plainly, it would be sensible to clarify the intention of any such proposal from the floor. Procedural motions proposed do not need be seconded. Despite the fact that a proposal from the floor would be unlikely to be carried if a seconder could not be found, it would be wrong to insist that it be seconded unless, unusually, the articles impose such a requirement.

Closure motion

A closure motion is a simple way of curtailing the debate on the question that is currently before the meeting. The chair or any member may simply propose 'that the question before the meeting should now be put to a vote' or words to that effect. In practice, the chair will only tend to propose a formal motion if he has attempted to wind up the debate and in doing so has encountered objections from the floor. It is certainly not necessary for the chair to propose a formal closure motion at the end of every debate.

If a closure motion is proposed from the floor, it is suggested that the chair may refuse to put the motion to the vote on the ground that it is an infringement of the rights of the minority. However, if, acting in good faith, the chair allows it to be put, the court will not intervene. No debate need be allowed on a closure motion, although it might be difficult to prevent objections from those who still wish to speak on the question before the meeting. If a closure motion is carried, the question before the meeting must be put to a vote immediately. If it is not carried, the debate should be allowed to continue.

Dealing with the business

As mentioned previously, there is a fundamental expectation that:

(a) the meeting will deal with all the business on the agenda in the order that it appears on the agenda;

(b) resolutions included in the notice will be put to the meeting in the form that they appear in the notice; and

(c) the meeting will continue until all the business has been dealt with.

The normal way to deal with business, is to propose and vote on a resolution. It is possible for more than one resolution to be proposed in connection with a single item of business. However, it is also possible to include items of business on the agenda merely to enable discussion and for no resolution to be proposed in connection with it.

Ordinarily, the chair would work his way through the agenda dealing with each item of business in the order that it appears and propose any resolutions connected with each item at the end of the discussion on the relevant item. Certain resolutions may also be the subject of proposed amendments, which would have to be dealt with before any vote on the substantive resolution. Any proposal to depart from these normal procedures ought to be agreed by the meeting (whether the proposal emanates from the chair or the floor). The normal way to obtain the consent of the meeting is to propose a procedural motion and to take a vote on it, although for certain less important matters the chair could obtain member's consent informally.

Departures from the norm would include proposals:

(a) to adjourn the meeting, thereby deferring consideration of the unfinished business but not preventing it from being dealt with if the meeting is reconvened;

(b) not to deal with an item of business in the order that it appears in the agenda, but to deal with it later , so to change the order of the business;

(c) that a matter remain on the table with a possibility of being restored at an alternative point in the meeting;

(d) not to deal with an item of business at all so to remove the item from the agenda completely with no prospect of it being restored in the future;

(e) not to put a substantive resolution to a vote; and

(f) not to put a question that is before the meeting to a vote, which could include an amendment.

Changing the order of business

Generally speaking, the chair would not need to propose a formal resolution to change the order of business. Typically, all the chair would need to do is explain why he is proposing to change the order and to ask whether there are any objections. If the reasons for the change of order make sense, there would not normally be any objections. However, if there are, then the chair may need to propose a procedural resolution that would achieve the desired effect.

Allowing a matter to lie on the table

A proposal that a 'a matter should remain on the table' enables that matter to be put aside for the time being without specifying when it will be dealt with or, indeed, how or whether it will be dealt with. Matters that remain on the table at a meeting still potentially form part of the business of the meeting. However, it may take an active decision for it to be restored to the agenda. Any member (or the chair) can propose at any time that it be restored. However, such a proposal may, in itself, end up being the subject of debate and, possibly, a procedural motion.

It is arguable that the chair should not close the meeting without determining how to deal with matters that still remain on the table or without offering members the opportunity to decide for themselves how to deal with them. Although the business has been removed from the agenda, the decision to restore it remains open. In other words, there is potentially unfinished business. Accordingly, it is advisable for the chair to formally dispose of it in some way before closing the meeting. One way of doing this would be for the chair to inform the members that unless there are any objections, he will close the meeting without dealing with a matter that remains on the table and to explain why. If nobody objects, the chair could safely declare the meeting closed. However, if a member does object, it will presumably be on the basis that they want to deal with the unfinished business that remains in a different way. Effectively, by objecting, they are proposing that the remaining business be restored to the agenda. Accordingly, the chair should allow that matter to be decided conclusively before closing the meeting, otherwise there is a danger that the members could continue to deal with the unfinished business without him.

Having said this, it is highly unlikely that the validity of the other proceedings would be affected if the chair failed to offer members the opportunity to decide how to deal with matters that remain on the table. Failure to deal with those matters properly will not affect the validity of resolutions and decisions that were made properly. The only real issue is whether the business of the meeting has been completed and whether the chair can properly declare the meeting closed.

It is, of course, possible that a member may suggest that a matter should be allowed to 'remain on the table' without understanding the full implications of what they are saying. It is also possible that all members may not understand the implications if such a proposal is put to a vote. Bearing this in mind, the chair probably ought to explain how such matters would normally be dealt with and seek confirmation from the member who made the proposal that this is what they intended, before putting any such proposal to a vote.

Removing items of business from the agenda completely

It may, of course, be desirable to remove an item of business from the agenda completely to preclude it from being raised or dealt with at the meeting at all. The traditional method of doing this is to propose a formal motion when that item of business is reached to move on to the next item of business. In truth, if that is all that is proposed, the members may not be very clear as to whether it is intended to return to the original item or if this would be possible. Accordingly, some sort of clarification would be required, preferably in the wording of the formal motion itself or, at the very least, in the explanation given by the chair. For example, it would be preferable to propose that the item of business be removed from the agenda to preclude any further discussion of it or decisions being made in connection with it at the meeting and that, if so agreed, the meeting should accordingly move on to the next item of business.

It is possible to propose such a motion at any time during discussion of an item of business, including during the discussion of an amendment. If the motion is carried, no further discussion or decision on the item of business (including any substantive resolutions included in the notice and any amendments proposed in connection with them) should be allowed at the meeting (or any adjournment thereof) as its effect is to remove the question from the scope of the meeting. The question can only be considered again if it is proposed at a subsequent meeting. If it is rejected, discussion on the main issue may continue.

More often than not, each item of business in the notice will be connected with only one substantive resolution. However, it is possible for a single item of business on the agenda to embrace the possibility of more than one resolution. In such circumstances, if the item of business is removed from the agenda, none of the resolutions can be proposed. If this is not what is desired, then some way must be found to prevent any decision being made on some, but not all, of the resolutions. One way of doing this is to clarify that, for the purposes of the proposal, each resolution is treated as a separate item of business and that the proposal only relates to one of those resolutions, which would then need to be clearly identified. Another way of dealing with it could be to propose, at the appropriate time, that the question before the meeting should not be put to a vote.

Not putting a question to a vote

A proposal not to put a substantive resolution to a vote can be dealt with simply by proposing that it should not be. The motion should clarify the resolution to which it refers. If that resolution is an item of business in itself, a decision not to put it to the vote effectively removes the whole item from the agenda. In other words, the effect is similar to a proposal to move on to the next item of business. However, if an item of business embraces the possibility of more than one substantive resolution, then a decision not to put one of those resolutions does not preclude the others from still being put.

If somebody were to propose that 'the question before the meeting should not be put', the chair would have to be careful to clarify what they meant, because it is possible that the substantive resolution is not actually the question that is before the meeting. The question before the meeting could be an amendment or some other type of procedural motion. Equally, if someone were to propose that a question 'be not now put' or 'be not put now', the chair would need to seek clarification as to whether they are proposing that it should not be put at all or that it should be put later, possibly after something else has been decided. Indeed, the chair could justifiably request that they clearly explain their proposal, using language that all attendees can understand.

That the matter be referred back to . . .

One of the ways in which a meeting could decide to dispose of an item of business is to refer the matter back to some other person or body. This does not tend to be something that is proposed as a formal motion at a general meeting, although it will commonly happen at board meetings. The normal course of events at general meetings is for the meeting to vote on the resolution, and if it is rejected, for the people who proposed it (typically the directors) to consider coming back with a revised proposal at a separate meeting called for that purpose. However, it is not beyond the realms of possibility that somebody (possibly the chair) may propose that a matter be referred back to another body (e.g. the board of directors) before a vote has actually been taken. The effect would be similar to a proposal not to put the matter to a vote. At a board meeting, a decision to refer a matter back to another person or body would typically be couched with certain conditions and reservations.

A proposal couched in similar terms and passed by the members as a formal resolution would not be binding on the directors because the members can only issue instructions to the directors by special resolution, and it is impossible to pass a special resolution without giving prior notice of it.

▓ Amendments

Dealing with amendments is one of the most difficult duties of the chair. Unless the articles require prior notice of amendments to be given, the chair will have to decide at the meeting whether to allow an amendment to be put to the meeting. If the chair wrongly refuses to admit an amendment, the resolution is liable to be declared invalid unless the articles provide some protection in this regard.

Consequences of wrongly refusing to submit

If the chair wrongly refuses to submit an amendment to a general meeting and the original resolution is passed without the inclusion of the amendment, the resolution will be invalid. It makes no difference whether the mover of the amendment contested the chair's ruling or left the meeting. Modern articles often provide that a resolution shall not be invalidated by any error in good faith on the part of the chair in ruling an amendment out of order (pcls 47(3), clg 33(3) and plc 40(3)). This type of provision can be viewed as a sensible precaution on the part of the company in view of the difficulties that can arise in this area. However, where the chair is found to have made a mistake, the courts are likely to apply a fairly restrictive interpretation of 'good faith'. The chair will, for example, be expected to have acted with scrupulous fairness and, if possible, taken any necessary advice.

Articles sometimes provide that no amendment shall be considered (except at the discretion of the chair) unless prior notice in writing of the proposed amendment has been given to the company. This type of article enables the chair to take considered legal or other professional advice before the meeting as to whether the amendment should be accepted.

Companies often find that they need to make amendments to resolutions themselves to correct clerical errors. Accordingly, it is not normally sensible for the articles to prohibit amendments altogether.

The model articles prescribed under the 2006 Act all include a provision which enables the chair to accept/propose amendments to resolutions proposed at a general meeting, but which requires members to give prior notice of amendments to ordinary resolutions and prohibits them from proposing amendments to special resolutions.

No such provision can be found in any version of Table A. Accordingly, the chair will be expected to make rulings on the validity of amendments proposed from the floor of which he has no prior notice.

Amendments to ordinary resolutions under the model articles

The model articles allow amendments to be made to ordinary resolutions proposed at a general meeting by ordinary resolution provided that the following conditions are satisfied:

(a) notice of the proposed amendment is given to the company secretary in writing by a person entitled to vote at the general meeting at which it is to be proposed not less than 48 hours before the meeting is to take place (or such later time as the chair of the meeting may determine); and

(b) the proposed amendment does not, in the reasonable opinion of the chair of the meeting, materially alter the scope of the resolution.

The requirements as to notice in (a) above apply to amendments proposed by the directors or by the members. Under the model articles, notice 'in writing' can be given in hard copy or electronic form (see the definition of writing in pcls, clg and plc 1). The requirement to give not less than 48 hours' notice will be satisfied even though some of those hours were part of a non-working day (e.g. for a meeting held on a Monday, the notice need only be given on the Saturday). The chair of the meeting is given discretion to accept amendments at shorter notice. However, written notice would still be required and an amendment could not, therefore, be proposed unless and until it is produced in writing.

The model articles provide that an amendment may only be made if it does not, in the reasonable opinion of the chair of the meeting, materially alter the scope of the resolution. An amendment is made by being put to, and passed by, the meeting. In normal circumstances, the only way the chair can prevent an amendment being made would be to refuse to allow it to be put to the vote at the meeting.

The question as to whether an amendment would materially alter the scope of a resolution will presumably fall to be decided by the usual common law rules. It should be noted that that the wording used in the model articles does not necessarily reflect the position under common law unless the 'scope of the resolution' is taken to be dependent on the scope of the notice given for that item of business in the notice of meeting.

It should also be noted amendments can be rejected on other grounds under common law and that the model articles do not necessarily restrict the chair from doing so on these other grounds.

The model articles provide that if the chair of the meeting, acting in good faith, wrongly decides that an amendment to a resolution is out of order, the chair's error does not invalidate the vote on that resolution (pcls 47(3), clg 33(3) and plc 40(3)). This saving would presumably apply to amendments which the chair has rejected on any grounds and not just those rejected on the grounds that they would have materially altered the scope of the resolution. However, it is worth pointing out that this saving does not apply to amendments which the chair wrongly allowed to be made which will, therefore, still be liable to challenge, notwithstanding the fact the chair acted in good faith.

Amendment of ordinary resolutions

An amendment to an ordinary resolution must be put to the vote unless it is:

- outside the scope of the notice of the meeting;
- irrelevant in so far as it bears no relation to the original motion or subject matter;
- redundant because its effect is simply to negate the resolution or to propose something which has already been resolved by the meeting;
- incompatible with a decision previously made by the meeting;
- vexatious (i.e. its sole purpose is to obstruct the transaction of business); or
- rejected by the chair under a discretion granted by the articles.

Any of the above amendments may be passed by an ordinary resolution of the meeting.

Outside the scope of the notice

Under the common law, amendments must be within the scope of the notice given for that item of business in the notice of meeting. The meeting may transact any business which is within the 'general nature' of the business set out in the notice. In deciding what the 'general nature' of the business in the notice is, the test is what a reasonable shareholder reading the notice would consider the business to be. The courts normally adopt a practical approach and, where there is any ambiguity, apply a restrictive interpretation to protect the absent shareholder.

A guide endorsed by the courts is that an amendment should not be allowed if it would have affected a member's decision to attend. For example, a resolution authorising the directors to allot shares could be amended to reduce the number they may allot, but not necessarily to increase it.

Ordinary and special business

As noted in the introduction to this section (Chapter 12) and Appendix 1, articles sometimes distinguish between 'ordinary' and 'special' business (e.g. reg. 52 of the 1948 Table A and the articles of many listed companies). Matters specified in the articles as 'ordinary' business may be considered at an AGM without prior notice having been given. These usually include:

- declaration of a dividend;
- consideration of the report and accounts;
- election of directors in place of those retiring; and
- appointment and remuneration of the auditors.

In effect, notice is deemed to have been given on any of these matters even if it is not included in the AGM notice. Thus, any resolution on these matters will be within the scope of the notice of the AGM. This also makes it more likely that an amendment to any such resolution will be within the scope of the notice, although this may be limited where the notice sets out the general nature of the resolutions to be proposed under these headings or sets out the resolutions in full. By default, any other business proposed at an AGM and all business proposed at a general meeting will be deemed to be 'special' business and, as such, the notice must specify the general nature of that business for it to be within the scope of the notice. Where articles adopt this formula it is usual for the AGM notice to distinguish between items which are proposed as ordinary business and those which are proposed as special business, and usual to dispose of the ordinary business before the special business.

The 1985 version of Table A requires the notice of a general meeting to specify 'the general nature of the business to be transacted' (reg. 38). The model articles rely on the statutory provision in this regard which provides that, in the absence of any other provision in a company's articles, the notice must state the general nature of the business (s. 311). In other words, under both the model articles and the 1985 Table A, all business is treated in the same way as special business.

Other reasons for rejecting amendments

An amendment need not be allowed if its effect is to negate the original resolution. The chair should refuse to put such an amendment and point out that those who support it can achieve the same result by voting against the original resolution. For example, an amendment may be proposed to a resolution authorising the board to fix the remuneration of the auditors which imposes a maximum sum.

But if the amendment proposes a limit of 1p, it effectively negates the resolution to authorise the board to fix the remuneration.

The chair can reject amendments if they seek to reopen business already settled at the meeting or they are incompatible with a previous decision of the meeting. The chair may sometimes do so where the proposed amendment is either obstructive, vexatious, dilatory or irrelevant (e.g. where the proposer is merely attempting to obstruct the conduct of the business by proposing a series of amendments).

Amending a resolution to appoint directors

Amendments to resolutions to appoint directors are probably the most common as shareholders often seek to propose a new person as a director, whether in place of, or in addition to, a nominated director. Unfortunately, this area is beset with difficulties. The principles outlined above in respect of ordinary resolutions apply and the basic question which must be considered is whether the amendment is within the scope of the notice. Before addressing this point, the chair should, however, check the following points which may prevent the amendment being put.

(a) The articles may fix (or determine the method of fixing) the maximum number of directors that may be appointed. If that maximum would be exceeded by passing the amendment, it can be rejected.

(b) The articles may require notice to be given to the company of the intention to propose someone as a director who is not recommended by the board (e.g. reg. 76 of Table A which requires notice to be given by a member not less than 14 nor more than 35 clear days before the date appointed for the meeting together with the particulars which would, if that person was appointed, be required to be included in the company's register of directors together with notice executed by that person of his willingness to be appointed). Assuming that the company receives no such notice from a member entitled to vote 14 clear days before the meeting, no-one other than a director retiring at the meeting or a person recommended by the board would be eligible for election as a director at the meeting.

(c) The articles may require prior notice to be given to the company of any amendments to be proposed at the meeting. If no such notice has been given, the chair may reject the amendment.

Amendment of special resolutions

Special resolutions may only be amended in very limited circumstances. Under the Act, a resolution passed at a meeting will not be a special resolution unless the notice of the meeting included the text of the resolution and specified the intention to propose it as a special resolution (s. 283(6)). Accordingly, if a special resolution is to be validly passed, the resolution as passed must be the same as that identified in the preceding notice. Inclusion in the notice of such words as 'with such amendments and alterations as shall be determined on at such meeting' would make no difference in this regard. However, a resolution as passed can properly be regarded as 'the resolution' identified in a preceding notice, even though:

- it departs in some respects from the text of a resolution set out in such notice (e.g. by correcting those grammatical or clerical errors which can be corrected as a matter of construction, or by reducing the words to more formal language); or
- it is reduced into the form of a new text, which was not included in the notice, provided only that in either case there is no departure from the substance.

In deciding whether there is complete identity between the substance of a resolution passed and the substance of an intended resolution as notified, there should be no room for the court to apply the *de minimis* principle or a 'limit of tolerance'. The substance must be identical. Otherwise the condition precedent to the validity of a special resolution as passed, imposed by section 283, namely that notice has been given 'specifying the intention to propose the resolution as a special resolution' is not satisfied.

It follows from the above propositions that an amendment to a previously circulated text of a special resolution can be properly put to and voted on at a meeting if, but only if, the amendment involves no departure from the substance of the circulated text, in the sense indicated above, with questions as to the notice given of the resolution being determined by reference to the notice and any circulars which accompany it.

It should be noted, however, that the above propositions may be subject to modification where all the members or a class of members, of a company unanimously agree to waive their rights to notice under section 283.

The 1985 Act makes similar provision with regard to the notice required to be given to members of extraordinary resolutions, which are preserved for certain purposes. Accordingly, the same principles will apply to amendments of such resolutions.

To eliminate any uncertainty with regard to amendments, companies sometimes adopt an article which disallows any amendment of extraordinary and special resolutions.

Amendment of special resolutions under the model articles
The model articles only allow an amendment to be proposed to a special resolution by the chair of the meeting at which the resolution is to be proposed. Any such amendment may be made by ordinary resolution but may not go beyond what is necessary to correct a grammatical or other non-substantive error in the resolution (pcls 47(2), clg 33(2) and plc 40(2)).

Amendment of resolutions requiring special notice

It is arguable that the common law rules on amending special resolutions may also apply to resolutions requiring special notice. Section 312 provides that where by any provision of the Companies Acts special notice is required of a resolution, the resolution is not effective unless notice of the intention to move it has been given to the company at least 28 days before the meeting at which it is moved (s. 312(1)). The company is then required under section 312(2) to give notice to the members of 'any such resolution in the same manner and at the same time as it gives notice of the meeting'. If a resolution to which these rules apply is amended, there is a danger that it is no longer the resolution of which special notice was given, and that it would, accordingly, be ineffective. For example, an amendment to a resolution to remove Mr Y as a director plainly cannot be amended to read to remove Mr X as a director, despite the fact that the removal of directors is within the scope of the notice. It is also arguable that the resolution should not be amended to propose the appointment of Mr Z as a replacement if it is agreed to remove Mr Y. That is not to say that a separate resolution to that effect could not be proposed if Mr Y is actually removed. However, the question as to whether this would be allowed would depend on the scope of the notice and any restrictions in the articles regarding the process for appointing directors.

Although the substance of an ordinary resolution for which special notice is required should not be amended, amendments can be made to rectify a clerical error (see above).

Procedure on an amendment

Under common law, an amendment may be moved at any time after discussion on the original motion has been invited by the chair and before the motion has been put to the vote. Where articles require prior notice of a proposed amendment, it will still be up to the person who notified it to propose the amendment at the meeting, although the chair of the meeting will have discretion to do so on their behalf. It is not necessary for an amendment to be seconded.

An amendment may alter the original motion by making deletions, additions or insertions. The proposal must be carefully drafted and, if necessary, the chair should assist the proposers in giving proper effect to their proposal.

For example, on a resolution 'to appoint ABC as auditors until the next AGM at which accounts are laid and to authorise the directors to fix their remuneration' the following amendment might be proposed:

> THAT the motion before the meeting be amended by deleting the word 'annual' and adding after the word 'remuneration' the words 'provided that the amount paid as remuneration shall not exceed £25,000'.

Order in which amendments are taken

A properly moved amendment must be considered and put to the meeting before the original motion.

There are no strict rules of debate that must be followed. However, it is normal for discussion to be restricted to the amendment itself until it has been properly dealt with. If it is carried, the chair should read out the amended motion and may invite discussion on it again before putting it to the vote. However, it may not be necessary to do so if, during the discussion of the amendment, all the relevant issues have already been discussed. If more than one amendment is proposed to the same motion, each amendment should be considered in the order in which it affects the motion. Where there are a series of amendments to a resolution, it is sensible for the chair to require a more structured debate which follows the amendments before the meeting and defers discussion of any other matters until the amendments have all been dealt with. Where the chair has refused to allow any debate on the main subject while an amendment is being considered, he clearly needs to afford members a subsequent opportunity to raise those matters, assuming that they are still germane to the resolution.

An amendment to an amendment may be proposed before the principal amendment is put to the vote. In these circumstances, the secondary amendment must be taken first. If it is carried, it must be embodied in the principal amendment which should then be read to the meeting before discussion is invited.

> For example, on a motion 'to appoint ABC as auditors until the next general meeting at which accounts are laid and to authorise the directors to fix their remuneration' the following amendments might be proposed:
>
> (a) to delete 'ABC' and to insert 'BCD';
> (b) to delete 'ABC' and insert 'BCD and XYZ';
> (c) to add after the word 'remuneration; the words 'provided that the amount paid as remuneration shall not exceed £25,000'.
>
> In the above scenario amendment (b) should be redrafted and proposed as an amendment to amendment (a) and dealt with first. If it is passed, amendment (a) (which would now read 'to delete "ABC" and to insert "BCD and XYZ"') should be put to the meeting, followed by amendment (c) which may no longer be appropriate if two different firms of auditors are to be appointed. It is feasible at this point that somebody may propose an amendment to amendment (c). If so, this should be considered first.

Dealing with common items of business

This section outlines the procedures for dealing with some of the more common items of business at general meetings as follows:

- laying of the report and accounts;
- approval of the directors' remuneration report of a quoted company;
- audit concerns raised by members of a quoted company;
- appointment and reappointment of auditors;
- auditors' remuneration;
- change of auditors;
- special notice and procedural requirements for certain appointments;
- auditors' liability limitation agreements;
- resignation of auditors;
- removal of auditors;
- dividends;
- appointment of directors;
- retirement by rotation,
- removal of directors;
- authority to enable a traded company to call meetings on less than 21 days' notice;
- directors' authority to allot shares;
- disapplication of pre-emption rights;
- market purchases of own shares; and
- role of the company secretary.

Report and accounts

The directors of a public company must lay its accounts and reports before the company in a general meeting (s. 437). The meeting at which the accounts and reports are laid is referred to in the Act as the 'accounts meeting'.

The directors of a private company are not required to lay the accounts and reports before the company in general meeting unless the articles of the company so require. Where this is the case, it cannot be assumed that any of the requirements of the Act relating to public companies apply in default and it is possible, as a consequence, that the exact procedures that must be followed by a private company will not be totally clear. For example, unless the articles say anything to the contrary, it would not be necessary for a private company to send members copies of the accounts at least 21 days before the meeting. The accounts would need to be sent before the meeting, probably at the same time as the notice or earlier. In addition, unless the articles make specific provision in this regard, there would probably be no fixed period within which the accounts should be laid.

Time for laying and delivering accounts – public companies

The accounts of a public company must be laid before the company in a general meeting before the end of the period for filing the accounts and reports in question, which for a public company is normally six months after the relevant year-end (s. 442). It should be noted that the period allowed for filing is subject to modification in certain circumstances (see below), and that where it is modified, it also directly affects the period allowed for laying the accounts.

Section 443 defines how to calculate the periods allowed for filing accounts and reports. In general, this is the same date the relevant number of months later. So, for example, if the end of the accounting reference period is 5 June, six months from then is 5 December. However, as months are of unequal length, there can be confusion as to whether six months from say 30 June is 30 December (exactly six months later) or 31 December (the end of the sixth month). Under the rule laid down in section 443, six months from 30 June will be 31 December.

It is no longer possible for a company with overseas interests to claim an automatic three-month extension of the period allowed for laying and delivering reports and accounts. However, it is still possible to make an application to the Secretary of State for a discretionary extension to the period for laying and delivery under section 442(5). This procedure is intended to be used in situations where there has, for example, been an unforeseen event, which was outside the control of the company and its auditors. It is highly unlikely that an extension would be granted under this procedure on the sole ground that the company has overseas interests. Applications must be made in writing, contain a full explanation of the reasons for the extension and the length of the extension needed.

If the first accounts of a newly incorporated public company cover more than 12 months, the period allowed for filing is six months from the first anniversary of incorporation of the company or three months from the end of the first accounting reference period, whichever is later (s. 442(3)). For instance, in the case of a public company incorporated on 1 March 2009 whose first accounting reference period ends on 30 June 2010, the filing deadline will be 30 September 2010 (i.e. three months after the end of the accounting reference period) not 1 September 2010 (i.e. six months after the first anniversary of incorporation) and not 31 December 2010 (the normal filing deadline under s. 442(2)).

The Act also includes a provision to ensure that a company does not immediately fall foul of the filing deadlines when it files a change of accounting reference date which has the effect of shortening the relevant accounting reference period. If in any year a company has shortened the relevant accounting reference period by filing a change of accounting reference date, the period allowed for filing is either the period applicable under the normal rules or three months from the date of the notice given to the Registrar under section 392, whichever is the later (s. 442(4)).

Listed companies must publish their accounts as soon as possible after the period end and, in any event, within four months of the period end (Disclosure and Transparency Rule 6.3). Publication is not the same as laying or delivering for which the usual time limits apply. Publication is the act of issuing, publishing or sending out copies of the accounts. If a listed company is unable to publish its accounts within the four-month time limit, it will need to obtain an extension from the UK Listing Authority.

It should be noted that all companies incorporated in the UK must also submit their accounts to Companies House within the specified time limit. Late filing of accounts incurs a late filing penalty.

Persons entitled to receive copies of the accounts and reports
Under the Act (s. 423(1)) every company must send a copy of its annual accounts and reports for each financial year to—

(a) every member of the company;
(b) every holder of the company's debentures; and
(c) every person who is entitled to receive notice of general meetings.

Under the Act (s. 423(2)) copies do not need to be sent to a person for whom the company does not have a current address. A 'current address' is one which has been notified to the company by the person as an address to which documents may be sent and where the company has no reason to believe that the documents will not reach them. By default, but not content, this could also include an email address.

In the case of a company without a share capital, copies of the accounts do not need to be sent to anyone who is not entitled to receive notices of general meetings (s. 423(4)).

The accounts of a private company must be sent out no later than the end of the period for filing accounts with Companies House or, if earlier, the date on which it actually files its accounts with Companies House (s. 424(2)).

A public company must comply with the requirement in section 423 to send a copy of the accounts to those entitled to receive one at least 21 days before the date of the relevant accounts meeting (i.e. the general meeting at which the accounts are to be laid) (s. 424(3)). Where copies of the accounts are sent out over a period of days (perhaps because of the sheer scale of the operation) they are deemed to have been sent out on the last of those days (s. 423(5)). It can be seen from this provision that the requirement to send the accounts at least 21 days before the meeting is not like the requirement to give notice. The accounts will be sent when they are actually sent by the company. This is reinforced by the fact that there is no hint that the clear days rule in section 360 applies.

If copies of the accounts and reports are not sent out in accordance with the above requirements, the company and every officer in default are liable to a fine (s. 425). However, if copies of the accounts and reports of a public company are sent out less than 21 days before the date of the accounts meeting, they will be deemed to have been duly sent if it is so agreed by all the members entitled to attend and vote at the meeting (s. 424(4)).

Precedent: Accounts – Agreement to Accept Accounts less than 21 days before General Meeting

We, the undersigned, being all the members of [name of company] entitled to attend and vote at the [annual] general meeting, convened for [date of meeting], hereby agree that copies of the documents required to be sent to us pursuant to section 423 of the Companies Act 2006 shall be deemed to have been duly sent for the purposes of sections 423 and 424 of that Act notwithstanding that they were sent less than twenty-one days before the date of the meeting.

[Date]

[Signatures]

In practice, it will be possible to obtain such agreement only in the case of public companies with relatively few members (e.g. public companies which are established as wholly owned subsidiaries) and not where the company is publicly traded.

It is arguable whether a public company can lay its accounts before the company in general meeting unless it has sent out the accounts at least 21 days before the meeting or obtained the consent of members for them to be treated as duly sent under section 424(4). There is no direct link between section 437 (public companies: laying of accounts) and sections 423 and 424 (circulation of accounts and reports). It is possible that the only consequence of failure to send out the accounts 21 days before the accounts meeting is that it renders the company and its officers liable to a fine if consent has not been obtained under section 424(4).

The safest assumption to make in this area is that a public company will not have complied with its obligation to lay accounts if the accounts have not been sent out at least 21 days before the meeting or the members entitled to attend and vote at the accounts meeting have not consented to treat the accounts as duly sent. If the company has not obtained the necessary consent and not complied with its obligation to lay the accounts, it will be guilty of an offence under section 438 for failing to lay its accounts and may also be guilty of an offence under section 425, although it is not clear whether the meeting before which the failure occurred would still be its accounts meeting if the accounts were not laid at it. According to section 437(3), the accounts meeting is the general meeting of the company at which the company's accounts are (*or are to be*) laid. Assuming that the company does not have time to hold another meeting to lay the accounts properly, the meeting at which they 'are to be laid' presumably includes the meeting where the company tried, but failed, to lay them.

Best practice is to ensure that copies of the accounts are circulated prior to the meeting to enable members to review their content before meeting. Where this distribution does not meet the 21-day rule, it is unlikely that there would be any consequences unless the lack of distribution was being deliberately done to conceal information.

Copies of the accounts must be sent in accordance with the company communications provisions of the Act. These rules require all documents or information to be supplied by the company in hard copy unless the member has agreed to some other form of delivery (e.g. by email or by the company making the accounts available on a website and notifying the member to that effect). Part 6 of Schedule 5 to the Act includes rules about the provision of copies of documents to joint holders and people who are entitled to shares as a consequence of the death or bankruptcy of the member, which apply in the absence of anything to the contrary in a company's articles.

Any member who elects to receive the accounts in electronic form may demand that the company provide him with a hard copy version free of charge (s. 1145). In addition, any member or debenture holder is entitled to be given a copy of the accounts without charge on demand, regardless of whether he is entitled to notice or not (ss 421 and 432). It does not matter that he has already had a copy. Failure to comply with such a demand within seven days renders the company and every officer liable to penalty.

Summary financial statements

A company may send a summary financial statement instead of the full report and accounts to any person entitled to a copy of the accounts under section 423, if that person agrees (s. 426). Copies of any summary financial statement must be sent to any such person in accordance with the provisions of sections 423 and 424.

Copies of any summary financial statement must be sent in accordance with the company communications provisions of the Act.

The information required to be included in summary financial statements and the acceptable methods of ascertaining shareholders' wishes regarding receipt of full accounts or the summary are contained in sections 427–429 and the Companies (Summary Financial Statement) Regulations 2008 (SI 2008/374).

A summary financial statement must include a summary auditors' report and, for quoted companies, a summary directors' remuneration report. It does not need to include a summary directors' report (although companies may voluntarily provide such a summary). However, it must include information on dividends paid and proposed as a note to the summary profit and loss account.

Summary financial statements should be approved by the board of directors and be signed on behalf of the board by a director (copies sent to holders must state the name of the person who signed on behalf of the board). Summary financial statements are not required to be filed with Companies House or laid before the members, but in the case of listed companies two copies should be sent to the UK Listing Authority (as they are communications with shareholders).

Earnings per share must be stated in any summary financial statement (LR, para. 9.8.13).

Notice

The notice of the general meeting must refer to the laying of the report and accounts unless they are to be laid at an AGM and the articles specify this as ordinary business (see, e.g., reg. 52 of the 1948 Act Table A). There is little to commend this practice and it is only likely to confuse shareholders. In practice, most companies set out the nature of the business in the normal manner.

Precedent: Notice of AGM for laying of the accounts

To receive the accounts and reports of the directors [and the auditors] for the year ended [date].

The UK Corporate Governance Code recommends that at any general meeting, the company should propose a separate resolution on each substantially separate issue, and should in particular propose a resolution at the AGM relating to the report and accounts (Code provision E.2.1). Best practice is that the resolution to receive or adopt the accounts should be separate from any resolution to approve the payment of the final dividend recommended by the directors.

Procedure at the meeting

Although section 437 does not require a resolution to receive the report and accounts to be put to the meeting, it is normal to do so as this is the standard way of putting business before the meeting. The requirement to lay the accounts is merely a device to ensure that the shareholders are given an opportunity to question the directors about the company's performance and their own performance as managers of the company. The wording of the resolution should not give the impression that the accounts and reports can be rejected or that they will not be laid if the members vote against the resolution. If a resolution on the accounts is lost, it does not alter the fact that they are the company's report and accounts or that they have been laid in accordance with section 437. Such a resolution would normally be interpreted as a vote of no confidence in the directors although they would not be under any obligation to resign. Thus, words such as 'to approve the accounts and reports . . .' and 'to lay the accounts and reports . . .' should be avoided.

Best practice is that when moving the adoption or receipt of the accounts, the chair should allow shareholders to raise questions on any item concerning the company's past performance, its results and its intended future performance.

Approval of a directors' remuneration report

Quoted companies are required to make detailed disclosures regarding directors' remuneration in a separate remuneration report and to put that report to a vote by shareholders (ss 420–422).

The remuneration report, often submitted by the remuneration committee of the company, must be approved by the board of directors and signed on its behalf by a director or secretary (s. 422), sent to members (s. 423) and filed at Companies House (s. 447).

Under section 439, quoted companies must give members notice of the intention to move an ordinary resolution at the meeting at which its accounts and reports are to be laid 'approving the directors' remuneration report for the financial year'. The existing directors (i.e. anyone who was a director immediately before the meeting) have a duty to ensure that the resolution is put to a vote at that meeting (s. 439(4)). However, section 439(5) specifies that no entitlement to remuneration is made conditional on the resolution being passed.

It should be noted that the remuneration report is often an agenda item that receives considerable focus and cause for discussion and the chair must balance the opportunity for members to comments with the wider agenda requirements. In addition, remuneration topics are frequently reported after the event and can have an impact on both the public perception of the company as well as a knock-on effect to its share price.

Audit concerns raised by members of quoted companies

Members of a quoted company satisfying the requirements of section 527 may require the company to publish on a website a statement by them relating to the audit of the company's accounts which are to be laid before the next accounts meeting (including the auditor's report and the conduct of the audit) or, where applicable, any circumstances connected with an auditor of the company ceasing to hold office since the previous accounts meeting at which accounts were laid. Should a valid request for the publication of such a statement be received, the company must, within three working days of receipt, publish the statement on a website and forward a copy to its auditors. Any statement published on a website under these rules forms part of the business which may be dealt with at the next accounts meeting.

Under section 529, a quoted company must in the notice it gives of the accounts meeting draw attention to the possibility of a statement being placed on a website in pursuance of members' requests under section 527 and the fact that it may not require members making such a statement to pay its expenses in doing so, and state that a copy of any such statement will be forwarded to its auditors and that any published statement will form part of the business which may be dealt with at the meeting.

Appointment and reappointment of auditors

A company must appoint auditors unless it is:

- exempt from audit as a dormant company under section 480;
- exempt from audit as a small company under section 480; or
- is exempt from the requirements of Part 16 of the Act under section 482 (non-profit making companies subject to public sector audit).

Appointment of auditors – private company

Auditors (or an auditor) of a private company must be appointed for each financial year of the company, unless the directors reasonably resolve otherwise on the ground that audited accounts are unlikely to be required (s. 485). For each financial year for which auditors are to be appointed (other than the company's first financial year), the appointment must be made before the end of the period of 28 days beginning with:

(a) the end of the period allowed for filing accounts for the previous financial year with the Registrar; or

(b) (if earlier) the day on which copies of the company's accounts for the previous financial year are sent out to members under section 423 of the 2006 Act.

The directors may appoint auditors:

(a) at any time before the company's first period for appointing auditors;

(b) following a period during which the company (being exempt from audit) did not have any auditor, at any time before the company's next period for appointing auditors; or

(c) to fill a casual vacancy in the office of auditor.

Precedent: Board resolution to appoint first auditors of a private company

THAT [name of auditors], of [address of auditors] be and are hereby appointed as the auditors of the company with effect from [date], at a fee to be agreed by the board [on the recommendation of the Audit Committee].

[Note: The directors may appoint the first auditors of the company or appoint auditors to fill a casual vacancy. Auditors appointed by the directors hold office, in the case of a private company, until the end of the first period for appointing auditors whereupon their reappointment will need to be approved by the members either at a general meeting or by written resolution.]

The members may appoint an auditor or auditors by ordinary resolution:

(a) during a period for appointing auditors;

(b) if the company should have appointed an auditor or auditors during a period for appointing auditors but failed to do so; or

(c) where the directors had power to appoint but have failed to make an appointment.

Precedent: Board resolution of a private company to [Re-]appoint auditors and fix their remuneration

THAT [name of auditors] be and are hereby appointed auditors of the company [and that for so long as they hold office as the company's auditors the directors be and are hereby authorised to fix their remuneration].

(Note: It is not necessary to say how long the appointment of the auditors shall last. If no term of office is specified, reappointment will normally be deemed under section 487. However, the resolution should authorise the directors to fix the remuneration of the auditors not just for the current financial year but also for any future years in which they are deemed to have been reappointed.)

If a private company fails to appoint auditors in accordance with section 485, the Secretary of State has default powers to appoint (s. 486). Where company fails to make an appointment before the end of the period for appointing auditors, the company must, within one week of the end of that period, give notice to the Secretary of State of that power having become exercisable.

Auditors of a private company hold office in accordance with the terms of their appointment, but do not take office until any previous auditor or auditors cease to hold office, and cease to hold office at the end of the next period for appointing auditors unless reappointed (s. 487).

Subject to the provisions of the Act concerning the removal and resignation of auditors, where no auditor has been appointed by the end of the next period for appointing auditors, any auditor in office immediately before that time is deemed to be reappointed, unless:

(a) he was appointed by the board; or

(b) the company's articles require actual reappointment; or

(c) the deemed reappointment is prevented by the members under section 488; or

(d) the members have resolved that he should not be reappointed; or

(e) the directors have resolved that no auditors should be appointed for the financial year.

An auditor of a private company is not deemed to be reappointed under the above provisions, if the company has received notices under section 488 from members representing at least 5% of the total voting rights of all members who would be entitled to vote on a resolution that the auditor should not be reappointed (or any lower percentage specified in the company's articles). The notice must be received by the company before the end of the accounting reference period immediately preceding the time when the deemed reappointment would have effect.

Appointment auditors – public companies

Unless exempt from audit, a public company is required to appoint auditors. A public company may be exempt from audit as a dormant company. The first auditors may be appointed by the directors. However, auditors so appointed must be reappointed at each general meeting at which accounts are laid (i.e. at the meeting known as the accounts meeting). They hold office until the end of the next general meeting at which accounts are laid (s. 489).

The directors may appoint the first auditors at any time before the first general meeting at which accounts are laid.

Precedent: Board resolution to appoint first auditors of a public company

THAT [name of auditors] be appointed auditors of the company to hold office until the conclusion of the next general meeting at which accounts are laid before the company [and that their remuneration be fixed by the directors].

(Note: The directors may appoint the first auditors of the company or appoint auditors to fill a casual vacancy. Auditors appointed by the directors hold office, in the case of a public company, until the next general meeting at which accounts are laid whereupon the members must either reappoint them or appoint new auditors.)

Auditors so appointed hold office until the conclusion of the first accounts meeting (i.e. the general meeting at which accounts are laid). If the directors fail to appoint the first auditors, the company in general meeting may do so (s. 489(4)).

Thereafter, auditors must be appointed or reappointed at each general meeting at which accounts are laid (s. 489(2) and (4)). The resolution to appoint auditors is usually passed after the accounts have been laid. The resolution should be worded so that the auditors are appointed until the conclusion of the next accounts meeting or the next general meeting at which accounts are laid rather than for a year or until the conclusion of the next AGM.

Precedent: Resolution to reappoint auditors at a general meeting

THAT [name of auditors] be and are hereby reappointed as auditors of the company from the conclusion of this meeting until the conclusion of the next general meeting before which accounts are laid [and that the directors be and are hereby authorised to fix their remuneration].

Precedent: Resolution of general meeting for appointment of auditors to replace retiring auditors

THAT [name of auditors] be appointed auditors of the company in place of the retiring auditors [to hold office from the conclusion of this meeting until the conclusion of the next general meeting before which accounts are laid] [and that the directors be and are hereby authorised to fix their remuneration].

Precedent: Resolution to remove and replace auditors

THAT [name of auditors] be removed from office as auditors of the company with immediate effect [and that [name of anew auditors] be appointed auditors of the company in their place to hold office until the conclusion of the next general meeting at which accounts are laid and that their remuneration be fixed by the directors].

If no auditors are appointed in accordance with section 489 before the end of the period for appointing auditors, the company must notify the Secretary of State who may appoint one or more persons to fill the vacancy (s. 490) and fix their remuneration (s. 492(3)).

A casual vacancy can be caused by the resignation or death of the existing auditor. The directors may fill any such vacancy in the office of auditor (s. 489(3)). Where they have not done so, the members may fill a casual vacancy (s. 489(4)). Resolutions for appointing a new auditor in such circumstances can mirror those provided above.

Auditors' remuneration

Generally speaking, the remuneration of auditors must be fixed by those who appoint them. If appointed by the directors, their remuneration must be fixed by the directors (s. 492(2)). If appointed by the Secretary of State, their remuneration must be fixed by the Secretary of State (s. 492(3)).

However, the remuneration of auditors appointed (or reappointed) by the members must be fixed by the members by ordinary resolution or in such manner as the members by ordinary resolution may determine (s. 492(1)). This is usually done at the same time as the appointment by authorising the directors to fix their remuneration. In the case of a private company, the initial resolution confirming the appointment of the auditors will usually authorise the directors to fix their remuneration not just for the current financial year but for all financial years where they are deemed to have been reappointed (see precedent above). Although section 492 envisages that the members themselves can fix the auditors' remuneration, this is not normally a practicable solution for either public or private companies. It will normally be difficult to predict the precise audit costs for the forthcoming year, not least because remuneration is deemed to include any of the auditors' expenses paid by the company (s. 492(4)). The members may only be able to fix the remuneration after the audit is complete. This is unlikely to be acceptable to the auditors as the members may not approve payment of the full amount. A resolution to approve the remuneration of auditors could, however, place some cap on the fees to be paid to them.

Change of auditors

Where a company wishes to change its auditors, it is normal to approach the existing auditors to see whether they would be prepared to resign voluntarily or agree not to seek reappointment. If they agree to resign, the procedures outlined above would apply, and the directors could then appoint new auditors to fill the resulting vacancy. Where the directors have filled a casual vacancy in this manner the appointment of the new auditors must be confirmed by the members before the end of the next period for appointing auditors under the special procedures set out below. These procedures must also be followed where the auditors have agreed not to seek reappointment at the end of their period of office. However, if the matter is urgent, perhaps because relations have irretrievably broken down, a general meeting could be held to remove the auditors by ordinary resolution before the end of their term of office (s. 510).

Special notice and procedural requirements for certain appointments

Certain special procedural requirements must be followed by both public and private companies for certain appointments. If these procedures are not followed, any appointment will be ineffective. Generally speaking, the circumstances in which these special procedures must be followed can be characterised as being where the members are asked to approve the appointment of new auditors in place of any auditors previously appointed by them. These circumstances can arise where it is proposed to appoint a person as auditor in place of a person whose office has expired (e.g. because of the resignation or removal of the previous auditors), or whose office is about to expire (e.g. because the auditors are not seeking reappointment). These circumstances will arise even where an appointment has been made by the directors to fill a mid-year casual vacancy (perhaps as a result of the resignation or removal of the previous auditors). In the case of both public and private companies, any such appointment must be approved by the members for the following financial year and, in the case of private companies, they are not deemed to be reappointed for these purposes.

In all of the above circumstances where the resolution is to be proposed at a general meeting of a company, special notice must be given of intention to propose the resolution at least 28 days before the meeting and a copy of it must be sent to the outgoing auditors forthwith (s. 515). If the resolution is to be proposed as a written resolution of a private company, a copy of the proposed resolution must also be sent to the outgoing auditors (s. 514). In both cases the outgoing auditor may make written representations (not exceeding a reasonable length) and request that these are also circulated to members of the company.

In the case of a written resolution of a private company, the outgoing auditor must make these representations within 14 days after receiving the notice of the resolution. If the auditor does so, the company must circulate the representations together with the copy or copies of the written resolution circulated in accordance with section 291 (written resolution proposed by the directors) or section 293 (written resolution proposed by the members). Where a private company has circulated representations by an outgoing auditor on such a resolution, the period allowed under section 293(3) for service of copies of the proposed resolution is 28 days instead of 21 days.

In the case of a resolution to be proposed at a general meeting of either a public or private company, the company must (unless the representations made by the outgoing auditor are received too late for it do so):

(a) in any notice of the resolution given to members, state the fact that representations have been made; and
(b) send a copy of the representations to every member of the company to whom notice of the meeting is or has been sent.

If a copy of the outgoing auditor's representations is not sent to members for any reason, they may insist that they be read out at the meeting. The outgoing auditor also has a right to be heard on the resolution whether or not their representations are read out at the meeting.

Under both the written resolution procedure and the special notice procedure any person claiming to be aggrieved can apply to the court to prevent the representations being sent to members or, where applicable, read out at the meeting on the grounds that the auditor is abusing his rights in order to secure needless publicity for defamatory matter.

The above rules also apply where it is proposed to fill a vacancy caused by the resignation of an auditor. Special notice of a resolution to remove the auditors before the end of their period of office is also required.

Approval of an auditor's limitation of liability agreement

A company is prohibited from indemnifying its auditor (whether in its articles or by an agreement) against claims by the company in the case of negligence or other default (s. 532). However, sections 534–538 of the Act permit auditors to limit their liability by agreement with the company. Such agreements are effective only to the extent that they are fair and reasonable. The court is empowered to substitute its own limitation if the agreement purports to limit liability to an amount that is not fair and reasonable in all the circumstances. Such a 'liability limitation agreement' can cover liability for negligence, default, breach of duty or breach of trust by the auditor. To be within the exception the agreement must:

(a) relate to the audit of one specified financial year; the limitation may be expressed in any terms, not necessarily as a fixed financial amount or a formula (s. 535 (2006)); and

(b) be approved by the members of the company (without which approval the agreement will not be effective).

The members of a private company can pass a resolution waiving the need for approval. The members of a private or public company can either pass a resolution before an agreement is signed approving its principal terms or can approve the agreement after it is signed. The resolution may be an ordinary resolution, unless a higher threshold is set in the company's articles. For this purpose the principal terms of a liability limitation agreement specify, or enable the determination of, the kinds of faults by the auditor that are covered, the financial year in relation to which those faults are covered and the limit on the auditor's liability. The members may, by passing an ordinary resolution, withdraw their approval of a liability limitation agreement at any time before entering into the agreement. If the company has already entered into the agreement, approval can be withdrawn, by ordinary resolution, only before the start of the financial year to which the agreement relates (s. 536).

A company is required to disclose any liability limitation agreement made with its auditor in accordance with any regulations made by the Secretary of State (s. 538). The Companies (Disclosure of Auditor Remuneration and Liability Limitation Agreements) Regulations 2008 (SI 2008/489) set out the detailed disclosure requirements. A company which has entered into a liability limitation agreement must disclose the principal terms of the agreement in a note to the company's annual accounts for the financial year to which the agreement relates, unless the agreement was entered into too late for it to be reasonably practicable for the disclosure to be made in those accounts, in which case it must be disclosed in the next annual accounts.

In July 2008, the Financial Reporting Council (FRC) published specific guidance on auditor liability limitation agreements which remains applicable. The FRC guidance:

(a) explains what is and is not allowed under the Companies Act 2006;

(b) sets out some of the factors that will be relevant when assessing the case for an agreement;

(c) explains what matters should be covered in an agreement, and provides specimen clauses for inclusion in agreements; and

(d) explains the process to be followed for obtaining shareholder approval, and provides specimen wording for inclusion in resolutions and the notice of the general meeting.

The guidance can be found at: www.frc.org.uk/getattachment/ec02c8ea-4c14-4349-9333-d655a5dd52f7/FRC-ALLA-Guidance-June-2008-final5.pdf

Resignation of auditors

Auditors may resign by depositing a notice in writing to that effect at the registered office of the company (s. 516(1)). However, the notice of resignation is not effective unless it is accompanied by a statement regarding the circumstances of the resignation prepared in accordance with section 519 (s. 516(2)). On receipt of a valid resignation, the company must file a copy of the notice (but not the accompanying statement) at Companies House within 14 days (s. 517).

Rights of resigning auditors

Where the auditor's notice of resignation is accompanied by a statement of the circumstances connected with his resignation under section 519 which must be circulated to the members by the company in accordance with section 520, the resigning auditor also has a right to deposit with his notice of resignation a requisition calling on the directors to convene a general meeting of the company to consider such explanation of the circumstances connected with his resignation as he may wish to place before the meeting (s. 518(1) and (2)).

Notwithstanding the fact that his statement of circumstances made under section 519 must be circulated by the company to its members, the resigning auditor is also given the right to require the company to circulate an additional statement (not exceeding a reasonable length) of the circumstances connected with his resignation before any meeting requisitioned by him or before any general meeting at which his term of office would have expired or at which it is proposed to fill the vacancy caused by his resignation (s. 518(3)). A resigning auditor is entitled to receive notice of these meetings under section 518(10)).

The company must comply with any such request to call a meeting within 21 days from the date of deposit and convene the meeting for a date not more than 28 days after the date on which the notice of meeting is given. Where the auditor has requested that a statement be circulated before a general meeting, the company must (unless the statement is received too late for it to comply) state in the notice of meeting that a statement has been made by the auditor and send a copy of that statement to every member of the company to whom notice of the meeting has been sent (s. 518(4)). The resigning auditors have a right to receive notice of and to attend and speak at any such meetings.

If the auditor's statement is received too late for circulation, the auditor may require it to be read out at the relevant meeting (s. 518(8)). The court may relieve the company of these obligations if it is satisfied that the auditors are using the provisions to secure needless publicity for defamatory matter (s. 518(9)).

Statement by auditor on ceasing to hold office

Where an auditor of a company ceases to hold office for any reason, he must deposit at the company's registered office a statement in accordance with section 519, which:

(a) in the case of an unquoted company, sets out the circumstances connected with his ceasing to hold office which he believes should be drawn to the attention of the members (in which case the company must circulate them to members in accordance with s. 520) or states that there are no circumstances in connection with his ceasing to hold office that need to be brought to the attention of members (in which case the statement does not need to be circulated by the company to its members); and

(b) in the case of a quoted company, sets out the circumstances connected with his ceasing to hold office, which the company must always circulate to members in accordance with section 520.

An auditor must deposit such a statement with his notice of resignation or, where he is not seeking reappointment, not less than 14 days after the time allowed for next appointing an auditor or, where he has ceased to hold office for any other reason (e.g. removal), 14 days after ceasing to hold office.

If the auditor's statement is one which must be drawn to the attention of members:

(a) the company must within 14 days of deposit of the statement either apply to the court for an order restraining publication or send a copy to every person entitled under section 423 to be sent copies of the statutory accounts (s. 520);

(b) the auditor must file a copy of his statement at Companies House. However, he is required to wait 21 days before doing so to ensure that anybody who wishes to do so has time to apply for a court order restraining publication of his statement. If, at the end of that 21-day period no such order has been served on him, he has a further seven days in which to file the statement at Companies House (s. 521); and

(c) both the auditor and the company may have a duty under sections 522 and 523 respectively to notify an appropriate audit authority.

Removal of auditors

A company's auditor may be removed before the end of his period of office by an ordinary resolution passed at a general meeting of the company (s. 510). It is not possible for a private company to pass such a resolution by written resolution (s. 288(2)).

Special notice must be given to the company at least 28 days before the meeting of the intention to propose a resolution to remove an auditor under section 510 (s. 511). On receipt of notice of the intended resolution, the company must immediately send a copy of it to the auditor proposed to be removed (s. 511(2)).

The auditor proposed to be removed may make written representations (not exceeding a reasonable length) to the company on the proposed resolution and demand that they be circulated to the members (s. 511(3)). Unless the representations are received too late for it to do so, the company must comply with such a demand and state in the notice of the resolution given to members that representations have been made (s. 511(4)). If the representations are not circulated to the members for any reason, the auditor may require them to be read out at the meeting (s. 511(5)). The court may relieve the company of these obligations if it is satisfied that the auditors are using the provisions to secure needless publicity for defamatory matter (s. 511(6)).

The auditor proposed to be removed will have the right under section 502(2) to receive notice of the meeting at which it is proposed to remove him and the right to attend and speak at that meeting on matters which concern him as the company's auditor (which will include his proposed removal). An auditor who is removed retains the rights conferred by section 502(2) in relation to any general meeting of the company at which his term of office would otherwise have expired or at which it is proposed to fill the vacancy caused by his removal (s. 513) and may attend and speak on matters that concern him as a former auditor.

An auditor who is removed from office must make a statement as to the circumstances connected with his removal at least 14 days after his removal (s. 519), which the company may in addition be required to circulate to the members (see previous section).

Dividends
Final dividend
Most articles provide that dividends may be declared by an ordinary resolution of the company in general meeting and that no dividend may exceed the amount recommended by the directors (pcls 30 and plc 70). Dividends can only be paid out of profits available for distribution (ss 829 to 853). In recommending the final dividend, the directors must ensure that there are sufficient funds available for distribution. It is, therefore, usual for the resolution to declare a dividend to be proposed at the general meeting at which the accounts have been laid. The wording of the notice with regard to dividends is usually very simple.

Precedent: Dividends – statement in directors' report

An interim dividend of [5] pence per share has been paid and the directors recommend a final dividend of [9] pence per share in respect of the year ended [date], making a total for the year of [14] pence per share. The proposed dividend will, if approved at the annual general meeting, be paid on [date] to shareholders on the register at the close of business on [date].

Precedent: Notice of resolution to declare a dividend:

To declare a dividend.

It is recommended that, at any general meeting, the company should propose a separate resolution on each substantially separate issue and should, in particular, propose a resolution at the AGM to receive or adopt the report and accounts. This should be separate from any resolution to approve the payment of the final dividend recommended by the directors.

Interim dividend

Older articles usually also provide that the directors may pay interim dividends without reference to the members, however, current model articles do not specifically include this provision. The directors should not pay a dividend unless it is clear that sufficient funds are available for distribution. They should also document the agreement to make the payment in the minutes of the relevant directors' meeting.

Precedent: Board resolution to pay an interim dividend

It was resolved:

THAT an interim dividend for the year ended [date] of [7] pence per share on the ordinary shares of [25] pence each be paid on [date] to shareholders registered at the close of business on [date].

Appointment of directors

Articles usually contain detailed procedures on the appointment of directors. Any natural or legal person may be appointed as a director. However, at least one director of a company must be an individual person (s. 155) and no director may be appointed who is under the age of 16 (s. 157).

Subject to these rules, at the present time, a company may be appointed as a director of another company, commonly known as a corporate director. However, as noted below, legislation is due to be enacted that abolishes the use of corporate directors except in limited circumstances. As such, it is advisable to only appoint individuals as directors to avoid any future need to amend or replace.

SBEE 2015

A general provision on the appointment of corporate directors is expected to come into force in the near future when s. 87 SBEE 2015 is scheduled to remove s. 155 and introduce new ss 156A–C. There are to be limited exceptions to the general prohibition on the appointment of corporate directors. Although the detailed guidance has not yet been published, the exceptions are expected to include appointments to listed groups, charities and trustee companies, amongst others. Any existing corporate director appointment not meeting one of the exceptions would automatically terminate 12 months after s 87 SBEE 2015 comes into force. At the time of writing, the amendment has not yet been implemented.

The method of appointment and the persons or body authorised to make the appointment may differ according to the type of appointment being made. The position under the model articles is simple. They provide that any person who is willing to act as a director and who is permitted by law to do so, may be appointed to be a director either by an ordinary resolution of the members or by a decision of the directors (pcls 17, clg 17 and plc 20). The position is not quite so simple under Table A.

Methods of appointing directors under the 1985 Table A

Type of appointment	Appointed by	Source
First directors	Subscribers to the memorandum	CA 2006, ss 9, 12 & 16
Additional directors	Board of directors	reg. 79
	Members	regs 76–78
Appointments to fill a casual vacancy	Board of directors	reg. 79
	Members	regs 76–78
Reappointment following retirement by rotation	Members	regs 72–75 and 78
Reappointment following retirement at first AGM after appointment	Members	regs 72, 78 and 79
Alternate directors	Directors	regs. 65 to 69

Procedure for appointment of directors

(a) Check articles for the method of appointment.
(b) If additional appointment, check that it will not cause the number of directors to exceed any maximum prescribed by the articles.
(c) Check compliance with any age requirements
(d) Check articles for any share qualifications.
(e) Obtain approval for the appointment at a board meeting or, as the case may be, at a general meeting (if a private company, members' approval may be obtained by written resolution).
(f) Notify appointment to Companies House within 14 days of appointment ensuring that the new director consented to act.
(g) Enter details of the new director in the register of directors.
(h) Remind director of any share qualification required by the articles.
(i) Request director to give general notice of any interest in contracts or proposed contracts with the company.
(j) Notify the company's bankers as appropriate.
(k) Obtain details of the director's PAYE coding and NI Number and instructions as to method of payment of remuneration.
(l) If appropriate, settle terms of service agreement (not to exceed two years without shareholder approval) and issue terms of reference or letter of appointment.
(m) Provide new director with any documentation (such as the company's articles, governance policies) and any necessary induction training.

Minimum and maximum number

The Companies Act 2006 provides that every private company (whether limited by shares, limited by guarantee or unlimited) must have at least one director and that every public company must have at least two (s. 154). Articles may require a higher number than the statutory minimum but not a lower number.

Articles may also specify the maximum number of directors who may be appointed or provide a mechanism for determining such a limit. Any appointment which would cause the number of directors to exceed that maximum will be invalid.

The model articles do not impose any maximum. Regulation 64 of Table A provides that the number of directors shall not be subject to any maximum unless the members determine otherwise by ordinary resolution. This is a rather ungainly provision. It is easy to imagine circumstances where the existence of a limit imposed by ordinary resolution might be forgotten as such a resolution does not operate to amend the articles and can only be proved by reference to the minutes of the general meeting at which it was passed (or the record of any relevant written resolution). It is better to fix a maximum by amending the relevant article. If, however, a maximum is imposed or changed by ordinary resolution under regulation 64, it is advisable to make a note referring to that resolution on the master copy of the articles. It may also be a good idea to make a note that no such resolution has ever been passed if, indeed, that is the case. Regulation 64 can also cause problems if the members vote to impose a maximum which is less than the number of directors currently holding office. It is doubtful whether such a resolution would have the effect of removing any of the directors unless special notice was given of a resolution to remove one or more of those directors in accordance with section 168. Such a resolution would, however, be effective in preventing any future appointments or reappointments in breach of the maximum.

First directors

Before a company can be registered, the subscribers to the memorandum (the people who will become the company's first members) must provide the registrar of companies with the name(s) and details of the first director(s). On incorporation, the people named as directors in the incorporation documents are deemed to have been appointed and no further action is required (s. 16). It is, however, standard practice to note in the minutes of the first board meeting the method by which they were appointed (see Chapter 8 Convening a Board Meeting). There is nothing to prevent the subscribers nominating themselves as the first directors.

If the articles require the directors to hold shares in the company, they may provide that they will cease to be directors if they do not satisfy that requirement within a certain period. The articles may also require the directors to satisfy other qualifications or provide for their removal from office on the happening of certain events.

Subsequent appointments

Subsequent appointments must be made in accordance with the procedures laid down in the company's articles of association and the requirements of the Companies Act 2006. The Act only interferes by providing:

- at least one of the directors must be an individual person (s. 155);
- a director must be at least 16 years of age (s. 157);
- that a motion for the appointment of two or more persons as directors of a public company by a single resolution at a general meeting shall not be valid unless the meeting agrees unanimously to a proposal that the resolution be proposed in that manner (s. 160);
- that details of appointments of directors must be entered in a register by the company and notified to Companies House, although failure to do so does not invalidate the appointment (ss. 162 to 167).

All other questions relating to the appointment of directors must be resolved by reference to the articles. This is one of the areas where articles are likely to differ from the norm and a careful examination of the relevant company's articles will be necessary to ensure that the correct procedures are followed. If the articles make no provision for the appointment of directors, appointments must be made by the members.

Appointment by the directors

Under the model articles, the directors may appoint new directors (pcls 17, clg 17 and plc 20). Under Table A the directors may appoint new directors either to fill vacancies or as additional directors (subject to any maximum fixed in accordance with the articles) (reg. 79). A vacancy arises where an existing director has died, resigned or has become disqualified from acting as a director. Such appointments should be made in accordance with the decision-making procedures for directors provided for in the company's articles.

Precedent: Board resolution to appoint an additional director – public company

THAT [name of new director] be appointed a director of the company with effect from [date] [and shall hold office until the next annual general meeting].

The model articles for private companies do not make any provision for retirement of directors whether by rotation or otherwise. Accordingly, a person appointed as a director of a private company will remain a director until they resign, are removed, or cease to hold office for any other reason.

The model articles for public companies require all the directors to retire at the company's first AGM and for the following directors to retire at every subsequent AGM (plc 21):

(a) all directors who have been appointed by the directors since the last AGM;
(b) any directors who were not appointed or reappointed at one of the preceding two AGMs.

Under Table A, directors appointed by the board must retire at the AGM following their appointment and offer themselves for election by the members (reg. 79). No less than seven nor more than 28 days before the meeting the company must give notice of any person retiring in this manner who is recommended by the directors for appointment or reappointment. The notice must include the details which would be required to be included in the register of directors if that person were to be appointed or reappointed (reg. 77). The purpose of this provision is to ensure that the directors cannot propose a person for appointment or reappointment without giving the members prior notice of his details (e.g. by including in the notice of the meeting an item of business to elect directors without naming them). If the company fails to give notice in accordance with regulation 77 the appointment will be invalid. If the members resolve not to reappoint a director, the director ceases to hold office at the conclusion of the AGM. Directors retiring in this manner are not taken into account in determining the directors who are to retire by rotation at the meeting.

A person appointed as a director of a private company to fill a casual vacancy may never be required to retire under this type of provision if the company never holds an AGM. If for any reason, one is subsequently held, directors appointed under regulation 79 should retire at that meeting and offer themselves for re-election.

Regulation 79 applies in respect of vacancies and appointments of additional directors. However, articles sometimes allow the directors to make appointments to fill casual vacancies only. In these circumstances, the directors may only appoint a person to replace a director who has died, resigned or been disqualified from acting as a director. They may not fill any vacancy which arises by virtue of the procedures on rotation of directors or any vacancy which arises because an appointment made for a fixed period has ceased (e.g. an appointment for a fixed term of one year or an appointment which ceases at the conclusion of the next AGM).

Where the articles restrict the powers of the directors to filling casual vacancies, the members retain the power to appoint additional directors.

Director appointment by the members

If the articles give the directors power to fill casual vacancies and appoint additional directors, the members will have no power to do so unless the articles make specific provision to that effect. The model articles allow the members of both public and private companies to appoint directors by ordinary resolution, whether as additional directors, to fill casual vacancies or otherwise.

Under Table A, the members can also appoint directors to fill casual vacancies or as additional directors by ordinary resolution at a general meeting (subject to any maximum) (reg. 78). However, under Table A, the members proposing the appointment must give the company prior notice of their intention to propose a person as a director who is not recommended by the board, not less than 14 days nor more than 35 days before the date of the meeting. The notice given to the company must include the details which would be required to be included in the register of directors if that person was appointed and notice signed by the person nominated of his willingness to act as a director (reg. 76). The purpose of regulation 76 is to prevent the members from relying on the inclusion in the notice of the meeting of an item of business to elect or re-elect directors in order to propose a person not recommended by the directors. It should be noted, however, that the fact that a member has given notice in accordance with regulation 76 does not guarantee that the proposal will be within the scope of the notice of the meeting.

Other methods of appointment

A company's articles may provide for different methods of appointment. For example, the articles could provide that directors may be appointed or removed from office by notice in writing signed by members holding a majority of the voting shares. This method is most likely to be used by subsidiary companies as it enables the parent company to make appointments without having to hold a meeting of the subsidiary.

A variation on this theme can be useful for joint venture companies where each of the partners in the joint venture is given the right to appoint a fixed number of directors (and replace them with others) by giving notice in writing. This can be achieved by having different classes of shares with each class having separate rights to appoint a fixed number of directors.

The articles of small owner-managed companies are frequently modified to ensure that the founders retain the right to participate in their management. Some amendment may be necessary even where all the company's shares are held equally by two people who are both appointed as directors. In particular, this may be required where the chair of the general meeting has a casting vote and could, therefore, appoint and remove directors against the wishes of the other member to gain management control. The simplest solution in these circumstances is to amend the articles to exclude the application of any article which gives the chair a casting vote.

Director retirement by rotation

The model articles for private companies make no provision for retirement by rotation. The model articles for public companies require all the directors to retire at the company's first AGM and for the following directors to retire at every subsequent AGM (plc 21):

(a) all directors who have been appointed by the directors since the last AGM;
(b) any directors who were not appointed or reappointed at one of the preceding two AGMs.

Directors who retire under this provision must retire from office and may (but need not) offer themselves for reappointment by the members.

The UK Corporate Governance Code recommends that all directors of listed companies should retire and offer themselves for re-election at least once every three years or, in the case of FTSE 350 companies, annually (see below). Although the Code does not have the force of law, most listed companies now comply with this recommendation in respect of both executive and non-executive directors.

Table A articles have a provision for directors to retire by rotation, although these are often excluded for owner-managed private companies, subsidiaries and joint venture companies. Particular attention should be paid to the articles of these companies to ensure that basic provisions are followed, including the numbers of directors required to retire on an annual basis which is calculated based on the size of the board.

Who is to retire?

The directors to retire by rotation will normally be those who have served longest since their last appointment or reappointment. Articles normally provide that, where the number who must retire is less than the number who are eligible under this rule because they were appointed or last reappointed on the same day, the selection of those to retire is to be determined by lot, unless they otherwise agree among themselves (in which case their unanimous agreement is required with respect to the decision or the method of reaching that decision). A lot may be performed by the drawing of straws or some other similar method of chance. It has been held that where the articles state that the matter is to be settled by ballot, this also means by lot rather than by any method of voting (*Eyre v Milton Proprietary* [1936] Ch. 244). This case is also authority for the fact that temporary directors (e.g. those appointed by the directors under regulation 79 and who must, therefore, automatically retire at the next following AGM) should not be included when calculating how many directors should retire under the rotation provisions.

UK Corporate Governance Code recommendations

The UK Corporate Governance Code (July 2018) (Provision 18) recommends that all directors should be subject to annual re-election. The board should set out in the papers accompanying the resolutions to elect each director the specific reasons why their contribution is, and continues to be, important to the company's long-term sustainable success.

Provision 19 also recommends that the chair should not remain in post beyond nine years from the date of their first appointment to the board. To facilitate effective succession planning and the development of a diverse board, this period can be extended for a limited time, particularly in those cases where the chair was an existing non-executive director on appointment. A clear explanation should be provided.

Notice and proxy forms

Unless the articles specify that the re-election of directors retiring by rotation at the AGM is part of the ordinary business of that meeting, it will normally be necessary for a company to indicate the general nature of the business in the notice. This can be done simply by stating as an item of business 'to re-elect directors retiring by rotation'. However, it is standard practice for the notice to name the directors who will be retiring and seeking re-election at the meeting. This should be expended upon by also providing a brief description of the relevant directors, including their relevant experience (not merely a list of other directorships they hold); the dates that they were first appointed to the board; and details of any board committees to which they belong. This could be done in any circular which accompanies the notice or in the directors' report if the accounts are sent to the members with the notice.

Listed companies must send proxy cards to members which allow them to indicate how their proxy should vote on every resolution (other than procedural resolutions) which will be put to the meeting (Listing Rule 9.3.6). If the resolutions to be proposed include the re-election of retiring directors and the number of retiring directors standing for re-election exceeds five, the proxy form may give shareholders the opportunity to vote for or against (or abstain from voting on) the re-election of the retiring directors as a whole but must also allow votes to be cast for or against (or for shareholders to abstain from voting on) the re-election of the retiring directors individually (Listing Rule 9.3.7).

The Act provides that a motion for the appointment of two or more persons as directors by a single resolution at a general meeting of a public company shall not be valid unless the meeting agrees unanimously to a proposal that the resolution be proposed in that manner (s. 160).

Failure to hold an AGM

If a company which is required to hold an AGM fails to do so, the directors who were due to retire at that meeting may be deemed to have retired at the end of the period during which the AGM was meant to be held. As private companies are no longer required to hold AGMs, this would not apply, unless the company's articles required the company to hold AGMs.

Removal of directors

The statutory rules on removal of directors apply to public and private companies alike and cannot be excluded by the articles. The articles may, however, provide an additional method of removal. If so, the members may use the statutory procedures or the additional method provided by the articles to remove a director.

The statutory procedures on removal are designed primarily to ensure that a simple majority of the members have the power to remove a director. This is a crucial safeguard for the members who might otherwise have little or no control over the directors. The statutory procedures also ensure that directors are given a fair chance to defend themselves against any proposal to remove them as directors. Directors are not normally afforded similar rights where an additional procedure is provided for by the articles.

This statutory power applies notwithstanding anything in the company's articles or in any agreement between the company and the director. Special notice is also required with respect to any resolution to appoint at the same meeting another person instead of a director removed under these statutory powers (s. 168(2)).

A vacancy caused by the removal of a director may, if not filled at the meeting at which he is removed, be filled as a casual vacancy (s. 168(3)).

A person appointed in place of a director removed under section 168 is treated, for the purpose of determining the time at which they or any other director is to retire, as if they had become a director on the same day on which the director whom they have replaced was last appointed (s. 168(4)).

Director's right to protest removal

Under the special notice rules, a resolution to remove a director under section 168 will not be effective unless notice of the intention to move it has been given to the company at least 28 days before the meeting at which it is moved (s. 312(1)). On receipt of a valid notice from a member, the company must immediately send a copy of it to the director concerned (s. 169(1)).

The director is entitled to be heard on the resolution at the meeting whether or not he or she is a member of the company (s. 169(2)), but is also allowed to make written representations (not exceeding a reasonable length). If the director makes written representations to the company in connection with the resolution and requests their notification to the members, the company must, unless the representations are received too late for it to do so:

(a) state in any notice of the resolution given to members that representations have been made; and

(b) send a copy of the director's representations to every member to whom notice of the meeting is sent (whether before or after receipt of the representations by the company) (s. 169(3)).

Special notice may be served on the company up to 28 days before the meeting. The company may not have time to wait for the director to make representations if it is to meet the deadline for giving notice of the meeting to the members. If notice of the meeting has already been given or if there is not sufficient time to have the notice reprinted, the company need not comply with subparagraph (a) above. However, even if the notice has already been sent, the company must still send a copy of the director's representations to each member (and bear the cost of doing so) unless it is impossible to deliver them to the members before the meeting.

If, for any reason, a copy of the director's representations is not sent to the members, the director may require them to be read out at the meeting. In these circumstances, the director still has a right to be heard on the resolution at the meeting (s. 169(4)).

The company or any other person who claims to be aggrieved may apply to the court for an order that the director's representations should not be sent to members or read out at the meeting on the grounds that the director is abusing the rights conferred by section 169 (s. 169(5)). The type of abuse envisaged here would include, but not necessarily be restricted to, matters such as securing needless publicity for defamatory matter.

Authority to enable a traded company to call meetings on less than 21 days' notice

The Companies Act 2006 originally enabled all public companies to call a general meeting (other than an AGM) on 14 clear days' notice. However, as a consequence of the EU Shareholders' Rights Directive, the Act was amended to require traded companies to call such general meetings on at least 21 clear days' notice unless certain conditions are complied with, in which case the company can hold general meetings (other than the AGM) with as little as 14 days' clear notice. One of those conditions is that the company must offer the facility for shareholders to vote by electronic means accessible to all shareholders. The other is that they must have obtained prior shareholder approval for the holding of general meetings at not less than 14 clear days' notice (s. 307A).

The resolution reducing the period of notice to not less than 14 days must be passed as a special resolution either at the immediately preceding AGM or at a general meeting held since that AGM (s. 307A(4)). However, in the case of a company which has not yet held an AGM, the resolution must be passed at a general meeting (s. 307A(5)).

Precedent: Special resolution to allow 14 days' notice of general meetings of a listed company

To authorise the calling of general meetings of the company (not being an annual general meeting) by notice of at least 14 clear days.

(Note: Unless this resolution is passed at every AGM of a listed company, the company will be required under section 307 to give 21 days' notice of all general meetings. The company must also offer the facility for shareholders to vote by electronic means accessible to all shareholders in order to call general meetings at less than 21 days' notice.)

Any such resolution is only valid up to the next AGM of the company and will need to be renewed in each succeeding year.

Directors' authority to allot shares

The directors of listed companies routinely request shareholders to renew their authority to allot shares at the AGM. Authority may be given to the directors to allot some or all of the unissued share capital by ordinary resolution in accordance (s. 551). Institutional investors impose certain conditions on the amount of shares over which they are willing to give authority to allot and generally insist that new issues of shares above a certain threshold be conducted on a pre-emptive basis (e.g. as a rights issue). Where shares are issued on this basis existing holders are offered the opportunity to subscribe for the shares. If they decide not to take up their entitlements, the shares are subsequently sold to the highest bidder through the market and original shareholder is paid the difference between the subscription price and the price obtained in the market.

Precedent: Resolution for directors' authority to allot shares

Ordinary Resolution:

(A) THAT the board be and it is hereby generally and unconditionally authorised to exercise all powers of the company to allot relevant securities (within the meaning of section 551 of the Companies Act 2006) up to an aggregate nominal amount of £...A... provided that this authority shall expire on ....*...... save that the company may before such expiry make an offer or agreement which would or might require relevant securities to be allotted after such expiry and the board may allot relevant securities in pursuance of such an offer or agreement as if the authority conferred hereby had not expired, and further,

(B) THAT the board be and it is hereby generally and unconditionally authorised to exercise all powers of the company to allot equity securities (within the meaning of section 560 of the said Act) in connection with a rights issue in favour of ordinary shareholders where the equity securities respectively attributable to the interests of all ordinary shareholders are proportionate (as nearly as may be) to the respective numbers of ordinary shares held by them up to an aggregate nominal amount of £...A... provided that this authority shall expire on the date of the next annual general meeting of the company after the passing of this resolution save that the company may before such expiry make an offer or agreement which would or might require relevant securities to be allotted after such expiry and the board may allot relevant securities in pursuance of such an offer or agreement as if the authority conferred hereby had not expired.

Institutional investors also impose a limit on the number of shares which may be issued under a routine section 551 allotment authority as a rights issue. The maximum limit is two-thirds of issued share capital. However, if the directors proceed to issue any more than one-third of the company's existing share capital in the following year, they are all expected to offer themselves for re-election at the next AGM.

Disapplication of pre-emption rights

Listed companies routinely request shareholders to approve a resolution to disapply the statutory pre-emption rights over some or all of the shares covered by the directors' authority to allot shares. This resolution must be passed as a special resolution in accordance with either section 570 or section 571.

Institutional investors impose limits on the amount of shares which may be issued on a non pre-emptive basis, but are prepared to disapply the statutory pre-emption rights over the whole of any allotment authority provided that any issue above that threshold is carried out on a pre-emptive basis in accordance with the requirements of the Listing Rules.

Precedent: Disapplication of pre-emption rights

Special Resolution:

Subject to the passing of the previous resolution, to authorise the board pursuant to section 570 of the Companies Act 2006 to allot equity securities (within the meaning of section 560 of the said Act) for cash pursuant to the authority conferred by the previous resolution as if sub-section (1) of section 561 of the said Act did not apply to any such allotment provided that this power shall be limited

(ii) to the allotment of equity securities in connection with a rights issue in favour of ordinary shareholders where the equity securities respectively attributable to the interests of all Ordinary shareholders are proportionate (as nearly as may be) to the respective numbers of Ordinary shares held by them and,

(ii) to the allotment (otherwise than pursuant to sub-paragraph (i) above) of equity securities up to an aggregate nominal value of £...B...

and shall expire {on the date of the next annual general meeting of the company after the passing of this resolution } save that the company may before such expiry make an offer or agreement which would or might require equity securities to be allotted after such expiry and the board may allot equity securities in pursuance of such an offer or agreement as if the power conferred hereby had not expired.

Market purchases of own shares

Many listed companies routinely request authority from shareholders at the AGM to enable them to make market purchases of their own shares. Under the Act, authority for such market purchases may be given by ordinary resolution. However, institutional investors expect listed companies to put forward any such proposal as a special resolution. Resolutions authorising the directors to make market purchases must comply with the requirements of section 701 and the Listing Rules. The directors do not have to exercise their authority to make market purchases and may only do so in accordance with the terms of the resolution approved by shareholders.

Precedent: Resolution – share buyback

Special Resolution: To authorise the company generally and unconditionally to make market purchases (as defined in section 693(2) of the Companies Act 2006) of ordinary shares with nominal value of [nominal value] each in the company, provided that:

(a) the company does not purchase under this authority more than [number] ordinary shares;

(b) the company does not pay less than [amount] for each share; and

(c) the company does not pay more for each share than 5% over the average of the middle market price of the ordinary shares for the five business days immediately preceding the date on which the company agrees to buy the shares concerned, based on share prices and currency exchange rates published in the Daily Official List of the London Stock Exchange.

This authority shall continue for the period ending on the date of the annual general meeting in 2011 or 15 [date], whichever is the earlier, provided that, if the company has agreed before this date to purchase ordinary shares where these purchases will or may be executed after the authority terminates (either wholly or in part), the company may complete such purchases.

The role of the company secretary at the meeting

The company secretary should first check that a quorum is present and then be ready to read the notice of meeting. If the meeting consents (and it usually does), this may be taken as read, since it will have been included in the report and accounts sent to all members.

The auditor's report must cover the accounts laid before the meeting and state the name of the auditor and, where the auditor is a firm, the name of the person who signed it as senior statutory auditor. This will, of course, have been included in the booklet containing the report and accounts.

The company secretary will assist the chair in counting the votes (if necessary) on a show of hands. This is not normally necessary, except in the case of a special resolution, where there might be some doubt about whether the necessary three-quarters majority of those attending and voting was achieved.

All proxies are entitled to speak at the meeting including demanding or joining in the demand for a poll vote on any resolution (ss 324 and 329). The company secretary will often oversee the process if a poll is demanded on any resolution, to be taken either at or after the meeting.

Conclusion

Events at the general meeting will dictate the requirements of the company and, as can be seen from this chapter, the inclusion of resolutions that may require polls or votes adds additional complexity to what is already a complex process.

Most meetings will run smoothly, acting as intended by giving members an opportunity to voice their views, concerns and comments. Where this becomes contentious or there is not a clear majority on any point, there is enormous benefit in being prepared for any eventuality and being able to react in a way that accords with both legislation and the articles of the company.

16 – After the general meeting

Actions and proceedings after a general meeting fall into the two categories of:

1 Administrative actions following the conclusion of the event, such as finalising the minutes and submitting documents to Companies House.
2 Remedies that can be taken that would make the meeting, or some of the business transacted at it, liable to challenge.

Given that remedies could make the meeting null and void, this will be covered first. Thereafter the practical aspects of concluding the meeting will be outlined, finishing with a brief guide to the actions that the company secretary should take after the general meeting has been held.

Shareholder remedies

Certain breaches of the statutory requirements relating to general meetings may make the meeting, or some of the business transacted at it, liable to challenge. These include:

- breach of statutory requirements;
- enforcement by reference to the articles;
- claims of wrong doing by the company, derivative claims;
- alteration of articles;
- unfairly prejudicial conduct; and
- application for winding up.

There are a number of other remedies, although these are rarely used other than in extreme circumstances.

In general, these post-meeting remedies are legal in nature and require court intervention. While they are covered here for reference, any action taken at this stage would clearly include the involvement of lawyers and other advisors.

Breach of statutory requirements

Meetings held and decisions made in breach of any statutory requirements are liable to be declared invalid. For example, a resolution which the Act requires to be passed as a special resolution will be invalid if it is only passed as an ordinary resolution. A general meeting called at less than the statutory minimum period of notice is liable to be declared invalid unless the members have consented to this shorter notice.

It might be thought that any such breach of a statutory requirement would automatically render a decision taken at a general meeting invalid. However, this will not necessarily always be the case where:

(a) the relevant statutory provision can be modified by a company's articles and the company complied with any relevant modification of that provision contained in its articles;

(b) the relevant statutory provision specifically provides that failure to comply shall not invalidate a decision (e.g. where a sole member fails to provide a written record of a decision which has effect as if taken at a general meeting); and

(c) the courts decide otherwise under a common law rule such as the principle of unanimous consent.

A breach of a statutory requirement may not be noticed until long after the general meeting took place, the decision was made, or may never be noticed at all. Even if the breach is noticed, it may be that there is nobody concerned enough to challenge the validity of the proceedings or the decision.

However, a person who has sufficient interest could challenge the validity of a decision in an attempt to prevent it from being implemented or taking effect. Generally speaking, this sort of action needs to be taken fairly promptly and the longer a person waits, the less inclined the courts become to intervene, particularly where intervention may prejudice the interests of innocent third parties. One of the ways the courts can avoid having to do this is by applying the principle of unanimous consent and by deeming the members to have acquiesced in an irregularity by failing to take action soon enough.

However, the courts are sometimes prepared to intervene long after the event if the breach is considered sufficiently significant (e.g. if there has been a breach of any of the procedural requirements for obtaining approval for an off-market contract for the purchase of own shares). The court will often declare such a resolution invalid, order the member whose shares were purportedly purchased to repay any money they received, and order that their name be restored to the register. The court will not normally have any qualms about doing this, particularly when a company is being wound up as insolvent, because the beneficiaries of such an order would be the creditors.

Although it may not always be possible to predict conclusively whether a breach of a statutory requirement will invalidate a meeting or a decision, it will render the meeting or the decision liable to challenge. This uncertainty is dangerous from the perspective of the company, its directors and, in some cases, the members. The occurrence of a breach can give rise to potential civil liabilities on the part of some or all of them. A company and its directors would not normally want this kind of uncertainty hanging over them and would normally want to take steps to rectify the breach once it becomes known.

In cases of doubt the company might even seek a court declaration that the decision-making process was valid. The danger of leaving the matter unsettled is that there might be an individual who has sufficient incentive to take action and such action may be commenced at a time that might be detrimental to the company (e.g. when they are tendering for a significant contract).

Very often that action will be taken by the company itself after a new board has been appointed or, where the company has become insolvent, the liquidator. In either case, the action may be taken to invalidate the decision(s) of a meeting that would have a detrimental impact on the company at such later stage.

Enforcement by reference to the articles

The provisions of a company's constitution bind the company and its members to the same extent as if there were covenants on the part of the company and of each member to observe those provisions. This creates a contract between the company and its members, the terms of which are contained in the company's constitution. Section 17 provides that, unless the context otherwise requires, references in the Companies Act to a company's constitution include the company's articles, and any resolutions and agreements to which Chapter 3 of Part 3 applies (i.e. resolutions and agreements which must be filed with the registrar).

The contract differs in a number of ways from normal contracts. Provision is made in the Act for its terms to be altered by a special majority as opposed to the consent of all the parties required to vary normal contracts.

A company can enforce its contract against its members and the members can enforce it against each other. The members can also enforce the contract against the company, but only in limited circumstances.

It has been held on a number of occasions that members may only enforce provisions in the articles which confer rights on them in their capacity as members. For example, a member cannot enforce a provision in the articles that he should be the company's solicitor but can enforce his right to vote under the articles.

In practice, a general meeting or the passing of a specific resolution at a meeting could, in theory, be challenged if it could, in some way, be seen to be actioned against the articles of the company

The second major exception for shareholders is that they may be able to bring personal actions for breaches of procedures, although the courts may consider these to be mere internal irregularities and not uphold the claim. As a general rule, the courts will not uphold a claim if it is clear that, even if the action is allowed, the majority would have still got their own way by following the correct procedures.

For example, a court may refuse to declare an adjournment passed on a show of hands invalid simply because the chair had improperly refused to allow a minority shareholder to demand a poll. Where, however, it is clear that the breach affected the outcome of the meeting, a court will allow an action to proceed (e.g. where the chair improperly excluded some votes cast by a proxy in favour of a resolution which would have been passed had they been accepted).

Derivative actions

The courts have applied a longstanding rule which limits the ability of shareholders to bring actions on behalf of the company (derivative actions) for wrongs done to the company. The rule is founded on two important principles. The first is that where a wrong is done to a company, only the company can take action against the wrongdoers and not individual members (the proper plaintiff principle). The second is that the will of the majority of the members should generally be allowed to prevail in the running of the company's business.

There are certain important exceptions to these principles, as follows:

1 The proper plaintiff in an action in respect of a wrong alleged to be done to a corporation is, prima facie, the corporation.
2 Where the alleged wrong is a transaction which might be made binding on the corporation and on all its members by a simple majority of the members, no individual member of the corporation is allowed to maintain an action in respect of that matter because, if the majority confirms the transaction, [the question is at an end]; or if the majority challenges the transaction, there is no valid reason why the company should not sue.
3 There is no room for the operation of the rule if the alleged wrong is ultra vires the corporation, because the majority of members cannot confirm the transaction.
4 There is also no room for the operation of the rule if the transaction complained of could be validly done or sanctioned only by a special resolution or the like, because a simple majority cannot confirm a transaction which requires the concurrence of a greater majority.
5 There is an exception to the rule where what has been done amounts to fraud and the wrongdoers are themselves in control of the company.

Ultra vires transactions

The exception to the rule that the majority cannot confirm an act which is ultra vires the company (i.e. beyond the capacity of the company as prescribed by the objects clause in the memorandum) is now qualified by section 239 which provides a procedure which enables the members to ratify acts of the directors (including those which are beyond the powers of the company) by ordinary resolution, albeit one where any votes in favour of ratification cast by a director (as a member of the company) or any connected persons are disregarded.

It should also be noted that section 40(4) specifically preserves a shareholder's right to bring a personal action against the company to restrain it from committing an ultra vires act.

Section 239 does not, however, allow a company to ratify transactions which are ultra vires because they are illegal (e.g. in breach of a statutory requirement) and a shareholder will be able to bring a derivative action against the wrongdoers on behalf of the company in these circumstances.

Special resolution procedures

Members can bring actions to restrain breaches of special majority procedures (whether they are contained in the Act or the articles) and to prevent the company from acting on resolutions passed as a result of such breaches. In *Edwards v Halliwell* [1950] 2 All ER 1064, the Court of Appeal declared a decision by a trade union to increase its membership fees invalid because a requirement in its constitution that a two-thirds majority of the members should agree had not been observed.

Statutory derivative claims

The Companies Act 2006 introduced a statutory procedure for derivative claims (and in Scotland, derivative proceedings). Under section 260 a member may bring proceedings in respect of a cause of action on behalf of a company seeking relief on behalf of the company. Such claims can be brought only in relation to a cause of action arising from an actual or proposed act or omission involving negligence, default, breach of duty or breach of trust by a director, former director or shadow director of a company.

The procedure for making an application in section 261 requires an initial petition to be made to the court for permission to proceed with the case. Section 262 enables a member to apply for permission to continue a claim brought originally by the company as a derivate claim where the company has failed to prosecute the claim diligently or the manner in which it has commenced the claim amounts to an abuse of the process of the court.

Section 263 sets out the grounds on which the court must decide whether permission to proceed with a derivative action should be given. Permission or leave must be refused if the court is satisfied:

(a) that a person acting in accordance with section 172 (duty to promote the success of the company) would not seek to continue the claim; or
(b) that the act or omission has been authorised by the company where the cause of action arises from an act or omission that is yet to occur; or
(c) that the act or omission was authorised by the company before it occurred, or has been ratified by the company since it occurred, where the cause of action arises from an act or omission that has already occurred.

In considering whether to give permission (or leave) the court must also take into account, in particular:

(a) whether the member is acting in good faith in seeking to continue the claim;
(b) the importance that a person acting in accordance with section 172 (duty to promote the success of the company) would attach to continuing it;
(c) where the cause of action results from an act or omission that is yet to occur, whether the act or omission could be, and in the circumstances would be likely to be authorised by the company before it occurs, or ratified by the company after it occurs;
(d) where the cause of action arises from an act or omission that has already occurred, whether the act or omission could be, and in the circumstances would be likely to be, ratified by the company;
(e) whether the company has decided not to pursue the claim; and
(f) whether the act or omission in respect of which the claim is brought gives rise to a cause of action that the member could pursue in his own right rather than on behalf of the company.

In addition, in considering whether to give permission (or leave) the court shall have particular regard to any evidence before it as to the views of members of the company who have no personal interest, direct or indirect, in the matter (s. 263(4)).

Fraud on the minority

Derivative actions were designed by the courts to enable members to bring an action on behalf of the company where the wrongdoers have committed a 'fraud on the minority' and control the company. The word 'fraud' in this context embraced a wider equitable meaning than deceit and in reality could be considered to be a wrong done to the company rather than to the minority.

The statutory procedure noted above probably enables a wider range of derivative claims to be brought on behalf of the company. However, at heart, their main purpose is still to provide redress where there has been a fraud on the minority.

Alteration of articles

The Act allows a company to alter its articles by special resolution (s. 21), subject to any entrenched provisions (see s. 22). However, this power of amendment must be exercised by the members in good faith for the benefit of the company as a whole. Hence, if the members have acted honestly in what they believe to be the best interests of the company, the court is unlikely to interfere.

It should be noted that, even though minority shareholders might not succeed under this heading, they could be entitled to relief under the unfair prejudice procedures set out below.

Unfairly prejudicial conduct

A member may petition the court for relief from unfairly prejudicial conduct under section 994. This statutory remedy has removed many of the obstacles which prevented minority shareholders from seeking relief under the common law. Any member may petition the court and the relief under section 994 is not restricted to minority shareholders although the court will not grant a majority shareholder a remedy if he can easily rid himself of the prejudice by using his majority shareholding.

Where the court is satisfied that a petition is well founded, it may make any order it thinks fit for giving relief in respect of the matters complained of (s. 996). The order may, for example:

- regulate the conduct of the company's affairs in the future;
- require the company to refrain from doing or continuing an act complained of;
- require the company to do an act which the petitioner has complained it has omitted to do;
- authorise civil proceedings to be brought in the name of and on behalf of the company by such person or persons and on such terms as the court may direct;
- require the company not to make any, or any specified, alterations to its articles without leave of the court;
- provide for the purchase of the shares of any members of the company by other members or by the company itself and in the case of a purchase by the company itself, the reduction of the company's capital accordingly.

The court may grant a petitioner relief under section 994 where the company's affairs are being (or have been) conducted in a manner which is unfairly prejudicial to the interests of its members generally or some of the members (including at least the petitioner), or where any actual or proposed act or omission of the company (including an act or omission on its behalf) is or would be so prejudicial (s. 994(1)).

According to a study undertaken on behalf of the Law Commission for its Consultation Paper No. 142 'Shareholder Remedies', the conduct which most petitioners (over 67%) complain of in cases brought under this heading is exclusion from the management of the company. It also reported that nearly 70% of petitioners seek an order for the purchase of their shares.

Relief has been given where a member who held 60% of a company's shares voted to allot himself new shares to increase his holding to 96% and reduce the holding of a minority shareholder from 40 to 4%. In this case the majority shareholder was ordered to purchase the minority shareholder's 40% holding at a price to be fixed by independent valuation.

Cases have also been brought successfully where there has been a deliberate diversion of the company's business by those in control to another business owned by them.

It has been held that a director's remuneration of over £350,000 over a 14-month period was plainly in excess of anything he had earned and was, therefore, unfairly prejudicial to the petitioner's interests. Excessive remuneration is often linked to the non-payment of dividends. However, the non-payment of dividends could in itself be unfairly prejudicial even though it affects all shareholders equally.

The courts are reluctant to grant relief for mismanagement. However, relief has been given for specific acts of mismanagement which had been repeated over many years and which the respondent had failed to prevent or rectify. A failure to provide information about how the company is being run to a person who has a right to be consulted on major decisions could constitute unfairly prejudicial conduct.

The Secretary of State may also petition the court for an order if it appears to him that a company's affairs are being or have been conducted in a manner which is unfairly prejudicial to the interests of its members or some of its members (s. 995).

Just and equitable winding up

Shareholders may in certain circumstances petition the court under section 122(1)(g) of the Insolvency Act 1986 for an order that the company be wound up on just and equitable grounds. Indeed, this is often pleaded in the alternative to a petition under the unfair prejudice procedures.

A member may petition for a winding up on just and equitable grounds if he can show any circumstances affecting him in his relations with the company or with the other shareholders for which winding up is a just and equitable solution. For example, in the case of *Ebrahimi v Westbourne Galleries Ltd* [1973] AC 360, the plaintiff and a Mr Nazar formed a private company to carry on a business, which they had previously done as equal partners, and were appointed the company's first directors. Shortly afterwards, N's son also became a director; between them, N and his son controlled the majority of votes at general meetings. All the company's profits were distributed as directors' remuneration and no dividends were ever paid. At a general meeting eleven years after incorporation, Mr Ebrahimi was removed as a director by N and his son in accordance with the statutory procedures. Mr Ebrahimi petitioned the court to wind up the company on just and equitable grounds and this was allowed even though N and his son had acted in strict accordance with the Act and the company's articles. Lord Wiberforce explained the meaning of 'just and equitable' by saying:

> The words are a recognition of the fact that a limited company is more than a mere legal entity, with a personality in law of its own: that there is room in company law for recognition of the fact that behind it, or amongst it, there are individuals, with rights, expectations and obligations inter se which are not necessarily submerged in the company structure . . . The

just and equitable provision does not . . . entitle one party to disregard the obligations he assumes by entering a company, nor the court to dispense him from it. It does, as equity always does, enable the court to subject the exercise of legal rights to equitable considerations; considerations, that is, of a personal character arising between one individual and another, which may make it unjust, or inequitable, to insist on legal rights, or to exercise them in a particular way.

The courts have also wound up companies under this heading where:

- it was no longer possible to achieve the purpose for which the company was formed;
- the company was promoted fraudulently; and
- the company was formed for an illegal purpose.

Other remedies

The remedies outlined above tend to be used as a last resort. The Act provides various other means by which shareholders may be able to reconcile their problems including in relation to the meeting itself or specific resolutions presented at a meeting. For example:

- The secretary of state has wide powers to appoint inspectors to investigate matters, which may have been drawn to his attention by a member (ss 431 and 442 of the 1985 Act). He may, as a result of these investigations, apply for a winding-up order under the Insolvency Act 1986 or petition for an order under the unfair prejudice rules in Part 30 of the Companies Act 2006.
- Shareholders representing a certain percentage of the total voting rights may require the directors to convene a general meeting and, if the directors fail to do so, may convene it themselves (ss 303–305).
- If for any reason it is impracticable to call a meeting of a company, or to conduct the meeting in the manner prescribed by the articles or the Act, any member may apply to the court for an order calling a meeting (s. 306).
- Members of any company may require the directors to circulate a statement in connection with any business to be proposed at a general meeting (ss 314–317).
- Members of a public company may require the company to give notice of AGM resolutions they intend to propose (s. 338).
- Resolutions varying class rights may be challenged by members holding not less than 15% of that class who did not vote in favour of the change (ss 633 and 644).
- Members may by ordinary resolution remove a director before the expiry of his term of office (s. 168).
- Application may be made to the court for an order that the company's register of members be rectified (s. 125).

- Members have various rights of inspection of company registers and the right to copies of them on payment of a fee.
- A company must send members copies of its accounts which must be prepared in accordance with the requirements of Part 15 of the Act.
- A company's accounts must be audited unless it is exempt as a small company or as a dormant company. However, even where the company is exempt, members holding just 10% of the shares or voting rights may require an audit (s. 476).

Post-meeting practicalities

Filing resolutions

The Act requires copies of certain resolutions to be filed with the registrar of companies at Companies House within 15 days of being passed. The resolutions which must be filed include:

(a) any special resolution (s. 29(1)(a));

(b) any resolution or agreement agreed to by all the members that, if not so agreed, would not have been effective unless passed as a special resolution (s. 29(1)(b));

(c) any resolution or agreement agreed to by all the members of a class of shareholders that, if not so agreed to, would not have been effective unless passed by some particular majority or otherwise in some particular manner (s. 29(1)(c));

(d) any resolution or agreement that effectively binds all the members of a class of shareholders though not agreed to by all those members (s. 29(1)(d));

(e) any extraordinary resolution (s. 380(4)(b) of the 1985 Act), including any such resolution passed pursuant to a provision in a company's memorandum and articles of association or any contractual provision (see para. 23 of Sch. 3 to the Third Commencement Order (SI 2007/2194) as amended by para. 2 of Sch. 5 to the Fifth Commencement Order (SI 2007/3495));

(f) an ordinary resolution under section 551 giving the directors authority to allot shares (s. 551 – formerly s. 80 of the 1985 Act);

(g) an ordinary resolution under section 601 authorising the transfer to a public company of a non-cash asset in initial period (s. 602);

(h) an ordinary resolution under section 622 authorising the redenomination of a company's share capital (s. 622);

(i) a resolution conferring, varying, revoking or renewing authority under section 701 (market purchase of a company's own shares) (s. 701(8) – formerly s. 166 of the 1985 Act);

(j) a resolution of the members under paragraph 10 of Schedule 5 to the 2006 Act (company communication provisions: deemed agreement of members to use of website);

(k) any resolution for voluntary winding up passed under section 84(1) of the Insolvency Act 1986;

(l) an ordinary resolution amending or revoking the authorised share capital clause in the memorandum of an existing company that is deemed to form part of its articles under section 28 (para. 42 of Sch. 2 to the Eighth Commencement Order (SI 2008/2860)); and

(m) an ordinary resolution of an existing or transitional company that the directors should have the powers given by section 550 of the Companies Act 2006 (power of directors to allot shares etc.: private company with only one class of shares) (para. 43 of Sch. 2 to the Eighth Commencement Order (SI 2008/2860)).

The following directors' resolutions must also be filed at Companies House within 15 days of being passed:

(a) a resolution of the directors in compliance with a direction under section 64 (change of name on secretary of state's direction – formerly s. 31(2) of the 1985 Act).

(b) a resolution of the directors of a public company under section 664 to re-register as a private company to comply with section 662 (formerly s. 147(2) of the 1985 Act;

(c) a resolution passed by the directors of an old public company under section 2(1) of the Companies Consolidation (Consequential Provisions) Act 1985 that a company should be re-registered as a public company;

(d) a resolution of the directors passed by virtue of regulation 16(2) of the Uncertificated Securities Regulations 2001 allowing title to the company's shares to be evidenced and transferred through CREST;

(e) a resolution of the directors passed by virtue of regulation 16(6) of the Uncertificated Securities Regulations 2001 preventing or reversing a resolution of the directors allowing title to the company's shares to be evidenced and transferred through CREST.

Where no authority is shown in the above lists, the requirement to file the resolution with the registrar can be found in the original section or paragraph which imposes the requirement for the resolution.

Documents to be incorporated in or accompany copies of articles issued by company

Section 36 (1) provides that every copy of a company's articles issued by the company must be accompanied by:

(a) a copy of any resolution or agreement relating to the company to which Chapter 3 applies (resolutions and agreements affecting a company's constitution) (see above);

(b) where the company has been required to give notice to the registrar under section 34(2) (notice where company's constitution altered by enactment), a statement that the enactment in question alters the effect of the company's constitution;

(c) where the company's constitution is altered by a special enactment (see section 34(4)), a copy of the enactment; and

(d) a copy of any order required to be sent to the registrar under section 35(2)(a) (order of court or other authority altering company's constitution).

The articles do not need to be accompanied by a copy of a document or by a statement if:

(a) the effect of the resolution, agreement, enactment or order (as the case may be) on the company's constitution has been incorporated into the articles by amendment; or

(b) the resolution, agreement, enactment or order (as the case may be) is not for the time being in force (s. 36(2)).

If the company fails to comply with this section, an offence is committed by every officer of the company (including any liquidator) who is in default (s. 36(3) and (5)).

Resolutions and other constitutional documents to be provided to members

Section 32(1) provides that any member may request the company to send him the following documents:

(a) an up-to-date copy of the company's articles;

(b) a copy of any resolution or agreement relating to the company to which Chapter 3 of the Act applies (resolutions and agreements affecting a company's constitution) and that is for the time being in force;

(c) a copy of any document required to be sent to the registrar under—
  (i) section 34(2) (notice where company's constitution altered by enactment), or
  (ii) section 35(2)(a) (notice where order of court or other authority alters company's constitution);

(d) a copy of any court order under section 899 (order sanctioning compromise or arrangement) or section 900 (order facilitating reconstruction or amalgamation);

(e) a copy of any court order under section 996 (protection of members against unfair prejudice: powers of the court) that alters the company's constitution;

(f) a copy of the company's current certificate of incorporation, and of any past certificates of incorporation;

(g) in the case of a company with a share capital, a current statement of capital;

(h) in the case of a company limited by guarantee, a copy of the statement of guarantee.

If a company fails to comply with such a request, an offence is committed by every officer of the company who is in default for which a fine may be levied (s. 32(3) and (4)). No time limit is imposed for satisfying such a request

Listed company requirements on resolution

Listed companies must forward to the UKLA (via the National Storage Mechanism) a copy of any resolution passed by the company other than a resolution concerning the 'ordinary business' at an annual general meeting (AGM) as soon as possible after the relevant meeting (LR 9.6.2). Listed companies must also notify a regulatory information service (RIS) as soon as possible after a general meeting of all resolutions passed by the company other than resolutions concerning ordinary business passed at the AGM (LR 9.6.18). In practice listed companies tend to file a copy all resolutions and announce the results of all resolutions, including those that may only concern the 'ordinary business' because the Listing Rules do not define what is meant by the 'ordinary business'.

Listed Company Reporting

A company must forward to the Financial Conduct Authority (FCA), for publication through the document viewing facility, two copies of all resolutions passed by the company other than resolutions concerning ordinary business at an AGM, as soon as possible after the relevant general meeting (LR 14.3.6(2)).

Example: London Stock Exchange – simple AGM reporting example

1   **Result of AGM**
Released 16:53 23-Mar-2020

23 March 2020

Hydro Hotel, Eastbourne, Plc

("Hydro Hotel" or the "Company")

Result of Annual General Meeting

Hydro Hotel, Eastbourne, Plc is pleased to announce that all the resolutions were duly passed at the one hundred and twenty fifth Annual General Meeting of the Company held today.

The Directors of Hydro Hotel accept responsibility for the content of this announcement.

Enquiries:

Member dissent – The Public Register

The Public Register was the world's first register tracking shareholder dissent in listed companies. It details companies in the UK FTSE All Share index who have received significant opposition from shareholders to a resolution or any resolution withdrawn before a shareholder vote.

This helps to identify which companies are acknowledging shareholder dissent and how they are addressing their shareholders' concerns.

The Investment Association included the idea of setting up a Public Register of shareholder votes in their response to the UK Government's Green Paper on Corporate Governance reform in 2017. In August 2017, the government asked the Investment Association to develop and maintain the Register, which includes:

- key details about the resolution (title, meeting date etc.);
- results of the shareholder vote (percentage of votes cast for and against, number of votes withheld, and percentage of the issued share capital voted);
- a link to the AGM/GM results, including any statement made by the board in response to the significant vote against at the time of the meeting – as required under provision E.2.2. of the UK Corporate Governance Code; and
- a link to any further announcements by the company in response to the dissent, including shareholder views and what the company has done or plans to do.

The Public Register provides companies with the opportunity to highlight to investors and other stakeholders the steps they have taken to engage with shareholders and understand their views in relation to the high vote against, as set out by the 2018 UK Corporate Governance Code.

When 20% or more of votes have been cast against the board recommendation for a resolution, the company should:

(a) explain, when announcing voting results, what actions it intends to take to consult shareholders in order to understand the reasons behind the result;
(b) publish an update on the views received from shareholders and actions taken by the company should be published no later than six months after the vote (the Update Statement); and
(c) provide a final summary in the annual report, or in the explanatory notes to resolutions at the next meeting, on whether the board has taken any action or proposed new resolutions following the feedback received.

Guidance notes that investors would like to see the following features in Update Statements. Statements should:

1 Be published as standalone statement. The disclosure should not be adjunct to other regulatory news or announcements.
2 Describe the original resolution and the voting outcome.

3   Describe the engagement the company has undertaken since the vote to understand the views of their shareholders, and provide a summary of the views heard.

4   Describe any actions taken by the company as a result of views heard from their shareholders. Where the company has decided not to take any further action, they should outline why this is appropriate in the company's circumstances.

5   Describe any future actions the company intends to take, including further engagement with shareholders, and reference to the final update to be included in the annual report.

6   Where the company has appeared on the Public Register for the same resolution in consecutive years, the statement should acknowledge and set out actions to address this.

The Public Register can be found at: www.theia.org/public-register.

Minutes

Every company must keep minutes of all general meetings held (including AGMs) (s. 355(1)(b)).

In relation to resolutions passed, meetings held or decisions made on or after 1 October 2007, the above records must be kept for at least ten years from the date of the resolution, meeting or decision (as appropriate) (s. 355(2)).

Records of resolutions passed, meetings held and decisions made before that date must be kept in accordance with the requirements of section 382 of the Companies Act 1985 (see Sch. 3, para. 40 to the Companies Act 2006 (Commencement No. 3, Consequential Amendments, Transitional Provisions and Savings) Order 2007 (SI 2007/2194)). This means permanently as section 382 of the 1985 Act made no provision allowing disposal of the records or minutes.

The company secretary (if any) and the directors can be fined for any default regarding compliance with the requirements of section 355 of the 2006 Act and section 382 of the 1985 Act relating to the maintenance of minutes.

Evidential status of general meeting minutes

Section 356 confers special evidential status on minutes kept in accordance with section 355. The minutes of proceedings of a general meeting, if purporting to be signed by the chair of that meeting or by the chair of the next general meeting, are evidence (in Scotland, sufficient evidence) of the proceedings at the meeting (s. 356(4)). Where there is a record of proceedings of a general meeting of a company, then, until the contrary is proved:

(a) the meeting is deemed duly held and convened;

(b) all proceedings at the meeting are deemed to have duly taken place; and

(c) all appointments at the meeting are deemed valid (s. 356(5)).

Section 382(4) of the 1985 Act makes similar provision regarding minutes of meetings kept in accordance with the requirements of that Act.

Approval and signature of minutes of general meetings

It is standard practice for the minutes of general meetings to be signed shortly after the meeting by the person who acted as the chair of the meeting. This is often done at the first available board meeting so as to allow the other directors to make any comments but also so that an entry may be made in the board minutes to the effect that they were duly signed. If this procedure is followed, it is not necessary to seek the approval of the members at the next general meeting nor, indeed, to refer to the minutes of the previous meeting at all.

If the person who acted as the chair of the meeting is unable or unwilling to sign the minutes, they should be signed by the chair of the next general meeting.

If it is not possible to adopt this procedure, then the minutes may need to be read at the next general meeting (they cannot be taken as read unless all the members have received a copy) and a resolution put to the meeting that they be approved.

The role of the company secretary after the meeting

The minutes of the meeting should be prepared. It is not always necessary for these to be sent out in draft to the directors for comments, since the minutes will usually cover only routine business or such other business as may have been specified in the notice convening the meeting.

If payment of a final dividend is approved at the meeting, the necessary arrangements must be put in hand for its payment. Depending on the payment date, this may simply be to release electronic transfers and mailing of cheques already prepared, or to take a cut of the register of members at the record date and calculate the amounts due to individual members.

Traded companies must make a market announcement via a RIS of all resolutions, other than ordinary resolutions at an AGM, approved by the shareholders at a general meeting (LR 9.6.18).

Registration of resolutions

As a final reminder, the resolutions that must be filed with the Registrar of Companies are specified in section 29, namely:

(a) any special resolution;
(b) any resolution or agreement agreed to by all the members of a company that, if not so agreed to, would not have been effective for its purpose unless passed as a special resolution;

(c) any resolution or agreement agreed to by all the members of a class of shareholders that, if not so agreed to, would not have been effective for its purpose unless passed by some particular majority or otherwise in some particular manner;

(d) any resolution or agreement that effectively binds all members of a class of shareholders though not agreed to by all those members; and

(e) any other resolution or agreement to which Chapter 3 of the Act applies by virtue of any enactment.

As can be seen, these include all special resolutions, as well as the ordinary resolutions to authorise the allotment of securities (s. 551(9)) and to authorise a market purchase of the company's own shares (s. 701(8)).

Copies of resolutions must be filed with the Registrar of Companies within 15 days of approval.

Failure to comply with these requirements is an offence committed by the company and every officer and, if found guilty, may result in a fine, with a potential default fine for continued contravention.

Conclusion

Actions after the meeting often become critical at a much later stage when an audit trail of resolutions is required or a healthcheck of statutory records is made. Ensuring that focus is given to the resulting actions ensures that the meeting is fully finalised, which is only really the case after all filings have been made, subsequent actions have been taken and the secretariat of a company moves back into their daily routine.

Rarely are the post-meeting shareholder remedies resorted to but, when they are, the fall out from the meeting needs to follow the requirements of legislation to enable as rapid a resolution as possible.

The vast majority of general meetings are completed in line with expectations, particularly in terms of actions at the meeting and following the agenda, albeit that adjournments are frequently accommodated for a number of diverse reasons. Rarely are actions taken after the meeting to make it null and void, although knowledge of the possibility, as explained herein, is beneficial.

Best practice following a formal meeting is to finalise any submissions and registrations, draft and circulate minutes for approval and ensure any other actions coming out of the meeting are progressed to completion. By undertaking this in a timely manner, future reviews, audits or data requests are easily accommodated.

17 – Section 3 conclusion

As can be seen from this section, the proceedings before, during and after a general meeting of a company can be extensive and, in certain respects, complex. The meeting itself can also be unpredictable despite what may have been considerable planning for every eventuality.

By having a clear framework and structure in place, the meeting should run smoothly, and any unexpected occurrences should be able to be accommodated. Although having noted this, it is clear from the content of this section, that there are many elements to a general meeting that must be identified and delivered. It is not surprising that the use of experts, such as registrars, to organise and host meetings has increased. This is particularly useful where this expert fulfils additional roles, such as maintaining the register of shareholders. As experts, they have an expertise in hosting meetings from across sectors and companies, both small and large and can ensure that the meeting runs as efficiently and effectively as possible. The content of this book can also be used as a useful guide to monitoring and having oversight of the activity of third-party meeting organisers.

However, as was noted in the section on meetings of directors, general meetings of a company are more than just the formal framework in which they sit and which has been documented here. The culture of the company, the actions of the board, the connectivity with the shareholders, all create the sense of both the company and the meeting. By having a clear and robust process for holding general meetings, the ethos of the business and the benefits of general meetings can be allowed to be visible. At its heart, a general meeting should be the meeting of a board and its shareholders who all have an ambition for the same thing: the success of the company.

Section 4
Other company meetings

18 – Section 4 Introduction

In addition to members, directors and committee meetings, there are many other formal and informal meetings that take place throughout a company. Some of these are aligned to the formal running of a company, although they are not documented in the Act or the articles of a company.

This section, will reflect on some of these meetings as well as those that are specific to certain types of companies.

In some larger companies, there are multiple classes of shares with broad numbers of members with different rights under the articles. Here, class meetings may be meetings of a specific class of members or the holders of a specific class of shares. A class meeting will typically be required where a company has more than one class of shares and proposes to vary the rights attached to a particular class, or where the articles provide that a transaction requires the separate consent of a meeting of the holders of a certain class of shares. Special procedures must be followed to vary the rights attached to different classes of shares. Additionally, the voting rights of classes of shares may differ according to the manner in which those rights are conferred and whether the articles make specific provision for variation of those rights.

Conversely, sole member and/or sole director companies have specific requirements under the Act and their articles. This chapter will clarify and confirm relevant requirements for both sole member and sole director companies, noting that a company with a sole member may also only have one director who is the member themselves. In this scenario, where their decision-making processes are personal and singular, it is even more important to understand and differentiate the different roles and their responsibilities in terms of decision making and the formal records required related to such decisions. This chapter will provide clarity on the quorum in these scenarios and record keeping, noting that the requirements for a sole member are greater than that for a sole director.

Dormant companies

Dormant companies (i.e. those that are no longer trading but, for a variety of reasons have not been liquidated) will continue to have reporting requirements to Companies House although it is unlikely that they will have many meetings, whether formal or not. In fact, the only formal meetings to be held may be to document the limited submissions required to Companies House or to start the winding-up process.

Where they are held, the same requirements for keeping minutes would apply to ensure there is an audit trail of director decisions. The formal liquidation process is defined by law and is not covered in this book while there is not a dedicated chapter for dormant companies given the limited meetings held. Where required, the contents of Chapter 20 on sole director and sole members is a beneficial reference point.

It should be noted that dormant companies that are subsidiaries may be exempt or excluded from the requirement to produce accounts (s. 394) or, where they are required to produce accounts, may be excluded or exempted from filing accounts (s. 448) and/or having their accounts audited (ss 480 and 481). These exemptions and exclusions are applicable in respect of a financial year if:

(a) the company is a subsidiary undertaking;
(b) it has been dormant throughout the whole of that year; and
(c) its parent undertaking is established under the law of a European Economic Area (EEA) State.

It should be noted that there are conditions attached to each that also need to be adhered to.

There are occasions, such as for the appointment of a new director, where even a dormant company may require a meeting to be held, given they are incorporated in the same way as any other company. In such cases, the Act, the articles of the company and the guidance in this book are applicable.

Special Purpose Vehicles

Special Purpose Vehicles (SPVs) are companies that are set up for a specific purpose, often holding assets ring-fenced away from the general trading and assets of a company or individual. Such companies are registered with Companies House and incorporated with model articles. Despite their limited purpose, they must operate in the same way as all other companies with model articles and have directors and members, albeit that the shares would not be traded.

One main difference of SPVs is that they are limited liability companies with the assets of the companies being the only security for recourse. In some scenarios, SPVs are used as the issuing vehicles for traded debt instruments, to enable the underlying assets backing the debt issuance to be ring-fenced and segregated from the asset originator. In these cases, while most focus is on the debt issuance itself, the legal entity that issues the debt must continue to maintain its legal standing through robust corporate record keeping and director approvals.

Directors of these types of companies are often as knowledgeable of the underlying debt issuance process as of company law and must maintain a segregation in their actions between debt related and those related to governance and the maintenance of the SPV itself. This can be even more blurred where the debt issuance requires a bondholder meeting (see below). In practice, maintenance of the SPV follows those requirements of a sole member company (see Chapter 20).

Meetings of bondholders

Companies that borrow via the debt capital markets through the issuance of debt will, as a result, also have bondholders with a vested interest in the company. Where a company borrows through issuance of a bond, this may be done directly in the name of the company or, as noted above, via an SPV. In both cases, there will be occasions where a formal meeting of the bondholders will be necessary to solicit bondholder consent for amendments.

These meetings are invariably called by the trustee of the bond issuance, with the knowledge and input, where required, of the company. In these cases, the bondholders can be considered as the equivalent of a member in terms of meeting procedures, with the process for convening meetings continuing to mirror that of general meetings, despite several attempts by the market to change it.

The first formal step of convening a bondholder meeting is for a notice to be published and communicated to all bondholders, giving not less than 21 clear days' notice of the date, time and place of the meeting and setting out the resolution(s) to be considered. So far, all in line with company requirements.

One area of difference is in respect of bondholder identification and bondholders. With only a few bearer bonds still in circulation, the vast majority are now held by custodians in clearing systems, primarily in Euroclear or Clearstream. These clearing systems have introduced unique identifiers for bondholders so that holders can be verified for bondholder meetings and voting therein. Sophisticated systems and technology have been implemented by specialist services providers acting as tabulation agents, often also providing bondholder identification and proxy services.

Despite the increased use of technology, physical meetings are invariably the norm for bondholder meetings. However, the advent of Covid-19 has re-ignited the need and acceptance for virtual meetings, thus potentially creating a framework for virtual front-end meetings that align to the technical advances supporting voting and identification. Initial steps include the encouragement of proxy voting in the notice of a bondholder meeting. Alongside this is a recognition that, while standard bond documentation does not expressly envisage virtual bondholder meetings, it does imply that a 'meeting' could include a meeting electronically as well as being in the same physical location.

One of the first virtual bondholder meetings held as a result of Covid-19 was in Singapore, and the resultant note, provided by Allen & Overy, gives a useful introduction to the practical implementation of virtual bondholder meetings, 'Bondholder meetings in the time of Covid-19: virtually ok?' (April 2020).

As can be seen, the mechanics of virtual meetings may not be expressly included in the bond documentation but, equally, they are not excluded. Typical documentation provides that the trustee may prescribe such further or other regulations concerning attendance and voting at meetings as it may see fit. Intended to capture changes in market practice, the impact of restrictions to meeting in person required due to Covid-19 provides a clear reason for implementing such changes. This usually does not require the consent of the issuing company; however, as a minimum, they should be consulted and notified.

Covid-19-related use of virtual bondholder meetings ensures that bondholders can continue to exercise their rights in the manner provided for in the documentation and, given the time sensitivities that some decisions may have, the flexibility of use is invaluable. The expectation, or at least hope, is that a pragmatic application of meeting requirements and use of existing technology will become the blueprint for future bondholder meetings.

Other meetings

Finally, there are other meetings held that sit alongside those of the company itself. These include the bondholder meetings noted above and other meetings including, but not limited to, those of:

- *The board of the company pension scheme, which administratively follows those of a meeting of directors with members being trustees of the pension scheme*: Attendance at meetings by expert legal, financial and investment advisors is standard. The law on pensions rapidly changes with this being a specialist area of knowledge. The pension scheme board are separate to the board of the company, albeit that they are funded by the company and the members of the pension scheme are past and present employees of the company.
- *A board of trustees representing employee owners*: The prevalence of employee-owned businesses across sectors and sizes of companies has increased since new legislation implemented in 2014, including notable names such as Richer Sounds and Aardman Animations which have transitioned to employee ownership in the recent past. In these scenarios, a majority of the shares of a company are owned by the employees, most frequently under a company trust structure. The legal entity owning the shares on behalf of the employees has a board of directors/trustees with the company constituted under model articles for a private company limited by shares. As such, requirements for director and general meetings are as defined in the relevant articles, which are often tailored to reflect the ownership of shares by the employees. Practicalities of meetings reflect the requirements of the act as, as such, the relevant chapters in this book are appropriate to refer to. It should be noted that these companies are, in turn, the shareholders of the company and, as such, have the same rights as members in the trading company.

Conclusion

This section of the book includes specific chapters on:

- class meetings;
- sole director/sole member companies; and
- committee meetings.

The final chapter in this section on committee meetings reflects the requirements of these types of meetings where the committee is constituted by the board under the articles of the company. Meetings of committees largely follow the same format as meeting of directors, with a few variances around their authority, agenda and meeting schedule. This chapter provides an insight into the membership and meetings of committees in general, with specific reference to the committees recommended for listed companies under the Financial Reporting Council (FRC) guidance, namely the audit, remuneration and nomination committees.

19 – Class meetings

Not all members of a company will necessarily have the same rights. Where this is the case, the company has different classes of members. The rights of each class of members will be specified in the articles. This may occur both in a company with a share capital and in a company limited by guarantee.

Class meetings are meetings of a specific class of members or the holders of a specific class of shares. Practically, the model articles (plc 42) clarify that, in relation to class meetings: 'the provisions of the articles relating to general meetings apply, with any necessary modifications, to meetings of the holders of any class of shares.'

A class meeting will typically be required where a company has more than one class of shares and proposes to vary the rights attached to a particular class or where the articles provide that a transaction requires the separate consent of a meeting of the holders of a certain class of shares.

Special procedures must be followed to vary the rights attached to different classes of shares. These differ according to the manner in which those rights are conferred and whether the memorandum or articles make specific provision for variation of those rights.

Classes of shares

The articles of a company with a share capital will normally provide that it may divide its share capital into shares of more than one class. This means that the company can issue different types of shares which each give their holders different rights. Shares which give their holders the same rights are deemed to be shares of the same class. Holders of a different class of shares will usually have different rights regarding dividends, voting at general meetings, participation in capital and surplus assets on winding up, or some other matter.

For the purposes of the Companies Acts shares are of one class if the rights attached to them are, in all respects, consistent. For this purpose, the rights attached to shares are not regarded as different from those attached to other shares if the only difference is that they do not carry the same rights to dividends in the 12 months immediately following their allotment. Hence, a new share issuance would be considered the same as the existing share class if the only difference is that dividend payments are not made in the first year of issuance.

Different classes of shares are usually given different designations (e.g. 'A' shares, 'B' shares, preference shares, etc.) in order to distinguish them from other shares with different rights. However, this will not always be the case and shareholders holding shares of the same name may have different rights and constitute a separate class. This may arise as a result of a separate shareholders agreement under which the shareholders agree to modify the rights of the respective shareholders.

The rights attached to shares are usually specified in the articles. The rights attached to shares can also be governed to a certain extent by the terms of issue.

The holders of all classes of shares are members of the company. They are, therefore, entitled to receive notice of general meetings of the company on an equal basis and may attend and vote at such meetings, unless their rights in this respect within the specific class of shares are withdrawn or restricted.

The most common classes of shares are:

- *Ordinary shares*: These are the shares which usually carry the right to vote at general meetings, to receive dividends, and to participate in any surplus when the company is wound up. Where a company has only one class of shares, these will normally be called the ordinary shares, if they are called anything at all.

- *Preference shares*: These shares usually carry preferential dividend rights, usually a fixed percentage of their nominal value, which must be paid out of profits available for distribution before dividends are paid to the ordinary shareholders. These rights are often cumulative, which means that any dividends payable to the preference shareholders which are in arrears must be paid before the ordinary shareholders are paid a dividend. The articles usually give preference shareholders the right to vote at general meetings if their dividends are more than six months in arrears, but not otherwise. If the company is wound up, preference shareholders will usually have the right to have their capital returned before the ordinary shareholders but are not usually entitled to share in any surplus.

- *'A' and 'B' shares*: Companies tend to use the designations 'A' and 'B' shares where the rights of the holders are almost identical except for one thing. In some cases, the rights of the 'A' and 'B' shareholders may appear to be identical in every respect. This can happen where they have been established as a different class purely to enable a different dividend to be declared on each class. 'A' and 'B' shares are commonly found in joint venture companies where each partner will hold a separate class of shares which gives them the right to appoint one or more directors but which otherwise have the same rights. Having two categories of ordinary shares may also be used to give a minority shareholder certain entrenched rights. For example, this may be applied when a founder has subsequently sold a majority holding in the company but has agreed as part of the sale to have certain retained rights, such as a potentially having enhanced voting rights on any resolution to remove them as a director.

■ *Non-voting shares*: These usually have the same rights as the ordinary shareholders to receive dividends, etc. However, they do not have the right to vote at general meetings and are primarily issued to enable holders to benefit from distributions but without the ability to control the business itself. These types of shares are becoming less prevalent as their value and inability to influence the company make them less valuable.

Variation of class rights

Given their importance and the interaction between classes, the rights attached to different classes of shares may only be varied in accordance with section 630 of the Act which provides safeguards to ensure that the interests of one class of shareholders are not prejudiced by another.

The section applies to any variation of the rights attached to any class of shares in a company having a share capital. It does not apply to the variation of the rights of different classes of members of a company limited by guarantee.

The rights attached to a class of a company's shares may only be varied:

(a) in accordance with any provision in the company's articles for the variation of those rights; or

(b) where the company's articles contain no such provision, if the holders of shares of that class consent to the variation in accordance with the requirements of that section.

The consent required for these purposes on the part of the holders of a class of a company's shares is:

(a) consent in writing from the holders of at least three-quarters in nominal value of the issued shares of that class (excluding any shares held as treasury shares), or

(b) a special resolution passed at a separate general meeting of the holders of that class sanctioning the variation (s. 630(4)).

It should be noted that the option to obtain consent in writing applies to both public and private companies and is not subject to the rules on written resolutions. A private company could, of course, also pass any special resolution as a written resolution.

Any amendment of a provision contained in a company's articles for the variation of the rights attached to a class of shares, or the insertion of any such provision into the articles, is itself to be treated as a variation of those rights (s. 630(5)). For the purposes of section 630 and (except where the context otherwise requires) any provision in a company's articles for the variation of the rights attached to a class of shares, references to the variation of those rights include references to their abrogation (s. 630(6)).

Special procedures

Subject to certain exceptions, section 334 applies the provisions of Part 13, Chapter 3 (resolutions at meetings) with necessary modifications to any meeting of the holders of a class of shares. One of the exceptions provided for in section 334(3) is that the provisions of section 318 (quorum) and section 321 (right to demand a poll) do not apply in relation to a class meeting held in connection with the variation of rights attached to a class of shares (but do apply in relation to a class meeting called for any other purpose).

Instead section 334 provides that at a class meeting of a company with a share capital held to approve a variation of class rights:

- the quorum for a meeting other than an adjourned meeting, is two persons present holding at least one-third in nominal value of the issued shares of the class in question (excluding any shares of that class held as treasury shares) (s. 334(4)(a));
- the quorum for an adjourned meeting is one person present holding shares of the class in question (s. 334(4)(b));
- for the purposes of the above quorum requirements, where a person is present by proxy or proxies, he is treated as holding only the shares in respect of which those proxies are authorised to exercise voting rights (s. 334(5)); and
- any holder of shares of the class in question present may demand a poll (s. 334(6)).

For the purposes of s section 334, any amendment of a provision contained in a company's articles for the variation of the rights attached to a class of shares, or the insertion of any such provision into the articles, is itself to be treated as a variation of those rights, and references to the variation of rights attached to a class of shares include references to their abrogation (s. 334(7)).

The provisions of section 334 with regard to the quorum can give rise to problems where the articles contain some other provision (e.g. where the articles provide for a quorum of ten at class meetings but make no provision as to the percentage of nominal value those members must hold). Read in isolation, the requirements of section 334 on the quorum at a variation of class rights meeting appear very stark. Unlike section 318 (quorum at general meetings), they are not expressed as being subject to the articles or as a minimum standard. This would seem to indicate that section 334 takes precedence over anything in the articles where a variation of rights is concerned. However, some modern articles of listed companies provide that the quorum for a variation of rights shall be one or more persons, instead of two, representing at least one third by nominal value. No doubt, such a provision was included in an attempt to reflect the fact that all the shares of a particular class may be held by a single person. It is slightly strange that the Act does not directly cater for this itself, although it does provide that the quorum at any adjourned meeting shall be one.

A single person may constitute a meeting where that person holds all the issued shares of a particular class.

A provision in a company's articles which purports to set a quorum of one at any variation of class rights meeting regardless of whether all the shares of a particular class are held by one person may fall foul of section 334 if the shares are held more widely. The only thing that might save such a provision is if it can be viewed as forming part of the provisions in the articles for the variation of class rights under section 630(2). Section 630(2) provides that rights attached to a class of shares may only be varied in accordance with the provisions in a company's articles for the variation of those rights or, where no such provision is made, if the holders consent to the variation in accordance with section 630. If a company's articles set out a full alternative procedure for the variation of class rights, they may override section 334, even though that procedure may involve the holding of a class meeting. If this is intended to be the case, it is by no means clear because section 334 is not expressed as being subject to section 630.

Proceedings at class meetings

Subject to certain exceptions, the provisions on meetings in Part 13, Chapter 3 (ss 301–335) apply with necessary modifications in relation to class meetings by virtue of section 334 (for a company with a share capital) and section 335 (for a company without a share capital).

However, the additional requirements relating to traded companies in sections 311(3), 311A, 319A, 327(A1), 330(A1) and 333A are disapplied in relation to class meetings of a company with a share capital by section 334(2).

Section 334(2A) clarifies that the notice requirements in section 307(1)–(6) apply in relation to a meeting of holders of a class of shares in a traded company rather than section 307A which deals with the notice requirements for general meetings of traded companies.

The following provisions are disapplied by section 334(2) (companies with a share capital) and section 335(2) (companies without a share capital) in relation to any class meeting:

- sections 303 to 305 (members' power to require directors to call general meetings); and
- section 306 (power of the court to order meetings).

In addition, sections 334(3) and 335(3) both disapply the following provisions but only in relation to a class meeting held in connection with a variation of rights (i.e. not in relation to a class meeting called for any other purpose):

Table showing the provisions of Part 13, Chapter 3 that apply to class meetings by virtue of ss 334 and 335

Section	Description	Companies with a share capital (s. 334)		Companies without a share capital (s. 335)	
		Variation of class rights meeting	Any other class meeting	Variation of class rights meeting	Any other class meeting
301	Resolutions at general meetings	Yes	Yes	Yes	Yes
302	Directors' power to call general meetings	Yes	Yes	Yes	Yes
303–305	Members' power to require directors to call general meetings	No (see s. 334(2))	No (see s. 334(2))	No (see s. 335(2))	No (see s. 335(2))
306	Power of court to order meeting	No (see s. 334(2))	No (see s. 334(2))	No (see s. 335(2))	No (see s. 335(2))
307	Notice required of general meetings	Yes	Yes	Yes	Yes
307A	Notice required of general meeting: certain meetings of traded companies	No (see s. 334(2A))	No (see s. 334(2A))	No (see note 1)	No (see note 1)
308	Manner in which notice to be given	Yes	Yes	Yes	Yes
309	Publication of notice of meeting on website	Yes	Yes	Yes	Yes
310	Persons entitled to receive notice	Yes	Yes	Yes	Yes
311	Contents of notice	Yes	Yes	Yes	Yes
311A	Traded companies: publication of information in advance of general meeting	No (see s. 334(2)(c))	No (see s. 334(2)(c))	No (see note 1)	No (see note 1)
312	Resolution requiring special notice	Yes	Yes	Yes	Yes
313	Accidental failure to give notice of resolution or meeting	Yes (except s. 311(3))	Yes (except s. 311(3))	Yes	Yes
314–317	Members' power to require circulation of statements	Yes	Yes	Yes	Yes
318	Quorum at meetings	No (see s. 334(3)–(5))	Yes	No (see s. 335(3) and (4))	Yes
319	Chair of meeting	Yes	Yes	Yes	Yes

319A	Traded companies: questions at meetings	No (see s. 334(2)(c))	No (see s. 334(2)(c))	No (see note 1)	No (see note 1)
320	Declaration by chair on a show of hands	Yes	Yes	Yes	Yes
321	Right to demand a poll	No (see s. 334(3) and (6))	Yes	No (see s. 335(3) and (5))	Yes
322	Voting on a poll	Yes	Yes	Yes	Yes
322A	Voting on a poll: votes cast in advance	Yes	Yes	Yes	Yes
323	Representation of corporations at meetings	Yes	Yes	Yes	Yes
324	Rights to appoint proxies	Yes	Yes	Yes	Yes
324A	Obligation of proxy to vote in accordance with instructions	Yes	Yes	Yes	Yes
325	Notice of meeting to contain statement of rights	Yes	Yes	Yes	Yes
326	Company sponsored invitations	Yes	Yes	Yes	Yes
327	Notice required of appointment of proxy	Yes (except s. 327(A1))	Yes (except s. 327(A1))	Yes	Yes
328	Chairing meetings	Yes	Yes	Yes	Yes
329	Right of proxy to demand a poll	Yes	Yes	Yes	Yes
330	Notice required of termination of proxy's authority	Yes (except s. 330(A1))	Yes (except s. 330(A1))	Yes	Yes
331	Saving for more extensive rights conferred by articles	Yes	Yes	Yes	Yes
332	Resolution passed at an adjourned meeting	Yes	Yes	Yes	Yes
333	Sending documents relating to meetings etc in electronic form	Yes	Yes	Yes	Yes
333A	Traded company: duty to provide electronic address for receipt of proxies etc	No (see s. 334(2)(c))	No (see s. 334(2)(c))	No (see note 1)	No (see note 1)

Note 1: None of the provisions relating to traded companies can apply to a company without a share capital as a traded company must, by definition, have voting shares which are traded on a regulated market.

- section 318 (quorum); and
- section 321 (right to demand a poll).

In both cases, for meetings held to consider a variation of class rights, sections 334 and 335 substitute a modified quorum requirement and a different rule on the right to demand a poll. These modified requirements do not apply in the case of a class meeting not called for the purpose of a variation of class rights but may still apply in the case of a resolution proposed at such a meeting even though that particular resolution does not relate to a variation of rights. Sections 630 to 640 (variation of class rights) will obviously not apply to any resolution that does not concern a variation of class rights. Although it is rare for such resolutions to be proposed or for class meetings to be held where a variation of rights is not on the agenda, it is not impossible.

Many of the provisions of Part 13, Chapter 3 that are deemed to apply to class meetings (whether in relation to a variation of rights or otherwise) state that they are capable of modification by a company's articles. If a company establishes more than one class of share or more than one class of member and wishes the provisions regarding general meetings in its articles to apply to any class meetings that may be required, it ought perhaps to clarify in its articles that the relevant provisions apply (with suitable modification where necessary). It is likely that this will be the case anyway. However, it is best not to leave such matters to chance.

It may not be possible to override the specific rules on polls and the quorum that apply in relation to a class meeting held to consider a variation of rights by sections 334 and 335.

Notice

Section 307 (which is applied by section 334 in relation to all class meetings) requires a company to give at least 14 days' notice of any class meeting to the holders of that class of shares. However, shorter notice may be given with the consent of members in accordance with section 307(4)–(6).

Precedent: Notice of class meeting

XYZ Limited

Notice is hereby given that a separate meeting of the holders of the six per cent £1 preference shares in the capital of the company will be held on [date] at [place] at [time] to propose the following resolution as an special resolution:

THAT this separate class meeting of the holders of the six per cent £1 preference shares in the capital of the company hereby sanctions [resolution being sanctioned] and hereby sanctions any variation, modification or abrogation of the rights and privileges attached or belonging to the six per cent £1 preference shares effected thereby or necessary to give effect thereto.

By order of the Board

[Signature]

Secretary

[registered office address]

[date]

Notes

1. Holders of 6% preference shares entitled to attend and vote at the meeting are entitled to appoint one or more proxies to attend and vote on their behalf. A proxy need not also be a member or a holder of 6% preference shares. Holders of 6% preference shares may appoint more than one proxy in relation to the meeting provided that each proxy is appointed to exercise the rights to a different 6% preference share or shares held by the member.
2. To be effective the form of proxy must be completed in accordance with the instructions and received by the company no later than 48 hours before the time for which the meeting is convened.

The notice must be given in either hard copy or electronic form or by means of a website (s. 308). If it is published on a website, the company must also comply with section 309.

Applying section 310 with suitable modification, unless the articles make some other provision, notice of a class meeting must be served on every director and every holder of shares of that class and any person entitled to a share of that class in consequence of the death or bankruptcy of the holder if the company has been notified of that entitlement. Most articles do make other provision regarding the service of notices and will often restrict the right to receive notice (e.g. to the first-named joint holder only).

The notice must state the date, time and place of the meeting (s. 311(1)) and, subject to anything to the contrary in the articles, the general nature of the business to be transacted. In practice, if a special resolution is to be proposed, the notice must also comply with the requirements of section 283(6) regarding the inclusion of the text of the resolution and specifying that it is to be proposed as a special resolution.

Accidental failure to give notice to one or more persons of a class meeting or a resolution to be proposed at such a meeting will not automatically invalidate the proceedings or the resolution (s. 313).

Where a company has given an electronic address in any notice calling a class meeting or any instrument of proxy or instrument of proxy in relation to that meeting, it is deemed to have agreed that any document or information relating to that meeting or proxies in relation to that meeting may be sent by electronic means to the address (subject to any conditions or limitations specified in the notice) (s. 333).

Right to call a class meeting

The holders of a class of shares have no statutory right to demand a class meeting (see s. 334(2)). However, there is no reason why a company's articles should not give them such a right.

Members' statements

The rules in sections 314 to 317 allowing members to require the company to circulate a statement in connection with a proposed resolution or other business to be considered at the meeting will also apply to class meetings with suitable modification.

Appointment of chair

Subject to the articles, any member or proxy elected by the members present at a class meeting may chair the meeting (ss 319 and 328). In practice, most articles provide that the chair of the board of directors or a director nominated by the board shall act as the chair of any meeting, and the class members will normally only be able to elect the chair in default of these provisions.

Quorum

Section 318 applies to any class meeting that is not held for the purpose of considering a variation of class rights. If variation of class rights is to be considered at a class meeting, the quorum requirements will be as stated in section 334(4) for companies with a share capital or section 335(4) for companies without a share capital.

Where a class meeting is held for some other purpose, the rule in section 318(1) will apply (with suitable modification) irrespective of anything contained in a company's articles. This rule provides that in the case of a private company limited by shares or by guarantee and only having one member, one qualifying person present at the meeting is a member. Whether this rule is capable of suitable modification for the purposes of class meetings is open to question.

The rule in section 318(2), which provides for a quorum of two in any other case, is expressed as being subject to the provisions of a company's articles.

Resolutions

Section 281 provides that a resolution of a class of members of a private company must be passed either as a written resolution in accordance with Chapter 2 of Part 13 or at a meeting of the members (to which the provisions of Ch. 3 of Pt 13 apply). A resolution of a class of members of a public company must be passed at a meeting of the members (to which the provisions of Chapter 3 and, where relevant, Ch. 4 of Pt 13 apply).

Where a provision of the Companies Acts requires a resolution of a class of members and does not specify what kind of resolution is required, an ordinary resolution will suffice unless the company's articles require a higher majority (or unanimity) (s. 281(3)).

An ordinary resolution of a class of members is one that is passed in accordance with section 282. A special resolution of a class of members is one that is passed in accordance with section 283.

Written resolutions

A resolution of a class of members in a private company can be passed by written resolution or at a general meeting (s. 281(1)). A written resolution of a private company has effect as if passed (as the case may be) by the company in general meeting or by a meeting of a class of members of the company (s. 288(5)).

Precedent: Written resolution of a class of members

...............................LIMITED

[Address]

Circulation Date: [Date].

We, the undersigned, being members of the Company eligible to vote on the proposals at the time and date of circulation, hereby pass the following resolution(s) as a written resolution in accordance with Chapter 2 of Part 13 of the Companies Act 2006:

As a Special Resolution

THAT ... ...

(Signatures)   (Date of signature)

Notes
1. Members may signify their agreement to the resolution by returning a hard copy of the resolution signed by them (or on their behalf) to the company at the address shown above. Agreement may also be signified by email as follows: ...

2. The proposed resolution(s) will lapse if not passed within the period of [28 days] beginning with the circulation date shown above.

(Note: The date of the resolution is the date when it was signed by the last member required to sign to pass the resolution by the requisite majority. Special care will need to be taken if the same written resolution is used to propose both a special resolution and an ordinary resolution. In those circumstances, it may be preferable to make the resolutions the subject of separate written resolutions.)

The provisions of Part 13, Chapter 2 (written resolutions) will apply to any such written resolution.

Voting

Subject to a company's articles, section 284(1) provides that on a vote on a written resolution:

- in the case of a company having a share capital, every member has one vote in respect of each share or each £10 of stock held by them; and
- in any other case, each member has one vote.

Subject to a company's articles, section 284(2) provides that on a vote on a show of hands at a meeting:

- every member present in person has one vote; and
- every proxy present who has been duly appointed by a member entitled to vote on the resolution has one vote.

Subject to a company's articles, section 284(3) provides that on a vote on a poll taken at a meeting:

- in the case of a company having a share capital, every member has one vote in respect of each share or each £10 of stock held by them; and
- in any other case, each member has one vote.

The other provisions of the Act on voting in sections 284 to 287 also apply to class meetings. These will apply to written resolutions of a class of members of a private company and class meetings, subject to any provisions in the articles. For example, articles usually contain provisions restricting the right to vote in certain circumstances.

If variation of class rights is to be considered at a class meeting, the rules regarding the right to demand a poll will be as stated in section 334(6) for companies with a share capital or section 335(5) for companies without a share capital. For any other class meeting, section 321 will apply and any provision of a company's articles will be void in so far as they do not comply with the minimum standards set out in that section.

Proxies and corporate representatives

Applying sections 334 and 335, class members have a right to appoint a proxy under section 324. The notice of any class meeting must contain a statement as to their rights to appoint a proxy (s. 325). If the company issues at its own expense invitations to members to appoint as a proxy a specified person or persons, the invitation must be issued to all the members of the class (s. 336). Any provision of a company's articles relating to the appointment of proxies will be void in so far as it would require any appointment or document to be received by the company or another person before the times set out in section 327. The provisions of section 330 on termination of a proxy's authority also apply.

A proxy may demand, or join in a demand, for a poll at a class meeting (s. 329). Nothing in sections 324 to 330 (proxies) prevents a company's articles from conferring more extensive rights on members or proxies (s. 331).

A corporation may authorise one or more persons to act as its representative at a class meeting (s. 323).

Attendance

In *Carruth v Imperial Chemical Industries Ltd* [1937] AC 707, the directors convened an extraordinary general meeting of the company and two class meetings to approve a reduction of capital. The meetings were held on the same day and at the same venue. As one meeting finished, the next was started; each meeting was attended by the holders of the other classes of shares. The resolution passed at one class meeting was challenged by a member of that class on the basis that people who were not members of that class were present at the meeting. The resolution was held to be valid and Lord Russell said:

> There are many matters relating to the conduct of a meeting which lie entirely in the hands of those persons who are present and constitute the meeting. Thus it rests with the meeting to decide whether notices, resolutions, minutes, accounts, and such like shall be read to the meeting or be taken as read; whether representatives of the Press, or any other persons not qualified to be summoned to the meeting, shall be permitted to be present, or if present, shall be permitted to remain; whether and when discussion shall be terminated and a vote taken; whether the meeting shall be adjourned. In all these matters, and they are only instances, the meeting decides, and if necessary a vote must be taken to ascertain the wishes of the majority. If no objection is taken by any constituent of the meeting, the meeting must be taken to be assenting to the course adopted.

Records of resolutions and minutes of meetings

Section 359 (records of resolutions and meetings of class of members) states that the provisions of Part 13, Chapter 6 (records of resolutions and meetings) apply, with necessary modifications, in relation to resolutions and meetings of holders of a class of shares, and in the case of a company without a share capital, a class of members, as they apply in relation to resolutions of members generally and to general meetings.

Accordingly, the following provisions of the Act apply, with necessary modifications:

- section 355 (records of resolutions and meetings etc.);
- section 356 (records as evidence of resolutions);
- section 357 (records of decisions by sole member); and
- section 358 (inspection of records of resolutions and meetings).

Classes of members in guarantee companies

A company limited by guarantee may have different classes of members. Typically, the company's articles will allow the board of directors to establish different classes of member with different rights. An example might be a sports club which has full members, weekend members and junior members. Unless the articles provide for a method of variation, the class rights can only be varied in accordance with section 631 (variation of class rights: companies without a share capital).

Variation of class rights: companies without a share capital

Section 631 deals with the variation of the rights of a class of members of a company where the company does not have a share capital. It provides that the rights of a class of members may only be varied:

(a) in accordance with provision in the company's articles for the variation of those rights; or
(b) where the company's articles contain no such provision, if the members of that class consent to the variation in accordance with section 631.

Section 631(4) provides that the consent required for these purposes on the part of the members of a class is:

(a) consent in writing from at least three-quarters of the members of the class; or
(b) a special resolution passed at a separate general meeting of the members of that class sanctioning the variation.

It should be noted that the option to obtain consent in writing in (a) above applies to both public and private companies and is not subject to the rules on written resolutions. A private company could, of course, also use a written resolution to pass the necessary special resolution for the purposes of option (b), whereas a public company would have to hold a meeting.

Any amendment of a provision contained in a company's articles for the variation of the rights of a class of members, or the insertion of any such provision into the articles, is itself to be treated as a variation of those rights (s. 631(5)). For the purposes of section 631, and (except where the context otherwise requires) any provision in a company's articles for the variation of the rights of a class of members, references to the variation of those rights include references to their abrogation (s. 631(6)).

Special procedures for variation of class rights meetings for companies without a share capital

Subject to certain exceptions, section 335 applies the provisions of Part 13, Chapter 3 (resolutions at meetings) with necessary modifications to any meeting of the holders of a class of shares. One of the exceptions provided for in section 335(3) is that the provisions of section 318 (quorum) and section 321 (right to demand a poll) do not apply in relation to a class meeting held in connection with the variation of rights attached to a class of shares (but do apply in relation to a class meeting called for any other purpose).

Instead section 335 provides that for a variation of class rights meeting of a company without a share capital:

- the quorum for a meeting other than an adjourned meeting, is two members of the class present (in person or by proxy) who together represent at least one-third of the voting rights of that class (s. 335(4)(a));
- the quorum for an adjourned meeting is one member of the class present (in person or by proxy) (s. 335(4)(b)); and
- any member of the class present (in person or by proxy) may demand a poll (s. 334(6)).

For the purposes of section 335, any amendment of a provision contained in a company's articles for the variation of the rights attached to a class of shares, or the insertion of any such provision into the articles, is itself to be treated as a variation of those rights, and references to the variation of rights attached to a class of shares include references to their abrogation (s. 335(6)).

Minutes and records

Section 359 provides that the provisions on records of resolutions and minutes of general meetings in Part 13, Chapter 6 of the Act apply (with necessary modifications) in relation to resolutions and meetings of:

(a) holders of a class of shares, and

(b) in the case of a company without a share capital, a class of members.

Accordingly, the following rules can be said to apply:

(a) A company must keep:
   (i) copies of all resolutions of a class of members or shareholders passed otherwise than at a class meeting (e.g. as written resolutions) (applying s. 355(1)(a));
   (ii) minutes of all class meetings (applying s. 355(1)(b)); and
   (iii) details of decisions taken by a sole (class) member provided to the company by the sole class member in accordance with s. 357 (applying s. 355(1)(c)).

(b) Any failure to do so is an offence for which any officer in default may be fined (applying s. 355(3) and (4)).

(c) Records kept in accordance with section 355 will be afforded special evidential status (applying s. 356).

(d) A sole member of a class may have to notify the company in writing of any decision he makes which could be taken at a class meeting and has effect as if agreed to at a class meeting (applying s. 357), although it has to be said that this section could be applied in a number of different ways.

(e) Any records kept under these rules must be made available for inspection (applying s. 358).

Conclusion

This chapter has specifically considered meetings of specific classes or shareholders. Most companies will not have split classes or, if they do, may not have the need for specific class meetings.

Where separate class meetings are required, it can be seen that the process for convening and holding such meetings mirrors that of general meetings of all members. The differences may be minimal and are often reflected in different voting rights or restrictions of voting when certain actions are outstanding, such as the payment of a dividend.

When holding a meeting of all members, it is beneficial to be mindful of the differences between and across classes so that these can be accommodated.

20 – Sole director and/or sole shareholder meetings

The Companies Act 2006 provides that, notwithstanding anything to the contrary in the articles of a private company limited by shares or guarantee having only one member, one member present in person or represented by a proxy or corporate representative shall be a quorum at general meetings of the company (s. 318(1)).

Equally, where there is only one director, any decisions taken in their role as a director should be documented as such to provide an audit trail for future reference.

This chapter will clarify and confirm relevant requirements for both sole member and sole director companies, noting that a company with a sole member may also only have one director who is the member themselves. In this scenario, it is even more important to understand and differentiate between the different roles and their responsibilities in terms of decision making and the records of such decisions.

Sole member

Where a company limited by shares or guarantee has only one member and that member takes any decision which may be taken by the company in general meeting, and which has effect as if agreed by the company in general meeting, they shall (unless that decision is taken by way of a written resolution) provide the company with details of that decision (s. 357). Failure to do so renders the sole member liable to a fine (s. 357(3) and (4)) but does not invalidate the decision (s. 357(5)).

A company must keep a record containing details of decisions taken by a sole member provided to the company by the sole member in accordance with section 357 (s. 355(1)(c)).

Precedent: Minutes of a general meeting of a single member company

XYZ LIMITED

Minutes of an extraordinary general meeting held at [place] on [date]

Present: [name] (Chairman)

In attendance: [name] (Company Secretary)

The chairman proposed as a [special] resolution:

THAT . . . .

After declaring an interest in the resolution to the extent that [nature of interest] this was passed by the sole member of the company as a [special] resolution of the company.

[Signature]

Chairman

In relation to decisions of a sole member made on or after 1 October 2007, the records must be kept for at least ten years from the date of the decision (s. 355(2)).

Records of decisions made by a sole member before that date must be kept in accordance with the requirements of the Companies Act 1985 which makes no provision allowing any of the records given to the company by a sole member under that section to be disposed of.

The company secretary (if any) and the directors can be fined for any default regarding compliance with the requirements of section 355 of the 2006 Act relating to the maintenance of these records although there is no equivalent penalty under the 1985 Act.

Confirmation of decisions

If the sole member of a company makes any informal decisions, they must provide the company with a written record of that decision, which the company must then keep.

Unanimous consent

Where a company has only one member it is, of course, much more likely that that member will make informal decisions which rely on the principle of unanimous consent for their validity. Recognising that this will be the case, the Act provides that whenever a sole member takes any decision which could have been taken by the company in general meeting and that has effect as if it had been agreed at a general meeting, they shall (unless the decision is taken by way of written resolution) provide the company with a written record of that decision (s. 357). In this sense, they are relying on decisions being approved as a majority decision.

Precedent: Record of decision by sole member of a company

XYZ LIMITED

Written record of a decision made by the sole member of the Company which could have been taken by the company in general meeting and has effect as if it were so taken.

The following resolution, having effect as an [ordinary/special] resolution, was approved on [date] by a decision of the undersigned sole member of the Company:

THAT . . . .

[Signature]

[Date]

A sole member who fails to comply with this requirement will be liable to a fine (s. 357(2) and (3)). However, failure to comply will not invalidate the decision of the sole member (s. 357(4)). The company must keep any record provided by a sole member in this regard for the same length of time as it would keep the minutes, had the decision been taken at a general meeting. Indeed, it would be normal for the records to be kept in much the same way as minutes and written resolutions.

Written resolutions

It is open to debate whether it is always advisable for the sole member of a company to rely on the principle of unanimous consent to validate informal decisions. As the Act requires a sole member to provide the company with a written record of any informal decisions, it would seem to be more sensible for them to make decisions by written resolution in accordance with the statutory procedures, and to obey all the conditions and limitations associated with those procedures. If something cannot be done by written resolution under the statutory procedures, it is possible that it cannot be done informally.

Although the statutory written resolution procedures do not apply to public companies, the sole member of a public company would be well advised to obey the same principles and limitations when making an informal decision that would apply if it was attempting to pass a written resolution under the statutory procedures. For example, it would not be sensible for the sole member of a public company to rely on an informal decision to remove a director as this cannot be done by written resolution of a private company.

Contract with sole member directors

Where a limited company having only one member enters into a contract with that sole member and they are also a director of the company, and the contract is not entered into in the ordinary course of the company's business, the company must, unless the contract is in writing, ensure that the terms of the contract are either:

(a) set out in a written memorandum; or
(b) recorded in the minutes of the first meeting of the directors of the company following the making of the contract (s. 231).

If a company fails to comply with this section an offence is committed by every officer of the company who is in default, who may be fined (s. 231(3) and (4)). However, failure to comply with this requirement in relation to a contract does not affect the validity of the contract (s. 231(6)), and nothing in section 231 should be read as excluding the operation of any other enactment or rule of law applying to contracts between a company and a director of the company (s. 231(7)).

Sole director

Quorum

The default figure of two for the quorum at meetings of directors found in most articles would seem to be wholly inappropriate for a private company with only one director.

Ideally, the articles should make alternative provision to cater for these circumstances. The model articles for private companies do so by disapplying the usual rules on directors' decision making where the company only has one director. In these circumstances the general rules do not apply and the director may take decisions without regard to any of the provisions of the articles relating to directors' decision-making (pcls 7 and clg 7). This almost certainly represents the common law position for companies whose articles do not make specific provision in this regard.

Nevertheless, a company with older articles may still prefer to make specific provision in its articles to clarify the position, either by following the format of the model articles mentioned above or by including specific language in the articles of the company.

Precedent: Wording for inclusion in articles to allow a sole director to act

The quorum for the transaction of business of the directors may be fixed by the directors and unless so fixed at any other number shall be two; but if and so long as there is a sole director, he may exercise all the powers and authorities vested in the directors by these Articles [and Table A; and Regulation 89 of Table A shall be modified accordingly]. A person who holds office only as an alternate director shall, if his appointor is not present, be counted in the quorum.

Declaration of interests

A sole director of a company that is only required by law to have one director is not required to make any declarations of interest under either sections 177 or 182 because both sections require the declarations to be made to the other directors of which there are none.

Minutes

As with decisions made by a sole member, decisions made by a director should also be recorded to provide an audit trail for future reference. Decision making and written records, in this sense, follow the general requirements of decisions made by a board of directors.

Conclusion

As can be seen, being a sole director or a sole shareholder may mean that an individual has sole responsibility within their remit. However, there remain certain actions that need to be taken to comply with legislation. Particularly where there is a single individual who is the director and shareholder of an operating company, especially one with employees, it is imperative that the two roles are distinguishable and that due records are kept of any decisions made. This audit trail of records not only ensures compliance with legislation, it also provides a record for future changes to the company structure, such as the appointment of additional directors, addition of new shareholders, the sale of the company or the purchase of another company.

21 – Committee meetings

Articles usually allow directors to delegate their powers to committees of directors. However, it should be noted that the board is not delegating their authority or responsibility and each committee remains responsible to the board.

Meetings of committees largely follow the same format as meeting of directors, with a few variances around their authority, agenda and meeting schedule.

The UK Corporate Governance Code recommends that all listed companies should establish an audit committee, a remuneration committee and a nomination committee. Increasingly companies are implementing committees for a wider range of requirements often driven by the sector that they act in or the circumstances of the particular company. These include Environmental, Social and Governance (ESG) committees, markets committees, risk committees and technology committees.

Committees can be set up at any time, for any purpose and for any tenure subject to the need identified by the board. They are frequently implemented to supplement the knowledge and experience of the board on a particular subject matter or to enable greater time to be focused on a specific area that would otherwise dominate board discussions. Each committee also reports back to the board on their progress and actions to support board oversight.

Establishing a committee of the board

The board can establish a committee to perform certain functions and authorise that committee to make decisions on its behalf. Directors can establish committees even if the articles do not allow them to delegate any of their powers to those committees. A committee could be established in these circumstances to make recommendations to the board on certain matters. This would not involve any delegation of powers, as long as the board makes the final decision on those matters. In practice, boards often establish committees for this reason, even in companies where the board is able to delegate its powers.

It is important to understand the distinction between duties and powers in this context. The board can delegate certain duties to a committee without necessarily giving the committee any decision-making powers. However, committees established solely to make recommendations to the board sometimes need to be given certain ancillary powers (e.g. to enable them to conduct an investigation prior to making their recommendations).

One might imagine that a committee of the board can only be established by a formal decision of the board. This is, of course, the way that board committees ought to be constituted. However, the courts are sometimes willing to recognise the fact that a committee has been established even though the board never made a formal decision to establish one. Judges sometimes use this technique to regularise decisions made by individual directors or a small group of them where there has been no formal delegation by the board, particularly where the other directors have absented themselves from the decision-making process in full knowledge that the affairs of the company are being managed by a small group of directors. In these circumstances, the courts may simply deem the other directors to have agreed to the establishment of the committee in view of the fact they did nothing to prevent the affairs of the company from being managed in this way.

However, it would be wrong to suggest that a small group of directors can constitute themselves as a committee and exercise the company's powers without board approval. Such behaviour would constitute a breach of duty (at least initially), and render them liable to possible legal action. If the other directors allowed such behaviour to go unchecked for too long, the courts might conclude that the arrangements had been sanctioned by them. However, it would be dangerous to rely on this.

The proper way to establish a committee of the board is by a formal resolution of the board. Such a resolution will need to deal with the committee's:

- membership;
- duties;
- powers (including any limitations on those powers); and
- constitution.

It may be possible to deal with all these matters in one simple board resolution. However, for standing committees, it is normal to pass a resolution establishing the committee's terms of reference (including its delegated powers) and to deal with appointments separately.

Which committees are board committees?

Before going any further, it is necessary to address what we mean when we refer to a board committee.

A company may have many forums and project teams, some of which may be referred to as committees. Typically, only a few of them will be board committees. The rest will just be committees established by executives and other employees for management purposes. It is important to be able to recognise which committees are board committees, because those must operate in accordance with the company's articles.

A board committee is one that has been established by the board, has clear delegated responsibilities and comprises a representative of the board in its membership. This membership may be a single director or more, but is not the whole board. Articles under Table A often state that the directors may delegate their powers to a committee of directors (reg. 72 of Table A). Where this type of wording is used, it has to be assumed that the committee must be made up exclusively of directors. Conversely, it is possible that, under the articles, the board can appoint a committee of directors that does not include any directors.

It should be noted that the 2006 Act model articles allow the directors to delegate their powers to any person or committee. They do not specify that the committee must be a committee of directors (see pcls 5, clg 5 and plc 5). Indeed, the model articles specifically provide that committees to which the directors delegate any of their powers must follow procedures which are based as far as they are applicable on those provisions of the articles which govern the taking of decisions by directors. However, they also provide that the directors may make rules of procedure for all or any committees, which prevail over rules derived from the articles if they are not consistent with them (pcls 6, clg 6 and plc 6). Accordingly, under the model articles, any committee to which the directors delegate any of their powers should be considered a committee of the board, even if it does not include any directors. It is important to note that this is only the case where the board has delegated any of its powers to that committee.

However, this raises the question as to whether there needs to be some form of direct delegation by the board and whether the same principles can apply where there has been some sort of sub-delegation of powers to a committee. Say, for example, the board delegates wide powers to the chief executive and those powers include the power to sub-delegate. And say, for example, the chief executive delegates some of his or her duties to a committee and gives the committee power to make decisions. Surely such a committee would not be treated as a committee of the board for the purposes of model articles. If it was, every committee in the company that has decision-making powers would have to be treated as a committee of the board. It would seem to be sensible to limit the application of the articles to committees that derive their powers directly from the board.

Model Articles (cl.5):

(1) Subject to the articles, the directors may delegate any of the powers which are conferred on them under the articles—

    (a) to such person or committee;

    (b) by such means (including by power of attorney);

    (c) to such an extent;

    (d) in relation to such matters or territories; and

(e) on such terms and conditions;
as they think fit.

(2) If the directors so specify, any such delegation may authorise further delegation of the directors' powers by any person to whom they are delegated.

(3) The directors may revoke any delegation in whole or part, or alter its terms and conditions.

The composition of the committee is particularly important where the board wishes to delegate any of its powers to the committee. The issue may not be at all relevant if the committee does not need to be given any delegate powers to perform its designated function (e.g. where the committee's sole function is to make recommendations to the board).

In practice, the executive committee may be nothing other than a sounding board for the chief executive, in which case it may not need to be given any delegated powers. It is normally the chief executive who makes the final decision on matters that come before the committee. Where this is the case, it is the chief executive who needs to be given delegated powers, not the committee. Indeed, in these circumstances, even though it may feel as though the executive committee has been established by the board, it is probably better to view it as a committee established by the chief executive for management purposes on the instructions of the board, rather than as a committee actually established by the board or a committee of the board.

If the articles do allow the directors to delegate their powers to a committee that is not made up exclusively of directors and the board does establish such a committee and authorises it to exercise certain delegated powers, the committee should be treated as a committee of the board and any relevant article provisions regarding the operation of board committees will apply to that committee.

In some cases, it might be better for a committee to be established under the direct authority of the board so that there is no doubt as to whether the articles are intended to apply to that committee. For example, it might be better to do this in order to establish a committee that is to act as a regional board or divisional board. It should not be forgotten that, under the model articles, the main board can establish constitutional rules for that committee which override the application of the articles.

Membership

In most cases, it will be preferable to appoint named individuals as members of a board committee. This will certainly be the case for standing committees such as the audit and remuneration committees which are usually comprised wholly or mainly of non-executive directors. However, it is possible to appoint post-holders rather than named individuals, for example the finance director on an audit committee. It may also be possible to establish a committee of 'any two directors' (or some other number), although this formula can cause some technical difficulties (see below).

One real benefit of implementing a committee is that non board members with specific expertise can be appointed as members. This ensures that the breadth and depth of knowledge is extended, thus enabling broader topic discussions and more in-depth knowledge to supplement and underpin decisions made at board level following submissions from committees.

There is no limit to the number of members a committee can have, or the ratio of either board members to non-board members or company employees to external representatives. Thus, membership of a committee can draw from a wider pool of potential candidates depending on the requirements and remit of the committee.

Tenure of committee membership should map that of the board to which it reports, noting as well that any board members who are also committee members should automatically terminate their committee membership at the same time as terminating their board membership. In addition, the composition of the committee members as a collective should be reviewed to ensure their skills remain relevant and that they continue to be able to commit sufficient time to contribute effectively. As part of this review, consideration should also be given to appointing additional members to refresh the membership and bring new skills and knowledge.

Committee membership

Anyone appointed to serve on a committee will be a member of the committee. Each committee member will have a right to attend and vote at committee meetings and to participate in any other decision-making processes that it may adopt. The right to vote and participate may, of course, be subject to certain restrictions under the articles (e.g. where a director is interested in a matter that is being addressed by the committee). Although, it is possible to appoint non-voting members, it is not normally necessary to do so. A committee can invite anyone to attend its meetings and allow them to make proposals and participate in its discussions. It is possible to make provision in the committee's constitution to clarify that certain people who are not committee members have something akin to a right to attend. It is rarely advisable to actually go so far as to give non-members an inalienable right to attend. Instead it is better to provide that they have a right to do so unless invited by the committee to leave.

The Listing Rules used to require directors to form the majority on board committees where the articles allowed co-opted members, and insisted that such committees act only where the majority of members present were directors. Although this rule was abolished in 1995, the articles of many listed companies still include such restrictions.

Committees of 'any two directors'

It is quite common for boards of directors to establish a committee of 'any two directors' or 'any three directors', etc. This method is most commonly used to allow directors to complete a transaction which the board has already authorised or to sign a document on behalf of the board. In such cases, it is arguable whether it is necessary to establish a committee. It would be sufficient for the board to resolve, for example, that any two directors be authorised to sign a certain document on behalf of the board.

The 'any two directors' method is slightly less satisfactory where the committee is to be given discretionary powers. The technique was used by the board of Guinness during its takeover of Distillers in the 1980s to appoint a committee of any three directors

> with full power and authority to settle the terms of the offer, to approve any revision of the offer which the committee might consider it desirable to make and [amongst other things] (vi) to authorise and approve, execute and do, or procure to be executed and done all documents, deeds, acts and things as they may consider necessary or desirable in connection with the making or implementation of the offer and/or the proposals referred to above and any revision thereof . . . (see *Guinness v Saunders* [1990] 1 All ER 654).

Appointing such a committee could be viewed as appointing the whole board as a committee and fixing the quorum at the number of directors specified. In theory, all the directors are potential members of such a committee and are therefore entitled to receive notice of its meetings. If it is possible to appoint a committee of any two directors, it must also be acceptable to appoint a committee of 'any two' of a number of named directors. The end result is, of course, the same as if the board had appointed a committee of, say, four named directors and specified the quorum as two. If the articles prevent the board doing this by the normal method, it must be doubtful whether it can achieve the same result by using the 'any two directors' method. It is worthy of note on this score that the articles of Guinness gave the board specific power to fix the quorum of committees of the board.

It is also questionable what the position would be if, say, four directors attended a meeting of a committee of 'any two directors'. Could they all vote? And what would happen if two were in favour and two opposed to a proposal? Which (if any) of the directors would constitute the committee? In *Guinness v Saunders*, Lord Templeman said, somewhat pointedly perhaps, that the three directors in that case 'constituted themselves as a committee'. Could three other directors have constituted themselves as a committee with the same powers?

In order to avoid these problems, some sort of control needs to be exercised on the calling of meetings of such a committee. Usually this will be the task of the person who prepares the documentation for the meeting. Indeed, it may be preferable to specify in the board resolution establishing such a committee that it may not meet unless the company secretary or some other specified person is present. These sort of safeguards may not be necessary where the committee is established to execute a document or perform some other mechanical process.

Committee of one

Articles often state that the directors may delegate their powers to a committee of one or more directors. Even if they do not specifically refer to a committee of one, any power to delegate to a committee is deemed to include the power to delegate to a committee consisting of only one director, unless the articles specify otherwise. This may be of relevance for companies with articles based on the 2006 Act model articles, none of which specifically state that a committee may consist of only one person.

Powers and duties

The extent of the powers delegated to a committee should be specified in the board resolution or the terms of reference approved by the board. To some extent, this will be apparent from the committee's duties or functions. However, it is safer to set out these powers explicitly. For example, if a committee is to be established to negotiate, agree and execute a contract for the purchase of a specified freehold property, it might be preferable to state explicitly that the committee has the power to appoint surveyors and solicitors and incur other costs which are necessary in the performance of its duties.

It may not be necessary to delegate any powers to a committee established solely to make recommendations to the board. Anybody may make recommendations to the board. Doing so is not something that requires any special powers. However, committees established for this purpose may also benefit from having certain incidental powers (e.g. to retain external professional advisers) and it is preferable to specify these powers at the outset. In these scenarios, where the committee has not been constituted to deliver on a particular action rather than have oversight of a specific area, it is best practice for the board to sign off on a clear terms of reference of the committee. In this way the deliverables, authorities, roles and responsibilities can be agreed by the board and understood by committee members.

Known as standing committees, it is normal to draft formal rules that are documented in a terms of reference. A standing committee is one which is established permanently to perform certain duties on a regular basis. Terms of reference for such committees are usually adopted by a specific board resolution. Named individuals are then appointed as members of such committees by separate resolution(s).

Terms of reference for each committee should be reviewed on a three-yearly basis to ensure they remain fit for purpose with annual oversight by the chairman of the board of directors.

Proceedings

The proceedings at committees of the board will be governed by the articles and in default by the common law of meetings. Articles usually provide that the proceedings at committee meetings shall be governed by the articles regulating the proceedings at board meetings so far as they are capable of applying.

The model articles adopt a formula using a wording that removes much of the doubt as to the power of the directors to override the provisions of the articles (pcls, clg and plc 6).

Model Articles: plc 6

1   Committees to which the directors delegate any of their powers must follow procedures which are based as far as they are applicable on those provisions of the articles which govern the taking of decisions by directors.
2   The directors may make rules of procedure for all or any committees, which prevail over rules derived from the articles if they are not consistent with them.

Conditions imposed by the board

As can be seen, the model articles allow the directors to make rules of procedure for all or any committees, which prevail over rules derived from the articles if they are not consistent with them (pcls, clg and plc 6(2)).

Although this would appear to give the board extraordinary latitude to override restrictions contained in the articles, it is suggested that the courts would not take kindly to any hint that committees have been formed with rules that enable them to do things that the board would not be empowered to do itself (e.g. by purporting to disapply for the committee any rule preventing a conflicted director from voting). It is easy to imagine in this regard that the courts could interpret the words 'rules of procedure' very narrowly in certain circumstances, but particularly where there is an alleged breach of duty by a director.

Appointment of chair

Under the normal formula where the articles governing the proceedings of the board also apply to committees unless the board decides otherwise, any provisions regarding the appointment of a chairman of the board would also apply to a committee. Under most articles this would enable the committee members to appoint (and remove) one of their number as chairman of the committee (pcls, clg and plc 12 and 6). Under the model articles, the board may nominate the chairman of the committee and in doing so can effectively override the committee's powers. A chairman appointed in this manner could not then be removed by the committee.

The chairman of any committee will have a casting vote if the articles confer a casting vote on the chairman of the board of directors, unless, of course, the board removes the casting vote as a condition on the exercise of the committee's powers.

Under some articles, the board may also appoint one or more deputy or vice chairmen to act in the chairman's absence. If the board fails to make provision in this regard with respect to a committee and the committee's quorum is such that meetings can still be held without the nominated chairman, the committee members present will have the power (e.g. in accordance with art. 12 of the model articles) to appoint one of their number to chair meetings in the absence of the nominated chairman.

Quorum

The common law rule is that a committee can only act if all its members are present. This rule can, of course, be modified by the articles. For example, the articles may give the board specific power to fix the quorum for board committees. Where this is the case, the common law rule will apply in default if the board fails to specify a quorum. Even though this may be what the board intended, it is preferable to state the quorum in the resolution appointing the committee or the terms of reference approved by the board.

The 2006 Act model articles definitely allow the directors to set the quorum of any committee and any decision they make in this regard will definitely override the common law rule and any other quorum that may have been fixed under the articles for the board, that would otherwise apply in default (see pcls, clg and plc 6(2)).

Where the common law rule applies, the directors can effectively reduce the committee's quorum by appointing less committee members. If they appoint five, all five have to participate in the committee's decisions. If they appoint four, all four must do so, and so on. If the board can vary the number of directors required to participate in the committee's decisions in this way, it would seem strange to say that they cannot appoint more committee members and specify that not all of them need to participate in the committee's decisions. However, it is submitted that this is what the position would be if the articles do not allow them to fix a different quorum for the committee.

It should be noted that delegation to a committee (or to an individual), by its very nature, can have the effect of allowing the directors to circumvent the usual quorum requirements for board meetings, particularly where the quorum for board meetings is set by the articles at a high figure. It is fairly obvious that the courts will not look kindly on any technique that the directors may use to circumvent the usual quorum requirements unless that technique is specifically allowed under the articles. In fact, the courts have, on occasion, refused to allow directors to do this even though it may appear to have been allowed under the articles (see below). The fact that they have done so, helps to explain why the board cannot assume that it has the power to fix the quorum for any committee unless there is something in the articles which specifically allows them to do so. It is fairly obvious that where the quorum for board meetings is set by the articles at quite a high figure, the directors are more likely to be tempted to try to establish a committee in order to circumvent their own quorum requirements. The courts are well aware of this and are likely to interpret the provisions of the articles fairly strictly when assessing whether this is allowed.

Indeed, as mentioned above, the courts are sometimes called to strike down something that appears to be allowed under the articles on the basis that the directors cannot delegate something to a committee merely to enable that committee to do something that the board was not capable of doing itself as a result of restrictions in the articles which prevented the directors from voting on or being counted in the quorum for matters in which they were interested. In this particular case, it would be obvious that the only reason why the board had established a committee was to circumvent the normal rules. The court judged this to be an abuse by the directors of their powers.

Quorum of one

The basic common law rule established in *Sharp v Dawes* is that in order to hold a valid meeting there must be a meeting of minds; in other words, there must be at least two people present who are entitled to attend and vote. However, even the common law recognises that a valid meeting can be held with only one person present where he or she is the only person entitled to attend and vote at meetings of that body (e.g. the sole holder of a class of shares).

In any case, if the articles allow the directors to fix a quorum of one at board meetings and provide that the regulations governing board meetings shall also apply to committee meetings, it would seem that they may also fix a quorum of one for a committee of more than one director.

Voting

Articles usually prohibit the directors from voting on any matter in which they have an interest. Model articles allow the directors to vote in certain limited circumstances where they are interested but otherwise imposes a general prohibition (pcls 14, clg 14 and plc 16). Committees to which the directors delegate any of their powers must follow procedures which are based as far as they are applicable on those provisions of the articles which govern the taking of decisions by directors (pcls, clg and plc 6(1)). This presumably includes the article provisions on directors' conflicts. The model articles also refer to committees of directors in the provision giving the chair power to decide whether or not a conflicted director may participate in the meeting (pcls 14(6), clg 14(6) and plc 16(5)).

Where non-directors are appointed as members of a board committee, it may be a good idea to clarify in the terms of reference their duties with regard to disclosure of interests and their right to vote on transactions in which they have an interest. Members of board committees who are not directors do not have a statutory duty to disclose such interests and articles on voting usually refer only to directors.

Articles sometimes provide that the majority of members present at a meeting must be directors where they allow non-directors to be appointed. This could also be included as a condition in the committee's terms of reference.

Under the common law, each member of the committee will have one vote. The articles may, however, make alternative provision with regard to board meetings and any such provisions may be adopted by default for committees by virtue of clauses like article 6 of the model articles. The most obvious example is where the articles provide for the appointment of alternate directors. If a director appoints another director as his or her alternate, the director so appointed will have two votes. Great care should, however, be taken where one or more directors have weighted voting rights in respect of the exercise by the board of certain powers and it is proposed to delegate those powers to a committee.

Disclosure of interests

It may not be sufficient for a director to declare an interest in a proposed transaction at a committee meeting for the purposes of section 177. The declaration must be made to the other directors (s. 177(1)) before the company enters into the transaction or arrangement (s. 177(4)). The requirement to make the declaration to the other directors means to the other members of the board rather than just to those serving on the committee.

A declaration of interest made at a committee meeting that is subsequently brought to the attention of the other directors will probably suffice for the purposes of section 177, provided that this happens before the transaction is entered into. This could be done in one of the ways permitted by section 177(2), although it should be noted that subsection (2) does not specifically require the declaration to be made in one of those ways. A declaration of interest recorded in the minutes of a committee which are circulated to the entire board or laid at a board meeting may suffice for these purposes, although it may be preferable for the declaration to be made in one of the manners explicitly allowed.

Where a committee has made a decision on a transaction or arrangement in which a director has declared an interest, it will be necessary to ensure that the company does not enter into that transaction or arrangement until the director has made the necessary declaration to the other directors. This will not be difficult where additional formalities are required. They can be delayed until the declaration has been properly made. However, there can be circumstances in which the committee's decision may create binding legal obligations on the part of the company, particularly where its decision relates to a proposal to enter into a contract with the director who declared the interest. In such circumstances it may be necessary to ensure that the committee's approval is made conditional on the necessary declaration having been made.

Where a committee has the ability to make decisions on behalf of the board, and the committee has members who are not directors, best practice would be for all committee members to note any conflicts of interests at the start of the meeting. This ensures that any further discussion including the non-directors has evidence and notice of such conflict. Merely restricting the voting to directors on any topic, whether in the committee or at board meetings themselves, would not avoid an interested party who is a committee member from influencing the voting through their contribution to the committee discussion and board submission, whether deliberately or inadvertently.

Alternate directors

There is no automatic right to appoint a proxy or an alternate at meetings of committees. The right to appoint an alternate depends entirely on the articles (plc 25–27). The model articles for public companies are not explicit in this regard but provide that alternates may act in relation to the taking of decisions by the directors in the absence of their appointor and, except where the articles specify otherwise, are deemed for all purposes to be directors (plc 25 and 26).

It is doubtful whether a person who is not a director but who is appointed as a member of a committee can appoint an alternate unless the articles specifically provide.

Written resolutions

Articles on directors' written resolutions or unanimous decisions often specifically extend this form of decision-making process to committees of the board. In the case of the model articles, the written resolution procedures will apply to committees by virtue of article 6 which applies the articles governing the taking of decisions by directors to committees.

Audit committee

Listed companies are required by the UK Corporate Governance Code and the Disclosure and Transparency Rules to establish an audit committee to perform certain duties.

UK Corporate Governance Code

Provision 24 of the UK Corporate Governance Code (2018) states that:

> The board should establish an audit committee of independent non-executive directors, with a minimum membership of three, or in the case of smaller companies, two. The chair of the board should not be a member. The board should satisfy itself that at least one member has recent and relevant financial experience. The committee as a whole shall have competence relevant to the sector in which the company operates.

Where a company has only a few independent non-executive directors, normally all of them will serve on the audit committee. If there are more independent non-executive directors than this, permitting selection from a larger group, three to five members is generally regarded as the optimum size for the committee.

Role of audit committee

The establishment of an audit committee is not intended to undermine the ultimate responsibility of the board for reviewing and approving the annual report and accounts and the half-yearly report. Rather, it is intended to ensure that the non-executive directors become actively involved in that process and have access to the resources necessary to enable them to make independent judgements. It also offers the auditors a direct link with the non-executive directors.

The Code defines the main roles and responsibilities of the audit committee (provision 25) as including:

- monitoring the integrity of the financial statements of the company and any formal announcements relating to the company's financial performance, and reviewing significant financial reporting judgements contained in them;
- providing advice (where requested by the board) on whether the annual report and accounts, taken as a whole, is fair, balanced and understandable, and provides the information necessary for shareholders to assess the company's position and performance, business model and strategy;
- reviewing the company's internal financial controls and internal control and risk management systems, unless expressly addressed by a separate board risk committee composed of independent non-executive directors, or by the board itself;
- monitoring and reviewing the effectiveness of the company's internal audit function or, where there is not one, considering annually whether there is a need for one and making a recommendation to the board;
- conducting the tender process and making recommendations to the board, about the appointment, reappointment and removal of the external auditor, and approving the remuneration and terms of engagement of the external auditor;
- reviewing and monitoring the external auditor's independence and objectivity;

- reviewing the effectiveness of the external audit process, taking into consideration relevant UK professional and regulatory requirements;
- developing and implementing policy on the engagement of the external auditor to supply non-audit services, ensuring there is prior approval of non-audit services, considering the impact this may have on independence, taking into account the relevant regulations and ethical guidance in this regard, and reporting to the board on any improvement or action required; and
- reporting to the board on how it has discharged its responsibilities.

Delegated powers

The primary purpose of the audit committee is not to exercise powers delegated by the board but to monitor and review matters connected with the financial statements and to make recommendations to the board arising from these activities. However, the committee may need to be given certain incidental powers to enable it to function effectively. These could include, for example, explicit powers of internal investigation and rights of access to any company information. In theory, this would enable the audit committee to cut through the usual chain of authority when conducting investigations. The committee will almost certainly need to be given power to retain independent professional advisers.

Statements in the annual report

The UK Corporate Governance Code requires the annual report of a listed company to contain a description of the work of the audit committee (provision 26), including:

- the significant issues that the audit committee considered relating to the financial statements, and how these issues were addressed;
- an explanation of how it has assessed the independence and effectiveness of the external audit process and the approach taken to the appointment or reappointment of the external auditor, information on the length of tenure of the current audit firm, when a tender was last conducted and advance notice of any retendering plans;
- in the case of a board not accepting the audit committee's recommendation on the external auditor appointment, reappointment or removal, a statement from the audit committee explaining its recommendation and the reasons why the board has taken a different position (this should also be supplied in any papers recommending appointment or reappointment);
- where there is no internal audit function, an explanation for the absence, how internal assurance is achieved, and how this affects the work of external audit; and
- an explanation of how auditor independence and objectivity are safeguarded, if the external auditor provides non-audit services.

It should be noted that the chairman of the audit committee should be in attendance at the annual general meeting to support any questions raised by members on the content of their statement in the annual report.

Disclosure and Transparency Rules/Audit Directive requirements

The UK Corporate Governance Code requirements on audit committees are also supplemented by certain mandatory requirements in the Disclosure and Transparency Rules (see DTR 7.1). These rules implement the requirements of the Audit Directive (2014/56/EU) and, subject to certain exceptions, apply to issuers whose transferable securities are admitted to trading and which are required to appoint a statutory auditor (DTR 1B.1.2).

The provisions of DTR 7.1 effectively replicate the provisions on audit committees in the UK Corporate Governance Code in that they require issuers to have a body which is responsible for performing the functions that an audit committee would typically carry out. At least one member of that body must be independent and at least one member must have competence in accounting and/or auditing (DTR 7.1.1), although the same member may satisfy both of these requirements (DTR 7.1.2).

The relevant body must, as a minimum (DTR 7.1.3):

(a) monitor the financial reporting process and submit recommendations or proposals to ensure its integrity;

(b) monitor the effectiveness of the issuer's internal quality control and risk management systems and, where applicable, its internal audit, regarding the financial reporting of the issuer, without breaching its independence;

(c) monitor the statutory audit of the annual and consolidated financial statements, in particular, its performance, taking into account any findings and conclusions by the Financial Reporting Council under article 26(6) of the Audit Regulation (537/2014/EU);

(d) review and monitor the independence of the statutory auditor in accordance with paragraphs 2(3), 2(4), 3 to 8 and 10 to 12 of Schedule 1 to the Statutory Auditors and Third Country Auditors Regulations 2016 (SI 2016/649) and article 6 of the Audit Regulation, and in particular the appropriateness of the provision of non-audit services to the issuer in accordance with article 5 of the Audit Regulation;

(e) inform the administrative or supervisory body of the issuer of the outcome of the statutory audit and explain how the statutory audit contributed to the integrity of financial reporting and what the role of the relevant body was in that process; and

(f) except when article 16(8) of the Audit Regulation is applied, be responsible for the procedure for the selection of statutory auditor(s) and recommend the statutory auditor(s) to be appointed in accordance with article 16 of the Audit Regulation.

In the Financial Conduct Authority's (FCA) view, compliance with the provision on audit committees in the UK Corporate Governance Code will result in compliance with the requirements of DTR 7.1 on audit committees (DTR 7.1.7).

Remuneration committee

The articles invariably give the board of directors the power to determine executive salaries and the members will normally have no direct say in the amount executives are paid. These arrangements are necessary because executive directors are usually employed under a service contract, the terms of which need to be settled before the executive joins the board. Members could be given a role in determining these salaries if the executive directors' contractual entitlements were made subject to the approval of the members in general meeting. However, any company which tried to impose such arrangements would probably find it impossible to recruit executives of desired calibre.

The usual procedure is, therefore, for the board to enter into a contract with the executive director on behalf of the company when it appoints him. If the director is subsequently dismissed (e.g. by the members at the next annual general meeting), he will be entitled to damages for breach of contract. The amount of damages will depend on the directors' remuneration but also on the period of notice the company is required to give under the contract.

UK Corporate Governance Code

The UK Corporate Governance Code (Principles P and Q) requires listed companies to have remuneration policies and practices which should be designed to support strategy and promote long-term sustainable success. Executive remuneration should be aligned to company purpose and values, and be clearly linked to the successful delivery of the company's long-term strategy. A formal and transparent procedure for developing policy on executive remuneration and determining director and senior management remuneration should be established. No director should be involved in deciding their own remuneration outcome.

In practice, listed companies are expected to establish a remuneration committee of independent non-executive directors, with a minimum membership of three, or in the case of smaller companies, two. In addition, the chair of the board can only be a member if they were independent on appointment and cannot chair the committee. Before appointment as chair of the remuneration committee, the appointee should have served on a remuneration committee for at least 12 months (Code provision 32).

The company chairman may serve on the remuneration committee provided that he is considered independent on appointment as chairman (but should not also chair the committee). Before appointment as chair of the remuneration committee, the appointee should have served on a remuneration committee for at least 12 months (Code provision 32).

The code requires the remuneration committee to set the remuneration of the executive directors and the chairman (Code provision 33), and it is recommended, as a general principle, that no director should be involved in fixing his or her own remuneration. If the chair serves on the committee, this does not necessarily present an insurmountable obstacle as the chair could absent himself from discussions regarding his own remuneration or fees. It does, however, imply that the chair should be treated as an executive for the purposes of remuneration even though he may be treated as a non-executive for other purposes.

When determining executive director remuneration policy and practices (Code provision 40) the remuneration committee should address the following.

- *Clarity*: Remuneration arrangements should be transparent and promote effective engagement with shareholders and the workforce.
- *Simplicity*: Remuneration structures should avoid complexity and their rationale and operation should be easy to understand.
- *Risk*: Remuneration arrangements should ensure reputational and other risks from excessive rewards, and behavioural risks that can arise from target-based incentive plans, are identified and mitigated.
- *Predictability*: The range of possible values of rewards to individual directors and any other limits or discretions should be identified and explained at the time of approving the policy.
- *Proportionality*: The link between individual awards, the delivery of strategy and the long-term performance of the company should be clear. Outcomes should not reward poor performance.
- *Alignment to culture*: Incentive schemes should drive behaviours consistent with company purpose, values and strategy.

Duties of the remuneration committee

The UK Corporate Governance Code requires the remuneration committee to be given delegated responsibility for setting the remuneration of all executive directors and the chairman, including pension rights and any compensation payments.

The committee is also expected to recommend and monitor the level and structure of remuneration for senior management. The definition of 'senior management' for this purpose should be determined by the board but should normally include the first layer of management below board level (Code provision 33).

Latest recommendations add that the remuneration committee additionally should review workforce remuneration and related policies and the alignment of incentives and rewards with culture, taking these into account when setting the policy for executive director remuneration.

Statements in the annual report

There should be a description of the work of the remuneration committee in the annual report (Code provision 41), including:

- an explanation of the strategic rationale for executive directors' remuneration policies, structures and any performance metrics;
- reasons why the remuneration is appropriate using internal and external measures, including pay ratios and pay gaps;
- a description, with examples, of how the remuneration committee has addressed the factors in Code provision 40 (see above);
- whether the remuneration policy operated as intended in terms of company performance and quantum, and, if not, what changes are necessary;
- what engagement has taken place with shareholders and the impact this has had on remuneration policy and outcomes;
- what engagement with the workforce has taken place to explain how executive remuneration aligns with wider company pay policy; and
- to what extent discretion has been applied to remuneration outcomes and the reasons why.

It should be noted that the chairman of the remuneration committee should be in attendance at the annual general meeting (AGM) to support any questions raised by members on the content of their statement in the annual report. Given this is the most read section of the annual report, it should be expected that questions will be raised of the committee, either directly or indirectly, on its statement and its work.

Delegating powers to the committee: articles of association

The UK Corporate Governance Code envisages that the board will delegate authority to the remuneration committee to determine executive remuneration. This contrasts with the approach taken in the Cadbury Report (in para. 4.42) that the remuneration committee should make recommendations to the board, with the board making the actual decision. Most listed companies' articles contain a general power enabling the board to delegate any of their powers to a committee of the board.

In the *Guinness* case it was held that a general provision in the articles allowing the board to delegate its powers to board committees did not extend to powers specifically given by the articles to 'the board' which the board would not otherwise have. Accordingly, in order to delegate the power to determine directors' remuneration to a committee of the board, it is essential that the articles allow the board to delegate not only its general powers but also any special powers, or specifically allow the board to delegate its power to fix directors' remuneration. If the articles do not allow such delegation, the decisions of the remuneration committee must be formally ratified by the board. Although this might constitute a technical breach of the UK Corporate Governance Code, it would not contravene the spirit if the board, as a matter of policy, adopted the recommendations of the remuneration committee without debate. This procedure would, however, raise questions as to whether the executive directors should vote on the recommendations of the remuneration committee. Clearly, they should not do so with regard to their own remuneration, and it may, accordingly, be necessary to have a separate vote on the committee's proposals for each director.

Nomination committee

All listed companies are required by the UK Corporate Governance Code to establish a nomination committee to lead the process for board appointments and make recommendations to the board. A majority of members of the committee should be independent non-executive directors. The chair of the board should not chair the committee when it is dealing with the appointment of their successor (Code provision 17).

Although the UK Corporate Governance Code does not provide any specific guidance on the matter, nomination committees rarely consist of more than three directors. If an executive director (or possibly the chairman) is a member, this will be the minimum number required to comply with the requirement that the majority of members are independent non-executive directors. This may put pressure on companies to categorise the chairman as an independent non-executive even though he or she may not meet all the independence criteria in the Code.

Role of the committee

According to the UK Corporate Governance Code, the role of the committee is 'to lead the process for board appointments and make recommendations to the board'.

Specifics around the tenure of board members provide a clear guidance for the committee in terms of board review noting that all directors should be subject to annual re-election. The board should set out in the papers accompanying the resolutions to elect each director the specific reasons why their contribution is, and continues to be, important to the company's long-term sustainable success (Code provision 18).

In addition, the chair should not remain in post beyond nine years from the date of their first appointment to the board. To facilitate effective succession planning and the development of a diverse board, this period can be extended for a limited time, particularly in those cases where the chair was an existing non-executive director on appointment. A clear explanation should be provided (Code provision 19).

Open advertising and/or an external search consultancy should generally be used for the appointment of the chair and non-executive directors. If an external search consultancy is engaged it should be identified in the annual report alongside a statement about any other connection it has with the company or individual directors (Code provision 20).

The nomination committee should also lead on the formal and rigorous annual evaluation of the performance of the board, its committees, the chair and individual directors. The chair of the board should be encouraged to have a regular externally facilitated board evaluation. In FTSE 350 companies this should happen at least every three years. The external evaluator should be identified in the annual report and a statement made about any other connection it has with the company or individual directors. The chair should act on the results of the evaluation by recognising the strengths and addressing any weaknesses of the board. Each director should engage with the process and take appropriate action when development needs have been identified (Code provisions 21 and 22).

Statement in annual report

The annual report should describe the work of the nomination committee (Code provision 23), including:

- the process used in relation to appointments, its approach to succession planning and how both support developing a diverse pipeline;
- how the board evaluation has been conducted, the nature and extent of an external evaluator's contact with the board and individual directors, the outcomes and actions taken, and how it has or will influence board composition;
- the policy on diversity and inclusion, its objectives and linkage to company strategy, how it has been implemented and progress on achieving the objectives; and
- the gender balance of those in the senior management and their direct reports.

It should be noted that the chairman of the nomination committee should be in attendance at the AGM to support any questions raised by members on the content of their statement in the annual report.

Minutes

Although, it is good practice for any committee to keep minutes of its proceedings, it is much more important to do so for board committees. Articles often require minutes of board committee meetings to be kept. Even where they do not, it is likely that the directors are required to do so under the Act.

The model articles for public companies are silent on the requirement for committees to keep minutes and it is debatable whether the requirements of section 248(1) under the Act requiring every company to record minutes of all proceedings at meetings of directors extends to meetings of committees of the board. However, given most board committees have representatives of the board within their membership, it is best practice to assume that this requirement extends to keeping minutes of all committee meetings. For consistency, best practice would also be to keep minutes and their format aligned to those of the board.

The model articles for private companies do, however, require the directors to ensure that the company keeps a record in writing, for at least ten years from the date of the decision recorded, of every unanimous or majority decision taken by the directors (pcls 15 and clg 15). They also require majority decisions to be taken at meetings or for them to be unanimous (pcls 7 and clg 7), and state that committees must follow procedures which are based as far as they are applicable on the provisions of the articles which govern the taking of decisions by directors (pcls 6(1) and clg 6(1)). Assuming that the directors do not override the rule regarding minutes and records of decisions in respect of a committee (which it seems they may do under pcls 6(2) and clg 6(2)), it would appear, therefore, that the model articles for private companies require minutes of committee meetings to be kept.

The model articles for public companies do not specifically require minutes to be kept of board meetings but do specifically require records of written resolutions to be kept (plc 18(4)). Accordingly, when the article regarding procedures at committee meetings (plc 6(1)) is strictly applied it would appear that committees are required to keep records of any written resolutions but not minutes of their meetings. It is doubtful whether this is intentional and it would be open to the directors to require committees to keep minutes of their proceedings.

In practice, where power to bind the company has been delegated by the board to a committee, it will be necessary to keep minutes of the proceedings of board committees as evidence that transactions have been duly authorised. Even if the Act does not confer special evidential status on the minutes of board committees, it is possible that the common law would do so.

Conclusion

Committees can bring value to the effectiveness of a company, whether their implementation is dictated by requirements under the Code or as best practice implemented by the company. Meetings of these committees should, if only for consistency, follow the same practices in terms of administration, record keeping, processes and procedures as the main board of the company.

To ensure there is a clear delineation of roles, responsibilities and deliverables, having a terms of reference in place for each committee agreed by and signed off by the board is invaluable. This gives clarity to members of the committee as well as serving as a reminder to board members that they have a forum where more in-depth knowledge and/or time can be applied to specific topics. Terms of reference and membership of committees should also be reviewed on a regular basis by the board to ensure that they remain fit for purpose reflecting any changes in the company, its strategy, its market or its environment.

When supporting or working in, or with, a committee, the requirements of meetings of the directors should be reviewed as a framework to be adopted, noting any additional reporting that may be required in the annual report which, by extension, includes reporting at the annual general meeting of the members.

22 – Section 4 conclusion

Section 4 introduced the meeting requirements for other forums that are still connected to meetings of the board and are required company meetings. In the introduction, other meetings were introduced, including bondholder meetings that, although they fall outside of direct legislation, still predominantly follow the requirements legislated in the Companies Act 2006.

What should be noted is that, where a meeting needs to be convened, the first consideration should be on what basis it is being called. Is it required to follow the Act plus the content of the articles of the company? If so, it should follow the guidelines included herein, alongside any company-specific processes and procedures that have been adopted.

The meetings included in this section as separate chapters reflect those that still fall under the umbrella of company meetings and, as such, have been explained in more detail. However, if in doubt, it is easiest to follow the framework for meetings of directors for formal internal meetings and of general meetings for meetings with shareholders.

Conclusion

Throughout this book the aim has been to present the legal framework within which company meetings must be held, whether included in the Act or the articles of the company. As has been noted, this is a framework to be adopted. However, there is sufficient flexibility to enable each company to adopt processes and procedures that reflect their specific requirements based on company culture as well the size of the board and the breadth of their shareholders.

The two main types of meeting should be remembered when convening, attending, supporting or documenting meetings of a company.

Firstly, those of internal meetings of directors or representatives on committees, and the requirements for these meeting to adhere to both legislation and the articles of the company. This is necessary even though they may be seen as solely internal meetings that are frequently purely operational in content. As can be seen, despite this, there are a myriad of rules and requirements that must be accommodated and met for a company to remain compliant in its internal governance.

Secondly, meetings with shareholders have a clear legal framework dictated by law and under the articles of the specific company. This framework must be adhered to but does give flexibility in certain areas to enable companies to adopt processes and procedures that meet their individual requirements. It should be remembered that there are two purposes for holding meetings with shareholders, whether these are formal large gatherings or more flexible in their approach. These two purposes are for the board to seek approval via resolutions for actions to be taken, and for shareholders to have an opportunity to hold the board to account. Both parties benefit from a successful business, with the general meeting being a joining together of two parties with separate needs but the same goal.

As can be seen from the content of this book, the legislation sitting behind companies is extensive and can be complex. It would be simple to fall foul of legislative requirements through a drive to maintain company processes in isolation; unfortunately, this may happen unconsciously. Mapping both legal requirements and company requirements is key to creating a formal but effective and efficient framework for meetings of a company, in all their guises. The challenge and aim should be to understand the requirements then adopt and apply these in a practical manner that meets the requirements of the company without distracting from the core purpose of the company. The hope is that the contents of this book go some way to supporting those who need to implement or apply processes and procedures surrounding the meetings of a company.

Appendices

Appendix 1 – Matters requiring members' approval

Description of resolution	Type	CA 2006
Articles		
Alteration of articles of association (Note 1)	Special	21(1)
Alteration of an entrenched article (Note 1)	Higher majority than a special	22
Company name		
Change of company name (Note 1) May also be altered by other means provided for by the company's articles (see s. 79).	Special	77
Resolution of a Welsh company that its registered office is to be situated in Wales (Note 1)	Special	88(2)
Resolution of a Welsh company that its registered office is to be situated in England and Wales (Note 1)	Special	88(3)
Re-registration		
Re-registration of private company as public (Note 1)	Special	90(1)
Re-registration of public company as private (Note 1)	Special	97(1)
Re-registration of private company as unlimited	Unanimous	102
Re-registration of unlimited company as limited (Note 1)	Special	105(1)
Re-registration of public company as private unlimited	Unanimous	109
Directors		
Removal of a director (Notes 4 & 5)	Ordinary	168(1)
Approval of a directors' long-term service contract	Ordinary	188(2)
Approval of substantial property transaction involving director	Ordinary	190(1) and (2)
Approval of a loan to a director	Ordinary	197(1) and (2)
Approval of a quasi-loan to a director	Ordinary	198(2) and (3)

Description of resolution	Type	CA 2006
Approval of loans or quasi-loans to persons connected with directors	Ordinary	200(2) and (3)
Approval of credit transaction in favour of director	Ordinary	201(2) and (3)
Approval of related loan, quasi-loan and credit transaction arrangements	Ordinary	203(1) and (2)
Affirmation of a transaction or arrangement entered into by a company in contravention of section 197, 198, 200, 201 or 203	Ordinary	214
Approval of payment for loss of office to director	Ordinary	217(1) and (2)
Approval of payment for loss of office to a director in connection with the transfer of an undertaking	Ordinary	218(1) and (2)
Approval of payment for loss of office to a director in connection with a transfer of shares in the company, or a subsidiary, resulting from a takeover bid	Ordinary	219(1) and (2)
Ratification by a company of conduct by a director amounting to negligence, default, breach of duty or breach of trust in relation to the company (Note 6)	Ordinary	239(2)
Making provision for employees on cessation or transfer of business	Ordinary	247
Election of a proxy as the chairman of a general meeting	Ordinary	328
Political donations		
Authorisation of political donations or expenditure	Ordinary	366
Accounts		
Public company required to lay its accounts before the company in general meeting (Note 2)	[Ordinary]	437
Approval of directors' remuneration report of a quoted company	Ordinary	439(1)
Auditors		
Appointment of auditors by the members of a private company	Ordinary	485(4)
Appointment of auditors by the members of a public company	Ordinary	489(4)
Resolution to fix remuneration of auditors	Ordinary	492(1)
Removal of auditors (Note 4)	Ordinary	510(2)
Authorisation by private company of liability limitation agreement with auditors	Ordinary	536(2)

Description of resolution	Type	CA 2006
Authorisation by public company of liability limitation agreement with auditors	Ordinary	536(3)
Withdrawal of authorisation of liability limitation agreement with auditors	Ordinary	536(5)
Share capital		
Authority for directors to allot shares (Note 1)	Ordinary	551
Disapplication of pre-emption rights by a private company with only one class of shares (Note 1)	Special	569(1)
Disapplication of pre-emption rights: directors acting under general authorisation (Note 1)	Special	570(1)
Disapplication of pre-emption rights (Note 1)	Special	571(1)
Disapplication of pre-emption rights: sale of treasury shares (Note 1)	Special	573(2) and (4)
Transfer to public company of non-cash asset in initial period (Note 1)	Ordinary	601
Sub-division or consolidation of shares	Ordinary	618(3)
Reconversion of stock into shares	Ordinary	620
Redenomination of share capital (Note 1)	Ordinary	622
Reduction of capital in connection with redenomination (Note 1)	Special	626(2)
Variation of class rights: companies having a share capital (Note 1)	Special	630(4)
Variation of class rights: companies without a share capital (Note 1)	Special	631(4)
Reduction of capital with solvency statement (Note 1)	Special	641(1) and 642
Reduction of capital (court procedure) (Note 1)	Special	641(1) and 645
Authorisation of the directors of a limited company to determine the terms, conditions and manner of redemption of shares (Note 7)	Ordinary	685(1) and (2)
Authority for off-market purchase of own shares (Notes 1 and 6)	Special	694(2)
Variation of contract for off-market purchase (Notes 1 and 6)	Special	697
Release of company's rights under contract for off-market purchase (Notes 1 and 6)	Special	700
Authority for market purchase of own shares (Notes 1 and 3)	Ordinary / special	701(1) and (4)

Description of resolution	Type	CA 2006
Payment out of capital for the redemption or purchase of own shares (Notes 1 and 6)	Special	713 and 716
Debentures		
Power to re-issue redeemed debentures	Ordinary	752(1)
Schemes of arrangement, mergers and divisions		
Scheme of arrangement	75% majority by value of each class	899
Approval of a merger of a public company	75% majority by value of each class	907
Approval of articles of new transferee company (merger)	Ordinary	912
Approval of a division of a public company	75% majority by value of each class	922
Approval of articles of new transferee company (division)	Ordinary	928
Takeovers,		
Opting in and opting out resolutions by listed companies in relation to impediments to takeovers (Note 1)	Special	966(1) and (5)
Electronic communications		
Approval required for deemed agreement of members of company etc to use of website (Note 1)	Ordinary	Sch. 5, para. 10

Insolvency	Type	IA 1986
Resolution to wind up voluntarily (Note 1)	Special	s. 84(1)
Authorise liquidator to transfer assets of company to new company in exchange for securities in the new company (Note 1)	Special	s. 110(3)
Resolution to be wound up by court (Note 1)	Special	s. 122(1)
Members' voluntary winding up, to sanction liquidator's proposals for a compromise with the company's creditors (Note 1)	Special	s. 165(2)

Requirements found in articles	Type	Model Articles
Directions to directors (Note 1)	Special	pcls 4, clg 4 and plc 4
Resolution to disapply article provision which would otherwise prevent a director from being counted as participating in, or voting at, a directors' meeting	Ordinary	pcls 14, clg 14 and plc 17
Appointment of director (Note 8)	Ordinary	pcls 17, clg 17 and plc 20
Issue of a new class of shares	Ordinary	pcls 22 / plc 43
Final dividend	Ordinary	pcls 30 and plc 70
Capitalisation issue	Ordinary	pcls 36 / plc 78
Adjournment of general meeting (Note 9)	Ordinary	pcls 41, clg 27 and plc 33

Common law	Type	
Procedural resolutions at general meetings	Ordinary	

Listed companies	Type	Listing Rules
Cancellation of primary listing (Note 1)	Special	LR 5.2
Employee share schemes and long-term incentive plans	Ordinary	LR 9.4
Class 1 transactions	Ordinary	LR 10.5
Reverse takeover	Ordinary	LR 5.6
Related party transactions	Ordinary	LR 11.1
Class approval for purchase of own shares (Note 1)	Special	LR 12.4.7

Notes

1. Resolution must be filed at Companies House and embodied in the articles.
2. The Act does not specifically require the company to put a resolution to the members regarding the accounts. However, this is the standard way of dealing with the requirement to lay accounts. Laying means to make them an item of business.
3. The Pre-emption Group Guidelines require listed companies to pass a special resolution.
4. A resolution which requires special notice to be given in accordance with section 312.
5. Articles cannot exclude the members' right to remove a director by ordinary resolution.
6. Special voting rules apply to these resolutions (see the relevant section of the Act).

7. Although this resolution is not required by the Act to be embodied in the articles, it is suggested that the company does so (particularly where the resolution has the effect of amending the articles).

8. Articles also usually allow appointments of directors to be made by the board.

9. The chairman of the meeting is also given power to adjourn in certain circumstances

Appendix 2 – Chair's scripts

This appendix includes specimen scripts for use by the chair at general meetings. The examples given include scripts for:

- an annual general meeting (this is merely provided as an example and will need to be modified to reflect the resolutions to be proposed) (see Script 1);
- delaying the meeting to allow members to register (see Script 2);
- dealing with overcrowding in the meeting room (see Script 3);
- delaying the meeting to allow members attending electronically to gain access (see Script 4);
- a poll called by the Chair or one demanded by a member (see Script 5);
- a resolution to adjourn (see Script 6);
- dealing with amendments (see Script 7);
- dealing with disruption (see Script 8); and
- proposing a formal closure motion to put the question to the vote (see Script 9).

1   Chair's script for annual general meeting

    Chair: Ladies and gentlemen, I am pleased to welcome you to the annual general meeting of [Company] and declare the meeting open. I propose to take the notice of the meeting as read.

              SHORT PAUSE TO SEE WHETHER ANYONE OBJECTS

    Chair: Thank you. Before we start the business of the meeting, I would like to take this opportunity to explain how voting will be conducted on the matters before the meeting today, the procedures we will be following to afford as many people as possible with the opportunity to speak and ask questions and various other matters concerning the conduct of the meeting. (*See notes 1 to 5*)

              EXPLAIN VOTING SYSTEM AND PROCEDURES FOR SPEAKING AND ASKING QUESTIONS, ETC. ADD ANY SPECIFICS FOR THOSE ATTENDING VIRTUALLY SUCH AS THEIR MICROPHONES BEING MUTED, HOW THEY CAN ASK QUESTIONS ONLINE, HOW THEIR VOTES WILL BE

COUNTED (INCLUDING IF THEY HAD TO BE SUBMITTED PRIOR TO THE MEETING)

Chair: If you have any questions about any of these procedures, please ask a member of the company's staff for assistance. [If you are attending virtually, there is online assistance available [insert where]). [If you have any questions about your shareholding, please speak to a member of the registration team on the registration desk either during or after the meeting.] [If you have any questions about any other matter not connected with the business of the meeting, please speak to [person or persons]].

Chair: I now turn to the business of the meeting.

Chair: And I call upon [name of auditor] to read the report of the auditors to the financial statements.

AUDITOR TO READ REPORT

Resolution 1: Report and accounts

Chair: Thank you. I now propose resolution 1 in the notice of meeting [and on your voting cards], namely:

THAT the report of the directors and the audited accounts for the year ended [date], now laid before the meeting, be received.

A copy of the report and accounts was sent to members with the notice of this meeting [and published on our website]. But before putting the resolution to the vote, I would like to draw your attention to certain matters in the report and accounts and update you on the company's performance since the end of the financial year. I will then invite questions & comments from the floor.

CHAIR TO MAKE STATEMENT

Chair: I now invite questions and comments from the floor on the report and accounts. I will also take questions on my statement. If you wish, you may direct your questions to [Mr Z], the Chair of the Company's Audit Committee, who is seated to my [left/right].

INIVITE [MR Z] TO STAND SO THAT MEMBERS CAN IDENTIFY HIM

Chair: If you have a question or a point to make, I would be grateful if you [could make yourself known to the staff at the question point nearest to you][raise your hand and wait until a member of staff has supplied you with a microphone]. Before asking your question, you should state your name and whether you are a shareholder or a proxy or corporate representative of a shareholder. If you are a proxy or representative, please state both your name and the name of the shareholder you represent. (*See note 5*)

INVITE QUESTION AND COMMENTS FROM THE FLOOR

Chair: If nobody has any further questions or points to make on the report and accounts (*slight pause*), I would now ask you to vote on the resolution before the meeting, namely:

THAT the report of the directors and the audited accounts for the year ended [date], now laid before the meeting, be received.

[Those in favour (*pause to count votes*) – those against (*pause to count votes*).

I declare the resolution carried.] (*see note 1*)

Chair: [The proxy votes submitted before the meeting are shown on the screen and were as follows: [proxy votes]] (*see note 3*)

Resolution 2: Directors' remuneration report

Chair: I now propose resolution 2 in the notice of meeting [and on your voting cards], namely:

THAT the Directors' Remuneration Report for the year ended [date] be approved.

Before inviting question and comments from the floor, I would like to invite [Mr Y], the Chair of the Company's Remuneration Committee to explain briefly how the committee works.

CHAIR OF REMUNERATION COMMITTEE TO MAKE REPORT

Chair: I now invite questions and comments on the Directors' Remuneration Report. You may direct any questions you have on the Report either to me or [Mr Z].

AFTER DEALING WITH QUESTIONS, IF ANY

Chair: I now put the resolution THAT the Directors' Remuneration Report for the year ended [date] be approved.

[Those in favour (*pause to count votes*) – those against (*pause to count votes*)

I declare the resolution carried.] (*see note 1*)

Chair: [The proxy votes submitted before the meeting are shown on the screen and were as follows: [proxy votes]] (*see note 3*)

Resolution 3: Dividends

Chair: I now propose resolution 3 in the notice of meeting [and on your voting cards], namely:

THAT the final dividend of [5.8p] per share recommended by the directors of the Company be declared payable on [date] to the holders of ordinary shares registered at the close of business on [date].

Does anyone have any questions or points to make on this resolution?

AFTER DEALING WITH QUESTIONS, IF ANY

Chair: I now put the resolution THAT the final dividend of [5.8p] per share recommended by the directors of the Company be declared payable on [date] to the holders of ordinary shares registered at the close of business on [date].

[Those in favour (*pause to count votes*) – those against (*pause to count votes*)

I declare the resolution carried.] (*see note 1*)

Chair: [The proxy votes submitted before the meeting are shown on the screen and were as follows: [proxy votes]] (*see note 3*)

Resolutions 4: Re-election of director

Chair: I now turn to the re-election of directors retiring by rotation (resolutions 4 and 5 in the notice of meeting [and on your voting cards]). As you may be aware, under the company's articles of association one third of the directors (including the executive directors) must retire each year and offer themselves for re-election [and that any director who has not been re-elected at either of the last two annual general meetings must retire and offer themselves for re-election]. This year the directors to retire by rotation are [name] and me. As I am one of the directors seeking reappointment, it would not be right for me to propose that resolution. I will therefore ask my colleague [name] to do so when we come to that item. However, before doing so I have pleasure in proposing:

THAT [name], a director retiring by rotation, be re-elected a director of the company.

Chair: [Name] has been a director of the company since [year]. [Other statement regarding [name]. Brief biographical details regarding [name] can be found on page [x] of the notice of meeting.

           INVITE QUESTIONS & COMMENTS

Chair: I now put the resolution to the meeting. Those in favour [pause to count votes] – those against [pause to count votes].

           I declare the resolution carried.

Chair: Thank you. [The proxy votes submitted before the meeting are shown on the screen and were as follows: [proxy votes]] (*see note 3*)

Resolutions 5: Re-election of Chair as a director

Chair: I now call upon [name] to propose the next resolution (resolution 5 in the notice of meeting [and on your voting cards].

[Name]:   Thank you, I propose:

           THAT [name of Chair], a director retiring by rotation, be re-elected a director of the company.

           INVITE QUESTIONS & COMMENTS

Chair: If there are no [further] questions, I now put the resolution to the meeting.

           [Those in favour (*pause to count votes*) – those against (*pause to count votes*)

           I declare the resolution carried.] (*see note 1*)

Chair: Thank you. [The proxy votes submitted before the meeting are shown on the screen and were as follows: [proxy votes]] (*see note 3*)

Resolution 6: Reappointment of auditors

Chair: The next resolution (resolution 6 in the notice) is:

           THAT [name of auditors] be reappointed auditors of the company to hold office to the conclusion of the next general meeting at which accounts are laid and that their remuneration be fixed by the directors and I ask [name of shareholder], a shareholder, to propose this resolution.

[Shareholder]: I propose the resolution.

Chair: Thank you. The reappointment of the auditors has been recommended by the Company's Audit Committee. If you wish, you may direct your questions to [Mr Z], the Chair of the Audit Committee, or to me. I can confirm that the Company is not proposing to adopt an auditors' liability limitation agreement as we do not feel it would be in the best interests of shareholders to do so.

INVITE QUESTIONS & COMMENTS

Chair: If there are no further questions or comments, I now put the resolution to the meeting, namely THAT [name of auditors] be reappointed auditors of the company to hold office to the conclusion of the next general meeting at which accounts are laid and that their remuneration be fixed by the directors.

[Those in favour (*pause to count votes*) – those against (*pause to count votes*)

I declare the resolution carried.] (*see note 1*)

Chair: [The proxy votes submitted before the meeting are shown on the screen and were as follows: [proxy votes]] (*see note 3*)

Resolution 7: Adoption of new Articles of Association

Chair: I now turn to the last item of business on the agenda for today's meeting, namely resolution 7. I therefore propose as a special resolution:

THAT the regulations in the document produced at the meeting, and signed by me so as to identify it, be adopted as the company's articles of association in substitution for and to the exclusion of all existing articles of association of the Company.

The reasons for recommending these alterations and their effect is explained on page [No.] of the notice of this meeting. In view of the number of changes it was decided that it would be easier to adopt new articles incorporating all of the changes to the existing articles. As the adoption of new articles is proposed, a separate resolution to renew the directors' authority to allot unissued shares in the capital of the Company will not be put to the annual general meeting. Instead, new allotment authority amounts have been inserted in the new articles of association and will become effective if the resolution to adopt the new articles is passed. The relevant amounts are set out on page [No.] of the notice.

I am happy to take questions on this item of business but may ask [name from the company's solicitors or the Company Secretary] to deal with any technical or legal points which arise.

INVITE QUESTIONS & COMMENTS

If there are no further questions, I now put the resolution to the meeting.

[Those in favour (*pause to count votes*) – those against (*pause to count votes*)

I declare the resolution carried.] (*see note 1*)

Chair: [The proxy votes submitted before the meeting are shown on the screen and were as follows: [proxy votes]] (*see note 3*)

Close the meeting

Chair: That concludes the business of the meeting and I thank you for your patience. Refreshments will now be served in [place]. All the directors will be available to answer any additional questions which you may have. We will be wearing [red badges/a buttonhole] so that you can identify us. Thank you. We look forward to seeing you next year.

Notes

1. ***Voting*** – Some companies now take all votes on substantive resolutions at general meetings on poll rather than on a show of hands. Other companies take a show of hands but automatically proceed to a poll on every substantive resolution. Other companies may utilise electronic voting methods. Where this is the case, the script will need to be modified accordingly. In some cases companies ask shareholders to complete the voting card on each resolution at the same time that it is put to the meeting (for example, the Chair may say 'I now invite members to vote on resolution number [x] on their voting cards, namely that ...'). In other cases, the Chair puts all the resolutions to the meeting at or near the beginning of the meeting and then invites question or comments on each item in turn. Some companies prefer to do this because it allows members to vote on all the resolutions immediately, enabling those who want to do so to enter their votes on the voting card and hand them in at any stage during the proceedings. Where this is done the Chair will need to explain the voting procedures at the start of the meeting.

2. ***Electronic voting*** – The Chair may also need to explain how any electronic voting methods should be used, and potentially include an initial test vote to ensure attendees can vote and that the results can be received. Such a test

vote would need to include a question that would return both yes/for and no/against answers from voters.

3. ***Disclosure of proxy votes*** – In the case of a listed company, the Chair may also need to disclose details of proxy votes submitted in advance by way of voting instructions on each resolution after any vote on a show of hands. The Chair may need to explain at the start of the meeting how these proxy votes will be disclosed, particularly if no votes are to be taken on a show of hands.

4. ***Conduct of the meeting*** – If the meeting is being held in more than one location, the Chair may need to explain how the proceedings will be managed. It may be preferable for a person at each subsidiary location to give a separate explanation simultaneously while the Chair is doing so at the main meeting location.

5. ***Questions*** – Shareholders of listed companies have something akin to a right to ask questions. Accordingly, the Chair should be careful to give adequate opportunity for them to do so.

2   Registration incomplete

Chair: Despite our best efforts to speed up registration there are still people who are waiting to register. I am told that registration is likely to be completed in about [15 minutes] and I therefore propose, with your consent, to delay the start of the meeting until [time].

IF ANYONE OBJECTS

Chair: There is room to accommodate everyone now waiting outside and I believe it would be courteous to them to wait [15] minutes so that they can be admitted.

Note: If necessary, temporary registration cards should be used so that those affected can be admitted. If a vote is required the votes of those with temporary cards could be taken by requiring them to register.

3   Room too small

Chair: Despite booking a room which we expected to be large enough, it is clear that not everyone can be accommodated in this room.

There are approximately [ ] people waiting to get in. People other than members present in person, by corporate representative or by proxy are reminded that they have no absolute right to be present at the meeting. In order to enable members who are outside to be accommodated in this hall, which is where the meeting is being held, it would be most helpful if about [ ] persons present who are not members or proxy holders or corporate representatives of members could volunteer to go to [another specified room]. [There is a one-way audio link so that those in the [specified room] will be able to hear the debate.]

IF ANNOUNCEMENT IS MADE AFTER TIME SET FOR THE MEETING

Chair: I propose, with your consent, to delay the start of the meeting until [ ] to enable everyone to get settled.

IF ANYONE OBJECTS

Chair: There is room to accommodate all members in this room and all non-members who cannot get into this room in the [ ] room. It would be courteous to those outside to wait [half an hour] to enable everyone to be accommodated.

Note: If after [fifteen minutes] non-members have left but registration is still not complete, temporary registration cards should be used so that those affected can be admitted. If a vote is required the votes of those with temporary cards should be taken by requiring them to register.

IF PEOPLE REFUSE TO MOVE OR THE ARRANGEMENTS FOR USING THE ROOM DO NOT WORK FOR ANY REASON

Chair: It is clear that not everyone can be accommodated in this room. Unfortunately, if this meeting is to proceed to business it will be necessary for at least [ ] non-members to leave the meeting to enable members and proxy holders outside this room to get in. Will these people please leave [and go to the [ ] room].

IF INSUFFICIENT NON-MEMBERS LEAVE

Chair: As non-members are unwilling to leave I propose to adjourn this meeting for [15] minutes while the stewards assist in accommodating them in the [ ] room. If insufficient non-members leave then this meeting cannot continue. If we have to reconvene this meeting further delay and additional expense will be incurred. This can be avoided if non-members (and that includes members of the press who are not themselves members) who have no entitlement to attend this meeting, now leave [and go to the [ ] room].

IF RESISTANCE IS ENCOUNTERED

Chair: In the circumstances I have no alternative other than to propose the adjournment of this meeting to an alternative venue [which we have arranged at [   ] on [   ] at [   ]]. In order to ensure a valid vote on the question of adjournment I ask again if non-members will please leave now. They should not miss anything as they will have the opportunity to attend the adjourned meeting if the vote to adjourn the meeting is passed.

IF NON-MEMBERS DO THEN LEAVE AND MEMBERS GET IN – PUT MOTION TO ADJOURN TO A VOTE. IF NECESSARY CALL A POLL

IF EVERYBODY IS STILL NOT ACCOMMODATED

Chair: There are still some members outside but I am going to put to the vote my proposal to adjourn to [   ] on [   ] at [   ] anyway. The stewards will attempt to count the votes of those outside.

IF THE VOTE IS LOST ON A SHOW OF HANDS, AN ATTEMPT SHOULD BE MADE TO PUT IT TO A POLL

Chair: I also adjourn the meeting on my own authority pursuant to the inherent power vested in me as Chair of this meeting. A further registration form will be posted to you to enable you to attend the adjourned meeting. [If you are uncertain whether you will be able to attend this meeting, proxy cards can be collected on the way out.] Proxies should be returned by [not less than 48 hours before the time of the adjourned meeting].

Notes:

4 VIRTUAL MEETING DELAY TO START

Chair: Despite our best efforts there are still people who are attempting to join our meeting electronically. I am told that our systems will enable full online attendance which is likely to be completed in about [10 minutes] and I therefore propose, with your consent, to delay the start of the meeting until [time].

Notes:

5 Poll procedures

Subject to the articles, the Chair has power to suspend the proceedings for the purposes of taking a poll on a resolution. If the demand for a poll is valid, the

poll is normally taken either immediately or at the end of the meeting after any other business has been concluded. A poll may need to be taken immediately because the nature of the business requires it (e.g. a poll on resolution to adjourn) or because the articles require all polls to be taken immediately. A poll called on an amendment will need to be taken before the vote on the substantive resolution. See further Chapter 15 on voting, adjournment and amendments.

5.A Poll called by Chair

Chair: In the circumstances, I exercise my right [under the articles] as Chair of the meeting to call a poll on the resolution. The poll will be conducted [immediately] [at the end of the meeting and in the meantime I will proceed with the remaining business of the meeting] [on [date], at [time] and [place] and in the meantime I will proceed with the remaining business of the meeting].

WHEN TIME FOR POLL, GO TO POLL PROCEDURE AT 5.C

5.B Demand by a member

Member(s): [Demand(s) a poll.]

Chair: [I should point out that proxies representing [number] of votes have instructed me to vote in favour of the resolution and that proxies have given me discretion as to how to vote in respect of [number] of shares, which I also intend to vote in favour of the resolution, giving a total of [number] of votes in favour. This represents [percent] of all of the proxy votes lodged when the [number] votes which proxies have instructed me to vote against the resolution are included. In view of the [considerable] level of support in favour of the resolution, it seems highly likely that it will be carried [by a significant majority/by the required majority of 75%]. As the conduct of a poll is a lengthy process, do those calling for a poll still feel that this is a worthwhile exercise?]

IF MEMBER STANDS DOWN

Chair: Thank you. I will proceed with the business of the meeting.

IF MEMBER PERSISTS

Chair: Under the Company's Articles of Association, a poll can only be demanded by the Chair or by [state relevant conditions].

Do you satisfy any of these conditions?

IF NO, RULE OUT OF ORDER AND:

(A) IF THE POLL WAS DEMANDED BEFORE A SHOW OF HANDS, PROCEED WITH THE VOTE ON A SHOW OF HANDS.

(B) IF THE POLL WAS DEMANDED AFTER A SHOW OF HANDS, STATE THAT THE RESULT OF THE VOTE ON THE SHOW OF HANDS STILL STANDS AND DECLARE THE RESOLUTION CARRIED [OR NOT CARRIED], WHETHER OR NOT THIS DECLARATION WAS PREVIOUSLY MADE

IF YES:

Chair: So that we can verify that the request is properly made, will you please provide your name(s) and details to the Company's Registrar.

IF VALID DEMAND FOR POLL ON RESOLUTION TO ADJOURN, GO TO 5.C

OTHERWISE

Chair: If the poll has been validly demanded, it will be conducted [immediately. Accordingly, I would ask members to be patient while we check whether the demand is valid.] [at the end of the meeting and I will explain the procedures when the time comes. In the meantime, I propose to proceed with the other business of the meeting] [on a later date which I will announce before the close of the meeting.]

IF NOT TO BE TAKEN IMMEDIATELY, RETURN TO MAIN SCRIPT

WHEN REMAINING BUSINESS COMPLETE, GO TO POLL PROCEDURE AT 5.C

5.C Conduct of poll

Chair: A poll on resolution [No.] [text of resolution] will now be conducted [by our Registrars] and I would ask the Secretary to describe the procedure for taking the poll.

Secretary: Please remain in your seats while the poll is being conducted. Polling cards will now be distributed.

On a poll each member present in person, by corporate representative or proxy has one vote for every share held. If you have already lodged a form of proxy you do not have to vote again now unless you wish to change the way you originally voted. If you do not wish to change your mind it will speed up the poll procedure if you do not vote again now.

A separate poll card should be used for each separate holding. If you are representing more than one holding, please ask for additional cards as necessary. If you are not authorised or do not want to vote all the shares owned by a member, you should indicate the number of shares to be voted in the appropriate box on the voting card. If you do not, all the shares registered in your name or in the name of the person you are representing will be included in the count. If two or more persons are jointly registered as shareholders, any one of them may vote either in person or by proxy. If more than one of the joint holders votes, then only the vote of the joint holder whose name appears first on the register of members will be counted.

Proxies and corporate representatives should complete a separate voting card and should provide their own details and the name of the member they represent. If requested to do so corporate representatives must be prepared to provide the registrars with some form of identification and their written authority to exercise the votes.

Note. Articles rarely require presentation of authority and it should only be insisted upon if a reasonable suspicion exists of wrongdoing.

Completed cards should be placed in one of the boxes at the exits from the hall. If you are unsure about how to complete the voting card or have any other questions about the poll procedures our staff will be pleased to answer your queries.

IN ADDITION TO CASTING HIS OWN VOTE (IF ANY), CHAIR SHOULD COMPLETE VOTING CARDS FOR AND AGAINST THE RESOLUTION IN ACCORDANCE WITH THE PROXIES HELD BY HIM.

AFTER A SUITABLE INTERVAL THE CHAIR SHOULD GIVE NOTICE OF HIS INTENTION TO CLOSE THE POLL

Chair: I intend to declare the poll closed in five minutes. Please ensure that your completed card has been handed in.

WHEN THE CARDS HAVE ALL BEEN HANDED IN

EITHER:

Chair: Thank you ladies and gentlemen, the poll is now closed. The voting cards will be processed by the scrutineers who will calculate the results of the poll as soon as possible. The results of the poll will be announced in this room but this will probably take about [ ] hours. I therefore adjourn the meeting pending the declaration of the result of the poll.

OR:

Chair: Thank you ladies and gentlemen. The poll is now closed. As the results of the poll will need to be checked, it will not be possible to know the result for some time. We expect that the result of the poll(s) will [be published on our website and in an announcement via our regulatory information service]. This concludes the business of the meeting and I now declare the meeting closed pending the calculation of the results. Thank you very much for attending.

Notes

1. **Virtual attendance and related actions** – Where members are able to attend virtually, the process for their response to a poll and how these will be processed should be included in the instructions.

6   Adjournment

6.A Proposal for Adjournment by the Chair

The motion for adjournment should include the day, time and place of the adjourned meeting or authorise the Board or the Chair to determine such matters. The Chair should give his views on or reasons for the proposal and invite debate from the floor.

The Chair has an inherent power, in limited circumstances, to adjourn the meeting if it is necessary to enable members to debate and vote on the business of the meeting (for example, if the room is too small to accommodate those entitled to attend or to deal with a disturbance).

If the meeting is adjourned, further proxies may become valid as the articles may allow proxies to be lodged up to 48/24 hours before the time of the adjourned meeting.

Chair: In accordance with Article [ ] of the Company's Articles of Association I propose that this meeting be adjourned:

■ [for [x] minutes]

■ [to [another place]]

- [until date, time and place]

- [indefinitely]

- [to a time, date and place to be fixed by the directors and notified to members].

AFTER DEBATE ENDS

I now propose to put the proposal to adjourn to the vote. Ladies and gentlemen the proposal is that the meeting be adjourned:

- [for [x] minutes]

- [to [another place]]

- [until date, time and place]

- [indefinitely]

- [to a time, date and place to be fixed by the directors and notified to members].
Will those in favour of the proposal to adjourn please raise their hands / [colour] voting cards.

Thank you.

Those against. Thank you.

IF VOTE CARRIED EITHER:

Chair: The proposal to adjourn the meeting has been carried.

This meeting stands adjourned:

- [for [x] minutes]

- [to [another place]]

- [until date, time and place]

- [indefinitely]

- [to a time, date and place to be fixed by the directors and notified to members].

IF VOTE NOT CARRIED:

Chair: I declare the resolution not passed on a show of hands and in accordance with article [No.] of the Company's Articles of Association I therefore exercise my right to demand a poll on the proposal to adjourn the meeting.

Note: The Chair should state how he intends to vote the proxies that he holds. When deciding how to cast the votes of proxies the Chair should consider the intentions of the shareholders who have appointed him as their proxy and act accordingly. Therefore, how the Chair votes will depend on the circumstances. If in doubt the Chair should seek advice on the matter.

THE POLL MAY NEED TO BE TAKEN IMMEDIATELY

GO TO POLL PROCEDURES AT 5.C.

6.B Proposal for adjournment from the floor

Member: I propose that the meeting be adjourned.

Chair: Are you a member, proxy or corporate representative?

IF NO:

Chair: Rule out of order.

IF YES:

Chair: I will ask the Registrars to verify your status. Will shareholders please bear with me while this exercise is completed.

Note: This must be done immediately – no other business can be carried out if a valid proposal to adjourn is outstanding.

IF STATUS IS NOT CORRECT:

Chair: The Registrars advise me that you do not have the required status to propose an adjournment. I therefore rule the proposed adjournment out of order. (Return to main script.)

IF STATUS IS CORRECT:

Chair: What exactly is your proposal? How long do you propose the adjournment should be for?

Member: [At least [No of days] – give reasons].

Chair: Would your proposal then be [for example, to adjourn for a minimum of [No of days] to a place, date and time to be fixed by the Board]?

Note: The Chair may have to assist the shareholders in formulating a suitable proposal.

Member: [Yes]

Note: The Chair should allow the Member to explain his point of view and allow debate on the motion generally.

Chair: I now propose to put the proposal to adjourn to the vote. Ladies and gentlemen, the proposal is that the meeting be adjourned [in accordance with the proposal agreed with the member]. Will those in favour of the proposal place please raise their hands/[colour] voting cards.

Thank you.

PAUSE TO ESTIMATE VOTES.

Those against. Thank you.

IF PROPOSAL IS CARRIED, CHAIR COULD CALL FOR A POLL:

Note: When deciding how to cast the votes of proxies, the Chair must consider the intentions of the shareholders who have appointed him as their proxy and act accordingly. Therefore how the Chair votes will depend on the circumstances. For instance, if the intention of the adjournment is to defeat the resolution, the Chair should cast the votes of those proxies who voted against the resolution in favour of the proposal to adjourn. If in doubt the Chair should seek advice on the matter.

Chair: In accordance with Article [No] of the Company's Articles of Association, I call for a poll on the proposal to adjourn the meeting. On this poll on the proposal to adjourn I am assuming that those members who have appointed me with a direction that I vote in favour of [resolution [   ]] [the resolutions proposed in the notice of meeting] approve of the conduct of the business before the meeting at this time.

Accordingly, I intend to cast those votes against the proposal to adjourn. I also propose to cast against the proposal those votes where I have been given a discretion how to vote. These amount in total to [   ] votes. [I intend to abstain] in relation to those members who have appointed me with a direction that I vote against [resolution [   ]] [the resolutions proposed in the notice of meeting].

GO TO POLL PROCEDURE AT 5.C.

IF PROPOSAL NOT CARRIED, PROCEED WITH BUSINESS OF MEETING

IF PROPOSAL IS NOT CARRIED BUT THERE IS A CALL FOR
A POLL FROM THE FLOOR:

Chair: A proposal to adjourn the meeting has been called for. Before I
explain the procedure I think the meeting should be aware that on
the poll I am assuming that those members who have appointed
me with a direction that I vote in favour of [resolution [   ]] [the
resolutions proposed in the notice of meeting] approve of the
conduct of the business before the meeting at this time.
Accordingly, I intend to cast those votes against the proposal to
adjourn. I also propose to cast against the proposal those votes
where I have been given a discretion how to vote. These amount
in total to [   ] votes. I intend to abstain in relation to those
members who have appointed me with a discretion that I vote
against [resolution [   ]] [the resolutions proposed in the notice of
meeting]. In view of the substantial majority of votes against the
proposal to adjourn and as the conducting of a poll is a lengthy
process, do those calling for a poll feel that this is a worthwhile
exercise?

IF PROPOSAL IS WITHDRAWN PROCEED WITH BUSINESS
OF MEETING

IF MEMBER PERSISTS, GO TO POLL PROCEDURE AT 5.B.

7   Demand for an amendment to a resolution

*An amendment to an ordinary resolution must be relevant to the resolution
and with the scope of the notice convening the meeting. Otherwise, it should
be ruled out of order. In addition, the amendment must not be so fundamental
as to destroy the intent of the original resolution. If it does, it should be ruled
out of order. A special resolution may only be passed in the form set out in the
notice, so any amendment (other than typographical or grammatical
corrections) should be ruled out of order.*

Chair: Can you tell me whether you are a member, proxy or a corporate
representative of a member.

IF NOT, PROPOSED AMENDMENT SHOULD BE RULED
OUT OF ORDER.

Chair: What is your full name and in what name is the shareholding
registered? I will ask the Registrars to verify your status. Will
shareholders please bear with me while this exercise is completed.

IF STATUS IS NOT CORRECT:

Chair: The Registrar advises me that you do not have the required status to call for an amendment so I must rule the proposed amendment out of order.

RETURN TO THE MAIN SCRIPT.

IF STATUS IS CORRECT.

Chair: The Registrar advises me that your status has been verified. Would you now please state precisely what your proposed amendment is.

Member: [............................]

Note: The Chair and the Secretary may need to assist the member in framing the amendment.

Chair: The proposal is that we amend Resolution [ ] to read as follows

[...........................]

Note: Chair gives his views on the amendment (taking advice as necessary) and invites debate from the floor, taking comments/ questions in turn. After debate ends, the Chair assesses the mood of the meeting and (if appropriate) asks whether in the light of the debate the person wishes to withdraw the proposed amendment. If the member does withdraw, return to the main script. If person does not withdraw, or there appears to be support for the amendment, the Chair should propose a vote.

Chair: I now put the proposal to amend the Resolution to the vote. The proposal is [repeat proposed amendment].

Those in favour of the proposal to amend the resolution please raise your hands/voting cards.

Thank you.

Those against?

IF AMENDMENT IS CARRIED, CHAIR MAY DEMAND A POLL.

Chair: In accordance with article [No.] of the Company's Articles of Association I exercise my right to demand a poll on the proposal to amend resolution [ ].

On this poll on the proposal to amend resolution [ ], I am assuming that those members who have appointed me with a direction that I vote in favour of the resolution which it is proposed to amend approve of the resolution in its existing form. Accordingly, I intend to cast those votes against the proposal to amend the resolution. I also propose to cast against the proposal those votes where I have been given a discretion how to vote. These amount in total to [ ] votes. I intend to abstain in relation to those members who have appointed me with a discretion that I vote against the resolution which it is proposed to amend.

GO TO POLL PROCEDURE AT 5.C

IF AMENDMENT NOT CARRIED, PROCEED TO A VOTE ON THE SUBSTANTIVE RESOLUTION UNLESS A POLL IS DEMANDED FROM THE FLOOR, IN WHICH CASE, PROCEED AS FOLLOWS.

Chair: A poll on the proposed amendment to resolution [No.] has been called for. Before I explain the procedure I think that the meeting should be aware that on the poll I am assuming that those members who have appointed me with a direction that I vote in favour of the resolution which it is proposed to amend approve of the resolution in its existing form. Accordingly, I intend to cast those votes against the proposal to amend the resolution. I also propose to cast against the proposal those votes where I have been given a discretion how to vote. These amount in total to [ ] votes. I intend to abstain in relation to those members who have appointed me with a direction that I vote against the resolution which it is proposed to amend. In view of the substantial majority of votes against the proposal to amend the resolution, and as the conducting of a poll is a lengthy process, do those calling for a poll feel that this is a worthwhile exercise?

Note: As regards proxy votes against the resolution, it is difficult to decide whether the Chair should vote them for or against the amendment. Accordingly, the safest course is to abstain. The proxy form should be drafted so as to give the Chair the discretion to vote as he thinks fit on other business at the meeting (including adjournments and amendments validly coming before the meeting). The Chair may wish to adopt the proposed amendment.

IF MEMBER WITHDRAWS:

Chair: As you have now decided not to call for a poll, I will proceed with the business of the meeting. I therefore intend to propose the resolution in its original format. Are there any more questions or comments on the main resolution?

RETURN TO MAIN SCRIPT

IF MEMBER PERSISTS, GO TO POLL PROCEDURE AT 5.B

8   Disruption

Chair: Would you please be quiet so that other members can be heard and the meeting can proceed.

Member: No [or equivalent]

Chair: If you do not stop, I will have to ask you to leave the meeting.

Member: No [or equivalent]

Chair: This behaviour is intolerable. With the consent of the meeting I propose to expel you from this meeting [pause to assess dissension]. [Mr X] would you please arrange for the stewards to escort this gentleman/lady from the meeting.

IF DISRUPTION IS SUCH AS TO REQUIRE A BRIEF ADJOURNMENT

Chair: It is quite impossible for this meeting to continue while this disruption is going on. In order to allow tempers to cool and to enable order to be restored, I declare this meeting adjourned for 15 minutes or, if necessary, until order has been restored.

Note: In the event that disruption comes from an external source – e.g. a fire alarm is set off – consult advisers. It may be possible to have a short interruption and avoid a full adjournment.

9   Vote on closure of the debate

Chair: We have now debated this proposal for [time] and I believe that despite the opposition of a small minority, most members would like now to vote on the resolution.

IF NO OPPOSITION, ANNOUNCE A VOTE ON THE RESOLUTION

IF THERE IS STILL OPPOSITION TO THIS

Chair: In the circumstances I formally propose the following procedural motion, namely:

"THAT the debate be closed and a vote be now taken on the resolution before the meeting".

No debate is allowed on such a motion. Accordingly, I will shortly be asking you to vote on the motion by a show of hands. If the motion is defeated, the debate on the main resolution will be allowed to continue. If the motion is carried, we will then proceed immediately with a vote on the main resolution before the meeting.

PROCEED TO VOTE ON A SHOW OF HANDS

Chair: I declare the motion carried. Accordingly we will now vote on the original resolution before the meeting.

IF CLOSURE MOTION IS NOT CARRIED, DISCUSSION ON THE RESOLUTION MUST BE ALLOWED TO CONTINUE

Appendix 3 – Specimen briefing document for AGM

1. **Location**
   The company's AGM will take place at [Venue], [Address]
   The areas being used are as follows:

Registration	Foyer, ground floor
Cloakroom	Foyer, ground floor
Shareholders' catering	[Room 1], third floor
Customer Enquiries	[Room 1], third floor
Shareholder Enquiries	[Room 1], third floor
Exhibition	[Room 2], third floor
Board members' lounge	[Room 3], third floor
Registrars' room	[Room 4], third floor
Organisers' office	[Room 5], third floor
Press office	[Room 6], third floor
Investor relations office	[Room 7], third floor
Researchers' room	[Room 8], third floor
AGM	[Room 9 and Room 2], third floor
Lunch	[Room 10], second floor

2. **Car Parking**
   Chauffeurs bringing directors and their guests to the AGM may drive onto the forecourt of the [Venue]. If chauffeurs remain with their vehicles, they may wait on the forecourt but otherwise they must leave the area for the duration of the AGM.

   There are no car parking facilities for company staff or shareholders on site, but there are car parks within walking distance at [locations].

3. **Timetable**
   [Day before AGM]
   Delivery and installation of stage set, display stands, question and answer system and exhibition panels throughout the morning.

14.00	Company staff arrive for familiarisation tours and briefing
14.30	Registrars' equipment delivery and installation
16.00	Lighting check

16.30	Company researchers arrive for briefing with Q & A personnel in [Room 8]
17.00	Directors arrive for rehearsals

[Day of AGM]

08.00	Chair's rehearsal
08.30	Company staff arrive
08.45	Security and fire safety briefing
09.30	All staff at their posts
09.45	All public areas to be ready
10.00	Doors open
10.55	Board escorted onto stage
11.00	AGM commences
13.00–13.30	AGM ends
13.30	Lunch commences
14.00	Displays dismantled and removed according to agreed delivery schedule
18.00	All company equipment to be removed from the building

4. **Security and Fire Safety Procedures**
    In the event of an emergency, the security personnel at [Venue] will take all necessary action. If a suspicious object is discovered or if there is any other security or safety problem, please contact the organisers' office in [Room 5] immediately. The organisers can then take steps to contact all the relevant authorities.

    Company personnel will be briefed by Venue staff on the fire alarm and safety procedures at the Security and Fire Safety Briefing on the morning of the AGM. The Venue has confirmed that there will be no fire alarm tests on the day of the AGM.

    In the event of a fire alarm or security alert, the chair will immediately adjourn the meeting [for a short period] in order to establish whether the Venue needs to be evacuated. If on the advice of Venue staff, it is recommended that the venue be evacuated, the chair will adjourn the meeting for [one hour] but also inform them that if it proves to be impossible to reconvene in [one hour] that the meeting will be adjourned until further notice. Members and guests will then be requested to leave the venue by the designated exits. Company personnel should assist and guide members and guests (particularly those who are disabled) to the exits.

    If it proves to be possible to re-enter the Venue and to reconvene the meeting within [one hour], Registration Personnel should only admit those who have the correct badges or who can prove their identity in some other way.

5.   **First Aid Procedures**
First aid staff from St John's Ambulance Brigade will be in attendance at the Meeting and there is a fully equipped first aid room on site. In the event of an emergency, please contact the St John's Ambulance Brigade representative in [Room 2] direct or contact the organisers' office in [Room 5].

6.   **Guidelines for [Company] Registration Personnel**
Registration is the point at which it is established whether people have the right to attend the meeting and also the means whereby shareholder attendance numbers are obtained. Company personnel are to follow the procedures set out below:

(a)   Shareholders should bring with them their admission card sent to them with the company's annual report. (Samples will be provided to company personnel involved.)

(b)   Shareholders producing such cards should be asked to hand you the card in return for which you should give them a yellow shareholder (voting) card and a folder containing the Chair's welcome letter and notice for the meeting. Shareholders are also to be provided with a badge. It is imperative that you obtain their admission card before handing them a shareholder badge card and folder. Thereafter, shareholders are free to make their way to the lifts for the exhibition and catering area and meeting room which are all on the third floor.

(c)   Shareholders who wish to bring a guest into the meeting with them can do so but the guest is to be given a shareholder guest badge together with a pink guest card (which is non-voting), and a folder.

(d)   Where two people are joint shareholders and both wish to attend, only the first named may have a yellow voting card, the second must be given a pink guest card and folder. Although the second shareholder is not technically a guest, this is the only practical way of preventing a double vote against a single holding.

(e)   Staff shareholders who only hold free and matching shares are not entitled to attend the meeting and any staff producing any blue card should be referred to [Registrars] personnel.

(f)   Institutional shareholders or corporate bodies are entitled to appoint a corporate representative to attend the meeting and vote on their behalf. Such corporate representatives should produce a letter of authorisation on their company letter heading to this effect. Such letters should be signed by their company secretary or director and strictly speaking should also bear their company's seal, but the latter is not always applied. If you consider this letter to be authentic hand the representative a shareholder badge, a yellow shareholder voting card and folder. If you are in any doubt refer the individual to [Registrars] personnel.

(g) Shareholders without admission cards or anyone who says they are a proxy, should be referred to the desks staffed by [Registrars] personnel.

(h) Likewise, there are separate registration procedures for the press and guests of the company who should be referred to the appropriate desk.

(i) Under no circumstances should anyone who does not have any means of identification be admitted. If in any doubt, refer to [Name] of [Registrars] who will contact security if necessary.

(j) Please retain all admission cards as the barcodes on these cards will be scanned by [Registrars] personnel during the meeting to enable an accurate count of shareholders attending.

7. Guidelines for [Registrars] Verification Personnel

Verification is the area which handles shareholders who cannot be admitted to the meeting directly through registration. Most of these will be shareholders who have forgotten their admission cards but there may also be proxies.

The clerical procedures are as follows:

(a) A person claiming to be a shareholder who has forgotten his voting card should be asked his name, address and number of shares. These details should be compared to the details on the computer and if the details agree the shareholder should be asked to sign the attendance record and is given a yellow shareholder voting card.

(b) A person claiming to be a proxy should be asked his name and that of the shareholder he represents. These details should be compared to the list of proxies provided and if the details agree the proxy should be asked to sign the attendance record and given a blue proxy card. Any proxy who is not on the list may not be admitted, except as a guest under certain circumstances.

(c) There will be separate registration procedures for people who are guests of the company or members of the press, and these people should be referred to the appropriate desk staffed by company personnel.

(d) Employees who hold free and matching shares or share options are not shareholders and may only be admitted to the meeting if they have stock as well. If such staff are insisting on admission it is suggested that you contact [Name] and the company's security adviser, who collectively will determine the appropriate course of action.

(e) At the end of the meeting the admission cards and signatures can be counted to establish how many people attended the meeting.

8. Guidelines for Press Registration

The company's press officer will brief the staff on the press desk as to the procedures to be adopted.

9. **Guidelines for Visitors' Registration**

   Staff on this desk will be provided with guest lists before the meeting. These lists will provide the names of the guests and their status, that is shareholder or guest, so that these staff may issue the appropriate cards, that is yellow or pink and folders.

10. **Displays**

    There will be a series of small displays at the back of the main auditorium for shareholders' general interest before and after the AGM. The displays cover the main businesses such as [. . .].

    Company personnel acting as stewards are to encourage shareholders to visit the display stands and models in the main auditorium. The doors to the main auditorium will be open at 1000 and a P.A. announcement will inform shareholders that the exhibition area is open.

11. **Customer and Shareholder Enquiries**

    There will be a customer enquiry desk situated in [Room 1] staffed by company personnel who will be pleased to answer queries on [. . .].

    Shareholders with enquiries relating to their shareholding should be directed to the shareholder enquiry desk situated [. . .]. This desk will be staffed by [Registrars] personnel and company personnel. Any documents on display at the meeting will be available for inspection by shareholders at this desk.

12. **Question Points**

    There will be four question points, two in [Room 1] and two in the auditorium, for any shareholder wishing to raise a question. Question should be registered in advance of the meeting as far as possible – details of this will be given to shareholders on their arrival. Included in the shareholders' folders will be a shareholder question card. The question card is for those shareholders who would prefer to receive a written answer – or if there is insufficient time for their question to be asked at the Meeting.

    A number of questions that shareholders may have can be answered either at the customer enquiry desk or the shareholder enquiry desk and personnel at the question points should direct them as necessary.

13. **Question and Answer Management System**

    The system consists of purpose-designed software running on a network of IBM compatible PCs. The configuration of the system consists of four question registration points, each with a computer and printer, two PCs and printers processing the answers to the questions and two further PCs outputting the next question (preview) or the 'on air' question (current). The system is split into four parts:

- front of house question registration points, two in [Room 1] and two in the auditorium;
- the research area behind the scenes;
- outputting information to the platform; and
- on stage equipment.

At each registration point there is a computer and printer. There will be two personnel, a computer operator and a member of company staff. The company employee is the first to meet the questioner. They make sure that he/she is entitled to ask a question (i.e. is a shareholder holding a yellow voting card). They should have sufficient procedural knowledge to be able to allocate the question to the correct resolution by reference to the Notice of Meeting.

Shareholders may need assistance to compose their questions and therefore company staff may wish to encourage questioners to draft questions on the pads provided at each point.

The question is then dictated to the computer operator. It is allocated a unique number which relates to the resolution to which it applies. Once the question has been entered, a print out of the question is provided for the questioner to keep. A badge is also generated with all the essential information on it (i.e. question number, resolution number and the question point in the auditorium from which it is to be asked).

The badge is marked with a colour sticker and worn by the questioner to aid his or her identification as the questioner by company personnel and [Event Organisers] staff marshalling questioners within the auditorium.

As the question is printed out for the questioner it is simultaneously networked to the research area, stored on the file server, and printed out on two-part paper. In the research area there would be a number of senior company representatives with their own co-ordinator. One copy of the question goes to the co-ordinator who will then decide which researcher will answer it and pass it on. The other copy is filed as a control by the question controller backstage in [Room 8].

Once the question has been answered, hopefully with bullet points provided by the researchers, it is collected by either of two computer operators who add the answers to the questions. Once the answer has been added the page is re-stored on the fileserver and printed out again, locally, on two-part paper. One copy is given to the question controller and the other held as a paper back-up.

The PCs and operators output to the stage. They will output the questions in the order called by the question controller. One PC is dedicated to previewing the next question, the other outputs the current question. At any time additional information can be added to the displayed page to cope with supplementary or non-pre-registered questions. Any alterations made on the screen will be reflected instantly on the on-stage monitors.

On the platform the Chair will have one monitor dedicated to the current question and one dedicated to the next question, or preview. Executive directors will have one monitor each with a switch to select 'next' or 'on-air' and non-executive directors will have one switchable monitor between the two.

14. Entrance to the Auditorium

Company personnel acting as stewards will monitor the admission of people entering the auditorium. Shareholders and their guests should have badges and have yellow or pink cards. Proxies should have a badge and blue card. Other personnel entering the auditorium should be wearing badges: either Company personnel, or [Registrars] personnel or representatives from the press or organisers.

15. Seating Arrangements

Seating for guests will be in the front row of the two seating blocks. Seating for questioners is in the back row of the two seating blocks, adjacent to the question points. Shareholders with pre-registered questions will be identified with badges and staff marshalling this area should seat questioners next to question point A or B in the auditorium as per the instruction on the badge. The question points are identified by overhead signs.

An area of the right side of the auditorium has been reserved for shareholders with wheelchairs and a signed area has been fitted with an induction loop system for the hard of hearing. Chairs will also be allocated for those accompanying the disabled.

Other shareholders may sit where they choose but, if possible, should be encouraged to sit near the front so that late arrivals sit towards the back. No special arrangements have been made for the press.

16. Annual General Meeting

The meeting will commence at 11.00. Prior to this background music will be played in the auditorium from 10.00. A short opening sequence of slides will be shown during this period. Once the meeting has commenced, company personnel may take their seats in the reserved area at the rear of the auditorium.

The finishing time of the meeting cannot be ascertained, but the anticipated time is between 13.00 and 13.30. At this time, **all** exhibition, registration and customer/shareholder enquiry personnel should resume their positions until the last shareholder leaves the building.

17. **Counting of Votes by a Show of Hands**

    [Registrars] personnel will be responsible for recording and counting the show of hands (i.e. by shareholders raising their yellow cards) if it is not clear whether the resolution has been carried or not. [Name] of [Registrars] will be positioned near one of the Question Points in the auditorium so as to communicate with the Chair.

18. **Poll**

    [Registrars] personnel are responsible for conducting a poll should the event occur. Again, [Name] of [Registrars] will be strategically placed near one of the question points so as to be able to communicate with the Chair as to the validity of the poll request. The detailed procedure on the conduct of a poll will be dealt with by the Company Secretary at the Meeting. Ballot boxes and poll cards will be stored under lock and key in the registrars' office and only brought out by [Registrars] personnel in the event of a poll.

19. **Organisers' Staff**

    The Company AGM is organised by the [Venue] and [Event Organisers]. As well as technical crew, stewards, caterers and security staff, the following people will be on duty throughout the day.

[Name]	event director	[Event Organisers]
[Name]	question controller	[Event Organisers]
[Name]	senior producer	[Venue]
[Name]	producer	[Venue]
[Name]	centre co-ordinator	[Venue]
[Name]	head of security	[Venue]

    In the event of any queries or problems, please go to the organisers' office in room 3/10 on the third floor. They are both linked to the other members of the crew by walkie-talkie and can issue instructions as required.

20. **Communications**

    The general telephone number for the [Venue] is [Tel. No.]. To contact representatives of the [Venue] or [Event Organisers], the direct lines to the Company AGM organisers' office are as follows:

    [Tel. No.] telephone   [Tel. No.] facsimile

    To contact [Company] staff, the direct lines to the investor relations office are as follows:

    [Tel. No.] telephone   [Tel. No.] facsimile

21. Catering

Shareholders will be served tea, coffee, orange juice or mineral water in [Room 1] before and after the AGM. The catering service will operate from 10.00 to 11.00 and 13.00 to 14.00.

Light refreshments will be served for the board in [Room 3] before and after the AGM.

Lunch will be served to invited guests in [Room 10] from 13.30 as a seated buffet.

Appendices

[Location Map of [Venue]]

[Plan of Registration Area (Room 1) and the Auditorium (Room 2 and Room 10)]

Appendix 4 – Companies Act 2006 provisions on meetings

PART 9: EXERCISE OF MEMBERS' RIGHTS (SS 145–153)

Effect of provisions in company's articles

Information rights

Exercise of rights where shares held on behalf of others

PART 13: RESOLUTIONS AND MEETINGS (SS 281–361)

Chapter 1: General provisions about resolutions

PART 37: COMPANIES: SUPPLEMENTARY PROVISIONS (SS 1143–1148)

Appendix 5 – Companies Act 1985 Table A: Contents and table of destinations

This annex shows the content and layout of the 1985 Table A and the location of any equivalent provisions in the Companies Act 2006 model articles for private companies limited by shares dated August 2013.

1985 Table A	2006 Act model articles for private companies limited by shares
1. Interpretation	1. Defined terms
	2. Liability of members
	21. All shares to be fully paid up
2–3. Share capital	22. Powers to issue different classes of share
4. Power to pay commissions	N/A – see ss 552 and 553
5. Company not bound by less than absolute interests	23. Company not bound by less than absolute interests
6. Share certificates	24. Share certificates
7. Replacement share certificates	25. Replacement share certificates
8–11. Lien 12–17. Calls on shares 18–22. Forfeiture	N/A
23–28. Share transfers	26. Share transfers
29–31. Transmission of shares	27. Transmission of shares 28. Exercise of transmittees' rights 29. Transmittees bound by prior notices
32–33. Alteration of share capital	N/A – see ss 617 and 618
34. Power to reduce capital	N/A – see s. 641
35. Power to purchase own shares	N/A – see s. 690
36. Extraordinary general meetings	N/A

1985 Table A	2006 Act model articles for private companies limited by shares
37. Calling general meetings	N/A – see ss 302–304
38. Notice of general meetings	N/A – see s. 307 (notice required), s. 311 (contents of notices of meetings) and s. 310 (persons entitled to receive notice of meetings)
39. Notice – accidental omission	N/A – see s. 313
40. Quorum – general meetings	37. Attendance and speaking at general meetings 38. Quorum for general meetings See also s. 318
41. Adjournment if no quorum present	41. Adjournment
42–43. Chairing general meetings	39. Chairing general meetings
44. Attendance and speaking by directors	40. Attendance and speaking by directors and non-shareholders
45. Adjournment	41. Adjournment
46. Voting: general 46. Demand for a poll 47. Declaration by the chairman of result on a show of hands 48. Demand for poll may be withdrawn 49. Method of taking poll	42. Voting: general 44. Poll votes See also s. 320 (declaration by chairman on a show of hands), s. 321 (right to demand a poll), s. 322 (voting on a poll) and s. 329 (right of proxy to demand a poll)
50. Chair's casting vote	13. Casting vote
51. Timing of certain polls 52. Notice of a poll	See Article 44(4) (Poll votes)
53. Members' written resolutions	N/A – see ss 288–300
54. Votes of members	N/A – see ss 284–287
55. Votes of joint holders	N/A – see s. 286
56. Voting by member subject to a mental health order	See Article 27(3) and Article 1 (definition of 'transmittee')
57. No votes on shares unless all moneys presently payable have been paid	N/A – all shares must be fully paid
58. Objection to qualification of any voter	43. Errors and disputes
59. Voting by proxies on a poll	N/A – see ss 284–287 and 322
60–62. Appointment of proxies 63. Determination of proxy	45. Content of proxy notices 46. Delivery of proxy notices
	47. Amendments to resolutions

1985 Table A	2006 Act model articles for private companies limited by shares
64. Number of directors	N/A
65–69. Alternate directors	N/A
70. Powers of directors	3. Directors' general authority 4. Shareholders' reserve power
71. Power to appoint agents 72. Delegation of directors' powers	5. Directors may delegate 6. Committees
73–75. Retirement of directors	N/A
76–78. Appointment by members 79. Appointment by directors	17. Methods of appointing directors
80. Retiring director continues in office until end of meeting	N/A
81. Disqualification and removal of directors	18. Termination of director's appointment
82. Remuneration of directors	19. Directors' remuneration
83. Directors' expenses	20. Directors' expenses
84. Directors' appointments	19. Directors' remuneration
85–86. Directors' interests	N/A – see ss 182–187
87. Director's gratuities and pensions	19. Directors' remuneration
88. Proceedings of directors	7. Directors to take decisions collectively 9. Calling a directors' meeting 13. Casting vote 16. Directors' discretion to make further rules
89. Quorum for directors' meetings 90. Continuing directors may act to fill vacancies or call a general meeting.	10. Participation in directors' meetings 11. Quorum for directors' meetings
91. Chairing of directors' meetings	12. Chairing of directors' meetings
92. Directors' acts valid notwithstanding any defects	N/A – see s. 161
93. Written resolution of directors	8. Unanimous decisions
94. Conflicts of interest – voting 95. Director not counted in the quorum if not entitled to vote. 96. Company may suspend or relax rules prohibiting a director from voting	14. Conflicts of interest

1985 Table A	2006 Act model articles for private companies limited by shares
97. Appointment of two or more directors to offices or employments with the company	N/A
98. Questions as to the right of a director to vote to be referred to the chairman of the meeting	See Article 14(7) (Conflicts of interest)
99. Secretary	N/A
100. Minutes	15. Records of [directors'] decisions to be kept See also s. 248 and ss 355–359.
101. The seal	49. Company seals
102. Declaration of dividends 103. Interim dividends 104. Apportionment of dividends 105. Non-cash distributions 106. Payment of dividends 107. No interest on distributions 108. Unclaimed distributions	30. Procedure for declaring dividends 31. Payment of dividends and other distributions 32. No interest on distributions 33. Unclaimed distributions 34. Non-cash distributions 35. Waiver of distributions
109. No right to inspect accounts and other records	50. No right to inspect accounts and other records
110. Capitalisation of profits	36. Capitalisation of profits
111–116. Notices	48. Means of communication to be used 29. Transmittees bound by prior notices
117. Winding up – distribution of assets	N/A
	51. Provision for employees on cessation of business
118. Indemnity	52. Indemnity 53. Insurance

Appendix 6 – Companies Act 2006 Model Articles: Contents and comparative location of provisions

Key to Table

* indicates that the relevant model articles shown in the same row are identical.

*¹ indicates that the relevant model articles shown in the same row are the same other than for the use of the word 'shareholder' in the model articles for private companies limited by shares where the word 'member' is used in the model articles for guarantee companies and the model articles for public companies.

Schedule 1 Regulation 2 Model articles for private companies limited by shares	Schedule 2 Regulation 3 Model articles for private companies limited by guarantee	Schedule 3 Regulation 4 Model articles for public companies
See Appendix 7	See Appendix 8	See Appendix 9
PART 1: INTERPRETATION AND LIMITATION OF LIABILITY 1. Defined terms 2. Liability of members	PART 1: INTERPRETATION AND LIMITATION OF LIABILITY 1. Defined terms 2. Liability of members	PART 1: INTERPRETATION AND LIMITATION OF LIABILITY 1. Defined terms 2. Liability of members
PART 2: DIRECTORS *Directors' powers and responsibilities* 3. Directors' general authority* 4. Shareholders' reserve power*¹ 5. Directors may delegate* 6. Committees*	PART 2: DIRECTORS *Directors' powers and responsibilities* 3. Directors' general authority* 4. Members' reserve power *¹ 5. Directors may delegate* 6. Committees*	PART 2: DIRECTORS *Directors' powers and responsibilities* 3. Directors' general authority* 4. Members' reserve power*¹ 5. Directors may delegate* 6. Committees*

Schedule 1 Regulation 2 Model articles for private companies limited by shares	Schedule 2 Regulation 3 Model articles for private companies limited by guarantee	Schedule 3 Regulation 4 Model articles for public companies
Decision-making by directors	*Decision-making by directors*	*Decision-making by directors*
7. Directors to take decisions collectively*	7. Directors to take decisions collectively*	7. Directors to take decisions collectively
8. Unanimous decisions*	8. Unanimous decisions*	8. Calling a directors' meeting
9. Calling a directors' meeting*	9. Calling a directors' meeting*	9. Participation in directors' meetings*
10. Participation in directors' meetings*	10. Participation in directors' meetings*	10. Quorum for directors' meetings
11. Quorum for directors' meetings*	11. Quorum for directors' meetings*	11. Meetings where total number of directors less than quorum
12. Chairing of directors' meetings*	12. Chairing of directors' meetings*	12. Chairing of directors' meetings
13. Casting vote*	13. Casting vote*	13. Voting at directors' meetings: general rules
14. Conflicts of interest*	14. Conflicts of interest*	14. Chairman's casting vote at directors' meetings*
15. Records of decisions to be kept*	15. Records of decisions to be kept*	15. Alternates voting at directors' meetings
16. Directors' discretion to make further rules*	16. Directors' discretion to make further rules*	16. Conflicts of interest
		17. Proposing directors' written resolutions
		18. Adoption of directors' written resolutions
		19. Directors' discretion to make further rules*
Appointment of directors	*Appointment of directors*	*Appointment of directors*
17. Methods of appointing directors*[1]	17. Methods of appointing directors*[1]	20. Methods of appointing directors
18. Termination of director's appointment*	18. Termination of director's appointment*	21. Retirement of directors by rotation
19. Directors' remuneration*	19. Directors' remuneration*	22. Termination of director's appointment*
20. Directors' expenses*	20. Directors' expenses	23. Directors' remuneration*
		24. Directors' expenses*

Schedule 1 Regulation 2 Model articles for private companies limited by shares	Schedule 2 Regulation 3 Model articles for private companies limited by guarantee	Schedule 3 Regulation 4 Model articles for public companies
		Alternate directors 25. Appointment and removal of alternates 26. Rights and responsibilities of alternate directors 27. Termination of alternate directorship
	PART 3: MEMBERS *Becoming and ceasing to be a member* 21. Applications for membership 22. Termination of membership	
PART 3: SHARES AND DISTRIBUTIONS *Shares* 21. All shares to be fully paid up 22. Powers to issue different classes of share*		PART 4: SHARES AND DISTRIBUTIONS *Issue of shares* 43. Powers to issue different classes of share* 44. Payment of commissions on subscription for shares
23. Company not bound by less than absolute interests*		*Interests in shares* 45. Company not bound by less than absolute interests*
24. Share certificates 25. Replacement share certificates		*Share certificates* 46. Certificates to be issued except in certain cases 47. Contents and execution of share certificates 48. Consolidated share certificates 49. Replacement share certificates

Schedule 1 Regulation 2 Model articles for private companies limited by shares	Schedule 2 Regulation 3 Model articles for private companies limited by guarantee	Schedule 3 Regulation 4 Model articles for public companies
		Shares not held in certificated form 50. Uncertificated shares 51. Share warrants
		Partly paid shares 52. Company's lien over partly paid shares 53. Enforcement of the company's lien 54. Call notices 55. Liability to pay calls 56. When call notice need not be issued 57. Failure to comply with call notice: automatic consequences 58. Notice of intended forfeiture 59. Directors' power to forfeit shares 60. Effect of forfeiture 61. Procedure following forfeiture 62. Surrender of shares
26. Share transfers 27. Transmission of shares 28. Exercise of transmittees' rights 29. Transmittees bound by prior notices		*Transfer and transmission of shares* 63. Transfers of certificated shares 64. Transfer of uncertificated shares 65. Transmission of shares 66. Transmittees' rights 67. Exercise of transmittees' rights 68. Transmittees bound by prior notices
		Consolidation of shares 69. Procedure for disposing of fractions of shares

Schedule 1 Regulation 2 Model articles for private companies limited by shares	Schedule 2 Regulation 3 Model articles for private companies limited by guarantee	Schedule 3 Regulation 4 Model articles for public companies
Dividends and other distributions 30. Procedure for declaring dividends 31. Payment of dividends and other distributions* 32. No interest on distributions* 33. Unclaimed distributions* 34. Non-cash distributions 35. Waiver of distributions*		*Distributions* 70. Procedure for declaring dividends 71. Calculation of dividends 72. Payment of dividends and other distributions* 73. Deductions from distributions in respect of sums owed to the company 74. No interest on distributions* 75. Unclaimed distributions* 76. Non-cash distributions 77. Waiver of distributions*
Capitalisation of profits 36. Authority to capitalise and appropriation of capitalised sums		*Capitalisation of profits* 78. Authority to capitalise and appropriation of capitalised sums
PART 4: DECISION-MAKING BY SHAREHOLDERS *Organisation of general meetings* 37. Attendance and speaking at general meetings* 38. Quorum for general meetings* 39. Chairing general meetings*1 40. Attendance and speaking by directors and non-shareholders*1 41. Adjournment*	*Organisation of general meetings* 23. Attendance and speaking at general meetings* 24. Quorum for general meetings* 25. Chairing general meetings*1 26. Attendance and speaking by directors and non-members 27. Adjournment*	PART 3: DECISION-MAKING BY MEMBERS *Organisation of general meetings* 28. Members can call general meeting if not enough directors 29. Attendance and speaking at general meetings* 30. Quorum for general meetings* 31. Chairing general meetings*1 32. Attendance and speaking by directors and non-members*1 33. Adjournment*

Schedule 1 Regulation 2 Model articles for private companies limited by shares	Schedule 2 Regulation 3 Model articles for private companies limited by guarantee	Schedule 3 Regulation 4 Model articles for public companies
Voting at general meetings 42. Voting: general* 43. Errors and disputes* 44. Poll votes*[1] 45. Content of proxy notices*[1] 46. Delivery of proxy notices* 47. Amendments to resolutions*	*Voting at general meetings* 28. Voting: general* 29. Errors and disputes* 30. Poll votes*[1] 31. Content of proxy notices*[1] 32. Delivery of proxy notices* 33. Amendments to resolutions*	*Voting at general meetings* 34. Voting: general* 35. Errors and disputes* 36. Demanding a poll 37. Procedure on a poll 38. Content of proxy notices*[1] 39. Delivery of proxy notices 40. Amendments to resolutions
		Restrictions on members' rights 41. No voting of shares on which money owed to company
		Application of rules to class meetings 42. Class meetings
PART 5: ADMINISTRATIVE ARRANGEMENTS 48. Means of communication to be used* 49. Company seals* 50. No right to inspect accounts and other records*[1] 51. Provision for employees on cessation of business*	PART 4: ADMINISTRATIVE ARRANGEMENTS 34. Means of communication to be used* 35. Company seals* 36. No right to inspect accounts and other records*[1] 37. Provision for employees on cessation of business*	PART 5: MISCELLANEOUS PROVISIONS *Communications* 79. Means of communication to be used* 80. Failure to notify contact details *Administrative arrangements* 81. Company seals 82. Destruction of documents 83. No right to inspect accounts and other records*[1] 84. Provision for employees on cessation of business*

Schedule 1 Regulation 2 Model articles for private companies limited by shares	Schedule 2 Regulation 3 Model articles for private companies limited by guarantee	Schedule 3 Regulation 4 Model articles for public companies
Directors' indemnity and insurance 52. Indemnity* 53. Insurance*	*Directors' indemnity and insurance* 38. Indemnity* 39. Insurance*	*Directors' indemnity and insurance* 85. Indemnity* 86. Insurance*

Appendix 7 – Model articles for private companies limited by shares

Model Articles for Private Companies Limited by Shares applicable for companies incorporated on or after 28 April 2013. This version was published on 10 October 2017 and last updated on 18 September 2018.

Later versions may be available at: www.gov.uk/government/publications/model-articles-for-private-companies-limited-by-shares

SCHEDULE 1 Regulation 2

MODEL ARTICLES FOR PRIVATE COMPANIES LIMITED BY SHARES
INDEX TO THE ARTICLES

PART 1
INTERPRETATION AND LIMITATION OF LIABILITY

PART 2
DIRECTORS
DIRECTORS' POWERS AND RESPONSIBILITIES

DECISION-MAKING BY DIRECTORS

PART 4
DECISION-MAKING BY SHAREHOLDERS
ORGANISATION OF GENERAL MEETINGS

VOTING AT GENERAL MEETINGS

PART 5
ADMINISTRATIVE ARRANGEMENTS

DIRECTORS' INDEMNITY AND INSURANCE

PART 1
INTERPRETATION AND LIMITATION OF LIABILITY

Defined terms

1. In the articles, unless the context requires otherwise—
   'articles' means the company's articles of association;
   'bankruptcy' includes individual insolvency proceedings in a jurisdiction other than England and Wales or Northern Ireland which have an effect similar to that of bankruptcy;
   'chairman' has the meaning given in article 12;
   'chairman of the meeting' has the meaning given in article 39;

'Companies Acts' means the Companies Acts (as defined in section 2 of the Companies Act 2006), in so far as they apply to the company;

'director' means a director of the company, and includes any person occupying the position of director, by whatever name called;

'distribution recipient' has the meaning given in article 31;

'document' includes, unless otherwise specified, any document sent or supplied in electronic form;

'electronic form' has the meaning given in section 1168 of the Companies Act 2006;

'fully paid' in relation to a share, means that the nominal value and any premium to be paid to the company in respect of that share have been paid to the company;

'hard copy form' has the meaning given in section 1168 of the Companies Act 2006;

'holder' in relation to shares means the person whose name is entered in the register of members as the holder of the shares;

'instrument' means a document in hard copy form;

'ordinary resolution' has the meaning given in section 282 of the Companies Act 2006;

'paid' means paid or credited as paid;

'participate', in relation to a directors' meeting, has the meaning given in article 10;

'proxy notice' has the meaning given in article 45;

'shareholder' means a person who is the holder of a share;

'shares' means shares in the company;

'special resolution' has the meaning given in section 283 of the Companies Act 2006;

'subsidiary' has the meaning given in section 1159 of the Companies Act 2006;

'transmittee' means a person entitled to a share by reason of the death or bankruptcy of a shareholder or otherwise by operation of law; and

'writing' means the representation or reproduction of words, symbols or other information in a visible form by any method or combination of methods, whether sent or supplied in electronic form or otherwise.

Unless the context otherwise requires, other words or expressions contained in these articles bear the same meaning as in the Companies Act 2006 as in force on the date when these articles become binding on the company.

Liability of members

2.   The liability of the members is limited to the amount, if any, unpaid on the shares held by them.

PART 2
DIRECTORS
DIRECTORS' POWERS AND RESPONSIBILITIES

Directors' general authority

3.   Subject to the articles, the directors are responsible for the management of the company's business, for which purpose they may exercise all the powers of the company.

Shareholders' reserve power

4.—   (1)   The shareholders may, by special resolution, direct the directors to take, or refrain from taking, specified action.

      (2)   No such special resolution invalidates anything which the directors have done before the passing of the resolution.

Directors may delegate

5.—   (1)   Subject to the articles, the directors may delegate any of the powers which are conferred on them under the articles—

        (a)   to such person or committee;

        (b)   by such means (including by power of attorney);

        (c)   to such an extent;

        (d)   in relation to such matters or territories; and

        (e)   on such terms and conditions;

        as they think fit.

      (2)   If the directors so specify, any such delegation may authorise further delegation of the directors' powers by any person to whom they are delegated.

      (3)   The directors may revoke any delegation in whole or part, or alter its terms and conditions.

Committees

6.—   (1)   Committees to which the directors delegate any of their powers must follow procedures which are based as far as they are applicable on those provisions of the articles which govern the taking of decisions by directors.

      (2)   The directors may make rules of procedure for all or any committees, which prevail over rules derived from the articles if they are not consistent with them.

DECISION-MAKING BY DIRECTORS

Directors to take decisions collectively

7.— (1) The general rule about decision-making by directors is that any decision of the directors must be either a majority decision at a meeting or a decision taken in accordance with article 8.

    (2) If—

        (a) the company only has one director, and

        (b) no provision of the articles requires it to have more than one director, the general rule does not apply, and the director may take decisions without regard to any of the provisions of the articles relating to directors' decision making.

Unanimous decisions

8.— (1) A decision of the directors is taken in accordance with this article when all eligible directors indicate to each other by any means that they share a common view on a matter.

    (2) Such a decision may take the form of a resolution in writing, copies of which have been signed by each eligible director or to which each eligible director has otherwise indicated agreement in writing.

    (3) References in this article to eligible directors are to directors who would have been entitled to vote on the matter had it been proposed as a resolution at a directors' meeting.

    (4) A decision may not be taken in accordance with this article if the eligible directors would not have formed a quorum at such a meeting.

Calling a directors' meeting

9.— (1) Any director may call a directors' meeting by giving notice of the meeting to the directors or by authorising the company secretary (if any) to give such notice.

    (2) Notice of any directors' meeting must indicate—

        (a) its proposed date and time;

        (b) where it is to take place; and

        (c) if it is anticipated that directors participating in the meeting will not be in the same place, how it is proposed that they should communicate with each other during the meeting.

    (3) Notice of a directors' meeting must be given to each director but need not be in writing.

    (4) Notice of a directors' meeting need not be given to directors who waive their entitlement to notice of that meeting, by giving notice to that effect to the company not more than seven days after the date on which the meeting is held. Where such notice is given after the

meeting has been held, that does not affect the validity of the meeting, or of any business conducted at it.

Participation in directors' meetings

10.— (1)   Subject to the articles, directors participate in a directors' meeting, or part of a directors' meeting, when—

    (a)   the meeting has been called and takes place in accordance with the articles, and

    (b)   they can each communicate to the others any information or opinions they have on any particular item of the business of the meeting.

  (2)   In determining whether directors are participating in a directors' meeting, it is irrelevant where any director is or how they communicate with each other.

  (3)   If all the directors participating in a meeting are not in the same place, they may decide that the meeting is to be treated as taking place wherever any of them is.

Quorum for directors' meetings

11.— (1)   At a directors' meeting, unless a quorum is participating, no proposal is to be voted on, except a proposal to call another meeting.

  (2)   The quorum for directors' meetings may be fixed from time to time by a decision of the directors, but it must never be less than two, and unless otherwise fixed it is two.

  (3)   If the total number of directors for the time being is less than the quorum required, the directors must not take any decision other than a decision—

    (a)   to appoint further directors, or

    (b)   to call a general meeting so as to enable the shareholders to appoint further directors.

Chairing of directors' meetings

12.— (1)   The directors may appoint a director to chair their meetings.

  (2)   The person so appointed for the time being is known as the chairman.

  (3)   The directors may terminate the chairman's appointment at any time.

  (4)   If the chairman is not participating in a directors' meeting within ten minutes of the time at which it was to start, the participating directors must appoint one of themselves to chair it.

Casting vote

13.— (1)   If the numbers of votes for and against a proposal are equal, the chairman or other director chairing the meeting has a casting vote.

(2) But this does not apply if, in accordance with the articles, the chairman or other director is not to be counted as participating in the decision-making process for quorum or voting purposes.

Conflicts of interest

14.— (1) If a proposed decision of the directors is concerned with an actual or proposed transaction or arrangement with the company in which a director is interested, that director is not to be counted as participating in the decision-making process for quorum or voting purposes.

(2) But if paragraph (3) applies, a director who is interested in an actual or proposed transaction or arrangement with the company is to be counted as participating in the decision-making process for quorum and voting purposes.

(3) This paragraph applies when—

(a) the company by ordinary resolution disapplies the provision of the articles which would otherwise prevent a director from being counted as participating in the decision-making process;

(b) the director's interest cannot reasonably be regarded as likely to give rise to a conflict of interest; or

(c) the director's conflict of interest arises from a permitted cause.

(4) For the purposes of this article, the following are permitted causes—

(a) a guarantee given, or to be given, by or to a director in respect of an obligation incurred by or on behalf of the company or any of its subsidiaries;

(b) subscription, or an agreement to subscribe, for shares or other securities of the company or any of its subsidiaries, or to underwrite, sub-underwrite, or guarantee subscription for any such shares or securities; and

(c) arrangements pursuant to which benefits are made available to employees and directors or former employees and directors of the company or any of its subsidiaries which do not provide special benefits for directors or former directors.

(5) For the purposes of this article, references to proposed decisions and decision-making processes include any directors' meeting or part of a directors' meeting.

(6) Subject to paragraph (7), if a question arises at a meeting of directors or of a committee of directors as to the right of a director to participate in the meeting (or part of the meeting) for voting or quorum purposes, the question may, before the conclusion of the meeting, be referred to the chairman whose ruling in relation to any director other than the chairman is to be final and conclusive.

(7) If any question as to the right to participate in the meeting (or part of the meeting) should arise in respect of the chairman, the question is

to be decided by a decision of the directors at that meeting, for which purpose the chairman is not to be counted as participating in the meeting (or that part of the meeting) for voting or quorum purposes.

Records of decisions to be kept

15.　　The directors must ensure that the company keeps a record, in writing, for at least 10 years from the date of the decision recorded, of every unanimous or majority decision taken by the directors.

Directors' discretion to make further rules

16.　　Subject to the articles, the directors may make any rule which they think fit about how they take decisions, and about how such rules are to be recorded or communicated to directors.

APPOINTMENT OF DIRECTORS

Methods of appointing directors

17.—　(1)　Any person who is willing to act as a director, and is permitted by law to do so, may be appointed to be a director—

　　　(a)　by ordinary resolution, or

　　　(b)　by a decision of the directors.

　(2)　In any case where, as a result of death, the company has no shareholders and no directors, the personal representatives of the last shareholder to have died have the right, by notice in writing, to appoint a person to be a director.

　(3)　For the purposes of paragraph (2), where 2 or more shareholders die in circumstances rendering it uncertain who was the last to die, a younger shareholder is deemed to have survived an older shareholder.

Termination of director's appointment

18.　　A person ceases to be a director as soon as—

　　　(a)　that person ceases to be a director by virtue of any provision of the Companies Act 2006 or is prohibited from being a director by law;

　　　(b)　a bankruptcy order is made against that person;

　　　(c)　a composition is made with that person's creditors generally in satisfaction of that person's debts;

　　　(d)　a registered medical practitioner who is treating that person gives a written opinion to the company stating that that person has become physically or mentally incapable of acting as a director and may remain so for more than three months;

　　　(e)　*[paragraph omitted pursuant to The Mental Health (Discrimination) Act 2013]*

(f) notification is received by the company from the director that the director is resigning from office, and such resignation has taken effect in accordance with its terms.

Directors' remuneration

19.— (1) Directors may undertake any services for the company that the directors decide.

(2) Directors are entitled to such remuneration as the directors determine—

(a) for their services to the company as directors, and

(b) for any other service which they undertake for the company.

(3) Subject to the articles, a director's remuneration may—

(a) take any form, and

(b) include any arrangements in connection with the payment of a pension, allowance or gratuity, or any death, sickness or disability benefits, to or in respect of that director.

(4) Unless the directors decide otherwise, directors' remuneration accrues from day to day.

(5) Unless the directors decide otherwise, directors are not accountable to the company for any remuneration which they receive as directors or other officers or employees of the company's subsidiaries or of any other body corporate in which the company is interested.

Directors' expenses

20. The company may pay any reasonable expenses which the directors properly incur in connection with their attendance at—

(a) meetings of directors or committees of directors,

(b) general meetings, or

(c) separate meetings of the holders of any class of shares or of debentures of the company, or otherwise in connection with the exercise of their powers and the discharge of their responsibilities in relation to the company.

PART 3
SHARES AND DISTRIBUTIONS
SHARES

All shares to be fully paid up

21.— (1) No share is to be issued for less than the aggregate of its nominal value and any premium to be paid to the company in consideration for its issue.

(2) This does not apply to shares taken on the formation of the company by the subscribers to the company's memorandum.

Powers to issue different classes of share

22.— (1) Subject to the articles, but without prejudice to the rights attached to any existing share, the company may issue shares with such rights or restrictions as may be determined by ordinary resolution.

(2) The company may issue shares which are to be redeemed, or are liable to be redeemed at the option of the company or the holder, and the directors may determine the terms, conditions and manner of redemption of any such shares.

Company not bound by less than absolute interests

23. Except as required by law, no person is to be recognised by the company as holding any share upon any trust, and except as otherwise required by law or the articles, the company is not in any way to be bound by or recognise any interest in a share other than the holder's absolute ownership of it and all the rights attaching to it.

Share certificates

24.— (1) The company must issue each shareholder, free of charge, with one or more certificates in respect of the shares which that shareholder holds.

(2) Every certificate must specify—

(a) in respect of how many shares, of what class, it is issued;

(b) the nominal value of those shares;

(c) that the shares are fully paid; and

(d) any distinguishing numbers assigned to them.

(3) No certificate may be issued in respect of shares of more than one class.

(4) If more than one person holds a share, only one certificate may be issued in respect of it.

(5) Certificates must—

(a) have affixed to them the company's common seal, or

(b) be otherwise executed in accordance with the Companies Acts.

Replacement share certificates

25.— (1) If a certificate issued in respect of a shareholder's shares is—

(a) damaged or defaced, or

(b) said to be lost, stolen or destroyed, that shareholder is entitled to be issued with a replacement certificate in respect of the same shares.

(2) A shareholder exercising the right to be issued with such a replacement certificate—

(a) may at the same time exercise the right to be issued with a single certificate or separate certificates;

    (b) must return the certificate which is to be replaced to the company if it is damaged or defaced; and

    (c) must comply with such conditions as to evidence, indemnity and the payment of a reasonable fee as the directors decide.

Share transfers

26.— (1) Shares may be transferred by means of an instrument of transfer in any usual form or any other form approved by the directors, which is executed by or on behalf of the transferor.

(2) No fee may be charged for registering any instrument of transfer or other document relating to or affecting the title to any share.

(3) The company may retain any instrument of transfer which is registered.

(4) The transferor remains the holder of a share until the transferee's name is entered in the register of members as holder of it.

(5) The directors may refuse to register the transfer of a share, and if they do so, the instrument of transfer must be returned to the transferee with the notice of refusal unless they suspect that the proposed transfer may be fraudulent.

Transmission of shares

27.— (1) If title to a share passes to a transmittee, the company may only recognise the transmittee as having any title to that share.

(2) A transmittee who produces such evidence of entitlement to shares as the directors may properly require—

    (a) may, subject to the articles, choose either to become the holder of those shares or to have them transferred to another person, and

    (b) subject to the articles, and pending any transfer of the shares to another person, has the same rights as the holder had.

(3) But transmittees do not have the right to attend or vote at a general meeting, or agree to a proposed written resolution, in respect of shares to which they are entitled, by reason of the holder's death or bankruptcy or otherwise, unless they become the holders of those shares.

Exercise of transmittees' rights

28.— (1) Transmittees who wish to become the holders of shares to which they have become entitled must notify the company in writing of that wish.

(2) If the transmittee wishes to have a share transferred to another person, the transmittee must execute an instrument of transfer in respect of it.

(3)   Any transfer made or executed under this article is to be treated as if it were made or executed by the person from whom the transmittee has derived rights in respect of the share, and as if the event which gave rise to the transmission had not occurred.

Transmittees bound by prior notices

29.   If a notice is given to a shareholder in respect of shares and a transmittee is entitled to those shares, the transmittee is bound by the notice if it was given to the shareholder before the transmittee's name has been entered in the register of members.

DIVIDENDS AND OTHER DISTRIBUTIONS

Procedure for declaring dividends

30.— (1)   The company may by ordinary resolution declare dividends, and the directors may decide to pay interim dividends.

(2)   A dividend must not be declared unless the directors have made a recommendation as to its amount. Such a dividend must not exceed the amount recommended by the directors.

(3)   No dividend may be declared or paid unless it is in accordance with shareholders' respective rights.

(4)   Unless the shareholders' resolution to declare or directors' decision to pay a dividend, or the terms on which shares are issued, specify otherwise, it must be paid by reference to each shareholder's holding of shares on the date of the resolution or decision to declare or pay it.

(5)   If the company's share capital is divided into different classes, no interim dividend may be paid on shares carrying deferred or non-preferred rights if, at the time of payment, any preferential dividend is in arrears.

(6)   The directors may pay at intervals any dividend payable at a fixed rate if it appears to them that the profits available for distribution justify the payment.

(7)   If the directors act in good faith, they do not incur any liability to the holders of shares conferring preferred rights for any loss they may suffer by the lawful payment of an interim dividend on shares with deferred or non-preferred rights.

Payment of dividends and other distributions

31.— (1)   Where a dividend or other sum which is a distribution is payable in respect of a share, it must be paid by one or more of the following means—

(a)   transfer to a bank or building society account specified by the distribution recipient either in writing or as the directors may otherwise decide;

(b) sending a cheque made payable to the distribution recipient by post to the distribution recipient at the distribution recipient's registered address (if the distribution recipient is a holder of the share), or (in any other case) to an address specified by the distribution recipient either in writing or as the directors may otherwise decide;

(c) sending a cheque made payable to such person by post to such person at such address as the distribution recipient has specified either in writing or as the directors may otherwise decide; or

(d) any other means of payment as the directors agree with the distribution recipient either in writing or by such other means as the directors decide.

(2) In the articles, 'the distribution recipient' means, in respect of a share in respect of which a dividend or other sum is payable—

(a) the holder of the share; or

(b) if the share has two or more joint holders, whichever of them is named first in the register of members; or

(c) if the holder is no longer entitled to the share by reason of death or bankruptcy, or otherwise by operation of law, the transmittee.

No interest on distributions

32. The company may not pay interest on any dividend or other sum payable in respect of a share unless otherwise provided by—

(a) the terms on which the share was issued, or

(b) the provisions of another agreement between the holder of that share and the company.

Unclaimed distributions

33.— (1) All dividends or other sums which are—

(a) payable in respect of shares, and

(b) unclaimed after having been declared or become payable, may be invested or otherwise made use of by the directors for the benefit of the company until claimed.

(2) The payment of any such dividend or other sum into a separate account does not make the company a trustee in respect of it.

(3) If—

(a) 12 years have passed from the date on which a dividend or other sum became due for payment, and

(b) the distribution recipient has not claimed it, the distribution recipient is no longer entitled to that dividend or other sum and it ceases to remain owing by the company.

Non-cash distributions

34.— (1) Subject to the terms of issue of the share in question, the company may, by ordinary resolution on the recommendation of the directors, decide to pay all or part of a dividend or other distribution payable in respect of a share by transferring non-cash assets of equivalent value (including, without limitation, shares or other securities in any company).

(2) For the purposes of paying a non-cash distribution, the directors may make whatever arrangements they think fit, including, where any difficulty arises regarding the distribution—

(a) fixing the value of any assets;

(b) paying cash to any distribution recipient on the basis of that value in order to adjust the rights of recipients; and

(c) vesting any assets in trustees.

Waiver of distributions

35. Distribution recipients may waive their entitlement to a dividend or other distribution payable in respect of a share by giving the company notice in writing to that effect, but if—

(a) the share has more than one holder, or

(b) more than one person is entitled to the share, whether by reason of the death or bankruptcy of one or more joint holders, or otherwise, the notice is not effective unless it is expressed to be given, and signed, by all the holders or persons otherwise entitled to the share.

CAPITALISATION OF PROFITS

Authority to capitalise and appropriation of capitalised sums

36.— (1) Subject to the articles, the directors may, if they are so authorised by an ordinary resolution—

(a) decide to capitalise any profits of the company (whether or not they are available for distribution) which are not required for paying a preferential dividend, or any sum standing to the credit of the company's share premium account or capital redemption reserve; and

(b) appropriate any sum which they so decide to capitalise (a 'capitalised sum') to the persons who would have been entitled to it if it were distributed by way of dividend (the 'persons entitled') and in the same proportions.

(2) Capitalised sums must be applied—

(a) on behalf of the persons entitled, and

(b) in the same proportions as a dividend would have been distributed to them.

(3) Any capitalised sum may be applied in paying up new shares of a nominal amount equal to the capitalised sum which are then allotted credited as fully paid to the persons entitled or as they may direct.

(4) A capitalised sum which was appropriated from profits available for distribution may be applied in paying up new debentures of the company which are then allotted credited as fully paid to the persons entitled or as they may direct.

(5) Subject to the articles the directors may—

    (a) apply capitalised sums in accordance with paragraphs (3) and (4) partly in one way and partly in another;

    (b) make such arrangements as they think fit to deal with shares or debentures becoming distributable in fractions under this article (including the issuing of fractional certificates or the making of cash payments); and

    (c) authorise any person to enter into an agreement with the company on behalf of all the persons entitled which is binding on them in respect of the allotment of shares and debentures to them under this article.

PART 4
DECISION-MAKING BY SHAREHOLDERS
ORGANISATION OF GENERAL MEETINGS

Attendance and speaking at general meetings

37.— (1) A person is able to exercise the right to speak at a general meeting when that person is in a position to communicate to all those attending the meeting, during the meeting, any information or opinions which that person has on the business of the meeting.

(2) A person is able to exercise the right to vote at a general meeting when—

    (a) that person is able to vote, during the meeting, on resolutions put to the vote at the meeting, and

    (b) that person's vote can be taken into account in determining whether or not such resolutions are passed at the same time as the votes of all the other persons attending the meeting.

(3) The directors may make whatever arrangements they consider appropriate to enable those attending a general meeting to exercise their rights to speak or vote at it.

(4) In determining attendance at a general meeting, it is immaterial whether any two or more members attending it are in the same place as each other.

(5) Two or more persons who are not in the same place as each other attend a general meeting if their circumstances are such that if they

have (or were to have) rights to speak and vote at that meeting, they
are (or would be) able to exercise them.

Quorum for general meetings

38.   No business other than the appointment of the chairman of the meeting is
to be transacted at a general meeting if the persons attending it do not
constitute a quorum.

Chairing general meetings

39.— (1)   If the directors have appointed a chairman, the chairman shall chair
general meetings if present and willing to do so.

(2)   If the directors have not appointed a chairman, or if the chairman is
unwilling to chair the meeting or is not present within ten minutes of
the time at which a meeting was due to start—

(a)   the directors present, or

(b)   (if no directors are present), the meeting, must appoint a director
or shareholder to chair the meeting, and the appointment of the
chairman of the meeting must be the first business of the
meeting.

(3)   The person chairing a meeting in accordance with this article is
referred to as 'the chairman of the meeting'.

Attendance and speaking by directors and non-shareholders

40.— (1)   Directors may attend and speak at general meetings, whether or not
they are shareholders.

(2)   The chairman of the meeting may permit other persons who are not—

(a)   shareholders of the company, or

(b)   otherwise entitled to exercise the rights of shareholders in
relation to general meetings, to attend and speak at a general
meeting.

Adjournment

41.— (1)   If the persons attending a general meeting within half an hour of the
time at which the meeting was due to start do not constitute a
quorum, or if during a meeting a quorum ceases to be present, the
chairman of the meeting must adjourn it.

(2)   The chairman of the meeting may adjourn a general meeting at which
a quorum is present if—

(a)   the meeting consents to an adjournment, or

(b)   it appears to the chairman of the meeting that an adjournment is
necessary to protect the safety of any person attending the
meeting or ensure that the business of the meeting is conducted
in an orderly manner.

(3) The chairman of the meeting must adjourn a general meeting if directed to do so by the meeting.

(4) When adjourning a general meeting, the chairman of the meeting must—

(a) either specify the time and place to which it is adjourned or state that it is to continue at a time and place to be fixed by the directors, and

(b) have regard to any directions as to the time and place of any adjournment which have been given by the meeting.

(5) If the continuation of an adjourned meeting is to take place more than 14 days after it was adjourned, the company must give at least 7 clear days' notice of it (that is, excluding the day of the adjourned meeting and the day on which the notice is given)—

(a) to the same persons to whom notice of the company's general meetings is required to be given, and

(b) containing the same information which such notice is required to contain.

(6) No business may be transacted at an adjourned general meeting which could not properly have been transacted at the meeting if the adjournment had not taken place.

VOTING AT GENERAL MEETINGS

Voting: general

42. A resolution put to the vote of a general meeting must be decided on a show of hands unless a poll is duly demanded in accordance with the articles.

Errors and disputes

43.— (1) No objection may be raised to the qualification of any person voting at a general meeting except at the meeting or adjourned meeting at which the vote objected to is tendered, and every vote not disallowed at the meeting is valid.

(2) Any such objection must be referred to the chairman of the meeting, whose decision is final.

Poll votes

44.— (1) A poll on a resolution may be demanded—

(a) in advance of the general meeting where it is to be put to the vote, or

(b) at a general meeting, either before a show of hands on that resolution or immediately after the result of a show of hands on that resolution is declared.

(2)   A poll may be demanded by—
    (a)   the chairman of the meeting;
    (b)   the directors;
    (c)   two or more persons having the right to vote on the resolution; or
    (d)   a person or persons representing not less than one tenth of the total voting rights of all the shareholders having the right to vote on the resolution.

(3)   A demand for a poll may be withdrawn if—
    (a)   the poll has not yet been taken, and
    (b)   the chairman of the meeting consents to the withdrawal.

(4)   Polls must be taken immediately and in such manner as the chairman of the meeting directs.

Content of proxy notices

45.— (1)   Proxies may only validly be appointed by a notice in writing (a 'proxy notice') which—
    (a)   states the name and address of the shareholder appointing the proxy;
    (b)   identifies the person appointed to be that shareholder's proxy and the general meeting in relation to which that person is appointed;
    (c)   is signed by or on behalf of the shareholder appointing the proxy, or is authenticated in such manner as the directors may determine; and
    (d)   is delivered to the company in accordance with the articles and any instructions contained in the notice of the general meeting to which they relate.

(2)   The company may require proxy notices to be delivered in a particular form, and may specify different forms for different purposes.

(3)   Proxy notices may specify how the proxy appointed under them is to vote (or that the proxy is to abstain from voting) on one or more resolutions.

(4)   Unless a proxy notice indicates otherwise, it must be treated as—
    (a)   allowing the person appointed under it as a proxy discretion as to how to vote on any ancillary or procedural resolutions put to the meeting, and
    (b)   appointing that person as a proxy in relation to any adjournment of the general meeting to which it relates as well as the meeting itself.

Delivery of proxy notices

46.— (1)   A person who is entitled to attend, speak or vote (either on a show of hands or on a poll) at a general meeting remains so entitled in respect of that meeting or any adjournment of it, even though a valid proxy notice has been delivered to the company by or on behalf of that person.

(2) An appointment under a proxy notice may be revoked by delivering to the company a notice in writing given by or on behalf of the person by whom or on whose behalf the proxy notice was given.

(3) A notice revoking a proxy appointment only takes effect if it is delivered before the start of the meeting or adjourned meeting to which it relates.

(4) If a proxy notice is not executed by the person appointing the proxy, it must be accompanied by written evidence of the authority of the person who executed it to execute it on the appointor's behalf.

Amendments to resolutions

47.— (1) An ordinary resolution to be proposed at a general meeting may be amended by ordinary resolution if—

(a) notice of the proposed amendment is given to the company in writing by a person entitled to vote at the general meeting at which it is to be proposed not less than 48 hours before the meeting is to take place (or such later time as the chairman of the meeting may determine), and

(b) the proposed amendment does not, in the reasonable opinion of the chairman of the meeting, materially alter the scope of the resolution.

(2) A special resolution to be proposed at a general meeting may be amended by ordinary resolution, if—

(a) the chairman of the meeting proposes the amendment at the general meeting at which the resolution is to be proposed, and

(b) the amendment does not go beyond what is necessary to correct a grammatical or other non-substantive error in the resolution.

(3) If the chairman of the meeting, acting in good faith, wrongly decides that an amendment to a resolution is out of order, the chairman's error does not invalidate the vote on that resolution.

PART 5
ADMINISTRATIVE ARRANGEMENTS

Means of communication to be used

48.— (1) Subject to the articles, anything sent or supplied by or to the company under the articles may be sent or supplied in any way in which the Companies Act 2006 provides for documents or information which are authorised or required by any provision of that Act to be sent or supplied by or to the company.

(2) Subject to the articles, any notice or document to be sent or supplied to a director in connection with the taking of decisions by directors may also be sent or supplied by the means by which that director has asked to be sent or supplied with such notices or documents for the time being.

(3) A director may agree with the company that notices or documents sent to that director in a particular way are to be deemed to have been received within a specified time of their being sent, and for the specified time to be less than 48 hours.

Company seals
49.— (1) Any common seal may only be used by the authority of the directors.

(2) The directors may decide by what means and in what form any common seal is to be used.

(3) Unless otherwise decided by the directors, if the company has a common seal and it is affixed to a document, the document must also be signed by at least one authorised person in the presence of a witness who attests the signature.

(4) For the purposes of this article, an authorised person is—

(a) any director of the company;

(b) the company secretary (if any); or

(c) any person authorised by the directors for the purpose of signing documents to which the common seal is applied.

No right to inspect accounts and other records
50. Except as provided by law or authorised by the directors or an ordinary resolution of the company, no person is entitled to inspect any of the company's accounting or other records or documents merely by virtue of being a shareholder.

Provision for employees on cessation of business
51. The directors may decide to make provision for the benefit of persons employed or formerly employed by the company or any of its subsidiaries (other than a director or former director or shadow director) in connection with the cessation or transfer to any person of the whole or part of the undertaking of the company or that subsidiary.

DIRECTORS' INDEMNITY AND INSURANCE

Indemnity
52.— (1) Subject to paragraph (2), a relevant director of the company or an associated company may be indemnified out of the company's assets against—

(a) any liability incurred by that director in connection with any negligence, default, breach of duty or breach of trust in relation to the company or an associated company,

(b) any liability incurred by that director in connection with the activities of the company or an associated company in its capacity as a trustee of an occupational pension scheme (as defined in section 235(6) of the Companies Act 2006),

(c) any other liability incurred by that director as an officer of the company or an associated company.

(2) This article does not authorise any indemnity which would be prohibited or rendered void by any provision of the Companies Acts or by any other provision of law.

(3) In this article—

(a) companies are associated if one is a subsidiary of the other or both are subsidiaries of the same body corporate, and

(b) a 'relevant director' means any director or former director of the company or an associated company.

Insurance

53.— (1) The directors may decide to purchase and maintain insurance, at the expense of the company, for the benefit of any relevant director in respect of any relevant loss.

(2) In this article—

(a) a 'relevant director' means any director or former director of the company or an associated company,

(b) a 'relevant loss' means any loss or liability which has been or may be incurred by a relevant director in connection with that director's duties or powers in relation to the company, any associated company or any pension fund or employees' share scheme of the company or associated company, and

(c) companies are associated if one is a subsidiary of the other or both are subsidiaries of the same body corporate.

Appendix 8 – Model articles for private companies limited by guarantee

Model articles for private companies limited by guarantee applicable for companies incorporated on or after 28 April 2013. This version was published on 13 September 2018 and last updated on 18 September 2018.

Later versions may be available at: www.gov.uk/government/publications/model-articles-for-private-companies-limited-by-guarantee

SCHEDULE 2 Regulation 3

MODEL ARTICLES FOR PRIVATE COMPANIES LIMITED BY GUARANTEE

INDEX TO THE ARTICLES

DIRECTORS' INDEMNITY AND INSURANCE

PART 1
INTERPRETATION AND LIMITATION OF LIABILITY

Defined terms

1.   In the articles, unless the context requires otherwise—

'articles' means the company's articles of association;

'bankruptcy' includes individual insolvency proceedings in a jurisdiction other than England and Wales or Northern Ireland which have an effect similar to that of bankruptcy;

'chairman' has the meaning given in article 12;

'chairman of the meeting' has the meaning given in article 25;

'Companies Acts' means the Companies Acts (as defined in section 2 of the Companies Act 2006), in so far as they apply to the company;

'director' means a director of the company, and includes any person occupying the position of director, by whatever name called;

'document' includes, unless otherwise specified, any document sent or supplied in electronic form;

'electronic form' has the meaning given in section 1168 of the Companies Act 2006;

'member' has the meaning given in section 112 of the Companies Act 2006;

'ordinary resolution' has the meaning given in section 282 of the Companies Act 2006;

'participate', in relation to a directors' meeting, has the meaning given in article 10;

'proxy notice' has the meaning given in article 31;

'special resolution' has the meaning given in section 283 of the Companies Act 2006;

'subsidiary' has the meaning given in section 1159 of the Companies Act 2006; and

'writing' means the representation or reproduction of words, symbols or other information in a visible form by any method or combination of methods, whether sent or supplied in electronic form or otherwise.

Unless the context otherwise requires, other words or expressions contained in these articles bear the same meaning as in the Companies

Act 2006 as in force on the date when these articles become binding on the company.

Liability of members

2.   The liability of each member is limited to £1, being the amount that each member undertakes to contribute to the assets of the company in the event of its being wound up while he is a member or within one year after he ceases to be a member, for—

(a)   payment of the company's debts and liabilities contracted before he ceases to be a member,

(b)   payment of the costs, charges and expenses of winding up, and

(c)   adjustment of the rights of the contributories among themselves.

PART 2
DIRECTORS
DIRECTORS' POWERS AND RESPONSIBILITIES

Directors' general authority

3.—   Subject to the articles, the directors are responsible for the management of the company's business, for which purpose they may exercise all the powers of the company.

Members' reserve power

4.—   (1)   The members may, by special resolution, direct the directors to take, or refrain from taking, specified action.

(2)   No such special resolution invalidates anything which the directors have done before the passing of the resolution.

Directors may delegate

5.—   (1)   Subject to the articles, the directors may delegate any of the powers which are conferred on them under the articles—

(a)   to such person or committee;

(b)   by such means (including by power of attorney);

(c)   to such an extent;

(d)   in relation to such matters or territories; and

(e)   on such terms and conditions;

as they think fit.

(2)   If the directors so specify, any such delegation may authorise further delegation of the directors' powers by any person to whom they are delegated.

(3)   The directors may revoke any delegation in whole or part or alter its terms and conditions.

Committees

6.— (1) Committees to which the directors delegate any of their powers must follow procedures which are based as far as they are applicable on those provisions of the articles which govern the taking of decisions by directors.

(2) The directors may make rules of procedure for all or any committees, which prevail over rules derived from the articles if they are not consistent with them.

DECISION-MAKING BY DIRECTORS

Directors to take decisions collectively

7.— (1) The general rule about decision-making by directors is that any decision of the directors must be either a majority decision at a meeting or a decision taken in accordance with article 8.

(2) If—

(a) the company only has one director, and

(b) no provision of the articles requires it to have more than one director, the general rule does not apply, and the director may take decisions without regard to any of the provisions of the articles relating to directors' decision-making.

Unanimous decisions

8.— (1) A decision of the directors is taken in accordance with this article when all eligible directors indicate to each other by any means that they share a common view on a matter.

(2) Such a decision may take the form of a resolution in writing, copies of which have been signed by each eligible director or to which each eligible director has otherwise indicated agreement in writing.

(3) References in this article to eligible directors are to directors who would have been entitled to vote on the matter had it been proposed as a resolution at a directors' meeting.

(4) A decision may not be taken in accordance with this article if the eligible directors would not have formed a quorum at such a meeting.

Calling a directors' meeting

9.— (1) Any director may call a directors' meeting by giving notice of the meeting to the directors or by authorising the company secretary (if any) to give such notice.

(2) Notice of any directors' meeting must indicate—

(a) its proposed date and time;

(b) where it is to take place; and

(c) if it is anticipated that directors participating in the meeting will not be in the same place, how it is proposed that they should communicate with each other during the meeting.

(3) Notice of a directors' meeting must be given to each director but need not be in writing.

(4) Notice of a directors' meeting need not be given to directors who waive their entitlement to notice of that meeting, by giving notice to that effect to the company not more than seven days after the date on which the meeting is held. Where such notice is given after the meeting has been held, that does not affect the validity of the meeting, or of any business conducted at it.

Participation in directors' meetings

10.— (1) Subject to the articles, directors participate in a directors' meeting, or part of a directors' meeting, when—

(a) the meeting has been called and takes place in accordance with the articles, and

(b) they can each communicate to the others any information or opinions they have on any particular item of the business of the meeting.

(2) In determining whether directors are participating in a directors' meeting, it is irrelevant where any director is or how they communicate with each other.

(3) If all the directors participating in a meeting are not in the same place, they may decide that the meeting is to be treated as taking place wherever any of them is.

Quorum for directors' meetings

11.— (1) At a directors' meeting, unless a quorum is participating, no proposal is to be voted on, except a proposal to call another meeting.

(2) The quorum for directors' meetings may be fixed from time to time by a decision of the directors, but it must never be less than two, and unless otherwise fixed it is two.

(3) If the total number of directors for the time being is less than the quorum required, the directors must not take any decision other than a decision—

(a) to appoint further directors, or

(b) to call a general meeting so as to enable the members to appoint further directors.

Chairing of directors' meetings

12.— (1) The directors may appoint a director to chair their meetings.

(2) The person so appointed for the time being is known as the chairman.

(3)   The directors may terminate the chairman's appointment at any time.

(4)   If the chairman is not participating in a directors' meeting within ten minutes of the time at which it was to start, the participating directors must appoint one of themselves to chair it.

Casting vote

13.— (1)   If the numbers of votes for and against a proposal are equal, the chairman or other director chairing the meeting has a casting vote.

(2)   But this does not apply if, in accordance with the articles, the chairman or other director is not to be counted as participating in the decision-making process for quorum or voting purposes.

Conflicts of interest

14.— (1)   If a proposed decision of the directors is concerned with an actual or proposed transaction or arrangement with the company in which a director is interested, that director is not to be counted as participating in the decision-making process for quorum or voting purposes.

(2)   But if paragraph (3) applies, a director who is interested in an actual or proposed transaction or arrangement with the company is to be counted as participating in the decision-making process for quorum and voting purposes.

(3)   This paragraph applies when—

(a)   the company by ordinary resolution disapplies the provision of the articles which would otherwise prevent a director from being counted as participating in the decision-making process;

(b)   the director's interest cannot reasonably be regarded as likely to give rise to a conflict of interest; or

(c)   the director's conflict of interest arises from a permitted cause.

(4)   For the purposes of this article, the following are permitted causes—

(a)   a guarantee given, or to be given, by or to a director in respect of an obligation incurred by or on behalf of the company or any of its subsidiaries;

(b)   subscription, or an agreement to subscribe, for securities of the company or any of its subsidiaries, or to underwrite, sub-underwrite, or guarantee subscription for any such securities; and

(c)   arrangements pursuant to which benefits are made available to employees and directors or former employees and directors of the company or any of its subsidiaries which do not provide special benefits for directors or former directors.

(5) For the purposes of this article, references to proposed decisions and decision-making processes include any directors' meeting or part of a directors' meeting.

(6) Subject to paragraph (7), if a question arises at a meeting of directors or of a committee of directors as to the right of a director to participate in the meeting (or part of the meeting) for voting or quorum purposes, the question may, before the conclusion of the meeting, be referred to the chairman whose ruling in relation to any director other than the chairman is to be final and conclusive.

(7) If any question as to the right to participate in the meeting (or part of the meeting) should arise in respect of the chairman, the question is to be decided by a decision of the directors at that meeting, for which purpose the chairman is not to be counted as participating in the meeting (or that part of the meeting) for voting or quorum purposes.

Records of decisions to be kept

15. The directors must ensure that the company keeps a record, in writing, for at least 10 years from the date of the decision recorded, of every unanimous or majority decision taken by the directors.

Directors' discretion to make further rules

16. Subject to the articles, the directors may make any rule which they think fit about how they take decisions, and about how such rules are to be recorded or communicated to directors.

APPOINTMENT OF DIRECTORS

Methods of appointing directors

17.— (1) Any person who is willing to act as a director, and is permitted by law to do so, may be appointed to be a director—

(a) by ordinary resolution, or

(b) by a decision of the directors.

(2) In any case where, as a result of death, the company has no members and no directors, the personal representatives of the last member to have died have the right, by notice in writing, to appoint a person to be a director.

(3) For the purposes of paragraph (2), where two or more members die in circumstances rendering it uncertain who was the last to die, a younger member is deemed to have survived an older member.

Termination of director's appointment

18.   A person ceases to be a director as soon as—

(a)   that person ceases to be a director by virtue of any provision of the Companies Act 2006 or is prohibited from being a director by law;

(b)   a bankruptcy order is made against that person;

(c)   a composition is made with that person's creditors generally in satisfaction of that person's debts;

(d)   a registered medical practitioner who is treating that person gives a written opinion to the company stating that that person has become physically or mentally incapable of acting as a director and may remain so for more than three months;

(e)   *[paragraph omitted pursuant to The Mental Health (Discrimination) Act 2013]*

(f)   notification is received by the company from the director that the director is resigning from office, and such resignation has taken effect in accordance with its terms.

Directors' remuneration

19.— (1)   Directors may undertake any services for the company that the directors decide.

(2)   Directors are entitled to such remuneration as the directors determine—

(a)   for their services to the company as directors, and

(b)   for any other service which they undertake for the company.

(3)   Subject to the articles, a director's remuneration may—

(a)   take any form, and

(b)   include any arrangements in connection with the payment of a pension, allowance or gratuity, or any death, sickness or disability benefits, to or in respect of that director.

(4)   Unless the directors decide otherwise, directors' remuneration accrues from day to day.

(5)   Unless the directors decide otherwise, directors are not accountable to the company for any remuneration which they receive as directors or other officers or employees of the company's subsidiaries or of any other body corporate in which the company is interested.

Directors' expenses

20.   The company may pay any reasonable expenses which the directors properly incur in connection with their attendance at—

(a)   meetings of directors or committees of directors,

(b)   general meetings, or

(c)   separate meetings of the holders of debentures of the company, or otherwise in connection with the exercise of their powers and the discharge of their responsibilities in relation to the company.

PART 3
MEMBERS
BECOMING AND CEASING TO BE A MEMBER

Applications for membership

21.   No person shall become a member of the company unless—

(a)   that person has completed an application for membership in a form approved by the directors, and

(b)   the directors have approved the application.

Termination of membership

22.— (1)   A member may withdraw from membership of the company by giving 7 days' notice to the company in writing.

(2)   Membership is not transferable.

(3)   A person's membership terminates when that person dies or ceases to exist.

ORGANISATION OF GENERAL MEETINGS

Attendance and speaking at general meetings

23.— (1)   A person is able to exercise the right to speak at a general meeting when that person is in a position to communicate to all those attending the meeting, during the meeting, any information or opinions which that person has on the business of the meeting.

(2)   A person is able to exercise the right to vote at a general meeting when—

(a)   that person is able to vote, during the meeting, on resolutions put to the vote at the meeting, and

(b)   that person's vote can be taken into account in determining whether or not such resolutions are passed at the same time as the votes of all the other persons attending the meeting.

(3)   The directors may make whatever arrangements they consider appropriate to enable those attending a general meeting to exercise their rights to speak or vote at it.

(4)   In determining attendance at a general meeting, it is immaterial whether any two or more members attending it are in the same place as each other.

(5)   Two or more persons who are not in the same place as each other attend a general meeting if their circumstances are such that if they have (or were to have) rights to speak and vote at that meeting, they are (or would be) able to exercise them.

Quorum for general meetings

24.   No business other than the appointment of the chairman of the meeting is to be transacted at a general meeting if the persons attending it do not constitute a quorum.

Chairing general meetings

25.— (1) If the directors have appointed a chairman, the chairman shall chair general meetings if present and willing to do so.

(2) If the directors have not appointed a chairman, or if the chairman is unwilling to chair the meeting or is not present within ten minutes of the time at which a meeting was due to start—

(a) the directors present, or

(b) (if no directors are present), the meeting, must appoint a director or member to chair the meeting, and the appointment of the chairman of the meeting must be the first business of the meeting.

(3) The person chairing a meeting in accordance with this article is referred to as 'the chairman of the meeting'.

Attendance and speaking by directors and non-members

26.— (1) Directors may attend and speak at general meetings, whether or not they are members.

(2) The chairman of the meeting may permit other persons who are not members of the company to attend and speak at a general meeting.

Adjournment

27.— (1) If the persons attending a general meeting within half an hour of the time at which the meeting was due to start do not constitute a quorum, or if during a meeting a quorum ceases to be present, the chairman of the meeting must adjourn it.

(2) The chairman of the meeting may adjourn a general meeting at which a quorum is present if—

(a) the meeting consents to an adjournment, or

(b) it appears to the chairman of the meeting that an adjournment is necessary to protect the safety of any person attending the meeting or ensure that the business of the meeting is conducted in an orderly manner.

(3) The chairman of the meeting must adjourn a general meeting if directed to do so by the meeting.

(4) When adjourning a general meeting, the chairman of the meeting must—

(a) either specify the time and place to which it is adjourned or state that it is to continue at a time and place to be fixed by the directors, and

(b)   have regard to any directions as to the time and place of any adjournment which have been given by the meeting.

(5)   If the continuation of an adjourned meeting is to take place more than 14 days after it was adjourned, the company must give at least 7 clear days' notice of it (that is, excluding the day of the adjourned meeting and the day on which the notice is given)—

(a)   to the same persons to whom notice of the company's general meetings is required to be given, and

(b)   containing the same information which such notice is required to contain.

(6)   No business may be transacted at an adjourned general meeting which could not properly have been transacted at the meeting if the adjournment had not taken place.

VOTING AT GENERAL MEETINGS

Voting: general

28.   A resolution put to the vote of a general meeting must be decided on a show of hands unless a poll is duly demanded in accordance with the articles.

Errors and disputes

29.— (1)   No objection may be raised to the qualification of any person voting at a general meeting except at the meeting or adjourned meeting at which the vote objected to is tendered, and every vote not disallowed at the meeting is valid.

(2)   Any such objection must be referred to the chairman of the meeting whose decision is final.

Poll votes

30.— (1)   A poll on a resolution may be demanded—

(a)   in advance of the general meeting where it is to be put to the vote, or

(b)   at a general meeting, either before a show of hands on that resolution or immediately after the result of a show of hands on that resolution is declared.

(2)   A poll may be demanded by—

(a)   the chairman of the meeting;

(b)   the directors;

(c)   two or more persons having the right to vote on the resolution; or

(d)   a person or persons representing not less than one tenth of the total voting rights of all the members having the right to vote on the resolution.

(3) A demand for a poll may be withdrawn if—
    (a) the poll has not yet been taken, and
    (b) the chairman of the meeting consents to the withdrawal.

(4) Polls must be taken immediately and in such manner as the chairman of the meeting directs.

Content of proxy notices

31.— (1) Proxies may only validly be appointed by a notice in writing (a 'proxy notice') which—

    (a) states the name and address of the member appointing the proxy;

    (b) identifies the person appointed to be that member's proxy and the general meeting in relation to which that person is appointed;

    (c) is signed by or on behalf of the member appointing the proxy, or is authenticated in such manner as the directors may determine; and

    (d) is delivered to the company in accordance with the articles and any instructions contained in the notice of the general meeting to which they relate.

(2) The company may require proxy notices to be delivered in a particular form, and may specify different forms for different purposes.

(3) Proxy notices may specify how the proxy appointed under them is to vote (or that the proxy is to abstain from voting) on one or more resolutions.

(4) Unless a proxy notice indicates otherwise, it must be treated as—

    (a) allowing the person appointed under it as a proxy discretion as to how to vote on any ancillary or procedural resolutions put to the meeting, and

    (b) appointing that person as a proxy in relation to any adjournment of the general meeting to which it relates as well as the meeting itself.

Delivery of proxy notices

32.— (1) A person who is entitled to attend, speak or vote (either on a show of hands or on a poll) at a general meeting remains so entitled in respect of that meeting or any adjournment of it, even though a valid proxy notice has been delivered to the company by or on behalf of that person.

(2) An appointment under a proxy notice may be revoked by delivering to the company a notice in writing given by or on behalf of the person by whom or on whose behalf the proxy notice was given.

(3) A notice revoking a proxy appointment only takes effect if it is delivered before the start of the meeting or adjourned meeting to which it relates.

(4) If a proxy notice is not executed by the person appointing the proxy, it must be accompanied by written evidence of the authority of the person who executed it to execute it on the appointor's behalf.

Amendments to resolutions

33.— (1) An ordinary resolution to be proposed at a general meeting may be amended by ordinary resolution if—

    (a) notice of the proposed amendment is given to the company in writing by a person entitled to vote at the general meeting at which it is to be proposed not less than 48 hours before the meeting is to take place (or such later time as the chairman of the meeting may determine), and

    (b) the proposed amendment does not, in the reasonable opinion of the chairman of the meeting, materially alter the scope of the resolution.

(2) A special resolution to be proposed at a general meeting may be amended by ordinary resolution, if—

    (a) the chairman of the meeting proposes the amendment at the general meeting at which the resolution is to be proposed, and

    (b) the amendment does not go beyond what is necessary to correct a grammatical or other non-substantive error in the resolution.

(3) If the chairman of the meeting, acting in good faith, wrongly decides that an amendment to a resolution is out of order, the chairman's error does not invalidate the vote on that resolution.

PART 4
ADMINISTRATIVE ARRANGEMENTS

Means of communication to be used

34.— (1) Subject to the articles, anything sent or supplied by or to the company under the articles may be sent or supplied in any way in which the Companies Act 2006 provides for documents or information which are authorised or required by any provision of that Act to be sent or supplied by or to the company.

(2) Subject to the articles, any notice or document to be sent or supplied to a director in connection with the taking of decisions by directors may also be sent or supplied by the means by which that director has asked to be sent or supplied with such notices or documents for the time being.

(3) A director may agree with the company that notices or documents sent to that director in a particular way are to be deemed to have been received within a specified time of their being sent, and for the specified time to be less than 48 hours.

Company seals

35.— (1) Any common seal may only be used by the authority of the directors.

(2) The directors may decide by what means and in what form any common seal is to be used.

(3) Unless otherwise decided by the directors, if the company has a common seal and it is affixed to a document, the document must also be signed by at least one authorised person in the presence of a witness who attests the signature.

(4) For the purposes of this article, an authorised person is—

(a) any director of the company;

(b) the company secretary (if any); or

(c) any person authorised by the directors for the purpose of signing documents to which the common seal is applied.

No right to inspect accounts and other records

36. Except as provided by law or authorised by the directors or an ordinary resolution of the company, no person is entitled to inspect any of the company's accounting or other records or documents merely by virtue of being a member.

Provision for employees on cessation of business

37. The directors may decide to make provision for the benefit of persons employed or formerly employed by the company or any of its subsidiaries (other than a director or former director or shadow director) in connection with the cessation or transfer to any person of the whole or part of the undertaking of the company or that subsidiary.

DIRECTORS' INDEMNITY AND INSURANCE

Indemnity

38.— (1) Subject to paragraph (2), a relevant director of the company or an associated company may be indemnified out of the company's assets against—

(a) any liability incurred by that director in connection with any negligence, default, breach of duty or breach of trust in relation to the company or an associated company,

(b) any liability incurred by that director in connection with the activities of the company or an associated company in its capacity as a trustee of an occupational pension scheme (as defined in section 235(6) of the Companies Act 2006),

(c) any other liability incurred by that director as an officer of the company or an associated company.

(2) This article does not authorise any indemnity which would be prohibited or rendered void by any provision of the Companies Acts or by any other provision of law.

(3) In this article—

    (a) companies are associated if one is a subsidiary of the other or both are subsidiaries of the same body corporate, and

    (b) a 'relevant director' means any director or former director of the company or an associated company.

Insurance

39.— (1) The directors may decide to purchase and maintain insurance, at the expense of the company, for the benefit of any relevant director in respect of any relevant loss.

(2) In this article—

    (a) a 'relevant director' means any director or former director of the company or an associated company,

    (b) a 'relevant loss' means any loss or liability which has been or may be incurred by a relevant director in connection with that director's duties or powers in relation to the company, any associated company or any pension fund or employees' share scheme of the company or associated company, and

    (c) companies are associated if one is a subsidiary of the other or both are subsidiaries of the same body corporate.

Appendix 9 – Model articles for public companies

Model articles for public companies applicable for companies incorporated on or after 28 April 2013.

Latest version available at: www.gov.uk/guidance/model-articles-of-association-for-limited-companies#examples-of-model-articles

SCHEDULE 3 Regulation 4

MODEL ARTICLES FOR PUBLIC COMPANIES
INDEX TO THE ARTICLES

PART 1
INTERPRETATION AND LIMITATION OF LIABILITY

PART 2
DIRECTORS
DIRECTORS' POWERS AND RESPONSIBILITIES

DECISION-MAKING BY DIRECTORS

PART 1
INTERPRETATION AND LIMITATION OF LIABILITY

Defined terms

1.   In the articles, unless the context requires otherwise—

'alternate' or 'alternate director' has the meaning given in article 25;

'appointor' has the meaning given in article 25;

'articles' means the company's articles of association;

'bankruptcy' includes individual insolvency proceedings in a jurisdiction other than England and Wales or Northern Ireland which have an effect similar to that of bankruptcy;

'call' has the meaning given in article 54;

'call notice' has the meaning given in article 54;

'certificate' means a paper certificate (other than a share warrant) evidencing a person's title to specified shares or other securities;

'certificated' in relation to a share, means that it is not an uncertificated share or a share in respect of which a share warrant has been issued and is current;

'chairman' has the meaning given in article 12;

'chairman of the meeting' has the meaning given in article 31;

'Companies Acts' means the Companies Acts (as defined in section 2 of the Companies Act 2006), in so far as they apply to the company;

'company's lien' has the meaning given in article 52;

'director' means a director of the company, and includes any person occupying the position of director, by whatever name called;

'distribution recipient' has the meaning given in article 72;

'document' includes, unless otherwise specified, any document sent or supplied in electronic form;

'electronic form' has the meaning given in section 1168 of the Companies Act 2006;

'fully paid' in relation to a share, means that the nominal value and any premium to be paid to the company in respect of that share have been paid to the company;

'hard copy form' has the meaning given in section 1168 of the Companies Act 2006;

'holder' in relation to shares means the person whose name is entered in the register of members as the holder of the shares, or, in the case of a share in respect of which a share warrant has been issued (and not cancelled), the person in possession of that warrant;

'instrument' means a document in hard copy form;

'lien enforcement notice' has the meaning given in article 53;

'member' has the meaning given in section 112 of the Companies Act 2006;

'ordinary resolution' has the meaning given in section 282 of the Companies Act 2006;

'paid' means paid or credited as paid;

'participate', in relation to a directors' meeting, has the meaning given in article 9;

'partly paid' in relation to a share means that part of that share's nominal value or any premium at which it was issued has not been paid to the company;

'proxy notice' has the meaning given in article 38;

'securities seal' has the meaning given in article 47;

'shares' means shares in the company;

'special resolution' has the meaning given in section 283 of the Companies Act 2006;

'subsidiary' has the meaning given in section 1159 of the Companies Act 2006;

'transmittee' means a person entitled to a share by reason of the death or bankruptcy of a shareholder or otherwise by operation of law;

'uncertificated' in relation to a share means that, by virtue of legislation (other than section 778 of the Companies Act 2006) permitting title to shares to be evidenced and transferred without a certificate, title to that share is evidenced and may be transferred without a certificate; and

'writing' means the representation or reproduction of words, symbols or other information in a visible form by any method or combination of methods, whether sent or supplied in electronic form or otherwise.

Unless the context otherwise requires, other words or expressions contained in these articles bear the same meaning as in the Companies Act 2006 as in force on the date when these articles become binding on the company.

Liability of members

2. The liability of the members is limited to the amount, if any, unpaid on the shares held by them.

PART 2
DIRECTORS
DIRECTORS' POWERS AND RESPONSIBILITIES

Directors' general authority

3. Subject to the articles, the directors are responsible for the management of the company's business, for which purpose they may exercise all the powers of the company.

Members' reserve power
4.— (1) The members may, by special resolution, direct the directors to take, or refrain from taking, specified action.
   (2) No such special resolution invalidates anything which the directors have done before the passing of the resolution.

Directors may delegate
5.— (1) Subject to the articles, the directors may delegate any of the powers which are conferred on them under the articles—
   (a) to such person or committee;
   (b) by such means (including by power of attorney);
   (c) to such an extent;
   (d) in relation to such matters or territories; and
   (e) on such terms and conditions;
   as they think fit.
   (2) If the directors so specify, any such delegation may authorise further delegation of the directors' powers by any person to whom they are delegated.
   (3) The directors may revoke any delegation in whole or part, or alter its terms and conditions.

Committees
6.— (1) Committees to which the directors delegate any of their powers must follow procedures which are based as far as they are applicable on those provisions of the articles which govern the taking of decisions by directors.
   (2) The directors may make rules of procedure for all or any committees, which prevail over rules derived from the articles if they are not consistent with them.

DECISION-MAKING BY DIRECTORS

Directors to take decisions collectively
7. Decisions of the directors may be taken—
   (a) at a directors' meeting, or
   (b) in the form of a directors' written resolution.

Calling a directors' meeting
8.— (1) Any director may call a directors' meeting.
   (2) The company secretary must call a directors' meeting if a director so requests.
   (3) A directors' meeting is called by giving notice of the meeting to the directors.

    (4)   Notice of any directors' meeting must indicate—
        (a)   its proposed date and time;
        (b)   where it is to take place; and
        (c)   if it is anticipated that directors participating in the meeting will not be in the same place, how it is proposed that they should communicate with each other during the meeting.
    (5)   Notice of a directors' meeting must be given to each director, but need not be in writing.
    (6)   Notice of a directors' meeting need not be given to directors who waive their entitlement to notice of that meeting, by giving notice to that effect to the company not more than 7 days after the date on which the meeting is held. Where such notice is given after the meeting has been held, that does not affect the validity of the meeting, or of any business conducted at it.

Participation in directors' meetings

9.— (1)   Subject to the articles, directors participate in a directors' meeting, or part of a directors' meeting, when—
        (a)   the meeting has been called and takes place in accordance with the articles, and
        (b)   they can each communicate to the others any information or opinions they have on any particular item of the business of the meeting.
    (2)   In determining whether directors are participating in a directors' meeting, it is irrelevant where any director is or how they communicate with each other.
    (3)   If all the directors participating in a meeting are not in the same place, they may decide that the meeting is to be treated as taking place wherever any of them is.

Quorum for directors' meetings

10.— (1)   At a directors' meeting, unless a quorum is participating, no proposal is to be voted on, except a proposal to call another meeting.
    (2)   The quorum for directors' meetings may be fixed from time to time by a decision of the directors, but it must never be less than two, and unless otherwise fixed it is two.

Meetings where total number of directors less than quorum

11.— (1)   This article applies where the total number of directors for the time being is less than the quorum for directors' meetings.
    (2)   If there is only one director, that director may appoint sufficient directors to make up a quorum or call a general meeting to do so.
    (3)   If there is more than one director—

(a)   a directors' meeting may take place, if it is called in accordance with the articles and at least two directors participate in it, with a view to appointing sufficient directors to make up a quorum or calling a general meeting to do so, and

(b)   if a directors' meeting is called but only one director attends at the appointed date and time to participate in it, that director may appoint sufficient directors to make up a quorum or call a general meeting to do so.

Chairing directors' meetings

12.— (1)   The directors may appoint a director to chair their meetings.

(2)   The person so appointed for the time being is known as the chairman.

(3)   The directors may appoint other directors as deputy or assistant chairmen to chair directors' meetings in the chairman's absence.

(4)   The directors may terminate the appointment of the chairman, deputy or assistant chairman at any time.

(5)   If neither the chairman nor any director appointed generally to chair directors' meetings in the chairman's absence is participating in a meeting within ten minutes of the time at which it was to start, the participating directors must appoint one of themselves to chair it.

Voting at directors' meetings: general rules

13.— (1)   Subject to the articles, a decision is taken at a directors' meeting by a majority of the votes of the participating directors.

(2)   Subject to the articles, each director participating in a directors' meeting has one vote.

(3)   Subject to the articles, if a director has an interest in an actual or proposed transaction or arrangement with the company—

(a)   that director and that director's alternate may not vote on any proposal relating to it, but

(b)   this does not preclude the alternate from voting in relation to that transaction or arrangement on behalf of another appointor who does not have such an interest.

Chairman's casting vote at directors' meetings

14.— (1)   If the numbers of votes for and against a proposal are equal, the chairman or other director chairing the meeting has a casting vote.

(2)   But this does not apply if, in accordance with the articles, the chairman or other director is not to be counted as participating in the decision-making process for quorum or voting purposes.

Alternates voting at directors' meetings

15. A director who is also an alternate director has an additional vote on behalf of each appointor who is—

(a) not participating in a directors' meeting, and

(b) would have been entitled to vote if they were participating in it.

Conflicts of interest

16.— (1) If a directors' meeting, or part of a directors' meeting, is concerned with an actual or proposed transaction or arrangement with the company in which a director is interested, that director is not to be counted as participating in that meeting, or part of a meeting, for quorum or voting purposes.

(2) But if paragraph (3) applies, a director who is interested in an actual or proposed transaction or arrangement with the company is to be counted as participating in a decision at a directors' meeting, or part of a directors' meeting, relating to it for quorum and voting purposes.

(3) This paragraph applies when—

(a) the company by ordinary resolution disapplies the provision of the articles which would otherwise prevent a director from being counted as participating in, or voting at, a directors' meeting;

(b) the director's interest cannot reasonably be regarded as likely to give rise to a conflict of interest; or

(c) the director's conflict of interest arises from a permitted cause.

(4) For the purposes of this article, the following are permitted causes—

(a) a guarantee given, or to be given, by or to a director in respect of an obligation incurred by or on behalf of the company or any of its subsidiaries;

(b) subscription, or an agreement to subscribe, for shares or other securities of the company or any of its subsidiaries, or to underwrite, sub-underwrite, or guarantee subscription for any such shares or securities; and

(c) arrangements pursuant to which benefits are made available to employees and directors or former employees and directors of the company or any of its subsidiaries which do not provide special benefits for directors or former directors.

(5) Subject to paragraph (6), if a question arises at a meeting of directors or of a committee of directors as to the right of a director to participate in the meeting (or part of the meeting) for voting or quorum purposes, the question may, before the conclusion of the meeting, be referred to the chairman whose ruling in relation to any director other than the chairman is to be final and conclusive.

(6)   If any question as to the right to participate in the meeting (or part of the meeting) should arise in respect of the chairman, the question is to be decided by a decision of the directors at that meeting, for which purpose the chairman is not to be counted as participating in the meeting (or that part of the meeting) for voting or quorum purposes.

Proposing directors' written resolutions

17.— (1)   Any director may propose a directors' written resolution.

(2)   The company secretary must propose a directors' written resolution if a director so requests.

(3)   A directors' written resolution is proposed by giving notice of the proposed resolution to the directors.

(4)   Notice of a proposed directors' written resolution must indicate—

(a)   the proposed resolution, and

(b)   the time by which it is proposed that the directors should adopt it.

(5)   Notice of a proposed directors' written resolution must be given in writing to each director.

(6)   Any decision which a person giving notice of a proposed directors' written resolution takes regarding the process of adopting that resolution must be taken reasonably in good faith.

Adoption of directors' written resolutions

18.— (1)   A proposed directors' written resolution is adopted when all the directors who would have been entitled to vote on the resolution at a directors' meeting have signed one or more copies of it, provided that those directors would have formed a quorum at such a meeting.

(2)   It is immaterial whether any director signs the resolution before or after the time by which the notice proposed that it should be adopted.

(3)   Once a directors' written resolution has been adopted, it must be treated as if it had been a decision taken at a directors' meeting in accordance with the articles.

(4)   The company secretary must ensure that the company keeps a record, in writing, of all directors' written resolutions for at least ten years from the date of their adoption.

Directors' discretion to make further rules

19.   Subject to the articles, the directors may make any rule which they think fit about how they take decisions, and about how such rules are to be recorded or communicated to directors.

APPOINTMENT OF DIRECTORS

Methods of appointing directors
20.   Any person who is willing to act as a director, and is permitted by law to do so, may be appointed to be a director—
(a)   by ordinary resolution, or
(b)   by a decision of the directors.

Retirement of directors by rotation
21.— (1)   At the first annual general meeting all the directors must retire from office.
(2)   At every subsequent annual general meeting any directors—
(a)   who have been appointed by the directors since the last annual general meeting, or
(b)   who were not appointed or reappointed at one of the preceding two annual general meetings, must retire from office and may offer themselves for reappointment by the members.

Termination of director's appointment
22.   A person ceases to be a director as soon as—
(a)   that person ceases to be a director by virtue of any provision of the Companies Act 2006 or is prohibited from being a director by law;
(b)   a bankruptcy order is made against that person;
(c)   a composition is made with that person's creditors generally in satisfaction of that person's debts;
(d)   a registered medical practitioner who is treating that person gives a written opinion to the company stating that that person has become physically or mentally incapable of acting as a director and may remain so for more than three months;
(e)   *[paragraph omitted pursuant to The Mental Health (Discrimination) Act 2013]*
(f)   notification is received by the company from the director that the director is resigning from office as director, and such resignation has taken effect in accordance with its terms.

Directors' remuneration
23.— (1)   Directors may undertake any services for the company that the directors decide.
(2)   Directors are entitled to such remuneration as the directors determine—
(a)   for their services to the company as directors, and
(b)   for any other service which they undertake for the company.

(3) Subject to the articles, a director's remuneration may—
   (a) take any form, and
   (b) include any arrangements in connection with the payment of a pension, allowance or gratuity, or any death, sickness or disability benefits, to or in respect of that director.
(4) Unless the directors decide otherwise, directors' remuneration accrues from day to day.
(5) Unless the directors decide otherwise, directors are not accountable to the company for any remuneration which they receive as directors or other officers or employees of the company's subsidiaries or of any other body corporate in which the company is interested.

Directors' expenses

24. The company may pay any reasonable expenses which the directors properly incur in connection with their attendance at—
   (a) meetings of directors or committees of directors,
   (b) general meetings, or
   (c) separate meetings of the holders of any class of shares or of debentures of the company, or otherwise in connection with the exercise of their powers and the discharge of their responsibilities in relation to the company.

ALTERNATE DIRECTORS

Appointment and removal of alternates

25.— (1) Any director (the 'appointor') may appoint as an alternate any other director, or any other person approved by resolution of the directors, to—
   (a) exercise that director's powers, and
   (b) carry out that director's responsibilities, in relation to the taking of decisions by the directors in the absence of the alternate's appointor.
(2) Any appointment or removal of an alternate must be effected by notice in writing to the company signed by the appointor, or in any other manner approved by the directors.
(3) The notice must—
   (a) identify the proposed alternate, and
   (b) in the case of a notice of appointment, contain a statement signed by the proposed alternate that the proposed alternate is willing to act as the alternate of the director giving the notice.

Rights and responsibilities of alternate directors

26.— (1)   An alternate director has the same rights, in relation to any directors' meeting or directors' written resolution, as the alternate's appointor.

(2)   Except as the articles specify otherwise, alternate directors—

(a)   are deemed for all purposes to be directors;

(b)   are liable for their own acts and omissions;

(c)   are subject to the same restrictions as their appointors; and

(d)   are not deemed to be agents of or for their appointors.

(3)   A person who is an alternate director but not a director—

(a)   may be counted as participating for the purposes of determining whether a quorum is participating (but only if that person's appointor is not participating), and

(b)   may sign a written resolution (but only if it is not signed or to be signed by that person's appointor).

No alternate may be counted as more than one director for such purposes.

(4)   An alternate director is not entitled to receive any remuneration from the company for serving as an alternate director except such part of the alternate's appointor's remuneration as the appointor may direct by notice in writing made to the company.

Termination of alternate directorship

27.   An alternate director's appointment as an alternate terminates—

(a)   when the alternate's appointor revokes the appointment by notice to the company in writing specifying when it is to terminate;

(b)   on the occurrence in relation to the alternate of any event which, if it occurred in relation to the alternate's appointor, would result in the termination of the appointor's appointment as a director;

(c)   on the death of the alternate's appointor; or

(d)   when the alternate's appointor's appointment as a director terminates, except that an alternate's appointment as an alternate does not terminate when the appointor retires by rotation at a general meeting and is then reappointed as a director at the same general meeting.

PART 3
DECISION-MAKING BY MEMBERS
ORGANISATION OF GENERAL MEETINGS

Members can call general meeting if not enough directors

28. If—(a)   the company has fewer than two directors, and

(b)   the director (if any) is unable or unwilling to appoint sufficient directors to make up a quorum or to call a general meeting to do so, then two or more members may call a general meeting (or instruct the company secretary to do so) for the purpose of appointing one or more directors.

Attendance and speaking at general meetings

29.— (1) A person is able to exercise the right to speak at a general meeting when that person is in a position to communicate to all those attending the meeting, during the meeting, any information or opinions which that person has on the business of the meeting.

(2) A person is able to exercise the right to vote at a general meeting when—
   (a) that person is able to vote, during the meeting, on resolutions put to the vote at the meeting, and
   (b) that person's vote can be taken into account in determining whether or not such resolutions are passed at the same time as the votes of all the other persons attending the meeting.

(3) The directors may make whatever arrangements they consider appropriate to enable those attending a general meeting to exercise their rights to speak or vote at it.

(4) In determining attendance at a general meeting, it is immaterial whether any two or more members attending it are in the same place as each other.

(5) Two or more persons who are not in the same place as each other attend a general meeting if their circumstances are such that if they have (or were to have) rights to speak and vote at that meeting, they are (or would be) able to exercise them.

Quorum for general meetings

30. No business other than the appointment of the chairman of the meeting is to be transacted at a general meeting if the persons attending it do not constitute a quorum.

Chairing general meetings

31.— (1) If the directors have appointed a chairman, the chairman shall chair general meetings if present and willing to do so.

(2) If the directors have not appointed a chairman, or if the chairman is unwilling to chair the meeting or is not present within ten minutes of the time at which a meeting was due to start—
   (a) the directors present, or
   (b) (if no directors are present), the meeting, must appoint a director or member to chair the meeting, and the appointment of the chairman of the meeting must be the first business of the meeting.

(3) The person chairing a meeting in accordance with this article is referred to as 'the chairman of the meeting'.

Attendance and speaking by directors and non-members

32.— (1) Directors may attend and speak at general meetings, whether or not they are members.

(2) The chairman of the meeting may permit other persons who are not—

  (a) members of the company, or

  (b) otherwise entitled to exercise the rights of members in relation to general meetings, to attend and speak at a general meeting.

Adjournment

33.— (1) If the persons attending a general meeting within half an hour of the time at which the meeting was due to start do not constitute a quorum, or if during a meeting a quorum ceases to be present, the chairman of the meeting must adjourn it.

(2) The chairman of the meeting may adjourn a general meeting at which a quorum is present if—

  (a) the meeting consents to an adjournment, or

  (b) it appears to the chairman of the meeting that an adjournment is necessary to protect the safety of any person attending the meeting or ensure that the business of the meeting is conducted in an orderly manner.

(3) The chairman of the meeting must adjourn a general meeting if directed to do so by the meeting.

(4) When adjourning a general meeting, the chairman of the meeting must—

  (a) either specify the time and place to which it is adjourned or state that it is to continue at a time and place to be fixed by the directors, and

  (b) have regard to any directions as to the time and place of any adjournment which have been given by the meeting.

(5) If the continuation of an adjourned meeting is to take place more than 14 days after it was adjourned, the company must give at least 7 clear days' notice of it (that is, excluding the day of the adjourned meeting and the day on which the notice is given)—

  (a) to the same persons to whom notice of the company's general meetings is required to be given, and

  (b) containing the same information which such notice is required to contain.

(6) No business may be transacted at an adjourned general meeting which could not properly have been transacted at the meeting if the adjournment had not taken place.

VOTING AT GENERAL MEETINGS

Voting: general

34. A resolution put to the vote of a general meeting must be decided on a show of hands unless a poll is duly demanded in accordance with the articles.

Errors and disputes

35.— (1) No objection may be raised to the qualification of any person voting at a general meeting except at the meeting or adjourned meeting at which the vote objected to is tendered, and every vote not disallowed at the meeting is valid.

(2) Any such objection must be referred to the chairman of the meeting whose decision is final.

Demanding a poll

36.— (1) A poll on a resolution may be demanded—

(a) in advance of the general meeting where it is to be put to the vote, or

(b) at a general meeting, either before a show of hands on that resolution or immediately after the result of a show of hands on that resolution is declared.

(2) A poll may be demanded by—

(a) the chairman of the meeting;

(b) the directors;

(c) two or more persons having the right to vote on the resolution; or

(d) a person or persons representing not less than one tenth of the total voting rights of all the members having the right to vote on the resolution.

(3) A demand for a poll may be withdrawn if—

(a) the poll has not yet been taken, and

(b) the chairman of the meeting consents to the withdrawal.

Procedure on a poll

37.— (1) Subject to the articles, polls at general meetings must be taken when, where and in such manner as the chairman of the meeting directs.

(2) The chairman of the meeting may appoint scrutineers (who need not be members) and decide how and when the result of the poll is to be declared.

(3) The result of a poll shall be the decision of the meeting in respect of the resolution on which the poll was demanded.

(4) A poll on—

(a) the election of the chairman of the meeting, or

(b) a question of adjournment, must be taken immediately.

(5) Other polls must be taken within 30 days of their being demanded.

(6) A demand for a poll does not prevent a general meeting from continuing, except as regards the question on which the poll was demanded.

(7) No notice need be given of a poll not taken immediately if the time and place at which it is to be taken are announced at the meeting at which it is demanded.

(8) In any other case, at least 7 days' notice must be given specifying the time and place at which the poll is to be taken.

Content of proxy notices

38.— (1) Proxies may only validly be appointed by a notice in writing (a 'proxy notice') which—

(a) states the name and address of the member appointing the proxy;

(b) identifies the person appointed to be that member's proxy and the general meeting in relation to which that person is appointed;

(c) is signed by or on behalf of the member appointing the proxy, or is authenticated in such manner as the directors may determine; and

(d) is delivered to the company in accordance with the articles and any instructions contained in the notice of the general meeting to which they relate.

(2) The company may require proxy notices to be delivered in a particular form, and may specify different forms for different purposes.

(3) Proxy notices may specify how the proxy appointed under them is to vote (or that the proxy is to abstain from voting) on one or more resolutions.

(4) Unless a proxy notice indicates otherwise, it must be treated as—

(a) allowing the person appointed under it as a proxy discretion as to how to vote on any ancillary or procedural resolutions put to the meeting, and

(b) appointing that person as a proxy in relation to any adjournment of the general meeting to which it relates as well as the meeting itself.

Delivery of proxy notices

39.— (1) Any notice of a general meeting must specify the address or addresses ('proxy notification address') at which the company or its agents will receive proxy notices relating to that meeting, or any adjournment of it, delivered in hard copy or electronic form.

(2) A person who is entitled to attend, speak or vote (either on a show of hands or on a poll) at a general meeting remains so entitled in respect of that meeting or any adjournment of it, even though a valid proxy notice has been delivered to the company by or on behalf of that person.

(3) Subject to paragraphs (4) and (5), a proxy notice must be delivered to a proxy notification address not less than 48 hours before the general meeting or adjourned meeting to which it relates.

(4) In the case of a poll taken more than 48 hours after it is demanded, the notice must be delivered to a proxy notification address not less than 24 hours before the time appointed for the taking of the poll.

(5) In the case of a poll not taken during the meeting but taken not more than 48 hours after it was demanded, the proxy notice must be delivered—

   (a) in accordance with paragraph (3), or

   (b) at the meeting at which the poll was demanded to the chairman, secretary or any director.

(6) An appointment under a proxy notice may be revoked by delivering a notice in writing given by or on behalf of the person by whom or on whose behalf the proxy notice was given to a proxy notification address.

(7) A notice revoking a proxy appointment only takes effect if it is delivered before—

   (a) the start of the meeting or adjourned meeting to which it relates, or

   (b) (in the case of a poll not taken on the same day as the meeting or adjourned meeting) the time appointed for taking the poll to which it relates.

(8) If a proxy notice is not signed by the person appointing the proxy, it must be accompanied by written evidence of the authority of the person who executed it to execute it on the appointor's behalf.

Amendments to resolutions

40.— (1) An ordinary resolution to be proposed at a general meeting may be amended by ordinary resolution if—

   (a) notice of the proposed amendment is given to the company secretary in writing by a person entitled to vote at the general meeting at which it is to be proposed not less than 48 hours before the meeting is to take place (or such later time as the chairman of the meeting may determine), and

   (b) the proposed amendment does not, in the reasonable opinion of the chairman of the meeting, materially alter the scope of the resolution.

(2) A special resolution to be proposed at a general meeting may be amended by ordinary resolution, if—

(a) the chairman of the meeting proposes the amendment at the general meeting at which the resolution is to be proposed, and

(b) the amendment does not go beyond what is necessary to correct a grammatical or other non-substantive error in the resolution.

(3) If the chairman of the meeting, acting in good faith, wrongly decides that an amendment to a resolution is out of order, the chairman's error does not invalidate the vote on that resolution.

RESTRICTIONS ON MEMBERS' RIGHTS

No voting of shares on which money owed to company

41. No voting rights attached to a share may be exercised at any general meeting, at any adjournment of it, or on any poll called at or in relation to it, unless all amounts payable to the company in respect of that share have been paid.

APPLICATION OF RULES TO CLASS MEETINGS

Class meetings

42. The provisions of the articles relating to general meetings apply, with any necessary modifications, to meetings of the holders of any class of shares.

PART 4
SHARES AND DISTRIBUTIONS
ISSUE OF SHARES

Powers to issue different classes of share

43.— (1) Subject to the articles, but without prejudice to the rights attached to any existing share, the company may issue shares with such rights or restrictions as may be determined by ordinary resolution.

(2) The company may issue shares which are to be redeemed, or are liable to be redeemed at the option of the company or the holder, and the directors may determine the terms, conditions and manner of redemption of any such shares.

Payment of commissions on subscription for shares

44.— (1) The company may pay any person a commission in consideration for that person—

(a) subscribing, or agreeing to subscribe, for shares, or

(b) procuring, or agreeing to procure, subscriptions for shares.

(2) Any such commission may be paid—

(a) in cash, or in fully paid or partly paid shares or other securities, or partly in one way and partly in the other, and

(b) in respect of a conditional or an absolute subscription.

INTERESTS IN SHARES

Company not bound by less than absolute interests

45.   Except as required by law, no person is to be recognised by the company as holding any share upon any trust, and except as otherwise required by law or the articles, the company is not in any way to be bound by or recognise any interest in a share other than the holder's absolute ownership of it and all the rights attaching to it.

SHARE CERTIFICATES

Certificates to be issued except in certain cases

46.— (1) The company must issue each member with one or more certificates in respect of the shares which that member holds.

(2) This article does not apply to—

(a) uncertificated shares;

(b) shares in respect of which a share warrant has been issued; or

(c) shares in respect of which the Companies Acts permit the company not to issue a certificate.

(3) Except as otherwise specified in the articles, all certificates must be issued free of charge.

(4) No certificate may be issued in respect of shares of more than one class.

(5) If more than one person holds a share, only one certificate may be issued in respect of it.

Contents and execution of share certificates

47.— (1) Every certificate must specify—

(a) in respect of how many shares, of what class, it is issued;

(b) the nominal value of those shares;

(c) the amount paid up on them; and

(d) any distinguishing numbers assigned to them.

(2) Certificates must—

(a) have affixed to them the company's common seal or an official seal which is a facsimile of the company's common seal with the addition on its face of the word 'Securities' (a 'securities seal'), or

(b) be otherwise executed in accordance with the Companies Acts.

Consolidated share certificates

48.— (1) When a member's holding of shares of a particular class increases, the company may issue that member with—

(a) a single, consolidated certificate in respect of all the shares of a particular class which that member holds, or

(b) a separate certificate in respect of only those shares by which that member's holding has increased.

(2) When a member's holding of shares of a particular class is reduced, the company must ensure that the member is issued with one or more certificates in respect of the number of shares held by the member after that reduction. But the company need not (in the absence of a request from the member) issue any new certificate if—

(a) all the shares which the member no longer holds as a result of the reduction, and

(b) none of the shares which the member retains following the reduction, were, immediately before the reduction, represented by the same certificate.

(3) A member may request the company, in writing, to replace—

(a) the member's separate certificates with a consolidated certificate, or

(b) the member's consolidated certificate with two or more separate certificates representing such proportion of the shares as the member may specify.

(4) When the company complies with such a request it may charge such reasonable fee as the directors may decide for doing so.

(5) A consolidated certificate must not be issued unless any certificates which it is to replace have first been returned to the company for cancellation.

Replacement share certificates

49.— (1) If a certificate issued in respect of a member's shares is—

(a) damaged or defaced, or

(b) said to be lost, stolen or destroyed, that member is entitled to be issued with a replacement certificate in respect of the same shares.

(2) A member exercising the right to be issued with such a replacement certificate—

(a) may at the same time exercise the right to be issued with a single certificate or separate certificates;

(b) must return the certificate which is to be replaced to the company if it is damaged or defaced; and

(c) must comply with such conditions as to evidence, indemnity and the payment of a reasonable fee as the directors decide.

SHARES NOT HELD IN CERTIFICATED FORM

Uncertificated shares

50.— (1)   In this article, 'the relevant rules' means—

    (a)   any applicable provision of the Companies Acts about the holding, evidencing of title to, or transfer of shares other than in certificated form, and

    (b)   any applicable legislation, rules or other arrangements made under or by virtue of such provision.

  (2)   The provisions of this article have effect subject to the relevant rules.

  (3)   Any provision of the articles which is inconsistent with the relevant rules must be disregarded, to the extent that it is inconsistent, whenever the relevant rules apply.

  (4)   Any share or class of shares of the company may be issued or held on such terms, or in such a way, that—

    (a)   title to it or them is not, or must not be, evidenced by a certificate, or

    (b)   it or they may or must be transferred wholly or partly without a certificate.

  (5)   The directors have power to take such steps as they think fit in relation to—

    (a)   the evidencing of and transfer of title to uncertificated shares (including in connection with the issue of such shares);

    (b)   any records relating to the holding of uncertificated shares;

    (c)   the conversion of certificated shares into uncertificated shares; or

    (d)   the conversion of uncertificated shares into certificated shares.

  (6)   The company may by notice to the holder of a share require that share—

    (a)   if it is uncertificated, to be converted into certificated form, and

    (b)   if it is certificated, to be converted into uncertificated form, to enable it to be dealt with in accordance with the articles.

  (7)   If—

    (a)   the articles give the directors power to take action, or require other persons to take action, in order to sell, transfer or otherwise dispose of shares, and

    (b)   uncertificated shares are subject to that power, but the power is expressed in terms which assume the use of a certificate or other written instrument, the directors may take such action as is necessary or expedient to achieve the same results when exercising that power in relation to uncertificated shares.

  (8)   In particular, the directors may take such action as they consider appropriate to achieve the sale, transfer, disposal, forfeiture,

re-allotment or surrender of an uncertificated share or otherwise to enforce a lien in respect of it.

(9) Unless the directors otherwise determine, shares which a member holds in uncertificated form must be treated as separate holdings from any shares which that member holds in certificated form.

(10) A class of shares must not be treated as two classes simply because some shares of that class are held in certificated form and others are held in uncertificated form.

Share warrants

51.— (1) The directors may issue a share warrant in respect of any fully paid share.

(2) Share warrants must be—
  (a) issued in such form, and
  (b) executed in such manner,
  as the directors decide.

(3) A share represented by a share warrant may be transferred by delivery of the warrant representing it.

(4) The directors may make provision for the payment of dividends in respect of any share represented by a share warrant.

(5) Subject to the articles, the directors may decide the conditions on which any share warrant is issued. In particular, they may—
  (a) decide the conditions on which new warrants are to be issued in place of warrants which are damaged or defaced, or said to have been lost, stolen or destroyed;
  (b) decide the conditions on which bearers of warrants are entitled to attend and vote at general meetings;
  (c) decide the conditions subject to which bearers of warrants may surrender their warrant so as to hold their shares in certificated or uncertificated form instead; and
  (d) vary the conditions of issue of any warrant from time to time, and the bearer of a warrant is subject to the conditions and procedures in force in relation to it, whether or not they were decided or specified before the warrant was issued.

(6) Subject to the conditions on which the warrants are issued from time to time, bearers of share warrants have the same rights and privileges as they would if their names had been included in the register as holders of the shares represented by their warrants.

(7) The company must not in any way be bound by or recognise any interest in a share represented by a share warrant other than the absolute right of the bearer of that warrant to that warrant.

PARTLY PAID SHARES

Company's lien over partly paid shares

52.— (1) The company has a lien ('the company's lien') over every share which is partly paid for any part of—

    (a) that share's nominal value, and

    (b) any premium at which it was issued, which has not been paid to the company, and which is payable immediately or at some time in the future, whether or not a call notice has been sent in respect of it.

(2) The company's lien over a share—

    (a) takes priority over any third party's interest in that share, and

    (b) extends to any dividend or other money payable by the company in respect of that share and (if the lien is enforced and the share is sold by the company) the proceeds of sale of that share.

(3) The directors may at any time decide that a share which is or would otherwise be subject to the company's lien shall not be subject to it, either wholly or in part.

Enforcement of the company's lien

53.— (1) Subject to the provisions of this article, if—

    (a) a lien enforcement notice has been given in respect of a share, and

    (b) the person to whom the notice was given has failed to comply with it, the company may sell that share in such manner as the directors decide.

(2) A lien enforcement notice—

    (a) may only be given in respect of a share which is subject to the company's lien, in respect of which a sum is payable and the due date for payment of that sum has passed;

    (b) must specify the share concerned;

    (c) must require payment of the sum payable within 14 days of the notice;

    (d) must be addressed either to the holder of the share or to a person entitled to it by reason of the holder's death, bankruptcy or otherwise; and

    (e) must state the company's intention to sell the share if the notice is not complied with.

(3) Where shares are sold under this article—

    (a) the directors may authorise any person to execute an instrument of transfer of the shares to the purchaser or a person nominated by the purchaser, and

    (b)   the transferee is not bound to see to the application of the consideration, and the transferee's title is not affected by any irregularity in or invalidity of the process leading to the sale.

(4)   The net proceeds of any such sale (after payment of the costs of sale and any other costs of enforcing the lien) must be applied—

    (a)   first, in payment of so much of the sum for which the lien exists as was payable at the date of the lien enforcement notice,

    (b)   second, to the person entitled to the shares at the date of the sale, but only after the certificate for the shares sold has been surrendered to the company for cancellation or a suitable indemnity has been given for any lost certificates, and subject to a lien equivalent to the company's lien over the shares before the sale for any money payable in respect of the shares after the date of the lien enforcement notice.

(5)   A statutory declaration by a director or the company secretary that the declarant is a director or the company secretary and that a share has been sold to satisfy the company's lien on a specified date—

    (a)   is conclusive evidence of the facts stated in it as against all persons claiming to be entitled to the share, and

    (b)   subject to compliance with any other formalities of transfer required by the articles or by law, constitutes a good title to the share.

Call notices

54.— (1)   Subject to the articles and the terms on which shares are allotted, the directors may send a notice (a 'call notice') to a member requiring the member to pay the company a specified sum of money (a 'call') which is payable in respect of shares which that member holds at the date when the directors decide to send the call notice.

(2)   A call notice—

    (a)   may not require a member to pay a call which exceeds the total sum unpaid on that member's shares (whether as to the share's nominal value or any amount payable to the company by way of premium);

    (b)   must state when and how any call to which it relates is to be paid; and

    (c)   may permit or require the call to be paid by instalments.

(3)   A member must comply with the requirements of a call notice, but no member is obliged to pay any call before 14 days have passed since the notice was sent.

(4)   Before the company has received any call due under a call notice the directors may—

    (a)   revoke it wholly or in part, or

(b) specify a later time for payment than is specified in the notice, by a further notice in writing to the member in respect of whose shares the call is made.

Liability to pay calls

55.— (1) Liability to pay a call is not extinguished or transferred by transferring the shares in respect of which it is required to be paid.

(2) Joint holders of a share are jointly and severally liable to pay all calls in respect of that share.

(3) Subject to the terms on which shares are allotted, the directors may, when issuing shares, provide that call notices sent to the holders of those shares may require them—

(a) to pay calls which are not the same, or

(b) to pay calls at different times.

When call notice need not be issued

56.— (1) A call notice need not be issued in respect of sums which are specified, in the terms on which a share is issued, as being payable to the company in respect of that share (whether in respect of nominal value or premium)—

(a) on allotment;

(b) on the occurrence of a particular event; or

(c) on a date fixed by or in accordance with the terms of issue.

(2) But if the due date for payment of such a sum has passed and it has not been paid, the holder of the share concerned is treated in all respects as having failed to comply with a call notice in respect of that sum, and is liable to the same consequences as regards the payment of interest and forfeiture.

Failure to comply with call notice: automatic consequences

57.— (1) If a person is liable to pay a call and fails to do so by the call payment date—

(a) the directors may issue a notice of intended forfeiture to that person, and

(b) until the call is paid, that person must pay the company interest on the call from the call payment date at the relevant rate.

(2) For the purposes of this article—

(a) the 'call payment date' is the time when the call notice states that a call is payable, unless the directors give a notice specifying a later date, in which case the 'call payment date' is that later date;

(b) the 'relevant rate' is—

(i) the rate fixed by the terms on which the share in respect of which the call is due was allotted;

          (ii) such other rate as was fixed in the call notice which required payment of the call, or has otherwise been determined by the directors; or

         (iii) if no rate is fixed in either of these ways, 5 per cent per annum.

  (3) The relevant rate must not exceed by more than 5 percentage points the base lending rate most recently set by the Monetary Policy Committee of the Bank of England in connection with its responsibilities under Part 2 of the Bank of England Act 1998(**a**).

  (4) The directors may waive any obligation to pay interest on a call wholly or in part.

Notice of intended forfeiture

58.   A notice of intended forfeiture—

  (a) may be sent in respect of any share in respect of which a call has not been paid as required by a call notice;

  (b) must be sent to the holder of that share or to a person entitled to it by reason of the holder's death, bankruptcy or otherwise;

  (c) must require payment of the call and any accrued interest by a date which is not less than 14 days after the date of the notice;

  (d) must state how the payment is to be made; and

  (e) must state that if the notice is not complied with, the shares in respect of which the call is payable will be liable to be forfeited.

  (f) 1998 c.11.

Directors' power to forfeit shares

59.   If a notice of intended forfeiture is not complied with before the date by which payment of the call is required in the notice of intended forfeiture, the directors may decide that any share in respect of which it was given is forfeited, and the forfeiture is to include all dividends or other moneys payable in respect of the forfeited shares and not paid before the forfeiture.

Effect of forfeiture

60.— (1) Subject to the articles, the forfeiture of a share extinguishes—

  (a) all interests in that share, and all claims and demands against the company in respect of it, and

  (b) all other rights and liabilities incidental to the share as between the person whose share it was prior to the forfeiture and the company.

  (2) Any share which is forfeited in accordance with the articles—

  (a) is deemed to have been forfeited when the directors decide that it is forfeited;

  (b) is deemed to be the property of the company; and

      (c)   may be sold, re-allotted or otherwise disposed of as the directors think fit.

(3)   If a person's shares have been forfeited—

      (a)   the company must send that person notice that forfeiture has occurred and record it in the register of members;

      (b)   that person ceases to be a member in respect of those shares;

      (c)   that person must surrender the certificate for the shares forfeited to the company for cancellation;

      (d)   that person remains liable to the company for all sums payable by that person under the articles at the date of forfeiture in respect of those shares, including any interest (whether accrued before or after the date of forfeiture); and

      (e)   the directors may waive payment of such sums wholly or in part or enforce payment without any allowance for the value of the shares at the time of forfeiture or for any consideration received on their disposal.

(4)   At any time before the company disposes of a forfeited share, the directors may decide to cancel the forfeiture on payment of all calls and interest due in respect of it and on such other terms as they think fit.

Procedure following forfeiture

61.— (1)   If a forfeited share is to be disposed of by being transferred, the company may receive the consideration for the transfer and the directors may authorise any person to execute the instrument of transfer.

(2)   A statutory declaration by a director or the company secretary that the declarant is a director or the company secretary and that a share has been forfeited on a specified date—

      (a)   is conclusive evidence of the facts stated in it as against all persons claiming to be entitled to the share, and

      (b)   subject to compliance with any other formalities of transfer required by the articles or by law, constitutes a good title to the share.

(3)   A person to whom a forfeited share is transferred is not bound to see to the application of the consideration (if any) nor is that person's title to the share affected by any irregularity in or invalidity of the process leading to the forfeiture or transfer of the share.

(4)   If the company sells a forfeited share, the person who held it prior to its forfeiture is entitled to receive from the company the proceeds of such sale, net of any commission, and excluding any amount which—

      (a)   was, or would have become, payable, and

(b) had not, when that share was forfeited, been paid by that person in respect of that share, but no interest is payable to such a person in respect of such proceeds and the company is not required to account for any money earned on them.

Surrender of shares

62.— (1) A member may surrender any share—

    (a) in respect of which the directors may issue a notice of intended forfeiture;

    (b) which the directors may forfeit; or

    (c) which has been forfeited.

  (2) The directors may accept the surrender of any such share.

  (3) The effect of surrender on a share is the same as the effect of forfeiture on that share.

  (4) A share which has been surrendered may be dealt with in the same way as a share which has been forfeited.

TRANSFER AND TRANSMISSION OF SHARES

Transfers of certificated shares

63.— (1) Certificated shares may be transferred by means of an instrument of transfer in any usual form or any other form approved by the directors, which is executed by or on behalf of—

    (a) the transferor, and

    (b) (if any of the shares is partly paid) the transferee.

  (2) No fee may be charged for registering any instrument of transfer or other document relating to or affecting the title to any share.

  (3) The company may retain any instrument of transfer which is registered.

  (4) The transferor remains the holder of a certificated share until the transferee's name is entered in the register of members as holder of it.

  (5) The directors may refuse to register the transfer of a certificated share if—

    (a) the share is not fully paid;

    (b) the transfer is not lodged at the company's registered office or such other place as the directors have appointed;

    (c) the transfer is not accompanied by the certificate for the shares to which it relates, or such other evidence as the directors may reasonably require to show the transferor's right to make the transfer, or evidence of the right of someone other than the transferor to make the transfer on the transferor's behalf;

    (d) the transfer is in respect of more than one class of share; or

    (e) the transfer is in favour of more than four transferees.

(6)   If the directors refuse to register the transfer of a share, the instrument of transfer must be returned to the transferee with the notice of refusal unless they suspect that the proposed transfer may be fraudulent.

Transfer of uncertificated shares

64.   A transfer of an uncertificated share must not be registered if it is in favour of more than four transferees.

Transmission of shares

65.— (1)   If title to a share passes to a transmittee, the company may only recognise the transmittee as having any title to that share.

(2)   Nothing in these articles releases the estate of a deceased member from any liability in respect of a share solely or jointly held by that member.

Transmittees' rights

66.— (1)   A transmittee who produces such evidence of entitlement to shares as the directors may properly require—

(a)   may, subject to the articles, choose either to become the holder of those shares or to have them transferred to another person, and

(b)   subject to the articles, and pending any transfer of the shares to another person, has the same rights as the holder had.

(2)   But transmittees do not have the right to attend or vote at a general meeting in respect of shares to which they are entitled, by reason of the holder's death or bankruptcy or otherwise, unless they become the holders of those shares.

Exercise of transmittees' rights

67.— (1)   Transmittees who wish to become the holders of shares to which they have become entitled must notify the company in writing of that wish.

(2)   If the share is a certificated share and a transmittee wishes to have it transferred to another person, the transmittee must execute an instrument of transfer in respect of it.

(3)   If the share is an uncertificated share and the transmittee wishes to have it transferred to another person, the transmittee must—

(a)   procure that all appropriate instructions are given to effect the transfer, or

(b)   procure that the uncertificated share is changed into certificated form and then execute an instrument of transfer in respect of it.

(4)   Any transfer made or executed under this article is to be treated as if it were made or executed by the person from whom the transmittee has

derived rights in respect of the share, and as if the event which gave rise to the transmission had not occurred.

Transmittees bound by prior notices

68. If a notice is given to a member in respect of shares and a transmittee is entitled to those shares, the transmittee is bound by the notice if it was given to the member before the transmittee's name has been entered in the register of members.

CONSOLIDATION OF SHARES

Procedure for disposing of fractions of shares

69.— (1) This article applies where—

    (a) there has been a consolidation or division of shares, and

    (b) as a result, members are entitled to fractions of shares.

(2) The directors may—

    (a) sell the shares representing the fractions to any person including the company for the best price reasonably obtainable;

    (b) in the case of a certificated share, authorise any person to execute an instrument of transfer of the shares to the purchaser or a person nominated by the purchaser; and

    (c) distribute the net proceeds of sale in due proportion among the holders of the shares.

(3) Where any holder's entitlement to a portion of the proceeds of sale amounts to less than a minimum figure determined by the directors, that member's portion may be distributed to an organisation which is a charity for the purposes of the law of England and Wales, Scotland or Northern Ireland.

(4) The person to whom the shares are transferred is not obliged to ensure that any purchase money is received by the person entitled to the relevant fractions.

(5) The transferee's title to the shares is not affected by any irregularity in or invalidity of the process leading to their sale.

DISTRIBUTIONS

Procedure for declaring dividends

70.— (1) The company may by ordinary resolution declare dividends, and the directors may decide to pay interim dividends.

(2) A dividend must not be declared unless the directors have made a recommendation as to its amount. Such a dividend must not exceed the amount recommended by the directors.

(3) No dividend may be declared or paid unless it is in accordance with members' respective rights.

(4) Unless the members' resolution to declare or directors' decision to pay a dividend, or the terms on which shares are issued, specify otherwise, it must be paid by reference to each member's holding of shares on the date of the resolution or decision to declare or pay it.

(5) If the company's share capital is divided into different classes, no interim dividend may be paid on shares carrying deferred or non-preferred rights if, at the time of payment, any preferential dividend is in arrears.

(6) The directors may pay at intervals any dividend payable at a fixed rate if it appears to them that the profits available for distribution justify the payment.

(7) If the directors act in good faith, they do not incur any liability to the holders of shares conferring preferred rights for any loss they may suffer by the lawful payment of an interim dividend on shares with deferred or non-preferred rights.

Calculation of dividends

71.— (1) Except as otherwise provided by the articles or the rights attached to shares, all dividends must be—

(a) declared and paid according to the amounts paid up on the shares on which the dividend is paid, and

(b) apportioned and paid proportionately to the amounts paid up on the shares during any portion or portions of the period in respect of which the dividend is paid.

(2) If any share is issued on terms providing that it ranks for dividend as from a particular date, that share ranks for dividend accordingly.

(3) For the purposes of calculating dividends, no account is to be taken of any amount which has been paid up on a share in advance of the due date for payment of that amount.

Payment of dividends and other distributions

72.— (1) Where a dividend or other sum which is a distribution is payable in respect of a share, it must be paid by one or more of the following means—

(a) transfer to a bank or building society account specified by the distribution recipient either in writing or as the directors may otherwise decide;

(b) sending a cheque made payable to the distribution recipient by post to the distribution recipient at the distribution recipient's registered address (if the distribution recipient is a holder of the share), or (in any other case) to an address specified by the distribution recipient either in writing or as the directors may otherwise decide;

(c) sending a cheque made payable to such person by post to such person at such address as the distribution recipient has specified either in writing or as the directors may otherwise decide; or

(d) any other means of payment as the directors agree with the distribution recipient either in writing or by such other means as the directors decide.

(2) In the articles, 'the distribution recipient' means, in respect of a share in respect of which a dividend or other sum is payable—

(a) the holder of the share; or

(b) if the share has two or more joint holders, whichever of them is named first in the register of members; or

(c) if the holder is no longer entitled to the share by reason of death or bankruptcy, or otherwise by operation of law, the transmittee.

Deductions from distributions in respect of sums owed to the company

73.— (1) If—

(a) a share is subject to the company's lien, and

(b) the directors are entitled to issue a lien enforcement notice in respect of it, they may, instead of issuing a lien enforcement notice, deduct from any dividend or other sum payable in respect of the share any sum of money which is payable to the company in respect of that share to the extent that they are entitled to require payment under a lien enforcement notice.

(2) Money so deducted must be used to pay any of the sums payable in respect of that share.

(3) The company must notify the distribution recipient in writing of—

(a) the fact and amount of any such deduction;

(b) any non-payment of a dividend or other sum payable in respect of a share resulting from any such deduction; and

(c) how the money deducted has been applied.

No interest on distributions

74. The company may not pay interest on any dividend or other sum payable in respect of a share unless otherwise provided by—

(a) the terms on which the share was issued, or

(b) the provisions of another agreement between the holder of that share and the company.

Unclaimed distributions

75.— (1) All dividends or other sums which are—

    (a) payable in respect of shares, and

    (b) unclaimed after having been declared or become payable, may be invested or otherwise made use of by the directors for the benefit of the company until claimed.

  (2) The payment of any such dividend or other sum into a separate account does not make the company a trustee in respect of it.

  (3) If—

    (a) twelve years have passed from the date on which a dividend or other sum became due for payment, and

    (b) the distribution recipient has not claimed it, the distribution recipient is no longer entitled to that dividend or other sum and it ceases to remain owing by the company.

Non-cash distributions

76.— (1) Subject to the terms of issue of the share in question, the company may, by ordinary resolution on the recommendation of the directors, decide to pay all or part of a dividend or other distribution payable in respect of a share by transferring non-cash assets of equivalent value (including, without limitation, shares or other securities in any company).

  (2) If the shares in respect of which such a non-cash distribution is paid are uncertificated, any shares in the company which are issued as a non-cash distribution in respect of them must be uncertificated.

  (3) For the purposes of paying a non-cash distribution, the directors may make whatever arrangements they think fit, including, where any difficulty arises regarding the distribution—

    (a) fixing the value of any assets;

    (b) paying cash to any distribution recipient on the basis of that value in order to adjust the rights of recipients; and

    (c) vesting any assets in trustees.

Waiver of distributions

77. Distribution recipients may waive their entitlement to a dividend or other distribution payable in respect of a share by giving the company notice in writing to that effect, but if—

  (a) the share has more than one holder, or

  (b) more than one person is entitled to the share, whether by reason of the death or bankruptcy of one or more joint holders, or otherwise, the notice is not effective unless it is expressed to be given, and signed, by all the holders or persons otherwise entitled to the share.

CAPITALISATION OF PROFITS

Authority to capitalise and appropriation of capitalised sums

78.— (1) Subject to the articles, the directors may, if they are so authorised by an ordinary resolution—

    (a) decide to capitalise any profits of the company (whether or not they are available for distribution) which are not required for paying a preferential dividend, or any sum standing to the credit of the company's share premium account or capital redemption reserve; and

    (b) appropriate any sum which they so decide to capitalise (a 'capitalised sum') to the persons who would have been entitled to it if it were distributed by way of dividend (the 'persons entitled') and in the same proportions.

  (2) Capitalised sums must be applied—

    (a) on behalf of the persons entitled, and

    (b) in the same proportions as a dividend would have been distributed to them.

  (3) Any capitalised sum may be applied in paying up new shares of a nominal amount equal to the capitalised sum which are then allotted credited as fully paid to the persons entitled or as they may direct.

  (4) A capitalised sum which was appropriated from profits available for distribution may be applied—

    (a) in or towards paying up any amounts unpaid on existing shares held by the persons entitled, or

    (b) in paying up new debentures of the company which are then allotted credited as fully paid to the persons entitled or as they may direct.

  (5) Subject to the articles the directors may—

    (a) apply capitalised sums in accordance with paragraphs (3) and (4) partly in one way and partly in another;

    (b) make such arrangements as they think fit to deal with shares or debentures becoming distributable in fractions under this article (including the issuing of fractional certificates or the making of cash payments); and

    (c) authorise any person to enter into an agreement with the company on behalf of all the persons entitled which is binding on them in respect of the allotment of shares and debentures to them under this article.

PART 5
MISCELLANEOUS PROVISIONS
COMMUNICATIONS

Means of communication to be used

79.— (1) Subject to the articles, anything sent or supplied by or to the company under the articles may be sent or supplied in any way in which the Companies Act 2006 provides for documents or information which are authorised or required by any provision of that Act to be sent or supplied by or to the company.

(2) Subject to the articles, any notice or document to be sent or supplied to a director in connection with the taking of decisions by directors may also be sent or supplied by the means by which that director has asked to be sent or supplied with such notices or documents for the time being.

(3) A director may agree with the company that notices or documents sent to that director in a particular way are to be deemed to have been received within a specified time of their being sent, and for the specified time to be less than 48 hours.

Failure to notify contact details

80.— (1) If—

(a) the company sends two consecutive documents to a member over a period of at least 12 months, and

(b) each of those documents is returned undelivered, or the company receives notification that it has not been delivered, that member ceases to be entitled to receive notices from the company.

(2) A member who has ceased to be entitled to receive notices from the company becomes entitled to receive such notices again by sending the company—

(a) a new address to be recorded in the register of members, or

(b) if the member has agreed that the company should use a means of communication other than sending things to such an address, the information that the company needs to use that means of communication effectively.

ADMINISTRATIVE ARRANGEMENTS

Company seals

81.— (1) Any common seal may only be used by the authority of the directors.

(2) The directors may decide by what means and in what form any common seal or securities seal is to be used.

(3) Unless otherwise decided by the directors, if the company has a common seal and it is affixed to a document, the document must also be signed by at least one authorised person in the presence of a witness who attests the signature.

(4) For the purposes of this article, an authorised person is—
   (a) any director of the company;
   (b) the company secretary; or
   (c) any person authorised by the directors for the purpose of signing documents to which the common seal is applied.

(5) If the company has an official seal for use abroad, it may only be affixed to a document if its use on that document, or documents of a class to which it belongs, has been authorised by a decision of the directors.

(6) If the company has a securities seal, it may only be affixed to securities by the company secretary or a person authorised to apply it to securities by the company secretary.

(7) For the purposes of the articles, references to the securities seal being affixed to any document include the reproduction of the image of that seal on or in a document by any mechanical or electronic means which has been approved by the directors in relation to that document or documents of a class to which it belongs.

Destruction of documents

82.— (1) The company is entitled to destroy—
   (a) all instruments of transfer of shares which have been registered, and all other documents on the basis of which any entries are made in the register of members, from six years after the date of registration;
   (b) all dividend mandates, variations or cancellations of dividend mandates, and notifications of change of address, from two years after they have been recorded;
   (c) all share certificates which have been cancelled from one year after the date of the cancellation;
   (d) all paid dividend warrants and cheques from one year after the date of actual payment; and
   (e) all proxy notices from one year after the end of the meeting to which the proxy notice relates.

(2) If the company destroys a document in good faith, in accordance with the articles, and without notice of any claim to which that document may be relevant, it is conclusively presumed in favour of the company that—
   (a) entries in the register purporting to have been made on the basis of an instrument of transfer or other document so destroyed were duly and properly made;

(b)   any instrument of transfer so destroyed was a valid and effective instrument duly and properly registered;

(c)   any share certificate so destroyed was a valid and effective certificate duly and properly cancelled; and

(d)   any other document so destroyed was a valid and effective document in accordance with its recorded particulars in the books or records of the company.

(3)   This article does not impose on the company any liability which it would not otherwise have if it destroys any document before the time at which this article permits it to do so.

(4)   In this article, references to the destruction of any document include a reference to its being disposed of in any manner.

No right to inspect accounts and other records

83.   Except as provided by law or authorised by the directors or an ordinary resolution of the company, no person is entitled to inspect any of the company's accounting or other records or documents merely by virtue of being a member.

Provision for employees on cessation of business

84.   The directors may decide to make provision for the benefit of persons employed or formerly employed by the company or any of its subsidiaries (other than a director or former director or shadow director) in connection with the cessation or transfer to any person of the whole or part of the undertaking of the company or that subsidiary.

DIRECTORS' INDEMNITY AND INSURANCE

Indemnity

85.— (1)   Subject to paragraph (2), a relevant director of the company or an associated company may be indemnified out of the company's assets against—

(a)   any liability incurred by that director in connection with any negligence, default, breach of duty or breach of trust in relation to the company or an associated company,

(b)   any liability incurred by that director in connection with the activities of the company or an associated company in its capacity as a trustee of an occupational pension scheme (as defined in section 235(6) of the Companies Act 2006),

(c)   any other liability incurred by that director as an officer of the company or an associated company.

(2) This article does not authorise any indemnity which would be prohibited or rendered void by any provision of the Companies Acts or by any other provision of law.

(3) In this article—

(a) companies are associated if one is a subsidiary of the other or both are subsidiaries of the same body corporate, and

(b) a 'relevant director' means any director or former director of the company or an associated company.

Insurance

86.— (1) The directors may decide to purchase and maintain insurance, at the expense of the company, for the benefit of any relevant director in respect of any relevant loss.

(2) In this article—

(a) a 'relevant director' means any director or former director of the company or an associated company,

(b) a 'relevant loss' means any loss or liability which has been or may be incurred by a relevant director in connection with that director's duties or powers in relation to the company, any associated company or any pension fund or employees' share scheme of the company or associated company, and

(c) companies are associated if one is a subsidiary of the other or both are subsidiaries of the same body corporate.

Appendix 10 – Checklist for annual general meeting

The checklist below gives an easy reference for those individuals tasked with the practicalities of convening a general meeting or for those with oversight of a third-party provider of services acting on behalf of the company.

Actions, dates, and practicalities should be checked against the Act, as well as the articles of the company, to ensure that they meet required protocols.

Date of meeting

- Calculate last date on which AGM must be held.
- Choose a suitable date or range of possible dates before the last date.
- Consult chair and other relevant personnel.
- Fix date and inform relevant company personnel and external advisers, e.g. registrars, auditors, solicitor, broker, PR consultants, etc.
- If a suitable opportunity arrives, inform the members.

Venue

- Estimate likely attendance numbers.
- Determine other requirements, e.g. location, cost, etc.
- Select and visit potential venues.
- Assess general suitability of each venue.
- Assess suitability for security purposes.
- Provisionally book preferred venue.
- Consult chair (and any other directors who wish to be consulted).
- If they approve, book venue and obtain confirmation of booking.
- Agree and sign contract.
- Obtain map of venue location and travel instructions.

Other arrangements

- Make arrangements for
  - catering (if required);
  - security and stewards;
  - audio visual equipment (if required);

- voting equipment (if required);
- printing of signs for AGM;
- stage design (if required); and
- display stands (if required).

Planning the AGM mailing

- Calculate last date notice must be sent out bearing in mind
  - notice requirements;
  - requirement for clear days' notice;
  - date notice deemed given if sent by post or electronically;
  - application of UK Corporate Governance Code recommendation;
- Set date for posting of notice and accounts (preferably before last date).
- If not possible within time limit, consider trying to obtain consent to short notice, otherwise change date of AGM.
- Set dates for:
  - final draft of notice;
  - finalisation of accounts and audit;
  - board meeting to approve accounts and convene AGM;
  - printing of notice, proxies, circulars, accounts and other documents to go with AGM mailing (inform printers);
  - printing of address labels (if by registrar, inform registrar stating where they are to be sent).

Drafting the notice, etc

- Prepare rough outline of business to be transacted at the AGM.
- If listed, check whether the notice and any accompanying circular will need to be approved by the UKLA before it is sent out.
- Check whether special notice is required for any resolution.
- Check type of resolution (Ordinary, Special) required for each item of business to be proposed.
- Calculate which (if any) of the directors must retire by rotation.
- Confirm that auditors are willing to be reappointed.
- Check whether directors' authority to allot needs to be renewed.
- Include any valid resolutions or statements submitted by members.
- Draft the AGM notice and circular.
- If a traded company, make preparations for publication of notice and other statements on website.
- Draft proxy cards and prepare website facilities for proxy appointments (if required).
- Draft attendance card (if required).
- Draft invitation to members to submit questions in advance (if required).

Board meeting to convene AGM and approve results and dividends

- Prepare and send out notice of board meeting including resolutions:
    - to approve report and accounts;
    - to authorise signing of accounts and reports;
    to recommend a dividend,
    - to convene the annual general meeting and approve business;
    - to authorise secretary to sign and send out notices, etc.;
    - to recommend the appointment of any directors (if articles require);
    - to approve the release of any preliminary announcement or results announcement (listed plc only);
    - nominate director to act as chair of the general meeting in the absence of the chair of the board.
- Immediately before meeting check again for any valid members' resolutions and include in papers put to the board.
- Hold board meeting and pass resolutions.

Immediately after the board meeting

- Release any preliminary announcement (listed plc only).
- Balance sheet signed by a director.
- Directors' report signed by a director or secretary.
- Auditors' report signed by auditors.
- Notice signed and dated by secretary.
- Calculate required number of copies of:
    - annual report (including extra copies);
    - notice, circular and proxy cards.
- Final proofs of report and accounts, proxy cards, notice, etc. sent to printers with instructions as to numbers required.

Sending out the notice

- Send report and accounts, notice, etc. to persons entitled to receive them.
- File annual report at Companies House.
- Send report and accounts to others on mailing list kept for that purpose.
- If a traded company, publish notice and other statements on website.
- Make available any website facilities for making proxy appointments.

Miscellaneous matters

- Make arrangements to enable the payment of the dividend (if subsequently approved).
- Calculate cut off time for valid proxies and, if necessary, inform registrars.
- Monitor proxies received.
- If necessary, contact major shareholders to encourage submission of proxies.

- At appropriate time on cut-off date for proxies prepare:
  - schedule of proxies appointed for the use of staff on the registration desk; and
  - schedule of voting instructions for the chair where the member has appointed chair as proxy.
- Print voting cards and poll cards (if required).

Preparations immediately before AGM

- Arrange for proposers and seconders of resolutions (as required).
- Finalise chair's agenda/script.
- Prepare AGM briefing document.
- If members were invited to submit questions in advance, prepare answers.
- Brief chair.
- Rehearse questions and answers.
- Allocate following duties to staff and brief accordingly:
  - registration;
  - poll;
  - roving microphone;
  - stewards and security.
- Rehearse AGM.
- Confirm final arrangements with venue, security staff, registrars, etc.
- Make arrangements for the release of an announcement if it is intended to reveal price-sensitive information at the meeting (listed plc only).

Day of the annual general meeting

- Things to take to the meeting:
  - directors' service contracts/non-executive directors' terms of appointment;
  - spare copies of report and accounts and notice;
  - chair's agenda/script (plus copies for other directors who are to propose resolutions);
  - questions and answers script;
  - memorandum and articles of association (indexed);
  - consolidated version of Companies Act 2006 (as amended);
  - a textbook on the law and procedures of meetings;
  - summary of proxies received;
  - original proxy forms and summary sheets;
  - register of members (usually supplied by registrar);
  - attendance sheets for members, proxies and corporate representatives, and guests;
  - notepads, pens and pencils;
  - name plates for top table and name badges;
  - reserved seats signs;

- – voting cards;
- – calculator with printed roll for counting votes on a poll;
- – telephone numbers of crucial participants.
- ■ Final briefing of staff.
- ■ Check that quorum present.
- ■ Open meeting and conduct business (see chair's scripts).
- ■ Record proceedings.

After the meeting

- ■ Prepare minutes for signature by chair.
- ■ Take actions required as a result of resolutions passed.
- ■ Authorise payment of dividend.
- ■ File any necessary copies of resolutions at Companies House.
- ■ Announce results of resolutions and send copies of resolutions sent to UK Listing Authority (listed plc only).
- ■ Publish the results of any poll on a website (quoted companies only).
- ■ Publish results of any independent report on a poll on a website.
- ■ Respond to shareholder questions raised at meeting.
- ■ Review the organisation of the AGM.
- ■ Book venue for next AGM.

Directory

References

Copland, James and Larcker, David F. and Tayan, Brian, *The Big Thumb on the Scale: An Overview of the Proxy Advisory Industry* (May 31, 2018).

Rock Center for Corporate Governance at Stanford University Closer Look Series: *Topics, Issues and Controversies in Corporate Governance*, No. CGRP-72; Stanford University Graduate School of Business Research Paper No. 18-27. Available at SSRN: https://ssrn.com/abstract=3188174

Tim Beech, Partner, Allen & Overy, *Bondholder meetings in the time of Covid-19: virtually ok? (15 April, 2020)*

Resources

ICSA knowledge, guidance and resources on governance can be found at: https://www.icsa.org.uk/

The Financial Reporting Council provides a number of corporate governance documents on their website at: www.frc.org.uk, including:

- UK Corporate Governance Code (2018) (the "Code")
- FRC Guidance for Board and Board Committees;
- FRC Guidance on Board Effectiveness
- The Wates Corporate Governance Principles for Large Private Companies;

The FCA Handbook can be found at: www.handbook.fca.org.uk/

The Public Register of Shareholder dissent can be found on the website of The Investment Association at: https://www.theia.org/public-register

For small and medium sized listed companies, reference and guidance on governance and company meetings can be obtained from the Quoted Companies Alliance www.theqca.com/

The Task Force on Climate-related Financial Disclosures: www.fsb-tcfd.org/about/

Links to the Walker Report review of corporate governance in UK banks and other financial industry entities published in 2019 can be found on the website of the ICAEW at: https://www.icaew.com/technical/corporate-governance/codes-and-reports/walker-report

Information on whistleblowing can be found on the website of Protect (formerly Public Concern at Work) at: https://protect-advice.org.uk/

The UK listing rules can be found at: https://www.handbook.fca.org.uk/handbook/LR.pdf

The complete UK Companies Act 2006 (with updates) can be found at: http://www.legislation.gov.uk/ukpga/2006/46/contents

Further information on GDPR can be found at the website of The Information Commissioner:https://ico.org.uk/for-organisations/guide-to-data-protection/guide-to-the-general-data-protection-regulation-gdpr/

Index